Contemporary Cases in U.S. Foreign Policy

From Terrorism to Trade

Third Edition

Ralph G. Carter, *Editor*
Texas Christian University

A Division of Congressional Quarterly Inc.
Washington, D.C.

CQ Press
1255 22nd Street, NW, Suite 400
Washington, DC 20037

Phone: 202-729-1900; toll-free, 1-866-4CQ-PRESS (1-866-427-7737)

Web: www.cqpress.com

Cover design: theDesignfarm
Cover photos: Brian Hagiwara/Brand X Pictures/Jupiterimages

∞ The paper used in this publication exceeds the requirements of the American National Standard for Information Sciences—Permanence of Paper for Printed Library Materials, ANSI Z39.48-1992.

Printed and bound in the United States of America

11 10 09 08 07   1 2 3 4 5

Cataloging-in-Publication Data available from the Library of Congress.
ISBN: 978-0-87289-472-3

Contents

Preface ix

Contributors xv

Introduction xxi
RALPH G. CARTER

PART I INTERVENTION POLICY

1 **The United States versus Terrorism: Clinton, Bush, and Osama Bin Laden** 1
RYAN C. HENDRICKSON AND FRÉDÉRICK GAGNON

The "war on terrorism" dates to the early 1990s and escalated with the 1998 bombings of the U.S. embassies in Kenya and Tanzania. The Clinton administration retaliated with missile attacks on targets in Sudan and Afghanistan thought to be affiliated with the al Qaeda network. In 2000, al Qaeda struck again, launching a suicide mission against the USS Cole *in Yemen. Following the attacks of September 11, 2001, the administration of George W. Bush launched a global campaign against Osama Bin Laden and the al Qaeda network.*

2 **The Return of the Imperial Presidency? The Bush Doctrine and U.S. Intervention in Iraq** 25
JEFFREY S. LANTIS AND ERIC MOSKOWITZ

After the fall of the Taliban and dispersal of al Qaeda forces in Afghanistan, the "war on terrorism" intersected with a long-standing desire among neoconservatives to overthrow Iraqi leader Saddam Hussein. To assuage opposition to war and to drum up public support, President George W. Bush decided to pursue a two-track policy of international diplomacy through the United Nations while also preparing for war. White House officials subsequently relied on their interpretation of the president's commander in chief powers, and the congressional authorization to use force, to conduct the war and the Iraq occupation with as little input from outsiders as possible.

3 Coca, Human Rights, and Violence: U.S. Foreign Policy toward Colombia 59
JENNIFER S. HOLMES

In Colombia, narco-trafficking permeates all levels of politics and society, complicating an ongoing struggle between the government and insurgents. Because of human rights violations, Congress attempted to use its power of the purse to attach conditions to Colombia aid. Yet after the attacks of September 11, 2001, George W. Bush administration officials declared the antigovernment insurgents "terrorists" and removed barriers to the use of aid to defeat them, including adding counterinsurgency tactics to the counternarcotics trafficking tactics already authorized.

PART II NATIONAL SECURITY AND DEFENSE POLICY

4 The Nuclear Standoff between the United States and Iran: Conflict, Misunderstandings, and Diplomatic Inflexibility 91
THOMAS PRESTON AND MICHAEL P. INFRANCO

For more than fifty years, U.S.-Iran relations have been plagued by policy conflicts heightened by mutual misunderstandings and suspicions. This history of poor relations worsened when Iran sought to develop nuclear weapons, alarming not only the United States but also the international community. Diplomatic efforts to resolve the concerns that Iran's nuclear program has generated have been frustrated by significant political intransigence on both the U.S. and Iranian sides.

5 The United States and North Korea: Avoiding a Worst-Case Scenario 121
PATRICK JAMES AND ÖZGÜR ÖZDAMAR

The Reagan administration and the U.S. intelligence community were surprised when satellite images revealed the construction of a nuclear reactor in North Korea in the 1980s. Diplomacy during the Clinton administration resulted in the 1994 Agreed Framework, which required that North Korea halt its nuclear program in return for being supplied with light water reactors and oil. After President George W. Bush labeled North Korea a member of an "axis of evil," relations quickly deteriorated. In 2003 North Korean officials acknowledged possessing nuclear weapons, greatly escalating the consequences of any policy mistake in dealing with the regime in Pyongyang. Only time will tell if a 2007 negotiated agreement will prove more successful than previous efforts.

6 **Anatomy of a Crash: Port Security and the 2006 Dubai Ports World Controversy** 151
DOUGLAS C. FOYLE

In late 2005, a company owned by the United Arab Emirates, Dubai Ports World, contacted the U.S. government regarding its plan to purchase a British firm that had been operating six major U.S. ports. George W. Bush administration officials convened as the multidepartmental Committee on Foreign Investment in the United States and approved the sale without advising either Congress or the president and apparently without considering how controversial turning over port operations to an Arabia-based firm would be in the era after September 11. Despite the president's subsequent defense of the sale as good for the United States, sufficient pressure was brought to bear to force the company to announce that it would sell the U.S. port operations to a U.S. buyer.

7 **NSA Eavesdropping: Unchecked or Limited Presidential Power?** 185
LOUIS FISHER

In December 2005, news reports revealed that after the September 11 attacks, the George W. Bush administration authorized the National Security Agency to eavesdrop on international telephone calls involving U.S. citizens or residents. Although the 1978 Foreign Intelligence Surveillance Act (FISA) had created a court specifically to issue secret warrants for such telephone intercepts, the administration chose not to seek warrants for its "Terrorist Surveillance Program." In 2006, a federal judge in Michigan ruled that the program violated both the Constitution and federal statutes. The Republican-controlled House and Senate proved unable to agree on the terms of an authorization of warrantless eavesdropping before the 2006 general election. Facing a Democratic-controlled Congress in 2007, administration officials indicated that they would seek such warrants from the FISA court in the future.

8 **Immigration Policy: U.S.-Mexican Relations Confront U.S. Political Realities** 217
MARC R. ROSENBLUM

When new presidents George W. Bush and Vicente Fox entered office, significant progress seemed likely on long-standing concerns about Mexican immigration into the United States. Not only did the September 11 terrorist attacks put off such policy discussions for years, but the "war on terror" made an already complex issue more complicated. Now border security involved potential terrorists, not just illegal immigrants. Huge public rallies in favor of immigration reform in 2006 reenergized the issue in the United States, but crosscutting pressures fragmented both political parties in Congress, making legislative resolution of the issue extraordinarily difficult.

PART III TRADE POLICY

9 **U.S. Steel Import Tariffs: The Politics of Global Markets** 249
ROBERT A. BLECKER

At the behest of special interests and in an attempt to gain political support in key states, the George W. Bush administration raised tariffs on imported steel in March 2002, putting the United States on a collision course with the European Union, Japan, and other steel producers. The World Trade Organization declared the tariffs illegal twice in 2003. A month after the second ruling, the administration lifted the tariffs, denying that it had bowed to international pressures and claiming instead that the tariffs had run their course. With global steel demand surging after 2004, even without the tariff protections U.S. steel manufacturers became profitable again, to the point that they became the targets of foreign-based mergers and acquisitions. The largest steel producer in the United States is now the U.S. subsidiary of a European conglomerate that includes six formerly separate U.S. steel-producing corporations.

10 **The Helms-Burton Act: Congress and Cuba Policy** 281
PATRICK J. HANEY AND WALT VANDERBUSH

Driven by partisan politics and an influential interest group, the Republican Congress sought to expand and codify the U.S. trade embargo against Cuba in 1995. A single deadly act by the Cuban government led President Bill Clinton to support the congressional initiative, but to the consternation of some members of Congress, he ultimately was able to circumvent some of the other restrictions on U.S. trade and contacts with Cuba. Opposition to parts of the law resulted in a split within the Republican Party. This break in Republican ranks led to the relaxation of some restrictions on trade with Cuba, and restrictions on travel by Americans to the island nation have been questioned. Given the importance of Florida in U.S. presidential elections and Fidel Castro's stature as a "lightning rod," U.S.-Cuba policy seems unlikely to diminish in political importance anytime soon.

11 **U.S.-China Trade Relations: Privatizing Foreign Policy** 305
STEVEN W. HOOK AND FRANKLIN BARR LEBO

Thirty years after the United States and China established economic relations, the two continued to exchange complaints about the other's trade practices. The Clinton administration's efforts to establish permanent normal trade relations between China and the United States and to support China's entry into the World Trade Organization pitted business-oriented groups against labor, environmental, and human rights organizations. China's image as a "strategic partner" during the

Clinton years changed to that of a "strategic competitor" during the administration of George W. Bush. The Bush administration has filed three formal complaints with the WTO about Chinese trade practices. Thus despite China's assurances that it would change its controversial trade practices to gain WTO entry, problems of U.S. access to Chinese markets continue.

12 The World Trade Organization and Tax Subsidies for Exports: Equal Competition or Corporate Welfare? 335
WENDY J. SCHILLER AND RALPH G. CARTER

For thirty years, Congress tried to "level the playing field" between U.S. corporations and their European competitors. With the 1995 creation of the World Trade Organization, European states finally had an entity that could authorize penalties against the United States for what the Europeans saw as unfair trade subsidies to U.S. corporations. Congressional efforts to avoid these WTO-sanctioned penalties were complicated by fundamental differences in what reformers wanted to accomplish, and by U.S. corporate heavyweights' lining up on both sides of the dispute. To have the penalties lifted, Congress eventually had to terminate these controversial corporate tax policies.

PART IV MULTILATERAL POLICY

13 The Kyoto Protocol and Beyond: The Politics of Climate Change 357
RODGER A. PAYNE AND SEAN PAYNE

International efforts to address global warming ran headlong into U.S. objections during the Clinton administration. Controversies ranged from whether there was a scientific basis for attributing global climate change to human activity to questions about the fairness and effectiveness of the means chosen to tackle the problem. Addressing global warming continues to pit environmentalists and advocates of apolitical science against those advocating continued U.S. economic growth and voluntary measures to stanch the emission of greenhouse gases. The reluctance of the George W. Bush administration to move in the direction of mainstream international opinion on this issue has motivated some U.S. states, cities, and corporate actors to adopt their own emissions reduction programs to move in the direction of, if not to comply with, the Kyoto Protocol's provisions.

14 The International Criminal Court: 105 Nations Join, but Not the United States 391
DONALD W. JACKSON AND RALPH G. CARTER

The Clinton administration was an early supporter of a permanent court to try individuals accused of war crimes, crimes against humanity, and genocide. When control over the court's agenda was not assigned to the UN Security Council, the U.S. position changed from support to active opposition. The International Criminal Court now exists and has issued its first indictments. The U.S. repudiation of the court stands as a continuing example of the unilateralism that critics say characterizes U.S. foreign policy. In light of the broad international support for the court, continuing U.S. opposition to it raises questions about U.S. commitment to the rule of international law.

15 **The Rights of Detainees: Determining the Limits of Law** 417
LINDA CORNETT AND MARK GIBNEY

What legal rights do detainees in the "war on terrorism" have? Does the executive branch have the authority to hold terror suspects without providing them access to the courts? The status of detainees pits those who stress wartime national security requirements against civil libertarians who claim that such detention violates the U.S. commitment to the rule of international law and the Constitution. Although the U.S. Supreme Court has ruled that detainees have some legal rights, Congress has sought to limit the courts' ability to interfere with the president's actions regarding the detention of terrorism suspects.

Conclusion 447
RALPH G. CARTER

Index 457

Preface

The terrorist attacks of September 11, 2001, and events thereafter demonstrate that post–cold war expectations for a more peaceful world built on a foundation of liberal democracies are, at best, premature. Military conflicts and national security issues continue to occupy the spotlight, while less-traditional foreign policy concerns have also emerged. Human rights, trade matters, and the U.S. role in the international community have moved to the forefront, as foreign policy making has become a much more complex and crowded affair than it was during the cold war.

Just as the types of foreign policy issues that seem important have changed, the relative roles played by different policymakers have been in flux as well. Although presidents still occasionally act unilaterally—as in decisions to use military force—presidential preeminence in overall foreign policy making has diminished. Domestic and international groups, nongovernmental organizations, and members of Congress now actively challenge the executive branch's ability to direct foreign policy. In the post–cold war period, public opinion also seems to play a greater role in policymakers' decisions.

This historic shift in the policy process raises a number of questions: Can international institutions contain terrorism or ethnic and religious violence? How can the United States protect its citizens and interests from global terrorist threats? Are unilateral U.S. responses appropriate for global threats? Will disgruntled domestic actors define new enemies or foreign policy challenges? Will the international economy be marked by trade wars between regions and free trade within them? What is more important to U.S. foreign policy: human rights or corporate profits and market share? These questions and similar concerns prompted the conception of this book.

Each of the fifteen case studies included here speaks to a foreign policy process that has become more open and pluralistic and deeply partisan. With the dramatic increase in the number of congressional subcommittees in the 1970s, followed by the explosive growth of the electronic media in the 1980s and 1990s, individuals and groups now have more points of access through which to participate in policymaking. New actors have their own needs, interests, and agendas. They are more partisan in their behavior as well, with Democrats and Republicans vying to put their own foreign policy agendas or policy alternatives forward. In short, U.S. foreign policy making now resembles U.S. domestic policy making: it is overtly political.

Most of the cases in this volume reflect the jurisdictional competition between the president and Congress (and at times the courts) over the control and direction of foreign policy in the contemporary era. Not only do members of the opposition party regularly challenge the president's foreign policy initiatives, but even members of his own party resist executive leadership when they think that the White House tramples on legitimate congressional responsibilities or that the public overwhelmingly opposes administration policies. Such circumstances have often led to "bad blood" between the branches, a situation that must strain the policymaking process. White House controversies—for instance, the Monica Lewinsky affair for Bill Clinton or multiple policy missteps for George W. Bush (for example, the inability to "win" the military occupation of Iraq and controversies within the Justice Department and its senior leadership, personified by former attorney general Alberto Gonzales)—further weaken presidential power. These themes combine to reveal the chinks in the presidential preeminence model of foreign policy making.

Using Case Studies in the Classroom

Although many excellent U.S. foreign policy texts exist, most fall short in their coverage of recent events and debates. This book aims to cover contemporary incidents, so that instructors can raise issues confronting today's policy makers. Each case study is an original work written expressly for this volume and is organized in a format that emphasizes the substance of events. A textbook's general description of the foreign policy making process simply cannot capture all of the intricacies, nuances, and subtleties involved in the events chronicled here. The cases starkly reveal the human dimension of policymaking and also help instructors show how administrations often take pains to attempt to do things differently than their predecessors. In addition to showing students the human, political, and organizational faces of policymaking, these case studies also introduce them to the wide variety of issues and actors of the post–cold war and post–September 11 period. Students are presented with a "good story," full of compelling characters and daunting challenges, and information on the relevance of issues and why particular policy choices were made.

The pedagogical benefits of the case study approach have spurred its use within the international studies community, joining military, business, public policy, and public administration schools that have long used this approach. For college graduates to compete and perform effectively in the real world, they must first see the world as it is. Simplified models of reality may be necessary at times, but they are rarely sufficient by themselves. Theoretical models alone do not capture the messy nature of foreign policy making. If instructors are to facilitate an understanding of the political arena, in which everything seemingly affects everything else, they must confront students with the policymaking dynamics that real-world cases illustrate. Were policymakers trying to make rational choices? Were they trying to balance power concerns on a regional or global basis? Were they more responsive to external threats or opportunities, or to internal political pressures at home? Were they reacting to widely shared perceptions of reality? Did analogies mold their decisions, or were they merely used to convey or defend decisions to the public? These and other theoretical concerns are addressed through the case study method.

Case studies also promote critical thinking and encourage active intellectual engagement. None of their recognized advantages can be realized unless students ask themselves why things occurred as they did. Reasoning, considering alternatives, deciding on one alternative rather than another, and communicating the reasoning behind a choice are skills that are integral to lifelong learning and success in any professional career.

Because different educational environments—for example, seminars versus large lecture courses, upper-level courses versus introductory classes—require different teaching approaches, this collection includes a number of aids to help students and instructors get the most out of each case study. "Before You Begin"—a series of critical questions at the beginning of each case—serves as a touchstone, giving students ideas to consider and later review. Each case includes a brief chronology that notes the important events covered and a list of key figures in the case. Our shared goal here is to walk a fine line: to encourage students to think without telling them what to think. To provide instructors with guidance in using the studies, the online, password-protected instructor's manual (**http://college.cqpress.com/ccusfp**) includes a section on the nuts and bolts of case-based teaching as well as separate entries for analyzing and discussing each case study.

The Cases

The case studies in this book were selected to illustrate two important realities of the post–cold war and post–September 11 period: (1) the range and diversity of the old and new issues facing U.S. foreign policy makers and (2) the variety of participants in the current policymaking process. The first set of cases concern the ongoing questions of when and how the United States should intervene militarily. Military interventions have always been considered "high politics"—decisions typically made in the White House. As the "war on terror," Iraq intervention, and Colombia intervention cases show, presidents still largely dominate these issues. However as always, domestic criticism arises swiftly if presidential policies are not seen as successful.

Changing national security and defense challenges prompted another set of cases: How to deal with nuclear weapons proliferation in North Korea, and potentially Iran, has bedeviled policymakers at both ends of Pennsylvania Avenue during the Clinton and Bush administrations. When the Bush administration decided to turn control of operations at six major U.S. ports over to a state-owned company based in Dubai, and when it chose to permit National Security Agency eavesdropping on the phone calls of some U.S. citizens, top administration officials thought they were doing the right thing. In both cases, however, the administration ran into a firestorm of protest in Congress. The issue of immigration reform also collided with national security concerns, in a case in which numerous Republican members of Congress argued that they were more concerned about national security in such matters than was President Bush.

Many observers predicted that the hallmark of the post–cold war period would be a new emphasis on trade and more cooperative international initiatives. The trade cases included here represent a diverse group of issues. The steel tariffs case illustrates the policymaking dynamics of a low-visibility issue in which officials below the level of the president, trade and industry representatives, and such international actors as the European Union and the World Trade Organization played important roles. The Helms-Burton Act highlights the influence of Cuban American groups and members of Congress on U.S. policy toward Cuba, as they struggled to maintain the U.S. embargo while others attempted to loosen it. The case of the Clinton administration's policy of engagement with China pits a variety of domestic groups (and their congressional advocates) against one another. In this case, business interests prevailed over the human rights, labor, and environmental groups lobbying to deny China permanent normal trade relations with the United States. Finally, the WTO trade subsidy case illustrates how difficult reconciling domestic and international economic imperatives can be, as well as what happens when members of Congress realize the policy opportunities that are available when they have a bill that must be passed.

The last set of cases focuses on the difficulties the United States currently faces in its dealings with a range of international organizations. Pressures from interest groups and Congress prevented the Kyoto Protocol on global warming from being submitted to the Senate for ratification. Congressional pressure and Defense Department concerns forced the Clinton administration to attempt to weaken the authority of the new International Criminal Court, against the wishes of more than one hundred other nations. Under the Bush administration, the policy of protecting U.S. soldiers and sovereignty against the court was strengthened. The final case study highlights the politics of the detention of people rounded up in the United States after the attacks of September 11; enemy combatants captured in Afghanistan and held at Guantanamo Bay, Cuba; U.S. citizens declared enemy combatants by the president; and detainees in U.S.-run prisons in Iraq. Whereas the Bush administration claimed that the president, as commander in chief, has the authority to deal unilaterally with the first three groups, the Supreme Court ruled otherwise, holding that such detainees could not be denied access to U.S. courts and lawyers. These are a few examples of the wide range and diversity of U.S. foreign policy making in the post–cold war and post–September 11 era.

Acknowledgments

As is usually the case in publishing, this book benefits from the efforts of many individuals. First, my thanks go to the authors of the case studies. Not only were they willing to write the studies requested, but they also graciously agreed to make the changes that the CQ editors and I suggested. Much appreciated is the timeliness with which they produced their chapters, particularly as the situations covered in some cases continued to evolve as they wrote. Second, a number of colleagues and friends provided valuable assistance at various stages of this process. I must thank Lynn Kuzma, James Lindsay, Brandon Prins, Helen Purkitt, and Michael Sullivan for their careful review of the initial book proposal. Jean Garrison, Karen Rasler, and Brandon Prins reviewed the entire first edition manuscript, and their constructive suggestions were deeply appreciated. Patrick Haney, Heidi Hobbs, Steven Hook, Jeffrey Lantis, James Scott, Doug Van Belle, and Dave Waselkow also provided valuable advice and assistance on the first edition of this work. A number of first edition users provided input that helped improve the second edition. They include Robert Bookmiller, Andrea Grove, Patrick Haney (again), Michael Kanner, Brian Kessel, Jeffrey Lantis (again), Kathryn Lee, Kenneth Schultz, and Robert

Sterken. A survey of users of the second edition provided significant input in reshaping the third edition. I thank all those who responded. Others who provided more specific feedback for the third edition included Polly Diven, Cooper Drury, Mark Gentry, Margaret Karns, Michael Schechter, Wendy Schiller, Carolyn Shaw, Jonathan Strand, and Peter Trumbore. Having good help when you need it is a treasure, and this book is better as a result of their respective contributions.

Luckily for me, the professionals at CQ Press have also been great partners. Charisse Kiino guided the first edition and the beginnings of the second. I appreciate all of her help and counsel. Michael Kerns then took up this project, and he was equally supportive and helpful. For the third edition, I've been wonderfully aided by both Charisse again and Dwain Smith. Careful copyediting by Nancy Geltman further improved the writing. Brenda Carter and Chris O'Brien spearheaded the European marketing of the book, which is deeply appreciated.

Finally, I must thank those closest to me. First, Nita has been wonderful throughout the long life of this project. Her advice, understanding, and encouragement, particularly on the many nights and weekends when I had to work, helped me keep my focus on the job at hand. Her consistent support has been instrumental to the successful completion of this project. I also need to thank my extended family and friends. They, too, have been supportive and understanding when my work pulled me away at times. I am truly fortunate to be surrounded by such caring individuals.

Contributors

ROBERT A. BLECKER is professor of economics at American University, Washington, D.C., where he received the University Faculty Award for Outstanding Teaching in 2005. His research interests include U.S. trade policy, the trade deficit, North American integration, exchange rates, and open economy macroeconomics. The author of *Taming Global Finance* (1999) and the coauthor of *Fundamentals of U.S. Foreign Trade Policy* (2nd ed. 2003), Blecker is on the editorial board of the *International Review of Applied Economics.* He received his PhD from Stanford University.

RALPH G. CARTER is a professor in and chair of the political science department at Texas Christian University. His research interests are U.S. trade, defense, and foreign policies and the domestic sources of policymaking, with particular attention to the role of Congress. He is the coauthor of *Choosing to Lead: Understanding Congressional Foreign Policy Entrepreneurs* (forthcoming) and *Making American Foreign Policy* (1994, 1996). Carter is a past president of both the International Studies Association's Foreign Policy Analysis Section and Midwest Region. He currently serves as one of the editors of *Foreign Policy Analysis* and is the 2006 recipient of the Quincy Wright Distinguished Scholar Award by ISA Midwest. He holds a PhD from Ohio State University.

LINDA CORNETT is associate professor of political science and director of international studies at the University of North Carolina, Asheville, where her classes include international organization and international law. She earned her bachelor's degree from Transylvania University, Lexington, Kentucky, and a master's and PhD in political science from the University of Washington, Seattle.

LOUIS FISHER is currently a specialist in constitutional law at the Law Library of the Library of Congress, after working for the Congressional Research Service from 1970 to 2006. He received his doctorate at the New School for Social Reseach in 1967 and is the author of many books, including *Presidential War Power* (2nd ed. 2004), *Constitutional Conflicts between Congress and the President* (5th ed. 2007), and (with David Gray Adler) *American Constitutional Law* (7th ed. 2007).

DOUGLAS C. FOYLE is associate professor of government at Wesleyan University, where he specializes in international relations and U.S. foreign policy. His research focuses on the connection between public opinion and foreign and national security policy. He is currently working on a book examining how impending elections affect the manner in which leaders confront international threats. He received his PhD from Duke University. Foyle is the author of *Counting the Public In: Presidents, Public Opinion, and Foreign Policy* (1999).

FRÉDÉRICK GAGNON is a lecturer and PhD candidate in the Department of Political Science at the University of Quebec at Montreal. He is a fellow at the Center for U.S. Studies of the Raoul Dandurand Chair, at the same university, and was visiting scholar at the Woodrow Wilson International Center for Scholars (Washington, D.C.) and at the Center for American Politics and Citizenship (University of Maryland) in 2006. His research and teaching interests focus on the U.S. Congress, American foreign policy, legislative-executive relations, congressional and presidential elections, and Quebec-U.S. relations. He is the author of a French-language textbook on the U.S. Congress (*Le Congrès des états-Unis,* 2006). His PhD dissertation focuses on the influence of the chairman of the Senate Foreign Relations Committee since 1945.

MARK GIBNEY is Belk Distinguished Professor at the University of North Carolina, Asheville. His teaching and research interests are in human rights, refugee protection, civil liberties, and international law and ethics. His recent publications include *Five Uneasy Pieces: American Ethics in a Globalized World* (2004), the edited volume *The Age of Apologies: Facing the Past* (forthcoming), and *International Human Rights Law: Returning to Universal Principles* (forthcoming).

PATRICK J. HANEY is professor of political science at Miami University, Oxford, Ohio. His teaching and research interests are U.S. foreign policy and crisis decision making. He is the author of *Organizing for Foreign Policy Crises: Presidents, Advisers, and the Management of Decision Making* (2002) and the coauthor (with Walt Vanderbush) of *The Cuban Embargo: The Domestic Politics of American Foreign Policy* (2005).

RYAN C. HENDRICKSON is associate professor of political science at Eastern Illinois University. His research and teaching interests focus on American military action abroad and multilateral diplomacy. He is the author of *Diplomacy and War at NATO: The Secretary General and Military Action after the Cold War* (2006) and *The Clinton Wars: The Constitution, Congress and War Powers* (2002). He received a PhD from the University of Nebraska, Lincoln.

JENNIFER S. HOLMES is an associate professor of political economy and political science at the University of Texas at Dallas. Her major area of research is violence and development, with an emphasis on Latin America and Southern Europe. She is the author of *Terrorism and Democratic Stability* (2001, 2006), *Terrorism and Democratic Stability Revisited* (forthcoming), and *Drugs, Thugs, and Development in Colombia* (forthcoming), and the editor of *New Approaches to Comparative Politics: Insights from Political Theory* (2003). Holmes's articles have been published in *Terrorism and Political Violence, Latin American Politics and Society, Bulletin of Latin American Research, International Journal of Social Economics, Studies in Conflict and Terrorism, International Journal of Public Administration,* and *Revista de Estudios Colombianos.*

STEVEN W. HOOK is associate professor of political science at Kent State University. He is the author of *National Interest and Foreign Aid* (1995) and *U.S. Foreign Policy: The Paradox of World Power* (2nd ed. 2008), the coauthor (with John Spanier) of *American Foreign Policy since World War II* (17th ed. 2007), and the editor of *Foreign Aid toward the Millennium* (1996) and *Comparative Foreign Policy: Adaptation Strategies of the Great and Emerging Powers* (2002). He is a past president of the Foreign Policy Analysis Section of the International Studies Association and the Foreign Policy Section of the American Political Science Association.

MICHAEL P. INFRANCO teaches seminars on global conflict and cooperation in the Honors College at Washington State University. His research interests include Middle Eastern politics, intergroup conflict and genocide, and East Asian security issues. In 2006, he retired as a lieutenant commander from the U.S. Navy Reserve; he holds a graduate diploma in National Security and Strategic Studies from the U.S. Naval War College (1996). Infranco is a combat veteran and has an expeditionary medal for his participation in Ernest Will missions in the Persian Gulf during the Iran-Iraq War. He has also participated in several international exercises and conferences, such as Ulchi Focus Lens 93 (defense of South Korea) and a Korean security conference at International Christian University in October 2003. He received his PhD from Washington State University in May 2005.

DONALD W. JACKSON is Herman Brown Professor of Political Science and director of the Center for Civic Literacy at Texas Christian University. His recent research has focused on transnational and international dimensions of the rule of law, especially on the protection of human rights. In 1998 he was an observer at the UN conference that led to the adoption of the Rome Statute and the creation of the International Criminal Court.

PATRICK JAMES is professor of international relations and director of the Center for International Studies at the University of Southern California (PhD, University of Maryland, College Park). James specializes in comparative and international politics. His interests include the causes, processes, and consequences of international conflict, crisis, and war. He also focuses on Canada, most notably with respect to constitutional dilemmas. James is the author of eleven books and more than one hundred articles and book chapters. Among his honors and awards are the Louise Dyer Peace Fellowship from the Hoover Institution at Stanford University; the Milton R. Merrill Chair in Political Science at Utah State University; the Lady Davis Professorship of the Hebrew University of Jerusalem; the Thomas Enders Professorship in Canadian Studies at the University of Calgary; the Senior Scholar Award from the Canadian Embassy, Washington, D.C.; the Eaton Lectureship at Queen's University in Belfast; and the Quincy Wright Scholar Award from the Midwest International Studies Association. He is a past president of the Midwest International Studies Association and the Iowa Conference of Political Scientists and currently is Distinguished Scholar in Foreign Policy Analysis for the International Studies Association (ISA). He is vice president, 2005–2007, and president, 2007–2009, of the Association for Canadian Studies in the United States, and vice president (2008–2009) of the ISA. James served a five-year term as editor of *International Studies Quarterly.*

JEFFREY S. LANTIS is associate professor of political science at the College of Wooster, Wooster, Ohio. His teaching and research interests include foreign policy analysis and international cooperation and conflict. A 2006 Fulbright Senior Scholar, he is the author of several books, including *The Life and Death of International Treaties* (forthcoming 2008), as well as numerous journal articles and book chapters. He is a past president of the Active Learning in International Affairs Section of the International Studies Association and coeditor of *The New International*

Studies Classroom: Active Teaching, Active Learning (2000). He earned his PhD from Ohio State University.

FRANKLIN BARR LEBO is an A.B.D. graduate assistant in the Department of Political Science at Kent State University, concentrating in transnational and comparative politics and policy. His research interests center on East Asia, along with matters pertaining to international peace and security. Lebo received his JD from the University of California, Hastings College of the Law and is a licensed attorney in the state of Ohio.

ERIC MOSKOWITZ is associate professor of political science at the College of Wooster, Wooster, Ohio. His research interests center on presidential decision making, the public policy–making process, and social and educational policy. He has also published on housing and neighborhood policy, the dynamics of racial politics in the United States, and contemporary U.S. decision making on foreign policy. He received his PhD from Indiana University.

ÖZGÜR ÖZDAMAR is an assistant professor in the Department of International Relations at the TOBB–University of Economics and Technology, Turkey. His research interests include foreign policy analysis, formal models of international relations, and energy security. He also specializes in Middle Eastern and Black Sea politics.

RODGER A. PAYNE is professor of political science at the University of Louisville and director of the Grawemeyer Award for Ideas Improving World Order. His research interests include U.S. foreign policy, global environmental politics, and democratization of international institutions. He is the coauthor (with Nayef H. Samhat) of *Democratizing Global Politics* (2004). He holds a PhD from the University of Maryland, College Park.

SEAN PAYNE is a doctoral student in the Department of Political Science at the University of Connecticut. His research interests include international relations theory, global environmental politics, global governance, and U.S. foreign policy.

THOMAS PRESTON is associate professor of political science at Washington State University and a Faculty Research Associate at the Moynihan Institute of Global Affairs at the Maxwell School, Syracuse University. His research interests focus on security studies, foreign affairs, and political psychology. He is the author of *From Lambs to Lions: Future Security Relationships in a World of Biological and Nuclear Weapons* (2007) and *The President and His Inner Circle: Leadership Style and the Advisory Process in Foreign Affairs* (2001) and coauthor of *Introduction to Political Psychology* (2004). He holds a PhD from Ohio State University.

MARC R. ROSENBLUM is associate professor of political science and Robert Dupuy Professor of Pan-American Studies at the University of New Orleans. His research interests are immigration policy and U.S.–Latin American relations. He is the author of *The Transnational Politics of U.S. Immigration Policy* (2004) and the coauthor (with Daniel J. Tichenor) of *The Oxford Handbook of International Migration* (forthcoming). He holds a PhD from the University of California, San Diego.

WENDY J. SCHILLER is an associate professor of political science at Brown University, Providence, Rhode Island. Her research interests are the U.S. Congress, interest groups, and political geography. She is the author of *Partners and Rivals* (2000) and coauthor (with Burdett Loomis) of the *Contemporary Congress* (5th ed.

2005). She has also published articles and book chapters on the modern and historical U.S. Senate and on congressional trade policy. She received her PhD from the University of Rochester.

WALT VANDERBUSH is associate professor of political science at Miami University, Oxford, Ohio. His research interests are Latin American political economy and U.S.–Latin American relations. He has written on labor, democracy, and neoliberalism in Mexico and with Patrick Haney is the coauthor of articles and of *The Cuban Embargo: The Domestic Politics of American Foreign Policy* (2005).

Introduction

Ralph G. Carter

When George W. Bush took office in 2001, significant international challenges greeted his new administration. Bush's generation had learned about foreign policy during the cold war, a period that focused on the Soviet-U.S. relationship and had as its overriding goal the prevention of nuclear war and possible global annihilation. The world had changed, however. In 1991 the Soviet Union broke into fifteen countries, challenging Russians and Americans to forge new, cooperative relationships while continuing to protect their national interests. What should new security arrangements entail? Should the United States offer foreign aid to Russia and the former Soviet republics? If so, how much, and under what terms? How could trade be structured to benefit all parties? Could the United States and these new countries be friends and competitors at the same time?

Without the glue of anticommunism as a bond, the United States and its traditional allies and trading partners faced the task of forging similar new cooperative relationships. Again, new questions arose: Should NATO continue to expand? What should the U.S. relationship be with the European Union? Were they friends or "friendly competitors"? What were the interests of the United States in Africa, Asia, and Latin America, and what should its relationships be with those nations?

Global issues also moved to the forefront of U.S. foreign policy. How should the United States react to terrorism, regional conflicts, the challenges involved in nation-building, attempted genocide, poverty, and threats to the environment? How much should the United States depend on international organizations in the pursuit of its goals? What place should international actors such as NATO, the United Nations, the World Bank, the World Trade Organization, and the International Monetary Fund have in U.S. foreign policy? Should the United States lead these international organizations, or should it act as a "first among equals" in a teamlike environment? As the international arena has changed, so has the U.S. foreign policy process. These changes in the internal policymaking process are as evident as the changes in the external environment. Understanding the dynamics of this process is the goal of this volume.

The "Old" Foreign Policy System

With the exception of a few periods of "thaw," the cold war dominated U.S. foreign policy from 1947 until the demise of the Soviet Union in late 1991. The threat of nuclear war between the U.S.- and Soviet-led blocs put a premium on national security policy, and U.S. foreign policy process evolved to meet that threat. As commander in chief, the president was at the heart of the process. Moreover, the National Security Act of 1947 gave the chief executive significant help by creating a unified Defense Department, the Central Intelligence Agency, the National Security Council, and the post of national security adviser.

Not surprisingly during that period, the focus of the policymaking process became the presidency and the executive branch. The process was well represented by the presidential preeminence model of foreign policy making, which views foreign policy as the result of decisions and actions by the president and his closest advisers and relevant other officials in the executive branch.[1] Other theoretical approaches were developed within the presidential preeminence model to reflect the processes by which presidential administrations made foreign policy. These included seeing their actions and decisions as

- optimal choices of a rational calculation of costs and benefits;
- choices between various bureaucratic routines appropriate to the situation; or
- the result of political processes played out within the administration by actors with differing degrees of power and interests in a particular issue.[2]

Members of Congress, interest groups, the news media, and the public were seen as playing little or no role in the making of foreign policy.[3]

The "New" Foreign Policy System

The post–cold war era triggered changes in the ways in which U.S. foreign policy is made. With the exception of the war power, the ability of the president to play a predominant role in shaping policy diminished, and the roles played by a host of other actors increased.[4] Two factors were crucial to these changes. First, the global economy became more interdependent, and decisions made elsewhere had greater influence on the United States. In short, "intermestic issues"—those that occur in the international environment but are reacted to as if they are domestic policy issues—are more common than was previously the case. Take, for example, the possible ways of formulating policy toward China: Should U.S. policy be defined primarily as national security policy, thus mobilizing the State and Defense Departments to rein in China's ability to threaten U.S. security interests? Should it increasingly be defined as trade policy, mobilizing officials in the Commerce Department, national and state chambers of commerce, trade groups, and U.S.-based multinational corporations that want to sell more to the enormous Chinese market? Should China policy be defined as "jobs policy," thus mobilizing members of the Labor Department and labor unions, whose members and leaders fear the loss of U.S. jobs to lower-paid Chinese workers? Should it be defined as human rights policy, thus mobilizing the State Department's under secretary for global affairs (under whose jurisdiction human rights issues fall) and such interest groups as Amnesty International, Human Rights Watch, and Freedom House? In short, how an issue is defined determines who will actively participate in its resolution.

Second, during the cold war, foreign and national security policy was deemed too important and too risky to let non-experts play a significant role. Primary policymakers included the president, his close White House advisers, and key officials from the foreign relations and defense bureaucracies—the members of the National Security Council and their staff, the State Department, the Defense Department, and the Central Intelligence Agency and other parts of the intelligence community. Congress and the public were generally relegated to supporting the actions of the White House, except in instances of a major policy mistake.

With the exception of protecting Americans from al Qaeda and its supporters, there is now no domestic political consensus regarding the central aims of U.S. foreign policy. More and more domestic actors can be expected to try to shape policy in the absence of widely shared norms that exclude their participation. Hence, one can expect more foreign policy activity by members of Congress, through legislation (whether an administration likes it or not) and other actions that administrations often resent (such as holding critical committee hearings, exercising oversight and monitoring the administration's foreign policy performance, requiring extensive briefings and reports by the administration, and making speeches critical of administration policy). Members of the opposition party in particular can be expected to challenge the president's foreign policy in terms of the ends pursued and the means employed.

Interest groups and other nongovernmental organizations will become more involved also, lobbying government officials on behalf of their policy preferences, using the print and electronic media to get their policy positions before the public and government officials, engaging in letter-writing campaigns to influence officials, using campaign contributions to help friendly officials win elections, and so on. Members of the media and other pundits will use their access to editorial pages, television, and the expanding constellation of news and information outlets to influence foreign policy in their preferred direction. Grassroots activists, public opinion pollsters, and others who claim to represent the public will also become involved. Even the ability of the president to control his own administration may weaken, as individuals in the bureaucracy become more active in policymaking or find themselves the targets of other actors.[5]

Thus, the unifying theme of this volume is that the U.S. foreign policy process is becoming more open, pluralistic, and partisan. It resembles more the decade leading up to World War II than the four decades that followed the war. One leading scholar summarizes the current period as follows:

> There now seems to be a *post–cold war dissensus* predicated on societal disagreement on the nature and extent of U.S. leadership, policy disagreement on the proper role, strategy, goals, and instruments of U.S. foreign policy, and procedural decentralization away from presidential leadership to more widely diffused involvement of actors from a wider circle of bureaucratic agencies, members of Congress, and nongovernmental actors.[6]

In short, the foreign policy process is becoming more like the domestic policy process, and thus it is becoming more political. As President Bill Clinton said in 1995, "The more time I spend on foreign policy . . . the more I become convinced that there is no longer a clear distinction between what is foreign and domestic."[7] More actors are involved, and they have their own foreign policy needs, interests, and agendas. Although the president still has impressive formal and informal foreign policy responsibilities and powers, he is now less able to dominate foreign policy processes and outcomes than was the case during the cold war.[8] Presidential foreign policy "wins" may be less frequent than in the past, and they will almost always represent hard-fought victories.

A number of other themes unify this volume. Jurisdictional competition between the president and Congress over the control and direction of foreign policy is commonplace. Even members of the president's own party resist his policies if they think the White House is trampling on the legitimate jurisdictional responsibilities of Congress to legislate policy or appropriate funds. The opposition party can be expected to challenge the president's wishes, and it does so in a number of cases. For example, during the 1990s, congressional Republicans developed a visceral dislike for President Clinton. It seemed that Republican Party leaders Trent Lott, Dick Armey, and Tom DeLay, along with powerful committee chair Jesse Helms, opposed anything Clinton supported. White House scandals, including the Monica Lewinsky affair and allegations of illegal campaign contributions, gave critics another reason to oppose Clinton's policy goals. The high-water mark of their opposition was Clinton's impeachment. More recently, the new Democratic-controlled Congress seems just as skeptical of the Bush administration, particularly when the White House refuses to share requested information and documents with Congress or invokes executive privilege in the face of congressional subpoenas to top administrative officials to testify under oath on Capitol Hill. Such bad blood between the branches strains the policymaking process. The themes discussed here reveal some of the chinks in the presidential preeminence model of policymaking.

The Case Study Approach

One often hears statements such as, "Today Washington announced . . ." or "The United States responded by . . ." Such pronouncements obscure the fact that individuals "announce" and decide how to "respond." Saying, "The United States decided to do X" is shorthand for the more accurate statement that a number of people acting in the name of the state decided to do X, usually for a variety of reasons. Case studies are perhaps the best way to illustrate how such individuals cooperate, conflict, and compromise to produce foreign policy.

The fifteen studies that make up this volume are teaching cases. The definition of a teaching case is that it tells the story of what happened, "who was involved, what they contended with, and, sometimes, how it came out." [9] Rather than provide analysis of why things happened as they did, teaching cases rely on the reader to determine why individuals took the stances or engaged in the actions discussed. They vividly illustrate how policymaking brings together individuals who see matters from different perspectives and who are motivated by an assortment of goals and objectives. Such cases also help show that these policymakers live in a political environment in which everything affects everything else; foreign policy decisions are not made in a vacuum. They affect and are affected by other foreign and domestic policy issues at the time the policy is devised and into the foreseeable future. Like the rest of the political process, foreign policy making can be a messy affair, and case studies help illustrate the process realistically.

An advantage of the cases in this book is their contemporary nature. Textbooks usually cover the broad themes and theoretical issues involved in foreign policy making, but they often do not present many contemporary illustrations of what happens or how things happen in the policymaking process. These cases focus on issues and events that confronted U.S. policymakers in the 1990s and into the 2000s. A second advantage of the studies here is their range. They were chosen to represent the array of external challenges and opportunities, substantive issues, internal political situations, and policymaking dynamics that seem likely to confront U.S. foreign policy makers repeatedly in the post–cold war and post–September 11 world.

Each case study offers a unique perspective on the events, issues, and policymakers involved, but beyond this uniqueness are patterns in the influences at work. Where do the causal factors for U.S. foreign policy arise? According to realists and neorealists, they arise beyond U.S. borders. These observers see foreign policy as a state's reaction to events taking place in an international system based on anarchy and lacking a strong legal structure. In essence, states can be expected to pursue their self-defined interests in ways that are, at least at some level, rational.[10] On the other hand, advocates of liberalism argue that what happens within a state's borders also matters, often as much as (or maybe more than) external situations facing policymakers. Thus for liberals and neoliberals, a central belief is that "*state structures matter:* the structure of their domestic governments and the values and views of their citizens affect their behavior in international affairs."[11] According to this point of view, one cannot ignore who is in the government, what they think, and what motivates them. Different administrations and Congresses will react differently to similar external events. The cases in this volume illustrate the importance of both external and internal factors and help in understanding what U.S. officials have been dealing with in the post–cold war and post–September 11 eras. In this respect, they provide a realistic understanding of how policy is actually made. They serve as reminders that people often have to make quick decisions based on less-than-complete information, and they help hone critical thinking skills in preparation for real-world situations.[12]

Each case opens with a section titled "Before You Begin," which poses questions about that particular case. These questions help in organizing thoughts and directing attention to important issues. All the cases follow a similar internal organization: the case is introduced, background information is provided, relevant events are related, and a conclusion is offered that should help readers identify some of the broader issues or themes involved. Each study is accompanied by a chronology of events and a list of key actors.

Case-based teaching requires class participation. Instructors ask questions, and students are expected to discuss what happened and, more important, determine why it happened as it did. Such active learning requires that students come to class prepared to contribute to an informed discussion of the case assignment, including putting themselves in the place of the major actors in order to assess issues and events: Why did policymakers do what they did? What internal or external factors affected their decisions? Was the option selected their only option? If not, why was that option chosen over others? What could be gained, and what could be lost? Students will get the most from this approach if they come to class having carefully thought about such things in addition to having reviewed the questions in "Before You Begin." Such preparation will make for a better understanding of the real world of foreign policy making.

As the cold war was ending, some observers of international politics began speculating about the nature of the post–cold war world. Many offered the optimistic assessment that international conflict would decline, and widely shared liberal values would become the new glue of international politics.[13] Violent conflict did not disappear, unfortunately, and not all people endorsed the same liberal values.[14] U.S. foreign policy still must deal with difficult issues involving the use of military force and how to protect national interests in an uncertain environment. The first three cases in this volume focus on U.S. decisions about whether and how to participate in military interventions. In chapter 1, Ryan Hendrickson and Frédérick Gagnon examine the efforts by the Clinton and Bush administrations to respond to the terrorist threat represented by Osama Bin Laden. In chapter 2, Jeffrey Lantis and Eric Moskowitz review the Bush administration's efforts to employ coercive diplomacy against the Iraq regime of Saddam Hussein. In chapter 3, Jennifer Holmes looks at the Clinton administration's efforts to stanch the flow of illegal drugs into the United States by helping the Colombian government fight drug traffickers—a decision that many believed risked U.S. involvement in Colombia's long-standing civil war—and how the Bush administration's "war on terrorism" affected U.S. policy toward Colombia.

The next five case studies examine national security and defense issues facing the United States. In chapter 4, Thomas Preston and Michael Infranco describe U.S. efforts to promote a negotiated settlement over Iran's nuclear weapons program, an approach made more difficult by U.S. unwillingness to talk to the

Iranians directly. In chapter 5, Patrick James and Özgür Özdamar examine the dynamics of the Clinton and Bush administrations' efforts to confront the threat of North Korean nuclearization. In chapter 6, Douglas Foyle reveals how a decision to allow an Arabia-based corporation to operate six of the busiest ports in the United States blew up in the face of the Bush administration. As a response to the global terrorist threat, the Bush administration's warrantless wiretapping of overseas phone calls made by U.S. citizens or residents is the focus of Louis Fisher's chapter 7. In chapter 8, Marc Rosenblum details the political dynamics behind efforts to reform U.S. immigration policy—both by those who wanted to tighten up the rules and by those who wanted to liberalize them.

Some observers thought the post–cold war world would be characterized by heightened international trade, so the next selection of case studies focuses on trade issues. In chapter 9, Robert Blecker illustrates how the U.S. steel industry sought to increase tariffs on imported steel and how the Bush administration responded. In chapter 10, trade issues involving friends and enemies are assessed by Patrick Haney and Walt Vanderbush in their examination of the 1996 Helms-Burton Act. This controversial legislation upset U.S. allies and trading partners by imposing more unilateral sanctions on the Castro regime in Cuba. A range of trade-related issues come to the fore in chapter 11, where Steven Hook and Franklin Lebo look at the impact of a wide array of interest groups in the Clinton and Bush administrations' decisions regarding trade with China. A thirty-year-long effort to "level the playing field" between U.S. and European corporations is the subject of chapter 12, in which Wendy Schiller and Ralph Carter illustrate how this policy ultimately failed in the face of economic threats sanctioned by the World Trade Organization.

A more liberal world would be one marked by a greater reliance on international organizations, institutions, and law. The last section of the book examines how U.S. approaches to multilateral policies mesh with the concerns of others in dealing with systemwide international issues. In chapter 13, Rodger Payne and Sean Payne focus on how the Clinton and Bush administrations dealt with the policy challenges presented by the Kyoto Protocol, the global climate change convention signed in 1997. In chapter 14, Donald Jackson and Ralph Carter illustrate the Clinton and Bush administrations' political dilemma when faced with the issue of how to react to the creation of the new International Criminal Court and the possibility that U.S. citizens might be tried before it for war crimes, crimes against humanity, and genocide. In chapter 15, Linda Cornett and Mark Gibney trace the evolution of Bush administration decisions concerning the detention of "enemy combatants" captured in the "war on terror" and the treatment of detainees in Iraq.

The cases here present the wide range of actors, interests, and issues in contemporary U.S. foreign policy. The conclusion returns to the book's primary unifying theme—that in the post–cold war period, U.S. foreign policy making is becoming increasingly open, pluralistic, and partisan. New issues have made their way onto the policy agenda, and many newcomers—agencies, interests, and constituencies—have become involved in addressing them. In short, U.S. foreign policy making looks increasingly like U.S. domestic policy making, and in a world marked by increasing interdependency among states, perhaps that is to be expected.

Notes

1. James M. Scott and A. Lane Crothers, "Out of the Cold: The Post–Cold War Context of U.S. Foreign Policy," in *After the End: Making U.S. Foreign Policy in the Post–Cold War World,* ed. James M. Scott (Durham, N.C.: Duke University Press, 1998), 1–25.

2. Graham Allison and Philip Zelikow, *Essence of Decision: Explaining the Cuban Missile Crisis,* 2nd ed. (New York: Longman, 1999).

3. See, for example, Samuel P. Huntington, *The Common Defense: Strategic Programs in National Politics* (New York: Columbia University Press, 1961); Roger Hilsman, *To Move a Nation* (New York: Doubleday, 1967); Morton Halperin, *Bureaucratic Politics and Foreign Policy* (Washington, D.C.: Brookings Institution Press, 1974); John Steinbruner, *The Cybernetic Theory of Decision: New Dimensions of Political Analysis* (Princeton, N.J.: Princeton University Press, 1974); Roger Hilsman, *The Politics of Policy Making in Defense and Foreign Affairs,* 2nd ed. (Englewood Cliffs, N.J.: Prentice Hall, 1990); and Allison and Zelikow, *Essence of Decision.*

4. See Ralph G. Carter and James M. Scott, "Taking the Lead: Congressional Foreign Policy Entrepreneurs in U.S. Foreign Policy," *Politics and Policy* (March 2004): 34–70; James M. Scott and Ralph G. Carter, "Acting on the Hill: Congressional Assertiveness in U.S. Foreign Policy," *Congress and the Presidency* 29 (Autumn 2002): 151–170; James M. Lindsay and Randall B. Ripley, "How Congress Influences Foreign and Defense Policy," in *Congress Resurgent: Foreign and Defense Policy on Capitol Hill,* ed. Randall B. Ripley and James M. Lindsay (Ann Arbor: University of Michigan Press, 1993), 17–35; James M. Lindsay, *Congress and the Politics of U.S. Foreign Policy* (Baltimore, Md.: Johns Hopkins University Press, 1994); and virtually all of the selections in Scott, *After the End.*

5. Scott and Crothers, "Out of the Cold"; James M. Scott, "Interbranch Policy Making after the End," in Scott, *After the End,* 389–407.

6. Scott, "Interbranch Policy Making after the End," 405.

7. Quoted in Ralph G. Carter, "Congress and Post–Cold War U.S. Foreign Policy," in Scott, *After the End,* 129–130.

8. See Carter, "Congress and Post–Cold War U.S. Foreign Policy"; Jerel Rosati and Stephen Twing, "The Presidency and U.S. Foreign Policy after the Cold War," in Scott, *After the End,* 29–56.

9. John Boehrer, quoted in Vicki L. Golich, "The ABCs of Case Teaching," *International Studies Perspectives* 1 (2000): 12.

10. There are lots of sources for realism and neorealism. For reasonably concise discussions of these topics, see David A. Lake, "Realism," in *The Oxford Companion to Politics of the World,* ed. Joel Krieger (Oxford: Oxford University Press, 1993), 771–773, or Allison and Zelikow, *Essence of Decision,* 30–33.

11. Allison and Zelikow, *Essence of Decision,* 39 (emphasis in original).

12. Laurence E. Lynn Jr., *Teaching and Learning with Cases: A Guidebook* (New York: Chatham House Publishers/Seven Bridges Press, 1999), 2.

13. See Francis Fukuyama, "The End of History?" *National Interest* 16 (Summer 1989): 3–16.

14. See Samuel P. Huntington, *The Clash of Civilizations and the Remaking of World Order* (New York: Simon and Schuster, 1996).

1 The United States versus Terrorism: Clinton, Bush, and Osama Bin Laden

Ryan C. Hendrickson and Frédérick Gagnon

Before You Begin

1. What is the traditionally accepted view of Congress's exercise of war powers during the cold war? How does that view compare to Congress's role leading up to military action in 1998 and 2001?
2. In the days prior to military action in 1998 and 2001, how did the diplomatic challenges differ for President Bill Clinton and President George W. Bush?
3. Is Congress's decision to endorse military action against those involved in the September 11, 2001, attacks a victory for Congress's war powers? If so, why?
4. Why does the director of the Central Intelligence Agency appear to play such a significant role in use-of-force decisions under Presidents Clinton and Bush?
5. Why does the national security advisor for Presidents Clinton and Bush appear to occupy a "privileged position" in terms of influencing the chief executive?
6. Did President Clinton's military action in 1998 have a "diversionary" intent? What evidence supports such a view? What evidence challenges it?

Introduction: Striking Back at Terrorism

The public, the media, and most members of Congress sometimes are not privy to the process in which U.S. foreign policy is made. Although President Bill Clinton and President George W. Bush are of different political parties, appear to have vastly different interests in policy matters, and certainly have divergent views of the appropriate role for the United States in international affairs, many similarities exist in the ways that they made decisions as commander in chief. On August 20, 1998, when Clinton launched missile strikes against alleged facilities of Osama Bin Laden in Sudan and Afghanistan, and on October 7, 2001, when Bush set in motion Operation Enduring Freedom against the Taliban and al Qaeda in Afghanistan, nearly all the critical military decisions were made by the executive branch. Unlike many other foreign policy issues in the post–cold war environment, the center of action concerning terrorism is the White House.

Background: Osama Bin Laden—The Man and His Mission

Prior to the Clinton administration's military strikes in August 1998, most Americans had never heard of Osama Bin Laden. He was, however, no stranger to the U.S. intelligence community. Bin Laden was born in 1957 into a wealthy, conservative family in Saudi Arabia with connections to the Al Saud, the Saudi royal family.[1] Bin Laden's first known foray into politics occurred in 1980, when he left Saudi Arabia to go to Afghanistan and support the *mujahidin,* the fighters who were resisting the Soviet takeover and occupation of Afghanistan with critical military assistance from the United States. Although the United States and Bin Laden were on the "same side" in Afghanistan, no hard evidence suggests that any U.S. government agency worked with or directly assisted him during that period.[2]

While in Afghanistan, Bin Laden assisted in the construction of roads and hospitals and provided some financial assistance to the rebels. His experience there, which may have involved combat, seems to have shaped his later belief that he and his movement could destroy a superpower through warfare.[3] Toward the end of the war, Bin Laden established an organization of radical Muslims that would become the foundation for al Qaeda, a network of supporters willing to advance their fundamentalist version of Islam using any means necessary.[4]

Bin Laden returned to Saudi Arabia in 1989, after the Afghan war ended. In 1991 Saudi officials seized Bin Laden's passport after he was caught smuggling weapons into the country from Yemen. He then moved to Sudan, where he invested heavily in its impoverished economy and developed a close relationship with Hassan al-Turabi, leader of the Sudanese National Islamic Front. Much of Bin Laden's financial support went toward Sudan's major export, gum, as well as pharmaceutical companies. He also assisted in the construction of an airport, a 750-mile highway, and a bank in the capital, Khartoum.[5]

During his years in Sudan, Bin Laden was suspected of being involved in a number of high-profile attacks around the world. The first occurred in 1992 in Aden, Yemen, when alleged Bin Laden associates planted a bomb in a hotel where American military personnel lived; the Americans left before the bomb exploded. Al Qaeda associates have also been connected to a 1994 attack on a Saudi National Guard station that resulted in the deaths of five American

The Clinton and Bush Administrations' Strikes against Osama Bin Laden

August 23, 1996 Osama Bin Laden issues his first *fatwa* against the United States.

February 23, 1998 Bin Laden issues his second *fatwa* against the United States.

August 7, 1998 Bombs explode at the U.S. embassies in Nairobi, Kenya, and Dar es Salaam, Tanzania.

August 14, 1998 Director of Central Intelligence George Tenet presents his agency's assessment that Bin Laden and his al Qaeda network were behind the attacks on the embassies.

August 17, 1998 President Bill Clinton admits to the nation that he misled the public about having an extramarital relationship with White House intern Monica Lewinsky.

August 19, 1998 While on vacation on Martha's Vineyard, Clinton speaks with national security advisor Samuel Berger and other senior advisers about possible strikes on Bin Laden.

August 20, 1998 In a 2:00 a.m. telephone conversation with Berger, Clinton authorizes strikes against Bin Laden. Missiles are launched on alleged al Qaeda sites in Afghanistan and Sudan.

Mid-September 1999 The Clinton administration initiates "the plan," consisting of broader covert operations intended to gather intelligence on Bin Laden and disrupt al Qaeda.

October 12, 2000 Al Qaeda launches a suicide boat attack against the USS *Cole* while it is docked in Aden, Yemen. Seventeen Americans are killed.

February 16, 2001 President George W. Bush, in cooperation with the United Kingdom, launches air strikes against Iraq for violations of the "no-fly" zone.

September 11, 2001 Al Qaeda operatives hijack four commercial aircraft, flying two into the World Trade Center towers and crashing another into the Pentagon. The fourth aircraft crashes in a field in Pennsylvania. The death toll is 2,995.

September 14, 2001 The Senate passes S.J. Res. 23, authorizing Bush to use all necessary and appropriate force against those associated with the September 11 strikes on the United States. The House of Representatives responds the following day by passing the resolution.

continued on the next page

continued from the previous page

September 15–16, 2001 President Bush holds meetings with foreign policy principals at Camp David to discuss military operations in retaliation for the September 11 attacks.

October 3, 2001 Uzbekistan signs on to allow U.S. military operations from its territory, the final logistical element in the U.S. plan for military action against the Taliban in Afghanistan.

October 6, 2001 Bush gives final approval for military action against Afghanistan.

October 7, 2001 The United States launches Operation Enduring Freedom against the Taliban and al Qaeda in Afghanistan.

December 7, 2001 The Taliban lose Kandahar, the last major city under their control.

military personnel. Four of five people arrested and beheaded by Saudi authorities for the bombings asserted that they had acted under Bin Laden's orders. Al Qaeda may have played a role in the 1996 Hizballah strike on Khobar Towers in Dhahran, Saudi Arabia, that took the lives of nineteen American soldiers. It has also been alleged that Bin Laden was involved in an aborted assassination plot against President Clinton in the Philippines in 1994.[6]

Bin Laden's network is believed to have had connections to the bombing of the World Trade Center in New York City in February 1993. Bin Laden followers from the war in Afghanistan were also convicted of an attempt to bomb U.S. passenger jets in 1995. His network was affiliated with a failed attempt to assassinate Pope John Paul II in 1995. The Islamic Group, which maintains an alliance with al Qaeda, claimed responsibility in 1997 for an attack in Egypt that claimed the lives of fifty-eight tourists. Although Bin Laden did not take responsibility for these actions, in multiple interviews he praised them and those who carried them out.[7] The State Department added al Qaeda to its list of terrorist organizations in 1997.

One of the first statements by Bin Laden to generate international attention occurred on August 23, 1996, when he publicly issued a *fatwa,* or decree (usually by a recognized religious leader), calling for a *jihad* (struggle or holy war) against the United States to oppose its military presence in Saudi Arabia that began with the 1991 Persian Gulf War.[8] He argued that Muslims had a legitimate right to drive the United States from the Islamic homeland, and he criticized Saudi Arabia for its alliance with the United States.[9] Under U.S. pressure, Bin

Laden was expelled from Sudan in 1996. He took refuge in Afghanistan, where he rekindled his friendship with Taliban leader Mullah Muhammad Omar.

In 1998 Bin Laden once again caught the eye of the world when on February 23 he issued a second *fatwa* in a fax to a London-based Arabic newsletter. In the communication, he made three central points: the United States should leave the Muslim holy land; the United States should end the "great devastation inflicted" upon the Iraqi people through its continuation of economic sanctions; and the United States was engaged in a religious and economic war against Muslims, while simultaneously serving Israel's interests vis-à-vis the Muslim world. Bin Laden called upon all Muslims to "kill the Americans and their allies—civilians and military," wherever possible.[10] Less than six months later, on August 7, 1998, his operatives bombed the U.S. embassies in Nairobi, Kenya, and Dar es Salaam, Tanzania. The attackers detonated two truck bombs minutes apart, killing 263 people, including 12 Americans. The strikes suggested a high degree of organizational capacity and a zeal uncommon among modern terrorists.[11]

Terrorism and Presidential Powers

The U.S. Constitution grants Congress the power to declare war, as well as other enumerated powers associated with the military. The president is given the explicit authority to act as commander in chief. Most constitutional scholars agree, however, that the president is empowered to use force without congressional approval to "repel sudden attacks" against the United States.[12] In other instances, the president must obtain Congress's approval prior to using force.

For much of U.S. history, Congress's war powers have been respected by the commander in chief.[13] With the cold war's onset and the widely accepted belief that the Soviet Union and communism represented a threat to the United States, the president's perception of his power as commander in chief became increasingly one of omnipotence. Since 1945 presidents have asserted broad military powers with few recognized limitations. Because Congress members agreed that communism should be checked, and because it was politically safer to let a president assume full responsibility for U.S. military endeavors, Congress often deferred to executive branch unilateralism in actions by the president as commander in chief.[14] This practice remained the norm until the 1973 passage of the War Powers Resolution, which was designed to reassert the authority that many felt Presidents Lyndon Johnson and Richard Nixon had usurped from Congress during the Vietnam War.[15] The resolution requires that the president "consult with Congress in every possible circumstance" prior to and after the introduction of U.S. forces into hostilities. The president must formally notify Congress within forty-eight hours of undertaking a use of force and must obtain Congress's approval within sixty days of the operation if it is ongoing; failing notification, U.S. troops must be withdrawn (P.L. 93-148). Despite its intent, the War Powers Resolution has been a failure. All presidents since 1973 have maintained that it is unconstitutional—arguing that it illegally limits their power as commander in chief—and Congress has often failed to enforce it.[16]

U.S. presidents have on occasion responded to terrorist threats with military force. In 1979, when Americans were being held captive by supporters of Ayatollah Ruhollah Khomeini at the U.S. embassy in Tehran, President Jimmy Carter planned a military rescue operation. No member of Congress was included in Carter's inner circle of decision makers.[17] In 1986, when President Ronald Reagan bombed Libya—including the compound of Libyan leader Mu'ammar Qadhafi—because of Libya's alleged involvement in an attack on a Berlin dance club frequented by Americans, a few members of Congress were informed of the forthcoming military action, but only three hours before the strikes occurred.[18] Both of these actions produced outrage among members of Congress who perceived them as violations of the War Powers Resolution, but no legislative remedies were undertaken to address their concerns. Like his recent predecessors, Bill Clinton also viewed his powers as commander in chief broadly, maintaining that congressional approval was not required for him to take military action.[19] Clinton's outlook is evidenced by U.S. military actions against Iraq, NATO air strikes in Bosnia and Kosovo, military deployments to Haiti and Somalia, and the use of force against Bin Laden, all of which occurred without specific congressional approval.

Clinton Strikes Bin Laden

Immediately after the August 1998 bombings of the U.S. embassies, experts from the Federal Bureau of Investigation (FBI) and the Central Intelligence Agency (CIA) rushed to East Africa to determine responsibility for the attacks. The evidence quickly pointed to Bin Laden. On August 14, Director of Central Intelligence (DCI) George Tenet presented his agency's analysis—a "judgment about responsibility"—to President Clinton. According to the CIA, additional evidence suggested that Bin Laden was planning another attack on Americans and that an important gathering of Bin Laden associates would take place in Afghanistan on August 20, 1998. At the meeting with Tenet, Clinton gave tentative approval to a military response and authorized his senior military advisers to move forward with operational plans.[20]

The bombings and their aftermath occurred at a difficult time for Clinton. On August 17, he testified to the Office of the Independent Counsel and a grand jury, by videoconferencing, that he had had an extramarital relationship with former White House intern Monica Lewinsky. Later that evening, in a national address, Clinton admitted that he had "misled" the American people about his relationship with Lewinsky.[21] After his address, Clinton and his family left for a vacation, but planning continued for military strikes against Bin Laden. On Wednesday, August 19, while on Martha's Vineyard, Clinton discussed the strikes with Vice President Al Gore. Senior leaders in Congress were also notified of possible military action. Throughout the day, Clinton spoke on four occasions by phone with his national security advisor, Samuel "Sandy" Berger, who was in Washington. In a call around 2:00 a.m. Thursday, Clinton gave final approval for the strikes.

Beginning on August 20 around 1:30 p.m. EST, seventy-nine cruise missiles were launched at targets in Sudan and Afghanistan from ships stationed in the Arabian and Red Seas. The Sudanese targets included the al-Shifa pharmaceutical plant, which the United States alleged was a chemical weapons factory. Six other sites were struck simultaneously in Afghanistan. Secretary of Defense William Cohen declared that al-Shifa was chosen because Bin Laden was heavily involved in Sudan's military-industrial complex and had an interest in acquiring chemical weapons.[22] The Pentagon added that Bin Laden had excellent relations with the Sudanese military and that the plant was heavily guarded by Sudanese soldiers. A senior intelligence official said that the CIA had found empta, a chemical compound used only in the production of chemical weapons, near the plant.[23] In discussing the sites hit in Afghanistan, General Henry Shelton, chairman of the Joint Chiefs of Staff, said that one "base camp" that served as the headquarters for Bin Laden's organization was struck. Other targets included a support camp, which served as a weapons storage facility, and four other weapons and tactical training camps.[24] It was later learned that Shelton and the joint chiefs had opposed one proposed target in Sudan and that it was eliminated from the military's list after Shelton protested. Otherwise, the joint chiefs supported the military action.[25]

Approximately twenty-five minutes after the strikes, Clinton addressed the nation, providing four justifications for his actions. First, he announced that "convincing evidence" pointed to Bin Laden's responsibility for the attacks on the embassies. Second, the president pointed to Bin Laden's history of terrorist activities. Third, Clinton argued that "compelling information" suggested that Bin Laden was planning another attack against the United States. Fourth, he said that Bin Laden sought to acquire chemical weapons.[26] In a second address to the nation later that evening, Clinton expanded on Bin Laden's previous declarations and activities and said that his senior military advisers had given him a "unanimous recommendation" to go forward with the strikes.[27] In mentioning the unanimous recommendation Clinton may have been anticipating the reaction from the public, 40 percent of whom believed that the Monica Lewinsky scandal may have influenced the decision to strike. Administration officials responded vehemently with denials that any link existed between the president's domestic troubles and the strikes at Bin Laden.[28] Though many Americans thought the "Lewinsky factor" may have entered into the decision to use force, 75 percent still supported the strikes.[29]

Consulting Congress

The night before the attacks, Berger phoned Speaker of the House Newt Gingrich, R-Ga., and Senate Majority Leader Trent Lott, R-Miss., and presented them with the evidence implicating Bin Laden. Senate Minority Leader Tom Daschle, D-S.D., also received a phone call before the strikes.[30] Berger attempted to call House Minority Leader Richard Gephardt, D-Mo., who was traveling in France. Clinton also phoned these leaders, with the exception of Gephardt, as he flew back to Washington to deliver his second address to the nation.[31] DCI Tenet notified, at minimum, Sen. Bob Kerrey, D-Neb., a member of the Senate Intelligence Committee, in advance of the strikes, which Kerrey strongly supported.[32] Other reports contend that Gingrich had been consulted and was privy to intelligence on Bin Laden before Berger's first phone calls were made.[33]

In retrospect, it is clear that the most senior leaders in Congress of both parties knew of the impending strikes. White House spokesman Michael McCurry purposely noted that all requirements of the War Powers Resolution were met, including its consultation mandate.[34] Clinton's actions were thus markedly different from those of other presidents who had used force against "terrorist actors," for example, Reagan's missile attack against Libya and Carter's attempted hostage rescue in Iran. In the aftermath of Clinton's strikes against Bin Laden there were no complaints about violations of the War Powers Resolution or Congress's war-making powers. Congress gave broad support to the president on constitutional grounds and, at the same time, played a tertiary role in the decision-making process for military action.

Although these strikes were the last overt military effort to kill Bin Laden before the terrorist attacks of September 11, 2001, the Clinton administration did not give up the hunt for Bin Laden.[35] Before Clinton left office, he authorized five different intelligence operations aimed at disrupting al Qaeda's planning and preempting terrorist activities.[36] Those plans depended heavily upon assistance from Afghan allies, who were providing intelligence and ostensibly carrying out military operations against Bin Laden.

The most comprehensive intelligence operation was known simply as "the plan" and went into effect around mid-September 1999. The plan sought to focus more attention on human intelligence gathering and expand the CIA's efforts to recruit well-qualified operatives who could be placed on the ground in Afghanistan to gather intelligence on Bin Laden. Another critical element of the plan was to develop and use the Predator, an unmanned aerial vehicle with intelligence-gathering and military strike capabilities. In 1999 the Predator was still in early development. From the inception of the plan until September 11, 2001, DCI Tenet did not deem the Predator capable of conducting military operations or of delivering its attached Hellfire missiles, although it had experienced some success in testing.[37] On at least two occasions before September 11, and perhaps a third, the Predator sighted Bin Laden.[38] Former counterterrorism coordinator Richard A. Clarke maintains that on Clinton's orders, the United States had submarines in place with cruise missiles ready for use against Bin Laden, but apparently not at times when "actionable intelligence" and military capability existed at the same time.[39] According to an Associated Press report, the CIA's inspector general later recommended that Tenet, as well as the leaders of the CIA's clandestine service and its counterterrorism center, be formally disciplined for failure to do more to protect the country from terrorist attacks before September 11, 2001.[40]

Tenet testified before the National Commission on Terrorist Attacks Upon the United States, or the 9/11 Commission, that prior to September 11 the United States was able to prevent a host of terrorist actions, including a number of "millennium plots." Tenet maintains that a strike against the U.S. embassy in Tirana, Albania, was prevented in 1998, as were plots to strike the U.S. embassy in Yemen in summer 2001 and an embassy in "a European capital."[41] There was not, however, enough intelligence to prevent the strike on the USS *Cole* in Yemen on October 12, 2000. As the destroyer was refueling in the port of Aden, a small boat pulled alongside it, and two men on a suicide mission detonated explosives that killed seventeen Americans and injured thirty-nine others. The CIA and FBI did not immediately blame the attacks on al Qaeda, but it was later determined that al Qaeda was responsible.

From a policymaking perspective, the bipartisan 9/11 Commission, which was established to review U.S. counterterrorism policies prior to September 11, made one especially important finding regarding the Clinton administration's counterterrorism policies: Senior officials of the National Security Council (NSC) and the CIA "differ[ed] starkly" in their assessment of the administration's objectives in regard to Bin Laden and therefore what types of actions they should be pursuing. NSC staffers, including Berger, maintained that the administration's policies were clear; authorization had been given to kill Bin Laden. In contrast, CIA officials asserted that the administration had sought the capture of Bin Laden and that only under certain conditions could he be killed.[42] Although misunderstandings or differences existed among key agencies regarding the effort to get Bin Laden, it is clear that the center of action for counterterrorism decisions and use of force was at the White House, with critical assistance provided by the CIA.

September 11: Authorization of Force and the War on Terrorism

President George W. Bush was made aware of the events that unfolded on September 11 while visiting with children at Emma E. Booker Elementary School in Sarasota, Florida. Upon hearing that an aircraft had crashed into the Pentagon, Bush later said, he thought to himself, "We're at war. . . . Somebody is going to pay."[43] After the session with the children ended, Bush's Secret Service detail quickly escorted him to Air Force One. As it was not considered safe to fly the president back to Washington immediately, Bush was flown to Barksdale Air Force Base in Louisiana, where he issued a short statement to the public. On the advice of the Secret Service and Vice President Richard Cheney, Bush then flew to Offut Air Force Base in Omaha, Nebraska. From there, Bush spoke by phone with members of his National Security Council, including DCI Tenet, who reported that Osama Bin Laden was behind the attacks.[44] By early evening, Bush was back at the White House, where deliberations began on how to address the crisis.

Before the September 11 attacks, Bush had already used force in one major military strike on Iraq. On February 16, 2001, his administration, in cooperation with the United Kingdom, had conducted air strikes on five Iraqi command and control stations, which included mostly radars and air defense systems. The administration justified these strikes as being in response to repeated violations of rules governing the U.S.-imposed northern and southern "no-fly" zones over Iraq. Twenty-four aircraft carried out the strikes, including six from the United Kingdom.[45]

Although the strikes received strong congressional support, it is noteworthy that the administration made the decision without consulting with Congress. At the time, there was no immediately perceived defensive need for the strikes. U.S. aircraft had definitely been fired upon while patrolling the no-fly zones, but the volleys posed a minimal threat to the aircraft and had become commonplace since December 1998, when President Clinton approved four days of strikes after Saddam Hussein's government refused to grant UN weapons inspectors access to parts of the country. Secretary Cohen had notified senior congressional leaders that the strikes were going to occur, but no member of Congress was involved in the actual decision to use force.[46] In this regard, the military planning stage in the Bush administration was similar to that in Clinton's, but different in terms of Bush's complete disregard for Congress prior to the strikes,[47] certainly a violation of the War Powers Resolution's consultation requirement.

The constitutional dynamics and the authority of the president to respond to the September 11 attacks with military action were considerably different from the February 2001 strikes on Iraq. Because the United States was directly attacked, most constitutional experts would concur that the Constitution allowed Bush, as commander in chief, to respond with force in defense of the nation. In addition, Article 51 of the United Nations Charter permits all member states to act in self-defense if attacked.[48] The Bush administration, however, quickly turned to Congress for formal authorization for the use of force. The public was strongly in favor of a military response, and by approaching Congress the administration could avoid raising constitutional questions about the legitimacy of its military actions. At the same time, legitimate constitutional questions existed in terms of whom the United States would be at war with. Part of the difficulty of this issue is that the enemy is not easily defined, identified, or targeted.

When Bush administration officials first met with congressional leaders and their senior staff members on September 12, congressional staffers were initially struck by the sweeping nature of the administration's force authorization proposal. Its request included the authority to "deter and pre-empt any future acts of terrorism or aggression against the United States" and essentially unrestricted financial resources for military responses, which would infringe on Congress's constitutional authority to appropriate money.[49] Key legislators, such as Senate Majority Leader Daschle and Sen. Robert C. Byrd, D-W.V., thought it was Congress's duty to avoid giving the president "a blank check to go anywhere, anytime, against anyone."[50] During deliberations over the language of the resolution, administration officials agreed to eliminate *pre-empt* and replace it with *prevent.*[51] The request for unlimited spending powers was deleted.[52] As of late evening on September 13, final agreement on the resolution language had not been reached.[53]

On the morning of September 14, Daschle and Senate Minority Leader Lott met with their respective caucuses. Later that morning, the Senate approved, 98–0, S.J. Res. 23 (P.L. 107-40), granting the president sweeping powers to initiate military action. The key provision of the resolution concerning force authorization stated,

> That the President is authorized to use all necessary and appropriate force against those nations, organizations, or persons he determines planned, authorized, committed, or aided the terrorist attacks that occurred on September 11, 2001, or harbored such organizations or persons, in order to prevent any future acts of international terrorism against the United States by such organizations or persons.

The process by which this resolution was crafted and eventually voted on is uncharacteristic in that it was not passed from a formal committee of the House or Senate, and there was no public debate on the constitutional merits of the resolution. The White House consulted with Congress and revised its original proposal based on congressional input, but all in private sessions. A day after the Senate approved the resolution, the House did so as well, in a 420–1 vote. Rep. Barbara Lee, D-Calif., was the only member of Congress who voted against the measure, maintaining that it provided a "blank check" to the president and granted him "overly broad powers."[54]

In most cases, senators and representatives commented on the resolution after the vote. A number of senior Democratic senators heralded the resolution as a victory for the principle of checks and balances. There is no doubt that Congress forced some important changes in the resolution's language, exercised and demanded its constitutional prerogatives on appropriations, and even inserted a reference to the War Powers Resolution. Congress also limited the administration's military response to only those "nations, organizations, or persons" associated with the September 11 attacks. These "congressional demands" were noted by senators Carl Levin, D-Mich., and Joseph Biden, D-Del., among others.[55] Regardless, the resolution language remains quite broad and grants considerable discretion to the president in determining who is responsible for the attacks and how an organization or individuals may be related to the events of September 11. It is easy to interpret the resolution in a number of equally legitimate ways. The process was constitutional, with the White House seeking congressional authority to act and the House and Senate voting to grant such authority. At the same time, however, some observers maintain that Congress abdicated much of its war power through the resolution's broad and ambiguous language and by granting the president excessive discretion as commander in chief.[56]

These interactions appear to be the last instance prior to the decision to use force against Afghanistan and al Qaeda when Congress played a substantive role. It is difficult to find any meaningful congressional input between the House vote on September 15 and the initiation of Operation Enduring Freedom on October 7, where a member of Congress had a role in determining whom to go to war against or when to respond militarily. On September 18, President Bush made clear his views on the constitutionality of his powers as commander in chief. With an approval rating at 90 percent, Bush expressed his appreciation to the leaders of the House and Senate for passing the resolution authorizing the use of force but noted, in the same manner as other presidents since World War II,

> I maintain the longstanding position of the executive branch regarding the President's constitutional authority to use force, including the Armed Forces of the United States and regarding the constitutionality of the War Powers Resolution.[57]

In short, although Bush welcomed the congressional support displayed in the passage of the resolution on force, in his view he did not need the resolution to act. This position echoes Vice President Cheney's conception of presidential war powers. Cheney agrees with many who believe the War Powers Act is unconstitutional and once said, "I don't think you should restrict the president's authority to deploy military forces because of the Vietnam experience."[58]

Whom to Strike

When administration officials first met with the president to discuss the September 11 attacks and devise a response, there was great confusion over what should be done.[59] As noted earlier, DCI Tenet reported almost immediately that Bin Laden was responsible for the attacks. Over breakfast on the morning of September 11, before the first plane hit the Twin Towers, Tenet had told former senator David Boren, R-Okla., that Bin Laden was his greatest security concern. As DCI during the Clinton administration, Tenet had warned Boren not to appear at any public New Year's celebrations because he feared a terrorist strike. According to Boren, Tenet was almost obsessed with Bin Laden during that period.[60]

After Tenet presented his conclusions to Bush cabinet officials, or "principals," differences in opinion immediately surfaced over where to direct a retaliatory attack. As the authorization proposal floated to congressional leaders made evident, the administration wanted broad powers to strike at any terrorist threat. In the first days after the attacks on the United States, Secretary of Defense Donald Rumsfeld and, to an even greater extent, Deputy Secretary of

Defense Paul Wolfowitz argued that this was an opportune time to think broadly about a military response not only against Bin Laden but also against Iraq.

The first weekend following the attacks, Bush convened the principals at Camp David to begin planning for a broad war on terrorism. On the first day of the meetings, Saturday, September 15, Rumsfeld and Wolfowitz pressed for making Iraq a target of the planned military response. Secretary of State Colin Powell made the case that Bin Laden should be the sole focus of the response, in part because he believed that international support existed for attacking Bin Laden but not Iraq. General Shelton was surprised that Iraq was even in consideration and also favored a military response only against Bin Laden. Tenet and Vice President Cheney focused their attention on Bin Laden. Andrew Card, White House chief of staff, also voiced the opinion that al Qaeda should be the target of the response.[61] Bush made the decision on September 15 to focus the administration's response on al Qaeda only. After Bush returned to the White House on Monday, September 17, he told his senior principals that Iraq would not be a target for a military response at that time. Former administration officials confirm that it was Bush's view that it was not the appropriate time to strike Iraq, although Bush felt that Iraq was somehow complicit in the September 11 attacks.[62]

Less is known about the personal views of National Security Advisor Condoleezza Rice, who appears to have been the president's central coordinator at planning sessions and who absorbed information and views and then consulted privately with Bush on the options. Rice appears not to have been engaged in the open debates over the targets but rather to have served as a meeting manager who tried to keep the principals and the president focused on their task. Said Bush of Rice, "I feel comfortable being—one of the things, I can be totally unscripted or unrehearsed with Condi. That's the nature of her job, is to absorb my—is to help, you know, kind of say, well, Mr. President I appreciate that point of view, and I think you ought to think this way a little bit."[63]

The personal relationship between Rice and Bush is similar to that between President Clinton and his national security advisor, Sandy Berger, prior to the August 1998 strikes on Bin Laden. Clinton consulted closely with Berger, more than with any other principal in the hours preceding the attacks. As Rice was to Bush, Berger was a close confidant of President Clinton and had a keen sense of how far and how fast to push the president for answers. Berger had developed a long-standing relationship with Clinton before Clinton became president, as Rice had with Bush.[64]

With Iraq no longer a target, and apparently with heavy input from George Tenet, the Taliban and al Qaeda were increasingly viewed as one entity, ending any lingering debate over who to strike. The Taliban had come to power in 1996 and governed Afghanistan under an extreme interpretation of the *sharia,* or Islamic law.[65] It provided sanctuary for Bin Laden in 1996, when he was expelled from Sudan, and protected him after the 1998 strikes on the U.S. embassies in East Africa. The Taliban also gave him communications equipment and security guards. In exchange, Bin Laden helped the Taliban train its military and expand its political control over Afghanistan, and he also provided financial assistance to Mullah Omar. It has been alleged that Mullah Omar and Bin Laden were so close that Omar took one of Bin Laden's daughters as one of his wives.[66]

On September 17, Bush instructed Colin Powell to issue an ultimatum to the Taliban: either turn over Bin Laden or face severe consequences from the United States. On Sunday, September 23, the CIA assessed that Mullah Omar would side with Bin Laden and refuse to give up the al Qaeda leader. That, indeed, was what happened.[67]

When to Attack

After they decided whom to attack, the question plaguing the Bush administration, and especially President Bush, was when, or more accurately, how quickly to initiate the strikes. In the first days after September 11, Secretary Rumsfeld offered that it would take at least sixty days to get the military in place and ready for a major offensive. General Tommy Franks, head of Central Command, concurred but more conservatively estimated that it could take several months.[68] President Bush wanted to be aggressive in time and strategy and avoid any comparison with President Clinton's military strikes, which he viewed as cautious and risk averse. He felt that Clinton's missile strikes amounted to little more than "pounding sand" with cruise missiles and instead wanted to engage the enemy aggressively.

Bush was attracted to one of the strategies presented by General Shelton. The plan Bush preferred entailed the launch of cruise missiles, air raids on Taliban and al Qaeda defenses, and the use of Special Operations Forces, and thus the insertion of "boots on the ground," all working in concert to combat al Qaeda and the Taliban. In addition, the CIA was to enlist the support of anti-Taliban groups in the northern and southern regions of Afghanistan to attack the Taliban with the assistance of special operations forces and CIA operatives.

Surprisingly, the Defense Department, to Rumsfeld's dismay, had no military plans on the books for attacking Afghanistan. Even as late as September 23,

Rumsfeld was still without a comprehensive war plan from the Pentagon.[69] That circumstance lends credence to the view that at least the Pentagon—and perhaps the entire Bush administration—had not previously considered the Taliban a major security threat to the United States, though the CIA had viewed al Qaeda and the Taliban as essentially inseparable.

As the military plans moved forward, the need for diplomatic allies in the Middle East quickly became clear. To insert special operations forces and to attack from the south, the United States needed access to military bases in the Persian Gulf. Oman, one of the best U.S. allies in the region, had assisted the Clinton administration with the use of its bases in the 1998 air strikes on Iraq. Oman had also helped the Carter administration when it attempted to rescue the American hostages from Iran in 1980. Although Oman did not immediately rush to assist the Bush administration, it ultimately agreed to lend its support, as did Bahrain and the United Arab Emirates. To Secretary Powell's surprise, Pakistani president General Pervez Musharraf, who had had friendly relations with the Taliban, agreed almost immediately to Bush's multiple diplomatic, intelligence, and military requests.[70]

The biggest operational and diplomatic obstacle was securing staging areas for combat and search and rescue operations north of Afghanistan. To obtain permission to operate from military bases in some of the former Soviet republics, the administration requested the assistance of Russian president Vladimir Putin in making diplomatic overtures in the region. Putin, who exercised considerable diplomatic influence with nearly all of the former republics, agreed on the condition that U.S. actions were only temporary and did not represent a long-term military presence in the region.[71]

This Central Asian element was the final piece of the puzzle needed before a military response could be initiated. Uzbekistan—whose president, Islam Karimov, did not have good relations with President Putin—was a preferred site. In responding to the U.S. request, Karimov used what diplomatic leverage he could. The Uzbeks initially demanded NATO membership, a $50 million loan, and what amounted to a full-fledged security guarantee from the United States. Rumsfeld traveled abroad on October 2 to meet with Karimov and other key leaders in the region. Although the United States did not grant Karimov's every wish, the Uzbeks signed on to assist the United States on October 3. The deal was sealed on Friday, October 5, when Rumsfeld appeared at a press conference in Tashkent, Uzbekistan, with Karimov. The secretary noted that the United States had a long-term interest in working with Uzbekistan, a statement that went beyond the immediate needs of the United States but was insisted on by

Karimov.[72] On the same day, General Franks told Bush that he was ready to begin full military operations. The following day, Rumsfeld returned to Washington and informed the president that the Pentagon was ready to initiate military operations. Bush then gave the final approval for action. The military launched its first strikes on the Taliban the following day, October 7. The Taliban regime was brought down 102 days after the terrorist attacks of 9/11, and American support for conduct of the war remained near 90 percent for the duration of the fighting in 2001.[73]

Conclusion: Presidential Leadership in the War on Terrorism

As of March 2007 Osama Bin Laden and Mullah Omar remained at large and were presumed to be somewhere along the Afghanistan-Pakistan border.[74] A large number of unverified claims about Bin Laden's death have been made over the last few years. Yet he continues to communicate through audiotapes sent to members of the Arab news media, and Mullah Omar's efforts to reorganize remnants of the Taliban in Afghanistan appear to be effective.[75] According to a former adviser to the special representative of the secretary general of the United Nations, "Afghanistan has stepped back from a tipping point. . . . the Taliban-led insurgency is still active on both sides of the Afghan-Pakistani border, and the frontier region has once again become a refuge for what President George W. Bush once called the main threat to the United States—'terrorist groups of global reach.'"[76] Moreover, reports indicate that a new generation of al Qaeda leaders, battle tested in places such as Afghanistan and Chechnya, has emerged in the Afghanistan-Pakistan border area to take operational control of the terror network.[77] Furthermore, al Qaeda continues to inspire, if not actively plan, attacks against Americans and their supporters in the Bush administration's war on terrorism. Attacks by Islamist jihadists to undermine the war in Iraq and to drive non-Muslims from Muslim lands have occurred in Europe, the Middle East, North Africa, and Southeast Asia.

In the Clinton and Bush administrations' military actions against al Qaeda, the White House has been the heart of the policymaking process, with limited formal input from others. This finding contrasts sharply with most other cases in this book—and in general with U.S. foreign policymaking in the post–cold war era—in which multiple bureaucratic officials, individual members of Congress, and individuals outside of government often play critical roles. Although Congress has considerable formal leverage through the War Powers Resolution and the Constitution to demand a substantive role for itself in matters concerning the decision to go to war, it is largely the president who controls the policymaking process regarding such a decision. Bush and Clinton, to different degrees, consulted with Congress, but in their formal communications with Capitol Hill, they asserted essentially unlimited powers as commander in chief, as had all presidents during the cold war.

The national security advisors of Clinton and Bush played key roles prior to the use of force. Sandy Berger and Condoleezza Rice, respectively, acted as primary confidants, consulting privately with the commander in chief. It appears that the national security advisor was the most trusted principal among all senior-level foreign policy decision makers in both administrations.

DCI Tenet was influential in defining the targets for the eventual military response. Tenet's presence and contributions were sought during times of crisis by Clinton and by Bush. DCIs had previously been central operators in planning military operations, as Allen Dulles was in the Bay of Pigs invasion in 1961, but it is difficult to find comparable recent examples. Following the recommendations of the 9/11 Commission, Congress adopted the Intelligence Reform and Terrorism Prevention Act of 2004, which created the position of director of national intelligence, or DNI.[78] Charged with coordinating the nation's intelligence community, the DNI seems likely to become a key figure of foreign policy decision making for the foreseeable future, as intelligence gathering to thwart terrorism will be central to U.S. national security for years to come. The fact that the first DNI, John Negroponte, resigned that position to take a lower-level position—the number-two position at the Department of State—suggests the significant organizational challenges of coordinating the nation's intelligence community.

The public widely supported the military actions of Clinton and Bush. Although many people suspected that Clinton's strikes on al Qaeda may have been a "diversionary military action" related to the Lewinsky scandal, his approval ratings remained high in the days following the strikes.[79] President Bush's political approval ratings soared soon after the September 11 tragedy and remained exceptionally high during the war in Afghanistan. The public has supported presidential leadership in the use of force against terrorists and has tacitly accepted that Congress's war powers have little relevance in such actions. Only time will tell whether the 2007 creation of a bipartisan Congressional Anti-Terrorism Caucus, a sixty-seven-member group led by Republicans Kay Granger of Texas and Sue Myrick of North Carolina and Democrats Bud Cramer of Alabama and Ben Chandler of Kentucky, will have any impact on congressional involvement in decisions to use force against terrorist targets.[80]

Key Actors

Samuel "Sandy" Berger National security advisor, principal adviser to President Bill Clinton leading up to strikes in 1998 against Osama Bin Laden and his network in Sudan and Afghanistan.

Osama Bin Laden Leader of al Qaeda, which was responsible for the bombings of U.S. embassies in Nairobi, Kenya, and Dar es Salaam, Tanzania, and the September 11 attacks.

George W. Bush President, principal decision maker for initiating Operation Enduring Freedom against the Taliban and al Qaeda in 2001 in Afghanistan.

Richard A. Clark Counterterrorism coordinator for Presidents Clinton and Bush.

Bill Clinton President, principal decision maker for strikes against Bin Laden in 1998.

Condoleezza Rice National security advisor, principal adviser to Bush in the lead-up to attacking the Taliban and al Qaeda in Afghanistan in 2001.

Hugh "Henry" Shelton Chairman of the Joint Chiefs of Staff under Clinton and Bush, provided Bush with options for striking the Taliban and al Qaeda after the September 11 attacks.

George Tenet Director of the Central Intelligence Agency under Clinton and Bush, exercised great influence in determining whom to strike after the September 11 attacks on the United States.

Paul Wolfowitz Deputy secretary of defense, most aggressive advocate for military strikes on Iraq immediately after September 11.

Notes

1. Osama Bin Laden's father came from Hadhramaut, an eastern province of Yemen known for its intense Wahhabism, a strict, conservative interpretation of Islam. The elder Bin Laden earned an estimated $5 billion in the construction business, and the Saudi monarchy was one of his chief clients. Two of his principal projects were the renovations of Islamic holy sites in Mecca and Medina.

The Al Sauds took power in the early 1900s, when King Abd al-Aziz enlisted the support of local followers of Wahhabism in taking control of the Arabian Peninsula from a rival family. In 1902 the king and his allies captured Riyadh, the Saudi capital (and later the birthplace of Bin Laden), and in 1923 declared the establishment of the Kingdom of Saudi Arabia. See Michael C. Hudson, *Arab Politics: The Search for Legitimacy* (New

Haven: Yale University Press, 1977), 171; John F. Burns, "Remote Yemen May Be Key to Terrorist's Past and Future," *New York Times,* November 5, 2000. Much of the information on Bin Laden's biography comes from Tim Weiner, "U.S. Hard Put to Find Proof Bin Laden Directed Attacks," *New York Times,* April 13, 1999, A1.

2. George Crile, *Charlie Wilson's War* (New York: Atlantic Monthly Press, 2003).

3. James S. Robbins, "Bin Laden's War," in *Terrorism and Counterterrorism: Under the New Security Environment,* ed. Russell D. Howard and Reid L. Sawyer (Guilford, Conn.: McGraw-Hill/Dushkin, 2004), 397.

4. See Vernon Loeb, "A Global, Pan-Islamic Network; Terrorism Entrepreneur Unifies Groups Financially, Politically," *New York Times,* August 23, 1998, A1. See also National Commission on Terrorist Attacks Upon the United States (the 9/11 Commission), "Overview of the Enemy," staff statement no. 15, June 21, 2004, www.9-11 commission.gov/hearings/hearing12/staff_statement_15.pdf.

5. See Weiner, "U.S. Hard Put," and Loeb, "A Global, Pan-Islamic Network." Loeb asserts that Bin Laden supported training camps in northern Sudan "for radicals from Egypt, Algeria, and Tunisia, as well as Palestinians" (A1).

6. Weiner, "U.S. Hard Put"; 9/11 Commission, "Overview of the Enemy"; Dan Eggen, "9/11 Panel Links al Qaeda, Iran: Bin Laden May Have Part in Khobar Towers, Report Says," *Washington Post,* June 26, 2004.

7. Loeb, "A Global, Pan-Islamic Network"; Robbins, "Bin Laden's War," 394.

8. *Jihad* is the religious duty to defend Islam against attack. This defense can come in many forms, including armed resistance.

9. "Saudi Militant Is Said to Urge Forced Ouster of U.S. Troops," *New York Times,* August 31, 1996, A2.

10. For a reprint and analysis of the declaration, see Magnus Ranstorp, "Interpreting the Broader Context and Meaning of Bin-Laden's Fatwa," *Studies in Conflict and Terrorism* 21 (1998): 321–330. See also Bernard Lewis, "License to Kill: Usama bin Laden's Declaration of Jihad," *Foreign Affairs,* November/December 1998, 14–19.

11. For the Federal Bureau of Investigation's executive summary of the attacks, made available to the public on November 18, 1998, see www.pbs.org/wgbh/pages/frontline/shows/binladen/bombings/summary.html.

12. Charles A. Lofgren, "War-Making under the Constitution: The Original Understanding," *Yale Law Journal* 81 (1972): 672–702.

13. Francis D. Wormuth and Edwin B. Firmage, *To Chain the Dog of War* (Urbana: University of Illinois Press, 1989).

14. Ryan C. Hendrickson, *The Clinton Wars: The Constitution, Congress and War Powers* (Nashville: Vanderbilt University Press, 2002).

15. Robert David Johnson, *Congress and the Cold War* (Cambridge: Cambridge University Press, 2006), 190–193.

16. Michael J. Glennon, "Too Far Apart: The War Powers Resolution," *University of Miami Law Review* 50 (1995): 17–31; Edward Keynes, "The War Powers Resolution: A Bad Idea Whose Time Has Come and Gone," *University of Toledo Law Review* 23 (1992): 343–362.

17. Sen. Robert C. Byrd, D-W.V., appears to be the only member of Congress Carter met with prior to the operation. On April 23, 1980, Carter asked him to come to the White House for discussion of the Iranian situation and revealed plans for a "covert operation" to rescue the Americans held hostage in Iran. Byrd returned home after the discussion and had "a troubled sleep." The following day he received an urgent call from

Secretary of State Cyrus Vance, who told him that "with reference to the operation which the President discussed with you yesterday, we have lost some helicopters—other helicopters are on their way back." That's when Byrd understood he had apparently been selected by Carter as the sole point of Hill contact for "consultation." Robert C. Byrd, *Losing America: Confronting a Reckless and Arrogant Presidency* (New York: Norton, 2004), 188–190. The absence of consultation within the administration prompted Cyrus Vance to resign. Robert A. Strong, *Working in the World: Jimmy Carter and the Making of American Foreign Policy* (Baton Rouge: Louisiana State University Press, 2000), chap. 9.

18. Pat Towell, "After Raid on Libya, New Questions on the Hill," *Congressional Quarterly Weekly Report,* April 19, 1986, 838.

19. Hendrickson, *The Clinton Wars,* 104.

20. "Press Briefing with National Security Advisor Berger on U.S. Strikes in Sudan and Afghanistan," August 20, 1998, http://secretary.state.gov/www/statements/1998/980820.html.

21. Bill Clinton, "Address to the Nation on Testimony before the Independent Counsel's Grand Jury," Weekly Compilation of Presidential Documents, August 28, 1998, 1638, available at www.gpoaccess.gov/wcomp/index.html; James Bennet, "Testing of a President: The Overview," *New York Times,* August 18, 1998, A1.

22. DefenseLINK News, "DoD News Briefing," August 20, 1998, www.defenselink.mil/news/Aug1998/t08201998_t820brfg.html.

23. DefenseLINK News, Background Briefing, "Terrorist Camp Strikes," August 20, 1998, www.defenselink.mil/news/Aug1998/x08201998_x820bomb.html.

24. Defense LINK News, "DoD News Briefing," August 20, 1998.

25. James Risen, "Question of Evidence: A Special Report," *New York Times,* October 27, 1999, A1.

26. Bill Clinton, "Remarks on Departure for Washington, D.C., from Martha's Vineyard, Massachusetts," Weekly Compilation of Presidential Documents, August 28, 1998, 1642.

27. Bill Clinton, "Address to the Nation on Military Action against Terrorist Sites in Afghanistan and Sudan," Weekly Compilation of Presidential Documents, August 28, 1998, 1643.

28. For example, see Secretary of State Madeleine Albright's statements, "Interview on NBC-TV *Today Show* with Katie Couric," August 21, 1998, http://secretary.state.gov/www/statements/1998/980821.html.

29. For polling data, see Marck Z. Barabak, "The Times Poll," *Los Angeles Times,* August 23, 1998, A1; Bruce Westbrook, "War or a 'Wag'?" *Houston Chronicle,* August 25, 1998, 1; Marcella Bombardieri, "Wagging Dog? Fine, Some Say," *Boston Globe,* August 22, 1998, A8.

30. Office of the Press Secretary, "Press Briefing by McCurry in Gaggle," August 20, 1998, www.clintonpresidentialcenter.org/legacy/082098-press-briefing-by-mccurry-in-gaggle.htm; see also Chuck McCutcheon, "Lawmakers Back Missile Strikes Despite a Bit of GOP Skepticism," *CQ Weekly,* August 22, 1998, 2289.

31. McCutcheon, "Lawmakers Back Missile Strikes."

32. "National Commission on Terrorist Attacks Upon the United States, Eighth Hearing," March 24, 2004, http://9-11commission.gov/archive/hearing8/9-11Commission-Hearing-2004-03-24.htm.

33. Office of the Press Secretary, "Press Briefing by McCurry in Gaggle"; see also McCutcheon, "Lawmakers Back Missile Strikes," 2289.

34. See Office of the Press Secretary, "Press Briefing by McCurry in Gaggle."

35. Questions later surfaced in the media concerning the wisdom of targeting the plant in Sudan, given its marginal, if not precarious, linkage to Bin Laden. Risen, "Question of Evidence."

36. Bob Woodward, *Bush at War* (New York: Simon and Schuster, 2002).

37. George Tenet, "Written Statement for the Record of the Director of Central Intelligence before the National Commission on Terrorist Attacks Upon the United States," March 24, 2004, http://9-11commission.gov/hearings/hearing8/tenet_statement.pdf.

38. Tenet maintains that it is likely that two sightings occurred, but Richard A. Clark, former counterterrorism coordinator, maintains that there were three occasions. "Testimony of Richard A. Clarke before the National Commission on Terrorist Attacks Upon the United States," March 24, 2004, 3, http://9-11commission.gov/hearings/hearing8/clarke_statement.pdf.

39. Ibid.

40. Katherine Shrader, "9-11 Attacks: Report Critical of CIA Officials," Associated Press, reported in *Fort Worth Star-Telegram,* August 26, 2005, 8A.

41. Tenet, "Written Statement," 21.

42. National Commission on Terrorist Attacks Upon the United States, "Intelligence Policy," staff statement no. 7, March 24, 2004, 8–9, http://9-11commission.gov/hearings/hearing8/staff_statement_7.pdf. Charles-Philippe David argues that the bureaucratic rivalries between Clinton's senior advisers and the absence of a clear plan to fight terrorism explain why the chase of Bin Laden was unsuccessful during the Clinton years. Charles-Philippe David, *Au sein de la Maison-Blanche. La formulation de la politique étrangère des Etats-Unis* (Sainte-Foy: Les Presses de l'Université Laval, 2004), 621. Other accounts of Clinton's efforts to find Bin Laden include Steve Coll, *Ghost Wars. The Secret History of the CIA, Afghanistan, and Bin Laden, from the Soviet Invasion to September 10, 2001* (New York: Penguin Books, 2004); and Richard Miniter, *Losing Bin Laden. How Bill Clinton's Failures Unleashed Global Terror* (New York: Regnery, 2003).

43. Quoted in Woodward, *Bush at War,* 17.

44. Ibid., 26–27.

45. Department of Defense, "Lt. Gen. Newbold on Military Strikes in Southern Iraq," transcript, February 16, 2001, www.defenselink.mil/news/Feb2001/ t02162001_t216iraq .html. See also James Dao and Steven Lee Meyers, "Attack on Iraq: The Overview; U.S. and British Jets Strike Air-Defense Centers in Iraq," *New York Times,* February 17, 2001, A1.

46. Hendrickson, *The Clinton Wars,* 155.

47. Dao and Myers, "Attack on Iraq."

48. One forceful advocate of this view is Robert F. Turner, "The War on Terrorism and the Modern Relevance of the Congressional Power to 'Declare' War," *Harvard Journal of Law and Public Policy* 25, no. 2 (2002): 519–537.

49. Quoted in David Abramowitz, "The President, the Congress, and Use of Force: Legal and Political Considerations in Authorizing Use of Force against International Terrorism," *Harvard International Law Journal* 43, no. 1 (2002): 73.

50. Sen. Tom Daschle (with Michael D'Orso), *Like No Other Time. The Two Years that Changed America* (New York: Three Rivers Press, 2003), 124.

51. Abramowitz, "The President, the Congress, and Use of Force," 73.

52. *Congressional Record,* September 14, 2001, S9424.

53. Dave Boyer, "Some Lawmakers Call for War on Terror," *Washington Times*, September 14, 2001, A13.

54. Barbara Lee, "Why I Opposed the Resolution to Authorize Force," *San Francisco Chronicle*, September 23, 2001. Lee's vote appeared to have little impact on her reelection effort, as she won 82 percent of the vote in the 2002 elections.

55. *Congressional Record*, September 14, 2001, S9416, S9417, S9423.

56. Nancy Kassop, "The War Power and Its Limits," *Presidential Studies Quarterly* 33, no. 3 (2003): 513–514. See also Frédérick Gagnon, "Dealing with Hegemony at Home: From Congressional Compliance to Resistance to George W. Bush's National Security Policy," in *Hegemony of Empire? The Redefenition of U.S. Power under George W. Bush*, ed. Charles-Philippe David and David Grondin (Aldershot: Ashgate, 2006), 95–96.

57. George W. Bush, "Statement on Signing the Authorization for Use of Military Force," Weekly Compilation of Presidential Documents, September 18, 2001, 37:1333, www.gpoaccess.gov/wcomp/index.html. For more on Bush's approval rating at the time, see Dana Milbank and Richard Morin, "Public Is Unyielding in War against Terror; 9 in 10 Back Robust Military Action," *Washington Post*, September 28, 2001, A1.

58. Quoted in Bob Woodward, "Cheney Upholds Power of the Presidency," *Washington Post*, January 20, 2005, A7.

59. Much of what is known about the White House deliberation comes from Woodward, *Bush at War*. In researching the book, Woodward had access to all the principal decision makers at the White House and conducted on-the-record interviews with Bush and others. At this time, Woodward's book remains one of the best publicly available sources on these deliberations. Other sources on the decision-making process during this period include Ron Suskind, *The Price of Loyalty: George W. Bush, the White House and the Education of Paul O'Neill* (New York: Simon and Shuster, 2004); and Richard A. Clarke, *Against All Enemies: Inside America's War on Terror* (New York: Free Press, 2004). O'Neill formerly served as Bush's Treasury secretary, and Clarke had been his counterterrorism coordinator.

60. Woodward, *Bush at War*, 3–4.

61. Ibid., 83–91.

62. Ibid., 99. Woodward's account squares with the recollection of former Treasury secretary Paul O'Neill. Although O'Neill states that he felt that the administration was consumed with toppling Saddam Hussein from the very first days of the administration, he too notes that a military strike on Iraq was removed from consideration at the Camp David meetings. See Suskind, *The Price of Loyalty*, 184–187.

63. Woodward, *Bush at War*, 158.

64. David Halberstam, *War in a Time of Peace: Bush, Clinton and the Generals* (New York: Scribner's, 2001), 404–409.

65. Shawn Howard, "The Afghan Connection: Islamic Extremism in Central Asia," *National Security Studies Quarterly* 6, no. 3 (2000): 28–29.

66. Robbins, "Bin Laden's War," 396. Tenet, "Written Statement," 6–7.

67. Woodward, *Bush at War*, 99, 121.

68. Ibid., 32, 43. For more details about Tommy Franks's role in the planning of the war, see General Tommy Franks, *American Soldier* (New York: HarperCollins, 2004), 255–262.

69. Ibid., 129.

70. Ibid., 115–117, 59.

71. Ibid., 117–118.

72. Ibid., 172, 199.

73. RAND Corporation, "Operation Enduring Freedom: An Assessment," Research Brief, 2005, 1, www.rand.org/pubs/research_briefs/2005/RAND_RB9148.pdf. See also Richard Morin and Claudia Deane, "Most Americans Back U.S. Tactics; Poll Finds Little Worry over Rights," *Washington Post,* November 29, 2001, A1.

74. Gretchen Peters, "Where Is Osama Bin Laden?" ABC News, September 8, 2006. See also William Schomberg, "Bin Laden Not Hiding in Pakistan: Prime Minister," *Washington Post,* January 25, 2007.

75. Hassan M. Fattah, "Bin Laden Re-emerges, Warning U.S. while Offering 'Truce,'" *New York Times,* January 19, 2006. See also Amir Shah, Associated Press, "Taliban Leader Said to Be Reorganizing Group," *Fort Worth Star-Telegram,* September 22, 2003, 6A.

76. Barnett R. Rubin, "Saving Afghanistan," *Foreign Affairs,* January/February 2007, 57.

77. Mark Mazzetti, "Terrorism: New Generation Is Taking Over al Qaeda," *Fort Worth Star-Telegram,* April 2, 2007, 11A.

78. P.L. 108-458. The 9/11 Commission recommendation reads as follows: "The current position of Director of Central Intelligence should be replaced by a National Intelligence Director with two main areas of responsibility: (1) to oversee national intelligence centers on specific subjects of interest across the U.S. government and (2) to manage the national intelligence program and oversee the agencies that contribute to it." *The 9/11 Commission Report* (New York: Norton, 2004), 411.

79. For an argument expressing doubt about the diversionary theory for these strikes, see Ryan C. Hendrickson, "Clinton's Military Strikes in 1998: Diversionary Uses of Force?" *Armed Forces and Society* 28 (2002): 309–332.

80. Maria Recio, "Granger Announces Anti-Terrorism Caucus," *Fort Worth Star-Telegram,* January 31, 2007, 4A.

2 The Return of the Imperial Presidency? The Bush Doctrine and U.S. Intervention in Iraq

Jeffrey S. Lantis and Eric Moskowitz

Before You Begin

1. Is the "imperial presidency" model being resurrected more than a decade after the end of the cold war?

2. Why did the Bush administration decide to invade Iraq and topple Saddam Hussein in 2003? How did the events of September 11 translate into justification in 2003 for a preemptive war against Iraq?

3. What leaders were particularly influential in shaping the decision to invade Iraq, and what domestic opposition did they face?

4. Why was it so difficult for Congress to oppose presidential plans for war?

5. During the year preceding the invasion of Iraq, why did the Bush administration disregard international criticism of its plan?

6. What are the long-term implications of the Bush doctrine of preemption for U.S. foreign policy?

Deterrence—the promise of massive retaliation against nations—means nothing against shadowy terrorist networks with no nation or citizens to defend. Containment is not possible when unbalanced dictators with weapons of mass destruction can deliver those weapons or missiles or secretly provide them to terrorist allies. . . . We must take the battle to the enemy, disrupt his plans, and confront the worst threats before they emerge. In the world we have entered, the only path to safety is the path of action. And this nation will act.

—President George W. Bush
2002 Graduation Speech at West Point

Introduction

The terrorist attacks of September 11, 2001, represented a watershed moment for United States foreign policy. September 11 enabled the executive branch to assume an unusual amount of influence over policymaking in the United States. President George W. Bush and his top advisers used that influence in a variety of ways, including implementing a new strategy calling for preemptive strikes against potential enemies. The United States would rely most often on the unilateral exercise of power rather, than on international law and organizations, to achieve its security objectives. Some observers suggest that the Bush doctrine, the larger war on terror, and the 2003 Iraq war represent the resurgence of the "imperial presidency."

Background: The Rise of the Imperial Presidency

Historian Arthur M. Schlesinger Jr. coined the term "imperial presidency" to describe the dominance of the executive branch in U.S. policymaking during the cold war. Schlesinger identified a pattern of steady accumulation of power in the executive branch, noting that this power grows "under the demand or pretext of an emergency." By the early 1970s, Schlesinger argues, "the American president had become on issues of war and peace the most absolute monarch (with the possible exception of Mao Tse Tung of China) among the great powers of the world." [1]

Another scholar, Michael Beschloss, argues, "The founders never intended to have an imperial president. Always worried about tyranny, they drafted a Constitution that gives the president limited authority and forces him to use his political skills to fight for influence as he squeezes laws out of Congress and prods the American people to think in new ways." [2] Schlesinger describes the rise of executive branch authority as "the appropriation by the Presidency, and particularly by the contemporary Presidency, of powers reserved by the Constitution and by long historical practice to Congress." [3]

Political winds shifted in the 1970s, however, as Americans grew weary of the war in Vietnam and, following the Watergate scandal, suspicious that presidents were abusing their powers. President Richard Nixon's resignation in 1974 marked the demise of the cold war imperial presidency. A resentful Congress and a mobilized nation consciously began to check the power of the executive branch. Succeeding presidents faced resistance from mobilized institutions that constrained their latitude in foreign policy decision making. When George W.

U.S. Intervention in Iraq

August 2, 1990 Iraq invades Kuwait.

August 8, 1990 President George H.W. Bush announces that the United States is sending troops to Saudi Arabia in response to the Iraqi invasion of Kuwait.

November 29, 1990 The UN Security Council passes a resolution authorizing the use of force against Iraq if it does not withdraw from Kuwait by January 15, 1991.

January 17, 1991 UN-sanctioned multinational forces launch an air war against Iraq.

February 24, 1991 After a six-week air campaign, the multinational forces launch a ground war against Iraqi forces.

February 28, 1991 With Iraqi troops in full retreat and decimated by a withering coalition attack, Bush decides to end the war for fear that the international community would view further action as an unjustified massacre.

March 1991 Iraq president Saddam Hussein brutally puts down a Shia revolt in southern Iraq and a Kurdish revolt in the north. After much criticism, the Bush administration sets up "no-fly" zones over Iraq to restrain further Iraqi military actions against these groups.

April 3, 1991 The UN Security Council passes Resolution 687, which requires the Iraqi government to allow international inspections of all its weapons facilities and to destroy all weapons of mass destruction (WMD).

December 1998 Iraq ends all cooperation with UN weapons inspections. Without Security Council approval, President Bill Clinton orders Operation Desert Fox, a four-day bombing campaign of Iraqi military installations.

September 11, 2001 In a coordinated attack by the al Qaeda network, two hijacked airplanes destroy the World Trade Center Towers in New York City and another crashes into the Pentagon outside Washington, D.C. A fourth hijacked plane crashes in Pennsylvania.

September 15, 2001 In a meeting of the war cabinet, Deputy Secretary of Defense Paul Wolfowitz proposes including Iraq as a target of the U.S. military response to the September 11 attacks. Secretary of State Colin Powell objects, arguing that an international coalition could only be built

continued on the next page

continued from the previous page

for an attack against the Taliban and al Qaeda in Afghanistan. Bush agrees that Afghanistan should be the immediate target, though he indicates that Iraq will be reconsidered later.

January 29, 2002 In the State of the Union address, Bush denounces Iraq, Iran, and North Korea as an "axis of evil." He declares that the United States will act preemptively against nations with WMD that threaten the United States. He focuses particularly on Iraq.

Summer 2002 Debate about regime change in Iraq rages in the Bush administration. The momentum for war appears to be growing.

August 5, 2002 In a meeting requested by Powell, the secretary of state warns Bush about the political and economic consequences in the Middle East if the United States unilaterally acts against Iraq. Powell suggests working with the Security Council to gain international backing.

Mid-August 2002 Bush agrees to engage in multilateral diplomacy as part of his strategy against Iraq.

September 12, 2002 Bush speaks to the UN General Assembly, calling on the body to preserve its integrity by enforcing its resolutions against Iraq.

October 11, 2002 Congress passes a joint resolution authorizing Bush to use any means he deems appropriate to enforce Security Council resolutions against Iraq and to defend U.S. national security.

November 8, 2002 The Security Council unanimously passes Resolution 1441, warning Iraq of serious consequences unless it submits immediately to unrestricted weapons inspections.

March 17, 2003 Bush declares that Hussein and his sons must leave Iraq within forty-eight hours or face military attack.

March 19–20, 2003 U.S. and coalition forces launch air and missile attacks on Iraq.

March 20, 2003 U.S. and coalition forces invade Iraq.

April 8–9, 2003 Baghdad falls to U.S. forces. A group of marines orchestrate the toppling of Saddam Hussein's statue in Firdos Square.

May 1, 2003 Bush lands on the USS *Abraham Lincoln.* Under a banner proclaiming "Mission Accomplished," he declares to the sailors on deck, and to millions of television viewers, that all major combat operations in Iraq have been successfully concluded.

June 28, 2004 Paul Bremer, head of the Coalition Provisional Authority, hands over sovereign authority to an interim Iraqi government led by Prime Minister Iyad Allawi.

December 15, 2005 Iraqis elect a permanent government, with the Shia-led United Iraqi Alliance winning a plurality of the seats.

April 22, 2006 Nouri al-Maliki, of the Shiite Dawa Party, is selected to be prime minister of the newly elected government.

December 6, 2006 The Iraq Study Group issues its report calling for an aggressive diplomatic effort and a phased withdrawal of American troops.

January 10, 2007 President Bush announces plans for a "New Way Forward," which includes a surge of 21,500 additional troops to Iraq.

Bush entered office, Beschloss characterized him as the United States' first truly "post-imperial president," given the controversy surrounding his election coupled with the relative peace in the world.

U.S. Foreign Policy after September 11

The attacks of September 11 became a catalyst for fundamental transformations in U.S. foreign policy. Leaders and the public came to grips with the fact that key tenets of cold war strategic culture were no longer adequate. The United States was vulnerable, and nuclear deterrence was rendered practically irrelevant by the new challenge. Shaping U.S. responses to the terrorist threat would call into question key concepts and practices in foreign affairs, including hegemony and multilateral cooperation.

Perhaps most significant, the Bush administration consciously decided to interpret September 11 as a transformative moment for the country. President Bush and his top advisers believed that the attacks represented a "moment of destiny" for the nation. Morever, they recognized that the attacks had reduced the public's resistance to risk taking and its casualty aversion. National Security Advisor Condoleezza Rice characterized this new era as similar to the period from 1945 to 1947, "in that the events so clearly demonstrated that there is a big global threat, and that it's a big global threat to a lot of countries that you would not have normally thought of as being in the coalition. That has started shifting the tectonic plates in international politics." She then stated that it was "important to try to seize on that and position American interests and institutions and all of that before they harden again."[4]

The Bush administration embraced the shift as an opportunity to define new avenues for foreign and security policy. In late September, Congress approved $40 billion in emergency spending to deal with the crisis. The president also received congressional support for a broadly worded resolution which authorized him "to use all necessary and appropriate force against those nations, organizations, or persons he determines planned, authorized, committed, or aided the terrorist attacks that occurred on September 11, 2001, or harbored such organizations or persons, in order to prevent any future acts of international terrorism against the United States by such nations, organizations, or persons."

Neither the resolution nor the spending measure prompted a great deal of congressional debate. Yet this was the beginning of what Ivo H. Daalder and James M. Lindsay have termed "a revolution in American foreign policy." Bush's advocacy of "the unilateral exercise of American power" and his emphasis on "a proactive doctrine of preemption and [de-emphasis of] the reactive strategies of deterrence and containment" were groundbreaking.[5]

Decision Making and the Iraq War

The idea to invade Iraq as part of a global war against terrorism was first raised with the president just four days after the September 11 attacks. The option was shelved at the time, but it remained under discussion in secret meetings over the next year. In fact, each time the Iraq option was discussed, it gained broader support inside the administration.[6]

On September 15, 2001, at Camp David, Maryland, President Bush held a meeting of his principal national security advisers: Rice, Vice President Richard Cheney, Secretary of State Colin Powell, Secretary of Defense Donald Rumsfeld, Deputy Secretary of Defense Paul Wolfowitz, Director of Central Intelligence (DCI) George Tenet, and Chairman Richard Myers of the Joint Chiefs of Staff. Rumsfeld and Wolfowitz reportedly brought along briefing papers that identified "three potential sets of targets: Taliban, al Qaeda, and Iraq," and Rumsfeld privately encouraged Wolfowitz to raise the idea of an attack on Iraq.[7] When given the opportunity, Wolfowitz forcefully argued that Iraqi president Saddam Hussein was a tyrant who represented a direct threat to U.S. national security, that his regime supported international terrorism, and that Iraq sought to develop weapons of mass destruction (WMD) that could be used against

U.S. allies, including Israel. Wolfowitz added that he believed there was a 10 percent to 50 percent chance that Saddam Hussein had actually been involved in September 11.[8]

Iraq had been a primary U.S. security concern since the conclusion of the Persian Gulf War in 1991. As part of Iraq's surrender, the United Nations conducted regular inspections of suspected WMD sites, but in 1998 Iraq ordered the inspectors out. Saddam Hussein had cracked down on insurgent groups and political opponents after the war, so the United States and its allies established "no-fly" zones over parts of northern and southern Iraq to help protect those groups. U.S. and British planes patrolled the zones from 1991 to 2003, engaging in periodic exchanges of fire with Iraqi antiaircraft missile batteries.

In spite of these concerns there was little support among the president's other advisers at Camp David for the Iraq option. When Wolfowitz continued to make his argument, Bush had his chief of staff, Andrew Card, take Wolfowitz aside to tell him to allow the discussion to move on to other more immediate policy alternatives.[9] Nevertheless, Bush reportedly told his national security advisor the next day that the first target of the war on terror was Afghanistan: "We're putting Iraq off," he said, "but eventually we'll have to return to that question."[10] On September 20, in a meeting with British prime minister Tony Blair at the White House, Bush made it clear that he was determined to topple Saddam Hussein eventually.[11]

In the meantime, the administration moved forward with plans to strike the Taliban and al Qaeda in Afghanistan. President Bush launched the war against Afghanistan with strong congressional and public support. U.S. and British troops, aided by forces from other countries, conducted a rapid series of campaigns against the Taliban. Special operations troops worked in consort with groups in the Northern Alliance and quickly took control of key regions of the country, including the capital, Kabul. By December 2001 the war in Afghanistan seemed effectively over, but al Qaeda leader Osama Bin Laden remained at large.

2002: A Year of Decision

Even before the war in Afghanistan wound down, battle lines had been drawn within the Bush administration over Iraq. Administration officials were divided into two camps: those who favored an invasion of Iraq and those who favored intensified efforts to contain Iraq.[12] In 2002, the camp supporting the invasion of Iraq included Rumsfeld, Cheney, and Wolfowitz. Also sharing their perspective were I. Lewis Libby, Cheney's chief of staff; Zalmay Khalilzad, deputy national security advisor on Iraq; Stephen Hadley, deputy national security advisor; and Wayne Downing, White House counterterrorism advisor. Some members of this faction had been involved for more than a decade in planning to topple Saddam. The call for an attack on Iraq was an important part of the agenda of a group of so-called neoconservatives, or "neocons," inside (and outside) the Bush administration, who were organized around a think tank called the Project for the New American Century (or PNAC).[13]

Secretary Rumsfeld sought advice on national security from the Pentagon's Defense Policy Board, a private group of consultants led by neoconservatives, which included former Pentagon official Richard Perle, former CIA director James Woolsey, and *Weekly Standard* editor William Kristol, the chair of PNAC. In February 1998 eighteen prominent neoconservatives from PNAC had sent President Clinton an open letter warning that Saddam Hussein posed an immediate threat to the United States and calling for U.S. support for a popular insurrection in Iraq. They called specifically for the Clinton administration to recognize the Iraqi National Congress, an exile group headed by Ahmed Chalabi, as the provisional government of Iraq.[14] Neoconservatives persuaded Congress to pass the Iraq Liberation Act in 1998, a "piece of legislation that made regime change in Iraq the official policy of the United States."[15] Many of those neoconservatives were later drafted by Cheney to serve in top positions in the Bush administration. They sought U.S. international hegemony and the democratization of the Middle East. In their calculation, the overthrow of Saddam might be the catalyst for such a revolution. The United States might even have to go to war against several states in the region to create a new regional order. Indeed, Perle argued that the United States could readily impose its will on Iran, Lebanon, and Syria by delivering "a short message.... 'You're next.'"[16]

During the presidential transition period in early January 2001, Cheney had set up a series of national security briefings for the president-elect. He specifically requested that the outgoing secretary of defense, William Cohen, make Iraq one of the centerpieces of his briefing.[17] After September 11, Secretary Rumsfeld created a new office in the Pentagon, the Counterterrorism Evaluation Group—later known as the Office of Special Plans—that was to provide the secretary with advanced analysis of intelligence on Iraq and links between Middle Eastern states and terrorist networks. Critics charged that this office was created to find evidence of what Wolfowitz and Rumsfeld already "believed to be true—that Saddam Hussein had close ties to al Qaeda, and that Iraq had an enormous arsenal of chemical, biological, and possibly even nuclear weapons that threatened the region and potentially, the United States."[18]

Dick Cheney was, "by common consent, the most powerful vice president in history."[19] And he seemed especially preoccupied with the September 11 attacks and possible links between Saddam Hussein and al Qaeda. Wolfowitz commented that Cheney was "someone whose view of the need to get rid of Saddam Hussein was transformed by September 11, by the recognition of the danger posed by the connection between terrorists and WMDs, and by the growing evidence of links between Iraq and al Qaeda."[20] Soon after September 11, "Cheney immersed himself in a study of Islam and the Middle East," meeting with scholars to discuss whether "toppling Saddam would send a message of strength and enhance America's credibility throughout the Muslim world."[21] His staff was also heavily focused on Iraq, working closely with Rumsfeld and the Pentagon in investigating links between Iraq and al Qaeda and building the case for war. Secretary Powell later said that he had "detected a kind of fever in Cheney. [Cheney] was not the steady, unemotional rock that he had witnessed a dozen years earlier during the run-up to the Gulf War. The vice president was beyond hell-bent for action against Saddam. It was as if nothing else existed."[22]

The group within the administration opposed to an outright invasion of Iraq included State Department officials, who became strong advocates of containment as an alternative, along with some military leaders. Powell was the leading voice for moderation in the cabinet during the winter months of 2001 and 2002. He was supported by Richard Armitage, deputy secretary of state, Richard Haas, the director of policy planning, and retired army general Anthony Zinni, the department's adviser on the Middle East. DCI Tenet also worried about the implications of an invasion for U.S. international security. The State Department officials argued that the United States should support a renewed international program of WMD inspections in Iraq and ideally should build a multilateral coalition of countries willing to authorize more stringent UN Security Council resolutions and possibly even threaten the use of force against Saddam Hussein's regime. Thus, while there was a growing consensus that the Iraqi leader should be removed from office, there remained significant disagreement on the means to that end.

Secret Plans

The two camps secretly debated Iraqi policy throughout the fall of 2001. Rumsfeld and Cheney reportedly kept Iraq alive in "freewheeling meetings of the principals," where they discussed possible ties between so-called rogue states, such as Iraq, and terrorist groups. One senior official said of those meetings, "The issue got away from the president. He wasn't controlling the tone or the direction. . . . [Some members of the administration] painted him into a corner because Iraq was an albatross around their necks."[23] Bush had a "eureka moment" in November 2001, when a series of events highlighted the danger that WMD could fall into terrorist hands. Pakistan took into custody several Pakistani nuclear scientists who had traveled to Afghanistan. Meanwhile British intelligence uncovered other Pakistani nuclear scientists willing to sell nuclear weapons components. The threat was further accentuated when a search of an al Qaeda safe house in Afghanistan found documents indicating that Bin Laden was trying to acquire WMD. Some administration officials quickly concluded that Iraq would be the most likely supplier of such weapons.[24]

On November 21, 2001, while the war in Afghanistan continued, the president ordered Secretary Rumsfeld and General Tommy Franks, head of Central Command, to begin secretly updating war plans for Iraq. Bush would later say that this order was "absolutely" the first step in taking the nation to war.[25] Between December 2001 and September 2002 Franks would meet with President Bush eight times to present ever more detailed Iraq war plans.

Bush's State of the Union address in January 2002 was one of his first major speeches to articulate the evolution of his foreign policy objectives. Behind the scenes, neoconservatives in the administration worked hard to shape the speech in a way that would lay the groundwork for a larger war on terrorism. One of the president's speechwriters was instructed in December 2001, "Make the best case for war in Iraq [in the address], but leave exit ramps."[26] In the address, the president's articulation of an "axis of evil"—Iran, Iraq, and North Korea—suggested that there were obvious enemies in the war on terror. A few weeks later, the president secretly directed the CIA to begin developing plans for supporting military efforts to overthrow the Iraqi regime. The CIA received almost $200 million for covert activities against Baghdad.[27] President Bush reportedly set a deadline of April 15, 2002, for his advisers to develop a "coagulated plan" for dealing with Iraq. He told top officials that he was ready to "take out Saddam."[28]

This new push to develop an operational plan led to serious debates in 2002 over the nature and scope of the operation. Administration officials discussed a number of options for toppling Hussein, including "providing logistical and intelligence help to [his] enemies in hopes of inciting a mutiny within his military circle; providing air and limited ground support for an assault by opposition groups; or an outright American invasion."[29] CIA officials informed the president that covert action alone could not achieve regime change in Iraq. Civilian leaders at the Pentagon and officials on the National Security Council favored an option in the spirit of the "Afghanistan model"—using several thousand Special Forces soldiers and concentrated airpower to support opposition groups' efforts to defeat the Iraqi army. Wolfowitz and Downing were among the most outspoken advocates for the plan, believing that light and technologically advanced forces could swiftly overrun Iraqi opposition.[30] At one point, Rumsfeld argued that perhaps as few as 125,000 troops could win the war.

The Joint Chiefs of Staff and General Franks argued strongly against the Pentagon's civilian leadership during this period. The military brass believed that any operation in Iraq would require overwhelming force to confront Iraq's established army. Military leaders were very concerned about Iraq's potential use of chemical or biological weapons and the possibility of prolonged urban warfare. They also questioned the reliability of the Iraqi National Congress as a leader of insurgent forces and the adequacy of plans for a postwar occupation regime. At one point General Franks articulated a plan calling for 380,000 troops for the invasion and occupation. "Nobody knew how long U.S. forces would need to be in Iraq, so CENTCOM war planners wrote that the occupation would last as long as ten years."[31] State Department officials joined the military brass in resisting a rush to invade.

To make matters worse, the National Security Council did not adequately manage the decision process. Critics charged that Rice was not sufficiently engaged in her management role, opting instead to serve as confidant to the president. According to one report,

> Rice has proved to be a poised and articulate defender of President Bush's policies. But her management of the National Security Council—the principal coordinator and enforcer of presidential decision-making—has come under fire from former and current administration officials and a range of foreign policy experts. From the start, the administration has been riven by ideological disputes on foreign policy. . . . A senior State Department official—voicing an opinion that few in the government disputed—said "if you want a one-word description of the NSC since January 21, 2001: dysfunctional."[32]

According to one assessment of the decision-making process, Cheney often teamed with Rumsfeld to "roll over national security advisor Rice and Secretary of State Powell" on Iraq policymaking.[33]

Finally, there was the issue of postwar planning for Iraq. Although the subject was just as important as war planning, it received far less attention in the buildup to the invasion. The State Department had begun a postwar planning initiative in 2002, but its efforts were quickly swept aside by the Pentagon leadership. Rumsfeld successfully argued that his department should be in charge of postwar planning and the occupation. The president signed National Security Presidential Directive NSPD-24 on January 20, 2003, establishing an Iraq Postwar Planning Office in the Defense Department.[34] Pentagon leaders effectively blocked input from other agencies. Retired general Jay Garner was appointed to head postwar planning initiatives, but months of preparation only revealed more potential problems of occupation, including security, infrastructure, and meeting basic needs for Iraqis.[35] One analysis from a planning simulation in Washington in late February 2003 warned, "Current force packages are inadequate for the first step of securing all major urban areas, let alone for providing interim police. . . . We risk letting much of the country descend into civil unrest [and] chaos whose magnitude may defeat our national strategy of a stable new Iraq."[36]

Looking back, an Army colonel on Garner's planning staff opined, "The overriding problem was that there was not one, single plan. There was no single document spelling out: This is your objective. This is who's in charge. These are priority tasks. These are the coordinating steps we will take to bring these all together."[37] And even though Rumsfeld had primary authority, through NSPD-24, the secretary seemed aloof and uninterested in postwar planning, while micromanaging the war plans.

The Hot Summer

Summer 2002 was a critical period for Bush administration decision making on Iraq, even as officials publicly maintained that there were no war plans on the president's desk. At graduation ceremonies at West Point on June 1, the president gave a speech that hinted that he had already made up his mind on Iraq. Bush said that history had issued its call to a new generation of military leaders. Faced with threats of attack from terrorist groups and rogue states, Bush argued,

> The gravest danger to freedom lies at the perilous crossroads of radicalism and technology. When the spread of chemical and biological and nuclear weapons, along with ballistic missile technology—when that occurs, even weak states and small groups could attain a catastrophic power to strike great nations. . . . They want the capability to blackmail us, or to harm us, or to harm our friends—and we will oppose them with all our power.[38]

The issue came to a head at an August 5 meeting of the National Security Council. General Franks briefed the president and his advisers on war plans for Iraq, including a new plan for faster mobilization and strikes. At the end of the briefing, Secretary Powell requested time alone with the president and Rice to address his reservations. Powell frankly expressed his concerns about all the potential negative consequences of an invasion of Iraq. He told the president, "You are going to be the proud owner of 25 million people. You will own all their hopes, aspirations, and problems. You'll own it all."[39] Powell and Armitage privately called this "the Pottery Barn rule: You break it, you own it." The secretary went on to warn that an attack on Iraq would "suck the oxygen out of everything. This will become the first term."[40] The best approach, Powell argued, was for the United States to push for UN and allied support.

President Bush, over the next few days, appears to have decided on some form of a two-track strategy. Track one would authorize military deployments and call-ups of reserves to amass troops in the Persian Gulf region for an attack against Iraq. Track two would focus on diplomacy at the United Nations. Should the UN efforts fail, the diplomacy would nevertheless help build international, congressional, and public support for track one.

The diplomatic track remained fairly controversial within the administration. Some officials, possibly including the president, simply "didn't believe diplomacy would or could take care of the threat Saddam posed. Going to the UN was a means, not an end."[41] Neoconservatives in the administration did not want the president to ask for another UN resolution creating new arms inspections in Iraq. They feared that Saddam would manipulate the inspection process and sidetrack U.S. efforts at regime change. Others in the Bush administration thought there was some chance that a refurbished United Nations inspection regime could work. State Department officials saw a new UN resolution as essential for any chance to disarm Iraq without a military invasion or, if that failed, for building an effective international coalition to support regime change. By late summer, the president seemed to accept the need for some diplomacy on Iraq at the United Nations, but he never clearly committed to asking the organization for a new resolution.

Given the disarray in the administration, it was no surprise that a public and media debate over the two tracks ensued. State Department officials leaked their concerns to the press, questioning whether an invasion had already been decided upon by the administration. Leading Republicans also began to question publicly the merits of a rush to invade. Brent Scowcroft, the national security advisor under the elder Bush, published an op-ed article critical of the current Bush administration.[42] Scowcroft warned that "an attack on Iraq at this time would seriously jeopardize, if not destroy, the global counter-terrorist campaign we have undertaken."[43] Republican leaders in Congress had concerns about whether the administration had adequately prepared the military or the public for the scope of the undertaking.[44]

In late August, invasion supporters pushed back. Rice gave an interview to the BBC in which she emphasized the growing moral imperative for the United States and its allies to topple Saddam: "This is an evil man, who left to his own devices, will wreak havoc again on his own population, his neighbors and if he gets weapons of mass destruction and the means to deliver them on all of us. There is a very powerful moral case for regime change."[45]

Vice President Cheney contributed to the war momentum, declaring in an August 26 speech to the convention of the Veterans of Foreign Wars, "We must take the battle to the enemy. . . . There is no doubt that Saddam Hussein now has weapons of mass destruction; there is no doubt that Saddam is amassing them to use against our friends, against our allies, and against us. . . . Many of us are convinced that Saddam will acquire nuclear weapons fairly soon."[46] Commenting on Cheney's speech, the *New York Times* reported, "Administration officials said that Mr. Cheney's views mirrored those of President Bush, and were part of an ongoing effort to convince the allies, Congress and the American public of the need for what the administration calls regime change in Iraq."[47]

Secretary Powell was blindsided by Cheney's bold assertions. Powell, who was on vacation, had not been briefed on the vice president's speech. He was particularly angered because weeks earlier the president's top advisers had unanimously agreed to take the Iraq issue to the United Nations.[48] Cheney's public assertion that inspections would not prevent Iraq from acquiring WMD was contrary to Bush's yearlong insistence that inspectors should be allowed to resume their work. Powell characterized Cheney's action as "a preemptive attack" on the policy process.[49]

Powell returned to Washington and requested another meeting with Bush to try to convince him of the need for the United States to work with the international community on the Iraq issue. He argued that the United States could gain international support by formulating a UN Security Council resolution to clamp down on Iraq and force compliance with UN demands.[50] The president reassured Powell that he would pursue a new round of diplomacy. The night before Bush's September address to the UN General Assembly, Powell convinced Rice that the president should include the following statement in his speech: "We will work with the UN Security Council for the necessary resolutions, but the purposes of the United States should not be doubted. The Security Council resolutions will be enforced."[51]

Bringing the War to the Home Front: Speaking with One Voice

By mid-August 2002 the public and Congress both sensed that war with Iraq was inevitable, but there was also deep-seated skepticism. Prominent congressional Republicans, including House Majority Leader Richard Armey, R-Texas, and senators Chuck Hagel, R-Neb., and Richard Lugar, R-Ind., questioned the wisdom of a unilateral, preemptive attack on Iraq. Other congressional representatives, back in their districts for the summer recess, were finding considerable uncertainty among their constituents. A *Washington Post*/ABC News poll showed slippage in public support for a war, and only 45 percent of the public thought Bush had a clear policy on Iraq.[52]

On August 26, the White House asserted that the president needed no authorization from Congress to pursue a preemptive attack against Iraq. Such a strike was validated by the president's constitutional role as commander in chief, the 1991 congressional authorization of the Persian Gulf War, and the 2001 congressional authorization to use force against those involved in the September 11 assault. One administration official said, "We don't want to be in the legal position of asking Congress to authorize the use of force when the president already has that full authority."[53] The administration also feared restrictions that Congress might impose on the president's flexibility to move against Iraq.

Many in Congress rejected the president's legal arguments. Sen. Arlen Specter, R-Pa., insisted that the war was "a matter for Congress to decide. The president as commander in chief can act in an emergency without authority from Congress, but we have enough time to debate, deliberate and decide."[54] Sen. Robert Byrd, D-W.Va., argued that the Persian Gulf War resolutions "ceased to be effective once Iraq capitulated to U.S. and allied forces in April 1991."[55] Sen. Max Cleland, D-Ga., maintained that the September 11 use-of-force resolution was "not some blank check to go after any terrorists in the world."[56] Others in Congress conceded the president's legal position but believed it would undermine the war's political support. Said Sen. John McCain, R-Ariz., "I believe technically the president is not required to come to Congress; politically, I believe it would be foolish not to."[57]

Significant congressional opposition (even among Republicans) coupled with volatile public attitudes ultimately led the White House to seek congressional approval to act against Iraq. The administration began to make its case to the nation and to Congress through frequent appearances by administration officials on Sunday morning talk shows, testimony at congressional hearings, and closed-door briefings for congressional leaders. On September 4, Bush met with a congressional delegation to make the case for the use of force against Iraq and to ask for an authorizing resolution. The president told the delegation that he wanted congressional approval soon—before the end of the October recess and before midterm elections—and without conditions.

The Search for Support

Bush's speech to the United Nations General Assembly on September 12 was designed to address both tracks of policy developed by the White House. While the president offered an olive branch—negotiations with the UN Security Council to reach a multilateral resolution of the Iraq situation—he also issued strong words of warning to Iraq and other nations. Marking the one-year anniversary of the September 11 attacks, he said,

> Our principles and our security are challenged today by outlaw groups and regimes that accept no law of morality and have no limit to their violent ambitions. . . . In one place—in one regime—we find all these dangers, in their most lethal and aggressive forms, exactly the kind of aggressive threat the United Nations was born to confront. . . . The conduct of the Iraqi regime is a threat to the authority of the United Nations, and a threat to peace. . . . Are Security Council resolutions to be honored and enforced, or cast aside without consequence? Will the United Nations serve the purpose of its founding, or will it be irrelevant?[58]

Bush's speech was met with mixed reviews around the world. Critics saw it as heavy-handed and confrontational; supporters saw it as concessionary. Eight weeks later, on November 8, the UN Security Council unanimously approved Resolution 1441, authorizing a new round of weapons inspections in Iraq under the direction of Hans Blix. In late fall 2002, dozens of UN inspectors returned to Iraq for the first time in four years.[59]

The UN address was a turning point for Bush in his efforts to build popular support at home for war. Major media outlets noted the overwhelmingly favorable congressional response to the speech and suggested that it had generated momentum for quick congressional approval of a resolution authorizing force.[60] The White House sent its formal draft of a resolution to Congress one week after the UN address. It authorized the president "to use all means that he determines to be appropriate, including force, in order to enforce the United Nations Security Council Resolutions ... [to] defend the national security interests of the United States against the threat posed by Iraq, and restore international peace and security in the region [the Middle East]."[61]

The draft had been designed to give the president maximum flexibility. Reaction in Congress was generally positive, though some were troubled by the breadth of the authority requested. In particular, the phrase "restore international peace and security in the region" raised the possibility of Congress authorizing the executive branch to undertake, at its discretion, other military interventions throughout the Middle East. The White House indicated a willingness to negotiate but insisted that Bush would not accept conditions that required another round of UN or congressional approval.

Momentum in Congress for a resolution seemed to wane in late September, when Democrats began to fear that the president's insistence on quick passage was being used for partisan advantage in the upcoming election. Senator Byrd spoke out against "the war fervor, the drums of war, the bugles of war, the clouds of war" and "this war hysteria [that] has blown in like a hurricane."[62] But a senior House Republican "gloated that Washington's preoccupation with Iraq will likely 'suck the oxygen' out of the Democrats' plans to focus the fall's election campaigns on domestic issues."[63]

Late September indeed witnessed a distinct shift in the Bush administration's campaign strategy. The White House was now focusing predominantly on national security and the war on terror. The *Washington Post*, in an analysis of recent Bush campaign speeches, noted that war and security made up more than two-thirds of the content and domestic issues less than one-fifth. Bush's strategy appeared to be having success, as a late September Gallup poll indicated a 16 percent shift during the month, with most voters more concerned about Iraq than the economy, despite a significant decline in both the stock market and consumer confidence.[64]

Some Democrats in Congress capitulated to the pressure. Several admitted to the *Washington Post* that many Democrats who opposed the president's confrontational strategy toward Iraq would "nonetheless support it because they fear[ed] a backlash from voters."[65] Others wanted to meet the president's deadline so as to eliminate the war as an election issue and be able to focus on more politically promising domestic issues. Sen. John Edwards, D-N.C., hoped, "In a short period of time, Congress will have dealt with Iraq and we'll be on to other issues."[66]

The tone of the Republican campaign eventually became so harsh that Democrats were forced to counterattack. On the campaign trail, both the president and the vice president suggested several times that congressional Democrats were not adequately concerned about national security.[67] Senate Majority

Leader Tom Daschle, D-S.D., angrily defended the patriotism of Democrats, charging, "This is politicization pure and simple."[68]

The White House continued its barrage of public events and interviews to convince the public of the danger of Iraq. A number of administration officials maintained that there was evidence linking Saddam Hussein to al Qaeda, culminating in Secretary of Defense Rumsfeld's assertion that U.S. intelligence analysts had "bulletproof" evidence of Iraq–al Qaeda links.[69] But Bush also sought to mollify Democrats at a September 26 meeting with congressional leaders. He publicly declared, "The security of the country is the commitment of both political parties."[70] The White House also circulated a new compromise resolution in Congress, with the regional security clause eliminated, language invoking the War Powers Act inserted, and a clause added requiring the president to inform Congress promptly of his determination that diplomatic efforts were insufficient.

The new version of the resolution was generally well received in Congress. Nonetheless, Sen. Joseph Biden, D-Del., and Senator Lugar, with the support of several other moderate senators, sought to narrow the resolution's justifications for war from the laundry list of UN resolutions to a single justification: Iraq's failure to destroy its WMD. Biden admitted, however, that he probably would vote for even an "imperfect" resolution so as not to undermine the president in the international arena. He added, "I just can't fathom the president going it alone. If I'm wrong, I've made a tragic mistake."[71] The White House saw making WMD the sole justification for war as too restrictive. Bush wanted the flexibility to remove Saddam Hussein from power regardless of whether he was disarmed. The president declared, "I don't want to get a resolution which ties my hands."[72]

House Minority Leader Richard Gephardt, D-Mo., also suggested revisions to the White House, which found his more minor reporting requirements far less restrictive than those of Biden and Lugar. On October 2, the White House announced that it had come to an agreement with Gephardt and the Republican Party leadership in the House on a new draft resolution. Gephardt explained his endorsement by arguing, "We had to go through this, putting politics aside, so we have a chance to get to a consensus that will lead the country in the right direction."[73] The agreement isolated Daschle, the only major congressional leader who had not come to terms with the White House, and diminished Biden and Lugar's bargaining position.

The reaction to the Gephardt-Bush accommodation was indicative of the splits within the Democratic Party. Some denounced Gephardt for selling out in the interest of his own 2004 run for the presidency, while others praised him for securing language acceptable to more Democrats. Rep. Martin Frost, D-Texas, chair of the Democratic Caucus, said, "It's clearly helped members in marginal districts and swing districts. It makes it clear Democrats are as concerned about Iraq as Republicans."[74]

Bush built on the momentum from the Gephardt agreement with a speech televised on October 7, in which he called for Congress to pass the authorizing resolution. He made the case that Iraq was an urgent threat "because it gathers the most serious dangers of our age in one place. Iraq's weapons of mass destruction are controlled by a murderous tyrant who has already used chemical weapons to kill thousands of people." In supporting the principle of a preemptive strike, he argued that "we cannot wait for the final proof—the smoking gun—that could come in the form of a mushroom cloud." Bush went on to say that passage of a resolution did not mean that war was imminent. Rather, a resolution would show "the United Nations and all nations that America speaks with one voice."[75]

The momentum of the Gephardt-Bush agreement and the October 7 speech seemed to sweep away much of the centrist opposition to the revised resolution. Two major Republican dissenters, Armey and Lugar, quickly fell into line with the president, and Daschle indicated that he too was now inclined to vote for the resolution. Within several days, others on the fence began to do the same. Sen. Evan Bayh, D-Ind., a strong supporter of regime change in Iraq and a cosponsor of the administration resolution, explained the Democratic shift: "The majority of the American people tend to trust the Republican Party more on issues involving national security and defense than they do the Democratic Party. We need to work to improve our image on that score by taking a more aggressive posture with regard to Iraq, empowering the president."[76]

On October 10, the House approved the resolution 296–133, with 127 Democrats and 6 Republicans opposed. The vote was less consensual than expected. Observers saw it as a sign of Democratic dissatisfaction with Gephardt's position and a reaction to the late release of a CIA letter concluding that Iraq was only likely to use WMD against the U.S. in response to an attack.[77]

Early the next day, the Senate voted overwhelmingly, 77–23, in support of the resolution. The most impassioned opposition of the day came from Senator Byrd, who deplored Congress's failure to be faithful to its constitutional duties, asserting, "We can put a sign on top of this Capitol: Gone home, gone fishing, out of business."[78] Senator Daschle summed up the case for supporting the president's resolution: "I believe it is important for America to speak with one voice at this critical moment."[79]

Final Preparations

The Bush administration publicly praised the congressional authorization vote and supported efforts by international weapons inspectors in Iraq (track two). Behind the scenes, however, the administration was heavily engaged in preparing for war in Iraq. As fall turned to winter, the United States prepositioned more than 100,000 troops in the Persian Gulf and began calling up National Guard and reserve units.[80] It appears that President Bush made his final decision to authorize the war in fall 2002, even as weapons inspectors continued their work in Iraq. In October the Joint Chiefs of Staff sent a strategic guidance memo to combat planning officers in the field telling them in essence that "a war with Iraq [should] be considered part of the war on terror."[81] CIA director Tenet was also convinced that war was inevitable based on a private conversation with the president in which Bush told him, "We're not going to wait." In a discussion with CIA officials on November 4, Tenet was "asked if it really looked like war with Iraq: "You bet your ass," Tenet said bluntly. "It's not a matter of if. It's a matter of when. The president is going to war. Make the plans. We're going."[82]

That winter the president was briefed on the contents of Iraq's 12,000-page declaration to the United Nations responding to WMD charges. The administration did not consider the response credible. Wolfowitz publicly stated that Iraq was not in compliance with international agreements on weapons inspections. He claimed that Iraq was demonstrating "a high-level commitment to concealing its weapons of mass terror." Wolfowitz added, "The threat posed by the connection between terrorist networks and states that possess weapons of mass terror presents us with the danger of catastrophe that could be orders of magnitude greater than September 11."[83] In early January 2003 the president told Rice privately, "This [international inspections] pressure isn't holding together. Time is not on our side here. . . . we're going to have to go to war." Rice interpreted this as the president's final decision: "He had reached the point of no return."[84]

The International Community and the Impending War

It seemed as if the world had come together following the attacks of September 11. U.S. allies in NATO invoked Article V of the Washington Treaty, defining the events as an attack on the security of the entire alliance. In the Afghan war, Europeans provided logistical support for operations, emergency food aid, refugee assistance, and troops for peacekeeping duties after the war.

International cooperation on Iraq was another matter, however. The UN Security Council's passage of Resolution 1441 in fall 2002 demonstrated the international community's shared commitment to counterproliferation initiatives. But U.S. perceptions of threats to their security and the perceptions of its allies now diverged. Members of the Bush administration, especially the neoconservatives, argued that terrorism, tyranny, and the spread of WMD were the fundamental threats to U.S security. Although sympathetic, other world leaders saw homeland security as economic stability and the management of ethnic and religious tensions. To them the most pressing issue in the Middle East continued to be the Israeli-Palestinian conflict, not regime change in Iraq.

Relations between the United States and its NATO allies soured in 2002, as the Bush administration pushed a more interventionist foreign policy around the globe. Faced with resistance to an invasion of Iraq, the Bush administration quickly demonstrated its willingness to go its own way on international security issues. On January 20, 2003, after intense debate, the Europeans made it clear that they would not go beyond Resolution 1441 to endorse an invasion of Iraq based merely on a lack of cooperation with weapons inspectors. Insiders have suggested that this was a turning point for Powell, who felt ambushed by the timing and intensity of international criticism. He seemed to gain new resolve in supporting President Bush's plan for war. On January 22, Secretary Rumsfeld characterized Germany and France as "old Europe," contending that the center of gravity in the NATO alliance was shifting to the east.[85] Rumsfeld's comment acknowledged the reality that the United States was receiving more offers of help from eastern European countries than from traditional NATO allies, but it also cast aspersions at those governments unwilling to support an invasion of Iraq.

On February 5, Powell outlined to the UN Security Council suspected WMD sites in Iraq and purported links between Saddam Hussein and al Qaeda. The world listened with interest, but European diplomats argued that Powell had presented no "new" evidence of Iraqi violations. Conservative American columnists were so frustrated that they bluntly warned that the United States should "stop pretending that Europeans and Americans share a common view of the world, or even that they occupy the same world."[86]

The Iraq War

On March 17, hours after dropping a plan to gain a Security Council resolution authorizing war against Iraq, President Bush issued a public ultimatum to Saddam Hussein: Go into exile within forty-eight hours or risk attack from the United States and its allies. The president made it clear that he expected war and believed that he could move forward confidently given his base of congressional and public support.[87] According to a CNN/*USA Today*/Gallup poll taken hours after the president's speech, 66 percent of Americans said they approved of the ultimatum and the choice of going to war against Iraq if Saddam Hussein did not leave office. In the same poll, 68 percent of respondents said that they believed the United States had done "everything in its power" to reach a diplomatic resolution.[88]

U.S. and coalition forces attacked beginning on March 20 (Baghdad time) and advanced rapidly.[89] The main contingent of ground troops invaded from the south, coupled with a massive aerial bombardment. Invading forces faced challenges such as bad weather, long and insecure supply lines, and hit-and-run attacks, but they made steady progress northward through the country.[90] In early April, U.S. and coalition forces rushed into Baghdad and forced a general surrender of Iraqi forces.[91] Many Iraqis and Americans celebrated, and there was a sense of optimism about the future. On May 1, aboard the USS *Abraham Lincoln*, President Bush stood before a banner proclaiming "Mission Accomplished" and declared the "end of major combat operations" in Iraq.[92]

War without End?

President Bush's victory speech to the American public on May 1 was meant to be a stirring message to the world; his administration's policy of preemptive attack had proved successful. Iraq had been liberated from a tyrannical dictator, and the threat of a rogue regime with WMD had been eliminated. The president's made-for-television spectacle was a powerful symbol of the modern imperial presidency.

But the war and its consequences proved more difficult to control than its imagery. U.S. soldiers and weapons inspectors entering the country in 2003 found no evidence of an active WMD program. Intelligence reports used by the Bush administration in making its case for urgent action proved false. Critics charged that the administration had "cooked the books" in favor of war. In particular, they asserted that the Pentagon's Office of Special Plans manipulated intelligence to influence public opinion and legitimate the administration's Iraq policies.[93] Weapons inspectors have never found any evidence of an active WMD program in Iraq and now believe that Iraq's past capacity did not survive the 1991 Persian Gulf War and subsequent international inspections.[94]

Furthermore, the limitations of postwar occupation planning soon became apparent. Many Bush administration officials erroneously believed that coalition forces would be greeted as liberators of Iraq, but the fall of Saddam Hussein did not trigger an outpouring of popular support. In addition, U.S. and allied forces were not deployed in sufficient numbers to provide security throughout the country. Jay Garner and his postwar administration arrived in Baghdad to find deteriorating conditions and very few resources with which to restore order. In the three weeks that followed the fall of the Iraq government, unchecked looting gutted almost every major public institution in Baghdad. When questioned about the chaos, an exasperated Rumsfeld said, "Stuff happens! Freedom is untidy."[95] Things quickly went from bad to worse, as an insurgency against coalition forces gained momentum.

In an effort to remedy this situation, Paul Bremer, an experienced diplomat, replaced Garner as head of the Coalition Provisional Authority in May 2003. While Bremer brought new resources to rebuild Iraq's infrastruction, he was also responsible for two of the most controversial occupation initiatives: the de-Baathification of the Iraqi government and the disbanding of the Iraqi army. These actions alienated hundreds of thousands of Iraqis and destroyed an indigenous Iraqi security force. Bremer's actions were part of Rumsfeld's plan to control postwar Iraq but had never been cleared at the interagency level. Critics have charged that these actions helped foment the popular insurgency that continues to plague Iraq today, and Garner, who warned Bremer about both of these policies before leaving Iraq, later called them "tragic decisions."[96]

Although "major combat operations" were over, attacks against coalition troops actually increased. More than a thousand U.S. soldiers were killed and several thousand were injured between spring 2003 and fall 2004. Facing the reality of the postwar occupation of Iraq, U.S. public opinion eroded. An April 2004 poll indicated that 46 percent of Americans believed that the United States "should have stayed out of Iraq." One year after the president's announcement of the end of major combat operations, his overall approval rating stood at 46 percent, down from a high of 89 percent just after the September 11 attacks.[97] But despite public doubts about the war, Iraq never became a central issue in the 2004 presidential election, perhaps because both Democratic nominees had voted to authorize the president's use of force in Iraq.

In spite of the change in public sentiment, President Bush and top officials maintained a resolute attitude. Indeed, the president was determined to proceed toward restoration of order in Iraq and the consolidation of democracy. Chairman of the Joint Chiefs of Staff Richard Myers observed:

> When any doubt started to creep into the small, windowless Situation Room, the president almost stomped it out. Whether it was alarming casualties, bad news, the current decision on the timing of Iraqi elections, some other problem, or just a whiff of one of the uncertainties that accompany war, the president would try to set them all straight. "Hold it," Bush said once. "We know we're doing the right thing. We're on the right track here. We're doing the right thing for ourselves, for our own interest and for the world. And don't forget it. Come on, guys."[98]

But the situation continued to worsen between 2004 and 2006, even as the Bush administration struggled to prop up a new unity government in Iraq. In late April 2004 the press received leaked accounts, and graphic images, of prisoner abuse by U.S. soldiers at the Abu Ghraib prison outside Baghdad. And attacks on U.S. troops continued to rise as the war lingered on. According to a May 2006 secret report by the intelligence division of the Joint Chiefs, the insurgency had gained momentum from 2004 to 2006. Attacks on coalition forces were at their highest point, more than 3,500, in May 2006. The report went on to predict, "Insurgents and terrorists retain the resources and capabilities to sustain and even increase current level of violence through the next year."[99]

With a growing and complex pattern of violence emanating from Baathist insurgents, Sunni jihadists, and Shiite militias, and with U.S. casualties and economic costs continuing to rise in Iraq during 2005 and 2006, political pressure for a new strategy became much more powerful. The White House reluctantly agreed in spring 2006 to the creation of a bipartisan, independent commission to reevaluate U.S. options in Iraq. To remain above partisan politics, the Iraq Study Group (ISG) headed by James Baker, former secretary of state in the elder Bush's administration, and Lee Hamilton, former Democratic representative and cochair of the 9/11 Commission, set its reporting date for after the 2006 elections. As the elections approached and problems in Iraq continued, Iraq became the dominant issue in the campaign and Republican prospects dimmed. A *New York Times*/CBS poll taken just before the election showed that the war in Iraq was the most important issue for voters. Thirty-four percent of the public believed the war should be Congress's first priority. No other issue even reached 10 percent in the poll. Moreover, only 29 percent of the respondents supported Bush's handling of the war in Iraq, and almost 70 percent believed that he had no plan to end the war.[100]

The election brought a stunning victory for the Democrats, who gained control of the Senate by a margin of 51–49 and the House 233–202. Not a single Democratic incumbent was defeated in the House. With the vote seen primarily as a referendum on Iraq, there was great expectation that the Baker-Hamilton commission might offer Bush an opportunity to build consensus around a new strategy for Iraq.

On December 6, 2006 the ISG issued its report. The opening sentence set the tone: "The situation in Iraq is grave and deteriorating." Despite its scathing critique of the situation, the report rejected drastic policy change in the form either of a significant increase in, or an immediate withdrawal of, U.S. troops. But it refused to accept staying the course, either. Instead, the report called for an aggressive diplomatic offensive involving all of Iraq's neighbors, internal political reform in Iraq, and a shift in the role of the U.S. military from direct combat to training Iraqi forces, with the goal, subject to conditions in Iraq, of removing U.S. combat forces by spring 2008.[101]

In public comments, President Bush acknowledged that the ISG report was "worthy of serious study," but he was clearly not comfortable with two of its most significant recommendations—negotiations that included Iran and Syria and setting a timetable for the removal of combat troops.[102] He indicated that he would wait for studies ongoing in his administration before making any decisions about future policy directions. In fact, in September 2006, concerned with both the security situation in Iraq and the political situation in the U.S., the administration had begun a review of Iraq policy. The review was kept secret because, "As the American elections approached, White House officials say, they believed it would amount to political suicide to announce a broad reassessment of Iraq strategy. But they recognized that unless they began such a review, they would be forced to accept the conclusions of the final report of the Iraq Study Group."[103]

Apparently by late September Bush had already decided that staying the course was no longer viable and that Donald Rumsfeld, a staunch defender of current policies, would be replaced, though that too would not be announced until after the election.[104] Immediately after the election, the pace of the administration's policy review quickened. Deputy National Security Advisor J. D. Crouch was tasked with coordinating reassessments already under way by the National Security Council, the Joint Chiefs of Staff, and the State Department. The goal was to complete the review by mid-December so as to have policy alternatives to compete with the ISG report. But the administration found it difficult to build a consensus on a new policy and soon announced that no new policy would be forthcoming before early 2007.[105]

Much of the military leadership, including the Joint Chiefs of Staff; General John Abizaid, head of Central Command; and General George Casey, commander of the coalition forces in Iraq, were highly resistant to any significant increases in troop levels.[106] They believed that an increase would only encourage the Iraqi government to postpone making necessary political, economic, and military reforms. On the other hand, National Security Advisor Stephen Hadley consistently supported a troop surge to regain control of the security situation in Baghdad, arguing that viable political reforms could not be achieved without that security.[107]

Bush had never seriously considered beginning to withdraw troops from Iraq. He had, however, briefly considered a plan by Iraqi prime minister Nouri al-Maliki to redeploy U.S. troops from the center of Baghdad and allow Iraqi forces to control the sectarian violence there. But Bush quickly concluded that Iraqi forces were incapable of the task and that the situation might rapidly degenerate. Thus, by early December Bush strongly leaned toward some type of surge.[108]

Bush was disappointed with the Joint Chiefs' opposition to such an increase. He was said to have come away from a meeting with them on December 13 thinking that the chiefs "were trying to manage defeat rather than find a way to victory."[109] Bush was quoted as warning them: "What I want to hear from you is how we are going to win . . . not how we're going to leave."[110] By the end of December, the Joint Chiefs, as well as Casey and Abizaid, were persuaded to accept a troop increase. For years Rumsfeld had rejected calls for an increase in the permanent force levels of the army and the marines. Bush now agreed to a permanent increase of 92,000 soldiers to relieve the stress on the military created by deployments in Iraq and Afghanistan.[111] Moreover, Bush accepted the military's request that the new Iraq policy include greater emphasis on economic development and political reform, as well as assurances from the Malaki government that it would provide sufficient Iraqi forces to assist American troops and that military operations would be permitted in Shiite neighborhoods. In the last week of December, General Casey submitted a request for two additional brigades of troops.[112]

In early January 2007, as the nation waited for Bush's Iraq policy address, word leaked out that Bush was removing his top diplomatic and military leadership in Iraq. The U.S. ambassador to Iraq, the commander of coalition forces in Iraq, and the head of Central Command were to be replaced. Perhaps most important, General David Petraeus, who had been responsible for revising the army's counterinsurgency policy and who enthusiastically supported a troop surge, was to be the new commander of forces in Iraq. A senior official in the administration commented, "The idea is to put the whole new team in at roughly the same time, and send some clear messages that we are trying a new approach."[113]

That "new way forward" was announced on January 10.[114] The president admitted that his old course had failed. But his new plan did not resemble the recommendations of the ISG report: there was no time frame for withdrawal or even reduction of troops, and there was no ambitious diplomatic initiative to draw Iraq's neighbors into a peace process. Instead, arguing that the mission in Iraq was too important to be abandoned, the president announced that five more brigades (about 21,500 combat troops) would be sent to Iraq. Most would be assigned to Baghdad, to control sectarian violence. Providing security within Iraq would become the primary goal of American forces. There would also be an extensive economic development effort to enhance the quality of life for Iraqis, and the Malaki government would be given a series of political reform benchmarks to achieve, although no clear negative consequences were spelled out for failure to achieve them.

Most Democrats and some Republicans in Congress denounced the increase as a rejection of both the bipartisan ISG recommendations and the public's will as expressed in the fall election. An overnight *Washington Post*/ABC News poll found that 61 percent of the public opposed the president's plan.[115] Congress struggled to respond to Bush's initiative, but congressional Democrats were divided. A number of recourses were considered, including a nonbinding resolution opposing the troop increase; a repeal of the original legislation authorizing the use of force in Iraq and its replacement with another, more narrowly drafted, conditional authorization; an appropriation of funds for the war that put conditions on the use of troops in Iraq, such as stipulating a deadline or goal for the removal of combat soldiers; and a refusal to appropriate any funds for the war in the next fiscal year.

Each of those options raised political, military, and constitutional problems. Some Congress members rejected a nonbinding resolution as a meaningless symbol that would do nothing to end the war. Others thought that placing restrictions, including time limits, in legislation not only would infringe on the president's consitutional role as commander in chief, but would put the military at risk by limiting the president's ability to make rapid adjustments to changes on the ground. Strong opponents of the war thought conditional appropriations would still let the war continue for too long. Furthermore, conditional legislation also had the liability of being subject to presidential veto. All sides agreed that Congress had the constitutional authority to refuse to appropriate any future funds for the war. Doing that, however, has the serious political liability of leaving members open to charges of failing to support the troops.

President Bush's need in spring 2007 for a $97 billion supplemental appropriation for the wars in Iraq and Afghanistan provided opponents with a vehicle to limit the combat role of American troops in Iraq. At the end of March 2007, after protracted debate within the Democratic Party, both the House and the Senate passed appropriations bills that set time limits on U.S. combat troops in Iraq.[116] Only two Republicans in each house supported the legislation. It was not clear whether a conference committee could bridge the differences between the two bills. But it was clear that with little Republican support Congress would not be able to override the president's threatened veto. And it was doubtful that Congress would allow the funding to lapse while troops were still on the ground.

Conclusion

The Iraq war has provided some important lessons for U.S. foreign policy in the post–9/11 era. In many ways, an ongoing war on terror lends itself to an imperial presidency. The Bush doctrine and the wars in Afghanistan and Iraq all suggest the ability of a very strong executive to dominate U.S. foreign policy decision making. The Iraq war and its aftermath also demonstrate some of the problems that result from executive branch dominance in foreign policymaking. A highly personalized and aggressive executive decision process, especially with an acquiescent Congress, can be prone to making decisions without an adequate range of information. The result can be a series of flawed decisions, including, in the case of U.S. military action against Iraq, underestimating the danger of intervening without adequate international support, failing to make adequate preparations for the occupation of Iraq, and only belatedly recognizing that the counterinsurgency strategy in effect was failing.

The constraints on an imperial president can be quite limited. Despite losing the 2006 election, Bush was still able to go against public opinion and impose a troop surge in 2007. The limits on Congress's ability to influence the situation were also seen in that decision. Party loyalty among Congress members of the president's party and the president's veto power normally limit Congress's ability to check the president. The most potent constitutional tool available to Congress, a funding cutoff, is under most circumstances too blunt a political tool to wield effectively. It may be that an imperial president can only be checked by his own electoral fate, the presidential two-term limit, or the abandonment of his cause by his own party. These are all slow processes.

The result has been an ill-conceived war going into its fifth year with no end in sight. By the end of 2006, the war had already cost the United States over $400 billion, with continuing costs, including refurbishing depleted military equipment and the long-term care of wounded veterans, estimated at two trillion dollars.[117] Casualties exceed 3,000 American troops killed and 20,000 wounded, plus the toll on Iraqi society of about 56,000 civilians killed, 1.6 million Iraqis internally displaced, and 1.8 million international refugees.[118]

Key Actors

George W. Bush President, saw the need after the September 11 attacks for the United States to adopt a policy of preventive strikes against nations that presented a potential security threat; believed that Iraq was such a threat.

Richard Cheney Vice president, strongly believed that Iraq, because it allegedly possessed weapons of mass destruction and had links to al Qaeda, posed an immediate threat to the security of the United States and that diplomacy would not produce an adequate response.

Stephen Hadley National security advisor in the second term of the Bush administration, was a strong proponent of a surge after the 2006 election.

Colin Powell Secretary of state, argued within the administration that the threat from Iraq could be contained with beefed-up UN weapons inspections and cautioned against the United States intervening militarily in Iraq without international support.

Condoleezza Rice National security advisor, central foreign policy adviser to President George W. Bush, but had difficulty coordinating the policy process within the administration because of strong and conflicting personalities and policy positions; became secretary of state in the second term.

Donald Rumsfeld Secretary of defense, argued that a transformed U.S. military with precision-guided munitions and a smaller, lighter strike force was the appropriate option to remove the allegedly imminent Iraqi threat.

George Tenet Director of central intelligence, was skeptical about the need for an invasion of Iraq but later provided intelligence reports that helped the president make the case for war.

Paul Wolfowitz Deputy secretary of defense, a long-time proponent of a preventive military strategy in general and the use of military force to achieve regime change in Iraq in particular.

Notes

1. Arthur M. Schlesinger Jr., *The Imperial Presidency* (Boston: Houghton Mifflin, 1973), ix.

2. Michael Beschloss, "The End of the Imperial Presidency," *New York Times*, December 18, 2000, A27.

3. Schlesinger, *The Imperial Presidency*, viii.

4. Nicholas Lemann, "The Next World Order: The Bush Administration May Have a Brand New Doctrine of Power," *New Yorker*, April 1, 2002, www.newyorker.com/fact/content/?020401fa_FACT1 (accessed January 12, 2004).

5. Ivo H. Daalder and James M. Lindsay, *America Unbound* (Washington, D.C.: Brookings Institution Press, 2003), 2.

6. Bob Woodward, *Plan of Attack* (New York: Simon and Schuster, 2004). See also Todd Purdum et al., *A Time of Our Choosing: America's War in Iraq* (New York: Times Books/Henry Holt, 2003).

7. Michael R. Gordon and Bernard E. Trainor, *Cobra II: The Inside Story of the Invasion and Occupation of Iraq* (New York: Pantheon, 2006), 16.

8. Bryan Burrough, Evgenia Peretz, David Rose, and David Wise, "The Path to War," *Vanity Fair*, May 2004, 236.

9. Bill Keller, "The Sunshine Warrior," *New York Times Magazine*, September 22, 2002, 48; Bob Woodward, *Bush at War* (New York: Simon and Schuster, 2002), 85.

10. Woodward, *Plan of Attack*, 26.

11. Burrough et al., "The Path to War," 238.

12. Lawrence F. Kaplan, "Why the Bush Administration Will Go After Iraq," *New Republic*, December 10, 2001, 21.

13. See its Web site at www.newamericancentury.org.

14. Chalabi was a controversial figure. Some hailed his stand for Iraqi freedom as heroic and referred to him as the "George Washington of Iraq," but critics charged that Chalabi was out of touch with popular sentiment in Iraq, having been out of the country for almost forty years; Seymour M. Hersh, "The Iraq Hawks," *New Yorker*, December 24, 2001, 58.

15. David Rieff, "Blueprint for a Mess," *New York Times*, November 2, 2003, A1.

16. Quoted in Robert Dreyfuss, "Just the Beginning: Is Iraq the Opening Salvo in a War to Remake the World?" *American Prospect*, April 1, 2003.

17. Woodward, *Plan of Attack*, 9.

18. Seymour M. Hersh, "Selective Intelligence?" *New Yorker*, May 12, 2003, www.newyorker.com/printable/?fact/030512fa_fact (accessed January 11, 2004).

19. Gordon and Trainor, *Cobra II*, 38.

20. Quoted in Michael Elliot and James Carney, "First Stop, Iraq," *Time*, March 31, 2003, 177; and Daalder and Lindsay, *America Unbound*, 130.

21. Daalder and Lindsay, *America Unbound*, 130.

22. Woodward, *Plan of Attack*, 175.

23. Glenn Kessler, "U.S. Decision on Iraq Has Puzzling Past," *Washington Post*, January 12, 2003, A1.

24. Elliot and Carney, "First Stop, Iraq," 172; Woodward, *Plan of Attack*, 45–47; Susan Page, "Iraq Course Set from Tight White House Circle," *USA Today*, September 11, 2002, 5A.

25. Woodward, *Plan of Attack*, 1–3.

26. Burrough et al., "The Path to War," 240.

27. Page, "Iraq Course Set," 5A–6A; Bob Woodward, *Bush at War* (New York: Simon and Schuster, 2002), 108, 329; Evan Thomas, "Bush Has Saddam in His Sights," *Newsweek,* March 4, 2002, 21.

28. Elliot and Carney, "First Stop, Iraq," 173.

29. Christopher Marquis, "Bush Officials Differ on Way to Force out Iraqi Leader," *New York Times,* June 19, 2002, A1.

30. Woodward, *Plan of Attack,* 72–73.

31. Gordon and Trainor, *Cobra II,* 26.

32. Glenn R. Kessler and Peter Sleven, "Rice Fails to Repair Rifts, Officials Say," *Washington Post,* October 12, 2003, A1.

33. Mark Hosenball, Michael Isikoff, and Evan Thomas, "Cheney's Long Path to War," *Newsweek,* November 17, 2003, 29.

34. Gordon and Trainor, *Cobra II,* 112.

35. Ibid., 127.

36. Quoted in Bob Woodward, *State of Denial* (New York: Simon and Schuster, 2006), 125.

37. Quoted in Gordon and Trainor, *Cobra II,* 129.

38. "President Bush Delivers Graduation Speech at West Point: Remarks by the President at the 2002 Graduation Exercise of the United States Military Academy," West Point, New York, June 1, 2002, www.whitehouse.gov/news/releases/2002/06/print/20020601-3.html (accessed January 22, 2004).

39. Woodward, *Plan of Attack,* 150.

40. Ibid.

41. John Diamond et al., "Bush Set Sights on Saddam after 9/11, Never Looked Back," *USA Today,* March 21, 2003, 8A.

42. Brent Scowcroft, "Don't Attack Saddam," *Wall Street Journal,* August 15, 2002, A14.

43. Todd S. Purdum and Patrick E. Tyler, "Top Republicans Break with Bush on Iraq Strategy," *New York Times,* August 16, 2002, A1.

44. Ibid.

45. Glenn Kessler, "Rice Lays Out a Case for War in Iraq," *Washington Post,* August 26, 2002, A1.

46. Elizabeth Pond, *Friendly Fire: The Near-Death of the Transatlantic Alliance* (Washington, D.C.: Brookings Institution Press, 2004); see also "Vice President Speaks at VFW 103rd National Convention," www.whitehouse.gov/news/releases/2002/08/20020826.html (accessed January 12, 2004).

47. Elizabeth Bumiller and James Dao, "Cheney Says Peril of a Nuclear Iraq Justifies an Attack," *New York Times,* August 27, 2002, A1.

48. Woodward, *Plan of Attack,* 161.

49. Woodward, *Bush at War,* 44.

50. Woodward, *Plan of Attack,* 167; Frontline, "The War Behind Closed Doors," www.pbs.org/wgbh/pages/frontline/shows/iraq (accessed September 8, 2004).

51. Frontline, "The War Behind."

52. Dana Milbank, "White House Push for Iraqi Strike Is on Hold," *Washington Post,* August 18, 2002, A1.

53. Mike Allen and Juliet Eilperin, "Bush Aides Say Iraq War Needs No Hill Vote," *Washington Post,* August 26, 2002, A1.

54. Ibid.

55. Miles Pomper, "Bush Hopes to Avoid Battle with Congress over Iraq," *CQ Weekly*, August 31, 2002, 2255.

56. Ibid.

57. Allison Mitchell and David Sanger, "Bush to Put Case for Action in Iraq to Key Lawmakers," *New York Times*, September 4, 2002, A1.

58. "President's Remarks at the United Nations General Assembly," www.whitehouse.gov/news/releases/2002/09/print/20020912-1.html (accessed July 31, 2003).

59. Bob Woodward, "A Struggle for the President's Heart and Mind," *Washington Post*, November 17, 2002, A1.

60. Allison Mitchell, "Bush's Address Draws Praise in Congress, but Doubts Linger," *New York Times*, September 13, 2002, A11; Dan Balz and Jim VandeHei, "Bush Speech Aids Prospect for Support by Congress," *Washington Post*, September 13, 2002, A32.

61. "Text of the Proposed Resolution," *Washington Post*, September 20, 2002, A21.

62. U.S. Congress, *Congressional Record*, September 20, 2002, 148:S8966.

63. Richard Cohen, "Between Iraq and a Hard Place," *National Journal*, September 14, 2002, 2621.

64. Dana Milbank, "In President's Speeches, Iraq Dominates, Economy Fades," *Washington Post*, September 25, 2002, A1.

65. Jim VandeHei, "Daschle Angered by Bush Statement," *Washington Post*, September 26, 2002, A1.

66. Milbank, "In President's Speeches."

67. Ibid.

68. VandeHei, "Daschle Angered."

69. Eric Schmitt, "Rumsfeld Says U.S. Has 'Bulletproof' Evidence of Iraq's Links to Al Qaeda," *Washington Post*, September 28, 2002, A9.

70. Todd Purdum and Elisabeth Bumiller, "Congress Nearing Draft Resolution on Force in Iraq," *New York Times*, September 27, 2002, A1.

71. David Nather et al., "'One Voice' Lost in Debate over Iraq War Resolution," *CQ Weekly*, September 28, 2002, 2500.

72. "Bush Rejects Hill Limits on Resolution Allowing War," *Washington Post*, October 2, 2002, A1.

73. Quoted in Louis Fisher, "Deciding on War against Iraq: Institutional Failures," *Political Science Quarterly* 18, no. 3 (2003): 403.

74. "For Gephardt, Risks and a Crucial Role," *Washington Post*, October 3, 2002, A1.

75. Karen DeYoung, "Bush Cites Urgent Iraqi Threat," *Washington Post*, October 8, 2002, A1.

76. John Cushman, "Daschle Predicts Broad Support for Military Action against Iraq," *New York Times*, October 7, 2002, A11.

77. "CIA Letter to Senate on Baghdad's Intentions," *New York Times*, October 9, 2002, A12.

78. Dana Milbank, "For Many, a Resigned Endorsement; Attack Authorized with Little Drama," *Washington Post*, October 11, 2002, A6.

79. James VandeHei and Juliet Eilperin, "House Passes Iraq War Resolution," *Washington Post*, October 11, 2002, A1.

80. Thom Shanker and Eric Schmitt, "Threats and Responses: The Pentagon; Rumsfeld Orders War Plans Redone for Faster Action," *New York Times*, October 13, 2002, A1.

81. Thomas Ricks, *Fiasco* (New York: Penguin, 2006), 66.

82. Woodward, *State of Denial,* 89.

83. Kathleen T. Rhem, "Wolfowitz: Disarming Iraq 'Crucial' to Winning War on Terror," American Forces Information Service, January 23, 2003, www.pentagon.gov/news/Jan2003/n01232003_200301238.html (accessed September 14, 2003).

84. Woodward, *Plan of Attack,* 254.

85. Department of Defense, "Secretary Rumsfeld Briefs at Foreign Press Center," January 22, 2003, www.pentagon.gov/news/jan2003/t01232003_t0122sdfpc.html (accessed September 14, 2003).

86. Robert Kagan, "Power and Weakness," *Policy Review* no. 113 (June/July 2002): 3.

87. Richard W. Stevenson, "Bush Gives Hussein 48 Hours, and Vows to Act," *New York Times,* March 18, 2003, A1.

88. CNN, "Poll: Two-Thirds of Americans Support Bush Ultimatum," www.cnn.allpolitics.printhis.clickability.com/pt/cpt?expire=1&fb=Y&urlID=5736455&action=cpt&partnerID=2001 (accessed May 6, 2003).

89. Ricks, *Fiasco,* 116.

90. For a detailed history of the Iraq War, see Anthony H. Cordesman, *The Iraq War: Strategy, Tactics, and Military Lessons* (Westport, Conn.: Praeger, 2003).

91. Thomas E. Ricks, "War Could Last Months, Officers Say," *Washington Post,* March 27, 2003, A1.

92. Editorial, "Elusive al Qaeda Connections," *New York Times,* February 14, 2003, A16.

93. Hersh, "Selective Intelligence?"

94. Burrough et al., "The Path to War," 294.

95. Harvey Rice and Julie Mason, "America at War; Anarchy Reigns in Baghdad," *Houston Chronicle,* April 12, 2003, 1.

96. Woodward, *State of Denial,* 219; see also Ricks, *Fiasco,* 158–165.

97. Richard W. Stevenson and Janet Elder, "Support for War Is Down Sharply, Poll Concludes," *New York Times,* April 29, 2004, A1; see also Marist College Institute for Public Opinion Poll, quoted in Kenneth T. Walsh, "A Case of Confidence," *U.S. News and World Report,* November 17, 2003.

98. Woodward, *State of Denial,* 371.

99. Quoted in Woodward, *State of Denial,* 472.

100. Adam Nagourney and Megan Thee, "With Election Driven by Iraq, Voters Want New Approach," *New York Times,* November 2, 2006, 1A.

101. Iraq Study Group, *Iraq Study Group Report* (New York: Vintage, 2006), xiii.

102. Peter Baker and Robin Wright, "Bush Appears Cool to Key Points of Report on Iraq," *Washington Post,* December 8, 2006, A1

103. David Sanger et al., "Chaos Overran Iraq Plan in '06, Bush Team Says," *New York Times,* January 2, 2007, A1

104. Ibid.

105. Michael Fletcher, "Bush Delays Speech on Iraq Strategy," *Washington Post,* December 13, 2006, A12

106. Sanger et al., "Chaos Overran Iraq Plan."

107. Glenn Kessler, "Bush's New Plan for Iraq Echoes Key Parts of Earlier Memo," *Washington Post,* January 11, 2007, A13

108. Michael Abramowitz and Peter Baker, "Embattled Bush Held to Plan to Salvage Iraq," *Washington Post,* January 21, 2007, A1

109. Ibid.

110. Sanger et al., "Chaos Overran Iraq Plan."

111. Ann Scott Tyson and Josh White, "Gates Urges Increase in Army, Marines," *Washington Post,* January 12, 2007, A14.

112. Abramowitz and Baker, "Embattled Bush."

113. Robin Wright and Michael Abramowitz, "Bush Making Changes in His Iraq Team," *Washington Post,* January 5, 2007, A1.

114. David Sanger, "Bush Adding 20,000 U.S. Troops," *New York Times,* January 11, 2007, 1.

115. Michael Abramowitz and Robin Wright, "Bush to Add 21,500 Troops in an Effort to Stabilize Iraq," *Washington Post,* January 11, 2007, A1

116. Jeff Zeleny and Robin Toner, "Democrats Rally Behind a Pullout from Iraq in '08," *New York Times,* March 9, 2007, 1; Robin Toner, "Democrats Unite around an Iraq Plan of their Own," *New York Times,* March 24, 2007, 1.

117. *Iraq Study Group Report,* 32.

118. Ibid., 4; see also the Brookings Institution Iraq Index for updated statistics on the situation in Iraq, www.brookings.edu/iraqindex.

3 Coca, Human Rights, and Violence: U.S. Foreign Policy toward Colombia

Jennifer S. Holmes

Before You Begin

1. What should the United States do about drug smuggling and the countries involved?
2. Did Plan Colombia help or hinder the U.S. goals of promoting trade, democracy, and regional stability in Latin America?
3. Do Colombia's concerns with its social stability and democracy conflict with the strategic or political concerns of the United States? Where do they converge, or where do they conflict?
4. Does U.S. policy address Colombian social stability and democracy? What concerns do U.S. lawmakers prioritize?
5. Why has U.S. aid to Colombia tended to be predominantly military in nature? Is this the most appropriate type of assistance?
6. Should human rights in Colombia be a prominent concern in crafting U.S. foreign policy where the drug trade is involved? Who is interested in this issue?
7. Is drug trafficking fundamentally a question of supply or of demand? Which aspect of the problem does U.S. policy address?
8. How did the September 11 attack on the United States alter the foreign policy of President George W. Bush toward Colombia?

Introduction: The Colombian Challenge

Colombia has been designated "public enemy number one" in the debate over illegal drugs in the United States. When Colombia reached its peak of cocaine production in 2001, it alone provided about 75 percent of all the cocaine consumed in the world. In 2003, 90 percent of all cocaine in the United States either originated in Colombia or passed through it.[1] Despite spending billions of dollars in a sustained effort to eradicate coca production, Colombia remains the world's leading producer and processor of cocaine. Opium poppies (used in heroin production) and marijuana are also grown in Colombia.

Recent U.S. presidents have attempted to deal with drug smuggling in various ways. President Ronald Reagan declared the drug trade a national security threat and launched his so-called war on drugs. Supplemented by First Lady Nancy Reagan's "Just Say No" domestic campaign against U.S. consumption of illegal drugs, his administration focused on production, processing, and trafficking abroad. Under President George Bush, the "Andean Initiative" provided some Latin American countries with military support, economic assistance, and law enforcement advice to curb production and trafficking. Countries that did not cooperate faced possible U.S. military intervention, as Panama experienced in 1989.[2] President Bill Clinton noted that drug production and trafficking put Colombia's progress in peril, while fueling addiction and violence in the United States and elsewhere.[3] Having reallocated some interdiction funds to programs targeting demand in face of substantial congressional resistance, in his second term Clinton shifted policy, reverting to a strategy aimed at supply. "Plan Colombia," a comprehensive strategy developed in coordination with the Colombian government, dramatically increased U.S. assistance, but it did not allow counternarcotics aid to be used directly for counterinsurgency purposes. Despite the restrictions on counterinsurgency aid, the increasing involvement by Washington heightened concerns within the human rights community and in Congress about U.S. involvement in the Colombian conflict. After the September 11 attacks, President George W. Bush adopted an approach overtly combining counterinsurgency and counternarcotic strategies in Colombia.

Background: The Colombian Producer State

Before the 1991 Constitution, political participation has been limited in Colombia, although it is one of Latin America's oldest democracies. After fighting a brutal civil war, the Liberal and Conservative Parties agreed to a power-sharing arrangement, known as the National Front, which lasted from 1958 until 1974. Until 1986, "adequate and equitable" representation was guaranteed to both parties. The dominance of these two left little room for other viable political parties under the National Front agreement, and since the 1960s successive Colombian governments have faced rebel insurgencies.[4] Since the 1970s Colombia has also been struggling against an illegal drug industry with expansive networks that have penetrated the economy and politics. Adding to the conflict are privately funded paramilitary armies with varying degrees of loyalty to the Colombian government and military.

The activities of the various guerrilla groups, drug cartels, and paramilitaries have made Colombia one of the most violent nations in the world. The damage

U.S. Aid to Colombia

1986 With congressional passage of P.L. 99-570, the United States adopts the process of certifying aid recipients on the basis of their efforts to stem the illegal drug trade. If not certified, countries risk forfeiting U.S. economic and military assistance.

1989 President George Bush's Andean Initiative provides Colombia and other South American nations with military and economic assistance and law enforcement advice to curb the production and trafficking of illegal drugs.

1994 Rumors circulate that Colombian president Ernesto Samper Pizano's election campaign had received millions of dollars from the Cali drug cartel.

1995 For the first time, Colombia fails to gain certification from the United States as a cooperating partner in the war on drugs. President Bill Clinton grants Colombia a national security waiver allowing the disbursement of U.S. aid.

1996 The United States decertifies Colombia but does not grant a national security waiver or impose sanctions.

1997 The United States decertifies Colombia and issues a list of drug-fighting measures that the Colombian government must implement in order to receive assistance, which is granted. The Leahy amendment is passed, restricting units of security forces from receiving U.S. aid if the secretary of state determines that the unit has committed human rights violations, a measure that threatens aid to Colombia.

1998 Colombia fails to gain certification but is issued its second national security waiver. Andrés Pastrana is elected president.

1999 The United States certifies Colombia as a partner in the war on drugs.

1999 Pastrana proposes Plan Colombia, a program to reduce drug cultivation, strengthen Colombia's political and judicial institutions, and gain the upper hand against the guerrillas opposed to the government. Pastrana's government seeks U.S. and international assistance to carry out the $7 billion program.

January 11, 2000 Clinton proposes $1.6 billion in aid for Plan Colombia.

March 30, 2000 The House of Representatives approves $1.7 billion in aid for Plan Colombia.

continued on the next page

continued from the previous page

June 22, 2000 The Senate approves $934 million in aid for Plan Colombia. House and Senate conferees agree on $1.3 billion with a certification provision.

August 2000 Clinton waives the requirement that Colombia meet human rights standards and implement drug-fighting measures before aid dollars and equipment can be released. Colombia is certified as a partner in the war on drugs.

January 18, 2001 George W. Bush assumes office as president.

September 11, 2001 Al Qaeda attacks the United States, flying hijacked passenger planes into the World Trade Center towers and the Pentagon.

February 20, 2002 Peace talks between the Colombian government and the FARC break down, and government forces reassert control over the land it had granted the organization.

August 2, 2002 P.L. 107-206 is passed, allowing Colombian counternarcotics aid to be used for counterinsurgency purposes. The Andean Trade Preference Act (P.L. 107-210) is renewed.

August 7, 2002 Alvaro Uribe Vélez takes office as president.

May 29, 2003 Bush designates the United Self-Defense Groups of Colombia (AUC) and the FARC as significant foreign narcotics traffickers.

February 2004 Forty leaders of the FARC and AUC are placed on the U.S. list of international drug traffickers.

March 2004 Bush proposes increasing the personnel cap for Plan Colombia to 800 soldiers and military advisers and 600 civilian contractors.

March 2004 President Uribe visits Washington and requests a new, multiyear counterinsurgency and counternarcotics package through 2009.

July 2004 The government begins peace talks with the AUC. AUC leader Mancusco addresses the Colombian Congress.

February 2006 Colombia and the United States sign a free trade agreement, but the U.S. Congress does not approve it.

May 2006 President Uribe is elected to a second term. The Colombian Constitution had been amended to allow presidential reelection.

December 2006 The Andean Trade Preference Act is extended through June 2007.

March 2007 The unfolding Colombian "paragate" scandal reaches Uribe's cabinet, forcing his defense minister to resign and implicating Colombia's army chief and head of domestic intelligence.

done to the country and the people has been horrendous. More than 2 million of Colombia's citizens have fled their country since 1985—a significant number in a nation of less than 42 million—and hundreds of bombings have rocked its cities. Four presidential candidates, half of the justices of a sitting Supreme Court, more than 1,200 police officers, hundreds of journalists and judges, and more than 300,000 Colombian civilians have been murdered since 1985.[5] Violence has become a pressing societal problem in Colombia, leading to the deaths of approximately 4,000 people and the displacement of 350,000 others from their homes each year.[6]

Politics and Drugs

Four major groups have been actively engaged in the Colombian violence. The largest and best equipped is the Revolutionary Armed Forces of Colombia (FARC). With some eighteen thousand members, the FARC wants to overthrow the government to create a democracy inspired by Marxist notions of social justice. The group finances its organization by extorting money from businesses, including from drug traffickers, in areas under its control. For a time, the second-largest group was the Nineteenth of April Movement (M-19), which formed in response to contested elections in 1970. In November 1985, M-19 seized the Palace of Justice in Bogotá and took the Supreme Court justices hostage. After a brief attempt to negotiate, the military stormed the building, killing most of M-19's leaders and half of the justices. In 1989 M-19's remaining leadership signed an agreement with the government of President Virgilio Barco Vargas to surrender their arms in return for their incorporation into civilian life. Today M-19 openly participates in the political system as the Democratic Alliance/M-19. The Army of National Liberation (ELN) is another, smaller guerrilla group involved in political violence. Its members number four thousand to five thousand and gained notoriety by bombing the pipeline that carries most of Colombia's export oil from the eastern plains to the Caribbean.[7]

In response to these guerrilla groups, paramilitary groups began forming. The most notorious confederation of paramilitaries is the United Self-Defense Groups of Colombia (AUC), which was led by Carlos Castaño. The fifteen thousand–strong AUC is funded by landowners, businessmen, and drug dealers[8] with the aim of protecting their lives and property from the guerrillas.[9] The group began reorganizing in 2002 in an effort to minimize human rights violations and its drug ties in preparation for talks with the government. In December 2002 the AUC declared a unilateral cease-fire with the government, and in 2003 some of its constituent groups began to disband. The leaders of the AUC promised to demobilize completely by 2005, but the process was continuing in 2007.[10] As peace talks progressed in 2004, however, the leaders responsible for purging the organization's drug funding either were assassinated (Rodrigo Franco) or disappeared (Carlos Castaño), creating uncertainty about the cohesion and motivation of the remaining AUC leadership. Concerns remain about whether or not paramilitaries are actually demobilizing and ceasing their violent activity. Suspicions remain about government complicity with paramilitary violence.

Colombian drug traffickers have also been involved in the violence plaguing the country. The drug trade in Colombia began with the small-scale cultivation of marijuana in the 1960s; by the 1970s some Colombians had begun to process and export cocaine. The necessary chemical supplies were imported from Europe, and cocaine paste was brought in from Peru and Bolivia. The final product was then smuggled into the United States. By 1982 the drug trade accounted for 10 percent to 25 percent of Colombia's exports. At that point, however, the trade did not appear to be a threat to Colombian democracy.[11]

A few groups initially controlled the trade. One of the major traffickers was the Medellín cartel, headed by Pablo Escobar and Jorge and Fabio Ochoa. The cartel was arguably at its strongest in the middle to late 1980s. When Escobar was killed in a shootout with Colombian police in December 1993, the Cali cartel took over most cocaine production. Less violent than the Medellín cartel, the Cali organization focused its attention on legalizing parts of its operations and moving into legitimate businesses. President Ernesto Samper Pizano was rumored to have received $6 million from legal Cali businesses during his 1994 campaign. Nevertheless, Samper pursued an antidrug strategy. The major cartel kingpins were all jailed by 1996, though they received relatively light sentences.[12]

In addition to the well-known Cali and Medellín cartels, many other independent organizations produced, refined, and smuggled drugs. Sometimes the smaller groups cooperated or coordinated their activities with the larger operations.[13] With law enforcement targeting the Cali and Medellín cartels, others quickly arose to meet demand. A large number of cocaine labs were destroyed and the eradication of opium was stepped up in 1996, but the successes were short-lived. In the words of David Gaddis, the resident U.S. Drug Enforcement Administration (DEA) chief in Colombia, "The head of the mother snake was chopped off . . . but now we have to chase baby poisonous snakes, which can be . . . just as venomous."[14] Between 1993 and 1999 the potential acreage of the coca harvest almost quadrupled.[15]

The business of drugs is far-reaching and complicated, and in the case of Colombia it has profoundly affected preexisting social dynamics. Before the emergence of drug trafficking, there had been an ongoing struggle between traditional landowners and popular groups concerning unused *latifundios* (large estates or ranches), demands by peasants for title to property, and disagreements over state-supported rural modernization programs. Until the 1970s the large landowners usually won in such disputes. The drug trade changed the pattern by introducing competition from the narco-traffickers into the mix. Many drug traffickers invested in land. They then sponsored armed groups to protect their landholdings from landless peasants and rebel groups. By the 1980s armed protection of haciendas was reinforced, "so that in the middle of that decade almost all of the struggle for land had been eliminated through a combination of military harassment and paramilitary terrorism" of the peasants.[16] The spread of the drug trade removed any obstacles before it, including judges, police, and so forth. The result was growth in criminal elements and a change in the dynamics of the traditional conflict over land.

The rise of the drug trade also affected the operations of guerrillas opposed to the government and their control over territory. Bloody conflicts between narco-traffickers and guerrillas are common in guerrilla-controlled areas that traffickers have taken over for cultivation and processing. When drug traffickers take control of land, they commonly create death squads to eliminate the guerrillas, terrorize the local population, and limit the effectiveness of government authority. In short, they reorganize society by eliminating the existing social structure and creating their own social order. In areas where guerrillas remain strong, a pragmatic relationship develops in which the producers and traffickers usually pay tribute to the guerrilla groups.[17]

Some have tried to characterize the guerrillas as little more than another drug cartel. For example, General Barry McCaffrey, President Clinton's director of the Office of National Drug Control Policy, called the FARC the "principal organizing entity of cocaine production in the world."[18] According to Marc Chernick, director of the Andean and Amazonian Studies Program at Georgetown University,

> Some have tried to obfuscate this issue by collapsing the two issues into one, saying that the guerrillas work with the drug traffickers and are therefore effectively "narco-guerrillas." However, this is a gross distortion of the situation in Colombia. The guerrillas do not constitute another "cartel." Their role in the drug trade is in extorting a percentage of the commercial transaction of coca and coca paste, just as they do with many other commercial products in the areas in which they operate, be it cattle, petroleum, or coffee.[19]

The nature of the trafficker-guerrilla relationship is significant because some policymakers have tried to link the guerrillas with the cartels in an effort to justify the use of drug war funds for counterinsurgency purposes. Regardless, drug-related violence and guerrilla operations make Colombia's problems harder to solve.

Controlling the Drug Trade and Violence

Since the late 1970s the Colombian government has tried to craft political and military solutions for the rebel and drug conflicts, but few of these efforts have enjoyed lasting success. President Julio César Turbay Ayala (1978–1982) relied on the military and paramilitary units to control guerrilla violence. President Belisario Betancur (1982–1986) initiated talks that resulted in the establishment of the leftist Unión Patriótica by former FARC members. Their demobilization was not accepted by all parties, and paramilitary groups killed more than six thousand Unión Patriótica members. From the perspective of the left, the government did little to protect the newly incorporated party or to pursue the paramilitaries that targeted its members. Consequently, a 1984 cease-fire agreement between the government and the FARC failed. Rural and urban violence escalated under President Virgilio Barco Vargas (1986–1990). President César Gaviria Trujillo (1990–1994) attempted to restart talks with guerrilla insurgents, holding extensive negotiations in 1991 and 1992, but the discussions did not produce an agreement.

The Colombian government's response to the drug trade has varied. The United States had demanded the right to extradite Colombian citizens and charge them in U.S. courts, on the grounds that the Colombian judicial system was too weak and corrupt to prosecute traffickers effectively. President Turbay signed an extradition treaty in 1979, but no extraditions were requested until the Betancur administration. Once extraditions began, they created cycles of drug violence, in which the narco-traffickers would attack government and public targets, followed by state retaliation, followed by more violence, and so on. The situation became so bad that President Gaviria halted the extraditions. In 1991 he tried a policy of voluntary submission to justice, by which drug traffickers would be allowed to legalize their assets if they pled guilty to a few offenses and agreed to serve short sentences. During the Samper administration (1994–1998), the Colombian Congress passed an asset forfeiture law and allowed the extraditions of drug traffickers to the United States to resume. Even so, Colombia's relationship with the United States was severely strained by allegations that Samper accepted drug-tainted campaign money.[20]

In 1998 newly elected president Andrés Pastrana (1998–2002) launched attempts to combat the drug problem and the guerrilla conflict. He initiated talks with the FARC and the ELN for the first time in eight years. Both were offered safe havens, free from government interference, as a precondition to the peace talks. The FARC received forty-two thousand square kilometers of land in the center of Colombia, and the ELN was to control approximately five thousand square kilometers, although that zone was never fully implemented because of local and paramilitary resistance. At the end of Pastrana's term, peace talks broke down and the safe havens were abolished. In 1999 Pastrana proposed a six-year program called "Plan Colombia," whose provisions included promoting alternative development in coca-growing areas, strengthening Colombia's political and judicial institutions, and regaining the initiative in the conflict with the guerrillas. The estimated cost of the program was more than $7 billion. The government committed $4 billion to the effort and requested aid from the international community, including the European Union and the United States.[21]

President Alvaro Uribe Vélez introduced the "Democratic Security and Defense Strategy" shortly after being elected in 2002. Its main goal was to restore the rule of law and a climate of security through a coordinated effort by the security forces and the judiciary. Uribe declared a "state of internal commotion"—essentially a state of emergency—which gave him emergency powers to deal with the immediate security situation, implemented a 1.2 percent war tax on assets, and proposed antiterrorism legislation. In general, Uribe pursued a hard line against drug and guerrilla violence. In March 2004 the government reintroduced the Search Bloc police unit to hunt drug traffickers in the south. It specifically targeted the Norte de Valle drug cartel in much the same way that government forces earlier went after the Medellín cartel.[22] Also in 2004 Uribe initiated peace talks with the AUC, granting it a zone free of government interference as a condition of the peace process. Uribe's government has extradited individuals to the United States for prosecution. With the concurrence of the Colombian Supreme Court, former Cali cartel leader Victor Patiño Fómenque was extradited in November 2002 to face drug charges in Florida, and in April 2002 for the first time a FARC member was extradited to the United States to face charges of murder in the 1999 deaths of three Indian rights activists.[23] Uribe was reelected in 2006.

Pre-Clinton U.S. Policy

There are two basic ways to fight drug use. One is to reduce the demand for drugs by increasing education and treatment programs. The other is to attack the supply by reducing drug production and targeting trafficking. Because Colombia is the main source of cocaine supplied to the United States, U.S. foreign policy toward Colombia has focused on supply-side tactics. A main component of this strategy has been tying aid, trade concessions, and external credits to the Colombian government's compliance with the U.S. goal of reducing the amount of coca cultivated and cocaine produced. This supply-side strategy has led to the militarization of antidrug campaigns.[24]

In 1989 the U.S. military presence in Colombia was minor, as was U.S. assistance. After drug traffickers assassinated Luis Carlos Galán, the leading presidential candidate, the United States decided to strengthen the Colombian military and jump-start the war on drugs. Within a day, President Bush announced the release of $65 million in stockpiled Defense Department weapons and supplies to Colombia. Congress quickly approved a $200 million line of credit from the U.S. Export-Import Bank to the Colombian military. Three weeks later, Bush announced that $261 million more in aid would be given to the Andean nations of Bolivia, Colombia, and Peru, as part of his Andean Initiative. By 1992 U.S.-Colombian efforts had begun to concentrate on attacking the drug traffickers and cartels directly by focusing on the kingpins instead of on crop eradication. As U.S. policy came to rely more heavily on military and police efforts to combat the traffickers, many observers, including the U.S. General Accounting Office, became concerned that the United States would be drawn into counterinsurgency operations in the long-standing conflict between the Colombian government and the rebels.[25]

In 1999, according to the State Department's Bureau for International Narcotics and Law Enforcement Affairs, U.S. drug policy in Colombia had three main goals: to eliminate the cultivation of illegal drugs, including opium, coca, and marijuana; to strengthen Colombia's ability to disrupt and dismantle major drug trafficking organizations and prevent their resurgence; and to destroy the cocaine and heroin processing industries.[26] These goals needed to be accomplished without undermining regional stability or the already embattled Colombian democracy.

The Clinton Drug Policy

When asked by an MTV interviewer during the 1992 presidential campaign if he had ever tried marijuana, candidate Bill Clinton responded that he had, but, as he put it, "I didn't inhale." Clinton's comment helped create distrust among many in Congress about the seriousness with which he would pursue an antidrug strategy. The distrust increased after December 7, 1993, when Clinton's surgeon general independently suggested that the government study the idea of legalizing some drugs as a way to reduce violent crime. The response from the White House to this comment was less than warm, with the president's press secretary stating that such a study was not even being considered.[27] It was too late, however; many thought that the administration did not take the drug problem seriously. Difficulties were already shadowing its drug policy.

Clinton initially pursued a different balance of supply-side and demand-side efforts. Between September 1992 and September 1995 Clinton reduced interdiction efforts and eliminated a thousand antidrug positions, shortened mandatory sentences for traffickers, and proposed cutting 80 percent of the staff of the Office of National Drug Control Policy and reducing the number of Drug Enforcement Agency agents by 227. Republicans viewed this policy as responsible for an increase in the supply of drugs from Colombia.[28] When they charged that Clinton's policy was evidence of a lack of commitment to an antidrug strategy, administration officials protested that the statistics they cited took the president's policy out of context. Robert Gelbard, assistant secretary of state for international narcotics and law enforcement affairs, clarified some of the funding reductions:

> The President's 1995 National Drug Control Strategy continues our shift in focus to the source countries, so we are taking a more surgical view of how to destroy major transit and transshipment operations. Both concentrations are occurring against the backdrop of enhanced efforts to strengthen antinarcotics institutions of cooperating countries so they can shoulder more of the drug control burden.[29]

The truth was that although some programs suffered cutbacks, others enjoyed an increase in funding. In 1993 the international counternarcotics budgets of most U.S. agencies were cut. Gelbard's budget, for example, was reduced by 30 percent. Overall, however, Clinton's aid request for drug control for fiscal year 1994 rose to $13.2 billion, an increase of $1.1 billion from the previous year. Five areas were to receive more money:

- Funding for drug prevention increased by $448 million.
- Funding for drug treatment programs increased by $360 million.
- Spending for drug-related criminal justice increased by $227 million.
- Funding for other international programs increased by $76 million.
- Funding for drug-related research increased by $27 million.

Funding for interdiction, however, was cut by $94 million, and antidrug intelligence programs were cut by $600,000. Some members of Congress, such as Rep. Donald Manzullo, R-Ill., believed that the cuts reflected a lack of emphasis on interdiction by the administration, even though Clinton's stated policy was to shift funding from "transit zone interdiction" to stopping production in the source countries.[30]

In addition to disagreements over the components of Clinton's antidrug strategy, many House Republicans were also angry at delays in delivering promised aid to Colombia. For example, Rep. Dan Burton, R-Ind., said, "It is unfortunate that the Congress has had to fight tooth and nail with the administration, from the State Department to the United States Embassy and our Ambassador in Bogotá, in an attempt to try to get some form of assistance down to the brave people who are fighting the war on drugs."[31] In another example, Burton, along with Ben Gilman, R-N.Y., and Dennis Hastert, R-Ill., was upset about the lack of aid, specifically, getting UH-1H "Huey" helicopters to the Colombian national police in a timely manner.

Clinton received high marks for appointing Barry McCaffrey, a retired four-star U.S. Army general, to head the White House Office of National Drug Control Policy, a move that many saw as an attempt by Clinton to build up his credentials in the war on drugs.[32] McCaffrey took over as "drug czar" in February 1996, but his appointment did not produce the positive effects the president had hoped for. In fact, McCaffrey contributed to interbranch squabbling by accusing some in Congress of attempting to micromanage U.S. foreign policy toward Colombia.[33] Adding to the dissension, others in the administration and elsewhere in government preferred different aid strategies. Secretary of State Madeleine Albright emphasized supporting the peace process with the guerrillas. Some in the Pentagon favored an approach that focused on the military, and many Republicans in Congress preferred more aid to the Colombian national police.[34]

Congressional opinion would ultimately be important in crafting policy. Not only did Congress's control over spending allow it to determine how much aid would be sent to Colombia, but it could challenge presidential decisions under a certification policy adopted in 1986 (P.L. 99-570) based on Section 490 of the Foreign Assistance Act of 1961. Amendment of the act gave Congress a more active role in forging policy in regard to drug-producing and drug transit countries. It required the president, on March 1 of each year, to select one of three options regarding countries known for substantial drug production or known to be transit points: (1) to certify a country as fully cooperating to meet the goals of the UN Convention against Illicit Traffic in Narcotic Drugs and Psychotropic Substances, also known as the Vienna Convention; (2) to decertify a country as uncooperative but grant it a national security waiver, so that it would not suffer sanctions; or (3) to decertify a country and impose sanctions. Sanctions could include an end to most U.S. aid and votes against loans for that country in multilateral economic and development organizations. Depending on the country, other sanctions could be imposed, such as the elimination of its sugar quota for the U.S. market or a cutoff of tourist visas to the United States. The president could also levy trade sanctions; for example, he could deny preferential tariff treatment granted by the Andean Trade Preference Act of 1991, increase tariffs generally, or withdraw the United States from any pre-clearance customs arrangements. Congress could overturn the president's decision within thirty days.[35] This policy lasted until 2002.

Until 1995 Colombia had always received full certification. In 1995 Sen. Jesse Helms, R-N.C., sponsored an amendment to prohibit federal aid to Colombia until it began to fight more effectively against drug production and corruption. Despite Helms's efforts, Colombia received a national security waiver that year. In 1996 Clinton again decertified Colombia, but sanctions were not applied, and the government received the year's aid allocation. President Samper's acceptance of Cali cartel money for his campaign seemed to be the reason for the decertification. In 1997 Colombia was decertified and given six months to improve its drug-fighting efforts before a decision on sanctions would be made. The United States demanded the extradition of Colombian nationals (especially the Cali kingpins), full implementation of asset forfeiture and money laundering laws, implementation of a bilateral agreement on maritime law enforcement (to aid in interdiction efforts), tightened security for Colombian prisoners, the use of more potent herbicides for drug crop eradication, and better efforts against corrupt officials.[36] Colombia did not meet the demands but received aid nonetheless.

Another notable event of 1997 was the passage of an amendment sponsored by Sen. Patrick Leahy, D-Vt. His amendment to the Foreign Operations Act for Fiscal Year 1998 stated, "None of the funds made available by this Act may be provided to any unit of the security forces of a foreign country if the Secretary of State has credible evidence that such unit has committed gross violations of human rights." Passage of the amendment was an acknowledgment of unofficial ties between the Colombian military and right-wing paramilitary groups in fighting the guerrillas, and it would later be included, in varying ways, in other security assistance programs in 1998, 1999, and 2000. Difficulty in applying it would arise, however, over the definitions and compositions of military units. Representative Burton, among others, criticized the administration for not granting Colombia a national security waiver in 1996 and 1997. Samper's term ended in August 1998, and that year Colombia failed certification but was granted a national security waiver. In 1999, 2000, and 2001, under President Pastrana, Colombia would again receive full certification.

Plan Colombia: Aid in 2000–2001

Congressional criticism followed President Clinton's Colombia policy into the new millennium. Some Republicans, such as Sen. Mike DeWine, R-Ohio, wanted to shift the balance of funding away from education and prevention and back to supply-side efforts. Congress (in P.L. 105-277) added $870.2 million in extra monies for the drug war for fiscal year 1999. Again, many Republicans accused Clinton of not taking the problem seriously enough.[37] Political pressure continued to build for a stronger U.S. response to the Colombian drug problem, culminating in U.S. support for Plan Colombia.

On January 10, 2000, Rep. Dennis Hastert, who was now Speaker of the House, gave a speech in Chicago to the Mid-America Committee for International Business and Government Cooperation on the need to increase funding to Colombia. "Aggressive diplomacy, military assistance, continued military cooperation, intelligence activities, and counterdrug assistance will be necessary if we are to deter this growing threat. . . . The Republican-led Congress stands ready to support such a comprehensive strategy, but time is not on Colombia's side."[38] Building on congressional support for Plan Colombia, the next day Clinton announced plans to increase aid to Colombia, proposing a $1.6 billion package designed to create two antidrug battalions (of one thousand troops each) within the Colombian military, control Colombian airspace, and wipe out coca fields.[39] The most expensive aspect of the 2000 plan was the allocation of sixty-three UH-1H Huey combat helicopters for use by antinarcotics forces in southern Colombia, where the FARC was strong.

Resistance

Criticism of the aid package focused on two matters. Many opponents were concerned that U.S. aid was being used for counterinsurgency purposes, thereby involving the United States in another country's civil war. Some critics asked why Plan Colombia focused counternarcotics actions in southern Colombia, a traditional rebel stronghold, instead of the northern regions, where paramilitaries sympathetic to the government were active in the drug trade. Brian E.

Sheridan, the assistant secretary of defense for special operations and low-intensity conflict, asserted that there was no evidence to support the suspicion that the true purpose of U.S. aid was to assist Colombia in its internal conflict. "We are working with the Colombian government on counternarcotics programs. We are not in the counterinsurgency business," contended Sheridan.[40] An earlier congressional staff report presented a somewhat different view:

> In the past, the United States has tried to describe a bright line separating counterdrug and counterinsurgency support to Colombia, with no direct assistance for counterinsurgency. That line remains in law. Circumstances, however, are pushing the limits, making it difficult on the ground to make distinctions between insurgents and traffickers.[41]

Others wanted to make sure that U.S. aid would not be used to benefit groups implicated in human rights violations. For example, Senator Leahy implored Clinton, "We at least need to see a concerted effort by the Colombian army to thwart the paramilitary groups, who are responsible for most of the atrocities against civilians, and a willingness by the Colombian armed forces to turn over to the civilian courts their own members who violate human rights."[42] Because of the complexity of the Colombia situation, it was impossible to ascertain with total certainty whether U.S. aid was being used for counterinsurgency efforts, at least indirectly. Part of the controversy involved whether the Colombian military had ties to paramilitary groups, such as Castaño's AUC, which was responsible for some 75 percent of the political killings. Human Rights Watch, in its *World Report, 2000,* documented ties between the Colombian army's Fourth Brigade and the Castaño group. Castaño's men were reportedly able to exchange civilian corpses for weapons from the brigade. The army would then dress the corpses as guerrillas and claim that they had been killed in combat.[43] The State Department, in its *1999 Country Reports on Human Rights,* acknowledged that Colombian "security forces actively collaborated with members of paramilitary groups by passing them through roadblocks, sharing intelligence, and providing them with ammunition."[44] Many human rights groups, as well as congressional Democrats, contended that the 2000–2001 aid package did not do enough to break these ties and prosecute those collaborating with the paramilitary groups.

In response to critics, the Clinton administration reduced the amount of aid requested for Colombia from $1.6 billion to $1.3 billion for 2000.[45] To appease the Pentagon, it dropped the request for sixty-three rebuilt, Vietnam-era Huey helicopters and requested instead thirty newer, more expensive, and more sophisticated Sikorsky UH-60 L Blackhawk helicopters for combating drug trafficking.[46]

Congressional Passage

Despite the vocal opposition of critics, the administration's modified proposal had solid support in the House among both the rank and file and the leadership. One of its most enthusiastic supporters was Speaker Hastert, who said, "The bill we're considering today is about our children and whether we want our children to grow up in a society free from the scourge of drugs."[47] It is safe to say that no representative wanted to be portrayed as condoning drug smuggling, but some spoke out against an aid package that seemed to move the United States closer to involvement in Colombia's internal conflict and did not sufficiently protect the human rights of Colombians. Rep. David Obey, D-Wis., invoked the Vietnam War: "This is the camel's nose under the tent for a massive long-term commitment to a military operation. I detest Vietnam analogies under most circumstances, but in this case there is a very real parallel."[48] Rep. Maxine Waters, D-Calif., objected for humanitarian reasons: "This bill gives money to drug traffickers who kill other drug traffickers and murder innocent civilians."[49] In the end, the House approved more aid for Colombia than the administration requested—$1.7 billion. On March 30, 2000, the House rejected an attempt to lower the amount by a vote of 239–186. It then passed the appropriations bill of which the Colombia aid was a part 263–146.[50]

Despite strong support and pressure for a large aid package in the House, the legislation faced problems in the Senate, with many senators fearing involvement in an escalating, Vietnam-like situation. Sen. Slade Gorton, R-Wash., and Sen. Paul Wellstone, D-Minn., led the debate in criticizing the Colombian military's human rights record, declaring that the aid package would pull the United States into Colombia's civil war.[51] Gorton stated, "There has been no consideration of the consequences, cost, and length of involvement. . . . This bill says let's get into war now and justify it later."[52] One of the concessions made to allay such fears was to limit the number of American military personnel in Colombia to five hundred at any one time, with exceptions made for carrying out a possible rescue mission.[53] The bill the Senate approved called for supplying Huey helicopters rather than the Blackhawks.[54]

The administration was not without supporters in the Senate, however. Majority Leader Trent Lott, R-Miss., called for giving Colombians "the aid they need, the equipment that they need to fight these massive narcotics traffickers themselves." Sen. Christopher Dodd, D-Conn., argued, "This package may not be perfect, but our delay in responding to a neighbor's call for help is getting old. . . . When we step up and offer the Colombian democracy a chance to fight for themselves, we're not only doing it for them, we're doing it for ourselves."[55]

On June 22 the Senate approved, 95–4, a Colombian aid package totaling $934 million, just slightly more than half of the $1.7 billion the House had approved. Later that day, House and Senate conferees met and split the difference between the two amounts.[56] The final package of $1.319 billion contained the requirement that the government of Colombia obtain a national security waiver to receive the aid if it could not meet six conditions:

- The president of Colombia must issue a written order requiring that all military personnel facing credible allegations of human rights violations be tried in civilian courts.
- The commander general of the Colombian armed forces must promptly suspend those members facing credible allegations of human rights violations or of participating in paramilitary groups.
- The Colombian armed forces must fully cooperate with the investigations of civilian authorities in the search for those accused of human rights violations.
- The Colombian government must actively prosecute in civilian courts paramilitary leaders and members and any military personnel who assist them.
- The Colombian government must craft a plan to rid the country of all coca and poppy production by 2005.
- The Colombian armed forces must develop and deploy a judge advocate general corps in field units to investigate military personnel misconduct.[57]

The majority of aid to Colombia under the 2000–2001 plan went to the police ($363.1 million) and the armed forces ($589.2 million). The remaining $238 million in the package went for alternative development, aid to the displaced, human rights, judicial reform, law enforcement, and peace efforts. The final package included the Blackhawks.[58]

But controversy did not end with the passage of the package. Clinton continued to be pressured to withhold aid because of human rights violations. Senator Wellstone wrote the president on July 28:

> At present, the President of Colombia has issued no directive requiring that Colombian armed forces personnel accused of human rights violations will be held accountable in civilian courts, nor has the Colombian military taken

the firm, clear steps necessary to purge human rights abusers from its ranks or ensure that its personnel are not linked to paramilitary organizations. . . . Given these facts, I believe your Administration cannot and should not certify Colombia to receive assistance under Plan Colombia.[59]

Representatives from thirty-three nongovernmental organizations, including Amnesty International, the Washington Office on Latin America, and numerous church groups, requested that Colombia not be certified because of its lack of compliance with the human rights provisions of Section 3201 of the supplemental aid package. In an open letter to President Clinton on July 31, the groups stated, "A certification or waiver that ignores this critical human rights situation will send a clear message to the Colombian government and security forces, at the outset of this major increase in U.S. military involvement, that the United States' commitment to human rights does not go beyond empty rhetoric."[60]

The groups further noted that the Colombian government had not met several of the conditions for receiving aid. First, officers with proven records of human rights violations and support for paramilitary groups had not been dismissed from duty or referred to civilian authorities for trial, despite credible accusations of army-paramilitary collusion. Second, the Colombian government had not enforced its own law that officers accused of human rights violations should be tried in civilian courts. Charges against those officers continued to be heard in the military courts, even though the Colombian Constitutional Court had ruled that human rights cases must be heard in civilian courts. Third, the groups charged that the Colombian government had not acted to restrain the paramilitary groups or protect the population from attacks. Their letter concluded, "We have raised serious questions about [the current aid policy's] efficacy as counter-narcotics policy. . . . It will be an unqualified disaster, however, if the human rights conditions prove meaningless at the very outset."[61] In the end, Colombia met only one of the U.S. requirements. Nevertheless, in August Clinton waived the requirement that the conditions of the aid be met, stating that the grave situation in Colombia dictated that aid could not be delayed any longer.[62] In this instance, drug control was the defining characteristic of the national interest; human rights were not.

Just a week after passage of the package, Speaker Hastert announced that he was reviewing a request for an additional $99.5 million in aid to Colombia to provide more aircraft, ammunition, and other equipment to the Colombian police. Seventeen conservative lawmakers, including Burton and Gilman, wanted more aid to the police to be included in the foreign assistance bill for the new fiscal year. They favored the police because they believed that they were less implicated in human rights violations and more effective at fighting drugs than the military.[63]

The Policy of George W. Bush

The September 11 attacks on the United States altered the atmosphere of debate about Colombia and U.S. policy toward it. What was previously viewed as a government under siege by internal forces was now viewed as an ally fighting terrorism from within. In an October 15, 2001, press conference at the Organization of American States, Francis X. Taylor, the State Department coordinator for counterterrorism, stated,

> The FARC, the AUC, and the ELN are on the [U.S. government's] list [of terrorist groups] because they participate in terrorist activities and they get the same treatment as any other terrorist group, in terms of our interest in going after them and ceasing their terrorist activities.[64]

Thus began the shift in U.S. policy toward Colombia.

Insurgency: The New Terrorism

In the new atmosphere of fighting terrorism, one observer noted, public "officials from both countries must frame Colombia's problems along antiterrorism lines to assume continued United States support."[65] This sentiment was verbalized by Secretary of State Colin Powell on October 25, 2001: "There's no difficulty in identifying [Osama Bin Laden] as a terrorist, and getting everybody to rally against him. Now, there are other organizations that probably meet a similar standard. The FARC in Colombia comes to mind." This change in perspective meant that the Bush administration would actively pursue a policy of blending counternarcotics aid with counterinsurgency aims, whereas the Clinton administration had attempted to separate the two activities. On Capitol Hill, Rep. Cass Ballenger, R-N.C., chairman of the House Subcommittee on the Western Hemisphere, stated on April 11, 2002, "Let's face it, the FARC, ELN and AUC are terrorists who support their activities with drug money. Although they do not have the reach of al Qaeda or Hamas, they do have international reach, which includes smuggling drugs out of Colombia and into the United States and Europe."[66]

Peace talks between the Colombian government and the FARC broke down on February 20, 2002, the day the FARC hijacked an airliner, taking its fifth member of Colombia's Congress hostage. At midnight, government forces began to reestablish authority in the area previously given over to FARC control as a precondition for peace talks. With the negotiations having failed, the presumption of FARC's desire for a peaceful resolution of the decades-old conflict evaporated, making the entire process appear insincere. The FARC accused the government of militarily blockading the zone and of not aggressively pursuing paramilitary groups, while the government accused the FARC of using the zone as a platform for promoting attacks.

Following the White House lead, the House of Representatives passed Resolution 358 on March 6, 2002, pledging "to assist the Government of Colombia to protect its democracy from United States–designated foreign terrorist organizations." This shift in rhetoric was followed by a change in policy. An August 2, 2002, emergency request for counterterrorism funding contained a clause allowing the Colombian government to use all current and previously appropriated counternarcotics assistance for counterinsurgency purposes in a "unified campaign against narcotics trafficking [and] against activities by organizations designated as terrorist organizations such as the Revolutionary Armed Forces of Colombia (FARC), the National Liberation Army (ELN), and the United Self-Defense Forces of Colombia (AUC)."[67] Thus, the previous distinction between counterinsurgency and counternarcotics activities was erased. Moreover, the Clinton-era policy of prohibiting intelligence sharing other than for counternarcotics purposes—as set out in Presidential Decision Directive 73—was revised to allow the sharing of paramilitary and guerrilla intelligence with Colombian officials, regardless of whether a drug connection existed.[68]

This shift intensified opposition from those who believed that the Colombian situation had the potential to become a Vietnam-like quagmire. "This is a major policy change.... We could find ourselves engulfed in a morass that would eat up American soldiers like we have not seen in years," warned Rep. Ike Skelton, D-Mo.[69] Rep. Jim McGovern, D-Mass., agreed: "The United States will be plunging head first into a grinding, violent and deepening civil war that has plagued Colombia for nearly four decades."[70] Opposition aside, the Bush administration has aggressively moved against drug and guerrilla leaders. On August 26, 2003, the former head of the Medellín cartel, Fabio Ochoa Vasquez, was sentenced to more than thirty years in federal prison by a federal judge in Miami.[71] On May 29, 2003, the FARC and the AUC had been designated by Bush as "significant foreign narcotics traffickers." In February 2004 forty leaders of the FARC and AUC were placed on the U.S. list of international drug traffickers. Several of them have been indicted in the United States.[72]

Continuing Plan Colombia 2002–2005: The Andean Regional Initiative and the Andean Counterdrug Initiative

The 2002, 2003, 2004, and 2005 aid packages are generally criticized by opponents for being too focused on military and counternarcotics assistance, with too little attention paid to social and economic conditions, human rights, and environmental concerns. President Bush's 2002 request for the Andean Regional Initiative (ARI)—his administration's funding program for Plan Colombia, launched in April 2001—totaled $882.29 million. Of this amount, Colombia was to receive $399 million, with $146.5 million allocated for socioeconomic aid and $252.2 million to military and police aid. The House (H.R. 2506) allotted the ARI $826 million, $52 million less than Bush's request. The House debate included three notable, unsuccessful amendments. Rep. Nancy Pelosi, D-Calif., proposed to cap Colombian military aid at $52 million and allocate the remainder to an infectious diseases child survival account. An amendment by Steven Rothman, D-N.J., proposed suspending fumigation efforts until they could be proved safe. An amendment by Rep. David Obey proposed to shift all ARI counternarcotics funding to domestic drug treatment programs. The Senate (S.R. 107-58) only allocated the ARI $698 million, $184 million less than Bush wanted. The bill included demands for verifying the safety of aerial fumigation and eradication programs and human rights certification.[73] In the end, the Bush administration received $782 million to pursue "strengthening democracy, regional stability, and economic development"[74] but was limited by three human rights conditions, including a second round certification for 40 percent of the aid and no national security waiver provision, a requirement that the State Department provide assurances about the safety of fumigation practices, and a cap of 400 U.S. military personnel and 400 civilian contractors to support Plan Colombia. The total for all programs to Colombia in 2002 was $367 million in military and police aid and $147 million in social and economic aid.[75]

President Bush's 2003 request included $979.8 million for the ARI, including $537 million for Colombia. In the end, Colombia received $284 million for eradication and interdiction programs and $149.2 million for social and economic programs and a renewed Air Bridge Denial Program (an air interdiction effort), all limited by human rights certification. In the supplemental fiscal 2003 Emergency Wartime Supplemental Appropriations Act (P.L. 108-11), Colombia received an additional $37 million for presidential security, police aid, support for displaced people, and aerial eradication programs. It also was granted $93 million to protect the Cano-Limon pipeline.[76] A two-stage human rights certification provision was included: 25 percent of the aid was held in two parts for the secretary of state's certification that Colombia was prosecuting human rights violators within the police and military and to ensure that the Colombian military had severed ties to the paramilitary organizations and was actively pursuing them. Another provision threatened to reclaim helicopters if they were used in support of paramilitary operations. The law also contained a provision for withholding 80 percent of the eradication budget until the State Department certified that health and environmental guidelines and standards were met. The 2003 aid program maintained the cap on 400 military personnel and 400 contractors for Plan Colombia. The unified campaign continued, but concern about a Vietnam-style entanglement was clear in the conference report. It warned that the authority to conduct a unified campaign "is not a signal . . . for the United States to become more deeply involved in assisting the Colombian Armed Forces in fighting the terrorist groups, especially not at the expense of the counternarcotics program, but to provide the means for more effective intelligence gathering and fusion, and to provide the flexibility to the Department of State when the distinction between counternarcotics and counterterrorism is not clear cut."[77] Making such distinctions continues to be difficult. In March 2007, the U.S. Embassy in Colombia confirmed a report that Colombian and U.S. troops had participated in an unsuccessful joint operation to rescue three U.S. military contractors held by the FARC since their surveillance aircraft went down in February 2004.[78]

For fiscal year 2004, President Bush requested $990.7 million for the ARI, with $731 million of the assistance set aside for the Andean Counterdrug Initiative (part of the ARI beginning with funds allocated in fiscal year 2002). Bush requested $463 million for Colombia, including $150 million for social and economic programs and $313 million for narcotics interdiction and eradication programs. The House (H.R. 2800) fully funded the ACI at $731 million. The Senate Appropriations Committee (S. B. 1426) allotted only $660 million. The House (H.R. 2673) raised the cap on the number of military personnel to 500 and maintained the unified campaign of counternarcotics and counterinsurgency aid.[79] The ACI was ultimately funded at $731 million, with Colombia receiving $332 million in military and police aid and $136 million for socioeconomic programs. The 2004 package retained the unified campaign language, maintained the cap on personnel at 400, and had similar human rights and fumigation certification provisions.

The 2005 request for the ACI, the last anticipated year of the original Plan Colombia funding, was $462.8 million, with approximately two-thirds going to police or military aid and the remaining third to economic or social development. The military cap was raised to 800 from 400, and the civilian to 600 from 400. Rep. Jan Schakowsky, D-Ill., charged, "It seems that the Bush administration's solution to dealing with the world is to deploy more U.S. soldiers and guns for hire, while refusing to seek real, lasting solutions."[80] The announcements coincided with a visit by President Uribe to Washington to ask the Bush administration and Congress for a new multiyear package of counterinsurgency and counternarcotics aid through 2009.[81] Additional 2005 funding included $348.3 million for the Colombian foreign military financing, antiterrorism, Department of Defense, and AirWing programs. The 2006 ACI funding was similar at $469.5 million, although the amount for alternative development increased slightly. Also included was $20 million in support for paramilitary demobilization, subject to certification by the secretary of state that the demobilized had actually renounced violence and were fully cooperating with the Colombian authorities. Additional 2006 funding included $247 million for the Colombian foreign military financing, DOD, and AirWing programs. During debate, Rep. Jim McGovern sponsored an amendment to H.R. 5308 that would have cut military aid to Colombia by $100 million. "This policy has failed as an antidrug policy. It has failed as a human rights policy, and it has failed to have any impact whatsoever in reducing the availability, price or purity of drugs in the streets of America."[82] Although the amendment failed 189–234, it reflects growing concern in the House. Leahy amendment human rights language and fumigation safety certification provisions were contained in both years' packages.[83]

Each year from 2002 to 2006, Secretary of State Powell, and later, Secretary of State Condoleezza Rice, certified that Colombia had met its human rights obligations. A portion of the aid package is withheld until the secretary of state certifies that human rights conditions have been met. Each time the country has been certified, however, congressional opponents and human rights groups have objected. The human rights debate became particularly heated in 2002, when a cable signed by former ambassador Myles Frechette surfaced detailing comments made in 1997 by Representative Hastert. In the cable, Hastert was quoted as telling Colombian police and military leaders that human "rights concerns were overblown" and decrying the "leftist-dominated" Congresses that "used human rights as an excuse to aid the left in other countries." A Hastert spokesman later tried to affirm his commitment to human rights but failed to reassure activists about the sincerity of Hastert's commitment to human rights in Colombia.[84] Human rights groups and their supporters ultimately succeeded in maintaining the restrictions in the law. One Colombian unit was decertified in 2003 because of the lack of an effective and transparent investigation into a 1998 incident in Antioquia, Colombia.[85]

Two additional policy changes occurred under George W. Bush. First, as during the Clinton administration, under President Bush trade politics has been linked to the fight against drugs in Colombia. In December 2001 the Andean Trade Preference Act expired. That act, which lowered tariffs on certain products from Andean countries, was an important part of the program to make legal crops an attractive alternative for Colombian farmers. Senate Majority Leader Tom Daschle, D-S.D., successfully pressed for a renewal and expansion of the act, which was passed in August 2002 (P.L. 107-210) with an expiration date of December 2006. Instead of preferring a permanent extension of the Andean Trade Preference Act, U.S. trade representative Robert Zoellick announced that the administration would pursue more comprehensive trade talks with Andean nations in 2004.[86] Bilateral agreements were signed with Peru in December 2005 and Colombia in July 2006, but neither has been approved by the U.S. Congress. Negotiations with Ecuador have stalled, and Bolivia prefers only an extension of the Andean Trade Preference Act. While the agreement was nearing expiration and the new bilateral trade agreements not yet ratified, the act was extended through mid-2007. Second, the drug certification policy changed in 2002 and 2003. Under the new law (P.L. 107-228, Section 706), the president submits to Congress by September 15 each year a list of major drug-producing or trafficking countries and, from among them, an additional list of countries that have "failed demonstrably . . . to make substantial efforts." These countries would potentially suffer sanctions. Moreover, the old prerogative of Congress to override the president's determinations has been eliminated. This modified U.S. certification process is now supplemented by an Organization of American States program, the Multilateral Evaluation Mechanism (MEM).[87]

The debate about the proper U.S. policy toward Colombia will likely intensify in the newly Democratic Congress. Even in 2002 there was talk of "Colombia fatigue" and the need for an "exit strategy" from Colombia.[88] Before the fall elections, many in Congress were ready to support changes; an amendment to H.R.5522 proposed shifting $30 million from aerial eradication in Colombia to global refugee relief. Amendment cosponsor Rep. Jim Leach, R-Iowa, said his support was based on "a belief that a military emphasis of this kind carries many counterproductive consequences." In response to statements that increased eradication was a sign of success, amendment sponsor Representative McGovern rebutted, "Yes, eradication has dramatically increased, but it has changed nothing."[89] Despite debate, ACI funding remained consistent with previous years at $465 million, with $306.5 million going to police and military and $151 million to social and economic development or rule of law programs. Democratic control of Congress after the November 2006 elections may influence Congress to a different mix of policies. At the same time, President Uribe began circulating a new six-year plan titled the Strategy of Strengthening Democracy and Social Development (2007–2013), which proposes a much heavier emphasis on social and economic programs, as opposed to military and police aid. Moreover, while paramilitary demobilizations were ongoing, new evidence emerged of ties between high-ranking Colombian officials and paramilitaries—as human rights groups have long alleged—in an unfolding scandal dubbed "paragate" by the media. As of March 2007, top officials or politicians charged and held for collaboration with paramilitaries include two top intelligence directors, one governor, six senators, two representatives, one former representative, and a colonel. Additionally, another former governor, a former representative, and a current representative are fugitives. Other top officials being investigated by the Colombian Supreme Court or attorney general include the general in charge of the army, six senators, five representatives, one governor, a former senator, and two former representatives. Although some believe that uncovering these ties demonstrates Uribe's resolve to eradicate paramilitary links, others worry about the depth of the scandal and Uribe's sincerity in prosecuting so many members of his governing coalition. These events may significantly change the tone of U.S. congressional debate in the future.

Conclusion: Supply or Demand—New Players, Unforeseen Events, and a New Agenda

President Clinton faced political pressure from Republicans in Congress and human rights groups as he crafted a drug policy toward Colombia. Originally Clinton tried to pursue a policy that included more demand-side efforts and a reduction in interdiction activities, but Republicans quickly attacked him, accusing him of being "soft on drugs." After trying to fashion a policy balance between supply and demand, Clinton acquiesced to Republican pressure and shifted priorities. Unwilling to weather conservative criticism of a new policy approach, he returned to a supply-side policy, symbolized by the appointment of General McCaffrey and the size of the 2000–2001 aid package. Clinton was also pressured by members of Congress and nongovernmental groups who feared that military aid to Colombia would result in more human rights violations. In the end, Clinton made concessions to both sides by increasing funds for the military and police and by including human rights provisions in aid packages.

President George W. Bush significantly changed U.S. policy, openly allowing counternarcotics aid to be used for counterinsurgency purposes. This shift reignited the debate about U.S. intervention in other countries' internal affairs and drew negative comparisons to the conflict in Vietnam. Human rights concerns persisted and were joined by worries about the effects of aerial eradication on the environment and people. The Republicans' loss of control of Congress may result in significant changes in U.S. policy toward Colombia, especially given the unfolding scandal in Colombia, which will bolster human rights–based concerns about U.S. military and police aid to the country.

The debate over Colombian drug policy exemplifies the conflict over intervention in Latin America in the post–cold war era and the increasing complexity of crafting foreign policy. Fighting communism in the region is no longer the priority; instead, new threats, such as the drug trade, are considered more important. Nonetheless, old concerns about entanglement and intervention remain. In addition, nongovernmental organizations, such as Amnesty International, are becoming more effective in making their voices heard in the policy debate and are making human rights an issue that Congress and the president cannot ignore. Whether human rights groups have succeeded in changing politics to include safeguarding civilians, or policies pay only lip service to that ideal, is debatable.

U.S. concerns about international terrorism have allowed governments to label people and organizations previously engaged in guerrilla campaigns, independence movements, and other strictly internal conflicts as terrorists. It is clear that no president can easily control the content of foreign policy. Political capital must be expended to promote the president's foreign policy agenda, as in other policy arenas. The present configuration of U.S. policy in Colombia demonstrates how lobbying by particular industries, nongovernmental activism, old-fashioned politics, and unforeseen events all shape foreign policy.

Key Actors

Cass Ballenger Representative, R-N.C., chairman of the House Subcommittee on the Western Hemisphere Affairs, headed efforts in the House to secure Colombian aid packages.

Dan Burton Representative, R-Ind., wanted Colombia to receive a national security waiver in 1996 and 1997 to allow U.S. assistance to be disbursed despite

Colombia's being denied certification as a partner in the war on drugs; supported more aid to the Colombian national police.

George W. Bush President, eliminated the distinction between counternarcotics and counterinsurgency assistance for Colombia.

Bill Clinton President, wanted to shift drug policy to strike a balance between suppressing demand and interdicting supply.

Ben Gilman Representative, R-N.Y., supported more aid to the Colombian national police.

Dennis Hastert Speaker of the House, R-Ill., strong proponent of additional military aid to Colombia.

Jesse Helms Senator, R-N.C., critic of aid to Colombia because of corruption in the Colombian government.

Patrick Leahy Senator, D-Vt., advocate of including human rights provisions in foreign aid bills.

Barry McCaffrey Retired U.S. Army general, director of the Clinton administration's Office of National Drug Control Policy; advocate for a supply-side approach to combat drug smuggling.

Jim McGovern Representative, D-Mass., critic of supply-side drug policy.

Andrés Pastrana Colombian president, struggled to regain confidence of the United States; devised Plan Colombia to deal with Colombia's drug and guerrilla problems.

Ernesto Samper Pizano Colombian president, plagued by allegations of ties to drug traffickers because of Cali cartel contributions to his electoral campaign.

Alvaro Uribe Vélez Colombian president, pursued hard-line approach against insurgents and narco-traffickers, pursued peace talks with the paramilitaries, requested a new U.S. multiyear aid package through 2009.

Paul Wellstone Senator, D-Minn., advocate of human rights in Colombia.

Notes

1. According to Paul E. Simons, acting assistant secretary of state for international narcotics and law enforcement affairs, in a hearing before the Senate Drug Caucus, 108th Cong., 1st sess., June 3, 2003, www.state.gov/g/inl/rls/rm/21203.htm.

2. For an excellent overview of U.S. drug policy from Nixon to Bush, see Bruce M. Bagley and William O. Walker, eds., *Drug Trafficking in the Americas* (Coral Gables, Fla.: University of Miami, North-South Center, 1996).

3. White House, Office of the Press Secretary, "Statement by the President (Plan Colombia)," November 10, 1999.

4. On contemporary Colombian history and politics, see Harvey Kline, *State Building and Conflict Resolution in Colombia, 1986–1994* (Tuscaloosa: University of Alabama Press, 1999).

5. Rafael Pardo, "Colombia's Two-Front War," *Foreign Affairs* 79, no. 4 (July/August 2000): 65.

6. Ingrid Vaicius and Adam Isacson, "The 'War on Drugs' Meets the 'War on Terror,' " *CIP International Policy Report*, February 2004, www.ciponline.org/colombia/0302 ipr.pdf.

7. Bruce Bagley, "Drug Trafficking, Political Violence and U.S. Policy in Colombia in the 1990s," *Mama Coca*, January 5, 2001, www.mamacoca.org/bagley_drugs_and _violence_en.htm.

8. "Carlos Castãno afirma que envi—instructores a las Autodefensas Unidas de Venezuela," *El Tiempo*, June 30, 2002. See Mauricio Aranguren Molina, "Las Autodefensas y el Narcotráfico," in *Mi confesión: Carlos Castãno revela sus secretos* (Bogatá: Oveja Negra, 2002).

9. Carlos Castãno, letter to Anne Patterson, U.S. ambassador to Colombia, October 26, 2001, www.semana.com/imagesSemana/documentos/aucannepatterson.doc.

10. EFE, "Colombian Paramilitary Group: We Are Ready to Demobilize," March 5, 2004.

11. Francisco Thoumi, "Why the Illegal Psychodelic Drug Use Industry Grew in Colombia," in Bagley and Walker, *Drug Trafficking in the Americas.*

12. Alejandro Reyes, "Drug Trafficking and the Guerrilla Movement in Colombia," in Bagley and Walker, *Drug Trafficking in the Americas.*

13. Fabio Castillo, *Los nuevos jinetes de la cocaína* (Bogotá: Oveja Negra, 1996).

14. Andrew Selsky, "Colombia DEA Chief Discusses Targets," Associated Press, January 23, 2004.

15. Department of State, *1999 International Narcotics Strategy Report.*

16. Reyes, "Drug Trafficking and the Guerrilla Movement in Colombia," 125.

17. Ibid., 122. See also Roberto Steiner, "Hooked on Drugs: Colombian-U.S. Relations," in *The United States and Latin America: The New Agenda*, ed. Victor Bulmer-Thomas and James Dunkerley (London: Institute of Latin American Studies, University of London, 1999), 171.

18. Scott Wilson, "U.S. Drug Chief Tries to Boost Colombian Resolve," *Washington Post*, November 21, 2000, A22.

19. House Committee on International Relations, *U.S. Narcotics Policy toward Colombia*, hearing, 104th Cong., 2d sess., 1996, 47.

20. For an in-depth overview of the responses to the guerrilla and drug conflict, see Reyes, "Drug Trafficking and the Guerrilla Movement in Colombia," and Steiner, "Hooked on Drugs."

21. A copy of Plan Colombia is available at www.usip.org/library/pa/colombia/ adddoc/plan_colombia_101999.html#pre.

22. Reuters, "Colombia Revives Cartel-Busting Police Squad," March 5, 2004.

23. Amanda Iacone, "Colombia's High Court Will Allow Cartel Figure's Extradition to U.S.," *Miami Herald*, November 22, 2002; and Jason Webb, "The Colombian Supreme Court Voted to Allow the Extradition of Victor Patiño Fómenque, a Notorious Cali

Cartel Chief Who Faces Drug Charges in South Florida," Reuters, April 23, 2002. Nelson Vargas Rueda of the FARC was returned to Colombia in mid-2004 after U.S. authorities determined that he was the wrong man. See Sibylla Brodzinsky and Jay Weaver, "U.S. Drops Case against Suspected FARC Guerrilla," *Miami Herald,* July 8, 2004.

24. Bruce M. Bagley, "Myths of Militarization: Enlisting Armed Forces in the War on Drugs," in *Drug Policy in the Americas,* ed. Peter Smith (Boulder: Westview Press, 1992).

25. General Accounting Office audits in 1992 and 1993 revealed that counternarcotics funds were being illegally used for counterinsurgency operations. The GAO concluded that this practice would likely continue because of the complexity of the Colombian situation. See Government Accountability Office, "The Drug War: Counternarcotics Programs in Colombia and Peru," T-NSIAD-92-9, Washington D.C., February 20, 1992; Government Accountability Office, "The Drug War: Colombia Is Implementing Antidrug Efforts, but Impact Is Uncertain," T-NSIAD-94-53, Washington D.C., October 5, 1993.

26. Bureau for International Narcotics and Law Enforcement Affairs, fact sheet, April 23, 1999.

27. Stephen Labaton, "Surgeon General Suggests Study of Legalizing Drugs," *New York Times,* December 7, 1993.

28. U.S. Congress, *Congressional Record,* June 21, 2000, S5509.

29. House Committee on International Relations, Subcommittee on the Western Hemisphere, *A Review of President Clinton's Certification Program for Narcotics Producing and Transit Countries in Latin America,* hearing, 104th Cong., 1st sess., 1995, 33.

30. House Committee on Foreign Affairs, Subcommittee on International Security, International Organizations, and Human Rights, *U.S. Anti-Drug Strategy for the Western Hemisphere,* joint hearing, 103rd Cong., 2nd sess., 1994.

31. House Committee on Government Reform and Oversight, Subcommittee on National Security, International Affairs, and Criminal Justice, *International Drug Control Policy: Colombia,* hearing, 105th Cong., 2d sess., 1998, 22.

32. See, for example, "Choice of General as Drug Fighter Gets Enthusiastic Response," *New York Times,* January 28, 1996.

33. Stanley Meisler, "House OKs $3.2 Billion Measure to Bolster the Fight against Drugs," *Los Angeles Times,* September 17, 1998, 8.

34. Miles A. Pomper, "Hastert Leads the Charge in Colombia Drug War," *CQ Weekly,* September 11, 1999, 2094.

35. "International Drug Trade and the U.S. Certification Process: A Critical Review," proceedings of a seminar held by the Congressional Research Service and prepared for the Senate Caucus on International Narcotics Control, 104th Cong., 2d sess., September 1996. The Andean Trade Preference Act of 1991 provided economic support to countries struggling to eliminate drug production by expanding the trade opportunities for legal crops. The ten-year program empowered the president to grant duty-free treatment to selected imports from Bolivia, Colombia, Ecuador, and Peru.

36. Statement by Assistant Secretary of State for Inter-American Affairs Jeffrey Davidow, *International Drug Control Policy: Colombia,* 19.

37. Jonathan Peterson, "Albright Pushes Anti-Drug Plan in Visit to Colombia," *Los Angeles Times,* January 15, 2000, A9. Despite Colombia's decertification, aid to its military and police had doubled from $68.6 million in 1993 to $136.4 million by 1997. (There had been decreases in 1995 and 1996 to $51.4 million and $73.9 million, respectively.) See also "Last Minute Spending Signals Shift in Drug War," *Congressional Quarterly Almanac,* 1998, 2–118.

38. Miles A. Pomper, "Clinton's Billion Dollar Proposal for Colombian Anti-Drug Aid Fails to Satisfy Republicans," *CQ Weekly,* January 15, 2000, 90.

39. Peterson, "Albright Pushes Anti-Drug Plan."

40. Larry Rohter, "Cocaine War: A Special Report; A Web of Drugs and Strife in Colombia," *New York Times,* April 21, 2000.

41. Senate Caucus on International Narcotics Control, *On Site Staff Evaluation of U.S. Counter-Narcotics Activities in Brazil, Argentina, Chile, and Colombia,* staff report, 105th Cong, 2d sess., January 28, 1998, 19.

42. Pomper, "Clinton's Billion Dollar Proposal," 91.

43. Human Rights Watch, *World Report, 2000,* www.hrw.org/wr2k.

44. Department of State, Bureau of Democracy, Human Rights, and Labor, *1999 Country Reports on Human Rights,* February 25, 2000, www.state.gov/www/ global/human_rights/99hrp_index.html.

45. Ester Schrader, "Congress Agrees on Funding for Colombia," *Los Angeles Times,* June 23, 2000, A1.

46. Tim Golden, "Colombia and Copters and Clash over Choice," *New York Times,* March 6, 2000.

47. Janet Hook and Ester Schrader, "Colombia Aid Package Gets House Approval," *Los Angeles Times,* March 31, 2000, A22.

48. Ibid.

49. Eric Pianin, "House Approves Additional $4 Billion for Defense; Nearing Passage, $12.6 Billion Emergency Spending Bill Has Funds for Colombia, Non-Emergencies," *Washington Post,* March 30, 2000, A6.

50. Hook and Schrader, "Colombia Aid Package." Included in the House bill was an endorsement of the administration's switch from the Huey helicopters to the Blackhawks. Intense lobbying efforts by the companies that make the helicopters helped influence the details of the final aid package. United Technologies, the Connecticut-based company that builds the Blackhawk, had contributed more than $700,000 to Republican and Democratic members of Congress between the 1996 and 1998 elections. Golden, "Colombia and Copters."

51. Karen DeYoung, "Colombia Aid Nears Approval in Senate; Lawmakers Back Bigger U.S. Military Role in Drug Fight," *Washington Post,* June 22, 2000, A1.

52. Anthony Lewis, "Abroad at Home: Into the Quagmire," *New York Times,* June 24, 2000.

53. Eric Schmitt, "$1.3 Billion Voted to Fight Drug War among Colombians," *New York Times,* June 30, 2000.

54. DeYoung, "Colombia Aid Nears Approval."

55. Ester Schrader, "Congress Agrees on Funding for Colombia," *Los Angeles Times,* June 23, 2000, A1.

56. Ibid.

57. Military Construction Appropriations Act, 2001, P.L. 106-246, Sec. 3201.

58. DeYoung, "Colombia Aid Nears Approval."

59. Available at www.ciponline.org/colombia/072801.htm.

60. Available at www.ciponline.org/colombia/073101.htm.

61. Ibid.

62. Marc Lacey, "Clinton Defends Colombia Outlay," *New York Times,* August 31, 2000, A1.

63. Eric Pianin and Karen DeYoung, "House Considers More Aid for Colombia; $99.5 Million Package Would Include Aircraft, Ammunition to Fight Drug War," *Washington Post,* September 9, 2000, A2.

64. Francis X. Taylor, press conference, Organization of American States, Washington, D.C., October 15, 2001, www.oas.org/OASpage/eng/videos/pressconference10_15_01.asf. The AUC was added to the list in 2001, but the ELN and the FARC were on the list even before September 11. They were officially designated as subject to Executive Order 13224 of September 23, 2001, on October 31, 2001. See www.fas.org/irp/news/2002/03/fr031902s.html.

65. Arlene Tickner, "Colombia and the United States: From Counternarcotics to Counterterrorism," *Current History,* February 2003, 81.

66. Rep. Cass Ballenger, R-N.C., "U.S. Policy toward Colombia," statement before the House Committee on International Relations, Subcommittee on the Western Hemisphere, 107th Cong., 2d sess., April 11, 2002, wwwc.house.gov/international_relations/107/ball0411.htm.

67. P.L. 107-206, H.R. 4775, http://frwebgate.access.gpo.gov/cgi-bin/getdoc.cgi?dbname=107_cong_public_laws&docid=f:publ206.107.pdf.

68. Vaicius and Isacson, "The 'War on Drugs' Meets the 'War on Terror.'"

69. Speech by Rep. Ike Skelton, *Congressional Record,* May 23, 2003, H2998.

70. Speech by Rep. Jim McGovern, *Congressional Record,* May 23, 2003, H2997.

71. Jerry Seper, "Colombian Drug Lord Draws 30 Years in Prison; Ochoa Reneged on Promise Not to Return to Narcotics Trade" *Washington Times,* August 27, 2003, 3A.

72. Treasury Department, "Treasury Takes Action against FARC/AUC Narco-Terrorist Leaders in Continued Effort to Halt Narcotics Trafficking," press release js-1181, February 19, 2004, www.ustreas.gov/press/releases/js1181.htm.

73. K. Larry Storrs and Nina M. Serafino, Congressional Research Service, *Andean Regional Initiative (ARI): FY 2002 Assistance for Colombia and Neighbors,* Report for Congress, October 31, 2001.

74. White House, Office of the Press Secretary, "Andean Regional Initiative," fact sheet, March 23, 2002, www.state.gov/p/wha/rls/fs/8980.htm.

75. Vaicius and Isacson, "The 'War on Drugs' Meets the 'War on Terror.'"

76. Paul E. Simons, acting assistant secretary of state for international narcotics and law enforcement affairs, in a hearing before the Senate Drug Caucus, 108th Cong., 1st sess., June 3, 2003, www.state.gov/g/inl/rls/rm/21203.htm.

77. K. Larry Storrs and Connie Veillette, Congressional Research Service, *Andean Regional Initiative (ARI): FY2003 Supplemental and FY2004 Assistance for Colombia and Neighbors,* Report for Congress, August 27, 2003, 4.

78. Associated Press, "U.S., Colombians Conduct Operation," *Fort Worth Star-Telegram,* March 11, 2007, 18A.

79. Storrs and Veillette, *Andean Regional Initiative.*

80. Bloomberg Newswire, *New York Daily News,* "Bush: Add Troops in Colombia," March 23, 2004.

81. Center for International Policy, "Plan Colombia 2?" press release, March 22, 2004, www.ciponline.org/colombia/040322memo.htm.

82. Speech by Rep. Jim McGovern, *Congressional Record,* June 28, 2005, HR 5308.

83. Connie Veillette, "Colombia: Issues for Congress" Congressional Research Service, Library of Congress, January 4, 2006, 24.

84. "Declassified Document Says Hastert Downplayed Human Rights Concerns in Colombia," *CongressDaily,* May 3, 2002.

85. State Department, Daily Press Briefing, January 14, 2003, www.stategov/r/pa/prs/dpb/2003/16641.htm.

86. Jerry Hagstrom, "Zoellick: Colombia, Peru, Ecuador and Bolivia Next FTAs," *CongressDaily,* November 18, 2003, 9.

87. Raphael Perl, "Drug Control: International Policy and Approaches," Congressional Research Service, Library of Congress, updated February 2, 2006.

88. Michael Shifter and Vinay Jawahar, "Latin America Daily Brief," *Oxford Analytica,* August 22, 2003.

89. Latin American Working Group, "House Increases Aid to Colombia before Uribe Visit, Senate Freezes Funds over Human Rights Concerns," June 13, 2006, www.lawg.org/countries/colombia/fy07debate.htm.

4 The Nuclear Standoff between the United States and Iran: Conflict, Misunderstandings, and Diplomatic Inflexibility

Thomas Preston and Michael P. Infranco

Before You Begin

1. What have been the trends and patterns in U.S.-Iranian relations over the past five decades? Why do history and context matter in foreign policy decision making as in U.S.-Iranian relations?
2. How does each actor, the United States and Iran, view the other, and are those perceptions accurate? Could the perceptions be changed?
3. What are the domestic political constraints preventing both countries from improving their relations or compromising on the nuclear issue?
4. How do the current war on terror and the occupation of Iraq affect U.S.-Iranian relations? Do they aggravate the current impasse in nuclear negotiations?
5. How has the election of Mahmoud Ahmadinejad affected U.S.-Iranian relations? Does the current Iranian political leadership bode well for the future of U.S.-Iranian relations?
6. What are the differences in the policy approaches and negotiating styles of the United States, the European Union, and Iran regarding the nuclear issue?
7. What are the roots of the Iranian nuclear program? What negotiating strategy may influence Iran to desist from developing nuclear weapons? Does it really matter, in terms of regional stability, whether Iran obtains nuclear weapons?

Introduction: The Axis of Evil and a Rush to Confront Iran over WMD

In his January 2002 State of the Union address, President George W. Bush characterized Iran, Iraq, and North Korea as an "axis of evil" intent on pursuing "weapons of mass destruction" (WMD), sponsoring terrorism, and committing aggression against the community of nations. The speech illustrated the administration's perception of these countries as "rogue states" and set the stage for confrontation with them over their nuclear ambitions. It stated an uncompromising position that actively sought "regime change" in all three countries through military, diplomatic, and economic means and U.S. insistence upon not rewarding their bad behavior by engaging in direct talks. As Washington implemented this policy approach—resulting in the invasion and occupation of Iraq, the inconclusive six-party talks over North Korea's nuclear program (which failed to prevent Pyongyang's first nuclear test in October 2006), and the long diplomatic standoff with Iran over its nuclear program—the policy's limitations grew increasingly apparent.[1] Not only did the U.S. policy often fail to accomplish its stated objectives (such as eliminating the North Korean and Iranian nuclear programs) and cause far greater regional instability than had existed before (as with Iraq's growing sectarian strife), but U.S. diplomatic flexibility to creatively resolve these disputes significantly decreased as a result of its uncompromising stance. Opportunities for negotiations between parties were not taken advantage of (or seriously considered), further reinforcing the negative political atmosphere between the actors and allowing the ongoing situations to continue deteriorating.

Complicating matters further was that the U.S.-Iranian nuclear standoff not only was affected by the current policy environment created by the Bush administration and Tehran, but also remained firmly embedded within the broader, historical context of U.S.-Iranian relations over the past sixty years. No foreign policy occurs in a historical vacuum. The deeper context colors the current conflict over Tehran's nuclear program and reinforces the preexisting, distinctive historical pattern between the United States and Iran of mutual antagonism, domestic constraints preventing improved relations, and ineffective statecraft narrowing diplomatic options. When those factors are combined with (1) Iran's understandable concern for its own security (given the example of Iraq and its placement within the "axis of evil"); (2) the potential of nuclear weapons to help deter American attack; (3) the political needs of both presidents, Bush and Ahmadinejad, to appear strong and to appeal to nationalism at home; and (4) the overextension of America's military in Iraq and Afghanistan, which limits its ability to take strong actions against Tehran, it becomes easy to see why the current standoff over Iran's nuclear program has become so enormously complex and difficult to resolve diplomatically.[2]

Background: Patterns of Intervention and Mutual Antagonism

A defining tendency in U.S.-Iranian relations has been a long-standing pattern of American intervention in Iran's domestic affairs. In 1953 the United

Timeline of U.S.-Iranian Relations and the Nuclear Issue

August 1953 A U.S.-supported coup overthrows democratically elected Iranian prime minister Mohammed Mossadeq and the pro-American Shah is restored to power.

1970s Shah of Iran institutes a nuclear program with both civilian and military components.

Mid-1978 through 1979 Iranian revolution overthrows the Shah, who is replaced by Ayatollah Khomeini.

October–November 1979 The Shah is admitted into the United States; Iranian students seize U.S. embassy in Tehran.

April 1980 The United States breaks off diplomatic relations with Iran; U.S. hostage rescue mission fails.

September 1980 Iraq invades Iran, beginning the Iran-Iraq War (1980–1988); the United States supports Iraq.

Mid-1985 Iran begins a secret centrifuge enrichment program.

1987 Iran acquires drawings of centrifuges and component parts from A. Q. Khan smuggling network.

May 1995 President Bill Clinton signs an executive order prohibiting trade with Iran.

August 1997 Moderate cleric and reformer Mohammad Khatami becomes president of Iran.

1999 After assembling and testing centrifuges, Iran enriches uranium for the first time.

June 2001 U.S. Senate extends economic sanctions on Iran an additional five years.

January 29, 2002 President George W. Bush's "axis of evil" speech.

August 14, 2002 Opposition group of exiles reveals that Iran has clandestine uranium enrichment facility and heavy water plant.

September 12, 2003 The International Atomic Energy Agency (IAEA) calls on Iran to suspend all enrichment-related activity.

October 21–23, 2003 Iran agrees to halt all enrichment and reprocessing activities after negotiations with France, Britain, and Germany.

March 13, 2004 IAEA criticizes Iran for failing to report centrifuge research or suspend all activities.

continued on the next page

continued from the previous page

April 29, 2004 Iran announces it is starting to convert uranium, the step preceding actual enrichment.

September 18, 2004 IAEA tells Iran to cease uranium conversion and implicitly threatens referral to UN Security Council.

November 15, 2004 After further negotiations with the European Union (EU), Iran agrees to cease uranium enrichment.

August 2005 Ahmadinejad becomes Iran's president, campaigning on a pro-nuclear platform.

September 2, 2005 IAEA announces that Iran has not fully cooperated with the agency, despite repeated requests and visits from inspectors.

January 12, 2006 Europeans call off nuclear talks with Iran.

February 4, 2006 IAEA board votes to report Iran to the UN Security Council.

April 11, 2006 Iran announces that it has succeeded in enriching uranium.

May 2006 Ahmadinejad sends his letter to President Bush.

June 2006 UN sanctions delayed to give Iran time to consider a new package of U.S. and European incentives to end its nuclear program; Iran rejects the proposal and is given an August 31 deadline to implement "full and sustained suspension" of its nuclear activities.

October 2006 North Korean nuclear test; Iran refuses to condemn it and sets up second centrifuge cascade.

December 2006 Security Council unanimously passes resolution banning import or export of materials and technology used in uranium enrichment, reprocessing, or ballistic missiles.

March 2007 Security Council unanimously passes resolution banning all arms exports to Iran and freezing assets of Iranians linked to its military or nuclear program.

April 2007 Ahmadinejad boasts Iran is capable of enriching uranium on an industrial scale.

States backed the overthrow of Iranian prime minister Mohammad Mossadeq's democratically elected government, an action sparked by Mossadeq's efforts to nationalize Iran's oil industry, taking ownership away from British companies. The United States subsequently reinstalled in power the autocratic Shah of Iran (who preserved foreign rights to Iran's oil fields). Although the United States saw Mossadeq's overthrow through the cold war lens of East-West competition and the need to prevent the spread of communism, to Iranians it epitomized U.S. interference in their internal affairs and imperial ambitions in their country. Hostility toward the United States for reinstalling the Shah continued long after his overthrow in the 1979 Iranian revolution. Indeed, it is revealing that a key Iranian demand during the subsequent hostage crisis, when militant students seized the American embassy and its staff, was an apology for the 1953 overthrow and a U.S. pledge never again to interfere in Iran's domestic affairs. Since that time, American policymakers have not restored diplomatic relations, have encouraged dissident groups, have spoken favorably of regime change, and have depicted Iran as a rogue state intent on shirking international law to advance its Islamic revolutionary agenda and destabilize the region. The Iranians have responded with unremitting hostility of their own, condemning the "Great Satan," pursuing improved military capabilities, and working to undercut American influence in the Middle East.

The origins of the conflict can be traced to the rise of the Shah of Iran, Mohammad Reza Pahlavi, who replaced his father on the Iranian throne during World War II. After he was deposed by the Iranian people during the early 1950s and Mossadeq elected, the Shah was returned to power in 1953 in a U.S.-backed coup.[3] In return for substantial American military and economic aid, the Shah provided both a steady stream of oil and an important pro-Western ally in the Persian Gulf to help block Soviet expansionism. Iran's strategic position and resources continued to make it a high-priority ally for American presidents throughout the Shah's reign. However, the Shah's rule was also marked by corruption, brutality, and political repression. The Shah's secret police and intelligence service, known at the SAVAK, was particularly hated by the population. It ruthlessly helped maintain the Shah's one-party rule through the torture and the execution of thousands of political prisoners, suppression of political dissent, and alienation of the religious masses.[4] U.S. training and support of the SAVAK served to further cultivate anti-Americanism in the decades prior to the Iranian revolution. Moreover, the Shah's efforts to modernize Iran and follow a Western model of development angered the country's conservative religious leaders, who saw Western influences as an affront to their fundamentalist Islamic faith.

Inspired by the fundamentalist cleric Ayatollah Ruhollah Khomeini, whose pro-Islamist and anti-Western message struck a special chord with the Iranian masses, violent demonstrations erupted throughout the country in mid-1978. By January 1979, the Shah (now terminally ill with cancer) abdicated his Peacock

Throne and went into exile, and Khomeini returned from exile. The Shah moved first to Egypt, then to Morocco, and by February 1979 was ready to accept an earlier American offer of asylum. On February 14, however, Iranian students "temporarily" overran the American embassy and held U.S. personnel for "several hours," prompting U.S. government concern for all the Americans there. When President Jimmy Carter's Special Coordinating Committee met to discuss the situation, it concluded that if the Shah was permitted to enter the country there might be an Iranian backlash that could threaten U.S. personnel in country. As a result, Carter decided to rebuff the Shah's request for admission into the United States, but administration officials remained split over the matter. Secretary of State Cyrus Vance argued against receiving the Shah, but National Security Advisor Zbigniew Brzezinski and a cadre of friends (including former secretary of state Henry Kissinger) pushed for the Shah's admission. Time and the Shah's health interceded in his favor, and Carter eventually acquiesced to the Shah's entry after being told that his life could only be saved by medical facilities in New York.[5] The Shah arrived in October 1979, received medical treatment, and was encouraged to leave. He eventually traveled to Egypt, where he died in July 1980. But the damage to U.S.-Iranian relations had been done. On November 4, 1979, thousands of Iranian students overran the U.S. embassy and seized 66 American hostages (53 of whom would be held for some 444 days).

The ensuing hostage crisis would humiliate and destroy the Carter presidency and cause a rupture in U.S.-Iranian relations that has lasted to the present day. The two countries still do not have diplomatic relations, and the twenty-seven-year freeze, in which the relationship has remained set in a mode of mutual hostility and antipathy, is the backdrop against which the current nuclear dispute is playing out. During the hostage crisis, U.S. efforts to negotiate with the Iranians were complicated by the fact that no one knew who had authority to discuss the hostages. Indeed, Iran's President Bani-Sadr negotiated with Carter for months before admitting he had no authority to release the hostages. Infuriated, Carter authorized a rescue mission, the ill-fated Desert One operation, which ended in disaster in the Iranian desert with a fatal collision between U.S. aircraft on an improvised runway. Despite all the sanctions the United States had to deliver, including freezing all Iranian assets, halting all military sales, breaking diplomatic relations, and so forth, Iran refused to budge on its demands that the United States release its assets, apologize for past misdeeds, and return the Shah (and later his wealth, after he died) to Tehran. Only the full-scale invasion of Iran by Saddam Hussein's Iraq in September 1980 (the start of a bloody eight-year war of attrition) and the election in November 1980 of Ronald Reagan, who had campaigned on a promise to unleash massive military retaliation on Iran if the hostages were not released, convinced the Iranians finally to resolve the crisis. Thus, on Carter's last day in office, in January 1981, the United States released a "ransom" of some of Iran's frozen financial assets, and the hostages were freed.

The War between Iraq and Iran

The U.S.-Iranian relationship continued to deteriorate during the Reagan administration, with the Americans throwing their support behind Iraq in its war with Tehran (even though Iraq was the aggressor). But with concerns about the spread of Iran's radical Islamist politics to the moderate, Sunni states of the Gulf, which the United States depended upon for oil (such as Saudi Arabia and Kuwait), Washington saw supporting Iraq as the lesser of two evils. The United States provided Iraq with economic support and military supplies, as well as sensitive satellite intelligence on Iranian military movements, while encouraging the wealthy Gulf states to bankroll the Iraqi war effort to the tune of hundreds of billions of dollars throughout the 1980s.[6] The Reagan team essentially established a long-term policy of containment of Iran, which subsequent administrations continued. Obviously, given the enormous casualties that the eight-year war inflicted on Iran, which some estimates place as high as one million, and its economic costs of upwards of $350 billion,[7] it is unsurprising that U.S. support for Saddam Hussein's Iraq created further hostility toward America among the Iranian people.

In several instances U.S. military forces engaged the Iranians during the conflict. For example, after Iranian attacks on Kuwaiti oil tankers (Kuwait supported Iraq), Reagan responded to requests for help by placing U.S. flags on Kuwaiti tankers and providing U.S. Navy escorts to convoy them through the Persian Gulf. Later, when the USS *Samuel B. Roberts* (FFG-58) struck a presumed Iranian mine in the Gulf during these convoys, Reagan ordered attacks against Iranian oil platforms, and U.S. forces sank several Iranian warships. Tensions between the U.S. and Iran rose still higher when the USS *Vincennes* mistakenly shot down an Iranian Airbus carrying nearly three hundred civilians in July 1988. To the Iranians the downing "was not a mistake, but a sign that the United States was taking off the gloves and preparing to bring its great power to bear in direct military confrontation with Iran in order to destroy the regime in Tehran."[8] With Iraq winning the conflict and its economy in shambles, Iran went to the

UN to negotiate a cease-fire with Iraq. The Iranian leadership's feelings toward America at that point were clear, with Khomeini, frustration boiling over, declaring, "God willing . . . we will empty our hearts' anguish at the appropriate time by taking revenge on the Al Saud [monarchy] and America."[9]

Relations remained frosty between Iran and the George H.W. Bush and Clinton administrations, both of which claimed that Iran was sponsoring terrorism (through its financial and military support of groups such as Lebanon's Hezbollah). Both suspected that Tehran might be pursuing nuclear weapons.

All U.S. and Iranian leaders must deal with the reality that domestic political constraints encourage hostile policies toward one another and that appearing tough toward the other is usually rewarded. It has also become a pattern of U.S.-Iranian relations that any move toward moderating the corrosive nature of the current relationship meets significant roadblocks. For example, in seeking to deter Iran from sponsoring terrorism abroad or pursuing WMD, President Clinton found himself caught between a desire to implement an anti-Iranian trade embargo during the mid-1990s and growing political pressure to pursue a more extreme, regime change policy. Following the pattern of Reagan's containment policy, Clinton hoped to separate the Middle East into friendly, moderate states versus the more radical, fundamentalist ones—thereby isolating Iran and putting pressure on it to alter its behavior. Clinton noted, "I am convinced that instituting a trade embargo with Iran is the most effective way our nation can help curb Iran's drive to acquire devastating [nuclear] weapons and its continued support for terrorist activities."[10] However, in the months leading up to the trade embargo vote, pressure increased on Clinton to adopt an even tougher policy. Aside from growing intelligence concerns about Iran's progress toward nuclear weapons (that were leaked to the press), Speaker of the House of Representatives Newt Gingrich, R-Ga., stated, "The eventual forced replacement of Iran's Islamic regime is the only long-term strategy that makes sense."[11] The United States adopted both the trade embargo and a policy implicitly supporting regime change.

In July 2001, prior to 9/11, the Senate approved legislation extending sanctions against Iran for another five years—a move that undercut efforts by moderate Iranian president Mohammad Khatami to improve relations with Washington and emboldened hard-liners. In October 2006, Congress passed and President Bush signed into law the Iran Freedom Support Act, which placed sanctions on countries that have helped Iran's nuclear program, even if the technical support was legal under the Nuclear Non-Proliferation Treaty (NPT).[12] Critics noted the similarity of this legislation to the 1998 Iraq Liberation Act, which helped to provide the Bush administration with some authority to take action in the buildup to the 2003 war. Thus, analysts worry that a U.S. administration seeking to launch an attack against Iran could cite the Iran Freedom Support Act. These concerns have some basis. The 2006 U.S. National Security Strategy identified Iran as the gravest threat to the United States. The *Weekly Standard* also published, in April 2006, an article advocating preemptive war with Iran. Written by former CIA specialist Reuel Marc Gerecht, a fellow at the conservative American Enterprise Institute, the piece argued that "diplomacy and sanctions are doomed to fail . . . [so that] letting Tehran actualize its nuclear weapons potential would be more threatening to the U.S. and to the world than the consequences of whatever it takes—even land invasion on the scale of Iraq."[13]

Lost Opportunities

It should be noted that in the months following the 9/11 attacks, the Bush administration had an opportunity to expand cooperation with the Khatami government. Khatami, a reformer, believed that a window of opportunity had opened. Mohammad Hossein Adeli, a deputy at the Iranian Foreign Ministry, began intense contacts with higher officials in the Iranian government. Adeli explains, "We wanted to truly condemn the [9/11] attacks but we also wished to offer an olive branch to the United States, showing we were interested in peace."[14] Adeli was even able to convince Supreme Leader Ali Khamenei that the proposals would be productive. A Khamenei assistant noted, "The Supreme Leader was deeply suspicious of the American government. . . . But [he] was repulsed by these [9/11] terrorist acts and was truly sad about the loss of the civilian lives in America."[15]

In the weeks following the September 11 attacks, American and Iranian representatives met several times in Switzerland. The Iranian delegation was pushing for action because it was opposed to the Taliban government and had supported elements of the opposition Northern Alliance (also an ally of the United States against the Taliban and al Qaeda). Jim Dobbins, President Bush's first envoy to Afghanistan, worked extensively with the Iranian diplomatic leader, Javad Zarif (a University of Denver graduate). Zarif was instrumental in convincing the Northern Alliance delegate, Yunus Qanooni, to accept Hamid Karzai, a Pashtun from the south, as the new president of Afghanistan and to form a coalition government. According to Dobbins, "The Russians and the Indians had been making similar points. . . . But it wasn't until Zarif took him aside that it was settled." Iran also committed five hundred million dollars to rebuild Afghanistan. A critical moment was approaching in which the United States and Iran had common interests and the will to open up dialogue on a number of issues, but a series of gaffes destroyed the moment. One week after the Iranian pledge to provide aid to Afghanistan, Iran was included in the "axis of evil" speech. Former Bush speechwriter Michael Gerson suggests that it was former national security advisor Condoleezza Rice's idea to add Iran to that speech. For Mohammad Adeli, the speech immediately marginalized the Iranian officials who were seeking better relations with the United States. Adeli comments, "The speech exonerated those [hard-liners] who had always doubted America's intentions."[16]

Even after the speech there were opportunities to progress with the talks. For instance, following the U.S. invasion of Iraq, Iranian officials proposed a swap of captured members of the Majahedin-e-Khalq (MEK), an anti-Iranian group in Iraq, for al Qaeda operatives held in Iranian jails. When the matter was broached at a White House meeting, Vice President Dick Cheney opposed the exchange, choosing to preserve "all our options." Iran, fearing the U.S. military presence on the adjoining border with Iraq, is reported to have offered to "disarm" Hezbollah and Hamas—the Lebanese and Palestinian military and political organizations, respectively—in return for a normalization of relations with the United States. Former secretary of state Colin Powell was dubious about these overtures but was unable to pursue them because of resistance within the Bush administration. "My position," according to Powell, "was that we ought to find ways to restart talks with Iran . . . but there was . . . reluctance on the part of the president to do that. . . . You can't negotiate when you tell the other side, 'Give us what a negotiation would produce before the negotiations start.'"[17]

In sum, domestic constraints on both sides have prevented progressive diplomacy between America and Iran. Since 1979, any U.S. president seeking to soften policy toward Iran, normalize relations, or engage in direct talks has risked attack by domestic opponents of such moves. Similarly, in Iran, limited efforts by two Iranian presidents—Rafsanjani during the 1990s and Mohammad Khatami prior to 2005—to improve U.S.-Iranian relations brought both men under attack at home from conservative clerics, who forced them to maintain the existing hostile pattern. Both sides are trapped with a hostile image of the other, locked into place like a bug in amber by the historical relationship they share and by strategic and political factors that make it almost impossible to escape. From the U.S. perspective, there are the issues of Iranian support for Islamic extremism and terrorism, its likely quest for nuclear weapons, and the lingering memory of the hostage crisis. For Iran, there is the constant memory of U.S. interference in its affairs through Mossadeq's overthrow and U.S. support of the Shah, its active support for Iraq's war against Iran during the 1980s, its containment policy of economic embargoes and calls for regime change from the Reagan administration onward, and the "axis of evil" charge by George W. Bush.

Iran's Nuclear Program

The Iranian nuclear program began during the mid-1970s under the Shah. He embarked on an ambitious effort involving establishment of a nuclear weapon design team and covert efforts to obtain the know-how and materials required, as well as plans to construct twenty-three nuclear power reactors.[18] The Shah openly remarked Iran would have nuclear weapons "without a doubt and sooner than one would think."[19] Documents found after the Iranian revolution revealed that the Shah's government and Israel discussed plans to adapt an Israeli surface-to-surface missile for use by Tehran to carry nuclear warheads.[20] Iran began a clandestine uranium enrichment program in 1985 and sought to develop a scientific cadre capable of pursuing a weapons program; 15,000 to 17,000 Iranian students were sent abroad to study nuclear-related subjects.[21] Iran also actively recruited nuclear technicians from the former Soviet Union and other countries, offering salaries of up to $20,000 a month to hire skilled (but impoverished) nuclear scientists.[22] In addition to building a gas centrifuge uranium enrichment program at Natanz, which International Atomic Energy Agency (IAEA) director general Mohamed El Baradei described as "sophisticated," Iran acknowledged intending to build both a forty-megawatt thermal heavy-water reactor at Arak and a fuel fabrication plant for the reactor at Esfahan.[23] The pilot plant at Natanz was designed to hold about one thousand centrifuges and produce ten to twelve kilograms of weapons-grade uranium per year. The main enrichment facility at Natanz was envisaged to hold up to 50,000 centrifuges and produce about five hundred kilograms of weapons-grade uranium annually (enough for twenty-five to thirty nuclear weapons per year). This facility, if operated at full capacity, could "produce enough weapons-grade uranium for a nuclear weapon in a few days."[24] In addition, Pakistan (through the illegal A. Q. Khan smuggling network) provided Iran not only with advanced centrifuge technology and advice, but also with essential data on bomb design.[25] In total, this infrastructure has the capability (if completed) to transform Iran rapidly into not only a nuclear weapon state, but one with a substantial arsenal. As the program's development demonstrates, Iran's interest in nuclear weapons has continued regardless of the nature of the current regime.[26]

Estimates within the U.S. intelligence community about Iran's nuclear program have varied widely (in some ways, mirroring the worst-case assumptions found in pre-war Iraqi WMD estimates). For example, the CIA reported in January 2000 that Iran might be able to make a nuclear weapon, but other intelligence agencies hotly disputed the claim.[27] Estimates of Iranian nuclear capabilities routinely overestimated the speed of Tehran's progress, with U.S. and Israeli intelligence in 1992–1993 predicting an Iranian nuclear bomb by 2002, and in 1995 predicting a bomb within "7–15 years."[28] Although a presidential commission reported in March 2005 that U.S. "intelligence on Iran is inadequate to allow firm judgments about Iran's weapons programs," an August 2005 National Intelligence Estimate (NIE) concluded that Iran was "determined to build nuclear weapons" but unlikely to possess them until 2010–2015.[29] But although the speed and scope of the program are subject to conjecture and debate, the intelligence services of Israel, Germany, Britain, and the United States all agree on the fundamental point that Tehran has "a long-term program to manufacture nuclear weapons."[30] In the views of many experts, Iran already possesses the basic nuclear technology, infrastructure, and expertise to build weapons and lacks only adequate stockpiles of fissile material to become a nuclear state.[31]

However, Tehran signed the Nuclear Non-Proliferation Treaty and placed its existing civilian nuclear power industry under IAEA inspection. As a result, Iran found itself not only under greater scrutiny from the IAEA but also subject to substantial supplier state restrictions on the importation of technology for its declared civilian nuclear power industry. By treaty, Iran is obligated to report all nuclear activities to the IAEA, and when rumors surfaced regarding a hidden program, Tehran (after intense outside pressure) was eventually forced to allow inspectors into the country in October 2003. Unfortunately for Tehran, the inspections revealed a long-running Iranian nuclear program that had effectively concealed itself from outside scrutiny for decades and which, unmolested, had the potential to provide it with substantial weapons capabilities. Although the U.S. position on Iran remained hostile, befitting Iran's status within the axis of evil, Britain, France, and Germany embarked on a three-and-a-half-year diplomatic effort to peacefully resolve the dispute over Iran's nuclear program.

The Nuclear Negotiations and Standoff (2003–2007)

Throughout, the Bush administration has viewed the diplomatic efforts with suspicion and emphasized the need to take an uncompromising approach toward Tehran and punish it at the UN with economic or military sanctions if it does not completely surrender its nuclear program. Moreover, the Bush administration strongly opposed offering any inducements to Iran to halt its activities.

In contrast, the Europeans have viewed diplomacy as the best way to resolve the dispute, to maintain international support for whatever sanctions might be necessary, and to avoid provoking a conflict that might cause Iran to leave the Nuclear Non-Proliferation Treaty and cease cooperation with the IAEA. Whereas the United States left the direct diplomatic efforts to the Europeans and refused to discuss incentives for Iran, it did not discourage Britain, Germany, and France from pursuing their efforts—judging that any later efforts to gain international support for harsher measures against Tehran would require an effort at diplomacy first (especially after the controversial lead-up to the Iraq war).[32]

Nevertheless, the Bush administration continued to demand that Iran be referred to the UN Security Council for sanctions and tried unsuccessfully to obtain the cooperation of reluctant allies, as well as the Russians and Chinese, to do so. But in November 2004 Iran accepted a European-brokered deal that temporarily froze its uranium enrichment program in return for future negotiations over possible incentives. This agreement, much to the chagrin of the Bush administration, effectively scuttled U.S. efforts to have the IAEA governing board refer Iran to the Security Council for possible sanctions.[33] Moreover, the agreement also greatly increased the political tensions between the United States and the Europeans. Having persuaded Iran to voluntarily (and temporarily) suspend its uranium enrichment activities, the Europeans argued that the next step was to provide Tehran with enough carrots (or inducements) to convince them to suspend their program permanently. From the European perspective, the Americans needed to join with them to offer not only economic incentives, but perhaps normalization of relations and security guarantees that "Iran would not be attacked or subverted" if it gave up its nuclear options. The Europeans also argued that Iran's right to peaceful uses of nuclear energy, guaranteed to it under the Nuclear Non-Proliferation Treaty, should be honored, as long as these were monitored by the IAEA to ensure compliance with peaceful use. Although they recognized that Washington would be unenthusiastic, the Europeans viewed this as the only viable path to both convince Iran to suspend is unmonitored program and maintain enough support among dubious members of the Security Council (such as Russia and China) to implement an agreement.[34]

In contrast, the United States still viewed such inducements as naïve and questioned whether the Iranians could ever be trusted to keep their end of any agreement.[35] Instead, the Bush administration maintained that the international community should unite to impose harsh sanctions on Iran (preferably at the UN, where economic as well as military actions could be imposed), with the goal of forcing Tehran's complete capitulation. Although the military situation in Iraq and the overstretched U.S. military had calmed talk of outright regime change in Iran over the issue, the Bush administration pointedly refused to remove the option of military strikes against Iran's nuclear facilities from the table.[36]

Over the ensuing months, however, negotiations failed to produce a breakthrough, as the Europeans and Iranians struggled without success to break an impasse over the details of a long-term agreement on economic inducements and security guarantees for Tehran.[37] With pressure growing on the United States to show some flexibility and commitment to the diplomatic efforts, the Bush administration reluctantly agreed to offer modest economic incentives to Iran in return for a European pledge to take the issue to the UN Security Council should the talks fail. Although the American incentives only came into play if Iran agreed to a permanent halt in uranium enrichment, they nevertheless represented a major policy shift by both the Bush administration (which had long opposed offering incentives) and the Europeans (who had been reluctant to discuss referring Iran to the UN for sanctions).[38] At the same time, Iran increased pressure on the Europeans by warning that it would soon revive its enrichment program and confirmed that it had converted thirty-seven tons of uranium ore concentrate into uranium tetrafluoride, a precursor to converting the material into the uranium hexafluoride gas that could be fed into centrifuges for enrichment. The Europeans responded by warning that such an action would violate the pledge Iran had made the previous year to temporarily freeze its enrichment program.[39] This brinksmanship by both sides eventually resulted, in May 2005, in an Iranian pledge to continue the temporary freeze on its nuclear activities, and that forestalled any move to refer Tehran to the Security Council.[40]

In June 2005, hard-line conservative Mahmoud Ahmadinejad was elected president of Iran, replacing the moderate reformist Khatami. And while maintaining that Iran's nuclear program was not intended to develop weapons, Ahmadinejad, even as he exited the polls on election day, left no doubt about his position on the issue, stating: "Nuclear energy is a result of the Iranian people's scientific development and no one can block the way of a nation's scientific development. . . . This right of the Iranian people will soon be recognized by those who have so far denied it."[41] Over the following months, Iran began to adopt a much tougher stance in its negotiations with the Europeans and the International Atomic Energy Agency. Although Ahmadinejad became the visible, public face of this more confrontational approach, he was not entirely responsible for the shift, since this policy is actually decided not by the president but by the supreme leader, Ayatollah Ali Khamenei.[42] Tehran not only refused to comply with the IAEA's demand to halt its uranium conversion program (which it had restarted in defiance of the agreement previously reached with Britain, Germany, and France) but stated that "making nuclear fuel for civilian purposes was its right under the Nuclear Nonproliferation Treaty."[43] By beginning work again at its uranium conversion facilities in Isfahan, where raw uranium is converted into a gas that can later be fed into centrifuges for enrichment, Iran explicitly rejected giving up its right to develop nuclear fuel indigenously.[44] Iranian officials warned the West that Iran would not negotiate over its uranium conversion plants but said it was still willing to discuss the uranium enrichment facilities at Natanz in future talks.[45] The governing board of the IAEA responded to the Iranian actions by setting a deadline of September 3, 2005, for Iran to "re-establish full suspension of all enrichment related activities."[46]

When Iran failed to comply with the new deadline, the United States and its European allies found their options limited. Although not immediately referring Iran to the UN Security Council, the United States and Europe sought a tough new IAEA resolution accusing Iran of "noncompliance" with treaties governing its nuclear program. Russia and China still objected to the IAEA draft proposal, since it signaled that Iran's case would eventually be sent to the Security Council—a step they were unwilling to take—and blocked this move to punish Iran. For its part, Iran continued to say it was willing to continue negotiations with the Europeans but did not back away from its earlier declaration that referral to the UN might lead to its withdrawal the Nuclear Non-Proliferation Treaty.[47] This long dance between Iran and the IAEA had been under way since inspectors first discovered that Iran was clandestinely enriching uranium in 2003. Between June 2003 and September 2005 the IAEA board passed seven resolutions criticizing Iran's activities and urging it to grant unfettered access to inspectors.[48] Still, although Iranian nuclear activities continued to be suspicious, the IAEA was unable to prove conclusively that Iran was pursuing a weapons program—despite its lack of cooperation with inspectors and its failure to provide a full accounting of its efforts to acquire centrifuges for uranium enrichment or an explanation for the discovery of recently produced plutonium, which was inconsistent with Tehran's claims that its plutonium separation experiments only ran between 1988 and 1993.[49] In the absence of conclusive proof, Russia, India, Brazil, South Africa, and many developing countries opposed U.S. and European calls for a referral of Iran to the Security Council, where sanctions (either military or economic) could be imposed.[50]

The inaccurate claims about Iraqi WMD that the Bush administration made prior to the 2003 invasion of Iraq—which were used as a justification for regime change—roused suspicions regarding U.S. motives, making the case more difficult. The prior case not only called into question American intelligence on Iran's actions, but also created a strong desire not to repeat the mistakes made in Iraq in a rush to punish Iran over its purported nuclear program. However, the Bush administration found help from an unlikely source in its effort to gain traction for a tougher approach to Iran—Mahmoud Ahmadinejad himself. During an ill-conceived speech at the United Nations, in New York in September 2005, Ahmadinejad stunned observers with a rambling, twenty-five-minute oration combining religious references with anti-American vitriol, conspiracy theories, and threats—along with a warning that in response to U.S. provocation "we will reconsider our entire approach to the nuclear issue."[51] The harsh, uncompromising nature of Ahmadinejad's speech cleared the path for a tougher negotiating approach to Iran and raised serious concerns among formerly sympathetic countries about Iran's nuclear intentions.

With international pressure on Tehran growing and the United States and the Europeans adopting a more united front on the nuclear issue, Ahmadinejad upped the ante in January 2006, announcing that Iran would reopen its massive uranium enrichment complex at Natanz after a fourteen-month halt in operations. That facility had sparked the original crisis over the Iranian nuclear program, when it was revealed in February 2003 and inspectors discovered plans for more than 50,000 centrifuges at the site—enough when fully constructed to produce fuel for up to twenty nuclear weapons per year. Not only did the United States and the Europeans send messages to Tehran warning against such a move, but Russia and China did so as well—a stark warning to Iran that the resistance of those two states to a referral to the Security Council might be fading.[52] Nevertheless, within days Iran broke open the internationally monitored seals on three of its nuclear facilities, clearing the way for uranium enrichment and derailing any new negotiations with the Europeans. Combined with Iran's harsh rhetoric, its actions met general condemnation by the international community. One European diplomat commented, "The Iranians have behaved so remarkably badly, it's hard to believe that the international community will do anything other than put them in front of the ultimate court of international public opinion (the UN Security Council). . . . That is where the Iranians are heading."[53] For their part, the Iranians defended their actions as peaceful and involving research activities permitted them under the NPT.[54] Later, during a press conference following a meeting with his French and British counterparts, the German foreign minister, Frank-Walter Steinmeier, noted, "Our talks with Iran have reached a dead end. . . . From our point of view, the time has come for the UN Security Council to become involved."[55]

Pressing its advantage, the United States announced that it fully supported the European action, with Secretary of State Condoleezza Rice declaring that Iran's actions "have shattered the basis for negotiation."[56]

In response, Iran warned the West that only diplomacy, not threats, could defuse the standoff over its nuclear program, and that any sanctions against it would force up world oil prices![57] Yet despite Iranian recalcitrance, and the rapprochement of the U.S. and European positions, Russia and China held firm to their posture of demanding that Iran freeze its nuclear activity but opposing bringing it before the Security Council.[58] Thus negotiations made no progress, and Iran was able to restart its uranium conversion operations at Isfahan in August 2005 and its enrichment operation at Natanz in January 2006. It still avoided referral because of Russian and Chinese concerns about ultimate U.S. intentions vis-à-vis Iran if the matter reached the Security Council. That being said, Iran's former negotiating partners in Europe (Britain, France, and Germany) felt betrayed by its actions and largely gave up on further talks. The United States and Europe sought to allay Russian concerns by stating that they would not press for immediate sanctions even if Iran was referred—an argument that failed to convince Moscow that Tehran would not terminate talks and expel international inspectors in response to such an action.[59] At the same time, Iran's supreme religious leader (and ultimate arbiter of the Iranian position), Ayatollah Khamenei, warned that the rest of the world cannot deter the will of the Iranian people to pursue their nuclear program and maintained that "the West knows very well that we are not seeking to build nuclear weapons."[60] Iran further warned that if taken to the Security Council, it would retaliate by banning UN inspectors from visiting its sites and fully resume uranium enrichment.[61]

Possibly in response to the renewed movement toward referring it to the Security Council, Iran turned up the heat still further in April 2006 by announcing that its nuclear engineers had advanced to "a new phase in the enrichment of uranium" and that it would now speed ahead to produce nuclear fuel on an industrial scale. In a nationally televised broadcast, Ahmadinejad declared that "Iran has joined the nuclear countries of the world," leading the White House to announce that the United States would work with the Security Council "to deal with the significant threat posed by the regime's efforts to acquire nuclear weapons." Given that earlier in the week President Bush had repeated that his "stated goal" was to not allow "the Iranians to have a nuclear weapon, the capacity to make a nuclear weapon, or the knowledge as to how to make a nuclear weapon," Ahmadinejad's announcement represented a serious setback for overall U.S. foreign policy.[62]

Although nuclear analysts quickly dismissed Iran's claims as exaggerated "political posturing," meant to invoke Iranian nationalism to firm up domestic political support for Ahmadinejad and convince the international community that Iran's nuclear advances were inevitable, that did nothing to reduce growing international concern about the program.[63] Iran refused to answer IAEA questions about the existence of a previously unknown, secret uranium enrichment program (based on P-2 centrifuges obtained on the black market through the A. Q. Khan network) unwisely disclosed by Ahmadinejad weeks earlier. Declaring that the new technology would increase fourfold the amount of uranium Iran could enrich, Ahmadinejad rejected a UN deadline to suspend the nuclear program and a proposal by Moscow to enrich uranium for Iran on Russian soil, and declared that sanctions would hurt Western nations more than Iran.[64] In response, the United States announced that it would ask the Security Council to require Iran to stop enrichment based on Chapter 7 of the UN Charter, the section making resolutions mandatory and opening the way for either sanctions or military action—a move still opposed by both Russia and China.[65]

Over the following months, with no movement on either the diplomatic or the sanctions front, the Europeans began pressing Bush to make a "dramatic gesture" to reenergize talks, rally world opinion against Iran, and avoid the United States' being blamed for not doing its utmost to defuse the crisis.[66] An eighteen-page letter from Ahmadinejad to Bush in May 2006, although filled with religious language and declarations that Western democracy had failed, was still seen by many foreign policy experts as an attempt by the Iranian leader to open up a new dialogue with the Americans.[67] After an internal White House debate, in which Secretary of State Rice overcame the skepticism of Vice President Cheney to convince Bush of the need for "a third option" apart from "either a nuclear Iran or an American military action," the president agreed to engage in substantive talks with Iran—the first major negotiations in the twenty-seven years since the hostage crisis. Although Cheney and other hard-line officials were "dead set against it" and preferred a strategy to isolate Iran enough to force "regime change," they were finally persuaded that if a military response was eventually necessary, it would be easier to gain international approval if efforts at negotiation preceded it.[68] As a result, in June 2006 punitive action by the Security Council was shelved until Iran had a chance to respond to a new package of incentives (still minus U.S. security guarantees) presented by the United States, Europe, Russia, and China.[69] Although the Iranians immediately stated that they would "not negotiate over our nation's natural nuclear rights," they struck a slightly conciliatory tone by noting that they were "ready to hold fair and unbiased dialogue and negotiations over mutual concerns within the context of a defined framework," and Ayatollah Khamenei (long an opponent of direct talks with Washington) gave his blessing to talks "if there was respect for mutual interests."[70] In response to the Iranian rejection of the package of economic incentives, the UN Security Council issued a call for Iran to implement a "full and sustained suspension" of its nuclear activities by August 31 or face sanctions.[71]

Iran ignored those calls, and after North Korea's nuclear test in October 2006, the EU supported limited UN sanctions against Iran after it had rejected suspending its enrichment program as a precondition for starting new talks.[72] The IAEA followed by reporting that Iran had successfully set up a second centrifuge cascade and was continuing to expand its enrichment capabilities, though IAEA Director El Baradei maintained, "The jury is still out on whether they are developing a nuclear weapon."[73] Although Iran suggested that "France organize and monitor the production of enriched uranium inside Iran" (a proposal rejected by the West as falling short of Security Council demands for a freeze on all nuclear activities), Tehran maintained its position that it would not comply with the UN demands and refused to condemn North Korea for its nuclear test.[74] Raising tensions further, Ahmadinejad declared in November 2006 that Iran's program was nearing the milestone of mastering the nuclear fuel cycle and that "we can have our celebration of Iran's full nuclearization this year."[75] The announcement increased Western concerns, since mastering the fuel cycle implies the ability not only to enrich uranium, but also to reprocess plutonium from spent fuel, potentially providing Iran with two sources of material for nuclear weapons.

Finally in December 2006 the Security Council unanimously passed a resolution against Iran, banning the import or export of materials and technology used in uranium enrichment, reprocessing, or ballistic missiles. Although the measure was softened to gain Russian and Chinese support (and excluded any sanctions against the Bashehr nuclear power plant being built by Russia in southern Iran), it still froze the assets of twelve Iranians and eleven companies involved in Tehran's nuclear and ballistic missile programs.[76] That led to friction with U.S. allies in Europe, who resisted subsequent Bush administration demands to increase financial pressure on Iran by curtailing exports, loan guarantees, and many business transactions because of their far greater commercial and economic ties with Tehran.[77] The Europeans believed they were being asked to sacrifice far more than the Americans for the sanctions (given limited U.S. business interests), and their resistance provided Tehran with a continued economic lifeline in the face of the UN penalties. For example, in February 2007

Russia announced that it would consider OPEC-like cooperation with Tehran on sales of natural gas, and President Putin observed that "the people of Iran should have access to modern technologies, including nuclear ones . . . they should choose a variant that will guarantee Iran access to nuclear energy" while complying with their NPT commitments to avoid weaponization.[78] One of the greatest hurdles for the United States in marshaling international support for harsh economic sanctions remains the reality that other states have tremendous economic interests in Iran and much to lose from such measures—ranging from the Russians and Chinese, who fear losing access to Iranian oil and gas, to the Europeans, who have long-standing business interests with Tehran.

Even so, in the face of Iran's continued defiance, the Security Council on March 24, 2007, unanimously passed Resolution 1747 barring all arms exports to Iran and freezing the financial assets of twenty-eight Iranians linked to its military and nuclear programs. This action provoked Khamenei to warn that were new sanctions passed, "Iran would strike back against any threats or violence." Not only, he said, was the nuclear program "more important than the nationalization of oil in 1958," but "if they want to treat us with threats and use of force or violence, the Iranian nation will undoubtedly use all its capabilities to strike the invading enemies."[79] Ahmadinejad warned that if pressure on Iran was not ended, he would consider halting all cooperation with the IAEA, observing that the West "should know that the Iranian nation will defend its right and that this path is irreversible."[80] According to Under Secretary of State Nicolas Burns, the United States was "trying to force a change in the actions and behavior of the Iranian government," and whereas the sanctions "immediately focused on the nuclear weapons research program," they were also "trying to limit the ability of Iran to be a disruptive and violent factor on Middle East politics."[81] Two U.S. carrier battle groups were sent to the Persian Gulf as a veiled threat to Iran. Nevertheless, in April 2007 Ahmadinejad boasted that Iran was capable of "enriching uranium on an industrial scale," with a newly operational site containing 1,300 centrifuges enriching small amounts of uranium at an underground facility in Natanz.[82] The United States intends to try gradually increasing the severity of sanctions against Iran, while refusing to take military options off the table, but Iran has shown no willingness to give in and has speeded up its installation of centrifuges. In fact, there is a growing likelihood of perhaps 8,000 (at the current rate of production) being added by the end of this year, which would be enough to enrich sufficient fissile material for a least two nuclear weapons a year.[83]

Conclusions and Policy Options

In the current impasse over Iran's nuclear program, it is clear that long-standing antagonisms between the United States and Tehran have created a situation in which neither side has "started from scratch" in its approach to the other. From the U.S. perspective, Iran is a radical state bent on spreading its religious extremism, destabilizing important U.S. allies, supporting terrorism, and (more significantly) seeking to acquire nuclear weapons capabilities under the guise of a civilian program. This perspective is strongly imprinted on the minds of U.S. policymakers, given the traumatic experience of the 1979 hostage crisis, Iranian religious leaders' "Great Satan" rhetoric, and Iran's general hostility toward the United States and its regional allies. The U.S. policy toward Iran, first adopted by the Reagan administration, has taken the form of an aggressive containment strategy that seeks to isolate Iran politically and economically, to limit its influence, and to moderate its behavior. The policy has led the United States to provide a great deal of military aid to Gulf allies (such as Saudi Arabia and Kuwait) to reduce their vulnerability to Iranian military threats; to try to cultivate pro-American relationships with states surrounding Tehran; and even to support Iraq in its war against Iran during the 1980s. The prospect of Iran's acquiring nuclear weapons is viewed with considerable alarm by Washington, which believes that it would allow Tehran to engage in nuclear blackmail within the region, threaten Israel, and seriously constrain U.S. freedom of action in its foreign and military policies vis-à-vis Iran. That Iran concealed some of its nuclear activity from IAEA inspectors and engaged in black market interactions with the A. Q. Khan nuclear network is considered evidence that Tehran is not pursuing peaceful, civilian nuclear energy and cannot be trusted with nuclear technology—voiding its legal rights to such capabilities under the NPT.

In contrast, Iran believes that it has been faced by an aggressive, imperialistic United States, seeking to dominate it politically and economically, for the past sixty years. From its installing the pro-American Shah and overthrowing the democratically elected Mossadeq in the 1950s (to ensure U.S. control over Iran's oil resources) and protecting the Shah after his overthrow and refusing to return him for trial, to its military and economic support of Iraq in a war that inflicted over a million casualties and its subsequent efforts to isolate Iran through economic sanctions, a deep well of historical experience suggests to Tehran that it faces a serious external security threat from Washington. Add to this the recent rhetoric about the need for "regime change" and its prominent listing among the axis of evil, and it becomes quite understandable why Tehran might believe that it needs a nuclear deterrent to defend itself against the world's lone remaining superpower. In addition, there is considerable nationalistic pride among the Iranian people that views Iran as a historic, legitimate great power in the region that, as such, deserves nuclear status. On a technical level, according to the NPT (which Iran signed), it is within its legal rights to develop peaceful, civilian applications of nuclear power, as long as these are monitored by the IAEA. The long-standing U.S. opposition to any Iranian nuclear projects, even the Russian-built Bushehr reactors in southern Iran, which were completely under IAEA supervision, is seen as clear evidence that the real U.S. policy is not based on pure proliferation concerns but is geared to prevent Iran from obtaining *any* nuclear technology at all.

Iran and the United States have deep-seated (and often well-grounded) suspicions about each other's motives, an unwillingness to put much faith in diplomacy (given those assumed motives), and tremendous levels of mutual antipathy. From a diplomatic standpoint, their history makes it difficult to engage in the kind of confidence-building measures routinely used in negotiations to show good faith and move parties toward tough policy compromises. Washington and Tehran each assume an inherent bad faith on the part of the other. Moreover, long-standing domestic political constraints, nurtured during their long, antagonistic relationship, make it difficult for leaders in either country to compromise or make diplomatic overtures to the other without being vulnerable to criticism at home. As a result, opportunities for engagement and compromise are dismissed or ignored (as occurred when reform-minded Iranian president Khatami put out feelers to improve U.S.-Iranian relations during the Clinton and Bush administrations), strengthening the views of hard-liners in both states that such efforts are pointless.[84] In essence, each sees only a reflection in the mirror of its own hostility to its opponent and lacks the perspective to understand the opponent's views as well.

Once this context is fully understood, it becomes easier to understand why the European-sponsored talks over the nuclear issue had difficulty gaining traction. Indeed, although Europe's diplomatic approach would be a reasonable one under normal circumstances, very little about the U.S.-Iranian relationship can be described as normal. Throughout the negotiations, Iran responded to EU initiatives with a wary eye on Washington. For its part, the United States initially opposed the European efforts, only grudgingly accepting them when the constraints imposed by its wars in Iraq and Afghanistan made military options increasingly problematic and Iran continued to build its nuclear facilities unabated. Bush refused to compromise on talking directly with Tehran (and rewarding its bad behavior) and continued a muscular containment policy, now intermingled with "regime change" rhetoric and military threats.

Iran sought to appear conciliatory in its negotiations with the EU to forestall U.S. efforts to bring it before the UN for sanctions. If Tehran is actually seeking a clandestine weapons capability, and because the Iranians witnessed a similar progression of U.S. policy toward Iraq in 2002–2003, the U.S. approach likely made it even more difficult for Iran to compromise and eliminate a program that might provide it with a deterrent in the absence of firm security guarantees from Washington. Yet, given the history of their relations, it is hard to imagine what guarantees the United States could have offered that Tehran would trust, just as it is difficult to envision a diplomatic settlement that Washington would trust. As the talks broke down and Iran restarted its uranium enrichment effort (and redoubled efforts to build its nuclear infrastructure), it is hardly surprising that Tehran's response to its referral to the UN Security Council and the subsequent sanctions has been outright defiance. That the debate has now moved in the direction preferred by the Americans all along—to the Security Council, which can punish Iran both economically and militarily—only reinforces Tehran's perception that the real U.S. agenda has been (and remains) regime change, and that makes the nuclear program even less negotiable.

Is there any way out of this impasse? Assuming that no extreme measures are taken militarily against Iran in the near future, it is possible that a change of U.S. administrations and continued weakening of Ahmadinejad's hold on the presidency (which, in the absence of an external threat unifying Iranians, has become increasingly unpopular) could soften the current standoff and allow compromises that might stabilize the situation. Even if Iran is unwilling to give up its nuclear capabilities completely (as is highly likely), a deal akin to the 1994 Agreed Framework with North Korea could slow the pace of Iran's nuclear development and allow diplomacy time to work (see chapter 5). Though that agreement was imperfect, without it the world would likely have seen either a general war on the Korean peninsula (which the Pentagon estimates would inflict a million casualties) or a North Korean regime with enough fissile material by 2007 for at least two hundred weapons.[85] Even though Bush's familiar strategy of refusing substantive negotiations and compromise with North Korea resulted in its restarting the Yongbyon reactor, reprocessing spent fuel rods, and testing a nuclear weapon, Pyongyang's likely arsenal of nine to twelve weapons (given its available fissile materials) is still far less than would have been the case without Clinton's Agreed Framework. So although Bush's strategy failed to produce his desired antiproliferation results in either North Korea or Iran, it is still possible to envision a return to an Agreed Framework–style compromise (which was the basis of European proposals during the early talks with Iran) that could defuse (though not completely solve) the crisis.

In addition to engaging in a diplomatic approach that does not require complete surrender by the other side as a starting point, it is important that military options (though perhaps not the threat of them) be taken off the table. Given that Iran is at least five to nine years away from developing nuclear weapons, precipitate military action is not called for at this point.[86] Moreover, the potentially extreme negative consequences of such action, given Iran's unquestioned ability to disrupt stability in both Iraq and Afghanistan, and the overstretched condition of the U.S. military in 2007, in which it lacks the long-term ability to maintain its current force levels in either theatre of operation, make it utterly unrealistic to consider options requiring substantial military conflict. Restored diplomatic relations between Washington and Tehran should not be dangled as some distant carrot but should be instituted to improve communications and contacts that have been largely silent for twenty-seven years. The European negotiations offered carrots rather than sticks to the Iranians, but with the United States waving a stick over their shoulders, their diplomacy failed.

Though the EU has now largely adopted the American view that diplomacy is ineffective and only sanctions will alter Iran's behavior, that approach promises to result in exactly the outcome the West least desires. Given the historical context and current strategic situation, without U.S. concessions that provide Iran a clearly decreased threat to its security (possibly tied to positive Iranian concessions on side issues, but not a demand for complete capitulation on the nuclear issue), the current pattern in the negotiations will be maintained. That pattern—of U.S./UN threats and sanctions, Iranian defiance, an inability to take strong UN action (because of U.S. military constraints and the unwillingness of veto-wielding Council members Russia and China to acquiesce to it)—will inevitably lead to more tension in the region, even greater hostility between the United States and Iran, and in the long run, an Iranian nuclear program outside of IAEA supervision that will provide Tehran with both civilian and military capabilities.

Key Actors

Mahmoud Ahmadinejad Iran's current president (2005–present), a conservative opposed to the societal reforms pushed by Khatami, has strongly pursued a more aggressive negotiating position in support of Iran's continued nuclear enrichment program, which he claims is for peaceful purposes.

George W. Bush U.S. president, has taken a hard line on negotiations with Iran over its nuclear program, demanding that Iran stop nuclear enrichment before negotiations may go forward.

Jimmy Carter U.S. president during the Iranian revolution and the hostage crisis.

Bill Clinton U.S. president, signed an executive order in 1995 prohibiting trade with Iran to force it to stop supporting terrorism and developing a nuclear weapons program.

Supreme Leader Ali Khamenei Iran's current supreme leader, wields tremendous power to step into the political process and make important decisions for the country. He has strongly supported Iran's nuclear program and has been largely opposed to normalizing relations with the United States.

Mohammad Khatami Iranian president (1997–2005), tried unsuccessfully to reform the political system and establish better relations with the West.

Ayatollah Ruhollah Khomeini Iranian revolutionary leader, became Iran's first supreme leader. His anti-Western policy became the inspiration behind the Iranian revolution and the storming of the American embassy in Tehran.

Ronald Reagan U.S. president, adopted a containment strategy versus Iran and supported Iraq in its war against Tehran (1980–1988).

Notes

1. Glenn Kessler and Peter Baker, "Bush's 'Axis of Evil' Comes back to Haunt United States," *Washington Post,* October 10, 2006, A12; Moshahed Hossein, "U.S. Strategy Tries to Isolate Iran," *Mahjubah, the Islamic Magazine for Women,* May 1995, web.archive.org/web/20030103132635/www.netiran.com.
2. See Thomas Preston, *From Lambs to Lions: Future Security Relationships in a World of Biological and Nuclear Weapons* (Boulder: Rowman and Littlefield, 2007).
3. See William J. Daugherty, "Jimmy Carter and the 1979 Decision to Admit the Shah into the United States," AmericanDiplomacy.org, January 2003, www.unc.edu/depts/diplomat/archives_roll/2003_01-03/daugherty_shaw.
4. GlobalSecurity.org, "Ministry of Security SAVAK," www.globalsecurity.org/intell/world/iran/savak.htm.
5. Daugherty, "Jimmy Carter."
6. John King, "Arming Iraq and the Path to War," March 31, 2003, www.parstimes.com/news/archive/2003/arming_iraq.html.
7. Farhang Rajaee, *The Iran-Iraq War: The Politics of Aggression* (Gainesville: University Press of Florida, 1993), 1.

8. See Daniel Yergin, *The Prize: The Epic Quest for Oil, Money, and Power* (New York: Touchstone, 1991), 766.

9. Ibid.

10. Hossein, "U.S. Strategy Tries to Isolate Iran."

11. Ibid.

12. Azar Nafisi, "The Veiled Threat," *The New Republic,* February 22, 1999, 27.

13. Ibid.

14. Michael Hirsh, Maziar Bahari, et al., "Rumors of War," *Newsweek,* February 19, 2007, 30.

15. Ibid., 31.

16. Ibid.

17. Ibid., 32.

18. Seymour M. Hersh, "The Iran Game," *New Yorker,* December 3, 2001, 42–50; Elaine Sciolino, "Nuclear Ambitions Aren't New for Iran," *New York Times,* June 22, 2003, WK 4.

19. Sciolino, "Nuclear Ambitions," 4.

20. Ibid.

21. Terrence Henry, "Nuclear Iran," *Atlantic Monthly,* December 2003, 45.

22. Ibid.; Jack Boureston and Charles D. Ferguson, "Schooling Iran's Atom Squad," *Bulletin of the Atomic Scientists* 60, no.3 (May/June 2004): 31–35.

23. David Albright and Corey Hinderstein, "Iran, Player or Rogue?" *Bulletin of the Atomic Scientists* 59, no.5 (September/October 2003): 54–56.

24. Ibid.

25. Hersh, "The Iran Game," 50; William J. Broad, David E. Sanger, and Raymond Bonner, "A Tale of Nuclear Proliferation: How Pakistani Built His Network," *New York Times,* February 12, 2004, A1.

26. For a detailed discussion of Iran's postrevolution pursuit of nuclear, biological, and chemical weapons, see Gregory F. Giles, "The Islamic Republic of Iran and Nuclear, Biological, and Chemical Weapons," in *Planning the Unthinkable: How New Powers Will Use Nuclear, Biological, and Chemical Weapons,* ed. James J. Wirtz, Peter R. Lavoy, and Scott D. Sagan (Ithaca, N.Y.: Cornell University Press, 2000), 79–103.

27. James Risen and Judith Miller, "No Illicit Arms Found in Iraq, U.S. Inspector Tells Congress," *New York Times,* October 3, 2003, A1.

28. Joseph Cirincione, *Deadly Arsenals: Tracking Weapons of Mass Destruction* (Washington, D.C.: Carnegie Endowment for International Peace, 2002), 257. Indeed, a January 2005 briefing to the Israeli Knesset by Meir Dagan, head of the Mossad intelligence agency, warned that Iran could build a bomb in less than three years and, if it successfully enriched uranium in 2005, could have a weapon two years later. See, BBC News, http://news.bbc.co.uk/go/pr/fr/-/2/hi/middle_east/4203411.stm, January 24, 2005. By August 2005, Israeli intelligence had adjusted its estimate to Iran's having the bomb as early as 2008, "if all goes well for it," but probably by 2012. Orly Halpern, "New Estimates on Iranian Nukes," *Jerusalem Post,* August 1, 2005, jpost.com/servlet/Satellite?pagename = Jpost/JPArticle/ShowFull&cid=1122776414371&p=1101615860782.

29. Douglas Jehl and Eric Schmitt, "Data Is Lacking on Iran's Arms, U.S. Panel Says," *New York Times,* March 9, 2005, A1; Steven R. Weisman and Douglas Jehl, "Estimate Revised on When Iran Could Make Nuclear Bomb," *New York Times,* August 3, 2005, A8. Agreeing with this assessment, London's International Institute for Strategic Studies concluded that Iran would not be expected to build nuclear weapons before the next decade.

Alan Cowell, "Nuclear Weapon Is Years off for Iran, Research Panel Says," *New York Times,* September 7, 2005, A11.

30. See Cirincione, *Deadly Arsenals,* 255. The IAEA, after two years of inspections, has stated it has not found evidence of any weapons program. See Jehl and Schmitt, "Data Is Lacking on Iran's Arms."

31. Cirincione, *Deadly Arsenals,* 255.

32. Steven R. Weisman, "U.S. in Talks with Europeans on a Nuclear Deal with Iran," *New York Times,* October 12, 2004, A16.

33. Elaine Sciolino, "Board Accepts Nuclear Vow by Iranians: A Tepid Resolution Angers U.S. Envoy," *New York Times,* November 30, 2004, A3.

34. Steven R. Weisman, "U.S. and Europe Are at Odds, Again, This Time over Iran," *New York Times,* December 12, 2004, A10.

35. Thom Shanker, Eric Schmitt, and David E. Sanger, "U.S. Wants to Block Iran's Nuclear Ambition, but Diplomacy Seems to Be the Only Path," *New York Times,* December 12, 2004, A10; and Weisman, "U.S. and Europe Are at Odds, Again."

36. Steven R. Weisman, "Bush Confronts New Challenge on Issue of Iran," *New York Times,* November 19, 2004, A1.

37. Elaine Sciolino, "Nuclear Accord Eludes Iran and Europeans," *New York Times,* March 24, 2005, A10.

38. David E. Sanger and Steven R. Weisman, "U.S. and Allies Agree on Steps in Iran Nuclear Dispute," *New York Times,* March 11, 2005, A1.

39. Steven R. Weisman, "Atom Agency May Be Asked to Meet on Iran Situation," *New York Times,* May 12, 2005, A12.

40. Elaine Sciolino, "Europe Gets Iran to Extend Freeze in Nuclear Work," *New York Times,* May 26, 2005, A1.

41. David E. Sanger, "Iranian Upset, U.S. Challenge," *New York Times,* June 26, 2005, A1.

42. Nazila Fathi, "Iran Tells Europe It's Devoted to Nuclear Efforts and Talks," *New York Times,* August 4, 2005, A6.

43. Nazila Fathi, "Iran Warns the West Not to Use the U.N. to Penalize It," *New York Times,* September 12, 2005, A7.

44. Nazila Fathi, "Iran Rejects European Offer to End Its Nuclear Impasse," *New York Times,* August 7, 2005, A11.

45. Nazila Fathi, "Iran's New Leader Turns to Conservatives for His Cabinet," *New York Times,* August 15, 2005, A3.

46. Thomas Fuller and Nazila Fathi, "U.N. Agency Urges Iran to Halt Its Nuclear Activity," *New York Times,* August 12, 2005, A8.

47. Steven R. Weisman, "West Presses for Nuclear Agency to Rebuke Iran, Despite Russian Dissent," *New York Times,* September 23, 2005, A6.

48. Mark Landler, "Nuclear Agency Expected to Back Weaker Rebuke to Iran," *New York Times,* September 24, 2005, A3.

49. Mark Landler, "U.N. Says It Hasn't Found Much New about Nuclear Iran," *New York Times,* September 3, 2005, A3.

50. Steven R. Weisman, "Wider U.S. Net Seeks Allies against Iran's Nuclear Plan," *New York Times,* September 10, 2005, A3.

51. Dafna Linzer, "Iran's President Does What U.S. Diplomacy Could Not," *Washington Post,* September 19, 2005, A12.

52. Elaine Sciolino, "Iran, Defiant, Insists It Plans to Restart Nuclear Program," *New York Times,* January 10, 2006, A11.

53. Steven R. Weisman and Nazila Fathi, "Iranians Reopen Nuclear Centers," *New York Times,* January 11, 2006, A1.

54. Ibid.

55. Richard Bernstein and Steven R. Weisman, "Europe Joins U.S. in Urging Action by U.N. on Iran," *New York Times,* January 13, 2006, A1.

56. Ibid.

57. "Iran Warns against Sanctions as Move in Nuclear Standoff," *New York Times,* January 16, 2006, A8.

58. Elaine Sciolino and Alan Cowell, "Russia and China Demand Iran Freeze Nuclear Activity, but Reject Referral to U.N.," *New York Times,* January 17, 2006, A9.

59. Steven R. Weisman, "West Tells Russia It Won't Press to Penalize Iran Now," *New York Times,* January 19, 2006, A6.

60. Nazila Fathi, "Iran's Ayatollah Affirms Peaceful Nuclear Plans," *New York Times,* January 19, 2006, A6.

61. Ibid.

62. Nazila Fathi, David E. Sanger, and William J. Broad, "Iran Reports Big Advance in Enrichment of Uranium: U.S. Warns of 'Significant' Arms Threat as Tehran Says It Will Defy the UN," *New York Times,* April 12, 2006, A1.

63. William J. Broad, Nazila Fathi, and Joel Brinkley, "Analysts Say a Nuclear Iran Is Years Away," *New York Times,* April 13, 2006, A1.

64. David E. Sanger and Nazila Fathi, "Iran Is Described as Defiant on 2nd Nuclear Program," *New York Times,* April 25, 2006, A6.

65. Elaine Sciolino, "U.N. Agency Says Iran Falls Short on Nuclear Data," *New York Times,* April 29, 2006, A1.

66. Steven R. Weisman, "U.S. Is Now Ready to Meet Iranians on Nuclear Plan," *New York Times,* June 1, 2006, A1.

67. Michael Slackman, "Iranian Letter: Using Religion to Lecture Bush," *New York Times,* May 10, 2006, A1; David E. Sanger, "U.S. Debating Direct Talks with Iran on Nuclear Issue," *New York Times,* May 27, 2006, A1.

68. David E. Sanger, "Bush's Realization on Iran: No Good Choice Left except Talks," *New York Times,* June 1, 2006, A8.

69. Thom Shanker and Elaine Sciolino, "Package of Terms (No Sanctions Included) for Iran," *New York Times,* June 2, 2006, A12.

70. Ibid.

71. Elissa Gootman, "Security Council Approves Sanctions against Iran," *New York Times,* December 24, 2006, A8.

72. "Europeans Back Gradual Steps against Iran's Nuclear Program," *New York Times,* October 18, 2006, A11.

73. David E. Sanger, "U.N. Official Says Iran Is Testing New Enrichment Device," *New York Times,* October 24, 2006, A8.

74. Elaine Sciolino, "Iran's Proposal to End Nuclear Standoff Is Rejected by the West," *New York Times,* October 4, 2006, A6; Navila Fathi, "Iran Defies Call to Drop Nuclear Plans," *New York Times,* October 13, 2006, A11.

75. William J. Broad and Nazila Fathi, "Iran's Leader Cites Progress on Nuclear Plans," *New York Times,* November 15, 2006, A8.

76. Gootman, "Security Council Approves Sanctions."

77. Steven R. Weisman, "Europe Resists U.S. on Curbing Ties with Iran," *New York Times,* January 30, 2007, A1.

78. Steven Lee Myers, "Pact with Iran on Gas Sales Is Possible, Putin Says," *New York Times,* February 2, 2007, A8.

79. Nazila Fathi, "Iran Says It Can Enrich Uranium on an Industrial Scale," *New York Times,* April 10, 2007, A3.

80. David E. Sanger, "Atomic Agency Confirms Advances by Iran's Nuclear Program," *New York Times,* April 19, 2007, A10.

81. Jon Sawyer, "War with Iran? Congress Says OK," *Los Angeles Times,* October 29, 2006, M1.

82. Sanger, "Atomic Agency Confirms Advances."

83. David E. Sanger, "Inspectors Say Iran Is Advancing on Nuclear Front, *International Herald Tribune,* May 15, 2007, A1.

84. See Tanyel Taysi and Thomas Preston, "The Personality and Leadership Style of President Khatami: Implications for the Future of Iranian Political Reform," in *Profiling Political Leaders: Cross-Cultural Studies of Personality and Behavior,* ed. Ofer Feldman and Linda O. Valenty, 57–77 (Westport, Conn.: Praeger, 2001).

85. See Preston, *From Lambs to Lions.*

86. Ibid.

5 The United States and North Korea: Avoiding a Worst-Case Scenario

Patrick James and Özgür Özdamar

Before You Begin

1. Why has North Korea been trying for more than two decades to achieve a nuclear weapons capability? What are the obvious and the more subtle reasons for such a venture?

2. What was the initial reaction of the George H. W. Bush administration to nuclear proliferation by North Korea? If incentive-based diplomacy had been pursued initially, would it have had a chance of resolving the issue before North Korea acquired nuclear weapons? If the United States had taken a harder line in the early 1990s, would North Korea have progressed further in producing nuclear weapons?

3. Was the "carrots" policy that President Bill Clinton pursued effective? What did former president Jimmy Carter contribute to U.S.–North Korean negotiations? Could the Clinton administration have achieved the same results without Carter's diplomatic efforts?

4. Is the Agreed Framework a good arrangement? What gains and losses did the United States experience as a result of the Agreed Framework? Did the benefits of the agreement exceed its costs?

5. Was the Agreed Framework sufficient to control North Korean nuclear proliferation? Could the United States have negotiated a better agreement? If so, how would it be different from the one reached?

6. What were congressional Republicans' criticisms of the Agreed Framework? Is the agreement an example of appeasement or of diplomatic and peaceful management of an international problem? With the framework, is the United States indirectly supporting an unfriendly regime or preventing a worst-case scenario? How different is the Agreed Framework from the February 2007 agreement at the six-party talks? If you think they are similar, what was the purpose behind the confrontation policy of the Bush administration, and what benefit did it achieve?

7. How did President George W. Bush's labeling North Korea a member of the "axis of evil" change U.S.–North Korean relations? How did five years of confrontation policy by the Bush administration contribute to security in East Asia and the

world? Who benefited most from the suspension of implemention of the Agreed Framework?

8. What is your opinion of the George W. Bush administration's approving the deal reached in February 2007? Is it another form of "appeasement" or a new hope for resolution of the issue? Does this deal send the wrong message to other states hoping to produce nuclear weapons?

9. Which of the foreign policy options available to present and future U.S. administrations would work best in dealing with North Korea? Would providing greater incentives to, and demanding more from, North Korea work more effectively than a hard-line approach? Is force the only viable option remaining?

Introduction: Surprising Intelligence

In March 1984 satellite images of North Korea revealed a nuclear reactor under construction at Yongbyon, 100 kilometers north of the capital, Pyongyang. The photographs shocked the Reagan administration, as this small but militarily powerful communist country in East Asia might be preparing to produce some of the world's deadliest weapons. The images also showed a reactor-type chimney rising from the site. In June 1984, additional intelligence identified a cooling tower, limited power lines, and electrical grid connections for the local transfer of energy. Analysts suggested that the reactor probably used uranium and graphite, both of which were available locally. This evidence, however, could not establish conclusively that North Korea had the capacity to produce nuclear weapons. Further intelligence in 1986, however, showed the construction of buildings similar to reprocessing plants used for separating plutonium, a step needed to produce atomic weapons. That same year, new photographs revealed circular craters of darkened ground, assumed to be the residue of high-explosive tests. The pattern suggested a technique used to detonate a nuclear device. A check of earlier photographs revealed the aftereffects of similar tests since 1983.[1]

When intelligence sources discovered construction in 1988 of a fifty-megawatt-capacity reactor—one much larger than the reactor photographed in 1984—the United States became even more alarmed. Estimates held that the older, smaller reactor could produce enough plutonium for up to six weapons a year, whereas the larger plant would make enough for up to fifteen weapons. Finally confident of the existence of a nuclear program, the administration of George H. W. Bush approached Soviet and Chinese officials in February 1989 and Japanese and South Korean authorities in May 1989 about putting pressure on North Korea to meet its obligations as a member of the International Atomic Energy Agency

U.S.–North Korean Relations

1977 The Soviet Union supplies North Korea with a small, experimental nuclear reactor.

March 1984 Satellite images of North Korea reveal a nuclear reactor under construction at Yongbyon, 100 kilometers north of the capital, Pyongyang.

1985 North Korea accedes to the Nuclear Non-Proliferation Treaty (NPT).

1988 U.S. intelligence identifies the construction of a large-capacity reactor in North Korea.

1989 The United States leads in calling on North Korea to meet its obligation to sign a safeguards agreement with the International Atomic Energy Agency (IAEA).

September 1991 The United States announces its withdrawal of tactical nuclear arms from the Korean Peninsula.

December 1991 North Korea and South Korea sign the Basic Agreement, concerning the end of hostilities between them, and the Joint Declaration on the Denuclearization of the Korean Peninsula, agreeing to forgo nuclear weapons–related activities.

January 1992 North Korea concludes a safeguards agreement with the IAEA.

1993 The crisis over North Korea's nuclear program escalates.

March 1993 Political and military issues erode North Korea's relations with South Korea and the United States. As a result, North Korea declares its intent to withdraw from the NPT in ninety days.

June 1993 The United States eases tensions with North Korea by offering to hold high-level talks on nuclear issues. The North suspends its withdrawal from the NPT.

January 1994 The CIA asserts that North Korea may have built one or two nuclear weapons.

June 13, 1994 North Korea announces its withdrawal from the IAEA.

June 15, 1994 Former president Jimmy Carter negotiates a deal in which Pyongyang confirms its willingness to freeze its nuclear program and resume high-level talks with the United States.

continued on the next page

continued from the previous page

June 20, 1994 The Clinton administration sends a letter to the North Korean government stating its willingness to resume high-level talks if the North Koreans proceed in freezing their nuclear program.

July 8, 1994 North Korean leader Kim Il Sung dies. He is succeeded by his son Kim Jong Il.

October 21, 1994 The United States and North Korea sign the Agreed Framework in Geneva. The agreement involves dismantling Pyongyang's nuclear program in return for heavy oil supplies and light water reactors.

March 1995 Japan, South Korea, and the United States form the Korean Peninsula Energy Development Organization (KEDO) as part of the Agreed Framework.

1996–2000 North Korea and the United States hold several rounds of talks concerning the North's missile program. Washington suggests that Pyongyang adhere to the Missile Technology Control Regime (MTCR). The talks prove unproductive.

August 1998 North Korea generates unfavorable international attention by testing the Taepo Dong I rocket, which flies over Japan. The missile has a range of 1,500 to 2,000 kilometers.

June 15, 2000 At a historic summit, North Korea and South Korea agree to resolve the issue of reunification for the Korean Peninsula.

June 19, 2000 Encouraged by the Korean summit, the United States eases sanctions on North Korea.

January 29, 2002 President George W. Bush labels North Korea a member of a so-called axis of evil. The North Korean government reacts negatively.

October 3–5, 2002 James Kelly, assistant secretary of state for East Asian and Pacific affairs, visits North Korea and informs officials that the United States is aware of its clandestine nuclear program.

October 16, 2002 North Korea admits to having had a clandestine program to enrich uranium (and plutonium) for nuclear weapons development.

November 2002 KEDO stops shipping oil to North Korea. The IAEA asks North Korea for clarification on its nuclear program.

December 2002 North Korea responds to KEDO's oil stoppage by restarting its frozen nuclear reactor and orders IAEA inspectors out of the country.

January 10, 2003 North Korea withdraws from the NPT.

April 2003 At a meeting held in Beijing with China, South Korea, and the United States, North Korea announces that it has nuclear weapons.

2003–2004 Negotiations involving China, Japan, North Korea, Russia, South Korea, and the United States fail to produce any effective results.

July 4–5, 2006 North Korea conducts seven missile tests, including a long-range Taepodong II.

July 15, 2006 The UN Security Council unanimously votes to impose sanctions that ban selling missile-related material to North Korea by all member states.

October 3, 2006 North Korea conducts its first nuclear detonation tests ever. The world condemns this provocative act.

October 14, 2006 The UN Security Council unanimously votes to impose both military and economic sanctions on North Korea to protest the nuclear tests.

January 2007 The United States bans export of iPods and cognac to North Korea as a part of the sanctions initiated by the UN.

February 13, 2007 Announcement from the six-party talks, continuing in Beijing, that North Korea has agreed to freeze its nuclear reactor in Yongbyon in return for economic and diplomatic concessions from the other parties.

(IAEA). The administration specifically wanted North Korea to sign a safeguards agreement allowing inspections of its nuclear facilities.[2] Thus began more than fifteen years of roller-coaster U.S.–North Korean relations concerning nuclear nonproliferation.

Background: North Korea's Nuclear Quest

The Korean Peninsula was ruled as a single entity from the time the Shilla Kingdom unified it in the seventh century until the end of World War II.[3] Japan colonized Korea in 1910, but when Japan surrendered in 1945, the Soviet Union and United States temporarily divided Korea at the 38th parallel. Thus a communist system evolved in the north, and a capitalist system in the south. Soon thereafter, the peninsula experienced the Korean War, one of the earliest and most intense confrontations of the cold war. Fought between communist North

Korea (Democratic People's Republic of North Korea, DPRK) and anticommunist South Korea (Republic of Korea, ROK) for domination of the peninsula, the war lasted from June 1950 to July 1953 and stands out as a major proxy war between the United States and Soviet Union.[4] The principal combatants included on one side Australia, Canada, South Korea, Turkey, the United Kingdom, the United States, and other allies under a UN mandate and on the other side North Korea and the People's Republic of China. The Soviet Union sided with North Korea, but it did not provide direct military support in the form of troops.[5] After some three years of fighting, a cease-fire established a demilitarized zone (DMZ) at the 38th parallel, a demarcation still defended by substantial North Korean forces on one side and South Korean and U.S. forces on the other. More than fifty years after the fighting, the adversaries have yet to sign a peace treaty.

North Korea is ruled by one of the last remaining communist regimes and has had only two leaders in more than a half-century: Kim Il Sung, from 1948 till his death in 1994, and his son Kim Jong Il, who succeeded him. The Korean Worker's Party of North Korea is the last example of a classic Stalinist, communist party. The regime in North Korea is extremely autocratic, and the country has perhaps the most closed political system in the world.[6] After decades of mismanagement, the North relies heavily on international food aid to feed its population and avert mass starvation.[7] It is estimated that nearly two million people may have died of famine from 1995 to 1998.[8]

Despite severe economic crises over the last two decades and widespread famine, North Korea continues to feed one of the largest armies, with more than a million personnel.[9] In addition to supporting such a vast military, the North is pursuing a nuclear program that appears to have started in the 1970s. North Korea's interest in nuclear power apparently began in the 1960s, when Kim Il Sung asked China to transfer nuclear technology to North Korea after China's first nuclear tests. Chinese leader Mao Zedong rejected such requests in 1964 and in 1974. The Soviet Union also refused to transfer nuclear technology to North Korea, but in 1977 the Soviets gave it a small, experimental reactor and insisted that it be placed under IAEA safeguards.[10] In all likelihood the North persisted in efforts to go nuclear for two primary reasons: the Korean War experience and South Korean efforts to obtain nuclear weapons. During the war, North Korea experienced the threat of U.S. nuclear power, a menace that remained in Pyongyang's consciousness after the war concluded. According to one observer, "No country has been the target of more American nuclear threats than North Korea—at least seven since 1945."[11] South Korea had attempted to gain nuclear weapons in the 1970s, but the United States prevented it from doing so. That venture by the South strongly influenced North Korean policymakers' security perceptions and pushed them toward seeking the nuclear option. In 1995 Walter Slocombe, U.S. under secretary of defense for policy in the Clinton administration, itemized the threats that North Korea's going nuclear poses, saying that it

- could be coupled with the oversized conventional force to extort or blackmail South Korea and greatly increase the costs of a war on the Korean Peninsula,
- could ignite a nuclear arms race in Asia,
- could undermine the Nuclear Non-Proliferation Treaty (NPT) and the IAEA safeguards system of inspections,
- could lead to the export of nuclear technologies and components to pariah states and terrorists worldwide, and
- could project the nuclear threat across most of Northeast Asia if the government was successful in upgrading missile delivery systems.[12]

For these reasons, nuclear proliferation by North Korea became one of the foremost foreign policy challenges for the United States in the late twentieth century, and it continues to be in the current century.

The Policy of George H. W. Bush

In the 1980s and early 1990s most senior officials in the first Bush administration—including National Security Advisor Brent Scowcroft, his deputy and later CIA Director Robert Gates, Secretary of State James Baker, Secretary of Defense Dick Cheney, and Under Secretary of Defense Paul Wolfowitz—believed that diplomatic means would not work with North Korea. Domestic political reasons, such as pressure to focus on the economy, along with Congress's and the foreign policy establishment's obvious distaste for dealing with North Korea, reinforced their reluctance to employ cooperative measures. Because Washington did not want to engage in diplomatic give-and-take, it adopted a crime-and-punishment approach that arguably led to crisis and subsequent deadlock.[13] In other words, from 1989 through 1992 the United States primarily, though not exclusively, used the stick rather than the carrot to deal with North Korea.

The Bush administration relied on the IAEA to monitor North Korea's nuclear program and the UN Security Council to enforce compliance with the

NPT, to which North Korea had acceded in 1985 on the advice of the Soviet Union.[14] Although Pyongyang was supposed to sign the IAEA safeguards treaty within eighteen months of signing the NPT, it delayed for six years and signed the agreement only in January 1992. In other words, through various actions (or inaction) the North Korean government gave the impression that it had an ongoing interest in producing nuclear weapons.

Efforts by the Bush administration significantly influenced North Korea's ultimate signing of the IAEA safeguards agreement. By 1990 South Korea and the United States both worried that North Korea might already have developed one or two nuclear weapons. Unknown to U.S. officials, Soviet intelligence also had been receiving signals about the North Korean project. A KGB document from February 1990 (revealed in 1992) suggested that the North actually had completed a bomb:

> Scientific and experimental design work to create a nuclear weapon is continuing in the DPRK. . . . According to information received, development of the first atomic explosive device has been completed at the DPRK Center for Nuclear Research, located in the city of Yongbyon in Pyongan-pukto Province. At present there are no plans to test it, in the interests of concealing from world opinion and from the controlling international organizations the actual fact of the production of nuclear weapons in the DPRK. The KGB is taking additional measures to verify the above report.[15]

Beginning in 1991, South Korea and the United States implemented different elements of an integrated political, economic, and military campaign designed to persuade North Korea to allow inspections of its nuclear facilities. U.S. actions appear, however, to have been somewhat ad hoc, developing according to circumstances,[16] most notably in reaction to getting nowhere by using the stick alone.

During 1991 U.S. strategy concerning North Korean nuclearization consisted of four primary elements. The first was an unequivocal statement of a reduced U.S. military position on the Korean Peninsula.[17] In 1990 the United States had initiated limited troop withdrawals from South Korea as part of its East Asian Strategic Initiative (and had taken steps to ease the trade embargo on the North). Then, in part because the cold war was coming to an end, the United States announced in September 1991 the withdrawal of nuclear warheads, shells, and bombs from South Korea.[18] Second, Washington reaffirmed its security relationship with South Korea, to convince the North Koreans that delaying inspections would gain them nothing; this was conceived as an assertive element to balance the more pacific announcement about its forces and nuclear arsenal. Third, the annual U.S.–South Korean Team Spirit Military Exercise, which had been condemned by North Korea as provocative, was suspended for a year. Fourth, U.S. officials agreed to begin direct talks with North Korea, albeit only for a single session, with more to follow if North Korea cooperated and allowed nuclear inspections.[19]

This diplomatic approach produced some relatively positive consequences. In December 1991 North Korea and South Korea began talks at the level of prime minister that resulted in two agreements, which were welcomed by the United States. The Basic Agreement, signed on December 10, appeared to provide a strong basis for ending hostility between the two Koreas. Its main terms are as follows:

- Mutual recognition of each other's systems and an end to mutual interference, vilification, and subversion
- Mutual efforts "to transform the present state of armistice into a solid peace," with continued observance of the armistice until this is accomplished
- A mutual commitment not to use force against each other and the implementation of confidence-building measures and large-scale arms reductions
- Economic, cultural, and scientific exchanges, free correspondence between divided families, and the reopening of roads and railroads severed at the border[20]

After signing the Basic Agreement, the North and South reached a nuclear accord in only six days. The Joint Declaration on the Denuclearization of the Korean Peninsula states that both countries agree not to "test, manufacture, produce, receive, process, store, deploy or use nuclear weapons" or "process nuclear reprocessing and enrichment facilities."[21]

In January 1992 North Korea concluded a safeguards agreement for inspection of its nuclear facilities by the IAEA, another result of diplomatic initiative. At the end of April, almost everything stood ready for inspections to begin at Yongbyon.

Some observers argue that the fundamental lesson from the negotiations was that diplomacy works when dealing with North Korea about its nuclear program, so such an approach should continue to be pursued. According to this line of argument, the gradual, nuanced strategy of pressure and incentives had persuaded the North to allow inspections.[22] Other observers argue, however, that the Bush administration had not provided any substantial incentive to the North to truly convince policymakers there to comply fully with the agreement. In fact, they say that the administration's handling of North Korea caused the deadlock that led to the more serious upheavals years later.[23] This line of argument also suggests that North Korea actually wanted to open direct talks with the United States, to obtain assistance to ameliorate its economic problems and to build light water reactors to solve its energy problem.[24] Quite possibly because of a reluctance to show the carrot, the Bush administration preferred to ignore North Korea's true goals.

Analysis of the situation in greater depth suggests that it is very likely that North Korea attempted to use its nuclear program as a bargaining chip to lure the United States into direct talks and into supplying it with light water reactors. The United States and South Korea, however, perceived the nuclear threat to be real. The differences between Washington's and Pyongyang's perceptions of the North's nuclear program stood during this phase as the main obstacles to a genuine resolution of North Korean nuclearization. Administration hawks—among them the national security advisor, Brent Scowcroft, and Under Secretary of State for Political Affairs Arnold Kanter—lobbied hard for military action against North Korea. In a more general sense, the administration had assembled a foreign policy team whose members believed that diplomacy would be wasted on North Korea because its leadership understood only the use of force. This view may have been indicative of a Munich syndrome, a disposition against appeasement of presumably dangerous states. Approaching elections also encouraged the Bush administration to play hardball with North Korea.

From Bush to Clinton

The agreements reached between the two Koreas, along with the North's announcement that it would allow IAEA inspections, represented two quite positive developments in terms of nonproliferation and peace on the Korean Peninsula. As early as February 1992, however, CIA Director Gates alleged—and, it turned out, with good reason—that the North had not been honest about its nuclear program. After Pyongyang accepted inspections, the head of the IAEA, Hans Blix, traveled to North Korea in May 1992 for a guided tour of its nuclear facilities in advance of the formal IAEA inspection teams. Although North Korea aimed to show Blix the most nonthreatening aspects of its program, large buildings suspected of being used for processing plutonium turned out to be exactly that. Blix's visit served to confirm suspicions that the North's nuclear weapons program might still be active. Later in 1992 the IAEA revealed that North Korea had not been truthful about its activities. Pyongyang had declared that it had processed ninety grams of plutonium for research purposes only. Analysis by the IAEA, however, revealed that it had processed plutonium at least three times—in 1989, 1990, and 1991. A sample of nuclear waste, supposedly from the separation process, did not match any of the separated plutonium, which led the IAEA to believe that more plutonium than was revealed had to have been produced. Neither the IAEA nor the CIA, however, could determine how much plutonium the North possessed at the time.[25]

In 1993 the dialogue between North Korea and the actors trying to denuclearize it began gradually to collapse. In January the IAEA began informing the international community that it might ask to inspect two other suspected North Korean sites, an unusual measure for the organization. The CIA provided the IAEA with photographs of certain sites that had not been inspected and that it thought might contain the hidden plutonium. North Korea, as anticipated, rejected further inspections on the grounds that the suspected structures were only conventional military buildings and that permitting further IAEA inspections would be a breach of sovereignty and a threat to North Korean security. The IAEA's desire for additional investigations isolated North Korea and set back the newly developing relations between Pyongyang and the world.

Despite the cooperation agreements between the North and South, by February 1993 growing evidence of the North's undocumented nuclear activities, combined with other events, reduced hopes for an amicable solution to the problem of North Korean nuclearization. In fall 1992 South Korea had revealed evidence of a North Korean spy ring in the ROK. The South Korean Agency for National Security Planning (ANSP) asserted that a conspiracy against the South—involving labor organizations and even lawmakers in the National Assembly—intended to disrupt its politics to facilitate unification with the North in 1995, an action that was viewed unfavorably in the South. The ANSP alleged that more than four hundred people were involved in the spy operation. North Korea, of course, rejected the allegations.

Although South Korea had a legitimate right to investigate espionage against it, the timing of the announcement could not have been worse in the context of long-term relations with the North. Bilateral talks and cooperation were canceled and their future prospects significantly damaged. As might have been expected, the suspended Team Spirit military exercises resumed. In spite of the spy ring incident, it is difficult to understand why South Korea and the United States would renew the military exercise. North Korea had long protested Team Spirit and had even used it as an excuse for delaying imminent IAEA inspections. Put simply, the gains hard won by diplomacy were lost as a result of the

Team Spirit exercises. In fact, just a day before the exercises began, the "Dear Leader," Kim Jong Il, heightened tensions all around when he ordered that "the whole country, all the people and the entire army shall, on March 9, 1993, switch to a state of readiness for war."[26]

Thus the diplomatic "spring" of 1992 gradually eroded in 1993. After six months of IAEA inspections, the North had obtained no tangible benefits from the process: no economic aid, no direct talks with the United States, no broader dialogue with the South, and no ability to verify that U.S. nuclear weapons had in fact been withdrawn from the South. The increasing demands from the IAEA and South Korea to allow short-notice inspections of virtually any military site in North Korea, combined with the spy ring incident and Team Spirit, led some observers to speculate that the South's moves were designed to force the North to back away from negotiations.[27] Despite all of these developments, it is not possible to place full blame for the disintegration of relations in 1993 with South Korea or the United States. The North had apparently violated international agreements and did not want to make additional concessions on denuclearization. The absence of any sign by the United States that it might be interested in rapprochement might also have contributed to the shift toward disintegrating relations. North Korea's actions ultimately influenced U.S. and South Korean policymakers to revert to a hard-line approach.

Withdrawal from the NPT and Reactor Refueling

The Clinton administration inherited a developing crisis in its first days in office. By January 1993, North Korea already had begun maneuvering around IAEA inspections. The administration did not, however, make any significant policy shifts, choosing instead to retain Bush administration policies, which stressed adherence to the NPT. This legalistic approach merely held that North Korea had certain obligations under the NPT and must therefore fulfill them. Direct talks with the North or benefits related to nonproliferation might come if the North complied with inspection requirements.

Secretary of Defense Les Aspin and officials from his office suggested initiating direct contact with Pyongyang in the form of a high-level delegation in early 1993 and offering the North Koreans concrete benefits as incentives to cooperate. They argued that if North Korea still refused to cooperate after getting the carrot, then the United States would use the stick of sanctions and possibly even military action. For the Clinton administration, this represented not appeasement but a rather balanced approach. One U.S. official described the policy as a "sugar-coated ultimatum."[28] President Bill Clinton did not pursue this option at first, however, because it seemed like rewarding the North for not doing something it should have already done. The conservative media and some members of Congress had been attacking the administration for its seemingly left-of-center disposition toward gays in the military, and conservatives argued that perceived weakness in dealing with North Korea was unacceptable among much of the public.

The first crisis for the Clinton administration was the one that began in March 1993 when, during the Team Spirit exercises, Pyongyang asserted that such operations endangered nonproliferation efforts and threatened its security and announced its opposition to additional nuclear inspections on its territory, claiming that the IAEA worked for U.S. interests. On those bases, in the same month, North Korea stated its intention to withdraw from the Nuclear Non-Proliferation Treaty in ninety days. Both the Clinton administration and the South Korean government of Kim Yong Sam were relatively new in March 1993 and not well prepared for such a development, but with the support of South Korea, the United States eased tensions by offering to hold talks with Pyongyang on nuclear issues. In return, North Korea suspended its withdrawal from the NPT in June. Thus the Clinton administration effectively adopted the Defense Department's previously articulated approach of direct, high-level talks, and North Korea attained one of its goals: to sit at the negotiating table with the United States. With this success, the North proposed to relinquish its entire nuclear program in return for light water reactors. The United States acknowledged the North's interest but then stated that it should first comply with IAEA inspections and renew its dialogue with South Korea. The dialogue with the United States continued in 1993 but did not resolve any existing problems. The IAEA continued to have difficulties with North Korea. The Board of Governors of the IAEA referred the issue to the UN Security Council and even claimed that it would be better for North Korea to be excluded from the NPT than to compromise the treaty's integrity.[29]

The North ignited another crisis as the international community discussed what to do about matters already under review: While ideas about how to punish North Korea for its nuclear program preoccupied leading members of the world community, Pyongyang declared in May 1994 that the reactor would be refueled. This meant removing the existing rods, from which weapons-grade plutonium could then be produced.[30]

The Carrot

In response to North Korea's decision to refuel, in early summer 1994 President Clinton threatened to halt the U.S. dialogue and impose economic sanctions, which would significantly damage the North's already terrible economy.

He also considered air strikes. The North announced that sanctions would mean war.[31] Before implementing punitive action, the administration decided to take a diplomatic tack. Former president Jimmy Carter had previously communicated to the White House his interest in visiting North Korea to seek a peaceful solution to the looming nuclear crisis. The Reagan and Bush administrations had earlier rejected his requests to travel to North Korea.[32] This time, however, Carter found support in the Oval Office. A White House official referred to Carter's visit as an opportunity for "a face-saving resolution" to the tensions.[33] Clinton did not designate Carter as an official U.S. representative, so he would travel to North Korea with the status of a private citizen. The State Department, however, briefed him and dispatched a career Foreign Service officer to accompany him. State Department spokesperson Michael McCurry pointed out that Carter would not be "carrying any formal message from the United States."[34]

The Carter mission had two primary goals: to defuse the immediate tensions related to the North Korean nuclear program and to jump-start the talks between the United States and North Korea. Carter left for Pyongyang on June 12, North Korea announced its withdrawal from the IAEA on June 13, and on June 16 the Clinton administration laid out its vision of economic sanctions. Madeleine Albright, the U.S. ambassador to the United Nations, called for restricting arms exports from North Korea, cutting UN assistance, and encouraging further diplomatic isolation. These measures would be followed by economic sanctions if the North did not comply with the IAEA inspection regime. Carter's diplomatic efforts, however, yielded positive results, with North Korea expressing a willingness to freeze its nuclear program and resume high-level talks with the United States. On June 20 the United States sent a letter to Pyongyang officially proposing such talks.[35]

The Carter visit elicited both praise and criticism. Conservatives perceived it as appeasement, and even some Democrats in the administration became outraged when Carter renounced the possible use of sanctions. One point cannot, however, be ignored: Carter's visit prevented the use of force and perhaps a war with enormous costs. According to one State Department official, "If Jimmy Carter had not gone to Korea, we would have been damned close to war."[36] If the prevention of war is the criterion of success, then at least for the short term Carter's mission must be regarded as a success indeed. Carter's efforts led both sides to conclude that negotiations constituted the best option available to them, but Kim Il Sung's death on July 8 delayed the start of talks that month. They instead began on August 5.

The Agreed Framework and KEDO

On October 21, 1994, the United States and North Korea signed the Agreed Framework to resolve the issues surrounding Pyongyang's nuclear program. The agreement included a bilateral structure for negotiations—which represented a major change in the nature of U.S.–North Korean relations—and was to be implemented in phases, allowing the two sides to assess each other's compliance at each step before moving on to the next. The Agreed Framework required North Korea to undertake the following:

- Eliminate its existing capability to produce weapons-grade plutonium
- Resume full membership in the NPT, including complying completely with its safeguards agreement with the IAEA, which mandates the inspectors to investigate suspected nuclear waste sites and to place any nuclear material not previously identified under IAEA safeguards
- Take steps to consistently execute the Joint Declaration on the Denuclearization of the Korean Peninsula
- Engage in a dialogue with the South

The Korean Peninsula Energy Development Organization (KEDO)—a consortium of Japan, South Korea, and the United States officially established in March 1995 to coordinate the agreement—was by 2003 to provide two 1,000 megawatt, light water reactor power plants (priced around $4 billion) and supply North Korea with 500,000 tons of heavy oil annually to compensate for the capacity forfeited by freezing its graphite-modulated reactors. The United States and North Korea agreed to open liaison offices in each other's capitals and reduce barriers to trade and investment. The United States also agreed to provide formal assurances that it would not threaten North Korea with nuclear weapons.[37] North Korean negotiator Kang Sok Ju remarked to his American counterpart, Robert Gallucci, that the North's bargaining chip was continuing production of plutonium and preventing IAEA inspections if the United States did not comply with the agreement. In turn, U.S. leverage rested on the prospect of establishing political and economic ties valuable to North Korea.[38]

The Agreed Framework was a loose agreement in the sense that its implementation was left to the states' own volition. Implementation initially ran rather smoothly. In August 1998, however, North Korea launched over Japan a Taepo Dong 1 rocket with a range of 1,500 to 2,000 kilometers. Pyongyang announced that the rocket had successfully placed a small satellite into orbit, but that claim was contested by the U.S. Space Command. Japan responded to this invasion of its air space by suspending the signing of a cost-sharing agreement for the Agreed Framework's light water reactor project until November 1998. The development came as a shock to the U.S. intelligence community, which admitted being surprised by North Korea's advances in missile-staging technology. On October 1, 1998, U.S.–North Korean missile talks held in New York made little progress. The United States requested that Pyongyang terminate its missile programs in exchange for the lifting of some remaining economic sanctions. North Korea rejected the proposal, asserting that the lifting of sanctions was implicit in the Agreed Framework.

On November 12, 1998, President Clinton appointed former secretary of defense William Perry as his policy coordinator on North Korea. A policy review that Perry undertook noted that the situation in East Asia was not the same as it had been in 1994, when the Agreed Framework was signed. He observed that the North's missile tests had substantially increased Japanese security concerns and that the passing of North Korea's leadership to Kim Jong Il had created further uncertainty. On a more positive note, the new South Korean president, Kim Dae Jung, had embarked on a policy of engagement with North Korea. Based on his policy review, Perry ultimately devised a two-path strategy. The first path involved a new, comprehensive and integrated approach to negotiations. In return for the North's full compliance with the NPT, Missile Technology Control Regime, and export of nuclear and missile technologies, Japan, South Korea, and the United States would reduce pressures that the North perceived as threatening. Perry argued that reduction of those threats would give the regime confidence about coexisting with other states in the region. If the North did as it should, according to Perry, the United States should normalize relations and relax sanctions.

Perry's second path focused on what to do if North Korea did not want to cooperate. If there was no chance of continuing relations with the North, the United States would sever relations, contain the threat, and enforce the provisions outlined in the first path.[39] Perry's report also observed that the North had complied with the NPT and had not produced plutonium in the preceding five years, which provided grounds for encouragement about the feasibility of the first path.

Overall, the first five years of the Agreed Framework reveal a mixed record. The North did not advance in producing nuclear weapons, but it did significantly improve its missile technology. The United States supplied crude oil as agreed, but the light water reactors remained far from being finished as scheduled. Maintaining the Agreed Framework was not to be an easy job.

The Critics

Clinton's policy of "engagement," in 1994 and later in his administration, met severe criticism in Congress and from conservative columnists. Critics argued that it was unacceptable to compromise with a so-called rogue state that threatened U.S. allies. From that point of view, unless the North capitulated, coercion in general, sanctions in particular, and even military action would be preferred to negotiation. Moreover, considering North Korea's economic problems, any deal effectively supported an already sinking regime. Putting together a deal such as the Agreed Framework, according to critics, was immoral and set a terrible precedent for other rogue states.[40] In an October 1994 letter to Clinton, four Republicans on the Senate Committee on Foreign Relations summed up the more critical view of policy at the time: "We are left wondering how to distinguish such a deal from U.S. submission to North Korean nuclear blackmail."[41] Other concerns focused on the timing of reciprocal concessions and actions under the framework.

Clinton administration officials and supporters of the Agreed Framework responded that although the United States made some concessions, the outcome, if successful, would meet U.S. strategic objectives. Key achievements for the United States as a result of the agreement were enumerated as follows: (a) being able to estimate the amount of plutonium produced by the North in the past and dismantling any nuclear weapons already produced; (b) convincing North Korea to halt its nuclear program; (c) keeping North Korea within the NPT and its safeguards agreement; (d) enticing the North out of international isolation; and (e) supporting stability and security in the region.[42]

Largely through Ambassador Galluci, the administration also countered the critics with six arguments. First, the framework did not amount to appeasement or, even worse, submission to blackmail because North Korea had made even more concessions than the United States. Second, the conditions the North agreed to fulfill met U.S. objectives, such as its remaining within the NPT and respecting obligations under the safeguards agreement. Third, the agreement pertained to the North's past nuclear program and aimed to find plutonium already produced. Fourth, whether Pyongyang met the requirements of the safeguards agreement could be verified by IAEA and U.S. assets, and no benefits would be provided before proof of full compliance. Fifth, the agreement needed to be viewed as a compromise, meaning that significant but not unreasonable costs were entailed to obtain such benefits as reduction of the threat of nuclear proliferation and instability in Northeast Asia. Sixth, the agreement set a precedent only to the degree that other situations involve similar elements, an unlikely event.[43]

The United States, like other great powers before it, has tended toward a basic action-reaction pattern: "Our first reaction to somebody's doing something we don't like is to think of doing something unpleasant to them."[44] In partial contrast to that generalization, the Clinton administration's Agreed Framework with North Korea on nuclear proliferation serves as an example of incentive-based diplomacy. Despite some legitimate criticisms, by signing the framework the United States accomplished its immediate goals at a bearable cost. The agreement, despite the political and financial problems of domestic criticism and the cost of supplying crude oil to North Korea, functioned until (for better or worse) President George W. Bush designated North Korea, Iraq, and Iran an "axis of evil" in 2002.

The Policy of George W. Bush

North Korea and the nuclear issue did not approach the top of the agenda for the first year of the administration of George W. Bush. Dialogue with the North slowed as the new administration took some time to review policy toward it in early 2001. Although Republicans, including some Bush aides, engaged in harsh rhetoric about the North, after three months of review, the president announced in June 2001 that his administration would stick with the basic outlines of the existing policy in the form of the Agreed Framework. Lobbying by Japan and South Korea, combined with Secretary of State Colin Powell's successful fending off of the more conservative Bush advisers, were influential in bringing about this decision.[45]

Although the administration reaffirmed its intent to supply the two light water reactors that the framework specified in return for North Korea's restraint of its nuclear development, it found domestic opposition to fulfilling that requirement difficult to bear. From the beginning of the administration, some members of Congress and commentators in academia and the media argued repeatedly that one of the two reactors should be replaced with a thermal power station. The reasoning was that nuclear weapons–grade plutonium could be extracted from them. Another, hidden reason might have been the increasing cost of the heavy oil the United States had provided to North Korea since 1995, and which it was slated to continue to provide until the new reactors were completed. Because of the financial and organizational problems related to KEDO, analysts expected the reactors to be finished around 2010.

Republican partisans, of course, did not want to fund a regime that they believed was hostile to the United States. The South Korean government, which bore 70 percent of the construction costs for the two reactors, maintained its opposition to their replacement with thermal power stations because (a) that would violate the most critical agreement between the United States and the North; (b) it would further delay the project and result in additional costs; and (c) it would be impossible for North Korea to extract plutonium of nuclear weapons grade from the light water reactors because, although extraction remains theoretically possible, it would not be able to obtain the extremely sophisticated reprocessing technology needed. North Korea also opposed such a change in the Agreed Framework. Although the Bush administration initially gave no indication of a significant change in U.S. policy, the simple act of reviewing the agreement was enough to upset the North. On March 17, 2001, the North Korean Central Broadcasting Station issued the following warning: "If the Bush administration feels it burdensome and troublesome to perform the Geneva Agreed Framework, we don't need to be indefinitely bound by an agreement that is not honored. We will go on our way in case the agreement is not honored."[46] *Rodong Sinmun,* the state-controlled newspaper, observed, "North Korea would take 'countermeasures' if the United States does not perform its obligations under the agreement. We will also demand compensation for the delay in construction of the LWRs."[47] At the end of 2001, there appeared to be reason to believe that bilateral talks would continue, although the North was suspicious of a renewed dialogue.

Another year of tense relations between the United States and North Korea unfolded in 2002. The attacks of September 11, 2001, on the United States transformed the Bush administration's foreign policy into one that would deal with unfriendly regimes more decisively, and if necessary, unilaterally and forcefully. The watershed event of 2002 for U.S.–North Korean relations occurred on January 29, when President Bush, in his State of the Union address, accused North Korea of being one of three members of a so-called axis of evil that threatened U.S. and even world security. In this highly controversial speech, Bush described North Korea as "a regime arming with missiles and weapons of mass destruction, while starving its citizens. . . . The United States of America will not permit the world's most dangerous regimes to threaten us with the world's most dangerous weapons."[48] Bush's speech sent shock waves around the world, as leaders waited to see what it might mean in practice.

Shortly after the speech, the State Department and the U.S. ambassador to South Korea, Thomas C. Hubbard, insisted that the president's statement did not represent a policy shift. The United States, according to them, remained fully open to resuming bilateral talks with North Korea without any preconditions.

North Korea, however, responded harshly and directly to the speech with rhetoric aimed to match Bush's:

> Mr. Bush's remarks clearly show what the real aim [*sic*] the U.S. sought when it proposed to resume talks with the DPRK recently. . . . We are sharply watching the United States [*sic*] moves that have pushed the situation to the brink of war after throwing away even the mask of "dialogue" and "negotiation." . . . The option to strike impudently advocated by the United States is not its monopoly.[49]

Thus, with Bush's speech and Pyongyang's reaction to it, what guarded hopes there were for a renewed diplomatic exchange between the United States and North Korea disappeared, at least for the foreseeable future.

In South Korea and Japan, various political groups accused the United States of destroying the North-South dialogue and threatening the peace in East Asia. Although the State Department, and Secretary Powell himself, asserted on several occasions that the United States was ready to resume a dialogue with North Korea at "any time, any place, or anywhere without preconditions," that did not convince the North Koreans.[50] A memorandum from President Bush stated that he would not certify North Korea's compliance with the Agreed Framework; because of national security considerations, however, Bush waived the provision that would have prohibited Washington from funding KEDO.[51] Continuation of that support under such hostile conditions, however, did not bring North Korea back to the negotiation table.

The United States warned North Korea in August 2002 to comply as soon as possible with IAEA safeguard procedures. The North replied that it would not do so for at least three more years. Developments that fall raised the tension between the United States and North Korea and led to the confrontation that continues today. In October, James Kelly, assistant secretary of state for East Asian and Pacific affairs, visited North Korea and presented U.S. concerns about its nuclear program as well as its ballistic missile program (which at the time the North Koreans themselves had delayed), export of missile components, conventional force posture, human rights violations, and overall humanitarian situation. Kelly informed Pyongyang that a comprehensive settlement addressing these issues might be the way to improve bilateral relations. North Korea called this approach "high-handed and arrogant" and maintained its noncooperative stance.[52]

More important, the United States announced on October 16 that North Korea had admitted to the existence of a clandestine program to enrich uranium (in addition to plutonium) for nuclear weapons, after Kelly had informed the North Koreans that the United States had knowledge of it. Such a serious violation of the Agreed Framework raised immediate and intense reactions around the world. In November, KEDO announced the suspension of oil deliveries, and the IAEA asked North Korea for clarification on its nuclear program. North Korea rejected these demands and announced that because of the halt to KEDO's supply of oil, it would reopen the frozen nuclear reactors to produce electricity. In December, North Korea cut all seals on IAEA surveillance equipment on its nuclear facilities and materials and ordered inspectors out of the country.

North Korea continued to abrogate its international agreements with the announcement of its withdrawal from the NPT on January 10, 2003. The following month, the United States confirmed that North Korea had in December restarted a nuclear reactor previously frozen by the Agreed Framework. The North also conducted two missile tests in February and March 2003.[53] Perhaps most ominous was an incident in which North Korea sent a fighter jet into South Korean airspace and shadowed a U.S. reconnaissance plane.[54]

Trilateral talks among China, North Korea, and the United States in April 2003 and six-party talks (with Japan, Russia, and South Korea) in September 2003 and February 2004 did not bring a resolution to the crisis.[55] Little was produced diplomatically in 2004 and 2005. Leaders of two nations occasionally railed against each other, while diplomats achieved next to nothing. In August 2004, in response to President George W. Bush's portraying Kim Jong Il as a "tyrant," North Korea described the president as an "imbecile" and a "tyrant that puts Hitler in a shade." Then on September 28, North Korea announced that it had produced another nuclear weapon from 8,000 spent fuel rods for self-defense against U.S. nuclear threats. On September 13, 2005, six-party talks resumed. On September 19, another "historic" statement was issued that North Korea agreed to give up its nuclear activity and rejoin the NPT. This time, the good atmosphere did not even survive a day: On September 20, North Korea declared it would not give up its nuclear program if light water reactors were not supplied, and that eventually ended the fifth round of six-party talks, without progress, a month later.[56]

The international community experienced a more turbulent year concerning the North Korean nuclear program in 2006. Two major acts by the DPRK shocked observers: On July 4 and 5, the DPRK test-fired seven missiles including a Taepodong-2, whose suspected range covers the western coast of the United States. The UN Security Council responded quickly, on July 15, 2006, with unanimous Resolution 1695, which demanded that North Korea return to the six-party talks without precondition, comply with September 2005 Joint Statement, "in particular to abandon all nuclear weapons and existing nuclear programmes," and return to the NPT and IAEA safeguards soon. In addition, the Security Council required all member states "to exercise vigilance and prevent missile and missile-related items, materials, goods and technology being transferred to DPRK's missile or WMD programmes."[57]

North Korea's response to the sanctions was even more provocative. On October 9, 2006, North Korea conducted its first nuclear weapon test ever. Sending shock waves around the world, the DPRK administration argued that the test was against "U.S. military hostility." The UN Security Council adopted Resolution 1718, condemning the action and demanding similar compromises from the DPRK. The UN also imposed military and economic sanctions.[58]

There were contending commentaries and intelligence about this test. On October 13, U.S. intelligence asserted that the air sample obtained from the test site contained radioactive material; yet the size of the explosion was less than one kiloton, which is quite small compared to nuclear detonations by other states, which usually ranged from ten to sixty kilotons.[59] On the other hand, a recent comment by CIA Director Michael Hayden suggests that the October 2006 test was a failure, and the United States does not recognize North Korea as a nuclear weapon–maintaining state.[60] Obviously, the DPRK conducted some kind of a nuclear detonation, but the success of the test is open to debate.

While the international community was upset by the latest developments in the DPRK's nuclear program and the failure of diplomacy at the six-party talks, the world was stunned, once again, with a new development: On February 13, 2007, "The Third Session of the Fifth Round of the Six-Party Talks" issued a statement that North Korea had agreed to a new arrangement. According to this, "yet another" historic agreement,

1. The DPRK will shut down and seal the Yongbyon nuclear facility in sixty days, including the reprocessing facility, and invite back IAEA personnel for monitoring and verifications.
2. The DPRK will discuss with other parties a list of all its nuclear programs.
3. The DPRK and the United States will start bilateral talks aimed at solving issues between them and advance toward full diplomatic relations. In this context, the United States will begin the process of removing the DPRK from its state-sponsor of terrorism list and terminate its application of the Trading with the Enemy Act to the DPRK.

4. The DPRK and Japan will start bilateral talks aimed at taking steps to normalize their relations.
5. The Parties agreed to send economic, energy and humanitarian assistance to the DPRK. Initially, 50,000 tons of heavy fuel oil will be given to DPRK within the next sixty days.[61]

Only time will show whether this deal will denuclearize the Korean Peninsula or be scrapped like its many predecessors. As of April 2007 there was already a serious disagreement about the DPRK's funds in China frozen by the United States. If the United States does not release the funds of Kim Jong Il's regime (U.S. $25 million), the agreement might go down the drain without being implemented at all. In fact, even if the North Korean funds are released, shutting down the Yongbyon nuclear facility before the deadline seems impossible. Marginal progress in implementing the February 2007 deal casts serious doubt on the future of the agreement.

Critics of George W. Bush's Policies

The international community welcomed the new, 2007 agreement, but it was publicly criticized by U.S. policymakers across the political spectrum. The most frequently expressed objection is that, despite the fact that Republicans have voiced their contempt for the Agreed Framework of 1994 for a decade, the new deal that the Bush administration agreed to looks almost identical to it; that is, North Korea will suspend its nuclear program by in return for economic and diplomatic incentives by the other parties. Perhaps the only difference is that now North Korea seems to have achieved greater nuclear capabilities than before. Therefore many analysts are asking what has been the use of the confrontation policy that the Bush administration has followed in the last five years, which simply gave North Korea additional time to build more weapons. As an example of where the international community is in terms of denuclearizing the peninsula, a South Korean regional expert's comment is informative: "We have lost four or five years and now we have to start again with North Korea—except the situation is worse because they have now tested a nuclear device."[62]

Critics of Bush administration were not the only ones dissatisfied with the agreement. John Bolton, a Republican and former U.S. ambassador to the UN, criticized the deal harshly: "It sends exactly the wrong signal to would-be proliferators around the world: If you hold out long enough and wear down the State Department negotiators, eventually you get rewarded. . . . It makes the [Bush] administration look very weak at a time in Iraq and dealing with Iran it needs to look strong."[63] Many Republicans in Congress also criticized the deal on similar grounds.

The Bush administration rejected the assertion that the agreement was an example of appeasement because it is based only on staggered incentives. That is, if North Korea does not fulfill the requirements, it will not receive any economic or diplomatic concessions. However, one should also remember that the heavily criticized Agreed Framework was based on similar terms. In sum, it could be argued that the confrontation policy of the Bush administration ended up favoring the North Korean regime.

Some analysts, on the other hand, hailed the agreement because it hints at a strategic move: the Bush administration decided to focus on Iran and go soft on North Korea; slowing down the North Korean program, and such a containment policy, may currently be the best option to deal with the DPRK. Of course, only time will tell whether U.S. policymakers are playing such a sophisticated game or simply agreed to those terms because they were alarmed by the nuclear tests of October 2006.

Conclusion: Options

North Korea's nuclear status has been an issue of varying salience in U.S. foreign policy for the last two decades. Presidents have used a range of tactics, from the stick to the carrot and varying combinations thereof, to cope with North Korea's quest for status as a nuclear power. It is not clear that any particular approach can be labeled an unqualified success. However, the dealings of various administrations with North Korea have one characteristic in common: their inclination to repeat same mistakes over and over again: "U.S. administrations have a tendency to start from scratch in their dealings with North Korea—and then relearn, step by step, the tortuous lessons."[64]

The George W. Bush administration significantly changed U.S. policy on North Korean nuclear proliferation, replacing engagement with confrontation, which led to the breakdown of bilateral relations and undermined the gains of the Agreed Framework of 1994. North Korea's uncompromising attitude and provocative behavior did not help the situation. Opponents of the Clinton administration's way of dealing with North Korea raised valid arguments concerning the likelihood that Pyongyang could be trusted to implement the framework and relinquish its quest for nuclear weapons. The Bush administration's undermining of the Agreed Framework without providing a better alternative, however, hurt the United States and its allies. As North Korean Vice Foreign Minister Kim Gye Gwan noted, North Korea can develop a nuclear arsenal without the limitations of any international agreement or monitoring: "As time passes, our nuclear deterrent continues to grow in quality and quantity."[65] Free from the limitations of the Agreed Framework, North Korea may have quadrupled its arsenal of nuclear weapons.[66] Of course the last deal, reached in February 2007, has some chance of success. Based on the record as of early 2007, however, the Bush administration's North Korea policy could not be considered successful.

None of the options for the future is without difficulties. One option is to do nothing: accept the North as a nuclear power (as is done with India, Israel, and Pakistan) and hope not to aggravate the situation. That entails the danger of North Korea's developing long-range missiles that can hit U.S. soil or its selling nuclear material to terrorists. Moreover, allowing the North to have nuclear weapons would set an unacceptable precedent for future cases of nuclear proliferation. Japan and South Korea, for example, might want to produce such weapons in response to the North Korean threat. The presence of multiple nuclear powers in Asia could lead to an enormously costly war in the region and place China in a difficult position in terms of choosing a side.

Second, the North Korean nuclear facilities could be destroyed, if that is still feasible strategically. Such an action might cause collateral damage and radioactive fallout over China, Japan, and South Korea. Third, sanctions and international pressure, led by China, Japan, Russia, and the United States, could eventually pressure North Korea into giving up its nuclear program. The North, however, already is being pressed hard, and escalation of such tactics could lead to another war on the Korean Peninsula.

The fourth option is trying to make the February 2007 deal work in a way that would provide assurances to the North Korean regime about its security and deliver the economic and diplomatic aid that the country desperately needs. This of course resembles Clinton administration policies, but the current situation requires the Bush administration to use more carrots or a bigger stick than before.[67] The conundrum for Bush is that although he has opposed the offering of carrots until 2007, sticks do not seem available for his use without risking a major war. Many policymakers around the world hope that the latest deal with North Korea will work smoothly this time. However, if the past is any guide to future, one should expect severe problems in implementation at each and every step. The likelihood of this deal also being scrapped is unfortunately very high, and making it work will require tremendous effort from the U.S. officials, North Korea's leadership, and the other parties involved.

Key Actors

George H. W. Bush First U.S. president to deal with North Korea as a nuclear problem, employed a confrontation policy and avoided direct talks.

George W. Bush President, publicly referred to the Korean leadership as part of a so-called axis of evil (along with Iran and Iraq), hastening the breakdown of relations and of implementation of the Agreed Framework.

Jimmy Carter President, actions as a self-appointed ambassador to help ease tensions between the United States and North Korea in summer 1994 led to a resumption of talks that produced the Agreed Framework.

Bill Clinton President, advocated engagement and direct negotiation with North Korea.

Robert L. Gallucci Ambassador-at-large and chief U.S. negotiator during the 1994 crisis with North Korea.

International Atomic Energy Agency UN agency that promotes safe, secure, and peaceful nuclear technologies for member states; active in keeping the North Korean nuclear program in check.

Kim Il Sung The "Great Leader" of North Korea from 1948 to 1994, chairman of the Korean Workers' Party, which has ruled the country for more than five decades.

Kim Jong Il The "Dear Leader" of North Korea since 1994, successor of Kim Il Sung, his father, and general secretary of the Korean Workers' Party and chairman of the National Defense Committee.

Korean Peninsula Energy Development Organization Grouping of Japan, South Korea, and the United States, established in 1995 to advance implementation of the Agreed Framework; was to provide North Korea with heavy fuel oil and light water reactors in return for dismantling its nuclear program.

William J. Perry U.S. North Korea policy coordinator and special adviser to President Bill Clinton, reviewed North Korean policy in 1999.

Notes

1. David Reese, *The Prospects for North Korea's Survival,* International Institute for Strategic Studies Adelphi Papers 323 (Oxford: Oxford University Press, 1998).
2. Ibid.

3. AsianInfo.org, "Korea's History/Background," www.asianinfo.org/asianinfo/korea/pro-history.htm.

4. Encyclopedia4u.com, "Korean War," www.encyclopedia4u.com/k/korean-war.html.

5. Wikipedia, "Korean War," http://en.wikipedia.org/wiki/Korean_War.

6. TheFreeDictionary.com, "Korean Communist Party," http://encyclopedia.thefreedictionary.com/Korean%20Communist%20Party.

7. Central Intelligence Agency, "North Korea," *World Factbook,* www.cia.gov/cia/publications/factbook/geos/kn.html.

8. May Lee, Associated Press, "Famine May Have Killed Two Million in North Korea," August 19, 1998, www.cnn.com/WORLD/asiapcf/9808/19/nkorea.famine.

9. Facts on International Relations and Security Trends, http://first.sipri.org/index.php.

10. Reese, *The Prospects for North Korea's Survival,* 42.

11. Leon V. Sigal, *Disarming Strangers: Nuclear Diplomacy with North Korea* (Princeton: Princeton University Press, 1998), 20.

12. Walter B. Slocombe, "The Agreed Framework with the Democratic People's Republic of Korea," *Strategic Forum 23* (Washington, D.C.: National Defense University, Institute for National Strategic Studies, 1995), www.ndu.edu/inss/strforum/SF_23/forum23.html.

13. Sigal, *Disarming Strangers.*

14. Ibid.

15. Michael J. Mazarr, *North Korea and the Bomb: A Case Study in Nonproliferation* (New York: St. Martin's Press, 1995), 56–57.

16. Ibid.

17. Ibid.

18. Curtis H. Martin, "The U.S.–North Korean Agreed Framework: Incentives-Based Diplomacy after the Cold War," in *Sanctions as Economic Statecraft: Theory and Practice,* ed. Steve Chan and A. Cooper Drury (New York: St. Martin's Press, 2000).

19. Mazarr, *North Korea and the Bomb.*

20. Reese, *The Prospects for North Korea's Survival,* 45.

21. Ibid., 46.

22. Mazarr, *North Korea and the Bomb.*

23. Sigal, *Disarming Strangers.*

24. In terms of nonproliferation, light water reactors are preferred to the North Korean graphite-modulated reactors because producing the necessary waste for the development of nuclear weapons is much more difficult.

25. Mazarr, *North Korea and the Bomb.*

26. Ibid., 98.

27. Ibid.

28. Ibid., 102.

29. Reese, *The Prospects for North Korea's Survival.*

30. Ibid.

31. Sigal, *Disarming Strangers.*

32. Rod Troester, *Jimmy Carter as Peacemaker: A Post-Presidential Biography* (Westport, Conn.: Praeger, 1999), 76.

33. D. Jehl, "U.S. Is Pressing Sanctions for North Korea," *New York Times,* June 11, 1994, A7, cited in Troester, *Jimmy Carter,* 76.

34. A. Stone, "Citizen Carter, the Statesman," *USA Today,* June 15, 1994, A4, as cited in Troester, *Jimmy Carter,* 76.

35. Troester, *Jimmy Carter.*

36. Sigal, *Disarming Strangers,* 132.

37. Thomas L. Wilborn, "Strategic Implications of the U.S.–DPRK Framework Agreement," U.S. Army War College, Washington, D.C., April 3, 1995, www.milnet.com/korea/usdprkp1.htm#B22.

38. Reese, *The Prospects for North Korea's Survival.*

39. William J. Perry, "Review of United States Policy toward North Korea: Findings and Recommendations," unclassified report, Washington, D.C., October 12, 1999, http://bcsia.ksg.harvard.edu/publication.cfm?program=CORE&ctype=book&item_ id=6.

40. Wilborn, "Strategic Implications."

41. Alfonse D'Amato, Jesse Helms, Mitch McConnell, and Frank Murkowski, October 19, 1994, in Wilborn, "Strategic Implications," 6.

42. Wilborn, "Strategic Implications."

43. Ibid.

44. R. Fisher, *International Conflict for Beginners* (New York: Harper and Row, 1970), as quoted in Martin, "The U.S.–North Korean Agreed Framework."

45. John Diamond, "On Foreign Policy Bush Moving to Clinton Views," *Chicago Tribune,* June 8, 2001.

46. Yonhap News Agency, *North Korea Handbook* (Armonk, N.Y.: M.E. Sharpe, 2003), 553.

47. Ibid.

48. Donald G. Gross, "Riding the Roller-Coaster," *Comparative Connections: An E-Journal on East Asian Bilateral Relations,* April 2002, www.csis.org/pacfor/cc/0201Qus_skorea.html.

49. Ibid., 1.

50. Arms Control Agency, "Chronology of U.S.–North Korean Nuclear and Missile Diplomacy," fact sheet, June 2003, www.armscontrol.org/factsheets/dprkchron.asp.

51. Ibid.

52. Ibid.

53. Ibid.

54. Donald G. Gross, "Tensions Escalate in Korea as the U.S. Targets Iraq," *Comparative Connections: An E-Journal on East Asian Bilateral Relations,* April 2003, www.csis.org/pacfor/cc/0301Qus_skorea.html.

55. Donald G. Gross, "In the Eye of the Beholder: Impasse or Progress in the Six-Party Talks?" *Comparative Connections: An E-Journal on East Asian Bilateral Relations,* April 2004, www.csis.org/pacfor/cc/0401Qus_skorea.html.

56. BBC News Web site. "Timeline: North Korea Nuclear Stand-Off," http://news.bbc.co.uk/2/hi/asia-pacific/2604437.stm (accessed April 9, 2007).

57. United Nations Web site. "Security Council Condemns Democratic People's Republic of Korea's Missile Launches," July 15, 2006, www.un.org/News/Press/docs/2006/sc8778.doc.htm.

58. "Resolution 1718 (2006)," IAEA News Center, October 14, 2006, www.iaea.org/NewsCenter/Focus/IaeaDprk/unscres_14102006.pdf.

59. Associated Press. "U.S. Confirms North Korea's Nuclear Test," October 16, 2006, www.iht.com/articles/ap/2006/10/16/america/NA_GEN_US_NKorea.php.

60. Lee Jin-woo, "U.S. Judges N. Korean Nuclear Test Failure," *Korea Times,* March 28, 2007, http://times.hankooki.com/lpage/nation/200703/kt2007032821284011990.htm.

61. Ministry of Foreign Affairs of PRC. "Initial Actions for the Implementation of the Joint Statement," February 13, 2007, www.fmprc.gov.cn/eng/zxxx/t297463.htm.

62. Jun Bong-geun, of the Institute of Foreign Affairs and National Security in Seoul, as quoted in "The End of a Long Confrontation?" by Charles Scanlon, BBC News, February 13, 2007, http://news.bbc.co.uk/2/hi/asia-pacific/6357853.stm.

63. "Rice Calls North Korean Deal 'Important First Step,'" CNN News, February 13 2007, www.cnn.com/2007/WORLD/asiapcf/02/13/nkorea.talks/index.html.

64. Scanlon. "The End of a Long Confrontation?"

65. Charles L. Pritchard, "What I Saw in North Korea," *New York Times*, January 21, 2004.

66. Ibid.

67. Wade L. Huntley, "Coping with North Korea," Foreign Policy in Focus policy report, February 2003, www.fpif.org/pdf/papers/PRkorea2003.pdf.

6 Anatomy of a Crash: Port Security and the 2006 Dubai Ports World Controversy

Douglas C. Foyle

Before You Begin

1. How safe are American ports? Would the Dubai Ports World deal change this level of safety? Why or why not?
2. Why did the DP World issue become a major controversy in February 2006? Should it have been? Why or why not?
3. How did the Bush administration, congressional Republicans, and congressional Democrats view the DP World issue? Why did they see it as they did?
4. How did the business community, public opinion, newspaper opinion, and other actors view the issue? What accounts for their attitudes?
5. Should the DP World takeover have been stopped? Why or why not?
6. What, if anything, does this case say about the ability of the United States to formulate foreign policy in the post-September 11 environment?

[Among security problems in American ports] who owns the management contract ranks near the very bottom.[1]

Stephen E. Flynn, Council on Foreign Relations
and retired Coast Guard commander, February 23, 2006

Ports are essentially the front line in the war on terror and on homeland security. And so allowing a foreign firm to operate a port is sort of like allowing a foreign firm to operate a U.S. military air field in a traditional conflict.[2]

Michael O'Hanlon, Brookings Institution,
February 13, 2006, on *Lou Dobbs Tonight*

Don't let them tell you this [Dubai Ports World purchase of P&O] is just the transfer of a title. Baloney. We wouldn't transfer title to the Devil; we're not going to transfer title to Dubai.[3]

Sen. Frank Lautenberg, D-N.J., February 27, 2006

Introduction: Significant National Security Threat or Politically Motivated Overreaction?

A radiological attack on New York might start innocuously enough at a factory in Surabaya, Indonesia. There, athletic shoes are loaded into a shipping container and the container sealed for transport to retail outlets throughout the United States. A truck picks up the container and drives to the port. With a bribe as an incentive, the truck driver takes a detour to a warehouse along the way. There, a small crew pries the container's door hinges loose, removes some of the shoes, and replaces them with a lead-shielded radiological "dirty bomb" before resealing the container. The driver then takes the now deadly container to the docks where it is loaded at a terminal (the place in a port where containers are transferred between ship and rail or truck) onto a container ship. After several transfers onto progressively larger ships, the container makes its way to New York. Since the company shipping the container has joined the U.S. Customs-Trade Partnership against Terror, the U.S. Container Security Initiative does not flag the container for inspection at the Port of New York. The container is unloaded at the port terminal directly onto a waiting truck, which drives through a radiation detection portal (which misses the shielded bomb) and takes it to a local distribution center. When the distribution center workers open the container door, a trigger sets off the bomb.

In addition to the deaths and damage the bomb causes and the radioactive material it spreads, more damaging in economic terms would likely be the government's response. With no way to discern where the security breach occurred, and with all in-place security measures having failed, pressure would likely mount to inspect *all* incoming containers, grinding the flow of containers on which the U.S. economy relies to a halt. Economic losses to the U.S. economy would mount rapidly. A temporary (a few days) system stoppage would cause potential losses of $58 billion. A more extensive stoppage could cause a global recession.[4]

In 2006, fears that a Dubai Ports (DP) World takeover of Peninsular and Oriental Steam Navigation Company (P&O), which held terminal operations leases at six ports on the U.S. East Coast, would leave a company owned by the Arab government of Dubai, one of the United Arab Emirates, in charge of port security gripped the American political system. In the post–September 11 context, would DP World's operation of American ports dramatically undermine American security and make a radiological attack more likely? Or would the purchase have only a negligible influence on American security? For three weeks, from mid-February to early March 2006, that debate dominated news coverage and public attention, until Dubai Ports World agreed to sell off its newly acquired American holdings.

The Dubai Ports World Takeover Controversy, October 2005–March 2006

October 17, 2005 Dubai Ports (DP) World approaches Treasury Department regarding Peninsular and Oriental Steam Navigation Company (P&O) purchase and is referred to Department of Homeland Security.

October 31, 2005 DP World buyout offer of P&O reported in the *Wall Street Journal.*

November 2, 2005 Department of Homeland Security (DHS) asks intelligence agencies for information on DP World.

November 29, 2005 P&O announces it will accept DP World buyout offer.

Early December 2005 DP World and P&O North America informally meet with CFIUS agencies.

December 15, 2005 DP World officially notifies CFIUS of P&O takeover and Exon-Florio 30-day review clock begins.

January 16, 2006 Committee on Foreign Investment in the United States (CFIUS) approves DP World takeover of P&O.

Late January 2006 Eller & Co. expresses opposition to deal in meetings with members of Congress.

February 11, 2006 Associated Press report on DP World Deal raising national security questions.

February 13, 2006 Senator Charles Schumer press conference, *Savage Report* radio show, and *Lou Dobbs Tonight* television show publicize DP World deal.

February 16, 2006 Bipartisan press conference by Senate and House members opposing deal.

February 16, 2006 President Bush first briefed on DP World deal.

February 19, 2006 DHS Secretary Michael Chertoff's Sunday morning talk show appearance exacerbates concerns regarding the deal.

February 21, 2006 Senate Majority Leader Bill Frist suggests deal should be placed on hold, then House Speaker Dennis Hastert suggests a moratorium on the deal until further investigation, and President Bush threatens to veto any congressional legislation affecting the deal.

continued on the next page

continued from the previous page

February 22, 2006 Rep. Sue Myrick's "HELL NO!" letter to President Bush.

February 23, 2006 DP World and White House announce DP World would "segregate" its U.S. operations.

February 26, 2006 DP World asks Bush administration to undertake 45-day investigation as provided by Exon-Florio.

February 27, 2006 Coast Guard intelligence report questioning DP World deal released.

March 2, 2006 News reports that Dubai International Capital's purchase of Doncasters Groups Ltd. triggers 45-day CFIUS investigation.

March 8, 2006 House Appropriations Committee votes 62–2 to block DP World takeover.

March 9, 2006 Oval Office meeting where Bush is told Congress will block the deal by veto-proof margins. Bush asks DP World to sell U.S. holdings; DP World announces it will sell U.S. holdings.

October 4, 2006 Bush signs fiscal 2007 DHS budget including increases for port security programs.

October 13, 2006 Bush signs Safe Port Act.

March 17, 2007 DP World finalizes sale of U.S. holdings to American Investment Group.

How did an obscure international business transaction, which few in Washington or the general public had heard about before mid-February, capture national headlines? In short, the DP World deal engaged a witch's brew of sensitive issues: national security versus economics, globalization versus economic security, Congress versus the president, foreign direct investment (FDI) versus economic nationalism, suspicions regarding a secret executive branch process to review foreign business takeovers, post–September 11 port security, the complexities of international container transport, port terminal operations, Arab stereotypes, and election year politics. Neither DP World nor the administration of President George W. Bush sensed the potential controversy until too late. But it took only three short weeks for a veto-proof congressional majority to convince DP World to cut its losses and for the Republican Bush administration to suffer a major political defeat at the hands of a Republican majority in Congress. Although the deal quickly dropped out of the headlines, we are left to ponder whether it unjustly fell victim to opportunistic politicians or the U.S. avoided a significant threat to its national security.

Background: A "Sunday Drive": DP World, Late 2005 through January 16, 2006

From the first word of DP World's possible takeover of P&O in late October 2005 through February 10, 2006, the scant news coverage of the deal focused on its business aspects. The first news report raising security concerns did not appear until February 11, and the first American editorial questioning the deal did not appear until February 14.[5] By that time, the seemingly mundane business deal had passed the U.S. governmental review process without top-level attention (the president and cabinet-level officials were not informed) and seemed destined for easy finalization.

The economic transaction itself was of the sort that appears nearly every day on the newspaper financial pages. On October 31, 2006, the *Wall Street Journal* reported that Dubai Ports World had made a buyout offer to port terminal operator Peninsular and Oriental Steam Navigation Company, and on November 29, P&O announced that it would accept the $5.7 billion offer.[6] P&O Ports North America, a P&O subsidiary that DP World would acquire as part of the purchase of the parent company, ran terminal operations in six American ports—Newark, Philadelphia, Baltimore, Miami, New Orleans, and Houston. If the deal closed, DP World would become the third-largest port operator in the world (up from the seventh), in its effort to build a broad business with global reach.[7]

P&O North America was a stevedoring company (a business hired by shipping lines to oversee the loading and unloading of ships at ports) and a terminal operator (which moves cargo onto trucks and rail cars).[8] The ubiquitous "intermodal shipping container" has had an enormous effect on the quintupling of international trade in the two decades prior to the DP World deal. The standard-sized, forty-foot-long boxes provide a significant advantage over previous methods because they can be easily transferred among truck, rail, and ship transport. By one estimate, what took twenty dockworkers all day a generation ago now takes twenty minutes and can be completed by just a handful of workers.[9] From a security perspective, containers do not easily yield to inspection because their sheer numbers—millions of containers are shipped each year—make manually opening them all infeasible, and remote sensing technology cannot yet accomplish a complete and thorough inspection. Yet despite the security risks, containers provide the foundation for the international trade system because their efficiencies have dramatically reduced the cost of shipping goods, as well as geographic constraints, allowing cheaper Asian labor markets such as Japan and China access to the American market.[10]

Most ports accommodate several different terminal operators. For example, in the Port of Los Angeles companies from Japan, China, Taiwan, Singapore, and Denmark operate terminals. The ports themselves are usually owned by a government entity, which leases terminals to operators to organize the loading and unloading of the containers from the ships, their storage for pickup, or their loading directly onto trucks or railcars. Upwards of 60 percent of all U.S. container terminals are operated by non-American companies.[11]

Regardless of who owns the port or terminal, members of the International Longshoremen's Association do the vast majority of the loading and unloading of the ships, railcars, and trucks. In the DP World case, the same longshoremen would move the containers before and after the transfer of ownership. Stevedores such as P&O provide a largely logistical service, ensuring that the container ships are unloaded quickly and that the containers are loaded onto trucks or railcars for the shipowner. Employees of the terminal operator rarely come into direct contact with the containers or even know what is in them.[12]

For example, the P&O terminal in Baltimore in spring 2006 would unload an average of three ships a day, employing 900 longshoremen to accomplish that task. As ships came in, P&O contacted the union hall where longshoremen awaited work. Longshoremen fitting the description of the tasks needed checked in with the longshoreman dispatcher, who scanned their identification cards. The computer then sorted them by seniority and issued passes for the docks. P&O employees managed the longshoremen, containers, and flow by telephone and e-mail from a location a quarter-mile from the docks.[13]

Only three stories and no editorials on the DP World/P&O transaction appeared in major American papers prior to February 12 (they focused on the business aspects).[14] But the ingredients for controversy lay right below the surface with the United Arab Emirates (UAE), Dubai, and DP World. Located on the southern edge of the Persian Gulf, the UAE was created in 1971 when seven tribal sheikdoms united into a rough confederation. For Americans, the UAE gained prominence after September 11: the funds to finance the attacks moved through its loosely regulated banking system, and two of the hijackers were UAE citizens. The UAE was one of a few nations to recognize Afghanistan's Taliban regime, and it appears to have played a major transit role in the A. Q. Khan nuclear smuggling network.

After the September 11 attacks, the UAE took measures to strengthen its banking regulations and terrorism laws. For the U.S. military, the UAE provided a deepwater port (operated by DP World), dry dock facilities for aircraft carriers and nuclear submarines, and air bases. In all, former U.S. ambassador to the UAE William Rugh concluded, "Across the board, the UAE is one of the region's strongest supporters of U.S. policy."[15]

Since the emirate of Dubai does not have the large oil and natural gas reserves of many Persian Gulf nations, it chose to develop a diversified economy, focused on enhancing its historical role as a regional trading hub, by emphasizing international shipping, banking, commerce, and tourism. This successful financial strategy left Dubai wealthy, with a burgeoning stock market, rising property values, and funds to invest overseas. On the other hand, Dubai likely provided a major transit point for Iran's efforts to acquire nuclear technology, as well as Pakistan's nuclear program.

The Dubai government owns Dubai Ports World which, at the time of the P&O acquisition, operated twenty-two port terminals around the globe and moved millions of containers per year. With a business plan set on expansion, DP World purchased P&O because, as a company spokesperson said, "We want to be in markets our customers [the container shipping lines] are telling us they are developing and that means a focus on India and China in particular, as well as the Middle East"; the U.S. ports were "not the focus of the acquisition."[16] But DP World's purchase would effectively place Dubai in charge of terminal operations at several major American ports, including those in the New York and Washington areas, and that would become the center of controversy in 2006.

The potential concerns about the UAE, Dubai, and DP World interacted with the controversial politics of foreign direct investment (FDI) and the U.S. government's review of foreign takeovers of domestic companies. "FDI" usually refers to a situation in which a nondomestic investor "exerts direct control" over a U.S business or firm.[17] FDI has been politically controversial in the United States, although most economists agree that it has contributed substantially to U.S. economic growth and prosperity.[18] Despite FDI controversies in the past (most recently focusing on Japan in the 1980s and China in the 2000s),[19] the U.S. economy in 2006 relied heavily on a continuing flow of foreign direct investment and other foreign capital to offset insufficient levels of savings available for domestic investment and to finance government budget deficits. Simplified, the United States must import capital from abroad equal to the trade deficit (the value of exports minus imports) and the government's budget deficit. In 2005, this balance of payments deficit was $800 billion, or roughly $2 billion per day. A shortfall in imported capital (because, for example, foreign investors decided that investment in the United States was no longer desirable, or the United States hindered the flow of investment through regulation) would risk undermining the economy by causing higher interest rates and declining investment, growth, and productivity.[20] For 2005, the contribution of foreign direct investment to the balance of payments totaled roughly $128.6 billion. The vast majority (97 percent) came from Europe (68 percent), Japan (14 percent), Canada (12 percent), and Australia (3 percent).[21]

Because of the economy's capital needs, the U.S. government has adopted a favorable attitude toward FDI. In 1983, President Ronald Reagan became the first president to favor FDI publicly, stating, "The United States believes that foreign investors should be able to make the same kinds of investment, under the same conditions, as nationals of the host country. Exceptions should be limited to areas of legitimate national security concern or related interests."[22] The long-running tension between this security caveat and economic need is at the center of the DP World controversy.

To monitor the balance between security and economic need the United States implemented a series of security reviews of FDI transactions. In 1975, President Gerald Ford created the Committee on Foreign Investment in the United States (CFIUS) to monitor and examine the flow of FDI. In 1988, Congress passed the so-called Exon-Florio amendment as part of the Omnibus and Competitiveness Trade Act of 1988, giving the president the authority to prohibit or suspend any foreign acquisition, merger, or takeover deemed a threat to national security. The law specifically allows the president to act when "(1) there is credible evidence that the foreign entity exercising control might take action that threatens national security, and (2) the provisions of law, other than the International Emergency Economic Powers Act[,] do not provide adequate and appropriate authority to protect the national security." The 1977 International Emergency Powers Act requires the president to return control of economic assets seized in an emergency to their previous owners once the emergency passes. President Reagan delegated his authority under Exon-Florio to the CFIUS process. CFIUS membership consists of the secretary of the Treasury as chair; the secretaries of state, defense, commerce, and homeland security (as of 2003); the attorney general; the director of the Office of Management and Budget; the U.S. trade representative; the chairman of the Council of Economic Advisers; the director of the Office of Science and Technology Policy; and the assistants to the president for national security affairs and economic policy.

The review process consists of two possible phases. After formal notification of a transaction, a 30-day review commences. If no national security problems emerge, or a national security mitigation agreement between the company and government addresses any security concerns within the 30 day period, CFIUS approves the transaction, and the process ends (with no formal report to the president). If national security concerns cannot be addressed within the 30-day review period, a 45-day investigation (an extended review) occurs. At the end of this period, a report is filed with the president (whether a national security mitigation agreement is reached or not). The president then has 15 days to approve the deal or not and report this action to Congress. In the P&O case, DP World agreed to a national security mitigation agreement during the 30-day review, and no 45-day investigation occurred. As amended in 1993 (the Byrd amendment), the law requires the 45-day investigation if "the acquirer is controlled by or acting on behalf of a foreign government; *and* the acquisition 'could result in control of a person engaged in interstate commerce in the U.S. that could affect the national security of the U.S.'"

The Exon-Florio amendment rather vaguely spells out the factors that may be used in evaluating a deal's national security effects, leaving wide latitude for interpretation. In fact, shortly before the DP World controversy, a September 2005 Government Accountability Office report concluded that the Treasury Department employed too narrow a definition of national security because it wanted to encourage foreign investment.[23] Since the Exon-Florio amendment passed in 1988, through the end of 2005, 1,593 notifications occurred, and the vast majority of the transactions were approved within 30 days. CFIUS only performed 25 investigations (the 45-day review). Of those 25, 13 of the business deals were withdrawn, and 12 reached a presidential decision. The president only rejected one deal during the entire period, a 1990 aerospace purchase by a company owned by the Chinese government.[24]

Before DP World completed its purchase of P&O, on October 17, 2005, the company informally approached the Treasury Department indicating its intent. Treasury referred DP World to the Department of Homeland Security (DHS) because of the port security issue.[25] On November 2, DHS asked U.S. intelligence agencies to report any information they had on the company. Assistant Secretary of Homeland Security for Policy Stewart A. Baker said that review revealed no "derogatory" information. In early December, before the start of the 30-day clock, DP World and P&O North America met with CFIUS agencies to provide information and smooth the review process. On December 15, the 30-day clock began, with DP World officially notifying CFIUS of the P&O purchase.[26]

The 30 day review led DHS to request several concessions from DP World as part of a national security mitigation agreement. DP World pledged to maintain the current management teams at the terminals (which would ensure that most were Americans), to continue participating in American security programs at the same level, and to give 30 days notice of any changes. In addition to designating an executive to act as a government liaison on security matters, Baker indicated, "they agreed to open their books, and give us access to records, without any formal legal process" and to cooperate on all matters related to port security. With DHS concerns met and no other CFIUS agencies raising objections, CFIUS approved the deal on January 16, 2006, within the 30-day review window. No officials higher than the assistant secretary level had knowledge of the deal, and Treasury officials intended to inform Congress of CFIUS's approval at its next quarterly meeting on CFUIS matters, on February 17.[27]

On Ramp: DP World Moves into the National Spotlight, January 17 to February 16

The efforts of the small Fort Lauderdale stevedoring firm Eller and Company provided the spark to move the DP World issue onto the front pages. Eller had partnered with P&O North America at the Port of Miami and concluded that DP World's takeover would negatively affect its business (the company feared a backlash from association with an Arab government). With the CFIUS process complete, Eller tried to sink the deal by lobbying senators and House members to stop it. It hired former drug industry lobbyist Joe Muldoon, who made the rounds of Congress, where he found that few had heard of the deal. Still, he pressed ahead and framed the issue in stark national security terms that would become familiar: "It's about foreign control over critical infrastructure—during wartime." Without Eller's actions, it seems unlikely that much attention would have gone to the deal. In fact, Israel Klein, spokesperson for leading deal opponent Sen. Charles Schumer, D-N.Y., commented that the company "was really the canary in the mineshaft for many people on the hill and in the media."[28]

On February 11, Eller's efforts to spotlight the takeover came to fruition with an Associated Press report that began, "A company in the United Arab Emirates is poised to take over significant operations at six American ports as part of a corporate sale, leaving a country with ties to the September 11 hijackers with influence over a maritime industry considered vulnerable to terrorism." The report noted that "critics of the proposed purchase said a port operator complicit in smuggling or terrorism could manipulate manifests and other records to frustrate Homeland Security's already limited scrutiny of shipping containers and slip contraband past U.S. Customs inspectors." Eller lawyer Michael Kreitzer was quoted in the article as saying, "When you have a foreign government involved, you are injecting foreign national interests. A country that may be a friend of ours today may not be on the same side tomorrow. You don't know in advance what the politics of that country will be in the future." Senator Schumer argued, "America's busiest ports are vital to our economy and to the international economy and that is why they remain top terrorist targets. Just as we would not outsource military operations or law enforcement duties, we should be very careful before we outsource such sensitive homeland security duties." Port security experts, on the other hand, found such claims dubious. Council on Foreign Relations port security expert Stephen Flynn observed, "Does [the DP World deal] pose a national security risk? I think that's pushing the envelope. It's not impossible to imagine one could develop an internal conspiracy, but I'd have to assign it a very low probability." Former State and Commerce Department official and Center for Strategic and International Studies fellow James Lewis concluded that the deal "doesn't offer al-Qaida any opportunities it doesn't have now." The docks would be unaffected, said Flynn, adding, "You're not going to have a bunch of UAE citizens working the docks. They're longshoremen, vested in high-paying jobs. Most of them are Archie Bunker-kind of Americans."[29]

The AP report set off a chain reaction that quickly moved DP World to the front page. White House officials, who were distracted by dealing with the aftermath of a hunting accident involving Vice President Richard Cheney, did not see the AP report, which appeared in the *Washington Post* on February 12; they missed the signs of the building storm.[30] As chair of the Democratic Senatorial Campaign Committee in 2006, with the charge of recruiting and supporting Democratic candidates for the Senate, Schumer realized the issue's potency as a campaign issue, as did the chair of the Democratic Congressional Campaign Committee (focused on winning House seats for the Democrats) Rep. Rahm Emanuel, Ill.[31]

Schumer began pressing the issue hard on February 13 with a series of press conferences, including one with the families of victims of the September 11 attacks. At the same time, conservative talk show host Michael Savage attacked the deal on his syndicated radio program. Savage recalled, "People were crazy about this. Even Bush supporters went nuts."[32] Even though "one of Bush's closest aides" heard the Savage show, the aide quickly dismissed it.[33] Lou Dobbs, a longstanding critic of outsourcing and big business, introduced his February 13 *Lou Dobbs Tonight* show on CNN by reporting, "A country with ties to the September 11 terrorists could soon be running significant operations at some of our most important and largest seaports with a full blessing of the Bush White House."[34]

Congressional Republicans quickly picked up on the political significance of the DP World takeover. Republican representatives Mark Foley, Fla., and Vito

Fossella, N.Y., criticized the deal on Savage's February 13 broadcast.[35] Foley and Rep. John E. Sweeney, R-N.Y., then used congressional hearings on February 15 to question Secretary of the Treasury John W. Snow and DHS Secretary Michael Chertoff on the deal.[36] Chairman of the House Homeland Security Committee Rep. Peter King, R-N.Y., called White House officials and urged them to undertake a more extensive review. The White House reassured King and told him to "go ahead" and raise his concerns in public.[37] Within a few days, the phones in congressional offices of both Democrats and Republicans were ringing off the hook.[38]

Politics affected the responses of both Democrats and Republicans in Congress. Democrats sensed an opportunity. Since September 11, Democrats had suffered the Republicans' use of national security as a political issue against them in the 2002 and 2004 national elections. With the UAE's links to terrorism and the September 11 attacks, harsh criticism of the DP World deal might allow Democrats to appear stronger on terrorism and national security than Bush. The issue also appealed to key Democratic constituencies. Protectionists opposed the deal simply because it was a foreign takeover, and big business critics could point to the secretive CFIUS approval process and the global business dynamics. Democrats such as Rep. Harold Ford, Tenn., who was running for the Senate, immediately began using the issue in television campaign ads. In Ford's ad he said, "President Bush wants to sell [six American ports] to the United Arab Emirates—a country that had diplomatic ties with the Taliban. . . . We shouldn't outsource our national security to anyone."[39]

On the Republican side, President Bush had recently reached his lowest public approval rating to that date, with only 39 percent of opinion poll respondents approving of the way he was handling his job as president, and 56 percent disapproving. Although Bush would not be running for reelection because of the two-term limit, congressional Republicans faced a tough 2006 election, and they feared that they might not retain their majority in Congress. With Bush becoming increasingly unpopular, in large part because of the ongoing Iraq war and the inept government response to Hurricane Katrina, Republicans saw the DP World issue as an opportunity to distance themselves from the Bush administration. As one House Republican put it, "It's not that we feel we now can [criticize the White House], it's that we feel we must."[40]

Institutionally, Congress had largely been subservient to the executive branch since the September 11 attacks. On a series of issues both domestic and foreign, Congress members believed that the executive branch had shut it out or limited congressional involvement. Finding out about a potentially controversial matter such as the DP World ports acquisition after the decision had already been made upset Republicans. Representative Foley complained, "We've defended them on wiretaps, we've defended them on Iraq, we've defended them on so many things he's tried to accomplish, that to be left out here supporting this thing in a vacuum is kind of offensive."[41]

Port security and DP World then moved to the top of the national agenda. While $18 billion had been spent on airport security after September 11, only $630 million had been spent on ports, and the U.S. Coast Guard estimated that $5.4 billion was needed over the next ten years for elementary items like fences and lighting alone. Responsibility for port and waterway security lies with the Coast Guard, which requires crew and cargo manifests ninety-six hours before a ship docks. However, maritime security consultant Kim Peterson concluded that the Coast Guard "doesn't have either the people or the necessary physical resources to provide the in-water patrols that are so desperately needed." With thousands of truckers entering ports every day (11,000 into and out of the Port of Los Angeles–Long Beach daily) using only a driver's license, "there is no way for the port to even know who is really on its property at any time" said port security expert Flynn.[42]

The Customs and Border Protection Agency runs two main programs to provide container security. First, the Container Security Initiative (CSI) places American inspectors in forty-two overseas ports (which together ship 80 percent of the containers coming to the United States) to examine cargo manifests of outgoing shipping. In addition, under the initiative the host country purchases scanning equipment and agrees to conduct inspections at U.S. request. Manifests are sent twenty-four hours before a ship is loaded and are examined for risk based on origin, route, sender, and irregular patterns. If flagged, a container can be screened by gamma-ray machines to view its contents. The Department of Energy is also installing radiation scanners in fourteen countries. This system allows the inspection of suspicious cargo overseas before it leaves for the United States. Ports must also follow the 2004 International Ship and Port Facility Security Code (adopted by the International Maritime Organization), requiring things such as fences to secure port perimeters and identification badges.[43] Second, the Customs-Trade Partnership against Terrorism (C-TPAT) is a voluntary program in which shipping companies implement certain security procedures in return for faster movement through customs. Each of the measures relies on the effectiveness of security overseas, and physical or gamma-ray inspections occur for only 5 percent to 10 percent of the estimated eleven million containers entering the United States in any year.[44]

Stephen Flynn notes that "the framework of these initiatives is well conceived, but there's not much muscle—or even skin—on them. . . . The ability of Customs and the Coast Guard to assess the risks in specific cases and to identify potential problems is weak. The information they get is entirely dependent upon what the ocean-shipping companies tell them." Gaps exist along the way at each step. Overseas, manifests might be inaccurate or incomplete (they might not match container contents and will not reveal that containers have been tampered with). They are "essentially secondhand declarations by importers that lack specifics" or back-up material, according to Flynn.[45] Sometimes flagged containers are sent to the United States before they can be inspected. The understaffed CSI program does not inspect 28 percent of the containers flagged for inspection. Gamma-ray scanners have a hard time penetrating dense material, and radiation detectors might not pick up highly enriched uranium (used for nuclear bombs), especially if it is shielded. In the United States, only about 200 of the 600 radiation portals (to scan for dirty bombs or a nuclear weapon) operate, so only 37 percent of containers are checked, while 12,400 handheld monitors (used to make up for the gap in portals) have error rates of 50 percent. Although 5,800 importers and ship terminal operators have signed on to the C-TPAT program, U.S. Customs has verified compliance for only one-third of them. The perimeters of U.S. ports are typically guarded by minimum wage, private security personnel with few cameras to detect intruders, and a security system designed to prevent theft rather than terrorism. Instead of using containers with sensors to indicate tampering, "What they use now is an easily tampered-with strip of aluminum," says port security expert Joe Bouchard. In Flynn's view, "port security today is still a house of cards."[46]

Despite these shortcomings, U.S. Customs and Border official Jay Ahern argues, "When you aggregate those layers, it is very difficult for someone to introduce something that causes a national security risk to this country. It is hardly a house of cards."[47] Nevertheless, throughout the DP World furor, public opinion, the media, and Washington politicians would behave as if serious port security problems did exist and DP World's purchase of P&O compounded the danger.

Acceleration: Bipartisan Opposition to Bush Veto Threat, February 16 to February 21

Once it appeared in the news media, bipartisan calls for further reexamination of the DP World transaction quickly emerged. At a February 16 press conference, Senator Schumer, along with senators Frank Lautenberg, D-N.J., Christopher Dodd, D-Conn., and Tom Coburn, R-Okla., and Republican House members Vito Fossella, Chris Shays, Conn., and Mark Foley, called for a deeper examination than had been completed under CFIUS.[48] In a letter to the Treasury Department, bipartisan leaders of the Senate Banking Committee described the CFIUS review as "cursory."[49] Representative King worried, "I am not convinced that the system that's used is satisfactory in a post-9/11 world. They just seem to do an analysis of what's known about the company—is there anything known showing that they're a threat?"[50]

The Bush administration believed the issue would soon go away. White House Chief of Staff Andrew H. Card Jr. first briefed the president about it on February 16, but Bush did not issue a comment until days later.[51] Instead, DHS Assistant Secretary Baker offered,

> This company will be subject to any U.S. laws that apply to port security, and will be obliged to have a port security plan that we will review. So, if there's a falloff in compliance on security here in the United States, we're not completely lacking in ability to respond to that. . . . So we do a lot of screening abroad, and our general experiences with [DP World] has been positive.[52]

Baker noted that although CFIUS did not complete an independent analysis because of the need to keep the potential transaction secret, "we did not find derogatory information in our review." Treasury Department spokesperson Brookly McLaughlin refused to provide any information on the CFIUS review, saying, "We as a general rule do not comment at all on any specific transactions."[53]

The administration would soon realize its mistake, but by then it was too late to put the toothpaste back in the tube. Representative Foley recalled, "It would have helped in a very extraordinary way for Bush to" speak out earlier on the issue and give the administration's position, since "he could have stymied the issue or at least clarified it." In retrospect, some blamed the administration's mishandling of the issue on the fact that Bush would not seek reelection again and his staff had lost its edge. Former Bush spokesperson Ari Fleischer said of the White House staff, "They have been there from the beginning; they are experienced, knowledgeable, and they know how things work and to get things done—but they are tired." Deputy Treasury Secretary Robert M. Kimmitt lamented, "We've learned from this that we have to make a more affirmative effort to give Congress the input they need to exercise their oversight function. Even in cases where the security work is done diligently and professionally, we need to make sure broader considerations are taken into account."[54]

Both DP World and the administration reacted slowly to the criticism. A few days after the February 16 press conferences, DP World sent advisers to the six American ports, and it planned to send DP World chief operating officer Edward H. Bilkey to Washington the next week to lobby Congress.[55] A few days later, Bilkey described the CFIUS review, saying, "There was no big deal about it. We complied with what the requirements were, and there was no problem." Kimmitt reported that "none of [the agencies involved in the CFIUS process] objected to the deal proceeding on national security grounds." The White House sent briefing teams to Congress, and DP World hired high-powered, bipartisan lobbying firms to help organize its public relations response.[56]

The initial public relations effort by DHS Secretary Michael Chertoff on February 19 only exacerbated problems. Chertoff's vague claims that the administration had followed a "rigorous process" and had "assurances in place," and that the deal was "appropriate from a national security standpoint," reassured no one, as the quality of the CFIUS review itself was under attack.[57] Representative King responded,

> I'm aware of the conditions, and they relate entirely to how the company carries out its procedures, but it doesn't go to who they hire, or how they hire people. They're better than nothing, but to me they don't address the underlying conditions, which is how are they going to guard against things like infiltration by al Qaeda or someone else[;] how are they going to guard against corruption?

Republican senator Lindsey Graham, S.C., called the deal "unbelievably tone deaf politically at this point in our history." Sen. Barbara Boxer, D-Calif., expressed her incredulity, saying, "It is ridiculous to say you're taking secret steps to make sure that it's okay for a nation that had ties to 9/11, [to] take over part of our port operations in many of our largest ports."[58]

Yet the opportunity still existed to quell the rising storm should some quiet deal be worked out. President Bush had not weighed in, and the top Republican leadership in the House and Senate had remained silent, making a face-saving alternative possible. However, that opportunity ended on February 21, when first Senate Majority Leader Bill Frist, R-Tenn., then House Speaker Dennis Hastert, R-Ill., and finally President Bush adopted clear, unequivocal, and contradictory positions.

Frist thought about his position strategically. If he was to control the issue in the future, he needed to stake out a position ahead of the pack. After giving the White House only one hour's notice, Frist came out publicly in favor of slowing the deal down, saying, "The decision to finalize this deal should be put on hold until the administration conducts a more extensive review of this matter. If the administration cannot delay this process, I plan on introducing legislation to ensure that the deal is placed on hold until this decision gets a more thorough review." His statement opened the criticism floodgate, since "a leading Republican, an ally of President Bush and a likely presidential contender in 2008" had now legitimized criticism from backbench Republicans.[59]

House Speaker Hastert, who had never opposed Bush on an important issue, added his voice to Frist's in a letter to Bush: "I am very concerned about the national security implications that this could have for the safety of the American people. Therefore, I believe there should be an immediate moratorium placed on the seaport deal in order to further examine its effects on our port security."[60]

With reporters saying that "they had seldom seen him so visibly angry, apparently provoked by the shock of House and Senate leaders lining up against him," Bush laid down his own marker on Air Force One, saying that if Congress passed legislation, "I'll deal with it, with a veto." He feared "mixed signals" if an Arab country were singled out and asked critics to "step up and explain why a Middle Eastern company is held to a different standard." Once the plane reached Washington, Bush explained, "If there was any chance that this transaction would jeopardize the security of the United States, it would not go forward. But I also want to repeat something again, and that is: This is a company that has played by the rules, that has been cooperative with the United States, a country that's an ally in the war on terror, and it would send a terrible signal to friends and allies not to let this transaction go through."[61]

Before his veto threat, in the words of White House spokesperson Scott McClellan, "One thing the president did . . . was go back to every cabinet member whose department is involved in this process and ask them, 'Are you comfortable with this deal going forward?' And each and every one expressed that they were comfortable with this transaction going forward." Bush administration officials also feared they would damage trade relations and harm the American economy if they terminated the deal. McClellan conceded, "We probably should have briefed Congress about it sooner."[62]

DP World tried to defend the deal. Bilkey stated, "We will continue to work with the U.S. government on maintaining the highest standards of security at U.S. ports, and will fully cooperate in putting into place whatever is necessary to protect the terminals"[63] P&O head of North American operations Michael Seymour pointed out that the same longshoremen would move the containers regardless of the terminal operator. And an unnamed UAE official stated, "Our track record speaks for itself. We have handed over a number of high-value Al Qaeda suspects either to their home countries or to the U.S."[64]

Full Throttle: "Hell No!" to 45-Day Investigation Offer, February 22 to February 26

After the president's veto threat, the editorial pages of the major papers and public opinion became engaged and the issue crossed the point of no return. Favoring the deal were the *Wall Street Journal*, the *Washington Post*, the *Los Angeles Times*, and the *Chicago Sun-Times*. The *Wall Street Journal* wondered why critics "believe Dubai Ports World has been insufficiently vetted," since none had "provided any evidence the Administration hasn't done its due diligence," and said that "the notion that the Bush Administration is farming out port 'security' to hostile Arab nations is alarmist nonsense." The *Washington Post*'s editorial began, "You know there's something suspicious going on when multiple members of Congress—House, Senate, Democrat, Republican, future presidential candidates of all stripes—spontaneously unite around an issue that none of them had known existed a week earlier." The *Post* concluded, "Clearly, Congress doesn't understand that basic principle [encouraging Arab countries to become economically and politically integrated with the rest of the world], since its members prefer instead to spread prejudice and misinformation." The *Los Angeles Times* labeled the "bipartisan hissy fit . . . neither serious nor welcome." The *Chicago Sun-Times* blamed the uproar on the "poor job the White House did in preparing Congress for the news and reassuring everyone that [the DP World deal] would in no way compromise their security." It noted that security would be run by the U.S. government and observed that "far from having shady connections to Arab extremists, the UAE has been a proven ally in the war against terrorism."[65]

In opposition were the editorial pages of both the liberal *New York Times* and the conservative *Washington Times*. The *New York Times* took the Bush administration to task for both port security and the DP World issue, arguing, "The Bush administration has done far too little to protect the nation's ports against terrorists. But it has taken that laxness to a new level by allowing a company from the United Arab Emirates to run significant operations at six American ports, including the Port of New York." It found that "putting port management in the hands of a country with such a mixed record [UAE 9/11 terrorists and banking system links to terrorism] in the war on terror is a step in the wrong direction." The *Washington Times* castigated the White House for "not listening to the congressional uproar over Dubai Ports World . . . despite its home country's glaring ties to international terrorism." The *Washington Times* asked, "Why must the United States let a state-owned firm from a hotbed of radicalism own the major ports of the Eastern seaboard?" Pointing directly to DP World, the paper argued that the company

> doesn't even have to be a willing collaborator to be a danger to the United States. All other things being equal, an Arabic company is easier for terrorists to penetrate than a British or American firm. . . .That would be possible even if the dockworkers are the same and even if most of the local management is exactly the same. . . . What happens if the government of the United Arab Emirates backs away from the counterterrorism support President Bush currently lauds it for?[66]

National columnists likewise provided a divided perspective. Liberal *New York Times* columnist Maureen Dowd found the whole decision the "same old pattern: a stupid and counterproductive national security decision is made in secret, blowing off checks and balances, and the president's out of the loop." Conservative *New York Times* columnist David Brooks attributed the criticism of DP World to "nativist, isolationist, mass hysteria." *Washington Post* columnist David Ignatius argued that the "worst thing that could happen to the United States, paradoxically, would be for the Arab and other foreign investors to take us at our xenophobic word and decide that America doesn't really want foreign investment."[67]

Former DHS inspector general Clark Kent Ervin thought that "we should all have deep concerns about [UAE's] links to terrorists," since the "Coast Guard merely sets standards that ports are to follow and reviews their security plans," whereas "meeting those standards each day is the job of port operators." On the other hand, former CFIUS head and assistant secretary of the Treasury for international affairs C. Fred Bergsten commented, "Nearly all objective observers . . . [agree the deal] will have no operational impact on the national security of the United States."[68]

The American business community worried that the DP World controversy might negatively affect trade and FDI. For example, a prominent business lobby, the U.S. Chamber of Commerce, urged caution in reacting to the deal and warned "lawmakers not to allow pockets of public hysteria . . . to stifle future foreign direct investment." It feared the reaction would "seriously damage U.S. relations with friendly countries in the Middle East and hamper our ability to promote trade and investment around the globe."[69]

Besides the deal's specifics, the issue seemed to capture the public's imagination for several overarching reasons. First, it opened the question of whether the Bush administration had done enough about port security since September 11.

Second, it touched on the question of whether the United States had opened itself too much to foreign investment and trade. Third, other economic vulnerabilities, such as the outsourcing of American jobs, particularly to Asia; the increasing number of immigrants from Latin America; and overall dependence on FDI, exacerbated those fears. Misperceptions that DP World would be in charge of security and cargo inspections at the ports, and ignorance of the fact that many ports were actually already run by foreign companies, compounded the worries.[70]

Once the firestorm among elites erupted, an activated public paid close attention and developed clear attitudes of its own. Although public opinion opposed the DP World deal, it continued to favor FDI at roughly the same level as ever. A March 12 poll by the Pew Center found that 41 percent of respondents followed news of the DP World deal "very closely" (trailing only the situation in Iraq, with 43 percent). In historical terms, that level of public interest made the DP World issue one of the top ten political issues of the previous two decades, behind such issues as the 2002 Supreme Court ruling on the Pledge of Allegiance (52 percent), the 1993 Clinton health care plan (49 percent), and the 1993 gays in the military controversy (45 percent), but ahead of the 2000 Elian Gonzalez debate (39 percent), the 1993 debate on NAFTA (39 percent), and the 2006 Bush authorization of domestic wiretaps (37 percent). Only 33 percent of Americans thought "investors from other countries owning companies in the U.S." was a "good thing" for the United States, while 53 percent found it a "bad thing." But that level of support is actually up from 1989, when 18 percent said FDI was a good thing and 70 percent said it was bad.[71]

Still, the public clearly opposed the DP World deal by wide margins. A February 27 CBS News poll found that an overwhelming 70 percent of the public opposed the United States letting "a United Arab Emirates company operate U.S. shipping ports" and only 21 percent favored it. A March 6 *Washington Post*/ABC News poll found that 23 percent of respondents thought "a company owned by the government of a nation called the United Arab Emirates . . . should be allowed to manage" the six U.S. ports, while 70 percent thought it should not be allowed to do so. A broader, March 2 CNN/*USA Today*/Gallup poll asked respondents whether the "federal government should allow companies" from a range of countries to "own cargo operations at U.S. seaports." Although the public thought the government should allow British companies (71 percent to 26 percent), respondents opposed allowing companies from France (45 percent to 50 percent), China (31 percent to 65 percent), and "Arab countries that are friendly to the United States" (40 percent to 56 percent) to do so.

A mid-March Pew poll found only 14 percent favoring "the government allowing this company [DP World] to operate U.S. ports" and 73 percent opposed. Still, according to the *Washington Post*/ABC News poll, the public held somewhat mixed attitudes about the motivations of deal opponents, 49 percent saying that the "elected officials who have been criticizing the Dubai Ports World takeover" mainly wanted to "use the issue for political advantage" while 37 percent thought the officials were mainly concerned about national security.[72]

Congress heard the public. Prominent Republicans, such as Sen. Trent Lott, R-Miss., and Speaker Hastert, heard strong opposition when home visiting constituents, as well as in e-mails and phone calls. Rep. Don Manzullo, R-Ill., said, "I got stopped all over the place. People are big-time upset." He said he hadn't heard as much negative reaction in a decade and found the level of response higher than in the Clinton impeachment. Even efforts by DP World to reassure the American public fell flat, as articulate company officials in Arab dress giving reassurances that they could handle security only increased public complaints to Congress.[73]

Spurred on by constituent opinion and undeterred by Bush's veto threat, the congressional opposition to the DP World deal continued unabated. Rep. Sue Myrick, R-N.C., wrote in a clipped letter to Bush, "Dear Mr. President: In regards to selling American ports to the United Arab Emirates, not just NO but HELL NO!" Constituents bombarded Republicans in Congress, urging them to oppose President Bush. Representative King noted that Congress was "responding to incredible local political pressure."[74]

In response, the White House briefed Congress on the deal's specifics, the CFIUS review and DP World's national security accommodations, the role that the Coast Guard and Customs Agency play in security, and the nature of port operations. Treasury Secretary John W. Snow also warned, "The implication of failing to approve this would be to tell the world that investments in the United States from certain parts of the world aren't welcome."[75] The general feeling among lawmakers was that the deal had not been examined to the extent necessary (they noted that the CFIUS committee had only met one time during the 30-day review) and that, in any event, the 1993 Byrd amendment required the 45-day investigation because DP World was owned by a foreign government.

Knowledgeable outside critics disagreed on the deal's security implications. Former anti-terrorist expert at the Treasury and DHS Joseph King suggested that DP World would be able to acquire visas for hundreds of its employees to relocate to the United States and that al Qaeda could pressure low-level officials to give visas to al Qaeda sympathizes who, once in the country, could gain access to other resources (driver's licenses, work permits, mortgages) that could assist terrorist operations. He also suggested that DP World's large volume of financial transfers to the United States could be used to bury transfers of funds from terrorist organizations. On the other hand, a banking official with a specialty in the maritime industry, Peter S. Shaerf, commented, "[DP World] have a sterling reputation. They have never done anything that would expose them in any way as a security risk. They run first-class ports."[76] Although former high-level customs official Robert C. Bonner characterized the deal's security risks as "greatly exaggerated" given that "Dubai . . . has been very supportive in the counterterrorism efforts," former CIA director James Woolsey warned, "The nature of these governments . . . can change at the whim of one individual. . . . so you don't want them controlling crucial infrastructure like ports."[77]

On February 23, the White House and DP World began to make concessions to the political pressure by making a coordinated announcement that DP World would "segregate" its U.S. operations and "not exercise control" over them until after further discussions between the administration and Congress. This concession came after Sen. John Warner, R-Va., and the Bush administration informed the company that more time was needed to stem the tide of congressional action.[78] DP World official Bilkey said, "We need to understand the concerns of people in the U.S. who are worried about this transaction and make sure that they are addressed to the benefit of all parties. Security is everybody's business."[79] Bush gave further assurances that, with the Coast Guard and Customs Agency in charge of port security, "People don't need to worry about security. This deal wouldn't go forward if we were concerned."[80] As for the U.A.E, Chairman of the Joint Chiefs of Staff Peter Pace said, "In everything that we have asked and worked with them on, they have proven to be very, very solid partners." Former U.S. ambassador to the UAE Theodore Kattouf said, "I think [rejecting the deal] would be seen as a real rebuff to a country that is sort of leading the way in the Middle East in terms of globalization and free trade."[81]

Congressional critics, for the most part, were not impressed with the delay. Speaker Hastert called it a "smart move," but Representative King complained, "If the company just thinks that by explaining the deal, or the administration thinks by explaining the deal, that Congress is going to get on board, I don't think so." Senator Schumer added, "If the president were to voluntarily institute the investigation and delay the contract, that would be a good step. But a simple cooling-off period will not allay our very serious concerns about this dubious deal."[82]

At a February 23 Senate Armed Services Committee hearing, the administration and Congress clashed over whether the law required the investigation or not. Sen. Robert Byrd, D-W.V. (author of the 1993 amendment), asked "why that investigation was not carried out." Deputy Treasury Secretary Kimmitt told Byrd, "We have a difference of opinion on the interpretation of your amendment," since the administration sees it "as being discretionary." Sen. Hillary Rodham Clinton, D-N.Y., read the law to Kimmitt, saying it "requires—requires—an investigation," to which Kimmitt replied, "We do not see it as mandatory . . . we didn't ignore the law. We might interpret it differently."[83]

On February 24 DP World, convinced that its offer to segregate its U.S. port operations was not settling the furor, embarked on an effort to work with congressional leaders to salvage the deal. Republican congressional leaders hoped to avoid legislative action to block the deal, but they feared giving the Democrats a campaign issue. In talks over February 24 and 25 with congressional leaders, including Senator Frist, DP World worked out an agreement by which it would "voluntarily" request that the Bush administration perform the more extensive, 45-day investigation and leaders in Congress would delay any vote to scuttle the deal until after the review. One individual involved with the talks commented, "Everybody needed a way to get off this train, and this seemed to be the best one."[84]

On February 26, DP World officially asked the Bush administration to undertake "the full 45-day investigation authorized under U.S. law," which would allow Bush to have the final decision. In response the Treasury Department, for the Bush administration, "welcomed" the action. Leading deal critics expressed caution and reserve. Senator Schumer desired an agreement in which Congress would have "the right of disapproval," and Representative King said, "I'm keeping [congressional approval of the deal] in reserve." Still, National Security Advisor Stephen Hadley said that the investigation was intended to reassure Americans, rather than truly investigate the deal, since Bush "thinks there are no outstanding security concerns."[85] White House Press Secretary McClellan, praised the "middle ground" the agreement had reached, said, "We believe the additional time and investigation at the request of the company will provide Congress with a better understanding of the facts, and that Congress will be comfortable with the transaction moved forward once it does."[86]

Spin Out: The Coast Guard Report to the House Vote Announcement, February 27 to March 7

Any optimism that the 45-day investigation would salvage the deal evaporated the next day, when on February 27 the Senate Homeland Security and

Governmental Affairs Committee released a December 13 Coast Guard intelligence assessment. The report stated, "There are many intelligence gaps, concerning the potential for DPW or P&O assets to support terrorist operations" that prevent a thorough evaluation of the deal, and "the breadth of the intelligence gaps also . . . [suggests] potential unknown threats against a large number of potential vulnerabilities." The Coast Guard attempted to minimize the concerns, saying that the preliminary evaluations "when taken out of context, do not reflect the full, classified analysis," which found that the deal "does not pose a significant threat to U.S. assets in ports." Assistant Secretary of the Treasury Clay Lowry said that the worries noted in the report "were addressed and resolved," but bipartisan congressional opposition accelerated with the report's release. Sen. Robert Menendez, D-N.J., exclaimed, "Since the president won't act to keep our ports safe, we will." Representative Foley added, "We have tried our best to support this administration at every turn, but to be blindsided by an issue of this magnitude demonstrates we have a lot of work to do."[87]

By March 1, congressional opposition had risen to a fever pitch, with bipartisan calls for an option for Congress to reject the deal at the end of the 45-day review. In the House, Representative King commented, "I think an investigation is clearly warranted, and Congress must stand ready to act pending the results of the investigation." In the Senate, Senator Schumer claimed bipartisan support for a move to give Congress "the right of disapproval" and indicated "we will seek a vote . . . to require it to happen."[88]

On March 2, a newspaper report that another Dubai company's (Dubai International Capital) purchase of an American company (Doncasters Groups Ltd., which made military parts) had triggered a 45-day review further aggravated the situation. Some wondered why there was a 45-day investigation for one deal but not the other, while still others complained that they heard about the purchase in the newspaper.[89] The UAE's support for the Arab boycott of Israel became another argument against DP World, as forty-one House Democrats wrote a letter to Bush indicating "deep concerns," and Republican Clay Shaw, Fla., added, "It certainly doesn't do them any good to have that boycott in place if they're trying to win favor with the United States."[90]

Legislative action on March 7 made the deal's demise inevitable. After a meeting of the House Republican leadership, Speaker Hastert endorsed an effort to block it. His spokesman, Ron Bonjean, said, "We do not believe the United States should allow a government-owned company to operate American ports." Chairman of the House Appropriations Committee Rep. Jerry Lewis, R-Calif., said that he would attach an amendment stopping the deal to a bill funding the Iraq conflict and Hurricane Katrina recovery. Republican leaders realized that should they fail to act, the Democrats would likely move in their stead and seize an important electoral advantage. House Majority Leader John A. Boehner, R-Ohio, observed, "This is a very big political problem. It is pretty clear to me that the House is going to speak on this sooner rather than later."[91] Representative King reported that he had counted a veto-proof 290 House members in favor of preventing DP World from taking over the American ports. Rep. Don Manzullo concluded that the deal was irrecoverable: "This duck is dead. Either the president finds a way to kill it or we'll have to ourselves. There is no out on this."[92]

DP World and the administration still expressed confidence in the face of the mounting opposition. White House spokesperson Dana Perino said, "There are a lot of conversations that are ongoing between the company and Congress and the administration and Congress."[93] Perino likely hinted at negotiations between DP World and Senators Frist, Warner, and Pete Domenici, R-N.M. As the deal's political support evaporated in the House, DP World proposed a series of actions to allay security concerns, such as giving DHS nearly total control over its U.S. operations, and pledged to install state-of-the-art radiation detectors and gamma-ray inspection machines at all current and future DP World ports at its expense (costing potentially $100 million). Events moved too quickly, and the offer did not become public until after the deal had collapsed. Noted Senator Frist's chief of staff, Eric Ueland, the offer "just came too late."[94]

Crash and Burn: The House Appropriations Vote and the DP World Pullout, March 8 and 9

On March 8, the House Appropriations Committee overwhelmingly approved Representative Lewis's amendment prohibiting the DP World deal in a bipartisan vote of 62–2.[95] Speaker Hastert endorsed the action, saying, "We will continue to use our best judgment on how to protect the American people." In the Senate, Schumer proposed a surprise amendment to a lobbying bill to ban the DP World deal, but Senate Republican leaders blocked a vote.[96] Public opinion seemed to drive the continued pressure. Rep. Deborah Pryce, R-Ohio, explained, "My phones are ringing off the hook every day. There's a strong feeling this was mishandled from the beginning." She reported the calls ran a hundred to one against DP World.[97] At this point, Senators Frist and Warner informed DP World that the company would be better served by selling off the U.S. holdings.[98]

With further congressional action barring the deal looking increasingly likely, top Republicans met with President Bush in the Oval Office on March 9 and told him the deal would fail. A person at the meeting said, "All we knew was that everyone was telling the company that this wasn't going to work as a matter of political reality." Senator Frist told Bush that he could only hold off a Senate vote for a few days while the full House was scheduled to vote the next week. Frist and Hastert told Bush that enough votes existed in both bodies to override his veto. One individual at the meeting characterized Bush's thinking, saying, "It was a tactical discussion at that point. Look, the president didn't fall off a turnip truck. He understood political reality." After the meeting Bush contacted Dubai, asking that it sell off the American port operations. After DP World decided to pull out of the deal, Senator Warner read a statement from the company that it would "transfer" the U.S. operations to "a U.S. entity." Afterward, Representative King described the White House officials he talked to later that day as "relieved."[99] One administration official said, "This was clearly not a business decision made by DP World. It was a strategic decision made by the UAE to avoid further damage." Said a senior Dubai official, "A political decision was taken to ask DP World to try to defuse the situation. We have to help our friends."[100]

Aftermath

Although the DP World controversy itself lasted only three weeks, its effects continue to today. On March 15, 2006, DP World clarified that it would be selling the U.S. port operations to "an unrelated U.S. buyer" after some questioned whether the ports would remain at least partially under DP World's control.[101] DP World agreed to sell its U.S. holdings to the insurance company American Investment Group in a deal that, when finalized on March 17, 2007, netted DP World a $400 million profit on the $1.2 billion sale.[102]

Right before the 2006 elections, the House, by a vote of 409–2, and the Senate on a voice vote passed the Safe Port Act, "to improve maritime and cargo security through enhanced layered defenses." It was signed into law by President Bush on October 13. The act requires radiation scanning of all containers at the top twenty-two ports in the United States by December 31, 2007, authorizes $443 million for CSI and $212 million for C-TPAT, orders DHS to develop a post-attack response and recovery plan in case the ports are attacked, sets deadlines for port worker identification and screening, and authorizes $2 billion in port security grants for 2007–2012. Speaking of the legislation, Representative King said, "This truly is a milestone in our mission to better secure the homeland. The American people demanded that Congress enact tough, no-nonsense homeland security legislation, and that is exactly what we have done." On October 4, President Bush signed the appropriations bill for DHS for fiscal year 2007, which included $4.3 billion for port, container, and cargo security, an increase of $400 million (16 percent) over fiscal 2006.[103] On December 7, the U.S. government announced that scans of all U.S.-bound containers for nuclear and radiological material would begin at six foreign ports beginning in February 2007. This action would cover roughly 7 percent of the eleven million containers shipped to the United States each year.[104]

Progress came more slowly on the CFIUS reform front. Although both the House and Senate passed legislation in 2006 reforming the system and giving Congress a larger role, agreement on differences between the bills could not be reached before the session ended. On its own, the Treasury Department gave the director of national intelligence a greater role in CFIUS reviews by having the director provide a report on each transaction; it also improved the congressional notification process. On February 28, 2007, the House passed, 423–0, a new version of CFIUS reform (H.R. 556) that establishes the organization in law, makes the national intelligence director a formal part of the process, designates the secretaries of commerce and homeland security as CFIUS vice chairs, requires a 45-day investigation for all transactions involving foreign governments, and expands the category of deals that might come under review to ones dealing with homeland security and critical infrastructure. The business community and the Bush administration supported the bill.[105] On June 29, 2007, the Senate passed the House CFIUS reform bill by unanimous consent. President Bush signed the bill into law on July 26.

CFIUS reviews have become more numerous and extensive. A January 2007 analysis by the National Foundation for American Policy concluded that "the process for securing approvals within CFIUS has grown more difficult for foreign investors, adding to uncertainty and increasing the regulatory risk associated with certain foreign acquisitions. Such uncertainty could inhibit investment in the United States. Reviews are taking longer, costs for companies have increased and CFIUS-imposed conditions are tougher." It reported that "in 2006, there were 113 filings (up 73 percent over 2005), seven second-stage (45-day) investigations (up 250 percent), and five withdrawals (up 150 percent) during the second-stage investigation period." In addition, CFIUS required more national security mitigation agreements (15 in 2006 compared to 13 in 2003– 2005).[106]

As the debate over the DP World deal and the U.S. government's response gripped the nation for a few weeks, it served to enhance the visibility of the port security problem, at least for a short time. It remains to be seen whether the government's response will result in safer port operations and prevent the type of radiological attack described at the beginning of this case, while ensuring the essential flow of goods and capital into the U.S. economy.

Key Actors

Edward H. Bilkey DP World chief operating officer. A well-respected American in the international shipping industry, he followed the CFIUS process but did not anticipate the negative political backlash in the United States.

George W. Bush President, favored the deal; did not see a national security threat; feared the UAE might reduce its cooperation in the war on terror if the deal were canceled; concerned that the controversy would reduce foreign direct investment in the United States.

Stephen E. Flynn Port security expert at the Council on Foreign Relations and former U.S. Coast Guard commander; thought that while port security needed significant improvement the deal did not threaten national security.

William (Bill) H. Frist Senate majority leader, R-Tenn., and potential 2008 presidential candidate; attempted to broker compromises to save the deal, but his early statement of opposition legitimized Republican opposition.

Peter T. King House member, R-N.Y.; leading deal opponent who saw the issue primarily in national security terms.

Charles E. Schumer Senator, D-N.Y., chair of the Democratic Senatorial Campaign Committee; opposed the deal and led the effort to publicize the DP World issue. He saw both a national security threat and a political opportunity to attack the Bush administration.

Notes

1. David E. Sanger, "Big Problem, Deal or Not," *New York Times,* February 23, 2006, A1.

2. *Lou Dobbs Tonight,* CNN, February 13, 2006, transcript 021301CN.V19 (accessed through Lexis-Nexis Academic).

3. John Cranford, "Defining 'Ours' in a New World," *CQ Weekly,* March 6, 2006, 592.

4. Scenario adapted from Stephen E. Flynn, "The DP World Controversy and the Ongoing Vulnerability of U.S. Seaports," remarks prepared for the House Armed Services Committee, March 2, 2006, www.cfr.org/publication/9998/. The $58 billion figure for a temporary slowdown comes from a simulation run by consulting firm Booz Allen Hamilton, www.boozallen.com/publications/article/1440496.

5. Ted Bridis, "UAE Co. Poised to Oversee Six U.S. Ports," Associated Press Online, February 11, 2006; "Port Insecurity," *New York Post,* February 14, 2006, 26.

6. Jason Singer, "P&O Attracts Buyout Overture amid Shipping-Industry Boom," *Wall Street Journal,* October 31, 2005, A3; Heather Timmons, "Dubai to Buy P&O, British Shipping Line, for $5.7 Billion," *New York Times,* November 30, 2005, C5.

7. Edward M. Graham and David M. Marchick, *U.S. National Security and Foreign Direct Investment* (Washington, D.C.: Institute for International Economics, 2006), 137; Jason Singer, "Dubai Ports World Is Close to Pact to Buy P&O for Over $5 Billion," *Wall Street Journal,* November 29, 2005, C5; Timmons, "Dubai to Buy P&O."

8. Dana Hedgpeth and Neil Irwin, "At Port of Baltimore, Debate Hits the Docks," *Washington Post,* February 26, 2006, A1.

9. Ibid.

10. This discussion is largely derived from Christian Caryl, "The Box Is King," *Newsweek International,* April 10, 2006 (accessed through Lexis-Nexis Academic).

11. Laura Meckler and Daniel Machalaba, "Port Deal: Not a Foreign Idea," *Wall Street Journal,* March 9, 2006, B1.

12. Hedgpeth and Irwin, "At Port of Baltimore"; Patrick McGeehan, "Work at Terminals Untouched by Firestorm of Security Debate," *New York Times,* February 23, 2006, A18.

13. Hedgpeth and Irwin, "At Port of Baltimore."

14. Alan Cowell and Heather Timmons, "Britain, the Continent and the Issue of Foreign Ownership," *New York Times,* December 1, 2005, C6; Singer, "Dubai Ports World Is Close to Pact"; Timmons, "Dubai to Buy P&O."

15. Bill Spindle, Neil King Jr., and Glenn Simpson, "Political Gulf: In Ports Furor, a Clash over Dubai," *Wall Street Journal,* February 23, 2006, A1.

16. Sources for the UAE, Dubai, and DP World background are Carl Hulse and Heather Timmons, "Lawmakers Plan for New Security Reviews," *New York Times,* March 3, 2006, A16; Spindle, King, and Simpson, "Political Gulf"; and Timmons, "Dubai to Buy P&O."

17. Graham and Marchick, *U.S. National Security and Foreign Direct Investment,* 2.

18. Edward M. Graham and Paul R. Krugman, *Foreign Direct Investment in the United States* (Washington, D.C.: Institute for International Economics, 1994); Graham and Marchick, *U.S. National Security and Foreign Direct Investment.*

19. For a history of FDI in the United States, see Graham and Marchick, *U.S. National Security and Foreign Direct Investment,* 2–32.

20. Ibid., 76–78.

21. Bureau of Economic Analysis, press release, March 14, 2006, www.bea.gov/newsreleases/international/transactions/2005/trans405.pdf; Organization for International Investment, "2005 Foreign Direct Investment Analysis," http://ofii.org/fdi.doc.

22. Graham and Marchick, *U.S. National Security and Foreign Direct Investment,* 33.

23. Elisabeth Bumiller and Carl Hulse, "Panel Saw No Security Issue in Port Contract, Officials Say," *New York Times,* February 23, 2006, A1; U.S. Government Accountability Office, "Defense Trade," GAO Report GAO-05-686, September 2005, www.gao.gov/new.items/d05686.pdf.

24. Michael Schroeder and Greg Hitt, "Congress May Fine-Tune Process to Vet Foreign-Investment Deals," *Wall Street Journal,* February 23, 2006, 12. This section relies on Committee on Foreign Investments in the United States (CFIUS), Office of International Affairs, U.S. Department of the Treasury, www.ustreas.gov/offices/international

affairs/exon-florio/, and Graham and Marchick, *U.S. National Security and Foreign Direct Investment,* 20–21, 34–40, 54–58.

25. Jim VandeHei and Paul Blustein, "Bush's Response to the Ports Deal Faulted as Tardy," *Washington Post,* February 26, 2006, A5.

26. Graham and Marchick, *U.S. National Security and Foreign Direct Investment,* 138; VandeHei and Blustein, "Bush's Response to the Ports Deal Faulted as Tardy."

27. "Dubai: Business Partner or Terrorist Hotbed?" *Wall Street Journal,* February 25, 2006, A9; Graham and Marchick, *U.S. National Security and Foreign Direct Investment,* 138; VandeHei and Blustein, "Bush's Response to the Ports Deal Faulted."

28. Greg Hitt and Sarah Ellison, "Abandon Ship: Dubai Firm Bows to Public Outcry," *Wall Street Journal,* March 10, 2006, A1; Neil King Jr. and Greg Hitt, "Small Florida Firm Sowed Seed of Port Dispute," *Wall Street Journal,* February 28 2006, A3, Richard Wolffe and Holly Bailey, "No Safe Harbor Here," *Newsweek,* March 6, 2006, 28. In addition to lobbying, Eller pursued legal cases in both the United Kingdom and United States to no avail.

29. Bridis, "UAE Co. Poised to Oversee."

30. Ted Bridis, "United Arab Emirates Firm May Oversee 6 U.S. Ports," *Washington Post,* February 12, 2006, A17; Wolffe and Bailey, "No Safe Harbor," 28.

31. Hit and Ellison, "Abandon Ship."

32. Sheryl Gay Stolberg, "How a Business Deal Became a Big Liability for Republicans in Congress," *New York Times,* February 27, 2006, A14.

33. Wolffe and Bailey, "No Safe Harbor," 28.

34. *Lou Dobbs Tonight,* February 13, 2006.

35. Stolberg, "How a Business Deal."

36. VandeHei and Blustein, "Bush's Response to the Ports Deal Faulted," A5.

37. "White House Is Urged to Review Dubai Deal," *Wall Street Journal,* February 16, 2006, A1; Wolffe and Bailey, "No Safe Harbor," 28.

38. Stolberg, "How a Business Deal."

39. "Macho Moms and Deadbeat Dads, the Politics of National Security," *The Economist,* March 11, 2006, 50.

40. Gloria Borger, "Trust Me? Yeah, Right," *U.S. News & World Report,* March 13, 2006, 37.

41. Stolberg, "How a Business Deal"; David S. Broder, "Republican Breakdown," *Washington Post,* March 10, 2006, A19.

42. Robert Block, "Security Gaps Already Plague Ports," *Wall Street Journal,* February 23, 2006, A12.

43. See the organization's Web site at www.imo.org.

44. Information on the port security section comes from U.S. Government Accountability Office, "Maritime Security," GAO Report GAO-05-448T, May 17, 2005, www.gao.gov/new.items/d05448t.pdf; Block, "Security Gaps Already Plague Ports," 12; Hassan M. Fattah and Eric Lipton, "Gaps in Security Stretch All along the Way from Model Port in Dubai to U.S.," *New York Times,* February 26, 2006, A26; David E. Kaplan, Alex Kingsbury, and Angie C. Marek, "The Ports in the Storm," *U.S. News & World Report,* March 6, 2006, 32, 35; Art Pine, "Port Protection Looks Overseas," *National Journal,* March 11, 2006.

45. Pine, "Port Protection Looks Overseas."

46. Fattah and Lipton, "Gaps in Security Stretch All along the Way"; Kaplan, Kingsbury, and Marek, "The Ports in the Storm," 35.

47. Fattah and Lipton, "Gaps in Security Stretch All along the Way."

48. "Terrorist Fears Spark Opposition to DP-P&O Deal," *Journal of Commerce Online,* February 16, 2006 (accessed through Lexis-Nexis Academic).

49. Hitt and Ellison, "Abandon Ship."

50. Paul Blustein, "Some in Congress Object to Arab Port Operator," *Washington Post,* February 17, 2006, A11.

51. VandeHei and Blustein, "Bush's Response to the Ports Deal Faulted."

52. Blustein, "Some in Congress Object."

53. Patrick McGeehan, "Despite Fears, a Dubai Company Will Help Run Ports in New York," *New York Times,* February 17, 2006, B1.

54. VandeHei and Blustein, "Bush's Response to the Ports Deal Faulted."

55. Ted Bridis, "Miami Partner Sues to Block Ports Takeover by Arab Company," Associate Press Wire Report, February 19, 2006 (accessed through Lexis-Nexis Academic).

56. Bumiller and Hulse, "Panel Saw No Security Issue"; Greg Hitt, Dennis K. Berman, and Daniel Machalaba, "Bush, Congress Head for Clash over Ports Deal," *Wall Street Journal,* February 22, 2006, A1.

57. David D. Kirkpatrick and Patrick McGeehan, "Pataki Joins Opposition to Takeover of Ports," *New York Times,* February 21, 2006, B3; Stolberg, "How a Business Deal."

58. Will Lester, "Lawmakers Deride Assurances on Arab Port Firm," *Washington Post,* February 20, 2006, A7.

59. Hitt and Ellison, "Abandon Ship"; David E. Sanger and Eric Lipton, "Bush Would Veto Any Bill Halting Dubai Port Deal," *New York Times,* February 22, 2006, A1.

60. Tim Starks, "Ports Deal on Hold," *CQ Weekly,* February 27, 2006, 550.

61. Craig Crawford, "Standing Firm on Shaky Ground," *CQ Weekly,* February 27, 2006, 562; Hitt, Berman, and Machalaba, "Bush, Congress Head for Clash," Sanger and Lipton, "Bush Would Veto."

62. Bumiller and Hulse, "Panel Saw No Security Issue"; Wolffe and Bailey, "No Safe Harbor."

63. Hitt, Berman, and Machalaba, "Bush, Congress, Head for Clash."

64. Paul Blustein and Eric Rich, "Security Programs, Union Would Stay at Ports," *Washington Post,* February 22, 2006, D1; Hitt, Berman, and Machalaba, "Bush, Congress Head for Clash"; Sanger and Lipton, "Bush Would Veto."

65. "Don't Scuttle Common Sense in Ports of Squall," *Chicago Sun-Times,* February 23, 2006, A39; "Port Hysteria," *Los Angeles Times,* February 22, 2006, B14; "Port Security Humbug," *Washington Post,* February 22, 2006, A14; "Ports of Politics," *Wall Street Journal,* February 22, 2006, A14.

66. "The Wrong Way to Guard the Ports," *New York Times,* February 16, 2006, A32.

67. David Brooks, "Kicking Arabs in the Teeth," *New York Times,* February 23, 2006, A27; Maureen Dowd, "G.O.P. to W: You're Nuts!" *New York Times,* February 22, 2006, A19; David Ignatius, "Taste of the Future," *Washington Post,* February 24, 2006, A15.

68. C. Fred Bergsten, "Avoiding Another Dubai," *Washington Post,* February 28, 2006, A15; Clark Kent Ervin, "Strangers at the Door," *New York Times,* February 23, 2006, A27.

69. Michael Schroeder and Greg Hitt, "Congress May Fine-Tune Process to Vet Foreign-Investment Deals," *Wall Street Journal,* February 23, 2006, A12; "U.S. Chamber Urges Caution as Debate over Port Deal Escalates," U.S. Chamber of Commerce press release, March 9, 2006, www.uschamber.com/press/releases/2006/march/06-44.htm.

70. Hitt and Ellison, "Abandon Ship."

71. "Dubai Ports Fallout," March 15, 2006, Pew Research Center, www.people-press.org.

72. "President Bush, the Ports, and Iraq," CBS News, February 27, 2006, www.cbsnews.com/htdocs/pdf/poll_bush_022706.pdf; *Washington Post*/ABC News Poll, March 6, 2006, www.washingtonpost.com/wp-dyn/content/politics/polls/; CNN/*USA Today*/Gallup Poll, March 2, 2006, http://i.a.cnn.net/cnn/2006/images/03/02/rel7a.pdf.

73. Hitt and Ellison, "Abandon Ship."

74. Jim VandeHei and Jonathan Weisman, "Republicans Split with Bush on Ports," *Washington Post*, February 23, 2006, A1.

75. Paul Blustein, "Ports Debate Reawakens Foreign-Investment Jitters," *Washington Post*, February 23, 2006, D1.

76. Ben White, "Uproar Surprised Dubai Firm," *Washington Post*, February 24, 2006, D1.

77. Kaplan, Kingsbury, and Marek, "The Ports in the Storm," 32; VandeHei and Weisman, "Republicans Split with Bush on Ports."

78. David S. Cloud and David E. Sanger, "Dubai Company Delays New Role at Six U.S. Ports," *New York Times*, February 24, 2006, A1; Greg Hitt, "Dubai Firm Seeks to Calm Furor over U.S. Ports," *Wall Street Journal*, February 24, 2006, A3.

79. White, "Uproar Surprised Dubai Firm."

80. Hitt, "Dubai Firm Seeks to Calm Furor."

81. David S. Cloud, "U.S. Sees Emirates as Both Ally and, since 9/11, a Foe," *New York Times*, February 23, 2006, A19.

82. Starks, "Ports Deal on Hold."

83. Dana Milbank, "Ports and a Storm," *Washington Post*, February 24, 2006, A2.

84. David S. Cloud and David E. Sanger, "Action on Port Deal Fails to Sway Critics," *New York Times*, February 25, 2006, A10; David E. Sanger, "Dubai Expected to Ask for Review of Port Deal," *New York Times*, February 26, 2006, A1.

85. David E. Sanger, "Dubai Deal Will Undergo Deeper Inquiry into Security," *New York Times*, February 27, 2006, A15.

86. Greg Hitt, "White House Agrees to Re-Examine Ports Deal," *Wall Street Journal*, February 27, 2006, A2; Jonathan Weisman, "Port Deal to Have Broader Review," *Washington Post*, February 27, 2006, A1.

87. Jonathan Weisman, "Coast Guard Saw 'Intelligence Gaps' on Ports," *Washington Post*, February 28, 2006, A4.

88. Paul Blustein, "Many in Congress Insist on Chance to Scuttle Ports Deal," *Washington Post*, March 2, 2006, A7.

89. Hulse and Timmons, "Lawmakers Plan for New Security Reviews."

90. Greg Hitt and King Neil Jr., "U.S. Opponents of Ports Takeover Cite Arab Boycott of Israel as Issue," *Wall Street Journal*, March 4, 2006, A4.

91. Carl Hulse, "G.O.P. Leaders Vowing to Block Ports Agreement," *New York Times*, March 8, 2006, A1.

92. Greg Hitt, "Push to Unwind Ports Deal Builds within Congress," *Wall Street Journal*, March 8, 2006, A4.

93. Hulse, "G.O.P. Leaders Vowing to Block Ports Agreement."

94. Neil King Jr., "DP World Tried to Soothe U.S. Waters," *Wall Street Journal*, March 14, 2006, A4.

95. Carl Hulse, "In Break with White House, House Panel Rejects Port Deal," *New York Times,* March 9, 2006, A20.

96. Carl Hulse, "A Rebellion in the G.O.P.," *New York Times,* March 9, 2006, A1.

97. Greg Hitt and Greg Jaffe, "Vote in Congress Boosts Opponents of U.S. Ports Deal," *Wall Street Journal,* March 9, 2006, A1.

98. Jonathan Weisman and Bradley Graham, "Dubai Firm to Sell U.S. Port Operations," *Washington Post,* March 10, 2006, A1.

99. Greg Hitt and Neil King Jr., "Dubai Firm Bows to Public Outcry," *Wall Street Journal* March 10, 2006, A1; King, "DP World Tried to Soothe U.S. Waters"; David D. Kirkpatrick, "How the Clock Ran Out on the Dubai Ports Deal," *New York Times,* March 10, 2006, A18; David E. Sanger, "Under Pressure, Dubai Company Drops Port Deal," *New York Times,* March 10, 2006, A1; Tim Starks, "Ports Deal Falls to Bipartisan Attack," *CQ Weekly,* March 13, 2006, 696.

100. Sanger, "Under Pressure, Dubai Company Drops Port Deal."

101. Paul Blustein, "Ports Deal Expected within 6 Months," *Washington Post,* March 6, 2006, D6.

102. "DP World Closes U.S. Ports Sale," *Wall Street Journal,* March 17, 2007; Heather Timmons, "Dubai Port Company Sells Its U.S. Holdings to A.I.G.," *New York Times,* December 12, 2006, C4.

103. Jonathan Weisman, "Internet Gambling, Ports Deals Reached," *Washington Post,* September 30, 2006, A8; Kathryn A. Wolfe, "Highlights of the Port Security Measure," *CQ Weekly,* October 9, 2006, 2708; Kathryn A. Wolfe, "Port Security Bill Includes Rider Targeting Internet Gambling," *CQ Weekly,* October 2, 2006, 2636; Kathryn A. Wolfe, "Port Security Legislation Clears," *CQ Weekly,* October 9, 2006, 2708; Patrick Yoest, "2006 Legislative Summary: Homeland Security Appropriations," *CQ Weekly,* December 18, 2006, 3333.

104. Spencer S. Hsu, "U.S.-Bound Cargo to Be Screened at Six Ports," *Washington Post,* December 8, 2006, A8.

105. Jim Abrams, "Bill on Foreign Investment Advances," *Washington Post,* March 1, 2007, D3; Neil King Jr. and Greg Hitt, "Dubai Ports World Sells U.S. Assets," *Wall Street Journal,* December 12, 2006, A2; Victoria McGrane, "2006 Legislative Summary: Foreign Investment Review," *CQ Weekly,* December 18, 2006, 3349; Victoria McGrane, "House OKs Foreign Investment Rewrite," *CQ Weekly,* March 5, 2007, 665.

106. David Marchick, "Swinging the Pendulum Too Far: An Analysis of the CFIUS Process Post-Dubai Ports World," National Foundation for American Policy, NFAP Policy Brief, January 2007, www.ofii.org/nfap.cfius.Brief.07.pdf.

7 NSA Eavesdropping: Unchecked or Limited Presidential Power?

Louis Fisher

Before You Begin

1. How does the Constitution balance the needs of national security against the rights and liberties of the individual?
2. In the field of national security, does the president possess "inherent" powers that are immune from legislative and judicial controls?
3. Which principles should guide government in balancing the need for national security wiretaps against the constitutional right of privacy?
4. If Congress legislates in the area of foreign intelligence surveillance and selects a procedure that is "exclusive," can the president ignore the statutory command?
5. Is it sufficient for the president to notify eight lawmakers and have them briefed about national security wiretaps conducted without a judicial warrant?
6. What role should federal courts play in supervising and approving national security wiretaps?

Introduction

On December 16, 2005, the *New York Times* reported that in the months following the September 11 terrorist attacks, President Bush secretly authorized the National Security Agency (NSA) to listen to international calls involving Americans and others inside the United States without a court-approved warrant. The agency had been monitoring international telephone calls and international e-mail messages over the past three years in an effort to obtain evidence about terrorist activity.[1]

NSA's statutory purpose, however, was to spy on communications abroad, not on American citizens or domestic activities. During the Nixon administration, it had crossed the line by engaging in domestic surveillance. After September 11, NSA violated the Foreign Intelligence Surveillance Act (FISA) of

Note: The views expressed here are those of the author and do not represent any government agency.

1978, which requires the executive branch to seek warrants from the FISA court to engage in surveillance in the United States. It raised the fundamental issue of whether the administration could violate statutory restrictions (FISA) by invoking "inherent" powers available to the president under Article II of the Constitution or even claim extraconstitutional powers.

Background: Previous Illegal NSA Activities

In 1967, when the U.S. Army wanted the NSA to eavesdrop on American citizens and domestic groups, the agency agreed to carry out the assignment. NSA began to put together a list of names of opponents of the Vietnam War. Adding names to a domestic "watch list" led to the creation of Minaret—a tracking system that allowed the agency to follow individuals and organizations involved in the antiwar movement.[2] NSA was now involved in a mission outside its statutory duties, using its surveillance powers to violate the First and Fourth Amendments.

On June 5, 1970, President Nixon met with the heads of several intelligence agencies, including the NSA, to initiate a program designed to monitor what the administration considered radical individuals and groups in the United States. Joining others at the meeting was Tom Charles Huston, a young attorney working at the White House. He drafted a forty-three-page, top secret memorandum that became known as the Huston Plan. Huston put the matter bluntly to President Nixon: "Use of this technique is clearly illegal; it amounts to burglary."[3] His plan required the NSA to use its technological capacity to intercept—without judicial warrants—the communication of U.S. citizens using international phone calls or telegrams.[4] Although Nixon, under pressure from FBI Director J. Edgar Hoover, withdrew the Huston Plan, the NSA had been targeting domestic groups for several years and continued to do so. Huston's blueprint, kept in a White House safe, became public in 1973, after Congress investigated the Watergate affair, and provided documentary evidence that Nixon had ordered NSA to illegally monitor American citizens. To conduct its surveillance operations, NSA entered into agreements with U.S. companies, including Western Union and RCA Global. U.S. citizens, expecting that their telegrams would be handled with utmost privacy, learned that American companies had been turning over the telegrams to the NSA.[5]

After the disclosure of the illegal NSA activities by the Church Committee, the agency supposedly underwent a sea change in attitude toward the statutory and constitutional issues and vowed to remain within the bounds of U.S. law.[6]

Timeline

October 25, 1978 Congress enacts the Foreign Intelligence Surveillance Act (FISA) to authorize and control national security surveillance.

September 11, 2001 Terrorists attack the United States, after which President Bush authorizes warrantless national security surveillance (called the Terrorist Surveillance Program, or TSP).

December 16, 2005 The *New York Times* breaks the story on the existence of TSP.

July 20, 2006 A federal district judge in California denies the government's motion to have a case dismissed that challenges the TSP.

July 25, 2006 A federal district judge in Illinois dismissed a lawsuit against a Bush administration program that involved the collection and monitoring of phone numbers.

August 17, 2006 A federal district judge in Michigan rules that the TSP violated the Constitution and federal statutes.

May 1, 2007 In congressional testimony, the director of national intelligence, Michael McConnell, appears to revive the administration's reliance on inherent powers after it had announced, earlier in the year, that it would abide by FISA.

Whatever lessons the agency learned in the 1970s were forgotten or subordinated decades later, especially in the period after September 11.

Establishing Limits on Wiretaps

Presidential authority to engage in eavesdropping for national security purposes without obtaining a warrant from a judge had never been properly clarified by statute or by judicial rulings. In this legal vacuum, presidents often expanded their powers in time of emergency. On May 21, 1940, on the eve of World War II, President Franklin D. Roosevelt sent a confidential memo to his attorney general, Robert H. Jackson, authorizing and directing him to obtain information "by listening devices" to monitor the conversations or other communications "of persons suspected of subversive activities against the Government of the United States, including suspected spies." Roosevelt told Jackson to limit these investigations "to a minimum and to limit them in so far as possible to aliens."[7]

In the landmark case of *Olmstead v. United States* (1928), the Supreme Court decided that the use of wiretaps by federal agents enforcing prohibition to monitor and intercept phone calls did not violate the Constitution. The Court reasoned that the taps—small wires inserted in telephone wires leading from residences—did not enter the premises of the home or office. Without physical entry there was neither "search" nor "seizure" under the Fourth Amendment.[8] This strained analysis drew a scathing dissent from Justice Louis Brandeis, who accurately predicted that technology would soon overwhelm the Fourth Amendment unless the Court met the challenge with open eyes.

Over the next few decades, federal courts wrestled with new forms of technological intrusion, ranging from "detectaphones" (placing an instrument against the wall of a room to pick up sound waves on the other side of the wall) to placing concealed microphones inside homes. Other variations of electronic eavesdropping blossomed. Police used "spike mikes," small electronic listening devices pushed through the wall of an adjoining house until they touched the heating duct of a suspect's dwelling. Law enforcement officers with earphones could listen to conversations taking place on both floors of the house.[9]

In 1967, the Supreme Court put a halt to these practices by returning to basic principles. By a 7–1 decision, it declared unconstitutional the placing of electronic listening and recording devices on the outside of public telephone booths to obtain incriminating evidence. Although there was no physical entrance into the area occupied by the suspect, the Court ruled that the individual had a legitimate expectation of privacy within the phone booth. In a decision broad enough to accommodate technological advances, the Court held that the Fourth Amendment "protects people, not places."[10] In response to this decision, Congress passed legislation in 1968 requiring law enforcement officers to obtain a judicial warrant before placing taps on phones or installing bugs (concealed microphones). If an "emergency" existed, communications could be intercepted for up to forty-eight hours without a warrant, in cases involving organized crime or national security. This legislation on wiretaps and electronic surveillance is often referred to as "Title III authority."

The 1968 statute established national policy on domestic wiretaps. The executive branch claimed that warrantless surveillances for national security purposes were lawful as a reasonable exercise of presidential power. A section of Title III stated that nothing in it limited the president's constitutional power to "take such measures as he deems necessary to protect the Nation against actual or potential attack or other hostile acts of a foreign power, to obtain foreign intelligence information deemed essential to the security of the United States, or to protect national security information against foreign intelligence activities." Nor should anything in Title III "be deemed to limit the constitutional power of the President to take such measures as he deems necessary to protect the United States against the overthrow of the Government by force or other unlawful means, or against any other clear and present danger to the structure or existence of the Government."[11] Congress, feeling an obligation to say something, chose general language to largely duck the issue. It would soon find it necessary to reenter the field and pass comprehensive legislation on national security surveillance.

What pushed Congress to act was a Supreme Court decision in 1972, which held that the Fourth Amendment required prior judicial approval for surveillances of domestic organizations.[12] The Court carefully avoided the question of surveillances over foreign powers, whether within or outside the United States. As to the language in Title III about national security wiretaps, the Court regarded that section as merely disclaiming congressional intent to define presidential powers in matters affecting national security and not to be taken as authorization for national security surveillances.

The FISA Statute

It was now necessary for Congress to pass legislation governing national security wiretaps. In 1973, in announcing a joint investigation by three Senate subcommittees, the lawmakers taking the lead explained, "Wiretapping and electronic surveillance pose a greater threat to the constitutional rights of American citizens than ever before. A recent survey of public attitudes shows that 75 percent of the American people feel that 'wiretapping and spying under the excuse of national security is a serious threat to people's privacy.'"[13] Extensive hearings were conducted to determine the procedures that would simultaneously protect security interests and individual rights. Legislation reported from the Senate Judiciary Committee in 1977 required the attorney general to obtain a judicial warrant authorizing the use of electronic surveillance in the United States for foreign intelligence purposes. Congress was filling a gaping hole. The federal government had never enacted legislation to regulate the use of electronic surveillance within the United States for foreign intelligence purposes, nor had the Supreme Court ever expressly decided the issue of whether the president had constitutional authority to authorize electronic surveillance without a warrant in cases concerning foreign intelligence.[14]

The bill enacted in 1978 was the Foreign Intelligence Surveillance Act. To provide a judicial check on executive actions, it created what is known as the FISA court. The chief justice of the United States would designate seven district court judges to hear applications for, and grant orders approving, electronic surveillance anywhere within the United States. After September 11, Congress increased the number of judges to eleven. No judge designated under this law "shall hear the same application for electronic surveillance under this Act which has been denied previously by another judge designated under this subsection." [15] The chief justice would also designate three judges from the district courts or appellate courts to make up a court of review with jurisdiction to review the denial of any application made under this statute.[16] Significantly, procedures under FISA "shall be the exclusive means by which electronic surveillance, as defined in section 101 of such Act, and the interception of domestic wire and oral communications may be conducted." [17]

The 1978 legislation required the government to certify that "the purpose" of the surveillance was to obtain foreign intelligence information. The USA Patriot Act of 2001 changed the requirements placed on federal officers when applying for a search order. The new language allowed application if a "significant purpose" was to obtain foreign intelligence information. The objective was to make it easier to obtain permission from the FISA court, not to bypass it altogether. Legislation after September 11 made other changes to FISA. Under the 1978 law, the attorney general could order emergency electronic surveillance without a warrant provided that he informed a judge having jurisdiction over national security wiretaps and obtained a warrant within twenty-four hours. Congress lengthened the emergency period to seventy-two hours in legislation reported by the Intelligence Committees.[18]

The Administration Responds to the Leak

The Bush administration could have chosen to say nothing about the leak in the *New York Times*; it could refuse either to acknowledge or deny the existence of the surveillance program. That approach is frequently used with leaks about other classified operations. In this case, the administration decided to have President Bush publicly defend the program as essential to the protection of U.S. security. One administration official explained that making the president the only voice "is directly taking on the critics. The Democrats are now in the position of supporting our efforts to protect Americans, or defend positions that could weaken our nation's security." [19] Sen. Patrick Leahy, ranking Democrat on the Judiciary Committee, responded to that tactic: "Our government must follow the laws and respect the Constitution while it protects Americans' security and liberty." [20]

During the operation of the NSA surveillance, the Bush administration offered to brief eight members of Congress and the chief judge of the FISA court.

The lawmakers (called the "Gang of Eight") included the chairs and ranking members of the two Intelligence Committees, the Speaker and minority leader of the House, and the Senate majority and minority leaders. Rep. Nancy Pelosi, Calif., at that time the Democratic leader in the House, acknowledged that she had been advised of the program shortly after it began and had "been provided with updates on several occasions."[21]

On December 17, 2005, in a weekly radio address, President George W. Bush defended what he called the Terrorist Surveillance Program (TSP). He acknowledged that he had authorized the NSA, "consistent with U.S. law and the Constitution, to intercept the international communications of people with known links to al Qaeda and related terrorist organizations."[22] His program was, in fact, inconsistent with, and in violation of, statutory law. Gradually it became clear that when President Bush referred to "U.S. law" or "authority," he meant law created within the executive branch, whether or not consistent with law passed by Congress. In his radio address, Bush underscored what he considered to be his independent constitutional powers: "The authorization I gave the National Security agency after September 11 helped address that problem [of combating terrorism] in a way that is fully consistent with my constitutional responsibilities and authorities."[23] He said he had "reauthorized this program more than 30 times since the September 11 attacks."[24] Bush expressed his determination to continue the program as "a vital tool in our war against the terrorists."[25]

In a news conference on December 19, Bush stated: "As President and Commander in Chief, I have the constitutional responsibility and the constitutional authority to protect our country. Article II of the Constitution gives me that responsibility and the authority necessary to fulfill it." He noted that Congress after September 11 had passed the Authorization for Use of Military Force (AUMF) to grant him "additional authority to use military force against Al Qaida."[26] Also on December 19, Attorney General Alberto Gonzales held a press briefing on the NSA program, claiming that "the President has the inherent authority under the Constitution, as Commander-in-Chief, to engage in this kind of activity."[27] When asked why the administration did not seek a warrant from the FISA court, which Congress created as the exclusive means of authorizing national security eavesdropping, Gonzales replied that the administration continued to seek warrants from the FISA court but was not "legally required" to do that in every case if another statute granted the president additional authority.[28] It was the administration's position that the AUMF provided that additional authority.

Gonzales emphasized the need for "the speed and the agility" that the FISA process lacked: "You have to remember that FISA was passed by the Congress in 1978. There have been tremendous advances in technology" since that time.[29] Why did the administration not ask Congress to amend FISA to grant the president greater flexibility, as was done several times after 1978 and even after September 11? Gonzales replied he was advised "that would be difficult, if not impossible."[30] Why not try and put the burden on Congress to pass legislation necessary for national security?

The Sole-Organ Doctrine

On January 19, 2006, the Office of Legal Counsel (OLC) in the Justice Department produced a forty-two-page white paper defending the legality of the NSA program. It concluded that the NSA activities

> are supported by the President's well-recognized inherent constitutional authority as Commander in Chief and sole organ for the Nation in foreign affairs to conduct warrantless surveillance of enemy forces for intelligence purposes to detect and disrupt armed attacks on the United States. The President has the chief responsibility under the Constitution to protect America from attack, and the Constitution gives the President the authority necessary to fulfill that solemn responsibility.[31]

Later in the paper, OLC linked "sole organ" to the 1936 Supreme Court decision of *United States v. Curtiss-Wright*.[32]

Nothing in the *Curtiss-Wright* decision supports exclusive, plenary, unchecked, inherent, or extraconstitutional powers for the president. The only question before the Court in that case was the constitutionality of Congress delegating part of its authority to the president to place an arms embargo in a region in South America. The case involved legislative power, not presidential power. In imposing the embargo, President Franklin D. Roosevelt relied solely on statutory—not constitutional—authority. His proclamation prohibiting the sale of arms and munitions to countries engaged in armed conflict in the Chaco region begins: "NOW, THEREFORE, I, FRANKLIN D. ROOSEVELT, President of the United States of America, acting under and by virtue of the authority conferred in me by the said joint resolution of Congress. . . ."[33] The issue in *Curtiss-Wright* was whether Congress could delegate legislative power more broadly in international affairs than it could in domestic affairs. In the previous year, the Court had struck down the delegation by Congress of domestic power to the president.[34] None of the briefs submitted to the Court in the *Curtiss-Wright* case discussed the availability of independent, inherent, or extraconstitutional powers to the president.[35]

Nevertheless, in his extensive dicta wholly extraneous to the legal issue before the Court, Justice Sutherland discussed the availability of inherent and extraconstitutional powers for the president in foreign affairs. His arguments draw from an article that Sutherland had published as a U.S. senator from Utah and from a book that he published in 1919. Sutherland's historical analysis has been dismissed as unreliable and erroneous by many scholars.[36] Sutherland's use of John Marshall's speech in 1800, referring to the president as "sole organ," is a glaring example of a statement made for one limited purpose taken wholly out of context to make the case for a proposition that Marshall never believed at any time in four decades of public life.

On March 7, 1800, in the House of Representatives, Marshall called the president "the sole organ of the nation in its external relations, and its sole representative with foreign nations."[37] The context of the speech demonstrates that his intent was not to advocate inherent or exclusive powers for the president. His objective was merely to defend the authority of President John Adams to carry out an extradition treaty. The president was not the sole organ in formulating the treaty, which required joint action by the president and the Senate. He was the sole organ in implementing it. Article II of the Constitution specifies that it is the president's duty to "take Care that the Laws be faithfully executed," and in Article VI, that all treaties made "shall be the supreme Law of the Land."[38]

Once on the Supreme Court as Chief Justice, Marshall held consistently to his position that the making of foreign policy is a joint exercise by the executive and legislative branches, whether by treaty or by statute, not a unilateral or exclusive authority of the president. With the war power, for example, Marshall looked solely to Congress—not the president—for the authority to take the country to war. He had no difficulty identifying which branch possessed the war power: "The whole powers of war being, by the constitution of the United States, vested in congress, the acts of that body can alone be resorted to as our guides in this enquiry."[39] In an 1804 case, Marshall ruled that when a presidential proclamation issued in time of war conflicts with a statute enacted by Congress, the statute prevails.[40]

In addition to these constitutional arguments, OLC looked to statutes as legal justification for NSA eavesdropping. It argued that "Congress by statute has confirmed and supplemented the President's recognized authority under Article II of the Constitution to conduct such warrantless surveillance to prevent catastrophic attacks on the homeland." In responding to the September 11 attacks, Congress enacted the AUMF to authorize the president to "use all necessary and appropriate force against those nations, organizations, or persons he determines planned, authorized, committed, or aided the terrorist attacks" of September 11, in order to prevent "any future acts of international terrorism against the United States."[41] Moreover, although FISA "generally requires judicial approval of electronic surveillance, FISA also contemplates that Congress may authorize such surveillance by a statute other than FISA," and the AUMF, OLC said, met that requirement.[42] Any congressional statute interpreted to impede the president's ability to use electronic surveillance to detect and prevent future attacks by an enemy "would be called into very serious doubt" as to its constitutionality. If this constitutional question "had to be addressed, FISA would be unconstitutional as applied to this narrow context."[43] According to this reading, statutory law could not restrict what the president decided to do under his Article II powers.

There is no evidence that any member of Congress, in voting on the AUMF, thought that it would in any way modify the requirements of FISA or give the president new and independent authority to conduct warrantless national security wiretaps. When Congress decides to amend a statute or grant new powers, it does so explicitly, not by implication. It is a canon of statutory construction that "repeal by implication" is disfavored. Changing law requires specific, conscious, and deliberate action by Congress.

A Hospital Visit

After initiating the Terrorist Surveillance Program, it was the policy of the administration to reauthorize it periodically after internal review of its legality. In March 2004, the Office of Legal Counsel concluded that the program had a number of legal deficiencies and recommended that it not be reauthorized until changed. The presidential order to reauthorize the program had a line for the attorney general to sign. Attorney General John Ashcroft and Deputy Attorney General James Comey agreed with the OLC analysis and recommendation. At that same time, Ashcroft was hospitalized with a serious illness, placed in intensive care, and had transferred the powers of attorney general to Comey until he could recover and resume the powers of his office.

On the evening of March 10, 2004, in his capacity as acting attorney general, Comey was heading home with his security detail about 8 o'clock. He received a call from Ashcroft's chief of staff that he had received a call from Mrs. Ashcroft, who understood that White House Counsel Alberto Gonzales and White House Chief of Staff Andrew Card were on their way to the hospital. Comey thought that Gonzales and Card, knowing of the legal objections that the Justice Department had raised to the TSP, might try to convince Ashcroft to reverse Justice's position and agree to sign the reauthorization form.

Comey called his chief of staff and told him to get as many of Comey's people as possible to the hospital immediately. He called FBI Director Robert Mueller and asked that he come to the hospital. With siren blaring, Comey's car reached the hospital, and he raced up the stairs to Ashcroft's room and found Mrs. Ashcroft standing by the bed. As Comey explained to the Senate Judiciary Committee on May 15, 2007, he was concerned that, given Ashcroft's illness, there might be an effort to ask him to sign the form and overrule what Justice had decided, when he was in no condition to do that.[44] Comey tried to get Ashcroft oriented to the issue, in preparation for the arrival of Gonzales and Card. He then went out in the hallway to call Mueller, who was on the way. Understanding the situation, Mueller directed FBI agents not to have Comey removed from Ashcroft's room under any circumstances. Shortly after that, OLC head Jack Goldsmith and a senior Justice official, Patrick Philbin, arrived and entered Ashcroft's room. Comey sat down in a chair at the head of Ashcroft's bed, Goldsmith and Philbin stood behind him, and Mrs. Ashcroft stood by the bed holding her husband's arm.

Within a few minutes Gonzales and Card entered the room. Gonzales, holding an envelope, told Ashcroft why they were there and why they wanted him to approve the reauthorization of the TSP. Ashcroft lifted his head off the pillow and defended the position that Justice had taken. He said his opinion did not matter because he was not attorney general. Pointing to Comey, he said he was the attorney general. Gonzales and Card, without acknowledging Comey, left the room. At that point Mueller arrived and Comey explained what had happened.[45]

Card then called Comey and told him to come to the White House immediately. Comey said that after the conduct he had just witnessed, he would not come without a witness. Card responded, "What conduct? We were just there to wish him well."[46] Comey called Solicitor General Ted Olson, explained the circumstances, and asked him to accompany him to the White House and witness what was said. Comey and Olson arrived at the White House that evening at 11 o'clock. Comey told the Judiciary Committee that he was very upset and angry because he thought Gonzales and Card had tried to take advantage of a very sick man who lacked the official authority to do what they asked of him.[47]

Card asked Olson to sit outside while he talked to Comey alone. Gonzales arrived and brought Olson into the room, and the four discussed the situation. Card said he had heard reports that there might be a number of resignations at the Justice Department over the incident. Comey concluded that he could not stay if the administration decided to engage in conduct that the Justice Department said had no legal basis.[48] Others prepared to resign included FBI Director Mueller, Comey's chief of staff, Ashcroft's chief of staff, and quite likely Ashcroft.[49] The mass resignations were averted when President Bush met with Comey and Mueller in the Oval Office two days later, in the morning, to receive a briefing on Justice's counterterrorism work. As Comey was leaving, Bush asked to see him privately in a separate room for about fifteen minutes, and Bush did the same with Mueller. The result of those two meetings was that Comey understood from Bush that he was to do "the right thing" as he saw it.[50] To Comey, that meant that Justice would not sign the reauthorization form until it was satisfied that the program had been sufficiently altered to pass legal muster. Pending the review by Justice, the White House went ahead with the TSP without the approval of Comey or the Justice Department.[51] After two or three weeks, and the acceptance of changes urged by Justice, the reauthorization form received the signature of the attorney general.[52]

Hayden's Testimony

Michael V. Hayden appeared before the Senate Intelligence Committee on May 18, 2006, to testify on his nomination to be Central Intelligence Agency (CIA) director. Previously he had served as NSA director at the time that the Terrorist Surveillance Program was initiated. At the hearing, Hayden defended the legality of the NSA wiretap program on constitutional, not statutory, grounds. He did not attempt to use the AUMF as legal justification. In recalling his service at NSA after September 11, Hayden told the committee that when he talked to NSA lawyers "they were very comfortable with the Article II arguments and the president's inherent authorities." When they came to him and discussed the lawfulness of the NSA program, "our discussion anchored itself on Article II."[53] The attorneys "came back with a real comfort level that this was within the president's authority [i.e., Article II]."[54] This legal advice was not put in writing, and Hayden "did not ask for it." Instead, "they talked to me about Article II."[55] There is no evidence that the NSA general counsel was asked to prepare a legal memo defending the TSP—no paper trail, no accountability, just informal talks.

Sen. Carl Levin, D-Mich., asked Hayden how he balanced security interests against liberty and privacy concerns. In initiating the TSP, he wanted to know, had Hayden understood that there was "at least a privacy concern there, whether or not one concludes that security interests outweigh the privacy concerns"? Hayden began by calling September 11 a watershed: "We were taking [steps] in a regime that was different from the regime that existed on 10th September." He gave an address on September 13 to NSA employees "about free peoples always having to decide the balance of security and their liberties, and that we through our tradition have always planted our banner way down here on the end of the spectrum toward security." He said "there are going to be a lot of pressures to push that banner down toward security, and our job at NSA was to keep America free by making Americans feel safe again. So this balance between security and liberty was foremost in our mind."[56] Levin tried to clarify his response: "Does that mean your answer to my question is yes?" Hayden replied: "Senator, I understand there are privacy concerns involved in all of this. There's privacy concerns involved in the routine activities of NSA."[57]

Hayden repeatedly claimed that the NSA program was legal and that the CIA "will obey the laws of the United States and will respond to our treaty obligations."[58] What did Hayden mean by "law"? National policy decided by statute or a treaty? Or a policy purely executive-made? During the hearing, he treated "law" as the latter—something that can be derived from Article II or inherent powers. "I had two lawful programs in front of me, one authorized by the president, the other one would have been conducted under FISA as currently crafted and implemented."[59] In other words, he had two avenues before him: one authorized by statutory law, the other in violation of it. He told one senator, "I did not believe—still don't believe—that I was acting unlawfully. I was acting under a lawful authorization."[60] He meant a presidential directive issued under Article II, even against the exclusive policy set forth in FISA.

Hearing Hayden insist that he acted legally in implementing the NSA program, a senator said, "I assume that the basis for that was the Article II powers, the inherent powers of the president to protect the country in time of danger and war." Hayden replied, "Yes, sir, commander in chief powers."[61] Hayden implied that he was willing to violate statutory law in order to carry out presidential law. After September 11, CIA Director George Tenet asked whether, as NSA director, he could "do more" to combat terrorism with surveillance. Hayden answered, "Not within current law."[62] In short, the administration knowingly and consciously decided to act against statutory policy. It knew that the NSA eavesdropping program it wanted to conduct was illegal under FISA but decided to go ahead.

At one point in the hearing, Hayden referred to the legal and political embarrassments of NSA during the Nixon administration, when it conducted warrantless eavesdropping against domestic groups. In discussing what should be done after 9/11, he told one group: "Look, I've got a workforce out there that remembers the mid-1970s." He asked the Senate committee to forgive him for using "a poor sports metaphor," but he advised the group in this manner: "Since about 1975, this agency's had a permanent one-ball, two-strike count against it, and we don't take many close pitches."[63] TSP was a close pitch. Perhaps with further disclosures one can say with confidence whether NSA took a close pitch and struck out.

Setbacks in Court

A number of private parties challenged the legality and constitutionality of NSA's eavesdropping. To show the injury necessary to have a case litigated, plaintiffs argued that the contacts they used to have with clients over the telephone were now impossible because of NSA monitoring. To maintain contact, they would have to travel to see clients personally, even in countries outside the United States. The government sought to have all such lawsuits dismissed on the ground that litigation would inevitably disclose "state secrets" injurious to the nation. That argument had been weakened when the Bush administration decided to publicly acknowledge the existence of the TSP and publicly defend its legality.

In a major case in California, decided on July 20, 2006, a U.S. District Court judge held that the state secrets privilege did not block action on the lawsuit and that plaintiffs had shown sufficient injury to establish standing. The judge denied the government's motion to have the case dismissed or go to summary judgment on the issue of the state secrets privilege. Under summary judgment, a court does not begin the time-consuming process of depositions and trial but rather goes immediately to the legal issue before it. As a result of the judge's rulings, the lawsuit was allowed to proceed—a significant defeat for the Bush administration.[64]

In this case, the plaintiffs alleged that AT&T and its holding company had collaborated with the NSA in conducting a massive, warrantless surveillance program that illegally tracked the domestic and foreign communications of millions of Americans. The plaintiffs charged violations of the First and Fourth Amendment of the Constitution, of FISA, various sections of other federal laws, and California's Unfair Competition Law. In attempting to have the case dismissed, the government advanced three arguments based on the state secrets privilege: "(1) the very subject matter of this case is a state secret; (2) plaintiffs cannot make a prima facie case for their claims without classified evidence and (3) the privilege effectively deprives AT&T of information necessary to raise valid defenses."[65]

To the court, the first step in determining whether a piece of information was a "state secret" was determining whether the information was actually a "secret."[66] The court pointed to public reports about the TSP in the *New York Times* on December 16, 2005. It noted that President Bush, the following day, confirmed the existence of the program and publicly described the mechanism by which the program was authorized and reviewed. Attorney General Gonzales had talked about the program in public briefings and public hearings, and the Justice Department publicly defended the TSP's legality and constitutionality. Based on this public record, the court said, "it might appear that none of the subject matter in this litigation could be considered a secret given that the alleged surveillance programs have been so widely reported in the media."[67]

The court recognized that just because a factual statement has been made public does not guarantee that the statement is true or that the activity was not a genuine secret. Even if a previously secret program has been leaked, verification of the program by the government could be harmful.[68] Also, media reports may be unreliable.[69] However, in this case the administration had "publicly admitted the existence of a 'terrorist surveillance program,' which the government insists is completely legal." Moreover, given the scope of the TSP, the court found it "inconceivable" that it could exist without the acquiescence and cooperation of a telecommunications provider. The size of AT&T and its public acknowledgment that it performs classified contracts and employs thousands who have government security clearances provided enough verifiable public information to avoid adopting the state secrets privilege as an absolute bar to litigation.[70] Under this reasoning, the court concluded that the plaintiffs were entitled "to at least some discovery."[71]

As to whether plaintiffs had shown injury, to establish standing and the right to sue AT&T, the court concluded that the plaintiffs "have sufficiently alleged that they suffered an actual, concrete injury traceable to AT&T and redressable by this court."[72] On those grounds, the court allowed the case to proceed to discovery, with each side at liberty to request additional documents to support its position.

A week later, the government prevailed in an NSA case decided in Illinois. A U.S. District Court dismissed a class-action lawsuit against a Bush administration program that involved the collection and monitoring of phone numbers rather than actual conversations (the program that the *New York Times* revealed in December 2005). The administration neither confirmed nor denied the existence of this program on phone numbers, and several telephone companies denied that they had given customer calling records to the NSA. The district judge noted that "no executive branch official has officially confirmed or denied the existence of any program to obtain large quantities of customer telephone records, the subject of the plaintiffs' lawsuit."[73] By invoking the states secrets privilege, the government this time prevented the plaintiffs from seeking additional facts or documents to establish that they had been harmed or would suffer harm in the future. The judge ruled that the plaintiffs could not seek relief in the courts and would have to seek redress from the political branches.

In the California case, the federal court merely let the case continue, without deciding on the merits. However, on August 17, 2006, District Judge Anna Diggs Taylor, in Michigan, ruled that the TSP violated the Constitution and federal statutes. Like the judge in California, Taylor took note that the existence of the program, the lack of warrants, and the focus on communications in which one party was in the United States had been admitted by the administration.[74] Contrary to the arguments of NSA, Taylor was persuaded that the plaintiffs were able "to establish a prima facie case based solely on Defendants' public admissions regarding the TSP."[75] As to injury, the plaintiffs had provided documentation that "they are stifled in their ability to vigorously conduct research, interact with sources, talk with clients and, in the case of the attorney Plaintiffs, uphold their oath of providing effective and ethical representation of their clients."[76] Plaintiffs cited additional injury by having to travel to meet with clients and others relevant to their cases.

The NSA argued in court that it could not defend itself "without the exposure of state secrets." Judge Taylor disagreed, pointing out that the Bush administration "has repeatedly told the general public that there is a valid basis in law for the TSP." Moreover, the NSA contended that the president has statutory authority under the AUMF and the Constitution to authorize continued use of the TSP, it and presented that case "without revealing or relying on any classified information."[77] Taylor found that the agency's argument that it could not defend itself in this case "without the use of classified information to be disingenuous and without merit."[78]

Judge Taylor next addressed the constitutional and statutory arguments presented by the plaintiffs, starting with the Fourth Amendment:

> The right of the people to be secure in their persons, houses, papers, and effects, against unreasonable searches and seizures, shall not be violated, and no Warrants shall issue, but upon probable cause, supported by Oath or affirmance, and particularly describing the place to be searched, and the persons or things to be seized.

She said that the Fourth Amendment was adopted "to assure that Executive abuses of the power to search would not continue in our new nation."[79] She cited cases that described a private residence as a place where society particularly recognizes an expectation of privacy. Other cases emphasized that executive officers of the government could not be trusted to be neutral and disinterested magistrates or the sole judges of the extent of their prosecutorial powers. Judicial scrutiny was necessary to protect constitutional values. In enacting FISA, Congress made many concessions to executive needs but still insisted on a body outside the executive branch—the FISA court—to provide independent review. All of the legislative concessions to executive flexibility "have been futile," she said, because the TSP "has undisputedly been continued for at least five years, it has been undisputedly been implemented without regard to FISA . . . and obviously in violation of the Fourth Amendment."[80]

Judge Taylor explained that unrestricted and unchecked use of search and seizure have over history had damaging effects on First Amendment rights of speech, press, and the ability of citizens to function effectively through organizations. FISA, she pointed out, explicitly admonished that "no United States person may be considered . . . an agent of a foreign power solely upon the basis of activities protected by the First Amendment."[81] President Bush, she concluded, "a creature of the same Constitution which gave us these Amendments, has undisputedly violated the Fourth in failing to procure judicial orders as required by FISA, and accordingly has violated the First Amendment rights of these Plaintiffs as well."[82]

The next constitutional issue explored was the principle of separation of powers. Judge Taylor recalled the Framers' resentment of the General Warrants authorized by King George III, which helped to precipitate the break with England. She cited the language of Justice Jackson in the 1952 steel seizure case that emergency power was consistent with free government "only when their control is lodged elsewhere than in the Executive who exercises them."[83] From Jackson again: "With all its defects, delays and inconveniences, men have discovered no technique for long preserving free government except that the Executive be under the law, and that the law be made by parliamentary deliberations."[84] Taylor concluded that President Bush, by acting in a manner forbidden by FISA, functioned outside the law decided by legislative deliberations and attempted to combine the powers of government into one branch.

The Bush administration defended the TSP by relying on the AUMF. Judge Taylor observed that the statute "says nothing whatsoever of intelligence or surveillance." She asked whether the authority for the TSP could be implied in the AUMF. In the cases of FISA and Title III on wiretaps, Congress had adopted those statutes "as the exclusive means by which electronic surveillance may be adopted." Prior warrants must be obtained from judges. FISA allowed for a fifteen-day exception in time of a declared war, but here the government argued that the TSP could function for more than five years without congressional authorization. The implication by the government that the AUMF somehow modified FISA, without direct and explicit amendment, said the judge, "cannot be made by this court."[85]

Did President Bush have some inherent power to authorize the Terrorist Surveillance Program? The government, Judge Taylor summarized, "appears to argue here that, pursuant to the penumbra of Constitutional language in Article II, and particularly because the President is designated Commander in Chief of the Army and Navy, he has been granted the inherent power to violate not only the laws of the Congress but the First and Fourth Amendments of the Constitution, itself."[86] She continued: "We must first note that the Office of the Chief Executive has itself been created, with its powers, by the Constitution. There are no hereditary Kings in America and no powers not created by the Constitution. So all 'inherent powers' must derive from that Constitution." The argument that "inherent powers justify the program here in litigation must fail."[87]

Finally, Judge Taylor addressed the government's argument that there were a number of practical justifications for the TSP, including the difficulty of obtaining judicial warrants in a timely manner. She noted that previous decisions by federal courts had rejected "practical arguments" used to justify emergency actions by executive officers, including the lack of judicial competence, the danger of security leaks, and unacceptable delay.[88] She observed that the government had not sought amendments to FISA to alleviate these practical problems. She found the government's argument for "speed and agility," as reason for bypassing statutory and constitutional requirements, to be "weightless."[89]

To summarize, Judge Taylor held that the TSP violated statutory law, the separation of powers doctrine, and the First and Fourth Amendments. Plaintiffs "have prevailed, and the public interest is clear, in this matter. It is the upholding of our Constitution."[90] The government appealed her decision to the Sixth Circuit.

Legislative Remedies

After the *New York Times* disclosed NSA's eavesdropping program, Congress drafted legislation to put the policy on firm legal footing. One element was to impose some type of legislative oversight to replace the skimpy "Gang of Eight" procedure that the Bush administration had followed.[91] However, the administration also was ready to use the *Times* disclosure to press for greater authority, claiming that FISA was out of date and had not kept pace with changing technology. Executive officials testified that it was impractical after September 11 to expect the administration to obtain individual warrants every time they needed to listen to a conversation of someone suspected of being connected with al Qaeda. They urged legislation to recognize by statute what they considered to be the president's inherent authority to conduct warrantless eavesdropping to collect foreign intelligence. Critics of this approach advised Congress that it would be better to have no legislative action than to grant the president such sweeping, unchecked power.[92]

By early March 2006, Republicans on the Senate Intelligence Committee said that they had reached agreement with the White House on proposed legislation to impose new forms of congressional oversight. The bill would allow wiretapping without warrants and increase the current three-day limit for emergency surveillance to forty-five days. If the administration found it necessary to exceed forty-five days, the attorney general would have to certify that continued surveillance was necessary to protect the country and explain why the administration would not seek a warrant. His statement would go to a newly created, seven-member "terrorist surveillance subcommittee" of the Senate Intelligence Committee, which would receive full access to details of the program's operations. Democrats attacked the bill as an abdication of legislative power and an offer to bless the NSA program before Congress, and the public, had understood its reach or manner of operation. Democratic senator John D. Rockefeller IV, vice chair of the Intelligence Committee, described the panel as "basically under the control of the White House."[93]

The seven members of the new subcommittee went to the White House to receive a two-hour briefing on the TSP and were scheduled to visit NSA to learn more. Under the rules set by the White House, the seven senators were not permitted to share what they learned with the other eight senators on the Intelligence Committee. Senator Rockefeller had traveled to NSA the previous week and spent almost seven hours getting information from more than a dozen NSA lawyers, policymakers, and technicians. He told reporters he learned more from that visit than from the White House presentation, which consisted of "flip-chart jobs and not very impressive."[94]

In an April 6 appearance before the House Judiciary Committee, Attorney General Gonzales seemed to suggest that warrantless wiretaps could be placed not only on international calls, with one party in the United States, but even on purely domestic calls if they were related to al Qaeda. In response to a question from Rep. Adam Schiff, D-Calif., as to whether the administration thought it had authority to listen to domestic calls without a warrant, Gonzales responded, "I'm not going to rule it out." In previous testimony, he said that the administration had rejected NSA spying on domestic communications because of the fear of public outcry. The Justice Department sought to downplay the significance of his remarks. At one point in the hearing, the Republican chair of the House Judiciary Committee, James Sensenbrenner, Wis., accused the administration of "stonewalling" in response to congressional requests for information.[95]

As debate on the legislation continued, the hope of reaching an early consensus vanished. Republican leaders thought there would be an advantage in passing legislation just before the November 2006 elections, to allow voters to compare the national security credentials of the two parties, but there were too many bills and too many contradictions. Opposition developed within Republican ranks to giving the president essentially unchecked power to conduct warrantless eavesdropping. The Senate bill crafted by Republican senator Arlen Specter, Pa., seemed to many to be too close to what the White House wanted. On the House side, debate was spread among six rival surveillance bills.[96] Strong objections were raised to allowing the FISA court to decide the constitutionality of the NSA program.[97] How would that be done? Secrets briefs submitted to the FISA court by the administration, followed by secret oral argument and eventually the release of a declassified, sanitized ruling? Why should constitutional issues be decided in that manner?

NSA prepared "talking points" to be used by Sen. Pat Roberts, Kan., Republican chair of the Intelligence Committee, to promote the administration's case. To Democrats, the NSA paper was offensive for its subjective and partisan tone, improperly inserting the agency into political matters that should be left to elected officials. For example, NSA suggested this language to Roberts: "I have been briefed on the Program and stood on the operations floor at NSA to see first-hand how vital it is to the security of our country and how carefully it is being run. . . . It is being run in a highly disciplined way that takes great pains to protect U.S. privacy rights. There is strict oversight in place, both at NSA and outside, now including the full congressional intelligence committees."[98]

With Congress about to recess for the elections, the differences between the various bills were too large to bridge. Members of both parties were reluctant to recognize Article II/inherent powers of the president to conduct warrantless wiretaps. It proved impossible to submit legislation to Bush for his signature.[99] The House managed to pass a bill, 232–191, but it was too unlike the Senate bill to permit quick resolution in conference committee.[100] Democratic victories in the November elections put an end not only to Republican control of Congress but to the Republican-drafted bills on national security surveillance.

Executive Self-Investigation?

With Congress conducting its own inquiry into the legality of NSA's program in spring 2006, there were calls for similar scrutiny within the executive branch. One agency to conduct a probe would have been the Office of Professional Responsibility (OPR) within the Justice Department. OPR looks into professional misconduct by government employees. Questions were raised whether Justice Department attorneys had played inappropriate roles in authorizing and overseeing warrantless electronic surveillance. In the past, OPR had access to information at the highest levels. No one could recall OPR having to shut down an investigation because of lack of clearance. This time, however, the administration decided to deny the necessary security clearances to those in the office to investigate the matter.[101]

In a Senate Judiciary Committee hearing on July 16, 2006, Attorney General Gonzales testified that President Bush had personally intervened to prevent OPR from conducting an inquiry into TSP activity. He was asked by Senator Specter: "Why wasn't OPR given clearance as so many other lawyers in the Department of Justice were given clearance?" Gonzales replied: "The president of the United States makes decisions about who is ultimately given access," and he made the decision "because this is such an important program."[102] A Justice Department official said that although some have questioned the legality of the TSP, there was never an issue of legal ethics, supposedly the jurisdiction of OPR. But Rep. Maurice Hinchey, D-N.Y., disagreed, saying that OPR was the appropriate agency to investigate the performance of lawyers who evaluated the surveillance program and whether they were manipulated.[103]

After the November elections shifted congressional control to the Democrats, the administration reversed its position on having the Department of Justice examine the NSA's program. Justice's inspector general, Glenn Fine, said he would investigate whether department lawyers had complied with legal requirements. No effort would be made to decide if NSA violated the Constitution or federal statutes. Other legal issues would be explored. Fine said that the White House had promised the necessary security clearances for his staff.[104]

Mid-Course Correction?

In the midst of troubling setbacks in federal courts, the administration announced in January 2007 that it would not continue to skirt the FISA court but would instead seek warrants from it, as required by statute. In a letter of January 17, Attorney General Gonzales informed the Senate Judiciary Committee that on January 10 a judge of the FISA court issued orders authorizing the government "to target for collection international communications into or out of the United States where there is probable cause to believe that one of the communicants is a member or agent of al Qaeda or an associated terrorist organization." As a result of those orders, "any electronic surveillance that was occurring as part of the Terrorist Surveillance Program will now be conducted subject to the approval of the Foreign Intelligence Surveillance Court."[105] This statement seemed to comply with FISA, but did it contemplate a one-time, blanket judicial approval for all future national security wiretaps within this category? Gonzales called these orders "innovative, they are complex, and it took considerable time and work for the Government to develop the approach that was proposed to the Court and for the Judge on the FISC to consider and approve these orders."[106] He concluded: "Under these circumstances, the President has determined not to reauthorize the Terrorist Surveillance Program when the current reauthorization expires."[107]

Aside from what appeared to be advance authorization for future national security wiretaps within the scope of the court's orders, the letter left unclear whether the administration was now relying solely on statutory authority or had kept in reserve its Article II, inherent power arguments. If it continued to believe in the latter (and there was no evidence that it found those arguments lacking in merit), the Gonzales letter offered a temporary accommodation, leaving open the reassertion of inherent powers if the administration decided that was best. For example, Gonzales said that President Bush "is committed to using all lawful tools to protect our Nation from the terrorist threat, including maximum use of the authorities provided by FISA and taking full advantage of developments in the law."[108] Presumably, the administration regarded the president's asserted inherent authority as a "lawful tool" because Gonzales said the TSP "fully complies with the law."[109] His language plainly states that the administration was not backing away from Article II claims of inherent power.

Press accounts largely interpreted the Gonzales letter as a repudiation of the TSP. In the *Washington Post,* Dan Eggen wrote that the Bush administration "has agreed to disband a controversial warrantless surveillance program run by the National Security Agency, replacing it with a new effort that will be overseen by the secret court that governs clandestine spying in the United States."[110] The title of his article, "Court Will Oversee Wiretap Program," suggested an ongoing, close judicial monitoring of warrants submitted to it, rather than what Gonzales appeared to describe: an advance, blanket authority for the type of national security wiretaps conducted under the TSP. Eggen spoke of "an abrupt reversal" by the administration rather than a partial and possibly temporary correction.[111]

Eggen explained that the new policy reflected the reality of the November 2006 elections, which gave Democrats control of both houses of Congress: "Administration officials suggested that the move was aimed in part at quelling persistent objections to the NSA spying by Democrats who now control Congress and that it is intended to slow or even derail challenges making their way through the federal courts." [112] A further advantage: obtaining approval from the FISA court would enable the Justice Department "to more easily use the information they obtain in future criminal prosecutions." Eggen correctly captured the ambiguity in the Gonzales letter. Executive officials would not say whether the administration would have to seek a warrant for each person to be monitored or whether the FISA court orders covered multiple cases. It was not even clear which FISA court judge issued the orders. Finally, the new orders from the FISA court did not mark a permanent reform. Officials told Eggen that the January 10 orders would expire in ninety days, leaving doubt both about their extension and possible modifications.[113]

Coverage by the *New York Times* also underscored the altered legal and political climate. The new Democratic-led Congress intended to hold searching investigations of the NSA program, including hearings within a few days to take testimony from Gonzales. A couple of weeks later the Sixth Circuit would hear arguments on the government's appeal from Judge Taylor's ruling declaring the TSP to be illegal and unconstitutional.[114] Exactly what the FISA court authorized remained classified. Justice Department officials told the *New York Times* that the orders were not broad approval of the TSP but rather a series of orders for individual targets.[115] Precisely what was ordered and what was not would remain private. The administration said it had briefed the full House and Senate Intelligence Committees in closed sessions. Rep. Heather Wilson, R-N.M., who served on the House committee, denied that such briefings had been held. Some sources said that congressional aides had been briefed without lawmakers present.[116]

Other news analyses reported dramatic departures in administration policy. The headline in a *New York Times* story read, "White House Retreats under Pressure." [117] A *Washington Post* article carried a similar message: "Bush Retreats on Use of Executive Power." The article overstated the administration's position, claiming that Bush officials "implicitly abandoned their argument that the president's inherent power under Article II of the Constitution was all the authority he needed." [118] The letter by Gonzales could be read just as easily to affirm that the Article II/inherent argument was still in place, to be invoked whenever the administration wished. Criticism by conservatives exaggerated what had happened. Mark Levin, on the *National Review* Web site, objected that the administration "is repudiating all the arguments it has made in testimony, legal briefs, and public statements."[119] Actually, the administration insisted that the TSP was legal then and legal now. The accommodation reached with a FISA court judge could be read as a tactical feint, jeopardizing none of the underlying Article II claims of power.

Some newspapers urged caution. An editorial in the *New York Times* warned that there "are still some big unanswered questions. For one thing, because the new warrant process is secret, we don't know whether the court has issued blanket approval for wiretapping, which would undermine the intent of the law, or whether the administration agreed to seek individual warrants."[120] Several days later the *Times* observed, "There is evidence that Mr. Bush got some broad approval for a wiretapping 'program' rather than the individual warrants required by law."[121]

The appearance by Gonzales before the Senate Judiciary Committee on January 18 provoked further confrontation. He would not agree to provide more documents to explain the decision.[122] He appeared to concede that the administration not only broke the law but knew it had done so: "The truth of the matter is we looked at FISA and we all concluded there's no way we can do what we have to do to protect this country under the strict reading of FISA."[123] There were reports that the FISA court orders would be shown to House and Senate leaders and selected committees, including Intelligence and Judiciary, although access by the latter seemed restricted to chairmen and ranking members.[124]

The tentative and possibly temporary accommodation by the administration undermined its position in court that the NSA cases should be considered moot and dismissed. Had the administration entered into a final and binding agreement, or one that could be revisited later and reversed? At a hearing on January 31, 2007, before the Sixth Circuit, one of the judges asked: "You could opt out at any time, couldn't you?" The deputy solicitor general acknowledged the possibility.[125]

Swerving Again: McConnell's Testimony

On May 1, 2007, Director of National Intelligence Michael McConnell testified before the Senate Intelligence Committee and signaled that the administration might not be able to keep its pledge to seek warrants through the FISA court. McConnell had served as NSA director from 1992 to 1996. On the one hand, his written statement appeared to endorse FISA as the foundation for conducting national security wiretaps. The pending bill, he said, "seeks to restore FISA to its original focus on protecting the privacy interests of persons in the United States."[126] He could not "overstate how instrumental FISA has been in helping the IC [intelligence community] protect the nation from terrorist attacks since September 11, 2001."[127] Yet he also stated that FISA's requirement to obtain a court order, "based on a showing of probable cause, slows, and in some cases prevents altogether, the Government's efforts to conduct surveillance of communications it believes are significant to the national security."[128] Could revision of FISA take care of these difficulties, or was McConnell hinting at a more fundamental problem beyond a statutory fix?

The Justice Department, in its testimony, alluded to what it considered to be the impractical requirement of obtaining a warrant from the FISA court for each national security surveillance. Critics of the administration

> argue that the Intelligence Community should be required to seek FISA Court approval each time a foreign target overseas happens to communicate with a person inside the United States. For reasons that I can elaborate upon in greater detail in closed session, this is an infeasible approach that would impose intolerable burdens on our intelligence efforts.[129]

Another signal that the administration's pledge in January 2007 to adhere to FISA court review would not be followed in each instance?

What happened at the hearing sheds light on these questions. Senior officials in the Bush administration told the committee that they could no longer pledge to seek warrants from the FISA court for a domestic wiretapping program. They argued that the president had independent authority under the Constitution to order this type of surveillance without warrants and without complying with statutory procedures. McConnell referred several times to Article II as a source of inherent presidential authority. When asked by Sen. Russ Feingold, D-Wis., whether the administration would no longer sidestep the FISA court, McConnell replied: "Sir, the president's authority under Article II is in the Constitution. So if the president chose to exercise Article II authority, that would be the president's choice." He wanted to highlight that "Article II is Article II, so in a different circumstance, I can't speak for the president what he might decide."[130]

Why would an administration witness tell a congressional committee that Article II is in the Constitution, and that Article II is Article II? Those are obvious—too obvious—points. The apparent message was that Congress can legislate as it likes, but the president need not comply, even if Article II of the Constitution directs the president to "take Care that the Laws be faithfully Executed." McConnell's testimony is similar to that of Michael Hayden, when he was nominated to be CIA director. Both men seemed to be coached to repeat the words "Article II, Article II, inherent, inherent," as though such assertions and claims stated with sufficient frequency would take on substance without further explanation. An assertion is an assertion until the witness develops a persuasive and informed argument, which neither McConnell nor Hayden attempted to do. Moreover, McConnell's testimony, or at least his oral remarks, seemed to undermine the administration's efforts to convince federal courts that pending challenges to the TSP were moot.

Conclusions

In times of emergency, government officials will push boundaries to do what they think is necessary. Sometimes their judgments are sound, persuading other branches of government, and the public, to register their support. On other occasions the zeal for quick action and prompt results runs roughshod over fundamental constitutional principles, placing in jeopardy the rights and liberties that government officials are sworn to respect and protect. The TSP was devised to circumvent what some executive officials saw as an outmoded FISA, but if that was their concern they could have come to Congress and asked for remedial legislation. Congress passed many emergency statutes in the months after September 11, including the AUMF and the USA Patriot Act. It would not have been difficult for the executive branch to persuade Congress to amend FISA to take into account technological changes after 1978. Many changes had indeed been made to FISA, including some after the September 11 terrorist attacks.

Instead of pursuing a legislative strategy, executive officials preferred to act unilaterally on the basis of inherent presidential power, a field of constitutional law filled with doubts, ambiguities, and open invitations to executive abuse. Advocating or depending on inherent presidential power always comes at the cost of checks and balances, separation of powers, and the kinds of structural safeguards the Framers adopted to ensure that a concentration of power does not endanger the liberties of citizens. The very purpose of a Constitution is to confer power and limit it. Inherent power, by definition, recognizes no limits. The principles of government announced in 1787 were sound then, when the Framers drafted the Constitution. They are even more crucial today, when governmental power has grown to dimensions that the Founders never imagined.

Key Actors

George W. Bush As president, he authorized warrantless national security surveillance after September 11 and decided not to comply with the exclusive procedures of the Foreign Intelligence Surveillance Act.

James Comey Deputy attorney general, acting attorney general during the illness of John Ashcroft.

Alberto Gonzales White House counsel at the time the warrantless surveillance was authorized; later became attorney general.

Michael V. Hayden NSA director at the time the Terrorist Surveillance Program was initiated.

Michael McConnell Previously NSA director and now the director of national intelligence; in that capacity oversees all intelligence agencies.

Notes

1. James Risen and Eric Lichtblau, "Bush Lets U.S. Spy on Callers without Courts," *New York Times,* December 16, 2005, A1.
2. James Bamford, *Body of Secrets: Anatomy of the Ultra-Secret National Security Agency* (New York: Random House, 2002), 428–429.
3. Keith W. Olson, *Watergate: The Presidential Scandal that Shook America* (Lawrence: University Press of Kansas, 2003), 16.
4. Bamford, *Body of Secrets,* 430.
5. Ibid., 431–439.
6. Ibid., 440.
7. Louis Fisher and David Gray Adler, *American Constitutional Law* (Durham: Carolina Academic Press, 2007), 736.
8. 277 U.S. 438 (1928).
9. Fisher and Adler, *American Constitutional Law,* 735–737.
10. *Katz v. United States,* 389 U.S. 347, 351 (1967).
11. 82 Stat. 214 (1968).
12. *United States v. United States District Court,* 407 U.S. 297 (1972).
13. "Warrantless Wiretapping and Electronic Surveillance," Report by the Subcommittee on Surveillance of the Senate Committee on Foreign Relations and the Subcommittee on Administrative Practice and Procedure of the Senate Committee on the Judiciary, 94th Cong., 1st Sess. 2 (February 1975) (Senators Edmund Muskie, Ted Kennedy, and Sam Ervin).
14. Ibid., 7, 9.
15. 92 Stat. 1788, sec. 103(a) (1978).
16. Ibid., sec. 103(b).
17. Ibid., sec. 201(f).
18. 115 Stat. 1402, sec. 314(a) (2001).
19. David E. Sanger, "In Address, Bush Says He Ordered Domestic Spying," *New York Times,* December 18, 2005, 30.
20. Ibid.
21. Ibid.
22. "Bush on the Patriot Act and Eavesdropping," *New York Times,* December 18, 2005, at 30.
23. Ibid.

24. Sanger, "In Address," 30.

25. Ibid.

26. *Weekly Compilation of Presidential Documents,* December 19, 2005, 1885.

27. Press briefing by Attorney General Alberto Gonzales and General Michael Hayden, principal deputy director for national intelligence, 2; available at www.whitehouse.gov/news/releases/2005/12/print/20051219-1.html.

28. Ibid.

29. Ibid.

30. Ibid., 4.

31. U.S. Justice Department, Office of Legal Counsel, "Legal Authorities Supporting the Activities of the National Security Agency Described by the President," January 19, 2006, 1.

32. Ibid., 6–7.

33. 48 Stat. 1745 (1934).

34. *Panama Refining Co. v. Ryan,* 293 U.S. 388 (1935); *Schechter Corp. v. United States,* 295 U.S. 495 (1935).

35. Louis Fisher, "Presidential Inherent Power: The 'Sole Organ' Doctrine," *Presidential Studies Quarterly* 37 (March 2007): 139, 144.

36. Ibid., 144–150.

37. 10 *Annals of Congress* 613 (1800), cited in *United States v. Curtiss-Wright Corp.,* 299 U.S. 304, 319 (1936).

38. Fisher, "Presidential Inherent Power," 140–142.

39. *Talbot v. Seeman,* 5 U.S. 1, 28 (1801).

40. *Little v. Barreme,* 2 Cr. (6 U.S.) 170, 179 (1804).

41. U.S. Justice Department, "Legal Authorities Supporting the Activities of the National Security Agency," 2.

42. Ibid., 2–3.

43. Ibid., 3.

44. Transcript of May 15, 2007 hearings on U.S. attorneys firings by the Senate Committee on the Judiciary, CQ Transcriptions. The transcript is not numbered but the remark by Comey appears on page 13.

45. Ibid., 14–15.

46. Ibid., 16.

47. Ibid., 17.

48. Ibid., 19.

49. Ibid., 20–21.

50. Ibid., 21

51. Ibid., 32.

52. Ibid., 43.

53. Hearing of the Senate Select Committee on Intelligence on the Nomination of General Michael V. Hayden to be Director of the Central Intelligence Agency, May 18, 2006, transcript, 35.

54. Ibid., 69.

55. Ibid.

56. Ibid., 32.

57. Ibid., 32–33.

58. Ibid., 74.

59. Ibid., 88.

60. Ibid., 138.

61. Ibid., 144.

62. Ibid., 68.

63. Ibid., 61.

64. *Hepting v. AT&T Corp.*, 439 F.Supp.2d 974 (N.D. Cal. 2006).

65. Ibid., 985.

66. Ibid., 986.

67. Ibid., 989.

68. Ibid., 990.

69. Ibid., 991.

70. Ibid., 992.

71. Ibid., 994.

72. Ibid., 1001. For newspaper stories on this decision, see Arshad Mohammed, "Judge Declines to Dismiss Lawsuit against AT&T," *Washington Post,* July 21, 2006, A9; John Markoff, "Judge Declines to Dismiss Privacy Suit against AT&T," *New York Times,* July 21, 2006, A13.

73. *Terkel v. AT&T,* 441 F.Supp.2d 899, 912 (N.D. Ill. 2006); Adam Liptak, "Judge Rejects Customer Suit over Records from AT&T," *New York Times,* July 26, 2006, A13; Mike Robinson, "Judge Dismisses Lawsuit on AT&T Data Handover," *Washington Post,* July 26, 2006, A6.

74. *American Civil Liberties v. National Sec. Agency,* 438 F.Supp.2d 754, 765 (E.D. Mich. 2006).

75. Ibid.

76. Ibid.

77. Ibid.

78. Ibid., 766.

79. Ibid., 774.

80. Ibid., 775.

81. Ibid., 776.

82. Ibid.

83. Ibid., 778 (citing *Youngstown Sheet & Tube v. Sawyer,* 343 U.S. 579, 652 (1952)).

84. Ibid. (citing 343 U.S. at 655).

85. Ibid., 779.

86. Ibid., 780.

87. Ibid., 781.

88. Ibid.

89. Ibid., 782.

90. Ibid.; Adam Liptak and Eric Lichtblau, "U.S. Judge Finds Wiretap Actions Violate the Law," *New York Times,* August 18, 2006, A1; Dan Eggen and Dafna Linzer, "Judge Rules against Wiretaps," *Washington Post,* August 18, 2006, A1.

91. David D. Kirkpatrick, "Republicans Seek to Bridge Differences on Surveillance," *New York Times,* March 1, 2006, A13.

92. Eric Lichtblau, "Administration and Critics, in Senate Testimony, Clash over Eavesdropping Compromise," *New York Times,* July 27, 2006, A19.

93. David D. Kirkpatrick and Scott Shane, "G.O.P. Senators Say Accord Is Set on Wiretapping," *New York Times,* March 3, 2006, A1.

94. Walter Pincus, "Panel on Eavesdropping Is Briefed by White House," *Washington Post,* March 10, 2006, A4.

95. Dan Eggen, "Warrantless Wiretaps Possible in U.S.," *Washington Post,* April 7, 2006, A3.

96. Jonathan Weisman, "Republican Rift over Wiretapping Widens: Party at Odds on Surveillance Legislation," *Washington Post,* September 6, 2006, A3.

97. Jonathan Weisman, "House GOP Leaders Fight Wiretapping Limits," *Washington Post,* September 13, 2006, A7.

98. *Congressional Record,* September 13, 2006, 152, S9451; Walter Pincus, "Democrats Call NSA's Input to Senate Panel Inappropriate," *Washington Post,* September 13, 2006, A7.

99. Keith Perine and Tim Starks, "House Panels Approve Surveillance Bill," *CQ Weekly,* September 25, 2006, 2556.

100. Eric Lichtblau, "House Approves Powers for Wiretaps without Warrants," *New York Times,* September 29, 2006, A18.

101. Scott Shane, "With Access Denied, Justice Dept. Drops Spying Investigation," *New York Times,* May 11, 2006, A24; "Justice on a Short Leash: Why Did the President Cut off Investigation of the NSA's Domestic Surveillance program?" (editorial), *Washington Post,* July 22, 2006, A16.

102. Neil A. Lewis, "Bush Blocked Ethics Inquiry, Official Says," *New York Times,* July 19, 2006, A14.

103. Ibid.

104. Dan Eggen, "Justice Dept. to Examine Its Use of NSA Wiretaps," *Washington Post,* November 28, 2006, A10; Eric Lichtblau, "Justice Official Opens Spying Inquiry," *New York Times,* November 28, 2006, A19.

105. Attorney General Alberto Gonzales to Senators Patrick Leahy and Arlen Specter, Chairman and Ranking Member of the Senate Committee on the Judiciary, January 17, 2007, 1.

106. Ibid.

107. Ibid., 2.

108. Ibid., 1.

109. Ibid.

110. Dan Eggen, "Court Will Oversee Wiretap Program," *Washington Post,* January 18, 2007, A1.

111. Ibid.

112. Ibid., A4.

113. Ibid.

114. Eric Lichtblau and David Johnston, "Court to Oversee U.S. Wiretapping in Terror Cases," *New York Times,* January 18, 2007, A1.

115. Ibid., A16.

116. Ibid.

117. Scott Shane, "White House Retreats under Pressure," *New York Times,* January 18, 2007, A16.

118. Peter Baker, "Bush Retreats on Use of Executive Power," *Washington Post,* January 18, 2007, A4.

119. Ibid.

120. "A Spy Program in from the Cold" (editorial), *New York Times,* January 18, 2007, A30.

121. "Retreat and Cheat" (editorial), *New York Times,* January 21, 2007, WK11.

122. David Johnston and Scott Shane, "Senators Demand Details on New Eavesdropping Rules," *New York Times,* January 18, 2007, A18.

123. Ibid. See also Dan Eggen, "Spy Court's Orders Stir Debate on Hill," *Washington Post,* January 19, 2007, A6.

124. Tim Starks, "Oversight Committees to Review Documents on NSA Wiretapping," *CQ Weekly,* February 5, 2007, 402; Mark Mazzetti, "Key Lawmakers Getting Files about Surveillance Program," *New York Times,* February 1, 2007, A11; Dan Eggen, "Records on Spy Program Turned over to Lawmakers," *Washington Post,* February 1, 2007, A2.

125. Adam Liptak, "Judges Weigh Arguments in U.S. Eavesdropping Case," *New York Times,* February 1, 2007, A11.

126. "Modernizing the Foreign Intelligence Surveillance Act," statement by J. Michael McConnell, Director of National Intelligence, before the Senate Select Committee on Intelligence, May 1, 2007, 1.

127. Ibid., 2.

128. Ibid., 5.

129. "The Need to Bring the Foreign Intelligence Surveillance Act into the Modern Era," Statement of Kenneth L. Wainstein, Assistant Attorney General, National Security Division, Department of Justice, before the Senate Select Committee on Intelligence, May 1, 2007, 8.

130. James Risen, "Administration Pulls Back on Surveillance Agreement," *New York Times,* May 3, 2007, A16.

8 Immigration Policy: U.S.-Mexican Relations Confront U.S. Political Realities

Marc R. Rosenblum

Before You Begin:

1. What is the U.S. national interest in immigration policy? Does immigration policy aspire to national goals, or are immigration interests primarily local and parochial?
2. Which interest groups care about immigration policy and why?
3. How are interest group policy demands regarding immigration related to traditional U.S. party cleavages? What makes partisan cleavages on immigration unlike those on other domestic and foreign policy issues?
4. What steps can countries of origin, such as Mexico, take to influence U.S. immigration policymaking? Under what conditions do efforts by countries of origin to influence U.S. immigration policy succeed? Have these conditions changed over time?
5. Do the United States and its Caribbean Basin immigration partners share common migration policy goals, or do their migration policy interests mainly conflict?
6. What are the consequences, for the United States and for Mexico and other Caribbean Basin states, of combining open trade and investment policies with restrictive migration controls? Is this combination of policy choices sustainable in the long run?

Introduction

Every twelve years, the U.S. and Mexican political calendars converge as their presidents' four- and six-year terms begin within a month of each other, and analysts on both sides of the border often see these double inaugurations as important opportunities to redefine and strengthen bilateral relations.[1] Optimism ran especially high in 2000–2001 when Mexico inaugurated its first democratically elected president, Vicente Fox of the National Action Party.[2] Like the new U.S. president, George W. Bush, Fox was a bilingual, former border state governor and business executive. He was also the first Mexican presidential candidate

Research for this chapter was supported by a Council on Foreign Relations International Affairs Fellowship, 2005–2006. The author thanks the Migration Policy Institute and the staff of Sen. Edward M. Kennedy, D-Mass., for cosponsoring the CFR fellowship.

to campaign systematically for votes in the United States. Fox returned to the United States in the fall as president-elect to thank his supporters. Bush broke with recent tradition by making Mexico (rather than Canada) the destination of his first foreign trip as president and then honored President Fox as his first state visitor to the White House.

The two presidents met a total of five times in 2001 alone and quickly agreed to make a priority of addressing the one bilateral issue that most threatened the relationship: migration. Immigration policy topped the agenda at a February summit in Guanajuato, Mexico, after which the two presidents directed Secretary of State Colin Powell and Attorney General John Ashcroft and their Mexican counterparts, Jorge Castãneda and Santiago Creel, to form a special working group to achieve "short and long-term agreements that will allow us to constructively address migration and labor issues between our two countries."[3] These efforts paid off by the September 2001 summit meeting in Washington, D.C.: Following the first-ever joint meeting of the full Mexican and U.S. cabinets, the presidents announced a framework for a breakthrough deal based on a new U.S.-Mexican guest worker program and the theme of "shared responsibility" for migration enforcement to preserve orderly migration flows.[4] The presidents also announced a new, bilateral public-private partnership, to be led by the Treasury and State Departments and their Mexican counterparts, to spur investment and growth in Mexican communities of origin as part of a long-term strategy to reduce emigration pressures.[5]

The September 11 attacks occurred five days later, moving migration negotiations to the back burner, and as of mid-2007, the first year of Bush's presidency represents the high-water mark for U.S.-Mexican relations, while broader efforts to reform America's immigration system appear to be stalled. The contrast between Bush's widely praised first trip to the region and his five-country tour in March 2007 is striking. Whereas press accounts of the earlier visit emphasized bilateral friendship and opportunities for greater cooperation,[6] coverage of the latter trip was devoted almost exclusively to protests—occasionally violent—at each of Mr. Bush's stops. The new Mexican president, Felipe Calderon, and Guatemala's President Oscar Berger were particularly critical of U.S. migration policy.[7]

Were the complaints warranted? Presidents Bush and Fox had raised expectations for a bilateral approach, and Bush recommitted himself to a guest worker program during his 2004 reelection campaign. Many Mexicans and Latinos within the United States were energized by the U.S. congressional immigration debate in the spring of 2006, when the Senate passed landmark leg-

U.S. Immigration Policy and U.S.-Mexican Relations

August 1942 United States and Mexico sign the "bracero" temporary labor migration (guest worker) treaty.

June 27, 1952 Congress passes the Immigration and Nationality Act (INA) over Truman's veto, sustaining national origins quota system, which favored northern and western Europe over other regions in the Eastern Hemisphere.

January 1954 U.S.-Mexican "showdown" on the border proves that Mexico is unable to prevent migration outflows; ushers in mature phase of the bracero program, with sharply curtailed rights for temporary workers.

September 1964 Bracero program terminated.

October 3, 1965 INA amended, replacing the national origins quota system with flat cap of 20,000 visas per country in the Eastern Hemisphere.

October 20, 1976 INA amended, extending the 20,000 visas per country quota to Mexico and other Western Hemisphere countries.

November 1, 1968 United States ratifies 1951 United Nations Convention on Refugees but does not change U.S. immigration law to reflect the convention's requirements.

March 17, 1980 Passage of the Refugee Act, bringing U.S. law into compliance with 1951 United Nations Convention on Refugees.

November 6, 1986 Passage of the Immigration Reform and Control Act (IRCA), increasing border enforcement, making it illegal to employ undocumented immigrants, and offering amnesty to some 3 million undocumented immigrants.

September 1993 Border Patrol initiates "Operation Blockade" around El Paso; "prevention through deterrence" strategy leads to border fencing and militarization of broad swaths of the U.S.-Mexico border since that time.

September 6, 2001 United States and Mexico sign Partnership for Prosperity, an agreement to target public-private investment toward Mexican emigration communities of origin; they announce plans to negotiate bilateral temporary worker agreement.

January 7, 2004 President Bush proposes general framework for comprehensive immigration reform.

April–November 2005 Three different Senate comprehensive immigration reform bills are introduced; Senate holds seven hearings on immigration reform.

continued on the next page

continued from the previous page

December 16, 2005 House of Representatives passes Border Protection, Antiterrorism, and Illegal Immigration Control Act of 2005.

March 27, 2006 Senate Judiciary Committee votes 12–6 to report the Comprehensive Immigration Reform Act of 2006 to the full Senate.

April 7, 2006 Senate fails to vote for cloture, terminating debate on the Comprehensive Immigration Reform Act of 2006 without taking substantive action on the bill.

May 15, 2006 Senate resumes debate on Comprehensive Immigration Reform Act of 2006.

May 25, 2006 Senate passes Comprehensive Immigration Reform Act of 2006.

June 19, 2006 House announces plans to hold field hearings instead of convening a conference committee to resolve differences between the House and Senate immigration bills.

October 26, 2006 Passage of Secure Fence Act, authorizing 700 miles of fencing at the U.S.-Mexico border.

January 23, 2007 President Bush highlights the need for comprehensive immigration reform in his State of the Union address.

February–May 2007 Senators from both parties join Secretaries Chertoff and Gutierrez in negotiations over comprehensive immigration reform.

May 17, 2007 Bipartisan group of senators and cabinet secretaries announce "grand compromise" on immigration reform.

June 7, 2007 Senate fails to support cloture, ending debate on Secure Borders, Economic Opportunity, and Immigration Reform Act of 2007.

June 26, 2007 Senate supports cloture on a motion to proceed, resuming debate on Secure Borders, Economic Opportunity, and Immigration Reform Act of 2007.

June 28, 2007 Senate fails to support final cloture motion, ending debate on Secure Borders, Economic Opportunity, and Immigration Reform Act of 2007.

islation to create new avenues for legal migration (permanent and temporary), move millions of existing undocumented immigrants into legal status, and strengthen enforcement at the border and within the United States. Yet the Senate bill also illustrated the limitation of U.S.-Mexican migration negotiations: The bill never made it to Bush's desk because the House passed a radically different bill and then refused to meet with senators to work out their differences. More generally, even though the citizens of Mexico and other countries of origin are the immediate subjects of U.S. immigration legislation, the history of immigration policymaking has often been written by Congress, not the president. As a result, efforts to link immigration to foreign policy compete with Congress's predominantly domestic approach to the issue.

Background: U.S. Immigration Policymaking 1940–2001

The U.S.-Mexican Bracero Program

Rules governing labor migration to the United States were highly restrictive in the decades prior to World War II, as most visas were reserved for the immediate family members of U.S. citizens, and no visas could be issued to contract workers. Restrictions against informal migration were strictly enforced during the Great Depression, including through mass deportations, leading to a net outflow of Mexican immigrants during the 1930s, the only such decade in the history of Mexico-U.S. migration. For these reasons, as the resurgent U.S. economy and the newly instituted military draft led to sharp agricultural labor shortages beginning in 1940, neither a formal nor an informal infrastructure existed to ensure the timely arrival of seasonal migrants to fill those jobs.

Agricultural groups lobbied Congress to restart a World War I–era program under which U.S. employers obtained temporary "guest worker" visas for Mexican laborers. Congress held extensive hearings on such a program during the spring of 1942 but deferred to the Roosevelt administration, which opposed it. Instead, responding to Mexican complaints about the earlier program, the Roosevelt administration initiated negotiations with Mexico to establish a bilateral guest worker program, in which Mexico would be in charge of recruiting workers and representing their interests in the United States. With Mexico threatening to ally with Germany, as the United States prepared to enter World War II,[8] U.S. negotiators were instructed to accommodate Mexican concerns about migrants' rights.[9] Mexico was reluctant to endorse labor outflows because of its own industrialization plans and drove a hard bargain.[10] The resulting agreement is unique in the history of regional relations: a document that favors Mexican over U.S. interests in almost every detail. In particular, Mexican workers (known as "braceros," as they worked with their *brazos*, or arms)[11] received a guaranteed minimum wage (unlike Americans), along with housing benefits, basic health care, and transportation costs. Mexico also insisted that contracts be signed by the U.S. government, with agricultural employers acting as subcontractors, and

Mexico blacklisted the state of Texas, where employers were considered especially likely to mistreat immigrant workers.[12]

The initial bracero agreement was revised a dozen times during the program's twenty-two-year history, and the program went through four distinct stages as a function of evolving policy preferences in Mexico and the United States and of ongoing negotiations between Congress, the president, and Mexico. Direct Mexican oversight of bracero contracts during World War II led to favorable bracero working conditions during the initial phase of the agreement and a rising chorus of grower complaints to Congress. Congress responded in 1948 by proposing legislation to reinstate a more pro-grower, World War I–style program, forcing Mexico to accept a scaled-back oversight role, with contracts signed directly by immigrants and their employers rather than by Mexico and the United States.

A third phase was initiated in 1951, when Mexico threatened to cut off guest worker outflows unless Congress agreed to reestablish state-to-state contracting and crack down on employers of undocumented immigrants (to force employers to participate in the more labor-friendly guest worker program). Congress met Mexico halfway, passing P.L.78, to mandate state contracting, and the so-called Wetback Bill, to make it illegal to aid or harbor undocumented immigrants, but also including the "Texas proviso" in the latter bill, over President Truman's objections, explicitly exempting employers of undocumented immigrants from prosecution under the law.[13]

Even so, growers continued to complain about Mexican oversight, and policymakers on both sides of the border objected (for different reasons) to ever-higher levels of undocumented immigration. Thus, in 1954, the pro-grower Eisenhower administration demanded substantial reductions in Mexican oversight authority. Mexico objected and threatened to prevent outflows in order to protect its role in the program. President Eisenhower called Mexico's bluff, however, directing U.S. agents to assist would-be border crossers, occasionally resulting in conflict between U.S. and Mexican border agents as each sought to pull workers to their side of the border.[14] Events quickly proved that ten years of bracero flows had reestablished sufficient linkages for migration to occur with or without Mexico's consent. The showdown at the border ushered in the "mature" stage of the bracero program, in which state-sponsored guest workers were stripped of virtually all legal protections and routinely exploited by unscrupulous employers. Bad publicity about the program, along with increasing sensitivity about worker and minority rights, caused the Eisenhower administration to require more humane treatment of guest workers beginning in the late 1950s, a trend that grew under John F. Kennedy before the program was terminated in 1964.

The Immigration and Nationality Act and Humanitarian Admissions

Legislation governing other migration to the United States operated on a separate track during these years, as Congress and the president clashed about policies governing humanitarian admissions and the balance between domestic and international determinants of migration policy. Congress followed Truman's lead on humanitarian admissions immediately after World War II, passing the Displaced Persons Acts of 1948 and 1950 and the Refugee Relief Act of 1953, eventually authorizing admission for about 420,000 Europeans displaced by the war. But Congress also passed the Internal Security Act of 1950, overriding Truman's veto. The law prohibited the admission of former members of the Communist Party, whom Congress viewed as threats to domestic security but Truman viewed as humanitarian cases who also offered valuable propaganda and intelligence resources in the emerging cold war. Truman also opposed Congress's Immigration and Nationality Act (INA) of 1952 on foreign policy grounds because the new law retained the discriminatory national origins quota system and failed to establish a quota for refugee admissions. But Congress again passed the law over the president's veto.

Tight quotas led to a foreign policy crisis in December 1956 when the Soviet Union invaded Hungary. Two hundred thousand refugees fled into neighboring Austria, but the INA limited U.S. immigration from Hungary to 756 visas per year. With Congress in recess, Eisenhower "paroled" 15,000 Hungarians into the United States over congressional objections, exploiting a loophole in the 1952 law that Congress intended to be applied on a case-by-case basis for individual migrants. By the time Congress reconvened, returning the refugees to Soviet-occupied Hungary was not a realistic option. Instead, Congress passed the 1957 Refugee-Escapee Act, authorizing Eisenhower's actions post hoc and establishing a precedent that individuals fleeing communist regimes could be admitted at the president's discretion.[15]

Political shifts after 1960 finally brought the domestic and international politics of migration policy into greater harmony. At the international level, the Kennedy administration sought to counter growing Soviet influence in Cuba, Vietnam, and throughout the developing world by more proactively reaching out to the third world, including through the Alliance for Progress in Latin America. At the domestic level, Kennedy and a coalition of northern Democrats and liberal Republicans supported the goals of the civil rights movement. For both of these reasons, the Kennedy administration proposed in July 1963 that the INA be revised to eliminate the national origins quota system, establish a permanent refugee quota, and liberalize employment-based admissions rules. Lyndon Johnson took up the cause in his 1964 and 1965 State of the Union addresses and reiterated Kennedy's themes of nondiscrimination in U.S. foreign policy in a special message to Congress accompanying his own legislative proposal in January 1965. Members of Congress viewed the issue in those terms as well, rejecting the 1952 INA as discriminatory and embracing the Kennedy-Johnson reform as a way to burnish the nation's image abroad.[16] After extensive hearings in both Houses during 1964 and 1965, Congress passed a revised set of amendments eliminating the national origins system and establishing a standing refugee quota as Kennedy and Johnson had requested.

U.S.-Mexican Migration Relations 1965–1980s

Migration nonetheless remained a contentious issue in U.S.-Mexican relations. The end of the bracero program in 1964 and the establishment of a universal, per-country admissions quota in 1968 (limiting family-based migration from Mexico for the first time) created an acute supply-and-demand problem for Mexicans seeking legal visas to enter the United States.[17] Mexico appealed repeatedly for a new guest worker program, but memories of the exploitative bracero program caused liberal and labor groups to oppose the proposals, while the willingness and ability of many Mexicans to migrate and work illegally in the United States meant that employers were satisfied with the status quo and thus did not lobby for new visas.

The tables turned following the oil shock of 1973. The Gerald Ford and Jimmy Carter administrations both approached Mexico about restarting guest worker flows in return for privileged U.S. access to Mexican oil. But by now Mexico was flush with oil wealth, and the nationalist Luis Echeverría and Jose Lopez Portillo administrations rejected those overtures.[18] The Carter administration also sought to provide extra visas to Mexican immigrants as part of a broader effort to strengthen U.S.-Mexico ties, but the Mexican visa proposal, like Carter's 1977 effort to pass immigration enforcement and visa reforms, was ignored by the Democratic Congress. As a result, Carter's legacy in this area was limited to his establishment in the White House of an Office of the U.S. Coordinator for Mexican Affairs and, with Jose Lopez Portillo, the establishment of a high-level U.S.-Mexico Consultative Mechanism to promote greater communication on energy, trade, and migration issues.[19]

By the 1980s, the combination of dramatic economic swings in Mexico, attractive job opportunities in the United States, and increasingly sophisticated transnational social networks had resulted in a well-developed system of undocumented Mexico-U.S. migration.[20] And whereas Carter had attempted—unsuccessfully—to use migration legislation as a tool of foreign policy in an effort to strengthen bilateral relations, attention to undocumented immigration instead exacerbated broader conflicts in bilateral relations during the 1980s.[21] Thus, members of Congress worried out loud that a wave of "feet people" were poised to invade the United States across the U.S.-Mexican border, and a Reagan administration official testified to Congress in the midst of the immigration debate that members of Mexican President Miguel de la Madrid's family were personally implicated in the drug trade. In this context, even though Sen. Alan Simpson, R-Wyo., made an explicit effort to solicit Mexico's input on pending migration reform legislation, Mexican officials refused an invitation to testify before Congress and remained disengaged from the U.S. policy debate. Likewise, when Congress passed the Immigration Reform and Control Act in 1986, the bill included provisions to strengthen border and worksite enforcement—finally overturning the "Texas proviso"—and an amnesty program for many undocumented immigrants, but it did not include language the Senate had approved two years earlier to expand Mexico's legal visa quota.[22]

Humanitarian Migration 1965–1980s

Humanitarian migration policies also remained contentious following passage of the 1965 amendments to the INA. The 1965 amendments established a standing Eastern Hemisphere refugee quota but restricted refugee admissions to about 10,000 people per year; it defined refugees exclusively as persons fleeing persecution from a communist regime or a country in the Middle East. This definition conflicted with the 1952 United Nations Refugee Convention, which defined refugees more broadly as persons fleeing their country of origin due to a well-founded fear of persecution on the basis of race, religion, nationality, or political beliefs.[23] The United States ratified the UN convention in 1968—making the United States one of the last advanced democracies to do so. But Congress failed to pass legislation bringing U.S. law into harmony with the UN language, and U.S. refugee admissions continued to prioritize diplomacy over humanitarian norms by admitting individuals from Soviet bloc states but denying admission to vulnerable refugees from authoritarian regimes allied with the United States.[24]

This two-track system became increasingly controversial during the 1970s, after the United States established a formal policy of admitting Cubans without any humanitarian test (the 1962 Migration and Refugee Assistance Act) but routinely denied admission to Haitians fleeing the repressive, but pro-American,

Duvalier regime in similar numbers and to thousands of people fleeing pro-American juntas in Greece, following the "Colonels' Coup" of 1967, and Chile following the Pinochet coup of 1973. Congress considered legislation throughout the late 1960s and early 1970s to adopt the UN's definition of refugees and establish more flexibility in the refugee quotas. But presidents argued in favor of the status quo, and the only legislative change came in 1976 when the INA was amended to extend the existing (that is, anticommunist) definition of refugees to include the Western Hemisphere.

A turning point came the same year, as the flight of 130,000 Indochinese "boat people" highlighted the inadequacy of the ad hoc system for "paroling" humanitarian refugees into the United States. Congress held extensive hearings in 1977–1978 and debated a pair of bills to require more formal executive branch consultation with Congress with respect to parolees, including a congressional veto over such admissions, and to establish clear numerical limits. The Carter administration consented—reluctantly—to a consultation process but adamantly resisted a congressional veto or hard quotas on both humanitarian and foreign policy grounds.

Finally, after extensive interbranch negotiations, the two sides agreed to the Refugee Act of 1980, which formally separated humanitarian and nonhumanitarian migration policy and established a formal legal framework for humanitarian admissions based on the UN's nonideological definition of refugees. The Refugee Act set a baseline quota of 50,000 refugees and required the president to formally consult Congress each year about how the visas were to be distributed. It also provided for additional emergency admissions at the president's discretion. The act anticipated that most humanitarian migrants would be admitted as refugees based on a proactive selection process through which individuals were resettled from UN-managed camps into the United States, but it also established a separate "asylum" category to provide for admission of individuals who meet refugee criteria and seek relief from within the United States rather than from abroad.[25]

The new asylum provisions were immediately put to the test. Just two weeks after the act was signed into law—and long before the executive branch drafted regulations to implement the new asylum provisions—the Cuban government opened the port of Mariel to people wishing to depart the island. One hundred twenty-five thousand "Marielitos" eventually came to the United States as part of this "Mariel boatlift," including about 3,000 criminals and mentally ill individuals who were essentially deported by Cuba to the United States. Thirty thousand Haitians also seized the opportunity to seek U.S. asylum. The Carter administration initially viewed the Haitians through a diplomatic, rather than a humanitarian lens, taking steps to interdict the Haitians at sea and prevent them from claiming asylum. But in May 1980 Carter established a special Cuban-Haitian entrant status, offering both groups a path to permanent U.S. residence.[26]

Seven months later the Reagan administration rejected Carter's approach and authorized a policy of mandatory detention for Haitians pending individual asylum hearings, few of which resulted in successful applications. The United States then negotiated a treaty with Haiti to permit U.S. inspections of Haitian vessels. Without waiting for a congressional response, Reagan signed an executive order requiring the Coast Guard to interdict Haitian boats and return any suspected asylum seekers to Haiti. The order contradicted the spirit of the 1980 act but succeeded in reducing Haitian asylum claims from 8,000 in 1981 to 134 in 1982.[27]

Many members of Congress objected to these policies, but interbranch conflict mainly focused on higher-profile disagreements over how the United States should respond to Central American refugees fleeing the U.S.-funded civil wars in El Salvador, Guatemala, and Nicaragua. The Refugee Act stipulated that refugee and asylum adjudication was to be based on a reasonable fear of persecution, without regard to the politics of the home country government. Yet the Reagan administration was reluctant to grant relief to applicants from El Salvador and Guatemala because doing so could suggest U.S. complicity with human rights violations, given the extensive U.S. support for those repressive regimes. Conversely, the administration was relatively open to admitting Nicaraguan refugees and approving Nicaraguan asylum claims, even though human rights organizations were less critical of the Nicaraguan regime.[28] Congress requested in 1980, 1981, 1983, and 1985 that the administration offer extended voluntary departure (EVD) status to Salvadorans, which would suspend deportations without a formal asylum hearing, but the administration refused. In 1986, House Democrats included EVD for Salvadorans and Nicaraguans as a provision in the Immigration Reform and Control Act (IRCA), defeating a Republican amendment to strike the provision during the IRCA floor debate by a two-vote margin (197–199). Nonetheless, with President Reagan threatening to veto the entire bill over EVD, House members agreed to drop the language during House-Senate conference negotiations, and the final bill made no mention of the issue.[29]

Immigration Policymaking after the Cold War

The end of the cold war was seen as a great opportunity to reorient U.S.-Latin American relations in general and U.S. relations with the high-emigration countries of the Caribbean Basin in particular.[30] Incoming presidents Carlos Salinas (December 1988) and George H.W. Bush (January 1989) moved quickly to repair bilateral relations, quickly producing the "Baker plan" for debt relief and eventually producing the breakthrough North American Free Trade Agreement (NAFTA) in 1992. Remaining sources of conflict seemed to fade away. President Bill Clinton signed the NAFTA (over the objections of most congressional Democrats) and convened a 1994 Summit of the Americas that included the head of state from every country in the hemisphere other than Cuba and produced a promise of a hemispheric free trade deal by 2005. Nicaragua's civil war ended with democratic elections in 1990, and El Salvador's civil war ended with a UN-monitored cease-fire in 1991. By the mid-1990s, Mexico was being praised by the Washington community as a model Latin American debtor-state, as it enthusiastically adopted neoliberal economic reforms and peacefully transitioned from a one-party system to a competitive democracy.

Initially, these improvements in regional relations seemed to lay the groundwork for improved regional migration relations as well, as Congress turned its attention from migration control efforts to modernizing the decades-old INA preference system. Congress passed the Immigration Act of 1990 with little fanfare, more than doubling quota numbers for legal permanent migration and dividing the preference system into separate family- and employment-based categories. In contrast with the 1980s, the problems of undocumented immigration and U.S.-Latin American relations did not figure prominently in the debate. Once again, congressional liberals attached an amendment granting EVD status to Salvadoran civil war refugees, and with the conflict winding down the Bush administration reluctantly allowed the measure to become law.[31]

Yet even as Bush and Clinton sought to strengthen regional relations in general, undocumented immigration inflows surged beginning in 1990, and the issue reemerged as a highly salient policy problem. By 1994, undocumented immigration was again the subject of inflammatory media attention, especially following California governor Pete Wilson's decision to support that state's controversial Proposition 187, denying social services to illegal immigrants.[32] Congressional Republicans also made migration a theme in their 1994 "Contract with America" campaign, and then candidate Pat Buchanan interjected migration into the 1996 presidential campaign.

Congress responded in 1996 with a trio of highly restrictionist laws: the Welfare Reform Act, which blocked *legal* immigrants from receiving welfare benefits (undocumented immigrants were already ineligible); the Antiterrorism and Effective Death Penalty Act, which tightened the asylum application process;

and the Illegal Immigration Reform and Immigrant Responsibility Act (IIRIRA), which increased funding for border enforcement, imposed stronger penalties on alien smugglers, and streamlined deportation and exclusion procedures into a single "removal" process. The new rules governing asylum hearings were applied retroactively, and their primary effect was to threaten with deportation 300,000 Salvadoran and Guatemalan civil war refugees who had registered with the INS as part of a legal settlement in 1990.

The legislation put President Clinton in an awkward position, caught between his outreach to Latin America and his effort to define himself as a "new Democrat," including by being tough on immigration.[33] Thus, while generally supporting all three pieces of legislation, Clinton responded to Mexican requests by demanding three important concessions from the Republican Congress: more moderate restrictions on migrants' access to welfare; a lower "deeming requirement," to make it easier for poor migrants to sponsor family members for new visas; and—through a veto threat—reversal of the "Gallegly amendment," which would have allowed states to deny undocumented immigrants access to public schools.[34] In addition, although the Clinton administration embraced "Operation Blockade" in 1993, to fortify the U.S.-Mexican border around El Paso, and more generally pursued a controversial strategy of "prevention through deterrence" that involved substantial new investments in personnel and military equipment at the U.S.-Mexican border,[35] the president also worked with Mexican Presidents Salinas and Ernesto Zedillo to create a number of new bilateral institutions designed to minimize the damage to relations from heavy-handed immigration enforcement.[36]

Clinton also responded to Central American lobbying efforts by introducing the Immigration Reform Transition Act, to exempt asylum applications already in the pipeline from IIRIRA's new restrictions. When Congress modified Clinton's bill and passed the Nicaraguan and Central American Relief Act (NACARA), however, it imposed a double standard: pending Guatemalan and Salvadoran applications would be considered under the old rules, as Clinton had proposed, but 5,000 Cubans and 150,000 Nicaraguans would be given a blanket right to adjust their status to legal permanent resident. Clinton reluctantly signed the bill but waited two years to approve regulations implementing the law. The regulations instructed asylum officers to consider Salvadoran and Guatemalan appeals on a case-by-case basis, as Congress had instructed, but—over Congress's objections—to reverse the normal burden of proof, ensuring that most of these applicants would be granted immigration relief.[37] NACARA's benefits were extended to certain Haitian asylum applicants under the 1998 Haitian Refugee Immigration Fairness Act (HRIFA), and the president offered additional benefits to Nicaraguans and Honduran immigrants affected by Hurricane Mitch in 1999.

Immigration Policy since September 11

President Bush Sets the Agenda

If the years after the dual inaugurations of George H. W. Bush and Carlos Salinas held reasons for optimism about integration and migration cooperation, balanced by new pressures for migration control, conflicting pressures were even more intense following the inaugurations of George W. Bush and Vicente Fox. On one hand, six years into the NAFTA period U.S.-Mexican trade and investment had doubled, and optimism ran high as two bilingual, former border state governors and business executives were poised to take office. Both presidents followed through on early pledges to make bilateral migration reform a priority, culminating with the September 2001 Partnership for Prosperity investment deal, aimed at reducing emigration pressures, and the framework agreement envisioning a broader migration deal that would include a Mexico-specific temporary worker program.

On the other hand, the September 11 attacks redefined prospects for bilateral cooperation. After decades of heavy-handed U.S. policies toward Latin America during and before the cold war, Mexicans and others in the region opposed the U.S. intervention in Iraq. Mexico's failure to support U.S. efforts to pass a United Nations Security Council resolution endorsing its military action, in March 2003, drove a significant wedge between the two states. Although Mexicans were initially tolerant of the post-September 11 suspension of migration talks, by the midpoint of Fox's presidency he was increasingly criticized for Bush's failure to follow through on bilateral immigration reform.[38]

Within the United States, immigration policy was subsumed into the war on terror. Just six weeks after the September 11 attacks, Congress passes the USA Patriot Act, a wide-ranging counterterrorism measure, which expanded domestic surveillance and enforcement against money laundering and eliminated barriers to communication among federal law enforcement agencies engaged in foreign and domestic investigations. Although never debated as an immigration bill, the Patriot Act also broadened the definition of terrorist activity for the purposes of immigration enforcement and authorized the indefinite detention of non–U.S. citizens. Five years later, Congress passed the REAL ID Act, with limited debate, by appending its provisions to a must-pass authorization bill. REAL ID emerged out of the 2004 Intelligence Reform Bill but eventually focused on three immigration-related provisions: expedited fence building along the U.S.-Mexico border, new restrictions on asylum admissions for "suspected terrorists," and new federal guidelines on the issuance of state driver's licenses, including a requirement that states verify individuals' immigration status prior to issuing licenses.

These enforcement provisions did not address the core immigration policy issues that had been discussed by Presidents Bush and Fox, nor did they in any way affect undocumented inflows or the availability of legal immigrant workers, the two issues that President Bush had identified in 2000 and 2001 as priorities. Thus, in January 2004 Bush held a press conference to place immigration policy back on the national agenda, announcing five core principles for immigration reform: tougher border security, a temporary worker program, temporary legal status for undocumented immigrants already inside the United States, incentives to promote return migration, and a path to permanent legal status and eventual citizenship for some immigrants who chose not to return.[39] The new proposal to "match willing workers with willing employers" became the de facto focus of a summit meeting with President Fox the following week,[40] and the president in his State of the Union address called on Congress to take up immigration reform.[41] Congress failed to do so in 2004, however, as most legislative business gave way to that year's presidential election. President Bush revisited the issue in his 2005 State of the Union address and in subsequent months by repeatedly identifying immigration, along with tax cuts and Social Security reform, as a top legislative goal for his second term.[42]

The Senate Judiciary Committee (Spring 2006)

The Senate took up this challenge, as three competing bills were filed, each of which shared the president's three-legged framework of enhanced enforcement at the U.S. border and worksites; new employment visas for "future flow" immigrants; and some form of legalization for existing undocumented immigrants.[43] The bills also differed in significant ways. The bill by John Cornyn, R-Texas, and Jon Kyl, R-Ariz., was the most restrictive of the three, offering strictly temporary visas to future workers and to existing undocumented immigrants but providing no new opportunity for either group to adjust to legal permanent status or eventual citizenship. In contrast, the proposal by John McCain, R-Ariz., and Edward Kennedy, D-Mass., as well as the one by Chuck Hagel, R-Neb., emphasized an eventual "path to citizenship" for guest workers and for existing undocumented immigrants who paid penalties and back taxes and maintained a clean record and steady employment in the future.[44] The Hagel and McCain-Kennedy bills also increased the number of permanent visas available to future immigrants, with Hagel focusing on high-skilled workers and McCain-Kennedy also expanding low-skilled employment and family-based flows. Judiciary Committee members Cornyn, Kyl, and Kennedy held seven hearings on the competing proposals between March and June 2005.

The Senate's work was sidelined in the fall as the Judiciary Committee (in charge of immigration policy) turned its attention to filling two Supreme Court vacancies, and the House stepped into the void by passing James Sensenbrenner's, R-Wis., H.R.4437,[45] a bill largely constructed by Bush administration officials in the Departments of Homeland Security and Justice. In contrast to the Senate's multiple hearings and extended debate (see below), the House moved quickly. The bill was introduced on December 6, marked up and reported by the Judiciary Committee two days later on a party-line vote, and then debated by the full House for just over a day before passing (239–182) in a mostly party-line vote on December 16. Also in contrast with the Senate, H.R.4437 restricted its attention to border and interior enforcement, without addressing future flows or legalizing existing undocumented immigrants. Instead, the House bill included extensive and controversial new provisions to restrict immigrants' access to courts, to expand the definition of "immigrant smuggling" to include acts of humanitarian assistance, and to turn civil immigration violations into felony criminal offenses.

Passage of H.R.4437 was a wake-up call to supporters of the Senate's more comprehensive approach, especially after the White House issued a strong statement of support for the Sensenbrenner bill during the House debate.[46] Thus, after completing its work on Supreme Court nominations in late January 2006, the Senate Judiciary Committee began marking up an immigration bill in February. Committee Chair Arlen Specter, R-Pa., drafted a "chairman's mark" (that is, a working draft of a bill not formally filed with the Senate clerk) as the starting point, borrowing employment-based visa language from the Hagel bill, enforcement provisions from the Cornyn-Kyl bill and from H.R.4437, and some details of a guest worker program from the McCain-Kennedy proposal, though without the McCain-Kennedy option for temporary workers eventually to adjust to U.S. citizenship. The proposal adopted a middle position on undocumented immigrants, proposing that they be eligible to remain in the United States indefinitely (in contrast with Cornyn-Kyl) but that they be denied the right eventually to become U.S. citizens (in contrast with McCain-Kennedy).

Specter's compromise failed to satisfy Kennedy and other advocates of "comprehensive reform," who held firm on a pathway to permanent citizenship and objected to Specter's inclusion of the new enforcement provisions from the Sensenbrenner bill, albeit in modified form. Seven of the eight Democrats on the committee and three of the ten Republicans—that is, a majority of the committee—supported the McCain-Kennedy approach to these issues.[47] But in a break with Senate tradition, Specter threatened to block any committee bill that lacked support from "a majority of the majority" on the committee. Four Republicans were reliable opponents of any legalization scheme or expansion in legal flows, and Specter's position therefore turned Senators Cornyn and Kyl into the swing voters whose support (along with Specter's) would make or break the "majority of the majority" condition.[48] Intense meetings were held throughout February and March among the Specter, Cornyn, Kyl, Kennedy, Dick Durbin, D-Ill., and Patrick Leahy, D-Vt., immigration staffs to try to forge a compromise, but differences over which undocumented immigrants and guest workers should qualify for citizenship could not be resolved.[49] Without a resolution of these long-term questions, the staff members found it impossible even to begin negotiating differences over interior enforcement provisions.

Two events in mid-March marked a turning point in the committee debate and shifted the focus from the backroom negotiations to the subcommittee markups. First, on March 16 Senate Majority Leader Bill Frist, R-Tenn., imposed a deadline on the Judiciary Committee by offering a bill of his own, which included all of the enforcement provisions in the chairman's mark but none of the new immigration benefits. Frist placed his bill on the calendar for March 28 and pledged to begin floor debate at that time if the Judiciary Committee had not reported a bill. With a recess scheduled the week of March 20, Frist's deadline seemed an impossible hurdle to overcome and a direct affront to Senator Specter and the rest of the committee. Second, in the week leading up to Frist's deadline, a million supporters of comprehensive immigration reform rallied around the country, including over half a million in downtown Los Angeles. The massive show of support—and of opposition to the House's enforcement-only bill—caused a perceptible shift in the debate when the committee reconvened, with California's Democratic senator Dianne Feinstein speaking eloquently, and for the first time, in favor of a McCain-Kennedy-style, broad legalization program for undocumented immigrants.

With Frist's deadline looming, Senator Specter scheduled a marathon markup session for March 27, pledging to keep the committee in session until a bill was agreed to. Sen. Sam Brownback, R-Kan., made a last-ditch effort to forge a compromise between supporters of the McCain-Kennedy bill and Senators Cornyn and Kyl, but when the effort showed no sign of progress Sen. Lindsey Graham, R-S.C., and committee Democrats circumvented the negotiations by forcing votes on a pair of amendments to replace Specter's temporary worker and legalization provisions with language from the McCain-Kennedy bill. In dramatic fashion, both amendments passed with identical 11–7 majorities (all eight Democrats plus the three supportive Republicans). Finally, after six days of markup and many months of work, Senator Specter backed down from his "majority of the majority" threat and joined the committee majority in the 12–6 vote to approve his amended bill.

The Senate Floor (Spring 2006)

The full Senate took up immigration reform two days later, with the committee bill offered as S. 2611, the Comprehensive Immigration Reform Act of 2006. Opponents of the bill introduced a series of amendments to strengthen immigration enforcement and narrow new immigration benefits. Senators Kyl and Cornyn, for example, offered an amendment denying legalization to undocumented immigrants with criminal records—a class the bill's supporters believed were already excluded under the committee's bill. A dispute arose over the meaning of the Kyl-Cornyn language, which the bill's supporters believed could deny legalization to hundreds of thousands of the bill's beneficiaries. Sen. Johnny Isakson, R-Ga., offered an amendment to require that implementation of the legalization and guest worker provisions could only be "triggered" once the president certified that the U.S.-Mexican border was "sealed and secured." Hard-liners saw this as consistent with the premise that comprehensive reform combined legalization and new legal flows with real enforcement, but supporters of the bill worried that the Isakson language established an impossible standard and that the new benefits would be postponed indefinitely.

The amendments placed the bill's supporters in a bind: passing either one struck at the heart of what reformers hoped to accomplish, but with a midterm election looming candidates feared that voting against the amendments would make them vulnerable to attack ads in the coming campaign. Kennedy and other supporters of the committee bill tried to organize votes to defeat the amendments, but the Democratic leadership overruled them and chose instead to exploit a procedural loophole to block the votes. Floor debate continued for another week, but discussion of immigration reform deteriorated into a partisan dispute over whether or not the amendments deserved a vote. Democrats attempted to salvage the bill by filing for cloture—a move that would limit additional amendments and force a vote on final passage—but the cloture move failed on a mainly party-line vote, and the Senate adjourned for its scheduled April recess without taking any substantive votes on the bill.[50]

Even as progress was derailed on the Senate floor, however, behind-the-scenes negotiations resumed. With support from the White House and Senator Frist, Republican Senators Hagel, Mel Martinez, Fla., McCain, and Graham sought a compromise with Democrats Kennedy, Barak Obama, Ill., and Ken Salazar, Colo., on a legalization program that would cover enough undocumented immigrants to satisfy Democrats while allowing Republicans to make good on their promise to oppose a broad "amnesty." In a late-night compromise, a two-track system was designed whereby aliens in the country for at least five years would be eligible for the McCain-Kennedy legalization procedure, but aliens with between two and five years of U.S. residence would be required to exit the United States, reenter as guest workers, and apply for green cards from an expanded pool of employment-based visas.[51] Democrats who opposed expanding the temporary worker program (already a source of contention) were mollified by offsetting cuts to visa numbers for new temporary worker flows and improved wage protections.

This "Hagel-Martinez" compromise brought together a bipartisan core group of members who pledged to place their common interest in comprehensive immigration reform ahead of partisan loyalties and to work together to defeat future "poison pill" amendments.[52] Public opinion polls reported unprecedented interest in the issue and a remarkably broad consensus in favor of the Senate bill.[53] Public demonstrations in favor of comprehensive reform continued, with more than three million people eventually marching in opposition to the House's enforcement-only approach and in support of the Senate bill. Broad-based support was reinforced by a broad left-right coalition of interest groups, which coordinated their lobbying activities and worked closely with the expanded McCain-Kennedy-Hagel-Martinez coalition throughout the debate.[54]

With the support of most Democrats and several additional Republicans, the pro-reform coalition fought off eight key amendments striking at the heart of the deal: a revised Isakson "trigger" amendment to link new immigration benefits to evidence of improved enforcement; a Kyl amendment to deny guest workers the ability to adjust to legal permanent status; a John Ensign, R-Nev., amendment to deny newly legal immigrants credit for their previously accrued Social Security benefits; a Saxby Chambliss, R-Ga., amendment to weaken wage protections for agricultural guest workers; a Cornyn amendment to weaken legal due process protections during the legalization process; a David Vitter, R-La., amendment to eliminate the legalization program; and a pair of Byron Dorgan, D-N.D., amendments to eliminate or phase out the temporary worker program.

The coalition also suffered a handful of defeats from the left (a pair of Jeff Bingaman, D-N.M., amendments to further reduce the size of the temporary worker program and to impose an absolute cap on employment-based permanent visas) and from the right (a Jeff Sessions, R-Ala., amendment to expand border fencing, a revised version of the earlier Kyl-Cornyn amendment to exclude certain immigrants from the earned legalization program, an Ensign amendment to deny newly legal immigrants access to the Earned Income Tax Credit, and a James Inhofe, R-Okla., amendment declaring English the official language of the United States). With these changes, the amended bill easily survived a cloture vote (73–25) on May 24 and passed the following day by a still-comfortable vote of 62–36.[55]

Bicameral Deadlock

The House and Senate bills differed in significant ways, and further progress would require negotiators to work out a compromise through a House-Senate conference committee.[56] Any sense of inevitability—or even probability—that that would happen evaporated within days of the Senate vote, when House leaders announced plans to hold field hearings rather than appoint conferees. Far from seeking common ground, the hearings—with titles such as, "What are the current risks of terrorists, narcotics smugglers, and human traffickers infiltrating the United States, and what role do secure identification documents play in limiting those risks? Does the Reid-Kennedy bill undermine efforts to limit those risks?"—widened the gap between the two chambers. The White House endorsed a final behind-the-scenes effort to circumvent the conference process through a new proposal sponsored by Rep. Mike Pence, R-Ind., and Sen. Kay Bailey Hutchison, R-Texas, but the Pence plan failed to pick up support in either chamber when sponsors of the House and Senate bills announced their opposition.

By the time Congress reconvened after its August 2006 recess, party leaders in both chambers had abandoned plans for a bicameral comprehensive reform bill. With the midterm elections looming, leaders felt compelled to "do something" in response to popular demands and settled for passage of the Secure Fence Act of 2006, a bill consisting of the border-area infrastructure language from the earlier House bill. While hard-liners were pleased that the chambers agreed to the more extensive border fencing provided by the House bill, they complained that the Bush administration was insufficiently committed to immigration control when the president's budget requested just half the amount Congress had authorized for fencing.

Conclusion: Continued Obstacles to Reform

U.S. regional relations since the cold war ended have been dominated by greater economic and political integration, and the NAFTA agreement is often held up as a model for the entire hemisphere. Immigration relations were a conspicuous outlier from this trend during the 1990s, as increasing trade and investment flows were met with a new focus on border enforcement and a broader trend toward the criminalization of undocumented migration. Why did Mexico drop out of the 2006 immigration debate after receiving so much attention from Bush in 2000–2001?

On one level, the failure to follow through on the promise of bilateralism should come as no surprise. As the preceding historical review suggests, the early years of the bracero program were uniquely characterized by bilateralism on migration policy. At the time, the United States needed Mexican support to restart migration flows and to ensure reliable access to Mexican labor during a period of war-induced shortages, and Mexico needed U.S. support to ensure that the state played a direct role in managing the program and in protecting the rights of Mexican workers within the United States. At other times, either the United States (1950s, 1960s) or Mexico (1970s) or both (1980s) have perceived their interests as best served by unilateral or even laissez-faire approaches to migration control, so that the objective conditions for a bilateral immigration deal have rarely been present.

Yet on another level, the failure of the United States and Mexico to follow through on the promise of 2001, reiterated in 2005, is surprising because the contemporary period resembles the early bracero years in that both Mexico and the United States have self-interested reasons to favor bilateralism. From the Mexican perspective, bilateralism is an attractive strategy for reducing the unacceptable level of violence at the U.S.-Mexican border, a top priority for a democratic Mexico eager to demonstrate its effectiveness. From the U.S. perspective, a bilateral deal offers the greatest promise with regard to both immigration control and the U.S. war on terror. And ruling factions in both countries see an immigration deal as an attractive way to solidify regional support for free markets and U.S. economic institutions.

Why, then, did the 2006 legislation fail to acknowledge Mexican concerns or move toward a Mexico-specific guest worker program such as Bush had previously proposed? Ultimately, the answer is that President Bush placed immigration on Congress's agenda but largely deferred to Congress on the specifics of an immigration proposal, and congressional immigration leaders view immigration from an overwhelmingly domestic perspective. Mexico's episodic efforts to influence U.S. immigration policy have been indirect (for example, mobilizing Mexicans within the United States or seeking to shape the public debate) or made through Mexican ties to the executive branch. As a result, Mexico has weak connections to U.S. congressional actors who are influential in the making of immigration legislation, and few Congress members gave any thought to opportunities for bilateralism as legislative details were finalized. Adding a Mexican dimension to the deal also would have created new sources of opposition to an already fragile compromise.

More generally, why did immigration reform efforts fail so spectacularly in 2006, despite widespread popular demands for reform and the rough popular consensus in favor of the Senate's reform bill? In short, reform efforts ran into a truism about immigration politics: that they are characterized by cross-cutting cleavages, which confound stable partisan coalitions. Democrats were divided between the desire to appeal to Latino voters, who favored generous comprehensive reform, and the desire to appear tough on national security by backing a House-style, enforcement-only bill. Some Democrats also objected to the Senate bill's temporary worker provisions, which labor unions traditionally have opposed. Republicans were even more divided. The president had made support for comprehensive immigration reform a central theme of his second term; national party leaders saw pro-immigrant reforms as a unique opportunity to solidify Bush's tentative gains with Latino voters; and traditionally Republican business and mainline religious groups were strong backers of the Senate bill. But grassroots social conservative groups like the Eagle Forum, anti-immigration advocates like the Federation for American Immigration Reform (FAIR) and the Minutemen, and evangelical groups like the Christian Coalition all brought significant restrictionist pressure to bear on Republican members, including a successful summer campaign to mail bricks (for building a border fence) to members of Congress.

Second, with the parties internally divided and elections looming, strategists on both sides of the aisle saw political reasons to block the Senate bill. Democratic leaders believed that the majority Republicans would be blamed if Congress failed to pass immigration reform, reinforcing the Democratic campaign theme of a "do-nothing" Congress. Republicans recognized that voters wanted action on immigration policy, but many considered the price of inaction to be lower than the price of supporting "amnesty," a term that hard-liners defined to include almost any policy short of mass deportation.

Third, immigration reform was undermined by President Bush's failure to exercise effective leadership on the issue. The president spoke out in favor of reform on a number of occasions, including in a rare prime-time address on May 15, timed to coincide with the start of the second round of Senate debate, but he never explicitly endorsed the Senate bill. More important, even when Bush did lobby reluctant senators in favor of the comprehensive reform bill, and when he lobbied both chambers to come together after passage of the Senate bill, his low approval ratings limited his leverage, and House members were unmoved by his efforts.[57]

Finally, what are the prospects for comprehensive immigration reform in the 110th Congress? Although immigration was not a dominant theme in the 2006 midterm elections, Democratic supporters of comprehensive reform defeated enforcement-only Republicans in thirteen of the fifteen races in which migration played a central role, and new Democratic majorities in both houses of Congress seemed to bode well for comprehensive reform efforts in 2007.[58] But efforts to draft a bipartisan, bicameral bill based on the 2006 Senate-passed language foundered when Senators McCain and Kennedy could not reach agreement on the details of a temporary worker program.[59]

Once again, the Senate Judiciary Committee became sidetracked, in this case by an evolving Justice Department scandal over the dismissal of U.S. attorneys. In contrast to the previous year, the Bush administration became highly engaged, sponsoring backroom negotiations among Democratic Senators Kennedy, Salazar, and Robert Menendez, N.J., and ten Republicans in an effort to craft a bipartisan deal that could garner broad Republican support. Democrats were skeptical that common ground could be found after the White House tapped Jon Kyl as the lead Republican negotiator, but Senator Kennedy committed himself to the negotiations after the primary Republican sponsors of the 2006 bill (John McCain, Arlen Specter, Lindsay Graham and Mel Martinez) signed a "Dear Colleague" letter pledging to filibuster any bill that did not emerge out of the bipartisan talks. This put Republican negotiators in a strong position, and the resulting legislative proposal was well to the right of the 2006 Senate-passed bill in its changes to permanent visa rules, temporary worker program, and worksite enforcement provisions. But in what the authors described as a "grand compromise" it also included more generous legalization provisions for undocumented immigrants than had passed the previous year (see Box 8.1).

The compromise was offered on the Senate floor in May 2007 as the Secure Borders, Economic Opportunity, and Immigration Reform Act of 2007. On the floor the bill was amended from the left (imposing a five-year sunset on the temporary worker program and cutting its size in half) and from the right (imposing additional enforcement "triggers" beyond those agreed to in the backroom negotiations, increasing penalties on legalizing immigrants, outlawing bilingual

Box 8.1 The Debate over Immigration Reform

Congressional debate about immigration reform during 2005–2007 focused on four key issues:

Legalization of Undocumented Immigrants

About 12 million undocumented immigrants live in the United States, including about 6 million undocumented workers, 5 percent of the U.S. workforce. Advocates of legalization argued that deportation of so many people would be too costly and too disruptive—for employers and for U.S. citizen relatives of the undocumented—to be practical. "Comprehensive" reform bills therefore proposed to allow undocumented immigrants to earn legal status by working and paying taxes, learning English and passing a civics test, and paying fees. Opponents criticized any path to legal status as "amnesty" and argued that it rewarded lawbreakers and was unfair to others waiting in line to enter legally. "Enforcement-only" bills therefore sought to deport the undocumented or to make their lives sufficiently unpleasant that they would leave on their own.

Temporary Workers

About 400,000 new, low-skilled, undocumented workers enter the U.S. workforce each year. Supporters of comprehensive reform argued that admitting a similar number of legal workers each year would reduce the "jobs magnet" that attracts undocumented immigrants. But critics from the left worried that *temporary* workers also would be easily exploited and pointed to the mature version of the bracero program as evidence. The 2006 Senate bills therefore would have allowed temporary workers eventually to transition to permanent legal status. The 2007 Senate bill would have required almost all temporary workers to return home after two years, a point of contention for both immigration advocates and immigrant employers.

Legal Permanent Visas

The United States issues about 800,000 "green cards" per year to the foreign families of U.S. citizens and legal permanent residents and to foreign workers when U.S. businesses cannot find an American worker to fill a particular position. Individuals with green cards may apply for U.S. citizenship after five years. The waiting lists for employment green cards may be as long as several years, and some family members must wait more than twenty years for a green card. The 2006 Senate bill would have doubled the number of family green cards available, to reduce this backlog and meet future demand, and would have more than doubled the number of employment-based cards. The 2007 Senate bill would have provided a temporary increase in family green cards to clear the existing backlog, and then eliminated most categories of both family and employment migration, replacing them with a point system that would provide green cards on the basis of immigrants' education and skills.

Enforcement

All of the Senate and House bills would have substantially increased fencing and use of military technology at the U.S.-Mexican border. And all would have established a universal electronic eligibility verification system (EEVS)—a system for employers to confirm workers' legal status by comparing their identity documents to a national legal worker database—but intense differences existed over how an EEVS should be structured. The House's Sensenbrenner bill also included numerous provisions to streamline immigration enforcement by reducing immigrants' access to courts and by imposing tougher penalties for migration-related offenses; these interior enforcement provisions and legal due process questions also became a source of controversy in the Senate debate.

ballots and other government documents, and stripping away important legal protections during the legalization process) during two weeks of Senate debate, leaving no one perfectly happy with the resulting product. Even so, pressure for reform—especially pressure from immigrant advocates demanding legalization on almost any terms—meant that the bill likely would have enjoyed the support of a similar group of forty or so Democrats and twenty or so Republicans had it come up for a vote.

Instead, in a process reminiscent of the April 2006 debate over S. 2611, negotiations broke down over a partisan dispute about the number of Republican amendments to be considered prior to a vote on final passage. Thus, when Senate Majority Leader Harry Reid, D-Nev., filed cloture to limit debate on the bill in June 2007, most Republican supporters maintained party discipline, joining the bill's Democratic and Republican opponents to defeat the cloture motion. Senators Kennedy and Kyl and other sponsors of the bill immediately returned to the negotiating table and struck a deal the following week on a list of eleven amendments from each party to be considered. They worked with leadership on both sides of the aisle to limit the debate to this list. With the agreement in place, on June 26, sixty-four senators supported a cloture motion to bring the bill back to the floor. Once again, however, controversy over the bill's contents and objections to the exclusive voting rules caused a majority to vote against a second cloture motion two days later that would have guaranteed a final vote on the bill. Fifteen Democrats joined thirty-eight Republicans in voting to kill the bill. While there was still a possibility that the House of Representatives would take up its own immigration measure after this book went to press, most analysts believed that the decisive Senate defeat marked the last chance for major immigration reform prior to the 2008 election.

Key Actors

George W. Bush President, placed immigration reform on the agenda in 2001, 2005, and 2007 but was criticized by supporters of reform efforts for failing to push hard enough to pass bills in 2006 and 2007.

Michael Chertoff Secretary of homeland security, key negotiator and spokesman for the Bush administration during debates over the Comprehensive Immigration Reform Act of 2006 (McCain-Kennedy bill) and the Secure Borders, Economic Opportunity, and Immigration Reform Act of 2007 (Kennedy-Kyl bill).

Vicente Fox President of Mexico (2000–2006), joined President Bush in pressing for immigration reform in 2001 but was sidelined from U.S. immigration debate after the September 11 attacks.

Carlos Gutierrez U.S. Secretary of Commerce, key negotiator and spokesman for the Bush administration during debate over the Comprehensive Immigration Reform Act of 2006 (McCain-Kennedy bill) and the Secure Borders, Economic Opportunity, and Immigration Reform Act of 2007 (Kennedy-Kyl bill).

Edward Kennedy Senator, D-Mass., coauthor of the Comprehensive Immigration Reform Act of 2006 (McCain-Kennedy bill) and the Secure Borders, Economic Opportunity, and Immigration Reform Act of 2007 (Kennedy-Kyl bill).

Jon Kyl Senator, R-Ariz., leading opponent of Comprehensive Immigration Reform Act of 2006 (McCain-Kennedy bill); coauthor of Secure Borders, Economic Opportunity, and Immigration Reform Act of 2007 (Kennedy-Kyl bill).

John McCain Senator, R-Ariz., coauthor of Comprehensive Immigration Reform Act of 2006 (McCain-Kennedy bill); supporter of the Secure Borders, Economic Opportunity, and Immigration Reform Act of 2007 (Kennedy-Kyl bill).

Ken Salazar Senator, D-Colo., primary Democratic cosponsor of the Comprehensive Immigration Reform Act of 2006 (McCain-Kennedy bill) and of the

Secure Borders, Economic Opportunity, and Immigration Reform Act of 2007 (Kennedy-Kyl bill).

James Sensenbrenner Representative, R-Wis., author of the Border Protection, Antiterrorism, and Illegal Immigration Control Act of 2005 (Sensenbrenner bill).

Arlen Specter Senator, R-Pa., primary Republican cosponsor of the Comprehensive Immigration Reform Act of 2006 (McCain-Kennedy bill) and of the Secure Borders, Economic Opportunity, and Immigration Reform Act of 2007 (Kennedy-Kyl bill).

Notes

1. See, e.g., Jorge I. Domínguez and Rafael Fernández de Castro, *The United States and Mexico: Between Partnership and Conflict* (New York: Routledge, 2002); Cathryn Thorup, "U.S. Policy toward Mexico: Prospects for Administrative Reform," in *Foreign Policy in U.S.-Mexican Relations,* ed. Rosario Green and Peter H. Smith (La Jolla: University of California, San Diego Center for U.S.-Mexican Studies, 1989), 129–157.
2. Robert Leiken, "With a Friend like Fox," *Foreign Affairs* 80, no. 5 (2001): 91–104.
3. White House, "Joint Statement by President George Bush and President Vicente Fox: Towards a Partnership for Prosperity," February 16, 2001, www.whitehouse.gov/news/releases/2001/02/20010220-2.html (accessed May 7, 2007).
4. The negotiating framework identified four goals: "matching willing workers with willing employers; serving the social and economic needs of both countries; respecting the human dignity of all migrants, regardless of their status; recognizing the contribution migrants make to enriching both societies; [and] shared responsibility for ensuring migration takes place through safe and legal channels." The high-level working group was instructed to work out the details for an agreement focused on border safety, a temporary worker program, and a strategy for legalizing the status of undocumented Mexicans in the United States. See White House, "Joint Statement between the United States of America and the United Mexican States" September 6, 2001, www.whitehouse.gov/news/releases/2001/09/20010906-8.html (accessed May 7, 2007).
5. White House, "Fact Sheet: Partnership for Prosperity," September 6, 2001, http://www.whitehouse.gov/news/releases/2001/09/20010906-7.html (accessed May 7, 2007). Analysts had long identified such a program as the most promising strategy for reducing undocumented outflows, though the politics of such a program are difficult because economic growth may increase emigration pressures in the short run, before reducing them in the long-run. See U.S. Commission for the Study of International Migration and Cooperative Economic Development (Asencio Commission), *Unauthorized Migration: An Economic Development Response* (Washington, D.C.: U.S. Government Printing Office, 1990).
6. Elliot B. Smith, "Neighborly Visit for Bush, Fox," *Chicago Sun Times,* February 18, 2001, A34.
7. James C. McKinley Jr., "From Mexico also, the Message to Bush Is Immigration," *New York Times,* March 14, 2007, A12.

8. In addition to a controversy about heavy-handed migration enforcement during the 1930s, bilateral relations were strained as a result of Mexico's 1938 expropriation of U.S. oil holdings. When the two sides were unable to agree on a compensation package for U.S. firms, the United States boycotted Mexican oil sales, and Mexico responded by boosting its exports to Germany.

9. U.S. Department of State, *Foreign Relations of the United States,* vol. 6 (Washington, D.C.: U.S. Government Printing Office, 1943), 538–544.

10. David Fitzgerald, "Inside the Sending State: The Politics of Mexican Emigration Control," *International Migration Review* 40, 2 (Summer 2006): 259–293.

11. "The Bracero Program," *Rural Migration News* 10, no. 2, April 2003, http://migration.ucdavis.edu/rmn/more.php?id=10_0_4_0 (accessed June 2, 2007).

12. On the bracero program and U.S.-Mexican relations generally, see Richard B. Craig, *The Bracero Program: Interest Groups and Foreign Policy* (Austin: University of Texas Press, 1979); Marc R. Rosenblum, "The Intermestic Politics of Immigration Policy: Lessons from the Bracero Program," *Political Power and Social Theory* 17 (2005): 141–184.

13. Kitty Calavita, *Inside the State: The Bracero Program, Immigration and the I.N.S.* (New York: Routledge, 1992); Stephen W. Yale-Loehr, "Testimony before the House Judiciary Committee, Subcommittee on Immigration," April 24, 2007, http://judiciary.house.gov/media/pdfs/Yale-Loehr070424.pdf (accessed May 7, 2007).

14. "Braceros Riot at the Border," *New York Times,* January 24, 1954, A10.

15. Gil Loescher and John A. Scanlan, *Calculated Kindness: Refugees and America's Half-Open Door, 1945 to the Present* (New York: Free Press, 1986); Daniel J. Tichenor, *Dividing Lines: The Politics of Immigration Control in America* (Princeton: Princeton University Press, 2002).

16. Cheryl Shanks, *Immigration and the Politics of American Sovereignty, 1890–1990* (Ann Arbor: University of Michigan Press, 2001).

17. Douglas Massey, Jorge Durand, and Nolan J. Malone, *Beyond Smoke and Mirrors: Mexican Immigration in an Era of Free Trade* (New York: Russell Sage Foundation, 2002).

18. Carlos Rico F, "Migration and U.S.-Mexican Relations, 1966–1986," in *Western Hemisphere Immigration and United States Foreign Policy,* ed. Christopher Mitchell (College Park, Pa.: Pennsylvania State Press, 1992), 3–25.

19. Salvador Campos Icardo, "Progress in Bilateral Relations," *Proceedings of the Academy of Political Science* 34, no. 1 (1981): 28–31; Thorup, "U.S. Policy toward Mexico."

20. Massey, Durand, and Malone, *Beyond Smoke and Mirrors.*

21. In particular, bilateral relations were strained by disagreements over conflicting U.S. and Mexican approaches to resolving civil wars in Nicaragua, Guatemala, and El Salvador; by Mexico's 1982 debt default and subsequent economic crisis; by the slow pace of Mexico's electoral reform; and by the conflict over the U.S. war on drugs. See Marc R. Rosenblum, *The Transnational Politics of U.S. Immigration Policy* (La Jolla: University of California, San Diego Center for Comparative Immigration Studies, 2004).

22. Ibid.

23. United Nations General Assembly, "Convention Relating to the Status of Refugees" (New York: United Nations), www.un.org/documents/ga/res/5/ares5.htm (accessed May 7, 2007).

24. Loescher and Scanlan, *Calculated Kindness*; Marc R. Rosenblum and Idean Salehyan, "Norms and Interests in U.S. Asylum Enforcement," *Journal of Peace Research* 41, no. 6 (2004): 677–697.

25. See Deborah E. Anker and Michael H. Posner, "The Forty-Year Crisis: A Legislative History of the Refugee Act of 1980," *San Diego Law Review* 19, no. 9 (1981): 1–89; and Loescher and Scanlan, *Calculated Kindness.*

26. See Alex Stepick, "Unintended Consequences: Rejecting Haitian Boat People and Destabilizing Duvalier," in *Western Hemisphere Immigration and United States Foreign Policy,* ed. Mitchell, 125–155.

27. Ibid.

28. See Loescher and Scanlan, *Calculated Kindness;* Rosenblum and Salehyan, "Norms and Interests"; and Lars Schoultz, "Central America and the Politicization of U.S. Immigration Policy," in *Western Hemisphere Immigration and United States Foreign Policy,* ed. Mitchell, 157–219.

29. See James G. Gimpel and James R. Edwards Jr., *The Congressional Politics of Immigration Reform* (Boston: Allyn and Bacon, 1999).

30. See Peter Hakim, "The Uneasy Americas," *Foreign Affairs,* March/April 2001, 46–61.

31. On the other hand, the president did threaten a veto in order to block a congressional effort to provide similar humanitarian relief to Chinese students in the United States at the time of the Tiananmen Square massacre. This contrast reflects a broader shift in the type of nonhumanitarian foreign policy bias seen in U.S. asylum enforcement—from cold war and military relations during the 1980s to economic relations during the 1990s. See Rosenblum and Salehyan, "Norms and Interests."

32. See, for example, Thomas Elias, "Proposition 187 Fans the Flames of Intolerance," *Houston Chronicle,* December 11, 1994, A1.

33. Clinton's pro-enforcement position was also a legacy of his experience as governor of Arkansas, where riots in 1980 by 21,000 Cuban Marielitos temporarily housed at Arkansas's Fort Chaffee contributed to Clinton's defeat in his gubernatorial reelection campaign.

34. The Gallegly amendment had passed by a comfortable margin of 257–163, and substantial presidential effort was required to strip the provision from the bill. See Rosenblum, *The Transnational Politics.*

35. See Deborah Waller Meyers, "U.S. Border Enforcement: From Horseback to High Tech," Migration Policy Institute Insight #7 (Washington, D.C.: Migration Policy Institute, 2005).

36. These efforts included a new U.S. border crossing card program for local migration, a bilateral "memorandum of understanding" emphasizing human rights over law enforcement, a joint training program for U.S. and Mexican border guards, "mechanisms of consultation" between U.S. enforcement agents and Mexican consuls to improve border-area bilateral communications, "border liaison mechanisms" to govern deportation procedures, and new programs to link migration control efforts to Mexican economic development programs. See Rosenblum, *The Transnational Politics.*

37. Ibid.

38. Jorge Castãneda, "The Forgotten Relationship," *Foreign Affairs,* May/June 2003, 67–81; Peter Hakim, "Is Washington Losing Latin America?" *Foreign Affairs,* January/February 2006, 39–53.

39. White House, "Fact Sheet: Fair and Secure Immigration Reform," January 7, 2004, www.whitehouse.gov/news/releases/2004/01/20040107-1.html (accessed May 7, 2007).

40. White House, "President Bush, President Fox Meet with Reporters in Mexico," January 12, 2004, www.whitehouse.gov/news/releases/2004/01/20040112-7.html (accessed May 7, 2007).

41. White House, "State of the Union Address," January 20, 2004, www.whitehouse.gov/news/releases/2004/01/20040120-7.html (accessed May 7, 2007).

42. White House, "State of the Union Address," February 2, 2005, www.whitehouse.gov/news/releases/2005/02/20050202-11.html (accessed May 7, 2007).

43. Senators John McCain, R-Ariz., and Edward Kennedy, D-Mass., introduced S. 1033 in March, the Secure America and Orderly Immigration Act. Senators John Cornyn, R-Texas, and Jon Kyl, R-Ariz., introduced S. 1438 in July, the Comprehensive Enforcement and Immigration Reform Act; and Sen. Chuck Hagel, R-Neb., introduced a package of four separate bills, S. 1916–S. 1919, in October.

44. The McCain-Kennedy bill offered "earned legalization" to immigrants who had been in the United States for at least two years, while Hagel's offer required five years of residency.

45. The Border Protection, Antiterrorism, and Illegal Immigration Control Act of 2005.

46. White House, "Statement of Administration Policy: H.R. 4437—Border Protection, Antiterrorism, and Illegal Immigration Control Act of 2005," December 15, 2005, www.whitehouse.gov/omb/legislative/sap/109-1/hr4437sap-h.pdf, (accessed May 28, 2007).

47. Sen. Diane Feinstein, Calif., was the only Democrat on the committee who opposed the McCain-Kennedy guest worker and legalization language. Among Republicans, Lindsay Graham. S.C., and Sam Brownback, Kan., were original McCain-Kennedy cosponsors, and Mike DeWine, Ohio, was a strong supporter.

48. Republicans Jeff Sessions, Ala., and Tom Coburn, Okla., were the two most reliable anti-immigration votes in the Senate, and Charles Grassley, Iowa, and Orrin Hatch, Utah, were also considered safe votes against comprehensive reform.

49. Republicans in these negotiations accepted the idea that some undocumented immigrants deserved a chance at legal status but proposed restricting the offer to the most extreme humanitarian cases and the most indispensable workers with specialized job skills. Republicans also wanted legalization cases adjudicated on a case-by-case basis. Democrats insisted that the vast majority of undocumented immigrants should be covered and that legalization should be offered on a categorical basis.

50. Six Democrats crossed party lines to vote against cloture. Even solid Republican supporters of comprehensive reform, such as John McCain and Lindsay Graham, voted against cloture based on their conviction that the Democrats were violating Senate norms by blocking votes on the disputed amendments.

51. These "touch-base returns" provided Republicans some political cover against the charge of amnesty because immigrants would reenter in legal status before getting on a path to citizenship. As in the Judiciary Committee and McCain-Kennedy bills, aliens in the country for less than two years were denied legalization.

52. The core group included Republican Senators Brownback, DeWine, Graham, Hagel, Martinez, McCain, and Specter and Democratic Senators Durbin, Kennedy, Lieberman, Conn., Menendez, Obama, and Salazar. The group met daily during the second floor debate to map out legislative strategy and to agree on coalition positions on each of the expected amendments.

53. A July Tarrance Group poll found that 11 percent of respondents identified candidates' positions on illegal immigration as the most important issue determining their vote in the fall, the highest figure ever reported on this question. Three separate polls conducted by CNN in April and May and by CBS in May found between 75 percent and 79 percent of respondents supporting the Senate's legalization provisions. Even strong majorities of Republican voters favored the Senate plan—75 percent in a June Tarrance Group poll—while only 47 percent supported the House's enforcement-only approach.

54. Key interest groups supporting the comprehensive Senate bill included the U.S. Chamber of Commerce, the Essential Workers Immigration Coalition (EWIC, itself a coalition of business groups employing low-skilled immigrant workers), the U.S. Conference of Catholic Bishops, the National Council of La Raza, the National Immigration Forum, the American Immigration Lawyers' Association, and the Service Employees International Union.

55. Four out of 43 Democrats crossed party lines to oppose the bill, and 23 out of 55 Republicans supported it; two Democrats were absent.

56. The House bill ran 256 pages in legislative format, compared to 795 for the Senate's. More fundamentally, while the bills included broadly similar enforcement provisions—increasing border infrastructure and personnel, strengthening document security, requiring employers to participate in an electronic employment eligibility verification system—the House bill made undocumented immigrants into felons, whereas the Senate offered them legal status. The Senate bill also promised a dramatic expansion in both temporary and permanent legal immigration, while the House offered none.

57. Nicole Gaouette, "House GOP Not Budging on Border," *Los Angeles Times,* May 24, 2006, A1.

58. Chris Dorval and Andrea LaRue, "Immigration Fails as Wedge Issue for GOP; Succeeds in Expanding Base for Democrats," Immigration 2006.org press release, November 8, 2006, www.immigration2006.org/index.html (accessed May 29, 2007).

59. Representatives Luis Gutierrez, D-Ill., and Jeff Flake, R-Ariz., introduced the compromise language, the Security through Regularized Immigration and a Vibrant Economy (STRIVE) Act of 2007, as H.R. 1645, but House leaders chose to postpone debate until after the Senate passed a bill.

9 U.S. Steel Import Tariffs: The Politics of Global Markets

Robert A. Blecker

Before You Begin

1. What factors accounted for the dramatic rise in U.S. imports of steel between 1995 and 2000, and how did the increased imports affect U.S. producers and consumers of steel?
2. How did the Clinton and Bush administrations respond to the steel industry's demands for import relief, and why were their responses so different?
3. How did domestic steel producers take advantage of U.S. international trade laws to protect their interests? What are the legal differences between "safeguard tariffs" and other trade remedies?
4. Why did President George W. Bush decide to impose safeguard tariffs on steel imports in March 2002, and why did he end those tariffs in December 2003?
5. How did the safeguard tariffs affect the U.S. steel industry and the U.S. economy as a whole? Were the tariffs justified? Why or why not?
6. How did foreign steel producers and U.S. steel consumers react to the tariffs? Why did the World Trade Organization rule that the U.S. steel tariffs were illegal?

Introduction

George W. Bush, like most U.S. presidents in recent decades, has portrayed himself as a strong supporter of free trade. Yet one of his most prominent trade policy decisions was the controversial imposition of tariffs on a significant portion of U.S. steel imports from March 2002 to December 2003. Bush approved these tariffs in accordance with the "safeguard" provision of U.S. trade law, officially known as section 201 of the Trade Act of 1974.[1] That legal provision, which is supposed to conform to the World Trade Organization Agreement on Safeguards, allows for the adoption of temporary import relief for a domestic industry, through tariffs or quotas, if increased imports have caused "serious injury" to the domestic producers—business firms and their workers—to give those producers a chance to adjust and improve their competitiveness.[2]

U.S. Steel Import Tariffs

1996–1998 U.S. steel imports rise rapidly, in large part as a result of the Asian financial crisis of 1997 and 1998 and a global glut of steel supplies. Although domestic demand for steel remained strong, imports captured a rising share of the U.S. market, causing prices to fall and companies to lose profits.

1998–1999 U.S. steel producers seek to "safeguard" import relief—tariffs or quotas—but are rebuffed by the Clinton administration. Instead, domestic firms file large numbers of antidumping and countervailing duty (antisubsidy) cases against foreign exporters of certain steel products. The U.S. International Trade Commission (ITC) votes in the industry's favor and imposes tariffs on imports of some of these products.

1999–2002 Thirty-one steel companies file for bankruptcy, and thousands of steel workers lose their jobs. Some of the bankrupt facilities reopen under new management.

July 2000 The Commerce Department issues *Report to the President: Global Steel Trade. Structural Problems and Future Solutions*, which analyzes the causes of the steel import surge and cites certain foreign countries for market-distorting practices that encourage artificially cheap exports.

June 2001 Responding to pressure from the steel industry, President George W. Bush requests the ITC to launch a safeguard investigation of all steel imports under section 201 of U.S. trade law.

September–October 2001 The ITC holds public hearings on steel imports and determines that they were "a substantial cause of serious injury" in sixteen out of thirty-three product categories, accounting for approximately 74 percent of steel imports.

December 2001 The ITC completes the "remedy phase" of its investigation and recommends a combination of tariffs and quotas on the sixteen types of steel imports determined to have caused serious injury to domestic producers.

March 2002 Bush imposes safeguard tariffs for three years and one day on most of the products recommended by the ITC but excludes numerous other products and many countries from the tariff remedy. Only about 24 percent of total steel imports by volume and 31 percent by value are covered by the tariffs.

June 2002 The World Trade Organization (WTO) creates a dispute resolution panel to hear complaints from the European Union (EU) and eight steel-exporting countries against the U.S. steel safeguard tariffs.

July 2003 The WTO panel rules that the U.S. steel tariffs are illegal under international trade agreements.

August 2003 The United States appeals the WTO panel's decision to the WTO Appellate Body, delaying enforcement of the ruling.

November 2003 The WTO Appellate Body upholds the WTO panel's ruling that the U.S. steel tariffs are illegal, thus allowing the affected steel exporters to impose retaliatory tariffs on an equal value of U.S. exports. The European Union and several nations threaten to impose tariffs on U.S. exports from politically sensitive states, such as Florida and the Carolinas.

December 2003 Bush decides to terminate the safeguard tariffs fifteen months ahead of schedule. He claims that they are no longer needed because they had achieved their purpose of helping the domestic industry to restructure and become more competitive.

U.S. steel producers had been calling for broad-based import relief since 1998, when the volume of steel imports reached what was then an all-time high of 41.5 million tons, representing a record 31.5 percent of the U.S. market.[3] When then-president Bill Clinton refused to support a safeguard remedy, the steel industry used other provisions of U.S. trade law to obtain protection from imports of particular steel products that were "unfairly traded" (illegally dumped or subsidized). Five months after taking office, however, in June 2001, President George W. Bush acceded to pressure from the industry and its congressional supporters and requested a safeguard investigation of all steel imports.[4]

Following the president's request, the U.S. International Trade Commission (ITC) conducted an investigation in which it determined that imports had seriously injured major parts of the U.S. steel industry. In December 2001 it recommended to the president a package of import relief covering most steel products.[5] Bush then exercised his legal authority to impose safeguard tariffs in March 2002, although he modified the ITC's recommended package by reducing the tariff rates, exempting certain countries, and granting exclusions for various products, leaving less than one-third of total U.S. steel imports covered by the tariffs.[6]

Almost immediately, the affected foreign countries—led by the European Union and Japan—appealed the tariff decision to a dispute resolution panel of the World Trade Organization (WTO). That panel issued a ruling against the U.S. decision in July 2003, finding that the United States had incorrectly applied the WTO safeguard agreement and that hence the U.S. tariffs were illegal.[7] The ruling gave the steel-exporting nations covered by the tariffs the right to impose retaliatory tariffs on an equal value of U.S. exports of other products. When the WTO Appellate Body upheld the panel's ruling, in November 2003, President Bush abolished the tariffs a month later.

The White House denied that the administration had bowed to the pressure of the WTO, however, claiming instead that the tariffs had worked and were therefore no longer needed. The reasons for Bush's decisions to impose the tariffs and later to revoke them can be understood by reviewing the causes of the steel import crisis and examining the economic interests, legal issues, and political factors that were at stake in the steel tariff dispute.

Background: The Origins of the Steel Import Dispute

U.S. steel companies have sought protection from imports repeatedly since the late 1960s, and they have been successful on many occasions.[8] The most recent episode began in the late 1990s, a period of rapid growth in the U.S. economy during which domestic demand for steel products reached a historic high of about 130 million tons per year from 1998 to 2000.[9] U.S. steel companies failed to benefit proportionately from the boom in demand, however, as imports increased their share of the domestic market and drove down domestic prices. Steel imports grew rapidly between 1995 and 1998 and remained high through 2000 (see Figure 9.1), while average prices of steel products fell sharply, especially in 1998–1999 and again in 2000–2001 (see Figure 9.2).[10] Although the recession of 2001 undoubtedly contributed to the further fall in steel prices in that year, the earlier declines were driven primarily by the high volume of low-priced imports.

Several factors combined to stimulate the rising volume of low-priced imports into the U.S. steel market in the late 1990s. To some extent, it was the culmination of a long-term trend in which more and more foreign nations developed export-oriented steel industries. The United States began to import significant quantities of steel from Western Europe and Japan in the 1960s and early 1970s and from newly industrializing, developing countries, including Brazil, Taiwan, and South Korea, in the late 1970s and 1980s. These sources of imports were then joined by formerly socialist, "transition economies," such as Russia, Ukraine, and China, which began exporting large volumes of steel in the mid-1990s.

Figure 9.1 Total Annual U.S. Steel Imports, 1990–2006

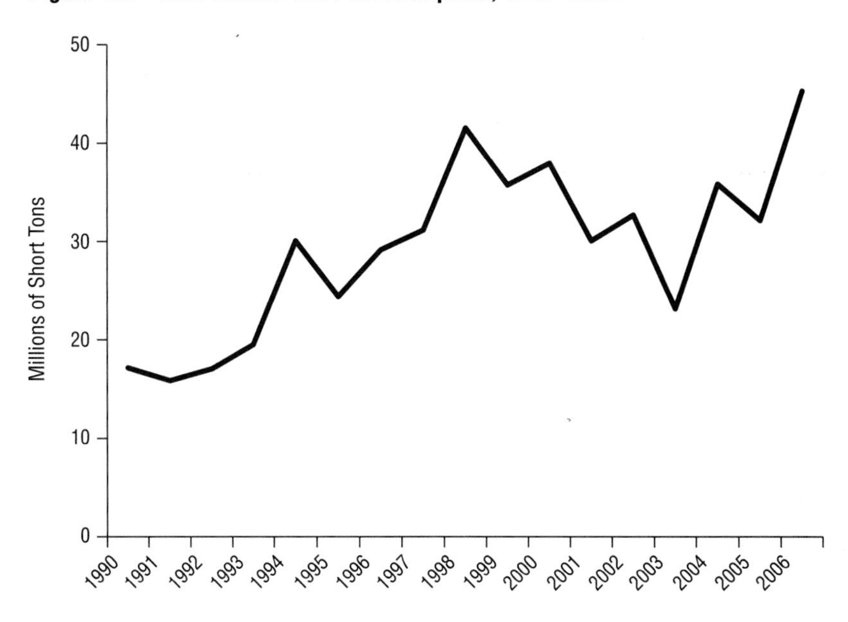

Source: American Iron and Steel Institute, *Annual Statistical Report, 2005,* and earlier issues. Data for 2006 are from idem, press release, January 30, 2007.

Along with this long-term increase in foreign steel-exporting capacity, two additional short-term factors contributed to the spike in U.S. steel imports in the late 1990s. First, economic downturns in other countries led to an international glut of steel that dramatically reduced steel prices worldwide. Many of the largest steel exporters—including the Western European nations, Russia, Ukraine, Argentina, Brazil, Japan, South Korea, and other East Asian countries—experienced periods of slow growth, severe recession, or even economic collapse in the latter half of the 1990s and early 2000s. The most significant single event was the Asian financial crisis of 1997–1998, which was followed closely by financial crises in Russia (1998) and Brazil (1999). As foreign demand for steel fell abruptly, a growing excess of supply depressed global steel prices, and low-priced imports took customers away from American firms in the U.S. market. The Asian crisis was the main reason why steel imports rose most rapidly and prices plummeted most sharply in 1998.

Second, the rising tide of steel imports was exacerbated by the appreciation of the U.S. dollar in international currency markets between 1995 and early 2002 (see Figure 9.3). Partly as a result of the "pull" of strong economic growth

Figure 9.2 Steel Price Index, January 1990–December 2003

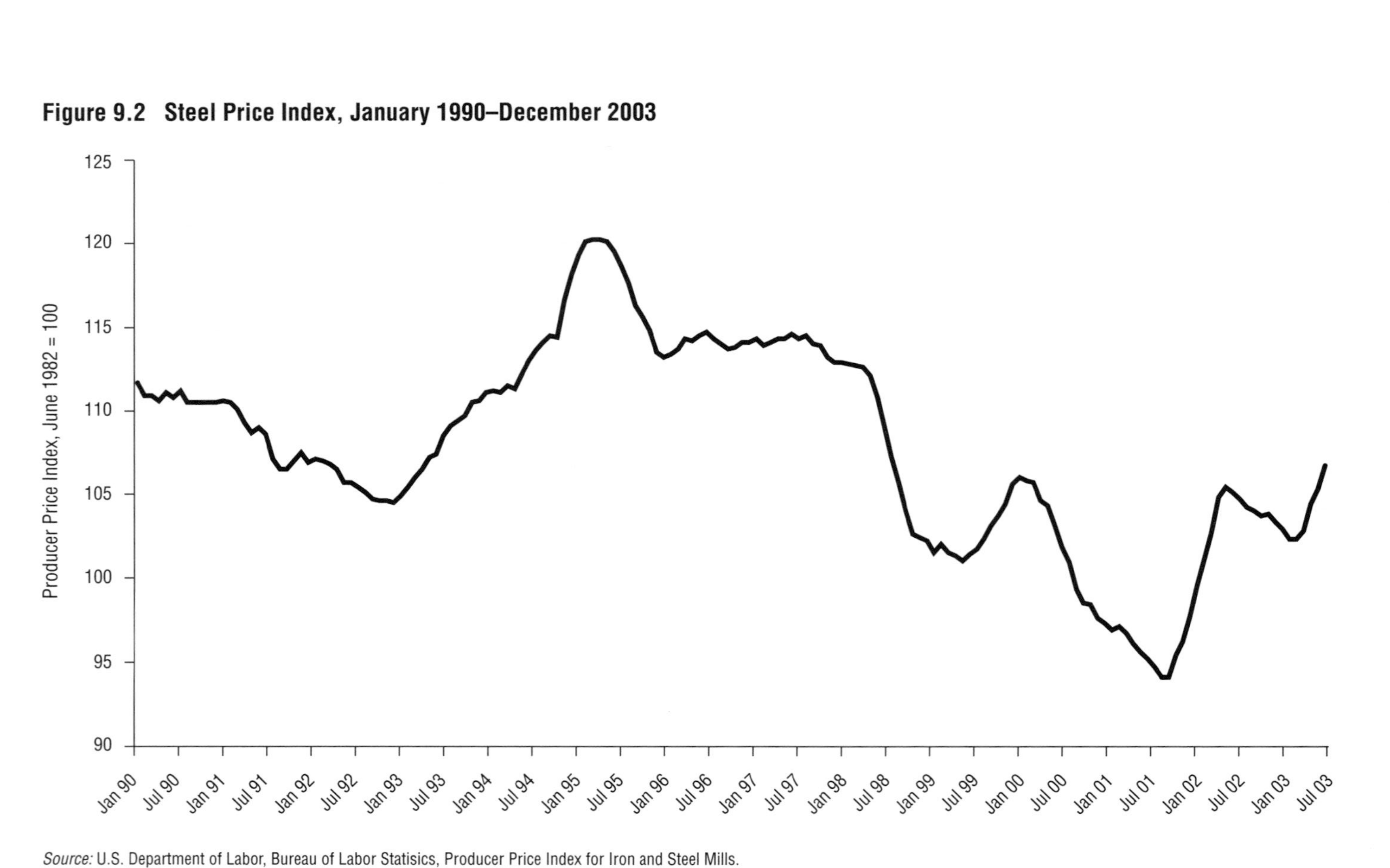

Source: U.S. Department of Labor, Bureau of Labor Statisics, Producer Price Index for Iron and Steel Mills.

Figure 9.3 Real Value of the U.S. Dollar, January 1990–December 2006

Source: Federal Reserve Statistical Release H.10, price-adjusted broad dollar index.

in the United States, and partly as a result of the "push" of financial crises and weak growth abroad, foreign investors poured funds into U.S. financial markets in the late 1990s, driving the dollar up in value. As foreign currency values declined relative to the dollar, most steel-exporting nations were able to slash their export prices in dollar terms without any reduction in revenue as measured in their home currencies. U.S. steel producers—like most other U.S. manufacturing producers—found themselves at an unexpected competitive disadvantage because of the increasing value of the dollar.[11]

In short, the main, immediate causes of the late 1990s surge in steel imports were excess global supplies and an overvalued U.S. dollar. Nevertheless, a number of other circumstances explain why the domestic U.S. steel industry was highly vulnerable to increased competition from imports. The industry is divided into older, "integrated" steel mills and newer "minimills." The integrated mills produce steel out of iron ore and other raw materials, in a multistep procedure involving blast furnaces (which transform iron ore into "pig iron"), steel furnaces (which transform the pig iron into raw steel ingots or slabs), and finishing equipment (which shapes the raw steel into usable forms, such as sheet, bar, rod, plate, and tubular products). The minimills, in contrast, skip the first step by using mostly steel scrap—recycled old steel—as a raw material, instead of iron ore, to feed into their steel furnaces. They also use smaller, electric-arc steel furnaces that melt the scrap metal and turn it into usable raw steel more cheaply than the integrated mills' equipment. In addition, many of the minimills employ nonunion labor, whereas most integrated mill workers are unionized. The minimills, therefore, typically have lower labor costs as well as lower capital costs.[12]

Furthermore, by the 1990s the major integrated companies, for example, U.S. Steel and the former Bethlehem Steel, had large numbers of retired workers to whom they had committed unfunded retirement benefits under old labor contracts. The companies thus had to devote part of their current revenue to paying pensions and health benefits for their former workers, who in many cases far outnumbered current workers because of the enormous shrinkage of employment in the industry since the early 1980s. Such "legacy costs" further swelled the labor costs of the integrated companies compared with those of the minimills. The integrated companies also suffered from outmoded management practices, bloated central office staffs, and rigid union work rules. All these factors meant that the minimills typically had lower overall production costs than the integrated mills and hence could make higher profits per ton on any products that both types of producers made. Alternatively, the minimills could charge lower prices and thus lure customers from the integrated companies.

In spite of these disadvantages, integrated steel companies have remained in business for several reasons. First, they produce a number of key product types that minimills cannot produce, such as larger-sized, flat-rolled sheets (needed for many automotive and machine products). Second, the supply of steel scrap is limited, so there is still a need for new steel made from iron ore. Third, the integrated companies have been modernizing their facilities and increasing their efficiency. Fourth, previous rounds of protection for U.S. steel producers helped keep the integrated companies operating in spite of their higher costs. By 2002 U.S. steel production was divided roughly fifty-fifty between integrated and minimill production, down from approximately sixty-forty in favor of integrated mills a decade earlier.[13]

As a result of increased import penetration in their vulnerable industry, many U.S. steel companies began losing money in the late 1990s, even though U.S. steel demand was high, the overall economy was growing rapidly, and most other U.S. businesses were quite profitable. In general, the integrated steel companies suffered absolute losses, while the more efficient, lower-cost minimills had significantly reduced profits. A total of thirty-one steel companies—among them some of the largest, including Bethlehem, National, and LTV—went bankrupt between 1999 and 2002.[14] Some of those were later bought out or reorganized, but others went out of business entirely. Meanwhile, steel employment fell from about 169,000 in 1996 to about 124,000 in 2002,[15] representing a loss of more than one out of every four jobs in the industry.

During the same period, U.S. consumers of steel—primarily "downstream" companies, which use steel in other products, such as automobiles, appliances, and farm equipment—benefited from the lower steel prices of the late 1990s. As import prices fell and more customers switched to imports, U.S. steel firms were forced to lower their prices to compete. Steel consumers therefore benefited from cheaper steel whether they bought imports or stuck with domestic products. Like the steel producers, however, steel consumers were also affected negatively by the rising dollar, which made U.S. exports less competitive and imports from foreign countries cheaper in all industries.

What distinguished the steel industry from many other U.S. manufacturing sectors was its strategic reaction to the challenge of falling import prices and rising import competition. For many U.S. industrial firms, the response was, "If you can't beat 'em, join 'em." Corporations in many U.S. manufacturing sectors were able to shut down or reduce their domestic production operations and replace them with imports from lower-cost sites abroad. For example, many automobile, electronics, and appliance manufacturers began to "outsource" more products (or parts and components) and to conduct more assembly operations in lower-wage countries such as Mexico and China. Many American workers in these industries were hurt, either losing their jobs or taking pay cuts in an effort to preserve their jobs. Because the companies could remain profitable by producing or sourcing elsewhere, they had little interest in seeking protection from cheaper imports.

Some U.S. steel manufacturers have used an outsourcing strategy. For example, many integrated companies import slabs of unfinished steel to use in domestic rolling and finishing mills, and some pipe and tube producers use imported steel sheet. But several factors limited the steel industry's ability to outsource in the late 1990s. Although foreign steel industries (especially in Europe and Latin America) had been consolidating into large, multinational companies for some time, most U.S. steel companies were still largely national in their scope and operations at the time of the steel crisis of 1998–2001. Lacking foreign affiliates or subsidiaries, they did not have foreign locations from which they could readily outsource.[16] Moreover, U.S. steel producers had a long history of relying on trade protection to cope with import crises. Although many minimills (especially the largest, Nucor) had not previously supported the protectionist policies that the integrated companies sought, by the late 1990s most minimills' attitudes had changed, and they joined their larger, older competitors in seeking import relief. For all these reasons, the vast majority of U.S. steel producers—companies and unions alike—sought protection under the nation's international trade laws.

Round One: Clinton's Response and the Fair Trade Laws

In the late 1990s, the steel industry—represented by company lobbyists and the United Steelworkers of America (USWA)—sought comprehensive import relief from the Clinton administration. President Clinton, however, was reluctant to support safeguard protection for several reasons. First, he had staked out a reputation as a committed free trader, having won passage of the North American Free Trade Agreement (NAFTA) in 1993 and approval of the WTO agreement in 1994. Clinton was a New Democrat who did not mind opposing such traditional Democratic Party constituencies as labor unions (which supported steel protection and opposed the NAFTA and WTO agreements), and he wanted to maintain his credentials as a supporter of open markets at home and abroad. He did not want to be seen as inconsistent in supporting protectionism for U.S. steel producers while advocating free trade for other industries and other countries.

Second, Clinton worried about the foreign policy repercussions if the United States were to launch a major protectionist initiative for its steel industry. Because he needed the support of many steel-exporting nations—including Japan, China, Russia, and the members of the European Union—in a variety of other foreign policy areas, Clinton was unwilling to anger them over trade in steel. Third, Clinton's economic advisers strongly opposed tariff protection for steel, partly because of their free trade principles and partly because they feared the negative effects that it could have on exporting countries whose economies were already hurting. Besides, the U.S. economy was generally booming in the late 1990s, unemployment was low, and steel imports seemed like a relatively minor problem.

Fourth, in terms of domestic politics, Clinton was a lame duck president, so reelection did not concern him. He could assume that labor unions would be likely to support the Democratic candidate for president in 2000 regardless of what he did or did not do for the steel industry. That assessment was borne out by the unions' support for Al Gore's ill-fated 2000 campaign, although one former economic adviser to Clinton later wondered whether his failure to support steel protection had hurt Gore in key steel states, possibly costing him the election.[17]

Still, Clinton had to offer the steel industry something to assuage its concerns. In August 1999 he announced a White House Steel Action Program, which included a Commerce Department investigation of "current subsidies given to [foreign] producers of steel and inputs for finished steel products and the extent to which government actions have led to other market-distorting trade barriers" in key steel-exporting countries.[18] This investigation culminated in the July 2000 *Report to the President: Global Steel Trade—Structural Problems and Future Solutions,* which largely supported the domestic industry's complaints that it had suffered from a significant surge in steel imports that had depressed prices and resulted in bankruptcies and layoffs. While noting the effects of the Asian financial crisis and depreciated foreign currencies, the report also concluded that the global steel market was characterized by "overcapacity" resulting from market-distorting policies practiced by a number of major steel-exporting nations, including the governments of Brazil, China, Russia, Japan, and South Korea.[19] For example, the report accused some of these countries of permitting their steel companies to engage in cooperative pricing practices, which are illegal under U.S. antitrust laws. Some countries were also accused of protecting their home steel markets, thus enabling their steel producers to sell at high prices at home while selling excess products at lower prices abroad, a practice known as "dumping."

The July 2000 report was a classic example of the Clinton administration feeling someone's pain but offering little more than a Band-Aid in response. The report recommended a number of well-intentioned but largely ineffective remedies for what it called the "steel import crisis": It recommended that government agencies do a better job of issuing "early warnings" by making more information about steel imports available more quickly. It also recommended that the United States attempt to negotiate with foreign countries to eliminate their alleged market-distorting practices. By the time Clinton left office six months later, nothing substantial had been accomplished in these negotiations. Otherwise the report merely promised that the Commerce Department would "ensure [that the] fair trade laws are responsive to crisis situations by expediting antidumping investigations."[20]

This last promise was essentially an open invitation to the domestic steel industry to take advantage of the so-called fair trade laws, which are an alternative means for an industry to obtain protection from imports in the absence of a section 201 safeguard remedy. The fair trade laws allow a domestic industry to obtain tariff protection if the industry is injured by "unfairly traded" imports—defined as imports that are either dumped (that is, sold below the exporters' home market prices) or illegally subsidized (that is, supported by subsidies that are forbidden by WTO rules).[21]

Once the Commerce Department determines that imports of a given product from certain countries are selling below their fair market value because of illegal foreign trading practices, the fair trade laws require a lower legal standard than in a safeguard investigation for proving that the domestic industry has been injured by the imports.[22] The lower standard can make it easier for the domestic industry to win tariff relief—antidumping duties in the case of dumping and countervailing duties in the case of subsidies—than it is to win safeguard tariffs. In injury investigations by the ITC in antidumping and countervailing duty cases, the industry only needs to prove that the unfairly traded imports from certain specific countries have been "a cause of material injury," whereas for safeguard cases the industry has to prove that total imports have been "a substantial cause of serious injury."[23]

Furthermore, when the domestic industry wins its argument in dumping and subsidy cases, the import relief is virtually automatic: Antidumping or countervailing duties are usually imposed to offset exactly the calculated effects of the dumping or subsidies on import prices.[24] In contrast, in a safeguard investigation, even if the domestic industry wins its injury case at the ITC, the application of a tariff or other remedy is entirely at the discretion of the president, who may refuse to impose tariffs or other protection regardless of the ITC's findings and recommendations. Thus, although under the law the U.S. steel industry could have filed for safeguard relief while Clinton was in office, it decided against doing so because he had not indicated that he would support safeguard tariffs.

Although domestic steel producers would have preferred across-the-board tariffs under the safeguard provision, they took the Clinton administration's hint and made extensive use of the fair trade laws from 1998 through 2000. During those years, the industry won twenty-three new antidumping and countervailing duty orders on individual products from specific countries and also won continuation of forty-six previous such orders that had undergone "sunset reviews" as required by the WTO agreement.[25] The filing of new fair trade cases peaked in 1999, causing imports to take a temporary dip that year before rising again in 2000 (see Figure 9.1). Also as a result of these cases, steel prices recovered somewhat in 1999, before falling again in 2000 and 2001 (see Figure 9.2). However, the tariff coverage that the industry obtained under the fair trade laws was limited to certain specific countries and products, and the industry also lost a number of fair trade cases during those years. U.S. firms also claimed that foreign exporters were circumventing antidumping orders through a variety of means, including transshipping through countries not subject to such orders, pricing-to-market behavior (essentially, absorbing part of the duties by lowering their export prices), and switching to downstream products not covered by duty orders. As the industry's losses continued to mount in 2000 and 2001, its interest in a broader safeguard tariff revived, but it took a change of administration to create a more receptive political climate in the White House.

Round Two: Bush's Tariff Decision and the Safeguard Investigation

When George W. Bush entered the White House in January 2001, the steel industry was already pressuring the new administration to launch the safeguard investigation that Clinton had refused to initiate.[26] Although Bush had run as a free trader, his unique political situation made him surprisingly receptive to the entreaties from embattled steel producers. Bush had lost the popular vote to Gore in 2000 in a virtual dead heat, but he won in the Electoral College after the U.S. Supreme Court halted vote recounting in Florida. As a result, Bush's political advisers were anxious to bolster his popular support. Many of the most hotly contested states in the 2000 election had been in the nation's industrial rust belt, where the steel industry is concentrated. Bush carried Indiana, Ohio, and West Virginia, but lost Pennsylvania, Michigan, and Illinois, mostly by thin margins.[27] According to some reports, during the 2000 campaign Vice President Dick Cheney had specifically promised West Virginia voters to help the steel industry.[28] Bush's political advisers were also concerned about the upcoming, 2002 midterm elections, in which the Republicans hoped to expand their razor-thin majorities in both houses of Congress, and these same steel-producing states would be major battlegrounds in those elections.[29]

Moreover, Bush may have had a special, personal motivation to show sympathy for the beleaguered steel industry and its workers. His father had been a one-term president, and one of the reasons why the elder George Bush lost the 1992 election was that he was perceived as unsympathetic to American workers who had lost their jobs in the recession and sluggish recovery of 1990 and 1991. The younger Bush presumably did not want to follow in his father's footsteps in this respect. By doing something to help the steel industry, Bush could show his sympathy for American workers, shoring up his own reelection chances for 2004, as well as helping Republicans in the 2002 congressional races.

Such electoral calculations were only part of the political picture. The Congressional Steel Caucus, a bipartisan coalition of senators and representatives from steel-producing states, was pressuring the administration for import protection. Members of the caucus had introduced legislation to roll back steel imports to their levels in the mid-1990s, in rather clear violation of U.S. trade agreements and WTO rules.[30] The support of these members of Congress was critical for the administration's other trade policy initiatives. Bush wanted congressional approval of trade promotion authority (TPA, formerly known as "fast track" authority), which enables the president to submit trade agreements to Congress for up-or-down votes without amendment. Bush sought TPA to strengthen his hand both in the upcoming Doha Round of WTO negotiations and in negotiating the proposed Free Trade Area of the Americas (FTAA) and other free trade agreements. By supporting a limited amount of steel protection through safeguard tariffs, Bush could fend off more drastic protectionist measures being considered by Congress and win votes for his other trade-promoting initiatives.

Meanwhile, the steel industry kept up the political pressure. Industry lawyers continued to file antidumping and countervailing duty cases at a rapid clip. The industry won an additional twenty-eight duty orders on various specific imported products in 2001, mostly based on petitions filed in late 2000 or early 2001, before the safeguard investigation began. Stand Up For Steel, a political action organization, mobilized unionized workers and their supporters to protest and lobby for steel protection. Behind the scenes, steel executives—many of them Republicans who had supported Bush in 2000—lobbied key administration officials for safeguard tariffs.[31]

Most of Bush's economic and foreign policy advisers reportedly opposed safeguard tariffs.[32] Nevertheless, in June 2001 the new president decided to follow the advice of his political advisers. He authorized Robert Zoellick, the U.S. trade representative at the time, to request that the ITC conduct a section 201 safeguard investigation and report back with recommendations.[33] Bush also declared that the United States would negotiate long-term reductions in steel capacity with other nations, and international meetings were held beginning in August 2001 to discuss such measures.[34] In terms of actual policy remedies, however, all attention was focused on the safeguard investigation.

At this point, Bush had not formally committed himself to approving tariffs or agreeing to any other remedy. The ITC would take several months to conduct its investigation, hold hearings, and issue its report, which would give the White House time to mull over the pros and cons of imposing tariffs. If the ITC made a "negative determination," ruling against the domestic industry, then the tariff issue would be moot. Nevertheless, the fact that the president had requested the safeguard investigation raised expectations that he would follow the ITC's recommendation if it made an "affirmative determination" in favor of tariff relief.

By the time the safeguard investigation began, however, the economic circumstances surrounding the steel industry had changed. Steel imports had declined slightly in 1999 and 2000 from their 1998 peak (see Figure 9.1), partly as a result of the antidumping and countervailing duties the domestic industry won under the fair trade statutes. Furthermore, by fall 2001 it was apparent that the U.S. economy had entered a recession, so overall demand for domestic as well as imported steel was shrinking rapidly. Evidence of a recession had been building for many months, and the terrorist attacks of September 11, 2001, worsened the economic downturn. Although the recession hurt steel producers, who continued to lose money and shed jobs, under U.S. law as well as WTO rules tariffs could not be used to offset injury caused by a recession.

These circumstances presented a dual challenge to the steel producers in their pursuit of safeguard tariffs. First, they had to prove that imports were at least as great a cause of their injury as the recession: under the provisions of section 201 imports are regarded as a substantial cause of serious injury to an industry only if there is no other factor that accounts for a greater share of the injury. Second, they had to argue that an import surge continued to injure their industry, even though imports had increased most rapidly in 1998 and were somewhat lower by 2000 (the last year covered in the investigation). Also, as is not the case in a fair trade investigation, in a safeguard investigation the domestic producers had to show that they would use the opportunity of temporary import relief to restructure and make themselves more competitive in the future.

On the other side, foreign steel exporters and U.S. consuming industries marshaled their arguments in opposition to safeguard tariffs. The opponents maintained that U.S. steel producers were mainly suffering from the recession, not imports. They charged that many of the industry's wounds were self-inflicted, the results of poor management, overgenerous labor agreements (especially the legacy costs of pensions and health care benefits for retired workers), and cutthroat competition between the minimills and integrated producers. Opponents pointed to the domestic industry's own problem of excess capacity, which they claimed resulted from the protection the industry had received in the past. In this view, more tariff protection for U.S. steel would only prevent the capacity reductions and restructuring that the industry needed, rather than encourage them.[35]

Especially vocal in opposing steel safeguard protection was the Consuming Industries Trade Action Coalition (CITAC), an organization formed by a number of prominent steel-purchasing corporations. CITAC launched a massive lobbying campaign that included economic studies purporting to show that steel protection would cause huge job losses in downstream, steel-consuming industries—far in excess of the jobs that would be saved in the steel industry—and would lead to increased costs for ultimate consumers of steel-containing products (for example, automobiles or farm equipment).[36]

Although some economists thought CITAC's estimates were exaggerated, conventional economic analysis generally showed that the costs of protection to consumers of imported products were greater than the sum of the benefits to the producers plus the tariff revenue to the government. Hence most economists opposed steel protection on principle. Industry defenders countered that the sector's losses from the import surge resulted from factors beyond its control and that the costs to consumers of protection for steel producers would merely offset the artificially low prices caused by the flood of imports and restore prices to more normal levels.

In the midst of this controversy, the ITC's professional staff of investigators gathered information from extensive surveys of producers, purchasers, importers, and foreign exporters for thirty-three categories of steel products. The commission then held several days of public hearings in September and October 2001. The ITC ultimately made an affirmative determination, finding that an import surge had been a substantial cause of serious injury, or threatened serious injury, for sixteen of the thirty-three product categories. Those sixteen categories were the largest part of the industry, accounting for roughly 74 percent of total steel imports.[37] Following further hearings in the remedy phase of the investigation, in December 2001 the ITC made a complex set of recommendations for various combinations of tariffs and quotas on imports of those sixteen types of products, with some ITC commissioners making conflicting recommendations.[38]

The ITC's findings in favor of the domestic industry—combined with the commissioners' divergent views on a remedy—threw the ball back into the president's court. Reportedly, the vast majority of his policy advisers—including Treasury Secretary Paul O'Neill, Commerce Secretary Don Evans, Secretary of State Colin Powell, Chairman R. Glenn Hubbard of the Council of Economic Advisers, and budget director Mitch Daniels, among others—strongly opposed the tariffs, while political advisers, including Karl Rove, favored them, and Zoellick, the U.S. trade representative, was willing to compromise with "political realities."[39] At one White House meeting, Vice President Cheney reportedly stated, "We can review this in eighteen months,"[40] referring to the legal provision for a midterm review of the tariffs that would provide an opportunity to reconsider them halfway through their three-year term. Cheney's point evidently was that if the political calculus changed, the decision could be reversed before the 2004 presidential election. Ultimately, politics won the argument, and on March 5, 2002, the president announced his decision in favor of tariff relief for a period of three years and a day.[41]

Although Bush's tariff plan was generally regarded as a victory for the steel industry, in reality it represented a compromise. The maximum tariff rate was set at 30 percent, below the 40 percent the industry sought, and imposed on only some products; rates were set lower for other products. All the tariffs were scheduled to be reduced each year for the next two years and phased out completely in March 2005. Furthermore, numerous types of steel imports, even within the categories designated for tariff protection, were excluded from the tariffs because customers claimed that they could not obtain adequate supplies from domestic producers (and for some products, no domestic supplies were available). A large number of countries were exempted from the tariffs, including NAFTA partners Canada and Mexico as well as most developing nations, which were small steel exporters. The major Asian steel producers—China, Japan, Korea, and Taiwan—were not exempted, however, and a few developing nations, including Brazil and Thailand, received only a partial exemption. Adding all these exclusions and exemptions to the fact that another seventeen types of products escaped tariffs because of the ITC's negative injury determinations, Bush's safeguard tariffs covered only 24 percent of total steel imports measured by volume and 31 percent measured by value.[42]

Economic Effects and Political Responses

Many economists, editorialists, and pundits criticized Bush for caving in to a special interest group by imposing the steel tariffs.[43] Yet, in a sense, Bush used the safeguard provision for its politically intended purpose: to buy off particular economic interests hurt by increased imports so as to preserve a larger political coalition in support of generally "liberal" trade policies, which in the trade arena means free trade policies, or open markets. In the short term, Bush succeeded in his immediate political objectives: The Congressional Steel Caucus stopped pushing for its more extreme remedies, and Congress passed TPA authorization in July 2002; caucus members' support was especially important in the close vote on TPA in the House.[44] Moreover, in the 2002 midterm elections the Republicans increased their majority in the House and regained control of the Senate (which they had lost briefly, when Republican senator James Jeffords of Vermont became an independent).[45] Although other issues, such as post–September 11 security concerns, obviously played a role in those elections, Bush's willingness to support an American industry and its workers can only have helped the Republicans' chances.

Abroad, however, the reaction was swift and negative. The foreign nations covered by the tariffs complained that the U.S. decision violated the WTO's rules for safeguard protection and that it was unfair for them to be singled out when so many other countries were exempted. In June 2002 the WTO created a dispute resolution panel to hear the complaint, which was officially filed by the European Union, Brazil, China, Japan, Korea, and three other nations. Most observers expected the WTO to rule against the United States, given its established interpretation of the safeguard rules, which is stricter than the U.S. ITC's interpretation of the standards for imposing tariff relief. The WTO dispute resolution process would, however, go on for several months, and even if the panel decided against the United States, the Bush administration could delay enforcement of a WTO ruling through an appeals process.

Foreign nations also complained loudly about U.S. hypocrisy on trade policy, arguing that the United States was restricting steel imports while urging other countries to make their markets more open to imports through new WTO negotiations and other trade initiatives, such as the proposed FTAA and Central American Free Trade Agreement (CAFTA). In trade policy, as well as in such foreign policy areas as global warming and national security, the Bush administration was accused of acting unilaterally and without adequate regard for U.S. allies. Yet many of the countries that complained loudly about Bush's steel tariffs maintained significant restrictions on their own steel imports or had been accused of unfairly aiding their steel exporters.[46] None of the countries had volunteered to undertake cooperative efforts to reduce global excess capacity in steel production, as both the Clinton and Bush administrations had recommended.

The ITC had to grapple with the actual economic effects of the tariffs when it conducted its legally mandated midterm review process—officially known as a section 204 monitoring investigation—between March and September 2003. Meanwhile, in response to pressure from steel-consuming industries, the House Committee on Ways and Means required the ITC to undertake a concurrent investigation into how the steel tariffs affected steel consumers and to report on that investigation—officially a section 332 fact-finding report, with no legally binding determinations—simultaneously with its section 204 report.

The ITC's findings in its joint 204/332 report of September 2003 were mixed. The ITC found that the steel industry's performance improved moderately in the year after tariff relief went into effect,[47] but that the lingering effects of the 2001 recession on downstream industries had hampered the industry's recovery by weakening demand. Steel prices increased enough to allow the major flat-rolled producers—integrated mills and minimills combined—to make small profits in the year after relief, as compared with the large losses they had suffered the preceding year.[48] Some of the price increases resulted from other factors, however, such as reduced supplies because of plant shutdowns at bankrupt steel firms. Overall, steel price increases in 2002 and 2003 were relatively moderate and merely brought prices back to where they had been in 1999 and 2000—not to the higher price levels of the mid-1990s (see Figure 9.2). The total number of jobs in the industry continued to shrink in spite of the tariff relief.[49]

As for the steel-consuming industries, the ITC found that they did pay more for steel as a result of the tariffs and that some steel purchasers reported shortages of particular steel products in the year following relief.[50] Nevertheless, the steel-consuming companies surveyed in the 332 investigation were about evenly divided on whether they had trouble obtaining steel supplies after the tariffs were imposed and whether they expected to lose profits if the tariffs were continued.[51] Overall these companies' total profits actually increased in the year following relief.[52] Employment in steel-consuming industries remained stable in the year following imposition of the tariffs, contrary to CITAC's predictions of large job losses.[53]

Although some steel-consuming firms may have experienced significant losses as a result of the safeguard tariffs, most steel consumers appear to have suffered only modest harm because steel prices increased only moderately while the tariffs were in effect. One subsequent study found that the safeguard tariffs had no statistically significant effect in raising prices and that the price increases of 2003 were entirely due to other factors, including rising demand at home and abroad, domestic plant shutdowns, and the decline in the dollar between 2002 and 2003.[54] By the time the tariffs were rescinded, in December 2003, steel prices were still about 7 percent *below* their average level in 1997, the year before steel imports peaked.[55] Taking account of the gains to steel producers and their suppliers, losses to steel consumers, and increased tariff revenue to the U.S. government, the ITC estimated that the steel tariffs caused a net welfare loss of $41.6 million,[56] a relatively tiny amount in an economy that had a gross domestic product of about $11 trillion in 2003.

If the tariffs had only modest effects, one reason may have been their partial nature. Because so many countries and products were excluded from the tariff remedy, imports were not reduced as much as the industry had hoped (and steel consumers had feared). For the largest product category (flat-rolled products), total imports actually increased 7.3 percent (from 16.0 to 17.2 million tons) in the year following relief, compared with the previous twelve months, because imports from countries not covered by the tariffs increased by more than imports from countries covered by the tariffs decreased.[57] With such incomplete import protection, it is no wonder that steel prices rose by less than the consumers feared (or the producers hoped) as a result of the safeguard tariffs.

The 204/332 report also covered the steel industry's efforts to restructure and modernize to become more competitive. Major consolidations occurred in the industry during the period after the tariffs went into effect: The largest firm (U.S. Steel) bought up the assets of another integrated company that had gone bankrupt (National); the newly formed International Steel Group (ISG) bought up the liquidated assets of three bankrupt companies (Bethlehem, formerly the second-largest producer, plus LTV and Acme) and later acquired two other companies (Weirton and Georgetown); and the largest minimill company (Nucor) bought up two smaller firms. U.S. Steel and ISG especially benefited from the government's creation of the Pension Benefit Guarantee Corporation (PBGC), which assumed the pension liabilities of the bankrupt steel companies (although it did not pay the health care benefits that had been promised to the retirees, who lost their health benefits).[58]

The USWA agreed to significantly more flexible work rules in new contracts with U.S. Steel and ISG, in exchange for company efforts to preserve jobs at the bankrupt mills (although it was understood that some jobs would necessarily be lost). The surviving companies also slashed management staff. Although many of the bankrupt mills were reopened under new management and new work rules, other mills closed forever. The steel industry argued that tariff relief had made all these changes possible by encouraging investors to invest in steel mills and unions to cooperate in changing work rules. The industry's critics countered that the changes had been forced on the industry by the rash of bankruptcies and that the tariffs prevented additional, necessary consolidations and capacity reductions from taking place.

Under the law, President Bush could have asked the ITC to recommend whether he should continue or terminate the safeguard tariffs, as part of its monitoring investigation. However, he did not make such a request, and in its September 2003 report the ITC presented its factual findings without making any policy recommendations. The president did not act immediately after receiving the ITC's 204/332 report. It was the WTO's final decision in favor of the steel exporters' complaint that eventually forced the Bush administration's hand.

The WTO Decision and Bush's Reversal

The WTO panel had ruled in July 2003 that the U.S. steel tariffs were illegal. The United States responded by appealing to the WTO Appellate Body in August. In November 2003 the WTO Appellate Body upheld the original panel's ruling.[59] Under the WTO agreement that went into effect in 1995 and was supported strongly by the United States, no additional appeal was available.

The WTO's ruling was based on the determination that the United States had misapplied the rules for safeguard tariffs. Whereas the ITC—following its own long-standing precedents in section 201 investigations—had viewed imports of most steel products as increasing during a five-year period of investigation (from 1996 through 2000), the WTO focused on the fact that imports increased the most in 1998 and subsequently fell. The WTO argued that a safeguard decision should be based on the most recent information available and that the problems of the U.S. steel industry in 2000 and 2001 could not be blamed on an import surge that had peaked in 1998. The WTO also faulted the United States on various procedural grounds, including that the ITC's analysis of the causation of injury by imports was not restricted to the limited group of exporting nations on which President Bush eventually imposed tariffs, as well as alleged irregularities in the ITC's voting procedures. Some of these arguments suggest that the United States would have had a stronger case if it had adopted safeguard tariffs in 1998 or 1999, under President Clinton, and if the tariffs had been applied to all steel-exporting nations. Of course, had such occurred, the WTO might still have overruled the tariffs on other grounds.

Under WTO rules, although the United States could not be forced to rescind its tariffs, the exporting nations had the right to impose retaliatory tariffs against U.S. exports of a value equal to the value of their affected steel exports if the United States refused to rescind the tariffs that had been found illegal. For example, the European Union announced its intention to retaliate on $2.2 billion worth of U.S. exports.[60] The Europeans, showing that they too could play the electoral politics game, cleverly focused on U.S. exports from politically sensitive states. For example, they threatened to impose tariffs on citrus fruit from Florida, textiles from the Carolinas, and agricultural products and farm equipment from the Midwest. This changed the political equation for the Bush administration, which feared that negative reactions from voters and politicians in those states could outweigh potential gains in steel-producing states if the tariffs remained in place.

In addition to the threat of retaliation, several other factors led the Bush administration to reconsider its previous support for steel tariffs. It had taken much criticism both at home and abroad for this apparent inconsistency in its support for free trade; abolishing the tariffs could assist in repairing the administration's free trade credentials and help boost faltering negotiations for a new WTO agreement and the FTAA.[61] Bush had also bruised many U.S. allies' feelings by going to war in Iraq in 2003; removing the steel tariffs might improve relations with countries such as France, Germany, and Russia, which had not supported the war. (It would also reward the British, who participated in the war.) On the domestic front, Bush's steel tariffs had not won him any union support, most business leaders outside the steel industry favored abolishing the tariffs, and steel executives would be likely to continue to support the Republicans anyway.

Having sold the world on the merits of WTO dispute settlement procedures, the U.S. government could not reject a WTO decision simply because it did not like it. The United States regularly files complaints with the WTO on behalf of U.S. firms or exporting interests, and it sometimes wins those cases. The Bush administration thus could not ignore a WTO ruling against the United States without encouraging other countries to do likewise when the WTO might rule against them. The economic situation also was changing in ways that could help the steel industry to improve its performance without tariff protection. By late 2003 the economic recovery was increasing demand for steel products at home, while the falling U.S. dollar was making U.S. steel products more competitive internationally.

Given all these factors, in December 2003 Bush announced that he was terminating the steel safeguard tariffs fifteen months ahead of schedule, in what the press noted was "a rare about-face for an administration not noted for reversing course."[62] Administration officials denied that they were responding to the WTO decision and threats of retaliation and instead tried to put a better spin on the termination of the tariffs by claiming that they had been successful and therefore were no longer needed. In a written statement, Bush announced, "I took action to give the industry a chance to adjust to the surge in foreign imports and to give relief to the workers and communities that depend on steel for their jobs and livelihoods. The safeguard measures have now achieved their purpose, and as a result of changed economic circumstances, it is time to lift them."[63]

Conclusion: Steel Politics after the Tariffs

Whether the steel safeguard tariffs were legally valid under either U.S. law or the WTO agreement is a matter that legal scholars can debate for some time to come. The economic effects of the tariffs are also subject to competing estimates and interpretations, although the safest conclusion is that both the benefits to the steel industry and the harm to steel consumers were relatively small compared with the hopes and fears that were expressed in advance by the competing interest groups. In the end, steel employment shrank in spite of the tariffs, perhaps somewhat less than it would have without them, but most of the jobs that were lost are unlikely to return. Many of them were eliminated to increase efficiency as producers restructured to become more competitive.

Bush's apparently inconsistent decisions—imposing tariffs in March 2002 and then revoking them in December 2003—are typical of the compromises involved in forging U.S. trade policies in the face of competing interests. As one textbook of U.S. foreign trade puts it, "trade policymaking involves reconciliation and trade-offs among a variety of economic goals and political necessities."[64] The specifics of Bush's tariff policy never satisfied anyone, however, inasmuch as supporters of steel import relief saw it as too little, while opponents saw it as too much. Nevertheless, Bush could claim to have gotten the best of both worlds politically. When the steel industry was reeling from the combined effects of increased imports and a recession in 2001 and 2002, he showed his concern for the industry and its workers by supporting a safeguard tariff. He was thus able to mollify congressional supporters of steel protection, while winning their votes for other trade policy initiatives (Congress later approved TPA,

CAFTA, and a few other trade agreements, but the FTAA negotiations broke down and never produced an agreement). Later, when faced with an adverse WTO ruling that threatened to spark retaliation by other countries, Bush could declare victory and abolish the tariffs. Thus, he could portray himself as committed to free trade in principle, while still helping the steel industry when it needed it the most (critics of his tariff decisions would argue that he was simply inconsistent).

Although most attention has been focused on the safeguard tariffs, antidumping and countervailing duties still applied to many types of steel imports after Bush revoked the safeguards in December 2003. At least one cause of the steel import crisis of 1998–2001 has subsequently been ameliorated: the fall in the dollar since its peak in February 2002 (see Figure 9.3) has helped all U.S. manufacturers, producers as well as consumers of steel, to compete internationally.[65]

Meanwhile, the global steel industry has changed in dramatic and unexpected ways since the U.S. safeguard tariffs were terminated. Led by surging demand in China and other Asian countries, global steel prices soared starting in 2004. As Figure 9.4 shows, the huge increases in steel prices in 2004–2006 dwarfed the small increase observed while the safeguard tariffs were in effect in 2002–2003.[66] With prices at record highs, and in spite of increased costs for raw materials and energy, steel companies around the world made record-breaking profits during these years. The U.S. steel industry, after losing money every year from 1999 through 2003, made net annual profits of about $3 billion in 2004 and 2005.[67] With the industry returned to profitability, the ITC eventually began to "sunset" some of the antidumping and countervailing duties that were still in effect. For example, duties on galvanized sheet and cut-to-length plate from fifteen countries were revoked in December 2006,[68] although similar duties remained in effect on other countries and products. Few new antidumping or countervailing duty petitions were filed by steel producers during this period, except for a few cases mostly involving imports from China.

During the boom in the world steel market, the global wave of steel industry consolidation finally washed up on American shores. The largest merger occurred in 2005, the multinational firm Mittal Steel (founded by Indian-born magnate Lakshmi N. Mittal and headquartered in Europe) acquired ISG, the company that earlier had bought up the assets of five former U.S. steel firms, along with another American company, Ispat Inland.[69] Mittal combined ISG and Ispat Inland into an American subsidiary called Mittal Steel USA, which immediately became the largest U.S. steel producer, surpassing the venerable

Figure 9.4 Steel Price Index, January 1990–December 2006

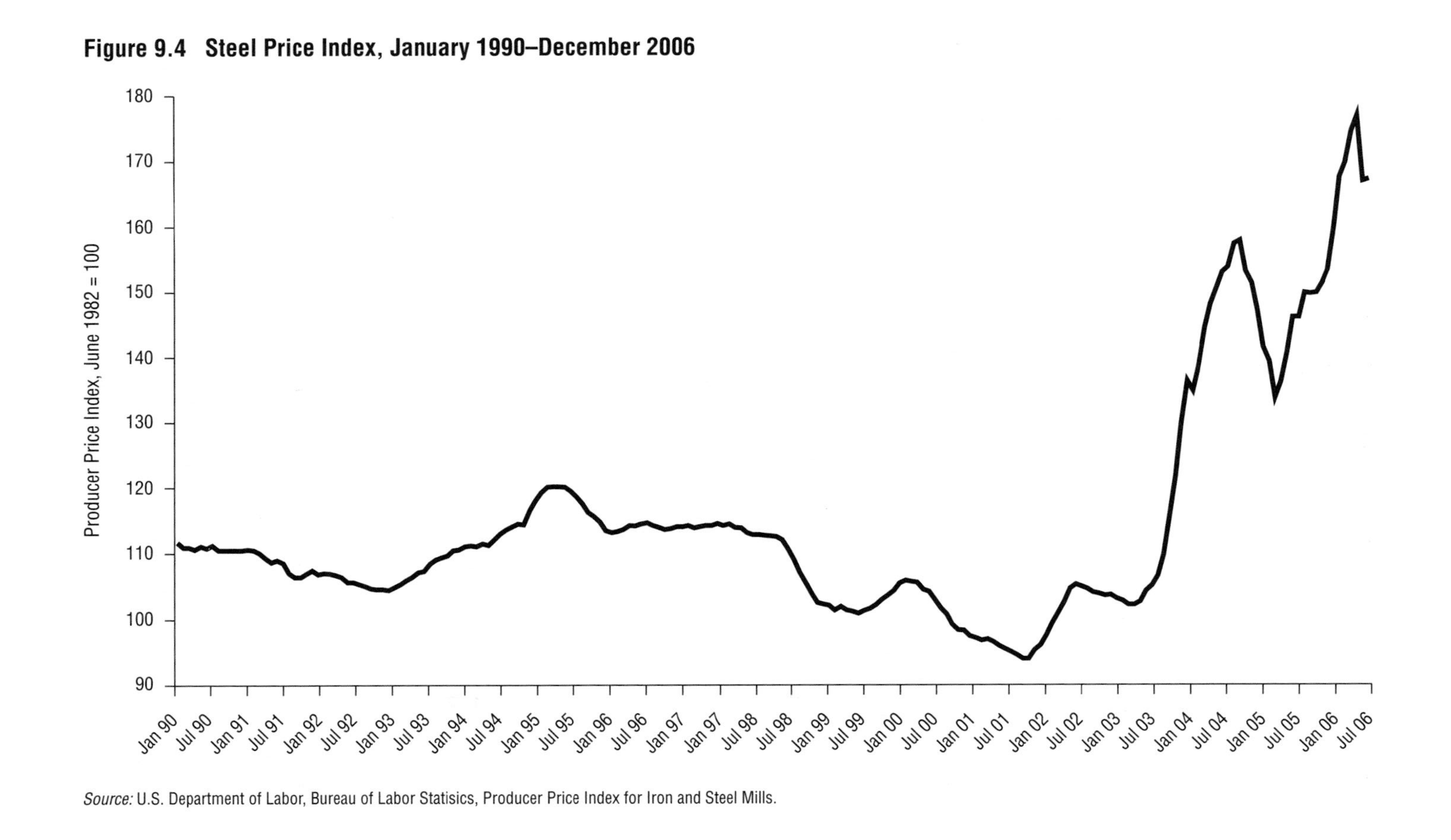

Source: U.S. Department of Labor, Bureau of Labor Statisics, Producer Price Index for Iron and Steel Mills.

U.S. Steel Corporation. Then, as of early 2007, Mittal Steel was in the process of merging with another Europe-based multinational, Arcelor, to form the world's largest steel company (Arcelor Mittal), which would have 320,000 employees (nearly three times the total employment in the U.S. steel industry) located in more than sixty countries around the world.[70]

Ironically, then, the U.S. steel industry became more "globalized" than ever before in the aftermath of one of the most protectionist episodes of modern times. Supporters of the safeguard tariffs would argue that they helped preserve the assets of the bankrupt steel companies that eventually were merged into Mittal Steel USA and other reorganized companies; critics would argue that the tariffs were unnecessary for this outcome. Whether the fact that the largest U.S. steel company is now owned by a foreign multinational (and many smaller ones are owned by other foreign companies) will influence the industry's future attitude toward seeking tariff protection remains to be seen. No one presently (as of 2007) knows how long the steel boom of 2004–2007 will last or how the restructured global industry will respond when the boom eventually ends.

Finally, the steel tariff episode raises important questions about the future role of international organizations such as the WTO. The WTO effectively forced the president of the United States to reverse a decision he had made based on U.S. trade laws—a fact that did not sit comfortably with critics of the WTO's powers and procedures. Defenders of the WTO argue that having a rules-based international trading system is preferable to letting countries, whether the United States or other nations, arbitrarily interfere with global commerce. Critics of the WTO counter that allowing an unelected international bureaucracy to undermine the decisions of elected national officials weakens political democracy. It is safe to predict that the steel safeguard tariffs will not be the last conflict between a U.S. trade policy decision and a ruling by an international trade authority that the United States helped to create.

Key Actors

American Iron and Steel Institute Organization of U.S. steel producers, most of whom strongly supported tariff protection.

George W. Bush President, initiated the steel safeguard investigation and imposed tariffs on steel imports but later revoked them.

Bill Clinton President, refused to call for a steel safeguard investigation.

Consuming Industries Trade Action Coalition Group of steel industry customers opposed to tariff protection for steel producers.

European Union Led the appeal of the U.S. tariff decision at the WTO.

Stand Up For Steel An industry-labor coalition active politically in support of steel protection.

United Steelworkers of America Union that represented most steelworkers and supported tariff protection.

U.S. International Trade Commission (ITC) Independent government agency that investigates allegations of injury to domestic industries caused by imports and analyzes other trade issues; it determined that steel imports were "a substantial cause of serious injury" to the U.S. steel industry.

World Trade Organization (WTO) International organization that ruled that the U.S. steel safeguard tariffs were illegal under international trade agreements.

Robert Zoellick U.S. trade representative in Bush's first term, representing him in trade negotiations, tariff cases, and at the World Trade Organization (he was named president of the World Bank in 2007).

Notes

The author wishes to thank Stephen D. Cohen and Kara Olson Reynolds for their helpful comments on an earlier version of the chapter.

1. See Stephen D. Cohen, Robert A. Blecker, and Peter D. Whitney, *Fundamentals of U.S. Foreign Trade Policy: Economics, Politics, Laws, and Issues,* 2nd ed. (Boulder: Westview Press, 2003), 153–158, for background on this legal provision, which was formerly called the "escape clause." See also the information about trade remedy investigations on the U.S. International Trade Commission Web site, www.usitc.gov.
2. A tariff—also sometimes called a "duty"—is a tax on imports. A quota is a quantitative restriction or limit on the volume of imports. Tariffs and quotas may be used separately or in combination.
3. Author's calculations based on data in American Iron and Steel Institute (AISI), *Annual Statistical Report, 2005,* table 1A, and earlier issues. These data are for total imports, including semifinished as well as finished products.
4. See Paul Blustein, "Bush to Seek Protection for U.S. Steel Firms," *Washington Post,* June 6, 2001, E1.
5. See U.S. International Trade Commission, *Steel,* investigation no. TA-201-73, pub. 3479, December 2001 (hereinafter ITC 201 Report).
6. The president's decision is summarized in U.S. International Trade Commission, *Steel: Monitoring Developments in the Domestic Industry,* investigation no. TA-204-9, and *Steel Consuming Industries: Competitive Conditions with Respect to Steel Safeguard*

Measures, investigation no. 332–452, 3 vols., pub. 3632, September 2003 (hereinafter ITC 204/332 Report), vol. 1, pp. overview I-5 to overview I-8.

7. See ITC 204/332 Report, vol. 1, overview I-9.

8. Regarding earlier steel import controversies, see Robert W. Crandall, *The Steel Industry in Recurrent Crisis* (Washington, D.C.: Brookings Institution Press, 1981); and Thomas R. Howell et al., *Steel and the State: Government Intervention and Steel's Structural Crisis* (Boulder: Westview Press, 1988). For broader perspectives on why the global steel industry has been the subject of so many trade policy disputes, see Robert A. Blecker, "Steel," in *The Princeton Encyclopedia of the World Economy,* ed. Kenneth A. Reinert and Ramkishen S. Rajan (Princeton: Princeton University Press, forthcoming 2008).

9. See American Iron and Steel Institute, *Annual Statistical Report, 2005,* and earlier issues. Apparent consumption, which AISI calls "apparent supply," is defined as domestic shipments plus imports minus exports (not including imports of semifinished products, which would otherwise be double-counted when they are transformed into finished steel products by domestic producers).

10. This figure ends in 2003 for a reason that will become clear later: The price increases in 2004–2006 were so big that they dwarf the earlier fluctuations, so in order to understand the steel crisis of 1998–2001 it is helpful to have a graph that shows the price declines of that period on a larger scale. See the concluding section and note 66 below for more details.

11. The rising value of the dollar accounted for an estimated 44 percent of the increase in steel imports between 1995 and 2000. See Robert A. Blecker, "Let It Fall: The Effects of the Overvalued Dollar on U.S. Manufacturing and the Steel Industry," unpublished report, American University, October 2002, nw08.american.edu/~blecker/research/dollpaper.pdf.

12. See Gary Clyde Hufbauer and Ben Goodrich, "Time for a Grand Bargain in Steel?" International Economics Policy Brief 02-1, Institute for International Economics, Washington, D.C., 2002, 3, www.iie.com.

13. See American Iron and Steel Institute, *Annual Statistical Report, 2002,* table 1B.

14. ITC 204/332 Report, vol. 1, vi and overview III-4.

15. U.S. Department of Labor, Bureau of Labor Statistics, data reported in AISI, *Annual Statistical Report, 2005,* table 1B.

16. Some foreign steel corporations were producing in the United States by the late 1990s, often through joint ventures with U.S. companies; these included Asian, European, and Canadian firms. However, few major U.S. steel firms had become multinational corporations with foreign operations (with the notable exception of U.S. Steel Corporation, which had invested heavily in Eastern Europe). Ironically, as a result of the steel crisis in the early 2000s, a number of major U.S. steel producers were later bought up by a large foreign multinational, Mittal Steel, as discussed in the conclusions to this chapter.

17. See David E. Sanger, "Backing Down on Steel Tariffs, U.S. Strengthens Trade Group," *New York Times,* December 5, 2003, www.nytimes.com; Sanger quotes Martin N. Baily, former chairman of the Council of Economic Advisers. This article notes that if Gore had carried just one more steel state—West Virginia—he would have won the electoral vote regardless of the outcome in Florida.

18. See U.S. Department of Commerce, International Trade Administration, *Report to the President: Global Steel Trade—Structural Problems and Future Solutions,* July 2000, www.ita.doc.gov/media/steelreport726.html, iii.

19. See ibid.

20. Ibid., 9.

21. For background on the fair trade laws, which (rather confusingly) are sometimes also referred to as the "unfair trade laws," see Cohen, Blecker, and Whitney, *Fundamentals,* 161–172, and the entries "Antidumping" and "Countervailing Duties" in Reinert and Rajan, eds., *Princeton Encyclopedia.* See also the information on trade remedy investigations on the ITC Web site, www.usitc.gov.

22. In a safeguard investigation, the main issue is whether imports are of a quantity that is large enough and rising sufficiently fast to cause serious injury, not whether they are selling at fair or unfair prices.

23. For details on these legal standards, see Cohen, Blecker, and Whitney, *Fundamentals,* 154–156, 165.

24. The only exception is that the administration may choose to negotiate a suspension agreement, in which the foreign country agrees to quantitative limits or price floors on its exports in exchange for suspension of an antidumping or countervailing duty order. This is most often done for politically sensitive countries, especially "non-market economies" such as Russia or China, and is entirely at the discretion of the White House. The vast majority of fair trade cases, however, are not settled by suspension agreements.

25. For a complete list of these cases, see ITC 204/332 Report, vol. 1, table overview I-7, overview I-10 to overview I-12. Most of the continued orders originated between 1992 and 1994, following the abolition of the Reagan-Bush voluntary restraint agreements with foreign exporters, an earlier program of negotiated steel protection that dated back to the 1980s.

26. Treasury Secretary Paul O'Neill warned Bush about these pressures at their first meeting in the Oval Office on January 24, 2001. See Ron Suskind, *The Price of Loyalty: George W. Bush, the White House, and the Education of Paul O'Neill* (New York: Simon and Schuster, 2004), 57–58.

27. See "David Leip's Atlas of U.S. Presidential Elections," www.uselectionatlas.org.

28. Suskind, *The Price of Loyalty,* 217.

29. Ibid. Suskind refers specifically to White House adviser Karl Rove.

30. See Hufbauer and Goodrich, "Time for a Grand Bargain," 6.

31. Suskind, *The Price of Loyalty,* 216–217, reports on some of these efforts.

32. See, for example, ibid., 218–220.

33. The Senate Finance Committee also officially requested the same type of investigation, as it is entitled to do under the law, but it did so only after the president's decision had already been announced. See ITC 204/332 Report, vol. 1, overview I-4.

34. See Blustein, "Bush to Seek Protection," on these initial meetings, and ITC 204/332 Report, vol. 1, overview IV-3, on meetings later conducted by the Steel Committee of the Organisation for Economic Co-operation and Development (OECD) between representatives of the United States, other member countries, and nonmember nations. Those meetings continued throughout 2003 but did not lead to any action.

35. See Hufbauer and Goodrich, "Time for a Grand Bargain"; and Dan Ikenson, "Steel Trap: How Subsidies and Protectionism Weaken the U.S. Steel Industry," Cato Institute, Washington, D.C., 2002, www.cato.org.

36. See Joseph F. Francois and Laura M. Baughman, "Costs to American Consuming Industries of Steel Quotas and Taxes," Consuming Industries Trade Action Coalition, Washington, D.C., 2001, www.citac.info.

37. See ITC, "ITC Details Its Determinations Concerning Impact of Imports of Steel on U.S. Industry," press release, October 23, 2001. For four of these categories, the ITC's vote was a tie (3–3), which counts as an affirmative vote (although this procedure has been challenged at the WTO).

38. See ITC 201 Report.

39. See Suskind, *The Price of Loyalty,* 218–220.

40. Ibid., 221.

41. Although Bush rejected some ITC commissioners' recommendations for quotas for various steel products, he did authorize a tariff rate quota—which applied a tariff only to imports over a quota limit—for one product: steel slabs, which can be used as inputs in domestic rolling mills. See ITC 204/332 Report, vol. 1, overview I-5. This was a concession to integrated mills that wanted to outsource production of basic steel and focus on the manufacture of finished steel products.

42. See Gary Clyde Hufbauer and Ben Goodrich, "Next Move in Steel: Revocation or Retaliation?" International Economics Policy Brief 03-10, Institute for International Economics, Washington, D.C., 2003, www.iie.com, 2. These percentages incorporate additional exclusions granted after the president's initial decision in March 2002.

43. For example, see Gary Clyde Hufbauer and Ben Goodrich, "Steel Policy: The Good, the Bad, and the Ugly," International Economics Policy Brief 03-1, Institute for International Economics, Washington, D.C., 2003, www.iie.com.

44. Hufbauer and Goodrich, "Next Move," 2. The vote in the House was 215–212, and the members of the Steel Caucus who voted in favor provided more than this three-vote margin of victory.

45. In January 2001 the Republicans had used Vice President Cheney's vote as president of the Senate to establish a 51–50 majority, in spite of having only 50 seats. Jeffords's switch from Republican to independent had given the Democrats a 50–49 majority (with Jeffords tacitly supporting the Democrats) until the 2002 elections created a clear Republican majority.

46. For example, the European Union has had its own antidumping duty orders on many steel imports. See also Department of Commerce, *Report to the President,* on Brazilian, Japanese, and Korean trade barriers.

47. Because the tariff remedy went into effect in March 2002, the ITC 204/332 Report used the unusual procedure of comparing data for the twelve-month period after the remedy (April 2002–March 2003) with the twelve-month period prior to the remedy (April 2001–March 2002). All subsequent references to "the year after relief" refer to a comparison of these time periods.

48. See ITC 204/332 Report, vol. 1, p. flat II-21, table flat II-15. Producers of other steel products experienced mixed financial results in the year following relief.

49. See ibid., vol. 2, pp. C-4 to C-38, tables C-1 to C-15.

50. See ibid., vol. 3, pp. 2–21 to 2-28 and 2-43.

51. See ibid., vol. 3, p. 2–22, table 2-9, and 5-2, table 5-1.

52. See ibid., vol. 3, p. 2–40, table 2-22.

53. Ibid., vol. 3, p. 2–50, table 2-30.

54. See Benjamin Liebman, "Safeguards, China, and the Price of Steel," *Review of World Economics (Weltwirtschaftliches Archiv),* vol. 142, no. 2 (July 2006): 354–373. Liebman identifies rising demand from China as a major factor inducing global steel prices to recover in 2003 and 2004. Note that the rise in steel prices toward the *end* of 2003 (as shown in Figure 9.2) cannot be attributed to the safeguard tariffs, because these had been *lowered* in April 2003 in accordance with the president's original tariff schedule. The decline in the value of the dollar during 2003 can be seen in Figure 9.3.

55. Calculated based on the underlying data in Figure 9.2.

56. ITC 204/332 Report, vol. 3, p. 4-4, table 4-2. This was the "central estimate" of a range of estimates based on alternative assumptions about the elasticity of steel import supply. For low elasticities, the ITC estimates show that the United States would have achieved a small net gain because the tariffs would turn the global terms of trade for steel in its favor.

57. See ibid., vol. 1, pp. flat II-22 to flat II-23. For other products, total imports did decline slightly, but in these sectors too there were large increases in imports from non-covered countries that partly offset the decreases from covered countries.

58. See ibid., vol. 1, overview III-12 to overview III-18; and David Moberg, "Remaking Steel without Throwing Its Retirees on the Slagheap," *American Prospect,* July/August 2003, 17–18. The PBGC also assumed the pension liabilities of some smaller bankrupt companies that were not bought up by U.S. Steel or ISG.

59. Paul Blustein and Jonathan Weisman, "U.S. Loses Appeal on Steel Tariffs," *Washington Post,* November 11, 2003, A1.

60. Ibid.

61. See Paul Blustein, "U.S. Trade Positions Shift according to Geography," *Washington Post,* November 14, 2003, E1.

62. Jonathan Weisman, "Bush Rescinds Tariffs on Steel," *Washington Post,* December 5, 2003, A1.

63. Quoted in Richard W. Stevenson and Elizabeth Becker, "Bush Avoids a Trade War by Lifting Steel Tariffs," *New York Times,* December 5, 2003. The phrase "changed economic circumstances" reflects language in U.S. trade law that can be used to legally justify early termination of a safeguard remedy.

64. Cohen, Blecker, and Whitney, *Fundamentals,* 3 (emphasis omitted).

65. The decline in the dollar from 2002 through 2006 shown in Figure 9.3 is mainly a result of its fall versus the major floating rate currencies, such as the euro, Canadian dollar, and British pound. The dollar has yet to decline significantly, however, versus the currencies of Japan and China, the two countries with which the United States has the largest trade deficits, as a result of currency manipulation by their governments. See Robert A. Blecker, "Why the Dollar Needs to Fall Further," *Challenge,* September/October 2003, 15–36.

66. This graph, which extends Figure 9.2 to 2006 (and has a different vertical scale), makes all the ups and downs in steel prices in the 1990s and early 2000s look small by comparison with the large increases that came later (in 2004–2006), which could lead one to question the significance of the price declines during the crisis of 1998–2001. But no one at that time anticipated the later spike in prices, which was historically unprecedented, so the apparently smaller fluctuations in steel prices prior to 2004 seemed large at the time. The steel price index fell by 11 percent from January 1998 to September 1999, then recovered by only 5 percent from September 1999 to May 2000, and finally dropped by another 11 percent from May 2000 to its lowest point in January 2002. The total decline of 17 percent from January 1998 to January 2002 contributed to huge financial losses in the steel industry and numerous bankruptcies, as discussed earlier. Perhaps what Figure 9.4 really shows is that, in retrospect, steel prices were relatively depressed throughout the 1990s and early 2000s.

67. American Iron and Steel Institute, *Annual Statistical Report, 2005,* Table 2. Profit data for 2006 were not available at the time of this writing.

68. See U.S. International Trade Commission, *Certain Carbon Steel Products from Australia, Belgium, Brazil, Canada, Finland, France, Germany, Japan, Korea, Mexico, Poland, Romania, Spain, Sweden, Taiwan, and the United Kingdom,* Volume I: Determination and Views of the Commission, Investigation nos. AA1921-127 (Second Review); 701-TA-319, 320, 325–327, 348, and 350 (Second Review); and 731-TA-573, 574, 576, 578, 582–587, 612, and 614–618 (Second Review); publication no. 3899, January 2007.

69. See Mittal Steel USA News Archives at www.steelnews.com/companies/producers/mittalusa.htm.

70. Information obtained from the Arcelor Mittal Web site, www.arcelormittal.com. Due to antitrust concerns, Mittal Steel USA was required to sell off its Sparrows Point, Maryland, steel mill, formerly one of the largest Bethlehem mills, to obtain U.S. government approval of the Arcelor-Mittal merger.

10 The Helms-Burton Act: Congress and Cuba Policy

Patrick J. Haney and Walt Vanderbush

Before You Begin

1. Who were the key participants in the debate over the Helms-Burton Act? What were their motivations? How did these actors and their methods differ from their cold war counterparts?

2. What role has the U.S. president traditionally played in determining U.S. foreign policy toward Cuba? What role did the president play in determining the course of Helms-Burton? What do the differences tell us about foreign policy making in the post–cold war era?

3. Describe the influence of the Cuban American National Foundation on Congress. How much influence has it had on legislation?

4. How did Congress gain momentum over U.S. Cuba policy? How did it lose it? Why did it regain momentum? What do you think of the behavior of Congress in this case?

5. Who ultimately "won" with the passage of Helms-Burton: Congress or the president? Why?

6. What was the political context within which Helms-Burton was crafted? How did U.S. policy toward Cuba change from the cold war to the post–cold war era?

7. What do you think about the efficacy of Helms-Burton and the U.S. embargo of Cuba? In what kinds of situations do you think economic sanctions would be a powerful instrument of foreign policy? When would you recommend their use? When would you not?

8. Are you surprised by the apparent continuity of Cuba policy from the Clinton to the Bush administration? Why or why not?

9. Do you think the ban on travel by U.S. citizens to Cuba should be lifted? Should the U.S. engage in trade with Cuba?

Introduction: Crafting Cuba Policy

On February 24, 1996, Cuban air force MiG fighter jets shot down two unarmed planes approaching Cuba from across the Florida Straits.[1] The planes were operated by members of the group Brothers to the Rescue, who fly over the waters separating Florida and Cuba looking for people fleeing Cuba by raft. Four Cuban Americans—three U.S. citizens and one U.S. resident—died in the attack. Brothers to the Rescue was also known to fly over Cuba from time to time to drop anti-Castro leaflets.[2] On March 12, President Bill Clinton signed into law the Cuban Liberty and Democratic Solidarity Act of 1996, or LIBERTAD, also called the Helms-Burton Act.[3] The measure tightened and codified into law the long-standing U.S. economic embargo of Cuba that had previously existed by executive order.

The road to Helms-Burton was not as simple as it might at first appear. Indeed, at one point Secretary of State Warren Christopher argued that he would urge President Clinton to veto the bill if it ever came before him, and he made that threat in reference to a weaker version of the bill than the one Clinton signed. This is the story of a bill that, with a little help from the Cuban air force, would not die and of the forces that crafted it.

Background: U.S. Cold War Policy and Cuba

Over the first two decades following the 1959 revolution that brought Fidel Castro to power in Cuba, U.S. presidents tightly controlled U.S. policy toward that island nation, largely through executive orders. When Castro consolidated power and joined forces with the Soviet Union, President Dwight D. Eisenhower imposed an embargo (excepting food and medicine) in 1960, and a year later he severed diplomatic relations. President John F. Kennedy tightened the embargo in 1962, banning Cuban imports and the reexport of U.S. goods to Cuba via third countries; in 1963 he prohibited travel by U.S. citizens to Cuba. U.S. policy toward Cuba in the 1960s and 1970s was quintessential cold war policymaking. That is, it was devised and directed by the president. Although President Gerald R. Ford opened secret talks with Cuba in 1974 about normalizing relations, and President Jimmy Carter reached a few agreements in 1977—including opening interest sections in Washington and Havana in lieu of formal diplomatic exchanges and allowing travel to Cuba by U.S. citizens—U.S.-Cuban relations remained in a deep freeze.[4]

The policy environment got even rougher in the 1980s. As a presidential candidate, Ronald Reagan made it clear that he saw Cuba as the source of U.S. difficulties in Latin America. "The troubles in Nicaragua [where communist Sandinistas were gaining power] bear a Cuban label. . . . There is no question but that most of the rebels are Cuban-trained, Cuban-armed, and dedicated to

U.S.-Cuban Relations and the Helms-Burton Act

January 1959 Revolutionary forces take over the Cuban government. The United States recognizes the new government.

October 1960 President Dwight D. Eisenhower imposes an embargo on Cuba, with food and medicine excepted, following Cuba's move into the Soviet orbit.

January 1961 Eisenhower severs diplomatic relations with Cuba.

February 1962 The United States bans Cuban imports and the re-export of U.S. products to Cuba from third countries.

February 1963 President John F. Kennedy prohibits travel to Cuba by U.S. citizens.

November 1974 President Gerald Ford authorizes secret talks with Cuban officials on normalizing relations.

August 1975 Ford eases the trade embargo by allowing U.S. subsidiaries based in third countries to trade with Cuba.

March 1977 President Jimmy Carter lifts the ban on travel to Cuba by U.S. citizens.

September 1977 The United States and Cuba each open interest sections in the other's capital.

May 1985 Radio Marti, a U.S.-sponsored radio operation, begins broadcasts to Cuba.

October 1992 Congress passes the Cuban Democracy Act prohibiting foreign-based subsidiaries of U.S. companies from trading with Cuba. President George H.W. Bush signs it.

February 1995 Sen. Jesse Helms, R-N.C., introduces the Cuban Liberty and Democratic Solidarity Act (LIBERTAD), also known as the Helms-Burton Act, which would allow U.S. citizens to sue foreign companies that profit from the use of seized property in Cuba. It also would deny entry into the United States of company executives who do business involving seized property.

April 1995 President Bill Clinton argues against passage of Helms-Burton on CNN.

September 21, 1995 The House of Representatives passes Helms-Burton by a vote of 294–130.

continued on the next page

continued from the previous page

October 1995 The Senate passes a version of Helms-Burton with controversial Titles III and IV omitted.

February 24, 1996 Cuban MiG fighters shoot down two planes belonging to the U.S.-based organization Brothers to the Rescue as they fly toward Cuba.

February 26, 1996 Clinton proclaims his support for Helms-Burton.

February 28, 1996 Congressional supporters of Helms-Burton meet with Clinton administration officials to negotiate final terms of the act.

March 12, 1996 Clinton signs Helms-Burton into law.

July 1996 President Clinton announces that he will waive implementation of Title III of Helms-Burton.

March 1998 Clinton announces new measures to facilitate visits to Cuba by U.S. citizens and the sale of medical products.

January 1999 Clinton announces additional measures to increase people-to-people contact between Cubans and Americans.

September 1999 The Ashcroft amendment, which would largely lift the embargo on food shipments to Cuba, passes the Senate but is blocked from the final agriculture appropriations bill by House opposition.

March 2000 The Senate Foreign Relations Committee votes to ease the embargo on the sale of food to Cuba.

October 2000 Clinton signs a bill allowing the sale of agricultural goods and medicine to Cuba but codifying restrictions on travel there by U.S. citizens.

July 2001 President George W. Bush announces that he will continue to waive Title III.

November 2001 President Fidel Castro announces in the wake of Hurricane Michelle that Cuba will buy $10 million in food and medical supplies from the United States.

July 2002 By a 262–167 vote, the House of Representatives votes to block the Treasury Department from enforcing restrictions on U.S. citizens' travel to Cuba.

September 2003 The House of Representatives votes 227–188 to block government spending to enforce travel restrictions to Cuba.

October 2003 The Senate votes 59–36 to block enforcement of travel restrictions (using the same language as the House).

November 2003 A Senate-House conference committee quietly removes the provision blocking Treasury Department enforcement of the travel ban from the spending bill to which it had been attached.

November 2004 Mel Martinez (R), having served as secretary of the Department of Housing and Urban Development, is elected to the U.S. Senate representing the state of Florida; Martinez becomes the fifth Cuban American member of Congress.

July 31, 2006 Because of illness, Fidel Castro temporarily transfers power to his brother Raul.

November 2006 Albio Sires is elected to represent New Jersey's thirteenth congressional district, the seat vacated by Robert J. Menendez (D) when he moved to the U.S. Senate; Sires becomes the sixth Cuban American member of Congress.

January 24, 2007 The Export Freedom to Cuba Act of 2007 (H.R. 654) is introduced by a bipartisan group of representatives in the House; it would lift restrictions on U.S. citizens and residents who wish to travel to Cuba. The Senate version (S. 721) is introduced by a bipartisan group of senators in March 2007.

creating another Communist country in this hemisphere."[5] The Reagan team favored an even stricter embargo and wanted other nations to join the United States in choking the Cuban economy and driving Castro from power. In Congress and among the public, however, there was little support for Reagan's view of Latin America.[6] Although Reagan pulled off a big victory at the polls in November 1980, he needed help lobbying Congress, especially the Democrat-controlled House of Representatives, and the public on this issue. As fate would have it, Miami-based Cuban Americans—who had been attempting to challenge Castro's regime for years—decided to take their political activities to Washington. The Cuban American National Foundation (CANF) was founded in 1980–1981 for the purpose of lobbying the government and the broader public on U.S. Cuba policy.[7]

CANF and its charismatic founder and leader, Jorge Mas Canosa, emerged as a powerful force in the 1980s. CANF worked with the Reagan administration to lobby Congress for a government-sponsored radio station aimed at Cuba. In October 1983 President Reagan signed into law the bill that established Radio

Marti, named after Cuban hero Jose Marti, who led the final push for Cuban independence from Spain starting in 1895. Radio Marti began broadcasting in May 1985. CANF would later follow this victory with the establishment of a TV station, TV Marti, which aimed its signals at Cuba in 1990. (The Cuban government jams most of the signals, but the broadcasts continue.) CANF also worked closely with the National Endowment for Democracy (NED), which was founded during the Reagan administration as a vehicle for government financial support for democracy movements around the world. CANF was also active in U.S. immigration policy with respect to Cubans fleeing the island and a host of other issues related to Cuba. Throughout the 1980s CANF became an increasingly powerful player in U.S. policymaking toward Cuba.

As the end of the cold war unfolded in Eastern Europe and the Soviet Union during the first part of George H. W. Bush's presidency, Cuba policy was moved to the back burner. It moved to the front burner during the latter part of the Bush administration for two reasons. First, Haitians fleeing their country en masse were being returned to Haiti, which raised the specter of a double standard vis-à-vis Cuban exiles, who were permitted easy entry to the United States.[8] Second, in 1991 a major legislative initiative on U.S. policy toward Cuba, the Cuban Democracy Act (CDA), was moving through Congress.[9] It is also important to note that in 1989 Cuban American Ileana Ros-Lehtinen, R-Fla., was sworn into the House of Representatives. Fellow Cuban Americans Lincoln Diaz-Balart, R-Fla., and Robert Menendez, D-N.J., joined her in 1993.

Post–Cold War Cuba Policy: The Cuban Democracy Act

The end of the cold war suggested two opposing directions for U.S. policy toward Cuba. On the one hand, a number of developments indicated that the embargo of the island should be lifted. The Soviet Union had ceased to exist, and Cuban troops stationed abroad had returned home. The Bush administration seemed to have little interest in Cuba given all that was changing around the globe. Many suspected that Bill Clinton had even less interest in maintaining the long-standing embargo.[10] On the other hand, with the cold war over and communism in retreat, some saw conditions as ripe to continue or even strengthen the embargo to finally force Castro from power; having lost its major trading partners, Cuba might even be more vulnerable to a tighter embargo.[11] Many members of Congress seemed attuned to the latter view.

With the demise of the Soviet Union, Cuba needed new trade relationships with the West, and that seemed to open the door for subsidiaries of U.S. companies in foreign countries to do business there. In response to this loophole in the embargo, for three years in a row, beginning in 1989, Sen. Connie Mack, R-Fla., proposed a bill prohibiting subsidiaries of U.S. firms from trading with Cuba. The Bush administration consistently opposed the so-called Mack amendment. Laying out the administration's reasoning in testimony before Congress in July 1991, Bernard Aronson, assistant secretary of state for inter-American affairs, argued, "The ban on subsidiaries of U.S. multinationals would create a foreign policy problem with a lot of allies who rightly believe that that would be an assertion of U.S. law into their territory and who would be prepared to retaliate in direct ways. Our analysis is that the benefits that we would gain in terms of embargo enforcement are relatively minimal."[12] Unable to overcome presidential opposition, the Mack amendment was easily defeated each time it was presented.

In early 1992 action on Cuba came from the other side of the aisle. Rep. Robert Torricelli, D-N.J., and Sen. Bob Graham, D-Fla., introduced the Cuban Democracy Act (CDA) in their respective chambers. The CDA had two tracks. One track sought—like the Mack amendment—to increase economic pressure on Cuba by prohibiting trade with foreign subsidiaries of U.S. companies and by making it more difficult for ships that had stopped in Cuba to enter U.S. ports. The other track tried to reach out to the Cuban people by facilitating communication and family visits to the island. CANF was a prominent player in the life of this bill, which was opposed by the Bush administration for the same kinds of reasons that it opposed the Mack amendment.

Representative Torricelli had developed close ties to CANF. Torricelli's New Jersey district had almost no Cuban Americans, but if he decided to run statewide for the Senate, Cuban American support throughout the state would be helpful. Among the original twenty-two House sponsors of the CDA, fourteen had received donations from CANF's political action committee of more than $1,000 each.[13] Bipartisan support in Congress notwithstanding, President Bush was probably going to veto the bill. In April 1992 Robert Gelbard, principal deputy assistant secretary of state for inter-American affairs, offered several objections to the CDA before Congress. Among the most important were that the bill would cause diplomatic problems for the United States and impinge "on the President's constitutionally mandated powers to conduct foreign affairs."[14]

With the November 1992 presidential election looming, and disappointed that the Bush administration was opposed to the Cuban Democracy Act, CANF leader Jorge Mas Canosa met with Rep. Stephen Solarz, D-N.Y., and apparently offered through him to help Bill Clinton's presidential campaign if Clinton would endorse the bill.[15] Clinton adviser George Stephanopoulos and Representative Torricelli negotiated a deal. With his campaign short on funds, and needing to be competitive in Florida against President Bush in the general election, candidate Clinton signed on in Miami: "I have read the Torricelli-Graham bill and I like it."[16] Clinton raised $275,000 from Cuban Americans in Coral Gables and Miami that day. Suddenly outflanked on the right on Cuba, the Bush camp tried to cut its political losses by working with Congress to fashion a CDA that the president could sign into law. In October 1992, just weeks before the election, Bush signed the Cuban Democracy Act. Although Clinton failed to carry Florida on his way to defeating Bush, he got many more Cuban American votes than Democratic candidate Michael Dukakis had received there in 1988. Clinton would win Florida in 1996.

Clinton supported the CDA from the outset of his administration, and he even argued that "no Democrat in my life time, in the White House at least, has come close to taking the strong position I have on this, agreeing with the Cuban-American community."[17] While Clinton supported continuing the embargo in public, a number of officials in the administration were asserting the need to reevaluate, if not change, U.S. policy toward Cuba. According to one administration critic, "On the entire Clinton foreign policy team—Bill (and Hillary); Anthony Lake and Richard Feinberg at the National Security Council; Warren Christopher, Strobe Talbott, and [Peter] Tarnoff at the State Department—there isn't one single person who favors a hard line against Castro."[18] Skepticism would grow when, in the summer of 1994, in the face of a large exodus of Cubans heading for Florida in boats, the administration reversed the nearly three-decade policy of automatically granting asylum to all arriving Cubans.[19] Beginning in the mid-1960s all Cubans fleeing the island had been immediately granted refugee status, allowing them to avoid the hearings that people fleeing other countries (such as Haiti) were required to have. Cuban Americans reacted to the new policy with shock and outrage.[20]

A New Initiative: Congress and Helms-Burton

The November 1994 elections resulted in Republican majorities in the House and Senate, a situation that would weaken the position of those in the Clinton administration interested in at least softening the embargo. The impetus for a new legislative initiative had begun to emerge even before the elections. Many on Capitol Hill were frustrated that Castro had survived the wave of democratization that had swept through Latin American countries such as

Chile, Guatemala, and Nicaragua in the late 1980s and early 1990s. Furthermore, some Republicans felt that Clinton was not doing enough to try to remove Castro from power. From the perspective of Dan Fisk, a former staffer for Sen. Jesse Helms, R-N.C., Clinton had run to the right of President Bush on the Cuban Democracy Act only then to ignore Cuba or send signals of possible rapprochement. The contrast of U.S. Cuba policy with Clinton's Haiti policy—on which Clinton invested significant time and resources and even committed the military in 1994 to help remove a dictator and restore democracy—also frustrated many in Congress. The view of some on the Hill was that Haiti and Cuba were both countries with dictatorships, but Clinton only seemed interested in dethroning the Haitian regime that refused to relinquish power after elections had been held. A key factor in the Haitian case, however, was the activism of the Congressional Black Caucus. Senator Helms and others decided that similar congressional activism was needed on Cuba.[21] It was in this context that the Cuban Liberty and Democratic Solidarity Act, LIBERTAD for short, and also known as Helms-Burton for its sponsors—Helms in the Senate and Dan Burton, R-Ind., in the House—began to take shape.

The proposed legislation picked up steam in early 1995 at the direction of Senator Helms, the new chair of the Senate Foreign Relations Committee. Dan Fisk was the point man on the legislation, the basic aim of which was to drive Castro from power. Fisk constructed the bill by bringing together all the pieces of Cuba legislation that had been floating around the Hill for years. He formed a coalition of staffers from the House and Senate to review those past initiatives and to draft the new bill.[22] Notably absent from the drafting coalition was CANF. Although it was the biggest and most important lobbying group in town on Cuba policy, and the drafting coalition wanted CANF's help in pushing the bill once it was drafted, Congress was growing more autonomous in matters concerning Cuba policy, in part because of its three Cuban American members.

The original idea was to tack Helms-Burton onto another bill, but pressure and momentum caused Senator Helms to unveil it as stand-alone legislation in February 1995. The bill included several controversial components to tighten and expand the embargo. Perhaps most controversial was the bill's Title III, which would give U.S. nationals the right to sue in U.S. courts foreign companies that "traffic" in "stolen property" in Cuba. For example, a foreign company doing business in Cuba on or with property of U.S. nationals that was seized following the revolution could be taken to court. This "extraterritorial" element of the bill was highly controversial. Its standing in international law was questioned by many, and it promised to pose diplomatic headaches for President

Clinton that were even bigger than the ones Bush had feared from the CDA. Canadian officials protested Title III by way of a strongly worded letter to the State Department in April, stating that it "would constitute an illegitimate intrusion upon third countries."[23] Also controversial was Title IV of the bill, which would deny visas to executives of foreign companies "trafficking" (doing business) in confiscated properties in Cuba. As Helms-Burton was moving through Congress in spring and summer 1995, others took more direct action to challenge Castro, with boats and small airplanes making periodic runs toward Cuba from Miami.

Hearings on Helms-Burton in the House were marked by suspicion about the Clinton administration's intentions toward Cuba. Administration witnesses were grilled about an article in the *Washington Post* claiming the existence of an internal National Security Council paper suggesting that the embargo be lifted.[24] This was compounded by leaks from the administration and from abroad to the effect that the Clinton team was considering loosening or lifting the embargo.[25] Clinton's unilateral move to lift the economic embargo against Vietnam and to normalize relations in 1995, plus his actions to reverse U.S. policy automatically granting asylum to fleeing Cubans during the 1994 immigration crisis, suggested to congressional proponents of the Cuban embargo that they might need to restrain the president. Representative Diaz-Balart, for example, was concerned that the administration was going to normalize relations with Cuba before political reforms were enacted there. He said that he had received a number of signals suggesting such a possibility, including a statement from a British diplomat who told him his government had been assured by Clinton officials that the president would normalize relations after the 1996 elections.[26]

The administration came out publicly against Helms-Burton. In an April 1995 interview on CNN, President Clinton argued that it was unnecessary because of the existing Cuban Democracy Act.[27] Under Secretary of State for Political Affairs Peter Tarnoff testified against the bill in the Senate, claiming that it would limit the president's flexibility in conducting foreign affairs. He, like Clinton, argued that the two tracks of the CDA were sufficient.[28] The day before the House vote, Secretary Christopher sent a letter arguing against the bill to Speaker Newt Gingrich, R-Ga. Christopher wrote that if Helms-Burton was passed he would urge the president to veto it on the grounds that it was too inflexible to allow the president to deal with rapidly developing situations, as might occur in Cuba. He also said that Title III was counterproductive.[29] The House passed Helms-Burton by a vote of 294–130 on September 21. The action then moved on to the Senate, where passage promised to be more difficult.

Since there was no "heavy-handed White House presence" against the bill, in the Senate its supporters did not think Helms-Burton was necessarily a "killer" for Clinton.[30] A former administration official confirmed that the administration's strategy was not to threaten a veto but rather to prevent the bill from ever getting to the president. The administration also tried to cultivate corporate opposition to the bill. On October 6, presidential chief of staff Leon Panetta and foreign policy advisers met with a group of about fifty U.S. business executives to discuss taking a trip to Cuba. The problem with such a visit was that according to Treasury Department regulations, only certain categories of U.S. citizens and residents could legally travel to the island. People receiving permission typically were journalists or academics.[31] To meet the restrictions, the executives were classified as "journalists." Among those making the trip, which included a meeting with Castro, were heads of Time Warner, Hyatt Hotels, General Motors, and Zenith.[32] Representative Diaz-Balart challenged the one-day trip: "There is an abhorrent, unscrupulous, carefully planned strategy by administration officials to use the business community as a means of putting pressure on Congress."[33] Sen. Phil Gramm, R-Texas, described Clinton's maneuvers as "putting out the welcome mat to Castro instead of tightening the noose around his aging neck."[34]

Despite a plea by Senator Graham in a "Dear Colleague" letter to Senate Democrats urging their support of the bill,[35] attempts to move Helms-Burton toward a Senate vote failed twice in mid-October 1995. As the White House strategy jelled and corporate opposition grew, support for Helms-Burton faltered. In the meantime Clinton moved forward on the two tracks of the CDA. He announced measures to expand contacts between Cuban and American residents, including opening news bureaus, relaxing travel restrictions, and allowing more activities in Cuba by nongovernmental organizations.[36] Unable to move the bill as drafted, the Senate removed Titles III and IV. Even though Helms-Burton had passed overwhelmingly in the House, the president seemed poised to win the showdown. Once Helms-Burton passed the Senate in its weakened form, it still appeared dead as it went to the conference committee for resolution of the differences between the House and Senate versions. The future of the embargo looked bleak to some.

While these events unfolded in Washington, activities in the Florida Straits caught everyone's attention. Brothers to the Rescue were regularly flying search missions over the waters between Cuba and Florida, but also reportedly flying over Cuba on occasion to drop anti-Castro leaflets. Tension over these flights was growing, as the Cuban government became increasingly angry. Matters reached a dramatic and tragic crescendo when jet fighters from the Cuban air force shot down two small, unarmed Brothers to the Rescue planes on February 24, 1996, breathing new life into the Helms-Burton Act.[37]

Helms-Burton's Second Chance

The downing of the Brothers to the Rescue planes produced strong reactions in Congress. Representative Ros-Lehtinen characterized the shooting as "an act of war" and called for a naval blockade.[38] On February 26, President Clinton condemned the attack and ordered a number of actions against Cuba. He also announced his intention to reach an agreement with Congress on Helms-Burton, as the advantage had now clearly shifted to the Hill.[39] At a strategy meeting the next day attended by Representatives Burton, Diaz-Balart, Patrick Kennedy, D-R.I., Menendez, Ros-Lehtinen, Torricelli, and others, Titles III and IV were reinserted in the bill. Diaz-Balart insisted that a new measure be added as well—codification of the embargo into law. This addition, inserted in Title I, would take the full body of the U.S. embargo policy toward Cuba, which existed by executive order, and make it law. Thereafter the embargo could only be lifted through repeal by Congress, making impossible a unilateral policy change such as Clinton implemented concerning Vietnam. Diaz-Balart told the gathering that he would insist on codification and that he wanted their support; they all agreed.[40]

From the perspective of congressional supporters of Helms-Burton, Clinton now had no choice but to accept LIBERTAD, which was "the only game in town."[41] A House staffer noted that the events in the Florida Straits "changed everything" and left the administration "no position to bargain."[42] Representative Kennedy argued, "Now is not the time to relax on Castro. Shooting down unarmed civilian planes is just one more in an escalating and disturbing pattern of human rights violations by the Castro regime, desperately clinging to power in its final days."[43] Diaz-Balart, adopting a populist tone at the same press conference, said, "Sometimes Main Street's got to . . . speak up and [tell] Wall Street where to go."[44] Even Richard Nuccio, the president's special adviser for Cuba policy, admitted that "President Castro created a veto-proof majority for the Helms-Burton bill."[45]

On the morning of February 28 in Representative Menendez's office, the coalition from the Hill met with several members of the administration, including Nuccio. Diaz-Balart recalls that the administration officials emphasized that they wanted to include in the legislation a waiver for Title III that would essentially allow the president to sign the bill but then waive its enforcement, at least temporarily, for reasons of national security. They negotiated most of the day. When the issue of codifying the embargo arose, the Clinton team objected on the grounds that it was new to the bill. Diaz-Balart then asked, "Well, are you going to lift the embargo?" When the Clinton team said that they would not, Diaz-Balart's response was, "Good, then we have no problem; next issue." This go-round recurred during the day, but Diaz-Balart contends that there was never any negotiation on this point and that the Clinton team seemed more concerned with Title III, for which they ultimately got a waiver. When it came time to negotiate on Title IV, for which the Clinton administration also wanted a waiver, Diaz-Balart recalled that Torricelli "played the bad guy and said there would be no waiver there." He further noted that the Clinton team had virtually no bargaining power and few options. "What were they going to do, veto a bill after a terrorist government's air force shot down American citizens? Not even Qadhafi has done exactly that."[46] Fisk confirmed that the deal was "you get waivers on Title III, and we get codification."[47]

The Clinton team then met to decide how to proceed. The group included Attorney General Janet Reno, Secretary of Defense William J. Perry, Secretary of State Christopher, Chairman of the Joint Chiefs of Staff General John M. Shalikasvili, Director of Central Intelligence John Deutch, and others. As they discussed the policy issues, none of them appeared to know about the codification provision; when they were told about it they objected on the ground that it took away too much prerogative from the president and might be unconstitutional. Political adviser Stephanopoulos and Chief of Staff Panetta overruled the policy staff and argued that Clinton should sign the bill because his administration could be weakened politically if he vetoed it after the dramatic event in the straits. Clinton's reelection prospects could also be hurt if he were to anger the politically strong Cuban American populations in Florida and New Jersey. When National Security Advisor Anthony Lake agreed, the policy discussion was over; political calculations carried the day. Rather than argue against codification, the Clinton team focused on the waiver to Title III, so that they could explain their reversal on the bill and salve the wounds of allies, who were not going to take well to Title III. They then agreed that Clinton would sign the bill.

Not everyone on Capitol Hill was happy about the deal. Rep. Charles Rangel, D-N.Y., assessed the new law, saying, "This bill has nothing to do with Castro; it has everything to do with our friends and our voters in Florida."[48] Sen. Christopher Dodd, D-Conn., warned that the bill "totally ties the hands of this president and future presidents to respond flexibly to change in Cuba when it comes."[49]

Rep. Lee Hamilton, D-Ind., shared Dodd's concern and argued that codification would "lock in the president of the United States in the conduct of foreign policy."[50] Beyond these concerns, critics of the bill continued to worry about how Helms-Burton would set the United States and its allies at odds over its extraterritorial provisions. Supporters argued that international opposition should not affect U.S. policymaking. Sen. Paul Coverdell, R-Ga., declared, "We can't retreat because this is disruptive to some of our European allies."[51] Representative Ros-Lehtinen added, "The United States must stop hiding behind international public opinion and stop wavering."[52] Representative Burton concluded that agreement on Helms-Burton "makes it clear that Fidel Castro and his blood-soaked, dictatorial, corrupt tyranny is about to end."[53] After the new bill passed both houses, Clinton signed Helms-Burton on March 12, 1996.

The Politics of U.S. Cuba Policy since Helms-Burton

A number of interesting developments followed the passage of Helms-Burton. As passed, the law allows the president to waive enforcement of Title III, (1) if the president deems the waiver "necessary to the national interests of the United States" or (2) if waiving it "will expedite a transition to democracy in Cuba."[54] In July 1996 President Clinton announced that although he would allow Title III to come into force on August 1, as the act specified, he would waive enforcement of that part of the measure for six months.[55] He thus put on notice companies doing business in Cuba with the seized property of U.S. nationals that they could end up in a U.S. court, although he delayed such legal action. He thereafter continued to invoke the waiver every six months. The framers of Helms-Burton thought that the president could not in good faith exercise the waiver because there was no transition to democracy under way in Cuba.[56] That Clinton did so frustrated Helms-Burton proponents.

There has been little action on Title IV since 1996. A small number of company executives have come under scrutiny for possible exclusion from entry into the United States, including individuals from the Canadian firm Sherritt International, the Mexican firm Grupo Domos, and the Italian company Stet International.[57] Only officials with Sherritt and the Israeli BM group have actually been barred,[58] though there has been speculation that the George W. Bush administration might increase activity on Title IV. Some had estimated that 100 to 200 foreign ventures under way in Cuba might be vulnerable under Helms-Burton's definition of "trafficking in confiscated property."[59] If the estimates are correct, enforcement efforts thus far would seem to be weak.

The bulk of the activity on Cuba policy since 1996 has been the expansion of the president's "licensing power" to relax some parts of the embargo. Although Helms-Burton froze all restrictions on trade and travel already in force, one part of the act, Section 112, gave the president limited licensing power to revise sanctions on family remittances—money that U.S. residents and citizens send to their families on the island—and travel to Cuba if specified steps are first taken by the Cuban government to liberalize political and economic life on the island (for example, releasing political prisoners). President Clinton used this licensing power provision to make a number of unilateral changes in policy. The first of these were announced just before Pope John Paul II visited Cuba in 1998 and included the resumption of direct humanitarian charter flights to Cuba, a higher remittance level ($300 per quarter), and easier shipping and sales of medicines and medical supplies to Cuba.[60]

A second set of changes followed in January 1999. Clinton expanded the use of remittances by allowing any U.S. resident to send money to Cuban families and independent organizations. He also sought to expand people-to-people contact through exchanges among academics, athletes (for example, allowing baseball games between the Baltimore Orioles and the Cuban national team), scientists, and others. He authorized the sale of food and agricultural products to independent family restaurants, religious groups, and private farmers. He permitted charter passenger flights to cities in Cuba other than Havana and from cities in the United States other than Miami. Finally, he pledged to establish direct mail service.[61]

Supporters of Helms-Burton were not happy with Clinton's actions. After the 1998 reforms, for example, Representative Diaz-Balart said, "We are not going to let Clinton proceed along the path of normalization."[62] Following the January 1999 reforms, Representative Ros-Lehtinen said, "We want to know where is the legal controlling authority that authorizes them to change the law. The way we read Helms-Burton, they do not have any such authority."[63] Frustration aside, there was little Congress could do to reverse Clinton's decisions.[64] In some ways, Clinton acted as if Helms-Burton never existed.

Other activity in Congress on U.S. Cuba policy centered around the efforts of the farm lobby to join forces with other business interests to weaken the embargo and allow increased sales of food to Cuba. A number of farm state senators (mostly Republicans) and farm groups, such as the American Farm Bureau Federation and the U.S. Grains Council, welcomed the limited sales of U.S. agricultural products to nongovernmental agencies and independent farmers and advocated even greater opening.[65] By the end of summer 1999, the momentum in the Senate to help distressed U.S. farmers by opening the Cuban market produced an amendment to the agriculture spending bill that would have largely lifted the embargo on food sales to Cuba. It would also have prohibited the president from imposing such bans in the future without the consent of Congress.[66] The measure was cosponsored by Nebraska Republican Sen. Chuck Hagel and one of the Senate's most conservative members, John Ashcroft, R-Mo. While the spending bill was sitting in the Senate-House conference committee, prominent nonagricultural business organizations, including the U.S. Chamber of Commerce, offered support for what was known by then as the Ashcroft amendment.[67] In the end, House opposition—largely from the Cuban American and Republican leaderships—kept the opening to Cuba out of the final bill.

In 2000, facing a third consecutive year of depressed global commodity prices, the farm lobby and its Senate allies resumed the battle to open the Cuban market. When Senator Helms dropped his opposition to easing the embargo to the extent of selling food and medicine for the Cuban people, the Senate Foreign Relations Committee voted in March to authorize such sales.[68] The Cuban American members of Congress and their allies fought hard in the House against a farm lobby that saw a potential $1 billion market in goods to Cuba.[69] The measure stalled during the summer, but by fall Congress had reached agreement on a bill that would allow Cubans to buy food and medicine from the United States. Iran, Libya, North Korea, and Sudan—countries also subject to U.S. economic sanctions—were affected by the new legislation as well. Of these five countries, however, only Cuba was denied the right to pay for goods with U.S. government credits or loans from U.S. banks. Congressional supporters of the embargo, especially the Cuban American members of Congress, were able to include in the bill a measure codifying all existing travel restrictions to Cuba. At the end of October, a little more than a week before the presidential election, Clinton signed the bill into law,[70] thus ensuring that future presidents would not be able to change travel restrictions without congressional approval.

When George W. Bush became president in January 2001 many observers assumed that Cuba policy in the executive branch would be driven by the president's desire to show appreciation to Cuban American voters whose support in south Florida had been pivotal in the election and the recount. Although codifications in 1996 and 2000 transferred much power over the embargo from the executive to the legislative branch, Bush could still reverse some of Clinton's policies, such as returning Cubans captured at sea to the island and the waiver of Title III. Bush, as of early 2007, had chosen not to reverse either policy. Although he did tighten the rules for family travel and remittances to Cuba as the 2004 elections approached, under George W. Bush's presidency the real action on U.S. Cuba policy took place in Congress.

A bipartisan group of legislators in the House and Senate, with views ranging across the political spectrum, continued to try to relax the embargo, particularly with respect to the ability of U.S. citizens to travel to the island. In 2001, 2002, and 2003 the House voted to prohibit the Treasury Department from spending money to enforce the travel ban. (U.S. nationals cannot spend money in Cuba legally without a license, so travel to Cuba is for all practical purposes banned for most Americans.) When the Senate voted to do the same in 2003, the days of prohibiting travel by U.S. citizens to Cuba seemed numbered. But the travel provision—passed by both houses with identical language—was quietly removed late one night by the House-Senate conference committee on the larger spending bill. The Republican sponsor of the move to end the travel ban, Jeff Flake, R-Ariz., described the maneuver: "Disgusting. Politics have triumphed again over principle. For the same reason we will never have a rational farm policy as long as presidential campaigns begin in Iowa, we will never have a rational Cuba policy as long as presidential campaigns are perceived to end in Florida."[71] However Flake kept trying. In December 2006, he and Rep. William Delahunt, D-Mass., led a delegation of ten members of Congress to Havana to press for additional Cuban support for reducing the U.S. trade and travel sanctions. While there, they met with Cuban government officials, foreign diplomats, and Cuba's Roman Catholic cardinal, Jaime Ortega.[72]

Conclusion: The Struggle to Control Cuba Policy

The post–cold war period in U.S.-Cuban relations began with a president who demonstrated little interest in changing policy toward the communist-led island. President George Bush's hand, however, was forced by the combined efforts of members of Congress, the Cuban American National Foundation, and an opportunistic opposing candidate in the 1992 presidential election. The resulting Cuban Democracy Act was the product of a variety of domestic political actors, operating openly in an election year to promote the tightening of the embargo even as international events might have favored a change of policy in a different direction.

The Helms-Burton bill that was enacted in 1996 was even more clearly driven by members of Congress dealing with a president whose decision making on Cuba policy was overwhelmingly based on electoral and other domestic political calculations. Republican members of Congress, led by Cuban American representatives from Florida, not only refused to defer to the chief executive in the wake of the downing of the Brothers to the Rescue planes, but they effectively usurped decision-making authority on Cuba from the president.

Since the signing of Helms-Burton, the cast of actors engaged in U.S. Cuba policy has continued to increase and has become more diverse. A range of economic interest groups, including the U.S. Chamber of Commerce and leading agricultural organizations, have promoted loosening the embargo. Farm state legislators on both sides of the aisle have supported them—from conservative Republican Senator Ashcroft, who put forward such a bill, to Sen. Tom Daschle, D-S.D., who traveled to the island in 1999, to Arizona's conservative Representative Flake. Former government officials working under the auspices of the Council on Foreign Relations have twice issued reports suggesting possible changes in the direction of more open relations with Cuba.[73] This impressive array of domestic political forces has yet to succeed in the face of the determined resistance of legislators led by Cuban American members of the House (and now Senate). A bit of a hole was opened in the embargo with the limited sale of food and medicine to Cuba. Recent attention has shifted somewhat to efforts to lift the travel ban, which have made strange allies of conservative Republicans and liberal Democrats but have so far been frustrated by the embargo hard-liners and the threat of a veto from the White House.

It is too early to tell if the Democratic takeover of the House and the Senate following the 2006 elections will shift the balance of power enough toward the pro-engagement forces to weaken or even end the embargo, but it is likely that the change in leadership, which includes a number of key committees, will provide new opportunities in this regard. Indeed, a new bill to end the travel ban, the Freedom to Travel to Cuba Act of 2007, is making its way through both houses with broad bipartisan support. The debate about U.S. policy toward Cuba is also being influenced by the resurgence of elected leaders of the left in Latin America, such as Hugo Chavez in Venezuela. Chavez has provided financial support for the Cuban economy, and the friendship between Presidents Chavez and Castro has been part of what some see as "Castro's comeback" in the region.[74] Even as that resurgence of leftist allies in Latin America has bolstered Castro's standing, the Cuban president's physical well being has been deteriorating. On July 31, 2006, Fidel temporarily transferred power to his brother Raul when he underwent intestinal surgery. Rumors about the severity of Fidel Castro's illness, his impending death, and the likelihood of instability or even significant reforms under Raul's leadership swirled in Cuba and Miami in the days and weeks that followed. In early 2007 there were signs that Fidel might in fact be recovering, and the transition to Raul's leadership seemed to have been quite smooth. If liberal Democrat Charles Rangel and conservative Republican Jeff Flake are successful with the Freedom to Travel to Cuba Act, Americans might soon be able to verify developments on the island for themselves (barring a presidential veto, of course).

As this case study suggests, U.S.-Cuban relations are rooted in the public struggles among a growing number of domestic political actors to shape a policy that once was almost exclusively driven by presidents debating the national interest with their advisers behind closed doors. And that policy struggle also takes place within the context of allies and neighbors and adversaries who have their own political struggles and interests that can affect the policy process inside the United States. And if past is prologue, as the presidential election of 2008 approaches, one thing is certain: Cuba policy, and the electoral votes in Florida, will be in play.

Key Actors

Brothers to the Rescue Group that sponsored two planes shot down by the Cuban air force in 1996 over the Florida Straits, an incident that changed the fortunes of the Helms-Burton Act.

Dan Burton Representative, R-Ind., cosponsor of the Helms-Burton Act.

Raul Castro Acting president of Cuba, brother of Fidel.

Hugo Chavez President of Venezuela, ally of Fidel Castro, leader of leftist and anti-U.S. movement in Latin America.

Bill Clinton President, initially opposed Helms-Burton but agreed to sign the bill after the downing of the Brothers to the Rescue planes.

Cuban American National Foundation Interest group that strongly supported the U.S. embargo against Cuba and lobbied for Helms-Burton.

Lincoln Diaz-Balart Representative, R-Fla., Cuban American sponsor of Helms-Burton and one of the leaders of the move to codify the U.S. embargo against Cuba.

Jeff Flake Representative, R-Ariz, supporter of more trade with Cuba and an end to the travel restrictions on visits to Cuba from the U.S.

Bob Graham Senator, D-Fla., supporter of Helms-Burton and sponsor of the Cuban Democracy Act of 1992.

Jesse Helms Senator, R-N.C., initiator and cosponsor of Helms-Burton legislation.

Ileana Ros-Lehtinen Representative, R-Fla., Cuban American supporter of Helms-Burton.

Robert Torricelli Representative, D-N.J., supporter of Helms-Burton and sponsor of the Cuban Democracy Act of 1992.

Notes

1. Much of the material for this case study has been adapted from Walt Vanderbush and Patrick J. Haney, "Policy toward Cuba in the Clinton Administration," *Political Science Quarterly* 144 (Fall 1999): 387–408. We would like to thank Ralph Carter, anonymous reviewers, and Amy Briggs for their helpful comments.

2. See Carl Nagin, "Backfire," *New Yorker,* January 26, 1998, 30–35.

3. 22 U.S.C. 6021 and following (H.R. 927, P.L. 104–114, March 12, 1996).

4. See the chronology of U.S.-Cuban relations, 1958–1999, at www. state.gov/www/regions/wha/cuba_chronology.html. See also Philip Brenner, *From Confrontation to Negotiation: U.S. Relations with Cuba* (Boulder: Westview Press, 1988); Gillian Gunn, *Cuba in Transition* (New York: Twentieth Century Fund, 1993); Donna Rich Kaplowitz, *Anatomy of a Failed Embargo: U.S. Sanctions against Cuba* (Boulder: Lynne Rienner, 1998); and William M. LeoGrande, "From Havana to Miami: U.S. Cuba Policy as a Two-Level Game," *Journal of Interamerican Studies and World Affairs* 40 (Spring 1998): 67–86.

5. Holly Sklar, *Washington's War on Nicaragua* (Boston: South End Press, 1988), 57.

6. Brenner, *From Confrontation to Negotiation*; Gunn, *Cuba in Transition*; Kaplowitz, *Anatomy of a Failed Embargo,* 117–143.

7. A number of different versions of the founding of CANF have appeared in the literature. For an analysis of these, see Patrick J. Haney and Walt Vanderbush, "The Role of Ethnic Interest Groups in U.S. Foreign Policy: The Case of the Cuban American National Foundation," *International Studies Quarterly* 43 (1999): 341–361.

8. House Committee on the Judiciary, Subcommittee on International Law, Immigration, and Refugees, *Cuban and Haitian Immigration,* hearing, 102d Cong., 1st sess., November 20, 1991.

9. House Committee on Foreign Affairs, Subcommittees on Europe and the Middle East and on the Western Hemisphere, *Cuba in a Changing World: The United States-Soviet-Cuba Triangle,* hearing, 101st Cong., 1st sess., April 30 and July 11 and 31, 1991, 154. For the first statement of the Cuban Democracy Act, see Robert G. Torricelli, "Let Democracy Shine through an Open Door," *Los Angeles Times,* August 18, 1991, M5.

10. For example, see Wayne Smith, "Shackled to the Past: The United States and Cuba," *Current History* 95 (February 1996): 49–54; Gail DeGeorge with Douglas Harbrecht, "Warmer Winds Are Blowing from Washington to Havana," *Business Week,* August 2, 1993, 42; Peter Hakim, "It's Time to Review U.S. Cuba Policy," *Brookings Review* 13 (Winter 1995): 47.

11. For example, see Susan Kaufman Purcell, "Cuba's Cloudy Future," *Foreign Affairs* 69 (Summer 1990): 113–130; and Purcell, "The Cuban Illusion: Keeping the Heat on Castro," *Foreign Affairs* 75 (May/June 1996): 159–161; Charles Lane, "TRB from Washington," *New Republic,* February 6, 1998, 6, 41; Michael G. Wilson, "Hastening Castro's Downfall," *Heritage Foundation Backgrounder,* July 2, 1992. For other views, see Bob Benenson, "Dissonant Voices Urge Clinton to Revise Policy on Cuba," *Congressional Quarterly Weekly Report,* August 24, 1994, 2498; Saul Landau, "Clinton's Cuba Policy: A Low-Priority Dilemma," *NACLA Report on the Americas* 26 (May 1993): 35–37; David Rieff, "Cuba Refrozen," *Foreign Affairs* 75 (July/August 1996): 62–75; Andrew Zimbalist, "Cuba, Castro, Clinton, and Canosa," in *Cuba in the International System,* ed. Archibald R.M. Ritter and John M. Kirk (New York: St. Martin's Press, 1995), 23–36.

12. House Committee on Foreign Affairs, *Cuba in a Changing World,* 128.

13. Peter H. Stone, "Cuban Clout," *National Journal,* February 20, 1993, 451.

14. House Committee on Foreign Affairs, *Consideration of the Cuban Democracy Act of 1992,* hearing, 102d Cong., 2d sess., April 8, 1992, 359.

15. Jane Franklin, *Cuba and the United States: A Chronological History* (New York: Ocean Press, 1997), 290.

16. Ann Bardach, "Our Man in Miami," *New Republic,* October 3, 1994, 20.

17. William Jefferson Clinton, "Media Roundtable on NAFTA," *Weekly Compilation of Presidential Documents,* November 12, 1993, 2350.

18. Elliott Abrams, "Castro's Latest Coup," *National Review,* June 12, 1995, 37.

19. Burt Solomon, "Clinton's Fast Break on Cuba . . . or Foreign Policy on the Fly," *National Journal,* September 3, 1994, 2044.

20. David Rieff, "From Exiles to Immigrants," *Foreign Affairs* 74 (July/August 1995): 87, describes Cuban Miami as "stupefied." See also Jonathan C. Smith, "Foreign Policy for Sale? Interest Group Influence on President Clinton's Cuba Policy, August 1994," *Presidential Studies Quarterly* 29 (1998): 207–220.

21. Dan Fisk, telephone interview, June 16, 1998.

22. Patrick J. Kiger, *Squeeze Play: The United States, Cuba, and the Helms-Burton Act* (Washington, D.C.: Center for Public Integrity, 1997), chap. 5. See also Dick Kirschten, "Raising Cain," *National Journal,* July 1, 1995, 1714–1717.

23. Steven Greenhouse, "Allies of U.S. Seek to Block Bill on Cuba," *New York Times,* April 13, 1995, A9.

24. See House Committee on International Relations, Subcommittee on the Western Hemisphere, *The Cuban Liberty and Democratic Solidarity (LIBERTAD) Act of 1995,* hearing, 104th Cong., 1st sess., March 16, 1995, 31–34.

25. Fisk, telephone interview; see also Senate Committee on Foreign Relations, Subcommittee on the Western Hemisphere and Peace Corps Affairs, *Cuban Liberty and Democratic Solidarity Act,* hearing, 104th Cong., 1st sess., May 22 and June 14, 1995, 76.

26. Rep. Lincoln Diaz-Balart, R-Fla., telephone interview, July 2, 1998.

27. William Jefferson Clinton, "Interview with Wolf Blitzer and Judy Woodruff on CNN," *Weekly Compilation of Presidential Documents,* April 14, 1995, 624–625. The compilations are available at www.access.gpo.gov/nara/nara003.html.

28. Senate Committee on Foreign Relations, *Cuban Liberty and Democratic Solidarity Act,* 16–30.

29. Kiger, *Squeeze Play,* 54.

30. Fisk, telephone interview.

31. For more detail on these regulations, see www.state.gov/www/regions/wha/cuba/travel.html.

32. Kiger, *Squeeze Play,* 54; Christopher Marquis, "New Clinton Strategy Eases Rules on Travel, Cultural Ties to Cuba," *Tampa Tribune,* October 6, 1995, 1; and Norman Pearlstine, "To Our Readers," *Time,* October 25, 1995, 4.

33. Mark Matthews, "Congress Divided on Clinton Move to Thaw Cuba Policy," *Baltimore Sun,* October 7, 1995, 9A.

34. William L. Roberts, "Clinton Draws Mixed Review on Cuba Policy," *Journal of Commerce,* October 10, 1995, 2A.

35. Pamela Falk, "U.S.-Cuba Deal Seems Close to Fruition," *Denver Post,* October 19, 1995, B7.

36. William Jefferson Clinton, "Remarks at a Freedom House Breakfast," *Weekly Compilation of Presidential Documents,* October 6, 1995, 1780–1781.

37. See Nagin, "Backfire."

38. Nancy Mathis, "New Sanctions against Cuba; U.S. Plans Action after 2 Civilian Planes Downed," *Houston Chronicle,* February 26, 1996, A1.

39. William Jefferson Clinton, "Remarks Announcing Sanctions against Cuba following the Downing of Brothers to the Rescue Airplanes," *Weekly Compilation of Presidential Documents,* February 26, 1996, 381–382; see also Nagin, "Backfire."

40. Diaz-Balart, telephone interview.

41. Fisk, telephone interview.

42. Steve Vermillion, Office of Rep. Lincoln Diaz-Balart, telephone interview, June 19, 1998.

43. Federal News Service, "Press Conference: Reaction to Cuban Shootdown of Civilian Aircraft," February 27, 1996.

44. Ibid.

45. Carroll J. Doherty, "Planes' Downing Forces Clinton to Compromise on Sanctions," *Congressional Quarterly Weekly Report,* March 2, 1996, 565.

46. Diaz-Balart, telephone interview.

47. Fisk, telephone interview.

48. "House, in 336–86 Vote, Passes Bill Increasing Economic Sanctions on Cuba," *Buffalo News,* March 7, 1996, 4A.

49. "Clinton, Congress, Agree on Bill to Hit Cuba," *Montreal Gazette,* February 29, 1996, B1.

50. "House, in 336–86 Vote."

51. Helen Dewar, "Clinton, Hill Agree on Cuba Sanctions; New Curbs May Be Enacted Next Week," *Washington Post,* February 29, 1996, A16.

52. Ibid.

53. Federal News Service, "Hearing of the House International Relations Committee: Cuba Shootdown Incident," February 29, 1996.

54. See the full text of the act at www.ustreas.gov/offices/eotffc/ofac/legal/statutes/libertad.pdf.

55. William Jefferson Clinton, "Statement on Action on Title III of the Cuban Liberty and Democratic Solidarity (LIBERTAD) Act of 1996," *Weekly Compilation of Presidential Documents,* July 16, 1996, 1265–1266.

56. See Jesse Helms, "Helms Slams Decision to Waive Cuba Provision," press release, July 16, 1996.

57. John Pearson, "Just Who's Getting Punished Here?" *Business Week,* international edition, June 17, 1996, 28. See also Juan O. Tamayo, "U.S. Poised to Bar Execs of Firm

Operating in Cuba," *Miami Herald,* July 3, 1999; and Tim Golden, "U.S., Avoiding Castro, Relaxes Rules on Cuba," *New York Times,* July 7, 1999, A1.

58. Michael E. Ranneberger, coordinator for the Office of Cuban Affairs, statement before hearings of the Subcommittee on the Western Hemisphere of the House International Relations Committee, March 24, 1999.

59. Craig Auge, "Title IV of the Helms-Burton Act: A Questionable Secondary Boycott," *Law and Policy in International Business* 28, no. 2 (Winter 1997): 575.

60. William Jefferson Clinton, "Statement on Cuba," *Weekly Compilation of Presidential Documents,* March 20, 1998, 475–476.

61. William Jefferson Clinton, "Statement on United States Policy toward Cuba," *Weekly Compilation of Presidential Documents,* January 5, 1999, 7–8.

62. Christopher Marquis, "U.S. to Cut Sanctions on Cuba," *Pittsburgh Post-Gazette,* March 20, 1998, A1. See also Steven Erlanger, "U.S. to Ease Curbs on Relief to Cuba and Money to Kin," *New York Times,* March 20, 1998, A1.

63. Juan O. Tamayo, "Eased Cuba Sanctions Questioned," *Miami Herald,* January 7, 1999, A12.

64. An attempt was made to form a presidential "blue ribbon" commission on U.S. Cuba policy, which may have suggested dropping the embargo, but a variety of political pressures stymied the effort in 1999. See, for example, Thomas W. Lippman, "Group Urges Review of Cuba Policy," *Washington Post,* November 8, 1998, A10, and the Web site of the National Bipartisan Commission on Cuba, http://uscubacommission.org.

65. Ann Radelat, "Farmers Hurting in Cuba, U.S. Want to Help Each Other," *St. Louis Dispatch,* February 7, 1999, B4.

66. Thomas W. Lippman, "Senate Votes to Lift an Embargo on Cuba; Measure to End Most Unilateral Export Bans Would Allow Food, Medicine Sales," *Washington Post,* August 7, 1999, A15.

67. Kevin G. Hall, "Outlook Brightens in Washington for Resuming Trade," *Journal of Commerce,* September 30, 1999, 4.

68. "Senate Panel Clears Sales of Food to Cuba," *Chicago Sun-Times,* March 24, 2000, 30.

69. Lizette Alvarez, "U.S. Farm Groups Join Move to Ease Cuba Embargo," *New York Times,* May 24, 2000, A10.

70. Edwin McDowell, "Correspondent's Report: Traveling to Cuba Is as Tricky as Ever," *New York Times,* November 5, 2000, sec. 5, p. 3.

71. Al Kamen, "Photo Op Becomes an Oops," *Washington Post,* November 14, 2003, A27.

72. Anita Snow, "U.S. Lawmakers Seek Better Ties with Cuba," *Fort Worth Star-Telegram,* December 16, 2006, 21A.

73. Bernard W. Aronson and William D. Rogers, *U.S.-Cuban Relations in the 21st Century: Report of an Independent Task Force Sponsored by the Council on Foreign Relations* (New York: Council on Foreign Relations, 1999); Bernard W. Aronson, William D. Rogers, Julia Sweig, and Walter Mead, *U.S.-Cuban Relations in the 21st Century : A Follow-on Report of an Independent Task Force Sponsored by the Council on Foreign Relations* (New York: Council on Foreign Relations, 2001).

74. Joseph Contreras, "Castro's Comeback," *Newsweek International,* March 20, 2006, 26–28.

11 U.S.-China Trade Relations: Privatizing Foreign Policy

Steven W. Hook and Franklin Barr Lebo

Before You Begin

1. In what ways did the U.S. policy of engagement with China reflect general changes in U.S. foreign policy after the cold war?
2. How did the composition of Congress and the world view of the president affect the prospects for trade "normalization" between the United States and the People's Republic of China (PRC)?
3. Which interest groups and nongovernmental organizations became active as advocates or opponents of closer economic relations between the two countries?
4. To what extent did the outcome of the debate on normalization of trade and U.S. support for China's entry into the World Trade Organization (WTO) reflect economic disparities between business interests and nonprofit, nongovernmental organizations?
5. What have been the key trends in China's trade relations, particularly those with the United States, since the PRC joined the WTO in December 2001? What has been the response of key government actors and interest groups to those trends?
6. What does this case tell us generally about the formulation and content of U.S. foreign policy after the cold war? Can the lessons from this case be applied to other foreign policy arenas, such as national security, particularly since the start of the global war on terror in September 2001?

Introduction: The Chinese Challenge

Exactly five years after the People's Republic of China (PRC) joined the World Trade Organization (WTO) on December 11, 2001, the U.S. government under George W. Bush concluded that the bilateral trade relationship remained "decidedly mixed."[1] On the one hand, China's "charm offensive" had been difficult to resist, as the dollar value of goods flowing between the two countries in 2006 reached a staggering $328 billion, which was ten times greater than in 1992.[2] On the other hand, despite sustained efforts to reduce China's barriers to trade and curtail governmental involvement in its economy, and amid recurring charges of human rights abuses in China, the number of matters still unresolved promised that the years ahead would be difficult for U.S.-China relations.

In early 2007, the Bush administration filed its third complaint against China before the WTO, this time charging that Chinese subsidies to its steel, wood, and paper industries provided unfair incentives for Chinese companies to purchase from domestic rather than U.S. producers.[3] This appeared to be just a warm-up to another potential WTO complaint, as the Bush administration launched a comprehensive review in 2007 of China's lax enforcement of intellectual property rights.[4] Despite implementing many reforms of its legal system, piracy remains rampant in China, with U.S. industry estimating that 85 percent to 93 percent of all copyright businesses in China engage in it.[5] "Piracy" includes the unauthorized reproduction and sale of many different goods, such as pharmaceuticals, chemicals, apparel, and foodstuffs; its annual cost to the American film industry alone was an estimated $2.7 billion in 2005.[6] But after China's accession to the WTO, bilateral negotiations were no longer the only forum through which the two global powers might resolve their disputes. Instead, the U.S. has turned to the formal dispute resolution procedures of the WTO. Although the effectiveness of the process has yet to be finally determined, this marks a change to the problem-solving options available to the trading giants.[7]

It would be a mistake to assume that only economic matters are relevant in this complex trading relationship. Other issues, such as China's relationship with Russia and North Korea's development of nuclear weapons and long-range missiles, have caused the United States to rethink its regional security strategy in East Asia. In this context U.S. officials have had to consider precisely what it means for China to be a "responsible stakeholder" in the international system.[8] That has translated, for instance, into U.S. pressure on China to support weapons nonproliferation efforts in its trading relationships with other states, such as Iran.[9] Likewise, the Bush administration determined that no longer was a policy of selective pressure for human rights observance possible in its dealings with the PRC. Rather, as Bush affirmed during his November 2005 visit to China, universal freedom, religious freedom, and democratization are now at the heart of U.S. policy in Asia.

To understand how this new relationship has evolved, in this case we explore the political process that led to establishment of permanent, normal trade relations (PNTR) between China and the United States and U.S. support for

U.S.-China Trade Relations

October 1949 Mao Zedong's communist forces defeat the Chinese nationalist government. The United States refuses to recognize the People's Republic of China (PRC), recognizing instead Nationalist Party exiles in Taiwan as the leaders of China.

February 1972 President Richard Nixon visits Beijing, initiating bilateral relations between the United States and the PRC.

September 1976 Mao dies.

1978 Deng Xiaoping launches a series of market-oriented economic reforms while maintaining strict control over the PRC's political system.

January 1979 President Jimmy Carter formally recognizes the PRC and abrogates the U.S. treaty with Taiwan.

June 1989 Government forces crush pro-democracy protesters in Tiananmen Square. The United States and other governments respond by imposing economic sanctions against China.

May 1994 President Bill Clinton adopts a policy of engagement toward China, arguing that closer economic relations are more likely than isolation to produce cooperation from Beijing.

February 1997 Jiang Zemin assumes leadership of the PRC and continues Deng's policies of economic reform and political repression.

1998 China applies for membership in the World Trade Organization (WTO).

November 1999 Clinton endorses China's entry into the WTO in return for a series of bilateral trade concessions from Beijing.

May 2000 By a vote of 237–197, the House of Representatives approves H.R. 4444, granting permanent normal trade relations (PNTR) to China.

September 2000 The Senate approves the China trade bill by a vote of 83–15.

October 2000 Clinton signs the legislation formally establishing normal trade relations between the United States and China.

November 2001 The WTO approves China's application.

December 2001 China officially joins the WTO.

continued on the next page

continued from the previous page

March 2002 President George W. Bush raises U.S. tariffs on foreign steel, prompting complaints by China and other steel producers and leading to possible sanctions by the WTO.

March 2004 U.S. Trade Representative Robert B. Zoellick files a case with the WTO alleging preferential treatment by China of domestic firms in the electronics industry. The case is subsequently settled outside of the WTO through bilateral negotiation.

2005 China overtakes Britain as the world's fourth-largest economy.

March 2006 U.S. Trade Representative Rob Portman files a case with the WTO alleging that unfair levying of import taxes on U.S. auto parts favors China's domestic manufacturers.

February 2007 U.S. Trade Representative Susan C. Schwab files a case with the WTO alleging preferential treatment by China of domestic firms in the steel, wood, and paper industries.

China's entry into the World Trade Organization. Both the Chinese leadership and the Clinton administration considered the two steps critical, and both considered Sino-American trade relations a high foreign policy priority. The administration of President Bill Clinton needed support from Congress to deliver the U.S. end of the bargain, however, and gaining it was hardly a sure thing. Private interest groups on both sides of the trade issue mobilized on behalf of their policy preferences as the legislative process unfolded. The mobilization of those interests and the uneven resources they brought to bear in shaping the U.S. decision played key roles in determining the outcome.

From its founding in 1949 through the end of the cold war, the PRC's relations with the United States were overshadowed by ideological competition and the East-West balance of power. China-U.S. tensions moderated in the 1970s, when the Nixon-Kissinger "opening" to China was followed by the rise of the reformist Deng Xiaoping as China's leader. Bilateral relations continued to be plagued, however, by U.S. complaints about China's repression of human rights, neglect of environmental problems, weapons transfers, and maintenance of protectionist trade policies. Conversely, Chinese leaders frequently opposed the United States at the United Nations and openly criticized Washington as "hegemonic."

Upon taking office in January 1993, President Clinton wanted to revive Sino-American relations. He sought specifically to "engage" the PRC, primarily through closer economic ties, in hopes that a more interdependent relationship would benefit U.S. firms and consumers while also eliciting greater cooperation from Beijing on issues of concern to Washington. Clinton's engagement strategy played an important part in his overall foreign policy, which shifted the nation's strategic focus from the military concerns of the cold war to the geoeconomics of a new era. In the president's view, the United States needed to exploit its status as the world's largest economy by making U.S. firms more competitive in the rapidly integrating global marketplace. Toward that end, the Clinton administration identified several "big emerging markets," including China, that warranted special attention in guiding U.S. foreign economic policy.[10]

Engagement required severing the link between China's human rights policies and its status as a trading partner. As Clinton stated in May 1994,

> That linkage has been constructive during the past year. But I believe, based on our aggressive contacts with the Chinese in the past several months, that we have reached the end of the usefulness of that policy, and it is time to take a new path toward the achievement of our constant objectives. We need to place our relationship into a larger and more productive framework.[11]

The president's policy was based on the neoliberal presumption that China's inclusion in global economic and political regimes would encourage Beijing to moderate its internal behavior and conform with international standards. The alternative policy of estrangement—isolating China diplomatically and economically—was viewed as less likely to produce compliance and restraint in Beijing. Beyond increasing bilateral trade and promoting restraint in China's behavior domestically, engagement raised the possibility of also eliciting China's cooperation in solving transnational problems.

A general shift in U.S. foreign policy in the 1990s produced concrete changes in policy formulation. During the cold war, the State and Defense Departments largely controlled the machinations of foreign policy. The end of the cold war not only altered the mission of those institutions, it also brought other agencies into the shaping of foreign policy. These included the Treasury and Commerce Departments, the Office of the United States Trade Representative, and a variety of federal agencies in law enforcement, environmental protection, and health and labor policy. As the foreign policy profile of these institutions grew, so did that of groups outside government in the United States and abroad. With a greater capacity to shape the U.S. foreign policy agenda, interest groups on both sides of the engagement debate mobilized in the late 1990s. Their efforts—often highly visible but frequently behind the scenes—typified the increased activism and policy advocacy of hundreds of organizations in myriad issue areas after the cold war.

Figure 11.1 Congress and Support for U.S.-China Trade

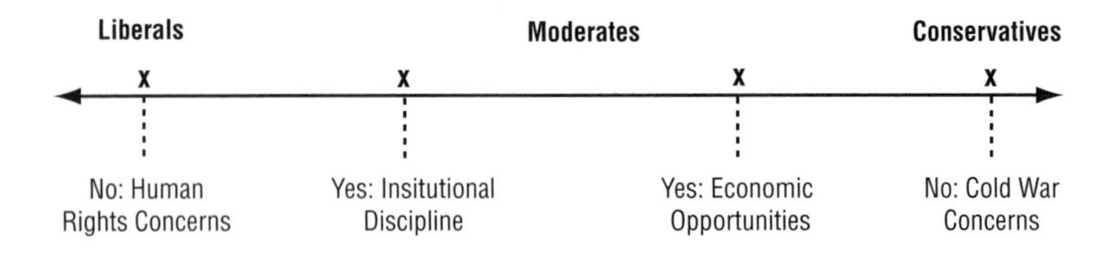

Business interests in particular benefited directly from the new opportunities inherent in the engagement policy. Dozens of U.S.-based multinational corporations praised and actively supported the strategy. From their perspective, China's population of more than 1.2 billion was a vast potential market for goods and services that could only be tapped if the governments of China and the United States maintained cordial relations. Echoing the Clinton administration's logic, they predicted that expanded economic contacts would force China's leaders to maintain stable relations overseas and to cooperate on political issues.

Many nonprofit nongovernmental organizations (NGOs), meanwhile, strongly opposed engagement. Human rights groups argued that Beijing should not be "rewarded" as long as it defied human rights standards. NGOs focused on the environment demanded that engagement only proceed after the Chinese government implemented stronger measures to protect air and water quality at home and embraced multilateral environmental initiatives overseas. Religious groups also became vocal on the issue, calling attention to the PRC's suppression of spiritual movements and religious institutions. U.S.-based labor groups weighed in, arguing that engagement would lead to the exodus of U.S. jobs and manufacturing capacity to the PRC.

This mobilization of interest groups occurred at a time when Congress was evenly split over China and highly polarized in general.[12] As Figure 11.1 illustrates, an ad hoc coalition of moderate Republicans and Democrats supported normalized trade with China, with overlapping but divergent priorities in mind: For moderate Republicans, the economic opportunities associated with gaining greater access to the world's largest market were compelling. Moderate Democrats thought engaging China through bilateral agreements and multilateral institutions would improve the chances for democratic reform and for gaining the PRC's cooperation in great power diplomacy. This consensus was threatened, however, by congressional critics at each end of the political spectrum. While conservative Republicans retained cold war–type hostilities toward Beijing's communist government and objected to its defiant stance on security issues, liberal Democrats opposed rewarding Chinese leaders who monopolized power, violated human rights, harmed the environment, and exploited labor.

Background: The Course of Sino-American Relations

This reshaping of U.S.-China trade relations occurred more than a half-century after the birth of the PRC in the mid-twentieth century. China, as the world's most populous state and its newest communist country, was then a primary source of concern to Washington. The Sino-Soviet friendship treaty of 1950 and the Korean War exacerbated U.S. apprehension, so that American leaders soon incorporated the PRC into the anticommunist containment policy designed in 1946 to prevent the spread of Soviet influence and power. Asia evolved as an arena of ideological competition in the 1950s and 1960s, with the wars in Korea and Vietnam taking center stage in the global cold war.[13] The United States refused to recognize the communist regime in Beijing and instead considered Nationalist Party exiles in Taiwan the true rulers of China. This policy of nonrecognition lasted until the 1970s, when the Nixon administration initiated bilateral relations with the PRC.

By the time Washington formally recognized the PRC in 1979, when Jimmy Carter was president, key changes in the economic structures of China had occurred. Following the death of Mao Zedong in 1976, Deng Xiaoping, a leader of the growing technocratic movement, assumed power and initiated a series of market-oriented economic reforms geared toward bringing China into the modern era.[14] In 1978 Deng began privatizing a small percentage of state-owned enterprises and overhauled the agricultural sector by permitting the sale of surplus commodities at market prices. The PRC under Deng continued to punish dissidents, however, and to deny political rights in general to the Chinese people.

When the United States recognized the PRC, it adopted a trade policy that required annual review of China's behavior in several areas, including foreign economic relations and the protection of human rights. The reviews rendered China's "most favored nation" (MFN) trade status—which allowed Beijing the same terms of trade accorded other major trading partners of the United States—dependent upon its overall behavior. The MFN reviews became an annual ritual in Congress and were routinely criticized by China's leaders. The Chinese felt that the PRC was being unfairly singled out among U.S. trading partners and that the United States was unduly interfering in their domestic and foreign affairs. Despite the PRC's widely publicized violations of human rights, Congress renewed its MFN trade status every year in the 1980s, largely because of the fast-growing trade between the two states and the rapid growth of the Chinese economy as Deng's economic reforms took effect.[15] Security concerns also figured in U.S. calculations; closer relations with China were seen as vital to containment of Soviet expansionism.

The Chinese government's assault on pro-democracy protesters in Tiananmen Square in June 1989 sparked renewed debate in Congress and the general public regarding human rights in China. Approximately 1,300 protesters were killed in the assault, and thousands more were arrested and imprisoned.[16] Questions regarding the government's treatment of political dissidents, its suppression of political and religious freedoms in Tibet, and its ongoing hostility toward Taiwan were also raised in Congress. Of additional concern to U.S. leaders was the Chinese government's conduct of bilateral trade with the United States. The Chinese domestic market had opened to some foreign goods, particularly high-technology products that facilitated the PRC's modernization drive. China, however, remained largely closed to foreign goods with equivalents that could be produced by Chinese workers. To gain access to Chinese consumers foreign companies had to establish joint ventures with Chinese firms.

U.S. complaints related to a wide range of barriers that prevented U.S.-based firms from competing in the PRC. The most common barriers were high tariffs, which averaged nearly 20 percent on all imports but were much higher on some goods, including automobiles and agricultural products. In addition, the Chinese government imposed a variety of nontariff barriers—such as quotas, import licenses, technical standards, and domestic content provisions—that further discouraged foreign competition. Corporate leaders also complained that the limited number of import-export companies in the PRC further impaired their ability to gain commercial licenses and establish transportation networks in the country.

In October 1991 the White House authorized the Office of the United States Trade Representative to launch the most sweeping market access investigation in that agency's history. In August 1992 the investigation confirmed a wide range of direct and indirect trade barriers hindering U.S. competition. The United States threatened to impose an unprecedented $4 billion in trade sanctions against Beijing if the protectionist measures remained in place. The threat of sanctions was dropped two months later, however, after Chinese officials promised to reform their trade policies and to make their regulations more transparent and understandable to foreign multinational corporations (MNCs) and governments. The symbiotic relationship of mutual need and opportunism between Washington and Beijing led to MFN renewals every year during the Bush administration.

Campaigning against President George H.W. Bush in 1992, Clinton vowed to make MFN status for China genuinely conditional. He viewed the human rights issue as central to U.S. foreign policy and demanded that China's MFN renewal be accompanied by strict legislation requiring reforms in Chinese law and in its behavior at home and overseas. Candidate Clinton promised to impose trade sanctions against China if its leaders did not adhere to internationally recognized standards of human rights. Clinton argued on the campaign trail that Bush had coddled the "butchers of Beijing" and tolerated their repressive rule and persecution of pro-democracy advocates.

Soon after the November 1992 elections, however, Clinton's approach toward China changed. As president he adopted a more cooperative stance based on closer economic ties between the PRC and the United States. Clinton then became a strong supporter of China's entry into the World Trade Organization, the global trade body whose open markets policy he strongly supported. In addition, Clinton endorsed the establishment of normalized trade relations to eliminate the annual reviews of China's MFN status.

Clinton's shift must be placed squarely within the context of the PRC's emergence as a global economic superpower. Between 1979 and 1999 real gross domestic product (GDP) in China grew at an annual rate of 9.7 percent, one of the fastest rates in the world.[17] Between 1978 and 1999 the country's annual trade volume increased in absolute terms from $21 billion to $361 billion. China had become the tenth-largest trading economy by 2000 and was projected by the World Bank to be second only to the United States in total trade by 2020. As China's trade steadily grew, it maintained a large trade surplus—estimated at $21 billion in 1999—and a level of foreign reserves that exceeded $150 billion by 2000. China also became the world's second-largest destination for foreign direct investment (FDI) in the 1990s, attracting more than $45 billion in 1998 alone, primarily from the United States and Japan. This trend reflected strong investor confidence in the sustainability of the Chinese economy, even as real growth in GDP slowed modestly and China's neighbors continued to recover from the regional economic crisis of 1997 and 1998. The scope of private investing in China widened throughout the decade, as the government loosened restrictions on capital transfers and became increasingly receptive to FDI, as well as portfolio investments (that is, trade in stocks, bonds, and international currencies).

The U.S. market was a major stimulant for the Chinese economy. In terms of bilateral trade, China exported more than $81 billion in goods to the United States in 1999. Of this total, $17 billion was in the form of manufactured goods. Footwear, office machines, telecommunications equipment, and apparel were the other major Chinese exports. Bilateral trade grew more lopsided during the 1990s, as China's trade surplus grew each year—from $10 billion in 1990 to nearly $70 billion by 1999. The United States exported just $13 billion in goods to the PRC in 1999, primarily in the form of aircraft, electrical machinery, fertilizers, computers, and industrial equipment.[18] Noticeably absent from this list are automobiles and agricultural products, both of which were subject to rigid trade barriers. It was argued that this would likely change if China were to be granted permanent normal trade relations with the United States. The Agriculture Department estimated that U.S. exports of wheat, rice, corn, cotton, and soybeans to China would increase by $1.5 billion annually between 2000 and 2009 if barriers were removed.[19]

The large and growing bilateral trade gap between Beijing and Washington stimulated protests by the U.S. government, which faced strong pressure from labor unions, farmers, and corporate leaders to reverse the imbalance. Many members of Congress and nonprofit NGOs, meanwhile, questioned why the United States continued to tolerate the Chinese government's ongoing violations of human rights, its neglect of environmental standards, and its transfers of military equipment to so-called rogue states. Their criticism was punctuated by the trade disparity, which only widened after the engagement policy was put into practice.

Clinton's Engagement Policy

While calling for improvements in the PRC's human rights record, Clinton argued that U.S.-China trade relations should not depend on political concerns. In May 1994 he renewed China's favorable trade status and by executive order proclaimed that future U.S. trade with China would not be linked directly to human rights. He predicted that U.S. engagement of the PRC, largely through closer economic ties, would elicit greater respect for human rights in China. Toward this end, the basis of U.S.-China trade would be redefined in legislation formalizing the change in policy. When Clinton announced this shift, the link between human rights and trade with China was effectively severed.[20] Concerns over China's human rights policies persisted, however, along with economic tensions. The next year, in 1995, China exported $48.5 billion worth of goods to the

United States, while receiving only $10 billion in U.S. imports.[21] The Clinton administration and Congress, which after the November 1994 midterm elections was dominated by the Republican Party, concluded that a trade war had to be avoided.

Debate over U.S.-China trade intensified in 1995. Human rights groups became more outspoken in February, when Human Rights Watch (HRW) released its annual report, concluding that Chinese officials had failed to improve their human rights record since Clinton's proclamation of the engagement policy. In addition to the human rights and labor groups pressuring Washington, U.S.-based multinationals, which had opposed isolating China for its human rights practices, now pushed for sanctioning China over its trade practices. The bilateral trade deficit had become a serious problem. U.S.-based music and software companies believed they had lost an estimated $500 million in potential profits since the early 1980s as a result of piracy of intellectual property. Even so, many of Clinton's economic advisers believed that a return to estrangement would be more harmful than the potential damage from the problems associated with engagement.

The controversy over intellectual property rights proved especially divisive. Washington threatened a 100 percent tariff on certain items if piracy continued. The result was a $3 billion package of sanctions. In retaliation, Beijing imposed higher tariffs against the U.S. automobile industry, which was already largely denied access to the Chinese market. The Chinese Civil Aviation Administration contracted with European aircraft manufacturers in a deal that exceeded $1.5 billion, spurning Boeing, which had taken its export monopoly in China for granted.[22] U.S. officials also expressed concerns about China's sales of nuclear technologies to developing countries, but the engagement strategy remained intact.[23]

After the death of Deng Xiaoping in February 1997, the new premier, Jiang Zemin, pledged to maintain Deng's formula of economic integration abroad and tight political control at home. Public opinion began to swing against engagement as Chinese officials continued to defy international human rights standards.[24] The PRC's burgeoning trade surplus with the United States provoked outrage among U.S. workers and trade unions. As a result, liberals motivated by human rights and conservatives opposed to the large U.S. trade deficit created ad hoc, anti-engagement coalitions (see Box 11.1). Clinton again argued that economic withdrawal from China would have disastrous consequences for the U.S. economy and would only make matters worse for Chinese dissidents and workers.

Box 11.1 Interest Groups in the U.S.-China Trade Relations Debate

Supporters	*Opponents*
Business groups	Human rights advocates
Transportation industries	Environmental groups
Telecommunications sector	Religious groups
Financial markets	Trade unions

Proponents of Engagement: Business Groups and MNCs

Outside the U.S. government, most advocates of the Clinton administration's engagement strategy were in the business sector. This was no surprise given the immense size of the Chinese consumer market, which remained largely untapped because of the incremental nature of the country's economic reforms and restrictions on foreign competition. Among the pro-engagement advocates were individual multinational corporations, trade groups, and multisector organizations such as the U.S. Chamber of Commerce. Much of their advocacy took the form of traditional lobbying, but they also committed large sums of money to support the reelection campaigns of like-minded members of Congress and to promote candidates challenging incumbents opposed to normalized trade relations between China and the United States. The groups were also able to advance their interests through soft money donations to the major political parties.

One of the first groups to promote expanded trade with China was the U.S.-China Business Council, which played an active role in commercial relations between Nixon's visit to China in 1972 and formal U.S. recognition in 1979. Created in 1973 as the National Council for U.S.-China Trade, this group consisted of about 270 corporate executives who maintained economic interests in China. In the late 1990s the council supported PNTR status for China and its accession to the WTO. A similar group, the Business Roundtable, composed of the chief executive officers of major U.S.-based multinationals, spent nearly $6 million on an advertising campaign to promote normalized trade relations. Another $4 million was budgeted for campaign contributions in 1996 and 1998 to congressional candidates supporting free trade with China.[25] The U.S. Chamber of Commerce also launched a major effort to support China's entry into the WTO and PNTR status.

Among the most active corporate supporters of normalized trade relations were the transportation industries, primarily aircraft and automotive firms, which eagerly sought greater access to the Chinese domestic market. Boeing was one of the earliest U.S. corporations to do business in China. Following Nixon's 1972 visit, the Chinese Civil Aviation Administration ordered ten passenger jets from the Seattle-based manufacturer. Since then, the Chinese government has purchased about 300 Boeing aircraft. Despite being snubbed in favor of European contractors in 1996, in 1998 Boeing held a 72 percent market share in China. Commercial flights to and from China increased by more than 20 percent annually from 1988 to 1998, so free trade with China would undoubtedly benefit Boeing.

Meanwhile, the "big three" U.S. automakers contributed large amounts of capital and time to the attempt to open the Chinese automobile market to foreign competition. The Chinese domestic auto market was still in the early stages of development in the 1990s, and importation of foreign-made cars was highly restricted. Nonetheless, the vast potential of the Chinese market attracted great attention from U.S.-based manufacturers. Private automobile purchasing in China grew more than 300 percent in the 1990s, but there remained a vast amount of room for growth in this sector.

General Motors (GM) was the most instrumental among U.S.-based automotive firms in developing the auto market in China. In 1997 GM entered into a joint venture with the Shanghai Automotive Industry Corporation that created nearly 2,000 manufacturing and administrative jobs. Together the companies invested $1.5 billion in the project.[26] Predictably, GM strongly supported normalized trade relations and China's entry into the WTO. The Chrysler Corporation, meanwhile, entered the Chinese market in 1987 by forming a partnership with Beijing Auto Works. The 1998 merger of Chrysler and Daimler Benz, the German automaker, was expected to increase the conglomerate's market share in China. By 2000, the Ford Motor Company had yet to maximize its potential in China. Although Ford had entered the Chinese automotive market before the 1949 revolution, its reentry was slow. Ford opened its first dealership on the mainland in 1993, but by 1998 it controlled less than 1 percent of the market in China.[27]

China, like much of the developing world, was also fertile ground for growth in the technology and communications sectors in the 1990s. In this respect U.S.-based corporations played a key role in facilitating China's development and application of information technologies, a cornerstone of its development strategy. The San Diego–based Qualcomm Corporation, for example, partnered with two of the three largest state-owned communications companies, China Telecom and China Unicom, in an effort to develop the Chinese wireless communications market. By 2000 only a small part of the market had been penetrated, but as sharing information becomes a necessity in the rapidly integrating business environment, the use of wireless phones and satellite communications networks will prove vital. Qualcomm's assistance helped standardize the industry by licensing intellectual property and creating a prototype system, Code Division Multiple Access, that all domestic telecommunications firms could use. Not only did Qualcomm reap royalties for its services, but its assistance also made wireless communications more accessible to the business sector. Other major communications and high-technology firms followed Qualcomm into China. Nortel, Motorola, and Lucent Technologies invested in joint ventures with Chinese counterparts. It was commonly estimated at the time that the total wireless market would exceed $16 billion in annual sales once fully exploited.[28]

Other proponents of normalized trade relations came from the financial markets, which may be viewed as something of a collective multinational corporation. Investors can be individual stockholders, corporations, brokerage firms, or mutual fund managers. Recipients of these private investments use the capital to develop new products, expand production, and open new retail outlets. As noted earlier, FDI and portfolio investments played a key role in spurring the PRC's economic growth. As more multinationals set up shop in China, even through the mandated joint ventures with Chinese firms, the country attracted additional private investment. As a result, leaders of U.S.-based financial institutions were among the most ardent supporters of normalized trade relations and Chinese entry into the WTO.

Opponents of Engagement: NGOs and Conservatives

Many conservative members of Congress argued that Clinton's engagement policy would merely reward a "revisionist" Chinese state bent on military expansionism at the expense of U.S. interests. In their view, a policy of isolating the PRC was preferable to one of actively engaging its government. Nonprofit NGOs were also active in the debate, their views in most cases differing strongly from the pro-engagement stance of business-related groups. Among other things, the groups demanded that political, environmental, and labor disputes between China and the United States be resolved before trade relations were normalized. The nonprofit NGOs were highly fragmented because of their wide range of interests and policy preferences. With more limited resources than the corporations and business groups, the NGOs faced an uphill battle in the policy debate. Nonetheless, they posed a strong challenge to the Clinton administration's engagement policy and were able to shape the terms of the legislation that Congress ultimately passed and President Clinton signed.[29]

Lacking the economic clout of business and trade groups, human rights organizations promoted their positions primarily through the release of detailed studies of the Chinese government's human rights conduct. Their reports were especially vital because of the severe press restrictions in the PRC, which prevented Chinese journalists from investigating and exposing human rights violations. In addition to its annual reports on human rights, Human Rights Watch published frequent studies that criticized the PRC's strict control of religion, the news media, and the private affairs of its citizens.[30]

Another human rights NGO that played a major role was Freedom House, based in New York City. Freedom House's annual reports, along with those published by Human Rights Watch, were closely monitored within the U.S. government, by corporate leaders, and by nonprofit interest groups. The reports were especially critical of the Chinese government's human rights policies; the PRC consistently received the group's lowest ranking in its annual surveys of political and civil rights. In its 1997–1998 report, Freedom House declared that the Chinese Communist Party "holds absolute power, has imprisoned nearly all active dissidents, uses the judiciary as a tool of state control, and severely restricts freedoms of speech, press, association, and religion."[31]

Amnesty International (AI) also published reports and sponsored demonstrations to draw attention to human rights abuses in the PRC. Most notably, AI launched a media campaign in 1999 commemorating the ten-year anniversary of the Tiananmen Square massacre and circulated a list of 241 political prisoners still detained by the Chinese government. Members of AI continued to write to political prisoners in China, as well as to government officials, urging the prisoners' release. While remaining nonpolitical, Amnesty International cited continuing human rights abuses as evidence that the engagement policy had failed.[32]

NGOs also expressed concern that the engagement policy ignored the environment in China, where air and water pollution had steadily worsened during the country's modernization drive. This trend was especially regrettable given that environmental quality was a noneconomic issue on which the Chinese and U.S. governments could potentially agree. China, however, made a Faustian bargain on the environment to achieve economic growth.[33] In particular, it relied on coal-burning power plants as the primary source of electricity, a practice that led to high levels of fossil fuel emissions that affected air quality far beyond China's borders. Greenpeace, arguably the most influential environmental group in the world, urged the U.S. government to include environmental provisions in any legislation to normalize trade relations and in any U.S. endorsement of Chinese entry into the WTO. Also of concern was the worsening water quality in the Dongjiang River, the Pearl River Delta, and the South China Sea. Greenpeace joined other environmental NGOs in opposing the massive Three Gorges Dam in Hubei Province, which was expected to force the relocation of two million people by 2009.

Most of these environmental concerns remained outside the PNTR and WTO debates, primarily because of the Chinese government's rejection of foreign interference in what it considered its sovereign authority over internal economic development. The environmental groups succeeded, however, in raising the profile of these issues and putting pressure on U.S.- and foreign-based corporations to consider the ecological effects of their projects in China. As in other parts of the world, the environmental groups were most effective in appealing directly to public opinion through Internet campaigns and the sponsorship of mass protests and demonstrations.[34]

Religious groups in the United States were also active in the debate over trade relations with China. Of particular concern to them was the persecution of individuals and groups that expressed support for religious principles and institutions. By their nature, such expressions are contrary to the ideology of the Chinese Communist Party. "Freedom of religion is under threat in China," proclaimed the United Methodist Church's General Board of Church and Society. "Catholic churches, mosques, Buddhist temples and indigenous religions are being harassed. . . . We call on Congress to vote against the extension of permanent normal trade relations to China until substantial improvements in religious freedom are achieved."[35]

The groups were particularly outraged at the Chinese government's outlawing in July 1999 of Falun Gong, a spiritual movement that promotes "truthfulness, benevolence, and forbearance," primarily through the ancient meditative practice of *qigong*. Government officials in China labeled Falun Gong a "cult" whose leaders were organizing politically, and illegally, in opposition to the Communist Party. An estimated 10,000 Falun Gong followers surprised Chinese authorities in April 1999 by surrounding the government compound in Beijing to protest their lack of official recognition. The group was officially banned in July, and Chinese authorities arrested large numbers of its followers, closed its facilities, and confiscated its literature.[36]

American labor groups were vocal in their opposition to engagement. These groups sought to sway public opinion against normalized trade relations with China through public information campaigns and public demonstrations. In an unusual show of unity, more than 10,000 labor union advocates from different industrial sectors held a rally in April 2000 at the U.S. Capitol. Their demonstration was designed to convince undecided members of Congress that public opposition to normalized trade relations was extensive and that normalized relations would have real human cost in the form of displaced workers. Their presence also reminded office seekers that the trade unions represented a large and potentially crucial voting bloc.

The AFL-CIO and the United Auto Workers (UAW) led in promoting the trade union position, often invoking reasons beyond the economic self-interest of their members. AFL-CIO president John Sweeney frequently spoke out against Chinese entry into the WTO and normalized trade relations. Testifying to Congress in March 2000, Sweeney argued that an affirmative vote on PNTR "would reward the Chinese government at a time when there has been significant deterioration in its abysmal human rights record."[37] The AFL-CIO devoted much of its lobbying effort—and its budget—to the China trade issue. Advertisements it ran in eleven congressional districts were crucial in garnering public support for its position. For its part, the UAW initiated a lobbying campaign to oppose PNTR for similar reasons and cited the use of child labor and forced labor by political prisoners as justification for a reversal in U.S. trade policy. Of particular concern to the UAW was the opposition of the Chinese government to the formation of independent trade unions in the country.

With the U.S. trade deficit widening in China's favor, labor leaders also argued that normalized trade relations would jeopardize the country's long-term economic growth and harm thousands of firms as well as workers. Labor cited piracy of intellectual property, global environmental destruction, and the treatment of workers in China as additional reasons to oppose PNTR and China's entry in the WTO. Their primary emphasis as they pressed the issue before Congress, however, was on the effects of normalized trade relations on their members. This appeal carried considerable weight among members of Congress who represented urbanized districts with large blue-collar populations.

Final Debates and Congressional Action

As the antagonists for and against engagement tussled, the U.S. government played a paradoxical role in informing the debate. While the White House promoted the cause of engagement, the State Department released annual reports that were consistently critical of the Chinese government. According to the department's 1999 report,

> The Government's poor human rights record deteriorated markedly throughout the year. The government intensified efforts to suppress dissent, particularly organized dissent. . . . Abuses included instances of extrajudicial killings, torture and mistreatment of prisoners, forced confessions, arbitrary arrest and detention, lengthy incommunicado detention, and denial of due process.[38]

The State Department's findings were affirmed by human rights NGOs. Freedom House's review of human rights in China during 1999 noted that Chinese "authorities escalated a crackdown on political dissidents, labor and peasant activists, and religious leaders."[39] To President Clinton, the arguments of the nonprofit NGOs and the State Department only strengthened his argument that the Chinese government should be engaged. Thus in 1999 and 2000 the president intensified his efforts to apply the engagement policy by supporting Chinese accession to the WTO and normalized trade relations between China and the United States.

China's Drive for WTO Membership

The WTO had barely come into existence when Chinese officials declared their interest in joining. They took the first step in that direction in 1995 by forming a working party to prepare a formal application. That part of the process was completed in 1998, after which China began formal negotiations for membership. All WTO applicants must undergo a two-part screening. First, they negotiate directly with the WTO on compliance with the trade body's regulations for open markets, protection of foreign firms and capital, and transparency of commercial regulations. These terms were originally set forth in the 1947 General Agreement on Tariffs and Trade (GATT), which was revised several times before becoming the World Trade Organization after the completion in 1994 of the Uruguay Round of global trade talks. In the second phase, WTO applicants negotiate directly with their primary trading partners. These bilateral negotiations are often the primary hurdle facing prospective WTO members. Chinese officials acknowledged that gaining the blessing of the United States would be its highest hurdle in the WTO accession process. Once applicants complete bilateral talks, they draft a protocol of accession to be considered by WTO member states (which numbered 135 at the time China's application was under review). Two-thirds of the states must approve the protocol for the applicant to gain entry into the organization.

Talks between Chinese and U.S. trade negotiators progressed early in 1999 despite a series of unrelated political controversies and diplomatic crises that strained relations. The full extent of the 1996 presidential campaign scandals over illegal contributions, many of which involved Chinese citizens, was widely known by 1998. The scandals provoked charges in Congress of undue Chinese influence in the Clinton administration. Making matters worse, U.S. bombers mistakenly destroyed the Chinese embassy in Belgrade in May 1999 as part of the North Atlantic Treaty Organization's effort to stem Serbia's crackdown against Kosovo. Chinese officials condemned the attack, and some even alleged that the bombing was deliberate. Trade talks were suspended for four months after the incident, and during that time the two governments again clashed over Taiwan's status, weapons proliferation in North Korea, and other regional issues.

These incidents compelled Clinton to step up his efforts to conclude a trade pact with China. Talks resumed in September 1999, leading to a comprehensive bilateral agreement that was signed by both governments in November. Under the terms of the deal, the United States endorsed China's WTO membership in return for a wide range of Chinese concessions on bilateral trade. Among other concessions, Chinese leaders agreed to

- allow full trading and distribution rights to U.S. firms doing business in China,
- reduce average tariffs on "priority" agricultural goods from 32 percent to 15 percent by 2004,
- phase out quotas on foreign versus domestically produced goods and suspend other nontariff barriers,
- permit greater access to the Chinese market by U.S.-based automobile companies by 2006, and
- improve the treatment of foreign firms operating in China.[40]

The Chinese government had long acknowledged that reaching a trade accord with the United States was essential if its goal of obtaining WTO membership was to be accomplished. If China had joined the trade body without a positive U.S. vote, its ability to play a meaningful role would have been greatly limited, and chronic differences between China and the United States would have remained. Thus the WTO served a useful function for U.S. officials, whose efforts to gain Chinese cooperation on bilateral trade had previously been frustrated.

While negotiating with the United States, Chinese officials were simultaneously engaged in trade talks with other industrialized countries in their drive for WTO accession. Of particular interest was the European Union, whose progress toward regional economic integration had taken a great leap forward in 1999 with the introduction of the euro as a common currency. Under the terms of the 1992 Maastricht Treaty, the major European states (except for the

United Kingdom) agreed to coordinate all facets of their fiscal and monetary policies. Such coordination included the conduct of trade relations, which the union would pursue with one voice. A "bilateral" trade deal between the European Union and the PRC was within reach, although EU members demanded many of the same market-opening concessions that China had granted the United States. The China-EU accord was reached on May 19, 2000, when the EU formally endorsed China's bid to join the WTO in return for promised reforms in the PRC's trade practices. Through this single agreement, Beijing garnered the blessing of France, Germany, Italy, and twelve other western European countries. The pact with the Europeans added momentum to China's drive for permanent normalized trade relations with the United States, an issue soon to be before Congress.

The PNTR Debate in Congress

Under U.S. law, Congress was not required to play a direct role in the bilateral negotiations on U.S. support for China's WTO membership. Congress was also not required to ratify the pact signed by President Clinton. That did not mean, however, that Congress was irrelevant to the process. To the contrary, given its other constitutional powers to regulate trade—specifically its authority to grant or deny "normal" status to U.S. trading partners—Congress effectively held the key to China's entry into the WTO. Furthermore, legislation passed during the cold war imposed explicit conditions on U.S. trade with communist states. Those conditions would violate the basic principle of the WTO that terms of trade among all its members be maintained consistently and unconditionally. For that reason, a bilateral trade agreement between the United States and China approved by both houses of Congress was the last major hurdle in Chinese membership in the multilateral WTO. The Clinton administration, therefore, directed its efforts early in 2000 toward gaining Congress's approval for PNTR with Beijing.

Clinton assigned lobbying duties to Secretary of Commerce William Daley and the deputy chief of staff, Stephen Ricchetti. The president also recruited former presidents Gerald Ford, Jimmy Carter, and George Bush to endorse the bill, along with Federal Reserve Chairman Alan Greenspan and leading foreign policy advisers in the State and Defense Departments. Clinton's sense of urgency owed much to the setbacks and frustrations that plagued his second term in office. His impeachment by the House of Representatives for the Monica Lewinsky sex scandal had crippled Clinton domestically. In foreign policy, his goal of achieving a comprehensive Middle East peace treaty was proving beyond reach, and his conduct of the military intervention in Kosovo received more criticism than praise. Clinton, therefore, looked to the China trade pact to define his legacy in foreign affairs.

Fortunately for Clinton, the political winds in Congress were in his favor. Under the trade bill introduced on May 15 in the House of Representatives (H.R. 4444), the United States would extend PNTR status to China upon its accession to the WTO. In approving the bill on May 17, the House Ways and Means Committee included an "anti-import surge" amendment that protected U.S. firms in the event of sudden increases in Chinese imports of specific commodities. The House Rules Committee further amended the bill on May 23. Among other provisions of the amended bill, a commission would be established to monitor and report on the PRC's human rights and labor practices. In addition, the U.S. trade representative would annually evaluate China's compliance with WTO regulations, and a special task force would confirm that Chinese exporters were not shipping goods manufactured by prison laborers to the United States. Finally, the House bill called for increased technical assistance to the PRC's efforts to enact legal reforms, and it urged the WTO to consider Taiwan's application to join the trade body immediately after China's accession.

Lobbying efforts peaked as the bill awaited a final vote in the full House. On the day before the vote was taken, about 200 business lobbyists met on Capitol Hill to coordinate their strategy for swaying undecided members.[41] On May 24, the House approved H.R. 4444 by a vote of 237–197. Although a majority of the 224 Republicans in the House voted for the bill, most of the 211 Democrats voted against it. Opponents came largely from urban areas with large populations of industrial workers and a strong labor union presence. On both sides of the aisle, support was primarily from members representing suburban or rural districts. Approval in the Senate was virtually assured, although its timing was uncertain given the Senate's approaching summer recess, other legislation on its schedule, and the distraction of a presidential election campaign.

Many prominent senators opposed the measure although Senate approval was considered a given. Sen. Paul Wellstone, D-Minn., for example, spoke out against normal trade with China because of the PRC's continuing repression of human rights and religious freedoms. Republican critics included Fred Thompson, R-Tenn., who sought without success to include an amendment that would link PNTR to Chinese restraint on nuclear weapons proliferation. Jesse Helms, R-N.C., chairman of the Committee on Foreign Relations, argued that PNTR status would reward Chinese leaders for maintaining the communist system he had long condemned. As in the House, supporters and opponents of PNTR crossed party lines to an extent otherwise unseen in the 106th Congress.

As the Senate vote approached in September 2000, the lobbying by interests on both sides of the China trade issue resumed, although with less intensity than before the House vote. Among pro-PNTR interest groups was the American Electronics Association, one of the largest and most influential high-tech trade associations in the United States, which stepped up its lobbying campaign in early September. Representing small and medium-sized industrial firms, the National Association of Manufacturers met with Senate Majority Leader Trent Lott, R-Miss., and Sen. John Breaux, D-La., and received their assurances that the bill would be approved. Once their position was made known, other business groups relaxed their lobbying efforts.[42]

The Senate was under strong pressure from the Clinton administration and business groups to pass the legislation without amendments. Clinton warned senators that amendments to the bill would force a new round of negotiations—first with the Chinese government and then with the House of Representatives. The outcome of those talks would be highly uncertain, and the legislation would be in the hands of a new Congress and a new presidential administration in 2001. The Senate soundly rejected a series of proposed amendments linking China's trade status to improvements in human rights, religious freedom, labor standards, and weapons proliferation. The final bill, identical to that passed by the House, moved quickly toward a vote on the Senate floor.

As expected, the Senate approved the measure on September 19 in an 83–15 vote and sent it to the White House for Clinton's signature. Again, support and opposition to the bill had crossed party lines to an unusual extent, with seven Democrats joining eight Republicans in opposing the legislation. Whereas the Democrats were primarily concerned with labor issues, Republican opponents most often cited the security threat posed by the PRC. Critics of China in both parties raised concerns about human rights. Clinton signed the legislation on October 10, and normalized U.S.-China trade relations became a reality.

Having gained the blessing of the world's foremost economic power, China joined the WTO on December 11, 2001. Its government then embarked on a series of economic reforms, to be phased in over the following decade, that would align the nation's trade policies with WTO standards and those of other member states. Among other commitments, Chinese officials agreed to reduce average tariff levels on industrial as well as agricultural goods by 2010. The PRC also pledged to limit subsidies for agricultural production, grant full trade and distribution rights to foreign enterprises, respect intellectual property rights, and open its banking system to foreign-based financial institutions. Taken together, once enacted these reforms would remove the barriers to the entry of goods, services, and foreign investments into China.

Conclusion: The Privatization of Foreign Policy

China's entry into the WTO was followed by rapid increases in its overseas trade. Between 2001 and 2005, China's overall trade nearly tripled, from $510 billion to $1.4 trillion.[43] The volume of Chinese imports and exports grew at roughly the same levels until 2005, when exports grew over the previous year by more than 28 percent, to $762 billion, whereas imports grew by only 18 percent, to $660 billion.[44] The Chinese economy's real growth, as measured by gross domestic product (GDP), continued at an annual rate of about 10 percent through 2006.[45] Such robust growth, which China had enjoyed in previous years while its neighbors endured a protracted economic crisis, also stood in stark contrast to the recessions experienced by Western economies, including that of the United States. Significantly, China had become the world's leading recipient of foreign direct investment by 2002, and despite a mild decrease in 2006 it retained its status as one of the top destinations for FDI.[46]

Among the key factors in this surge in China's global trade was the United States, whose imports from China grew by approximately 140 percent, from $100 billion in 2000 to an estimated $244 billion in 2005.[47] Exports from the United States to China also increased during the period, from $16 billion to about $42 billion. The growth in U.S. exports was welcomed in Washington, but the resulting trade deficit of approximately $202 billion, the largest ever recorded between two trading partners, fueled widespread complaints and renewed charges that China was shirking its commitment to open markets.[48] According to the Office of the United States Trade Representative, in many economic sectors China by 2006 "continues to pursue problematic industrial policies that rely on trade-distorting measures such as local content requirements, import and export restrictions, discriminatory regulations and prohibited subsidies, all of which raise serious WTO concerns."[49] As noted in the introduction, the United States filed three complaints with the WTO against China; a fourth complaint concerning intellectual property rights seemed just around the corner early in 2007.[50]

The large and protracted trade imbalance has provided ammunition to U.S. critics of normalized trade relations and China's WTO membership. These critics also have emphasized the most recent human rights reports, which indicated little or no improvement in China's record since it joined the WTO. Freedom House, for example, concluded in its 2006 report that life in China is still "marked by ongoing governmental control and repression of political dissent."[51] According to Catherine Baber of Amnesty International, "China's so-called economic 'miracle' comes at a terrible human cost—rural migrants living in the cities experience some of the worst abuse in the work place."[52]

American importers in particular have had a difficult time ensuring that workers' rights are not abused, as many factories in China have simply developed more sophisticated methods for hiding violations.[53] Labor unions in the United States claimed that such findings prove that Clinton's logic of inducing reform in China through engagement was unfounded. The AFL-CIO unsuccessfully petitioned the administration of George W. Bush in 2004 to put greater pressure on China, and it submitted a new petition to the White House early in 2006 that was also rejected.[54] As the secretary-treasurer of the AFL-CIO responded to this latest rejection, "It's a travesty that after five years of failed trade policy that have contributed to the loss of almost three million U.S. manufacturing jobs . . . the Administration continues to take no meaningful action to support America's workers or stop the abuse of workers in China."[55]

Despite these findings, pro-engagement groups in the United States continue to favor closer bilateral trade ties with China. The U.S. Chamber of Commerce, for example, asserted with regard to enforcing antipiracy laws, "Our message in China is not only to encourage the central government to stiffen penalties and step-up enforcement, but also that we are willing to work cooperatively with them to get it done."[56] Similar conclusions were drawn by the U.S.-China Business Council and other trade groups with a material stake in bilateral trade.[57] Those views were largely accepted by the administration, whose trade representative, Susan C. Schwab, continued to favor closer trade ties in 2007 despite recognizing both progress and "backsliding" in China's attempts to comply with the commitments made during the PNTR and WTO negotiations.[58]

Although the continued centrality of the bilateral trade relationship between the United States and China is beyond dispute, China's global ambitions are much broader than this picture might suggest. The PRC has adopted international engagement as a key component of its own foreign policy agenda and has demonstrated a willingness to deal not only with the democratic allies of the United States, but with more controversial governments in Iran, Syria, and Libya.[59] In addition to ongoing tensions with Japan, China has begun to emerge as a competitor of the United States in Asia, as evidenced by its 2005 participation in the East Asian Summit with sixteen regional powers and its signing of a free trade agreement with the Association of Southeast Asian Nations (ASEAN) in November 2004. Other examples of China's expanding global reach, which is often aimed at satisfying its voracious energy appetite, include a liquid natural gas agreement with Australia, negotiations with African states rich in resources such as the Sudan, and energy agreements with Venezuela and Brazil.[60] Without a doubt, Clinton's neoliberal engagement strategy has resulted in a much stronger Chinese economy with profound global implications.

The continuing debate over U.S.-China trade relations serves as a microcosm of a larger phenomenon in the formulation of post–cold war U.S. foreign policy. A variety of new issues, actors, and policy calculations emerged in the 1990s to replace the challenge that the Soviet Union formerly posed. Of particular concern to this study is the heightened stature of foreign economic relations on the policy agenda of the first post–cold war administration. With the easing of security concerns, U.S. leaders identified competitiveness in the rapidly integrating global economy as a pressing national interest. A related trend was the growing role of international and domestic nonstate actors seeking to promote their interests in this more fluid, pluralistic environment. The global war on terror, while altering the strategic environment since September 2001, has not altered this more general shift in world politics.

All these elements greatly complicate the U.S. policymaking environment, which had already been altered by the diffusion of foreign policy responsibilities beyond the State and Defense Departments. As the foreign affairs bureaucracy has grown to empower economic-oriented agencies, such as the Treasury and Commerce Departments, the opportunities for private interest groups to penetrate the policymaking process have greatly increased. This trend is reflected in Congress, whose committees concerned with foreign economic relations are a focus of heightened interest group lobbying and political pressure. The outcome of this legislative process reflects the more complex setting in which "intermestic" issues—those crossing foreign and domestic boundaries—dominate the agenda. In this respect, the debate over U.S.-China trade relations typifies the new era in U.S. foreign policy after the cold war.

Key Actors

Amnesty International Nongovernmental organization, opposed to the Clinton administration policy of engagement with China because of Beijing's political repression of dissidents.

Bill Clinton President, an advocate of engagement and normalized trade relations with China.

General Motors Corporation The largest U.S.-based automaker and a proponent of normalized trade relations with China; involved since 1997 in a joint venture with Shanghai Automotive Industry Corporation.

Human Rights Watch Nongovernmental organization whose annual reports highlighted ongoing political repression in China despite closer economic relations with the United States.

Qualcomm Corporation A San Diego–based business, proponent of normalized trade relations with China; partnered with two Chinese companies to modernize the country's telecommunications network.

John Sweeney AFL-CIO president, an outspoken opponent of normalized trade relations on the basis of Chinese trade restrictions, the country's human rights record, and the potential loss of jobs in the United States.

United Methodist Church Issued a report condemning the Chinese government's crackdown on religious freedom and opposing closer trade relations.

U.S.-China Business Council An industry-based group strongly in favor of engagement.

Notes

1. Office of the United States Trade Representative, "2006 Report to Congress on China's WTO Compliance," December 11, 2006, 3.

2. David J. Lynch, "Force of China's Impact Grows in USA; After Only Five Years in WTO, Country Has Made Its Mark on U.S. Economy," *USA Today,* December 12, 2006, 1B. See also Kerry Dumbaugh, Congressional Research Service, "China-U.S. Relations: Current Issues and Implications for U.S. Policy," September 22, 2006, 13.

3. David Armstrong, "United States Complains to WTO about China; Asian Country's Government Allegedly Subsidizing Many Companies in Order to Keep Exports Cheap," *San Francisco Chronicle,* February 3, 2007, C1. For background information on the second case the U.S. filed against China on March 30, 2006, over the alleged unfair levying of import taxes on U.S. auto parts, see Office of the United States Trade Representative, "United States Files WTO Case against China over Treatment of U.S. Auto Parts," March 30, 2006, www.ustr.gov/Document_Library/Press_Releases/2006/March/United_States_Files_WTO_Case_Against_China_Over_Treatment_of_US_Auto_Parts.html.

4. Derwin Pereira, "U.S. Review of Copyright Piracy Set to Rock China Ties; U.S. May Involve WTO if China Does Not Enforce Intellectual Property Rights, Says Official," *Singapore Press,* February 17, 2007.

5. Office of the United States Trade Representative, "United States Files WTO Case," 76.

6. Pereira, "U.S. Review of Copyright Piracy"; see also U.S. Chamber of Commerce, "The Battle against Counterfeiting and Piracy," March 27, 2007, www.uschamber.com/publications/weekly/commentary/070327.htm.

7. U.S.-China Business Council, "U.S. Trade Policy toward China," October, 2006, www.uschina.org/statistics/tradetable.html; see also Singapore Press Holdings Limited, "Will WTO's China Case Take the Heat off Bush? WTO Action against China Could Help Ease Pressure to Take a Tougher Approach against China," *Business Times Singapore,* February 13, 2007.

8. Dumbaugh, "China-U.S. Relations," 3–5.

9. Ibid., 20.

10. Jeffrey E. Garten, *The Big Ten: The Big Emerging Markets and How They Will Change Our Lives* (New York: Basic Books, 1997).

11. White House, Office of the Press Secretary, press conference transcript, May 26, 1994.

12. For an elaboration on this domestic balance of power, see the various essays in Scott Kennedy, ed., *China Cross Talk: The American Debate over China Policy since Nationalization* (Lanham, Md.: Rowman and Littlefield, 2003).

13. For an elaboration, see Steven W. Hook and John Spanier, *American Foreign Policy since World War II,* 15th ed. (Washington, D.C.: CQ Press, 2000), 68–79.

14. See Andrew Nathan, *China's Transition* (New York: Columbia University Press, 1997).

15. China's economic output grew by an average of 10 percent annually in the 1980s, with much of this growth based on foreign commerce. See Claude E. Barfield, "U.S.-China Trade and Investment in the 1990s," in *Beyond MFN: Trade with China and American Interests,* ed. James R. Lilley and Wendell L. Willkie II (Washington, D.C.: AEI Press, 1994), 63.

16. William R. Keylor, *The Twentieth Century World: An International History,* 3rd ed. (New York: Oxford University Press, 1996), 479–480.

17. The figures in this section are derived from Wayne M. Morrison, Congressional Research Service, "China-U.S. Trade Issues," July 20, 2000, 2–5.

18. U.S. Census Bureau, Foreign Trade Division, *U.S. Trade Balance with China,* May 7, 2000, www.census.gov/foreign-trade/balance/c5700.html.

19. Department of Agriculture, Economic Research Service, "China's WTO Accession to Significantly Boost U.S. Agricultural Exports," press release, February 2000.

20. See Hook and Spanier, *American Foreign Policy,* 361–363.

21. John T. Rourke and Richard Clark, "Making U.S. Foreign Policy toward China in the Clinton Administration," in *After the End: Making U.S. Foreign Policy in the Post–Cold War World,* ed. James M. Scott (Durham, N.C.: Duke University Press, 1998), 203.

22. Ibid., 208.

23. During a November 1997 visit to the White House, Jiang Zemin agreed to halt the sharing of nuclear technology with Iran, among other concessions. A similar concern among congressional critics involved the Clinton administration's support for sharing satellite launch technology with China. White House officials certified in May 1999 that such technology exports to China would not harm U.S. firms in this sector or threaten U.S. strategic interests.

24. For a review of the shift in public opinion and its relationship to Sino-American relations, see "Support for NTR/MFN Status," *Americans on Globalization: A Study of Public Attitudes,* Center on Policy Attitudes, University of Maryland, College Park, March 28, 2000, www.pipa.org/OnlineReports/Globalization/appendixa/appendixa .html.

25. Susan Schmidt, "Businesses Ante Up $30 Million," *Washington Post,* October 26, 2000, A26.

26. China Business World Online News Service, "Joint Venture Project with GM," February 25, 1997, www.cbw.com/business/quarter1/automoti.htm.

27. Richard Pastore, "Motorskills: Emerging Markets," *CIO Magazine Online,* September 15, 1998, www.cio.com/archive/enterprise/091598_ford.html.

28. Lester J. Gesteland, "Foreign Firms to Benefit from China Unicom U.S. $16 Billion CDMA Market," *China Online,* December 13, 1999.

29. For more information regarding the impact of NGO pressure on government policies, see Margaret E. Keck and Kathryn Sikkink, *Activists beyond Borders* (Ithaca, N.Y.: Cornell University Press, 1998).

30. For recent critiques, see Human Rights Watch, "China: Release Whistleblowing Doctor. Year-Long Pattern of Harassment Comes to Light," June 10, 2004, http://hrw.org/english/docs/2004/06/10/china8794.htm; and idem, "China: Stifling the Memory of Tiananmen," June 4, 2004, http://hrw.org/english/docs/2004/06/03/china 8732.htm.

31. Freedom House, *Freedom in the World, 1997–1998* (Piscataway, N.J.: Transaction Publishers, 1998), 190–191.

32. *Amnesty International Annual Report, 1999: China,* www.amnesty.org/ailib/aireport/ar99/asa17.htm.

33. Elizabeth Economy, "Painting China Green," *Foreign Affairs* 78 (March/April 1999): 16.

34. For examples of environmental NGOs' Internet lobbying activities, see the Greenpeace Web site, www.greenpeace.org, and that of the Sierra Club, www.sierra club.org.

35. United Methodist Church, General Board of Church and Society, "An Appeal of Conscience by Religious Leaders to Members of the U.S. Congress," September 19, 2000, www.umc-gbcs.org/issues/letter.php?letterid=42.

36. While most religious groups opposed the engagement policy, some sided with the Clinton administration in arguing that toleration of faith would be more likely once the PRC became more integrated in the global economy. One example was a Quaker group, the Friends Committee on National Legislation, which became active during the 1990s on many aspects of Sino-American relations.

37. Federal News Service, "Prepared Testimony of John J. Sweeney before the Senate Finance Committee," March 23, 2000.

38. State Department, Bureau of Democracy, Human Rights and Labor, *Country Reports on Human Rights Practices, 1999,* February 25, 2000, www.state.gov/www/global/human_rights/1999_hrp_report/china.html.

39. See the Freedom House Web site, www.freedomhouse.org.

40. Wayne M. Morrison, National Council for Science and the Environment, "U.S.-China Trade Issues," CRS Issue Brief for Congress, January 3, 2001, http://cnie.org/nle/econ-35.html.

41. Anne E. Kornblut, "House OK's Normalizing China Trade, Bipartisan Vote Praised and Assailed," *Boston Globe,* May 25, 2000, A1.

42. Edward Daniels, "Manufacturing Advocate Confident China Trade Bill Will Pass," States News Service, August 23, 2000.

43. U.S.-China Business Council, *U.S.-China Trade Statistics and China's World Trade Statistics,* www.uschina.org/statistics/tradetable.html (accessed April 5, 2007).

44. Ibid.

45. U.S.-China Business Council, *PRC Economic Statistics,* www.uschina.org/statistics/economy.html (accessed April 5, 2007).

46. U.S.-China Business Council, "Foreign Investment in China," February, 2007, www.uschina.org/info/forecast/2007/foreign-investment.html.

47. U.S.-China Business Council, *U.S.-China Trade Statistics and China's World Trade Statistics.*

48. Amid these complaints from Washington, interestingly, increasing discontent in China over the status of the trade relationship also grew, as the United States was seen more and more as a brake on China's otherwise unrestrained growth.

49. Office of the United States Trade Representative, "2006 Report to Congress on China's WTO Compliance," December 11, 2006.

50. The first complaint against China filed in 2004 with the WTO involved the semiconductor industry; it was settled through bilateral negotiation. Armstrong, "United States Complains to WTO about China."

51. Freedom House, *Freedom in the World, 2006 Edition—Country Report: China (2006),* http://freedomhouse.org/template.cfm?page=22&year=2006&country=6941.

52. Amnesty International, press release, "China: The Human Cost of the Economic Miracle," March 1, 2007, http://web.amnesty.org/library/Index/ENGASA170092007?open&of=ENG-CHN.

53. Dexter Roberts and Pete Engardio, "Secrets, Lies, and Sweatshops," *Business Week,* November 27, 2006.

54. AFL-CIO, *The AFL-CIO's Worker's Rights Case against China, Global Economy,* www.aflcio.org/issues/jobseconomy/globaleconomy/chinapetition.cfm (accessed April 5, 2007).

55. AFL-CIO, "Statement by AFL-CIO Secretary-Treasurer Trumka on Bush Administration's Rejection of 301 Petition against Chinese Government," July 21, 2006, www.aflcio.org/mediacenter/prsptm/pr07212006a.cfm.

56. U.S. Chamber of Commerce, "The Battle against Counterfeiting and Piracy."

57. U.S.-China Business Council, "USCBC Urges Senate to Take Balanced Approach to China Trade Relationship," March 27, 2006, www.uschina.org/public/documents/2007/03/sfc-testimony-press-release.html.

58. Susan C. Schwab, "The President's Trade Policy Agenda," Policy Brief, Office of the United States Trade Representative, Washington, D.C., March 1, 2007, www.ustr.gov/assets/Document_Library/Reports_Publications/2007/2007_Trade_Policy_Agenda/asset_upload_file629_10624.pdf.

59. Dumbaugh, "China-U.S. Relations," 16.

60. Ibid., 13–18.

12 The World Trade Organization and Tax Subsidies for Exports: Equal Competition or Corporate Welfare?

Wendy J. Schiller and Ralph G. Carter

Before You Begin:

1. What is an international trade "subsidy," and how does it create conflicts between countries? How did a "DISC," an "FSC," and the exemption from taxes of "extraterritorial income" each qualify as a trade subsidy when they were in fact tax provisions?

2. How does the shift from the General Agreement on Tariffs and Trade (GATT) to the World Trade Organization (WTO) change the nature of trade negotiations among countries? What power does the WTO have that GATT did not?

3. Were there any other issues besides taxes that caused conflict in trade negotiations between Europe and the United States between 1995 and 2005?

4. Why did corporate tax policy create a rift among Republicans in Congress? Why did the House and Senate produce very different bills on this subject?

5. How did corporations influence the U.S. response to rulings on unfair trade practices? Did they appear to have a different effect on Congress than on the president? What role did geographic location play in the provision of benefits to businesses in the legislation that ultimately passed?

6. How does the story of corporate tax subsidies illustrate the extent to which the United States now has a globally interdependent economy?

Introduction: What's Fair?

In the early twenty-first century, Congress tried once again to fix a thirty-year-old foreign trade problem. Previous Congresses had exempted U.S. corporations from taxation on the income they earned on exports abroad. Not only were such exemptions good politics at home, but they also helped offset several economic advantages that European governments provided to their corporations. The exemptions made the economic competition for sales abroad appear to be a more even contest. However, two different international trade organizations twice ruled that such exemptions are illegal.

In its effort to promote the rule of law and regularization of global trade, the U.S. government's position was to abide by such rulings. At the same time, U.S. policymakers wanted to find a formula for corporate taxation that would make U.S. products more competitively priced on the world market and would even that playing field. Reconciling these two aims was challenging enough, but the resulting legislation became bogged down by competing proposals for solving the problems. For one group of policymakers, the legislation needed to address global competitiveness issues, making it easier for U.S. multinational corporations to compete abroad through both exports and foreign operations. This group's primary aim was to help U.S. corporations, wherever they operated. To others, the major goal of the legislation was to provide corporate tax benefits at home, so as to create more U.S. jobs. In their view, encouraging exports was a fine goal, but it was equally important, if not more so, to try to keep jobs here.

Background: United States–European Union Foreign Trade Competition

After World War II, the Bretton Woods economic system fixed the value of the dollar at $35 per ounce of gold. That static price made sense when the United States had the most robust economy in the international system. However by the early 1970s, the United States faced growing economic problems. Trying to pay for both the Vietnam War and expanding domestic programs had strained the U.S. economy, resulting in an overpriced dollar. An overpriced dollar meant that U.S. goods exported to foreign markets became prohibitively expensive, and that led to a drop in consumption of U.S. goods abroad. In 1971, President Richard Nixon tried to remedy the situation by proposing a comprehensive set of economic reforms, which included taking the United States off the gold standard and letting the value of the dollar float against other currencies. Congress ultimately passed the reforms in the Revenue Act of 1971.

An important but frequently overlooked component of the reforms was the creation of Domestic International Sales Corporations (DISCs).[1] Lawmakers viewed DISCs as a way to address the inequity in the way that U.S. and European governments taxed corporate income. Europeans typically relied on territorial tax systems, taxing the income generated by corporations at home but not taxing their income generated abroad.[2] In contrast, the U.S. tax code applied to corporate income no matter where it was earned. Thus most European corporations paid taxes only on income generated domestically, but U.S. corporations

The WTO and Export Tax Subsidies

1971 President Richard Nixon signs the Revenue Act of 1971 into law, which creates a corporate tax break, Domestic International Sales Corporations (DISCs), for corporations that do business overseas.

1976 The General Agreement on Tariffs and Trade (GATT) rules that DISCs unfairly subsidized exports to varying degrees and that the United States is out of compliance with international trade rules. The U.S. appeals the ruling.

1981 The GATT again rules that DISCs are an unfair trade subsidy to corporations.

1984 Congress passes the Deficit Reduction Act and includes Foreign Sales Corporations (FSCs) as a replacement for DISCs.

1995 The European Union (EU) replaces the European Community, and the World Trade Organization (WTO) replaces the GATT as the governing structure for global trade.

1997 The EU files a formal complaint with the WTO charging that FSCs are an illegal trade subsidy.

1999 The WTO rules that FSCs are an unfair trade subsidy, and the U.S. appeals the ruling.

February 24, 2000 The WTO rejects the U.S. appeal.

November 15, 2000 The FSC Repeal and Extraterritorial Income Exclusion Act of 2000 is signed into law. This bill creates a new corporate tax break, extraterritorial income (ETI), as a substitute for the FSC.

January 2001 The EU files suit with the WTO charging that the ETI tax break is an illegal trade subsidy.

August 20, 2001 The WTO rules against the U.S. by determining that the ETI provisions still apply to exports and as such constituted an illegal export subsidy.

April 11, 2003 Representatives Crane, R-Ill., and Rangel, D-N.Y., introduce the Job Protection Act, to repeal the ETI provisions and give tax breaks to corporations regardless of the amount of goods they export.

July 25, 2003 Rep. Bill Thomas, R-Calif., chair of the House Ways and Means Committee, introduces H.R. 2896, the American Jobs Creation Act, which would repeal the ETI provisions and give corporations tax breaks on profits from exported goods.

continued on the next page

continued from the previous page

September 18, 2003 Sen. Charles Grassley, R-Iowa, chair of the Senate Finance Committee, introduces his own corporate tax bill, S. 1637, the Jumpstart Our Business Strength Act (JOBS).

October 2, 2003 The Senate Finance Committee approves Grassley's bill by a vote of 19–2.

October 28, 2003 The House Ways and Means Committee approves the Thomas bill (H.R. 2896) by a party-line vote of 24–15.

March 1, 2004 The European Union carries out its threat and imposes tariff barriers on U.S. goods.

March 3, 2004 The Senate takes up S. 1637 in response to the EU's actions, but the bill stalls over controversial amendments unrelated to the tax provisions.

May 11, 2004 The Senate finally passes S. 1637 by a vote of 92–5.

June 17, 2004 The House of Representatives passes a revised version of H.R. 2896 by a vote of 251–178.

September 29, 2004 Members from the House and Senate begin meeting in conference to agree on a single compromise version of the American Jobs Creation Act.

October 7, 2004 The House of Representatives passes the compromise version American Jobs Creation Act by a vote of 280–141.

October 11, 2004 The Senate passes the compromise version of the American Jobs Creation Act by a 69–17 vote.

October 22, 2004 President Bush signs the American Jobs Creation Act.

July 22, 2005 The WTO announces its decision that the long transition periods built into the American Jobs Creation Act had not brought U.S. tax policies into compliance with international trade rules. The EU threatens to impose sanctions on U.S. goods again, and the U.S. appeals this ruling.

February 2006 The WTO rejects the U.S. appeal.

May 10, 2006 The House of Representatives passes H.R. 4297, the Tax Increase Prevention and Reconciliation Act of 2005, which brings the U.S. into compliance with the WTO ruling, by a vote of 244–185.

May 11, 2006 The Senate passes H.R. 4297 by a 54–44 vote.

May 17, 2006 President Bush signs H.R. 4297 into law.

paid income taxes on both their domestic and foreign sales. In the eyes of U.S. lawmakers, these differential tax systems produced an uneven playing field, in which European corporations got tax breaks on their exports but U.S. corporations did not.[3] Such uneven competition was not a major concern of U.S. policymakers in the 1950s, when the U.S. economy was far larger than that of Europe and the U.S. government's goal was to promote European economic growth and recovery from World War II. But by the 1970s, Europe had recovered to the extent that those European advantages hurt their American competitors. Now something needed to be done.[4]

The creation of DISCs was also an effort to address the broader problem of the move to manufacture goods in foreign countries. Prior to 1971, U.S. law allowed U.S. corporations to delay indefinitely paying taxes on the income that their operations in other countries generated. This quirk in the tax code produced an incentive for U.S. corporations to move operations abroad, rather than expand at home and simply export more finished products overseas. In a key way then, the U.S. tax code favored exporting U.S. jobs over exporting U.S. goods. By routing exports through the newly created DISCs, however, U.S. corporations could indefinitely defer between 16 percent and 33 percent of their export income from federal income tax. To lawmakers, the result was a "win-win" situation: U.S. corporations benefited from a more level playing field with their European competitors, and they had an incentive to export goods rather than jobs.[5]

Europeans did not take long to respond to this new law, which they viewed as an unfair trade practice. Two months after it passed, Belgium, France, and the Netherlands exercised their right under the General Agreement on Tariffs and Trade (GATT—an international organization created in 1947 to reduce tariffs and promote free trade)[6] and filed for consultations with the United States over what they saw as an illegal export subsidy. The process of consultations was an informal negotiation between countries to try to resolve differences before launching a formal hearing.

By May 1973 it was clear that consultations alone could not solve the dispute. The Europeans charged that DISCs were an illegal export subsidy, and the Americans countercharged that European territorial tax systems were an illegal export subsidy. In November 1976, the GATT panels ruled that both the European territorial systems and the U.S. DISCs unfairly subsidized exports to varying degrees. The United States was willing to accept the GATT ruling against the DISCs, if the Europeans accepted the GATT ruling against their territorial systems. However, Belgium, France, and the Netherlands refused.[7]

Both sides pursued the case, and in 1981 the GATT panels further ruled that the tax incentives available through the DISCs were illegal export subsidies (because they were created solely to reduce taxes on profits from exports) but that territorial tax systems were generally acceptable (because they did not exist solely to reduce taxes on profits from exports). Facing sanctions from the Europeans in the form of barriers to their exports, U.S. corporations sought relief from Congress. In the Deficit Reduction Act of 1984, Congress created Foreign Sales Corporations (FSCs) to replace DISCs.[8] U.S. corporations could now create FSCs in places such as Guam, the Virgin Islands, and Barbados and exempt from U.S. income taxes between 15 percent and 30 percent of their earnings on exports routed through those corporations. The only requirement to qualify for this benefit was that at least 50 percent of the product had to be made in the United States, so as to help staunch the flow of jobs overseas. Europeans were not happy with the creation of FSCs, but they let the matter drop, mainly because they believed that they would not get a better solution by extending the battle at GATT.[9]

Enter the European Union and the World Trade Organization

More than a decade later, the global trade landscape had changed in very important ways. In 1995, the European Community was replaced by the European Union (EU), and GATT was replaced by the World Trade Organization (WTO), an international organization with the ability not only to make and administer trade rules, but also to enforce them. Believing that they might finally be able to eliminate FSCs, the EU filed a complaint with the WTO in 1997.[10] In 1999, the WTO ruled that FSCs created an unfair trade subsidy, since they existed solely for the purpose of sheltering exports from taxation. It authorized retaliatory tariffs unless the United States changed the policy.[11] The WTO rejected the Clinton administration's appeal on February 24, 2000.

The WTO decision had very serious economic ramifications for U.S. tax policy. Over the previous sixteen years, U.S. corporations had benefited greatly from the FSC provision. For example, in 1998 alone, Boeing saved $130 million in tax payments under the program; Cisco Systems saved $55 million, and Monsanto saved $29 million.[12] Because the stakes for corporations were so high, any attempt by Congress or the administration to change or eliminate the FSC program would face strong opposition. The WTO decision would no doubt produce an intense political battle on Capitol Hill.

In April 2000, the Clinton administration notified the WTO that the United States would abide by its ruling banning FSCs, but it would do so in a way that

Box 12.1 Key Terms

Tariff Tax imposed on goods that are exported to another country. The country that receives the goods collects the tax when the goods reach their destination. Tariffs increase the price of exported goods to a foreign producer as well as the consumer. They create an advantage for domestic producers of the same goods by protecting the domestic market from cheaper imported goods.

Trade subsidy Financial support to domestic producers that enables them to export goods at a lower cost.

Domestic International Sales Corporations (DISCs) Separate corporations through which U.S. businesses could route their exported goods; they could indefinitely defer between 16 percent and 33 percent of export income generated by DISCs from federal income tax.

Foreign Sales Corporations (FSCs) Separate corporations residing outside the U.S., in places such as Guam, the Virgin Islands, and Barbados. U.S. businesses could exempt between 15 percent and 30 percent of their earnings on exports routed through these corporations from U.S. income taxes. The only requirement to qualify for this benefit was that least 50 percent of the product be made in the USA.

Extraterritorial income (ETI) U.S. corporate income generated by exported goods or foreign operations (overseas production and sales), which was granted the same tax break as FSCs.

General Agreement on Tariffs and Trade (GATT) An international treaty created in 1947 to reduce tariffs and promote free trade.

European Union (EU) Group of European countries that agree to abide by one set of economic and trade policies.

World Trade Organization (WTO) Governing structure for global trade in which all members agree to abide by rulings and pay penalties for violating fair trade practices.

Ways and Means Committee Congressional committee with jurisdiction over taxation and trade in the U.S. House of Representatives.

Finance Committee Congressional committee with jurisdiction over taxation and trade in the U.S. Senate.

Conference committee A specially formed committee, with members of both the House and Senate, to negotiate a single compromise version of bills that pass both chambers.

Committee chair The formal head of a congressional committee and always a member of the majority party.

Ranking member The most powerful minority-party member on a congressional committee.

did not harm U.S. corporations in their competition with their European counterparts. Administration officials said that the goal would be to produce new laws that reduced taxes on both the exports and the foreign operations of U.S. corporations and their overseas subsidiaries.[13] Moving swiftly, Rep. Bill Archer, R-Texas, chair of the House Ways and Means Committee, introduced the FSC Repeal and Extraterritorial Income Exclusion Act of 2000.[14] Following the Clinton administration's logic, this bill abolished FSCs and extended the tax breaks to all extraterritorial income, thereby including both exports and foreign operations (thus seemingly mimicking European territorial tax systems). The bill passed the House on September 13, by a 315–109 vote, and passed the Senate by unanimous consent on November 1. President Bill Clinton signed it on November 15, 2000.

It only took the EU two days to file a formal challenge with the WTO over the extraterritorial income (ETI) provisions in the bill.[15] On August 20, 2001, the WTO once again ruled against the United States, determining that the ETI provisions still applied to exports and thus constituted an illegal export subsidy. This time, it was up to President Bush to appeal the ruling, but the WTO rejected the appeal on January 14, 2002. The EU then asked for permission to impose retaliatory tariffs against U.S. goods, on an increasing, sliding scale, to the tune of $4 billion per year.[16]

Rep. Bill Thomas, R-Calif., who had succeeded Archer as chair of the Ways and Means Committee, introduced legislation in July 2002 to try to forestall punitive tariff increases by the EU. His goal was to revamp the entire corporate tax structure to make U.S. firms more competitive internationally, and he proposed the elimination of ETI provisions altogether. Thomas's bill provoked a swift reaction from the National Foreign Trade Council, a group of export-oriented businesses, which claimed that its benefits would not equal the tax savings from the current system that would be lost.[17] Moreover, major U.S. exporters, such as Microsoft, Boeing, and Caterpillar, objected strongly to any change in the system that now benefited them so well, and they recruited House Speaker Dennis Hastert, R-Ill., and Ways and Means Committee member Rep. Jennifer Dunn, R-Wash., to support their position. With such powerful opposition, Thomas's bill was stopped in its tracks in summer 2002.[18]

On August 30, 2002, a WTO arbitration board gave final approval for the $4 billion in retaliatory tariffs.[19] U.S. Trade Representative Robert Zoellick warned that the retaliatory tariff increase would be like "dropping a nuclear bomb" on international trade because it would imperil the European sales of giant U.S. corporations such as Microsoft and Boeing.[20] But the tariff increases would not take effect until March 1, 2004, and that gave the United States some time to try to find an alternative solution.[21]

At that point, trade relations between the EU and the United States were already tense because of other types of subsidies that were in dispute. The United States had already protested against European trade barriers to U.S.-produced bananas, hormone-added beef, and genetically modified foods, including soybeans and corn. Now U.S. officials became increasingly worried about the competition to Boeing from the multinationally owned Airbus corporation, which had recently eclipsed Boeing in annual commercial jet sales. The U.S. position was that Boeing needed tax subsidies to offset the research and development subsidies that Airbus received from its home governments (the United Kingdom, France, and Germany).[22] For their part, Europeans were troubled by President Bush's March 2002 imposition of tariff increases on imported steel (see chapter 9).[23]

2003—Congressional Conflict over Corporate Tax Breaks

With the 2004 imposition of trade sanctions looming, Congress again took up the issue of corporate tax breaks. One side, led by Ways and Means Chair Thomas, rallied behind his original proposal to repeal the ETI provisions and replace them with tax cuts applied to both corporate exports and income from overseas subsidiaries. The other side was led by two other Ways and Means heavyweights: Philip Crane, R-Ill.—the committee's number-two majority-party member—and Charles Rangel, D-N.Y.—the ranking minority-party member. The Crane-Rangel bill favored an approach that cut income taxes for all domestic U.S. manufacturers, regardless of whether they exported goods or not, thus providing benefits that might translate into more jobs for Americans at home.[24]

Representatives Crane and Rangel got ahead of Thomas by introducing their bill, H.R. 1769, the Job Protection Act of 2003, on April 11, 2003. Because of the claim that it would allow domestic manufacturing firms to maintain or expand their existing operations, the Crane-Rangel bill attracted wide support; 177 House members signed on as cosponsors.[25] Once again Speaker Hastert expressed his opinion on the issue by signaling his approval of the Crane-Rangel bill over the Thomas proposal. Recall that the Speaker was a key opponent of the Thomas bill in its earlier incarnation. Hastert had local reasons to support the Crane-Rangel bill because major corporations from his home state of Illinois—such as Boeing and Caterpillar—strongly favored it.[26] Other corporate backers of the Crane-Rangel bill included Microsoft, Motorola, and United

Technologies. Corporate lobbyists spent millions of dollars touting the job protection and job creation aspects of the Crane-Rangel bill, and a study by the consulting firm PriceWaterhouseCoopers was produced to show how many jobs would be jeopardized in each congressional district if the tax cut in the Crane-Rangel bill was not enacted.[27]

Chairman Thomas was behind, but when you are the chairman of the committee, the game is never over this early. Thomas introduced a revised version of his previous measure, H.R. 2896, the American Jobs Creation Act, on July 25. Thomas had heavyweight corporate backers for his bill as well, including Exxon Mobil, General Motors, Ford Motor Company, Texas Instruments, and Coca-Cola, all of which supported its proposed revision of international taxation rules. Both sides of this debate were thus well represented by lobbyists, reflecting the facts not only that bottom-line corporate profits were involved, but also that corporate leaders felt omitted from the large individual tax cuts enacted in 2001 and 2003.[28] In their eyes, a change in corporate tax policy was overdue.

The jockeying for support between the Thomas camp and the Crane-Rangel camp was intense, and Chairman Thomas had the advantage of the institutional power to offer fellow committee members side benefits to win their support. For example, committee member Rep. Nancy Johnson, R-Conn., was undecided between the two bills, but her district included United Technologies, which was constantly reminding her of its support of the Crane-Rangel bill. Thomas tried to win her vote by offering to include in the bill a research and experimentation tax credit that she had long championed. Rep. Phil English, R-Pa., had previously introduced legislation to allow U.S. corporations to pay reduced income taxes, for one year only, on their foreign earnings. Thomas folded that provision also into his bill, thereby picking up English's vote and the support of corporations (including computer firms Dell and Hewlett-Packard and such drug companies as Eli Lilly and Merck) that had lobbied hard for the provision.[29] Thomas approached other members as well, offering favorable consideration for their policy projects unrelated to the tax measure in return for their support.[30] Thomas recognized that persuading Speaker Hastert to support his bill was key to its success, so he pointed out that the new version of the bill included $100 billion in domestic tax breaks for U.S. corporations that his 2002 version did not include. By adding provisions that favored domestic manufacturers, Thomas was able to convince Speaker Hastert that his bill was as beneficial to Caterpillar as the Crane-Rangel bill, and Hastert publicly changed his position and endorsed the Thomas bill on October 2, 2003.[31]

On the other side of the Capitol, the chairman of the Senate Finance Committee, Sen. Charles Grassley, R-Iowa, introduced his own version of a corporate tax break bill, S. 1637, the Jumpstart Our Business Strength Act (JOBS), on September 18, 2003. It was a very different bill from the one offered by Chairman Thomas. Grassley's bill also proposed to eliminate the ETI provision in the tax code but to replace it with a straight deduction of 9 percent on corporate profits from domestic production. U.S. firms that had manufacturing operations overseas would have a smaller tax break through 2013.[32] Grassley argued that his bill had essentially the same effect as the Thomas bill but with smaller overall budget consequences. In other words, it would put less of a drain on the U.S. Treasury.

The Grassley bill had a bipartisan group of eight cosponsors, including the ranking minority-party member of the Finance Committee, Sen. Max Baucus, D-Mont., and the Senate minority-party leader, Tom Daschle, D-S.D.[33] Sen. Ernest "Fritz" Hollings, D-S.C., had introduced S. 970, which was identical to the Crane-Rangel bill, on May 1, with eight cosponsors, but it was clear early on that his bill would not get far.[34] Given Grassley's position as Finance Committee chair and his bipartisan support, his bill would be the center of debate in the Senate. The Senate Finance Committee approved the Grassley bill by a vote of 19–2 on October 2; two conservative senators, Jon Kyl, R-Ariz., and Don Nickles, R-Okla., voted against the bill, saying that it favored some companies over others.[35] The Finance Committee reported the bill to the full Senate on November 7, but it would be almost four months before it would be debated on the Senate floor.

Meanwhile, back in the House of Representatives, the Ways and Means Committee approved Thomas's revised bill by a party-line vote of 24–15 on October 28, 2003. In doing so, the committee rejected Rangel's efforts to make the bill's provisions more similar to those of the Crane-Rangel bill. The committee also adopted an amendment by Rep. Jim McCrery, R-La., to provide tax benefits to mutual fund companies selling their products abroad. The bill even addressed a brewing controversy of the time by specifying that firms such as Bechtel and Halliburton could not qualify for the manufacturing tax credits for their operations in Iraq.[36]

However, getting the bill to the House floor proved politically difficult. Not only did House Democrats prefer the Crane-Rangel version because it promised more jobs at home, but so did a bloc of twenty House Republicans led by Donald Manzullo, R-Ill., chair of the House Small Business Committee. If House Democrats and Manzullo's twenty Republicans voted together to oppose the revised Thomas bill, it would not get the 218 votes needed to pass. As Manzullo said, "A bill like that should not be taken to the floor. Members who have lost factories in their district should not be put in the position of voting for a bill like this."[37] House Majority Leader Tom DeLay, R-Texas, said that the bill would come to the House floor "when it's ripe" and that he hoped that would occur before the House adjourned for Thanksgiving.[38] That time did not come, despite the fears of major exporting corporations as the 2004 deadline for European retaliation against U.S. products fast approached. As Calman J. Cohen, president of the Emergency Committee for American Trade (representing large exporters such as Caterpillar, John Deere, and Cargill), put it, "The retaliatory threat is real, and the cost would be severe."[39]

2004—Resolving Differences to Achieve Final Passage

The European Union held true to its threat and imposed retaliatory tariffs on March 1, 2004.[40] According to congressional staffers, many of their congressional bosses were surprised by the EU's actions. They had not thought the EU would actually be willing to impose the increases, but their assessments were wrong. Tariffs were raised on specific items including timber and paper products (affecting California, Maine, Mississippi, Kentucky, and Wisconsin), tourism and travel products (California), textiles (the Carolinas), thoroughbred horses (Kentucky), motorcycles (Wisconsin and Pennsylvania), leather products (Maine and Wisconsin), citrus (Florida), and iron and steel (Ohio, Pennsylvania, and West Virginia). The increases began at 5 percent per month (or an estimated $16.5 million for March 2004) and were scheduled to increase one percentage point each month. The total for 2004 was projected at over $300 million, and the increases would continue until the rate reached 17 percent and the total reached $4 billion per year.[41]

The European Union was very strategic in its imposition of the tariff increases. Some large exporters, such as Boeing and Caterpillar, were specifically exempted from the increases for the simple reason that Europeans needed their products too much. However other U.S. exports were purposely targeted for increases, with an eye to maximum political impact in a presidential election year. Targeted products came from states that leaned heavily Republican or states with large numbers of Electoral College votes. Because the Republicans held control of the Congress and the White House, the EU calculated that targeting businesses in their backyards would put maximum pressure on the government to change trade-related corporate tax policies.

The Senate was the first to respond to the European Union's actions by bringing the Grassley bill up on the Senate floor on March 3, 2004. During the Senate debate, a major conflict erupted over an amendment offered by Sen.

Tom Harkin, D-Iowa, which tried to block the Bush administration from changing the rules on overtime pay for millions of workers. Not wanting to allow a vote on such a politically charged issue in an election year, Senate Republicans withdrew the entire bill from the Senate floor on March 24.[42] On April 5, the Senate resumed consideration of the bill, only to be sidetracked once again by the overtime amendment. On May 4 the Senate returned to the bill and allowed a version of the Harkin amendment to be added to it.[43] Finally on May 11, the Senate passed the Grassley bill by a vote of 92–5. Sen. Jon Corzine, D-N.J., said, "It's got plenty of things in there . . . I'd like to pocket veto. But we need to get the tariffs removed."[44] The impact of Senate passage was clear to EU Trade Commissioner Pascal Lamy, who said, "It goes without saying that the moment WTO-compliant legislation becomes law, the EU will immediately repeal the countermeasures."[45]

At this point, in the House, Ways and Means Chairman Thomas was rewriting every provision in the prior year's bill in an effort to pick up more votes. The most significant additions included a tobacco buyout whereby tobacco farmers would see their seventy-year-old federal price support program end but would also be freed from the existing production quotas. If they chose to leave tobacco production, their transition to other products would be eased by guaranteed government payments totaling $9.6 billion over five years (paid for by the U.S. tobacco industry through federal cigarette taxes). These tobacco changes helped pick up votes from numerous southern representatives. Thomas also included a state sales tax deduction from federal income taxes for people living in states that relied on state sales taxes rather than state income taxes (including Texas, Florida, Alaska, Washington, Nevada, South Dakota, and Wyoming).

As Thomas was rewriting his bill, lobbyists continued to press for tax breaks for their clients. The biggest corporate lobbyist, General Electric (GE), threw its efforts behind the revised Thomas bill, which now included a provision that would produce nearly $2 billion a year in tax breaks, almost all going to GE. GE now stood to gain more in tax benefits under the new law than under the current ETI provisions. According to Wayne State University tax law professor Michael J. McIntyre, "This is the definition of corporate welfare."[46] However, as Thomas said in response to the committee's critics, "There is room for purists, but none of them are chairmen of committees."[47] As a result of these changes, the Ways and Means Committee approved Thomas's bill on June 19, 27–9, with all twenty-four Republican members voting for it, as well as three Democrats.[48]

The newly revised Thomas bill had similar success on the House floor, passing the House 251–178 on June 17. In addition to the expected Republican support, forty-eight Democrats chose to vote for the bill. Twenty-eight Democrats from tobacco districts or states with sales taxes but not income taxes voted for it. Most of the other twenty Democrats voting for the bill did so because of the bill's tax cuts on manufacturing income, which they saw as job-protecting measures in rust belt states like Michigan, Ohio, and Pennsylvania.[49]

The next step in the legislative process was appointing members from the House and Senate to meet in conference to iron out their differences and agree on one final version of the bill. The Senate reached a snag in its attempts to appoint conferees when two influential senators, Edward Kennedy, D-Mass., and Mike Dewine, R-Ohio, objected to the tobacco provisions in the House bill. To appease them, Sen. Bill Frist, R-Tenn., the Republican majority leader, and Senator Daschle, the Democratic minority leader, agreed to bring the Grassley bill back to the floor and add an amendment to enhance the regulatory power of the Food and Drug Administration over tobacco products. As a result of this compromise, the Senate finally voted to appoint conferees and begin negotiations with the House on July 15, 2004.[50]

The Last Stage

Although the two versions of the legislation were ready for conference committee action after July 15, election year politics delayed matters. House Republican leaders feared that their Democratic colleagues would consume valuable time on the House floor with multiple, nonbinding motions instructing House conferees on how to resolve their differences with the Senate's bill. Not only could such motions be expected to be played for maximum political advantage back home in an election year, but they could also clog the legislative calendar, thereby making it hard for all House members to get home in time to do some serious campaigning before the November election.

In early September, Senator Grassley further complicated the matter by announcing that he would delay legislation extending middle-class tax cuts that were due to expire, a measure that was a priority for the Bush administration and virtually all Republicans, until the WTO-mandated repeal of the ETI tax breaks was accomplished. Mindful of the impact, growing each month, of the EU's retaliatory tariff increases on Midwestern agricultural exports, Iowa's Grassley wanted to ensure that the ETI provisions were repealed as soon as possible. Senators Grassley and Frist met with Chairman Thomas on September 20 to discuss an agreement on the two versions of the bill. In a key development, Thomas agreed to move a $12.9 billion package of business tax breaks that were expiring or about to expire out of his bill and into the bill extending the middle-class tax cut. Although many differences remained between the House and Senate versions of the ETI measure, removing that $12.9 billion in lost revenues made it easier to meet the Senate's demand that all new tax breaks be offset by revenue increases.[51]

When the House and Senate conferees began meeting on September 29, Thomas was determined to get the ETI provisions repealed and to protect the tax provisions he saw as essential to making U.S. multinational corporations more competitive overseas—whether in terms of exports or overseas operations. To preserve those priorities, virtually everything else was negotiable.[52] Thomas agreed to expand the legislation to accommodate the Senate's addition of small business class-S corporations, sole proprietorships, partnerships, and cooperatives to the traditional class-C corporations his version had included.[53] Thomas took some chances with the Senate's version of the bill. He dropped the Senate's restriction on the tax benefits applying to the oil and gas industry, restaurants, the electricity and utility industries, media outlets, and the entertainment industries.[54] However, the most important chances he took involved the tobacco and overtime pay issues. Because House Majority Leader DeLay objected so strongly to the provision allowing FDA regulation of the tobacco industry, Thomas got it removed from the final version of the bill. He also managed to eliminate Harkin's amendment preventing the Bush administration changes in the rules governing overtime pay. His hope was that all the extra tax breaks spread throughout the bill would make it too attractive to vote against in an election year. His assessment proved correct.[55]

This legislation began as an effort to satisfy the WTO by repealing the $58 billion in ETI tax breaks in prior law and replacing them with tax breaks for traditional manufacturing industries, which had lost 2.9 million jobs since July 2000.[56] In the end, there was something in this nearly $150 billion, 276-provision, 633-page-long bill for everyone: tax breaks for restaurant owners; shipbuilders; those involved in the horse and dog track gambling industry; movie makers; the railroad industry; those who made fishing tackle boxes, bows and arrows, and sonar fish finders; tobacco growers; those living in states without state income taxes; NASCAR track owners; and those involved in producing ethanol.[57] As Rep. Ron Lewis, R-Ky., said, "In the end, Chairman Thomas had everyone in checkmate. The political pressures were [such] that they couldn't move."[58]

The conference committee's bill reached the House floor on October 7 and passed easily, 280–141. The Senate proved more difficult, as those who had not gotten what they wanted in the bill tried to recover what was lost. Sen. Mary Landrieu, D-La., tried to reattach her priority concern—a $2 billion tax credit making it possible for employers to keep on their payrolls employees currently serving in the National Guard or military reserves in Iraq and Afghanistan. She dropped her opposition to the conference version when the Senate voted to attach her proposal to another bill pending Senate consideration.[59] Harkin objected that both the FDA regulation of the tobacco industry and his ban on changing overtime pay rules had been dropped. The Senate satisfied him by passing those measures as separate bills (S. 2974 and S. 2975, bills which the House chose not to consider). With those objections removed, the Senate passed the bill on October 11, by a 69–17 vote. The Senate then adjourned so members could go home and campaign for reelection, and President Bush signed the American Jobs Creation Act on October 22, 2004.[60]

Sen. Max Baucus, the ranking Democrat on the Senate Finance Committee, was quoted as saying, "This bill's not perfect, but we all say many, many times we should not let perfection be the enemy of the good. It's very clear the pluses outweigh the minuses."[61] Others did not agree. According to Robert Bixby, executive director of the Concord Coalition, a group dedicated to fiscal prudence and reducing the nation's deficit, the WTO-mandated ETI tax break repeal was "a legitimate problem they needed to address, and they used that legitimate problem to drag all these goodies over the finish line. This is a very cynical conclusion to this Congress."[62] Rangel agreed, saying, "It's Christmas in October for multinational companies and lobbyists with friends in high places."[63] Senator Kennedy called it "a lobbyist's dream and a middle-class nightmare," and Sen. John McCain, R-Ariz., said it was the "worst example of the influence of special interests that I've ever seen."[64]

In the months after the bill was passed, it was unclear whether it accomplished the original desired result. Two days after Bush signed the bill, the EU announced it would temporarily lift the retaliatory tariff increases it had imposed. According to Pascal Lamy, outgoing EU trade commissioner, the decision was only temporary because Congress chose to phase out the tax breaks over time and to "grandfather" tax benefits to certain businesses (such as aircraft manufacturers) that operated on the basis of very long term contracts. The EU's position was that the tax breaks should have been terminated rather than phased out, and that it would take the time needed to determine whether to pursue another WTO complaint. EU policymakers were also irritated that the Bush administration had filed a complaint with the WTO over British, French, and German subsidies to the Airbus corporation, while Boeing continued to benefit from the grandfather clauses in U.S. tax law and from the EU's own exemption of Boeing aircraft from its retaliatory tariff increases. However, the Bush administration officials argued that that was an illegal subsidy for exports, too.[65]

Conclusion: A Final Resolution?

On July 22, 2005, the WTO announced its decision that the long transition periods built into the American Jobs Creation Act had not brought U.S. tax policies into compliance with international trade rules. As a result, there was a possibility that the EU might reimpose the $4 billion per year retaliatory tariff increases it had ended in 2004.[66] On September 30, 2005, the WTO panel decision was circulated to all members, confirming the illegality of both the transitional phase-out period and the grandfather clauses. In the words of EU Trade Commissioner Peter Mandelson,

> The EU welcomes the WTO's clear language and conclusions. It has been confirmed that the U.S. has yet to comply with previous WTO rulings. The EU appreciates that the U.S. Congress has repealed the original FSC tax scheme. However, despite European opposition, the U.S. Congress chose to perpetuate the prohibited tax subsidies through a transition period and the permanent "grandfathering" of existing contracts. These provisions, which are now contained in the American Jobs Creation Act, are unacceptable in view of the large benefits involved. We estimate these advantages, for example, to add up to over $750 million for Boeing alone. This is striking because the U.S. is asking European companies to abide by the WTO definition of subsidies regarding grants to Europe's civil aircraft sector. I hope that the U.S. authorities will choose to act consistently in this matter.[67]

In February 2006, a U.S. appeal of this WTO decision was rejected.[68] Determined to finally resolve the problem, Chairman Thomas selected as his vehicle the highly popular bill extending $70 billion in individual tax cuts for five years (the Tax Increase Prevention and Reconciliation Act). To this bill he added a component that rescinded the American Job Creation Act's phase-in provisions and the grandfathering of prior contracts.[69] The House passed the bill on May 10, 244–185; the Senate passed it on May 11, 54–44; and President Bush signed it on May 17, 2006.[70] The firms primarily affected by repeal of those provisions were Boeing, General Electric, and American International Group, which would now have to pay nearly $500 million more in taxes. However, both GE and AIG stood to benefit from a $4.8 billion tax break in the American Jobs

Creation Act for companies with overseas finance divisions, so the chief victim of Thomas's action seemed to be Boeing.[71]

With that, the WTO mandate to end illegal U.S. export subsidies was finally satisfied, but questions continue as to whether U.S. and European corporations compete on a level playing field. Clearly each country—the United States or the countries that make up the European Union—wants to protect and preserve its competitive advantage when trading goods. But the old rules of the game have been altered by the continuous expansion of the global economy. After all, it was not until 1995 that the United States even agreed to part of an international organization that had real enforcement powers over U.S. business practices and tax policy. Our own free trade policies have encouraged U.S. corporations to "go global," and that makes all countries more interdependent with the world economy than ever before. The difficulty arises when the global interest directly conflicts with a country's individual interest. It is then that we learn whether the playing field is truly fair.

Key Actors

Phil Crane Representative, R-Ill., the second-ranking majority-party member on the Ways and Means Committee; he was considered an expert on trade policy and wanted to create more U.S. jobs.

Tom Daschle Senator, D-S.D., Senate minority leader from 1994 to 2001 and again from 2002 to 2004; he tried to find compromises between Senate and House versions of the legislation.

Emergency Committee for American Trade Coalition that lobbied on behalf of large U.S. corporations, such as John Deere and Caterpillar, to preserve their benefits under U.S. tax law where possible.

Bill Frist Senator, R-Tenn., Senate majority leader from 2002 to 2006; he tried to find compromises between Senate and House versions of the legislation.

Charles Grassley Senator, R-Iowa, chair of the Senate Finance Committee; wanted to improve U.S. economic competitiveness abroad without increasing the federal budget deficit any more than necessary.

Tom Harkin Senator, D-Iowa, stalled the corporate tax bill in the Senate in a dispute about overtime pay regulations.

Dennis Hastert Representative, R-Ill., Speaker of the House of Representatives from 1998 to 2006; wanted to protect the interests of major Illinois corporations such as Boeing and Caterpillar.

Pascal Lamy European Union trade commissioner; saw U.S. corporate income tax breaks as illegal trade subsidies.

Charles Rangel Representative, D-N.Y., was the ranking member on the Ways and Means Committee; wanted to create more U.S. jobs.

Bill Thomas Representative, R-Calif., chaired the Ways and Means Committee from 2000 to 2006 and wanted to improve U.S. economic competitiveness abroad.

Notes

1. David L, Brumbaugh, "A History of the Extraterritorial Income (ETI) and Foreign Sales Corporation (FSC) Export Tax-Benefit Controversy," Congressional Research Service, November 9, 2004, www.taxhistory.org/thp/readings.nsf/cf7c9c870b600b9585256df80075b9dd/d1e0dcc337b8048385256f860068159e?OpenDocument.
2. Also, European value-added taxes (VAT) were built into the cost of products at each major phase of production. These taxes were routinely rebated to foreigners who filled out the appropriate paperwork.
3. Brumbaugh, "A History."
4. David L. Aaron, "Heading Off a Trade War," *Washington Post,* September 7, 2001, A29.
5. Brumbaugh, "A History."
6. CIESIN Thematic Guides, "General Agreement on Tariffs and Trade," www.ciesin.columbia.edu/TG/PI/TRADE/gatt.html.
7. Ibid.
8. "Foreign Sales Corporations, 2000," www.irs.gov/put/irs-soi/00fscart.pdf; also Suanne Buggy, "Foreign Sales Corporations," *Export America,* December 2000, 32–33, www.ita.doc.gov/exportamerica/Volume%202/December2000/FSC.pdf.
9. Brumbaugh, "A History."
10. Ibid.
11. "Corporate Tax Changes Stall," *Congressional Quarterly Almanac Plus 2003,* vol. 59, 108th Congress, 1st Sess. (Washington, D.C.: Congressional Quarterly, 2004), 17-12.
12. Ibid.
13. Brumbaugh, "A History."
14. See thomas.loc.gov, 106th Congress, for details on the Archer bill.
15. Ibid.; Brumbaugh, "A History."
16. Ibid.
17. Ibid.
18. Paul Blustein, "EU Told It Can Slap Duties on U.S. Goods," *Washington Post,* August 31, 2002, E1.
19. Brumbaugh, "A History."
20. William Drozdiak, "EU May Hit U.S. with $4 Billion in Penalties," *Washington Post,* August 21, 2001, E1.
21. "Corporate Tax Changes Stall."

22. Robert Samuelson, "The Airbus Showdown," *Washington Post*, December 8, 2004, A31.

23. Paul Blustein, "U.S., EU Reduce Trade Tensions," *Washington Post*, May 3, 2002, E1.

24. "Corporate Tax Changes Stall," 17-13.

25. See thomas.loc.gov, 108th Congress, for details on the Crane-Rangel bill.

26. Ibid.

27. Juliet Eilperin, "WTO Ruling on U.S. Tax Breaks Ignites Lobbying Battle: Issue Divides Domestic Firms, Multinationals," *Washington Post*, July 6, 2003, A7.

28. Ibid.; Jonathan Weisman, "Congress Weighs Corporate Tax Breaks," *Washington Post*, October 14, 2003, E1.

29. Weisman, "Congress Weighs."

30. Eilperin, "WTO Ruling."

31. "Corporate Tax Changes Stall," 17-13.

32. Stephen J. Norton, "Corporate Tax Overhaul Battle Being Fought on Two Fronts," *CQ Weekly Online*, October 3, 2003, 2428–2430.

33. See thomas.loc.gov, 108th Congress, for details on the Grassley bill.

34. See thomas.loc.gov, 108th Congress, for details on the Hollings bill.

35. Norton, "Corporate Tax Overhaul."

36. "Corporate Tax Changes Stall," 17-14.

37. Ibid.

38. Jonathan Weisman, "EU Trade Negotiator Unyielding on Subsidies," *Washington Post*, November 5, 2003, E1.

39. Ibid.

40. "Corporate Tax Breaks Enacted," *Congressional Quarterly Almanac Plus 2004*, vol. 60, 108th Congress, 2nd Sess. (Washington, D.C.: Congressional Quarterly, 2005),13-3.

41. George Will, "Irony and Steel," *Washington Post*, November 16, 2003, B7; Jonathan Weisman, "EU to Begin Sanctions on Some U.S. Goods," *Washington Post*, February 27, 2004, E1; Helen Dewar, "Overtime Pay Battle Threatens Trade Bill," *Washington Post*, March 24, 2004, A4; Jonathan Weisman, "Tax-Bill Standstill Leaves Businesses Hanging," *Washington Post*, April 9, 2004, E1.

42. Jill Barshay, "Corporate Tax Bill Stalls in Senate; House Mulls Altering Its Version," *CQ Weekly Online*, March 26, 2004, 741–742.

43. See thomas.loc.gov, 108th Congress, for details on the floor debate of the Harkin amendment to the Grassley bill.

44. Jill Barshay. "House Thickets Await Tax Bill after Solid Senate Victory." *CQ Weekly Online*, May 14, 2004, 1132–1136.

45. Ibid.

46. Jeffrey H. Birnbaum and Jonathan Weisman, "GE Lobbyists Mold Tax Bill," *Washington Post*, July 13, 2004, A1.

47. "Corporate Tax Breaks Enacted," 13-7.

48. Ibid.

49. Ibid.

50. Jill Barshay, "Corporate Tax Bill Inches Closer to Law with Senate Consensus on Tobacco; Though Cost Remains a Divisive Issue," *CQ Weekly Online*, July 16, 2004, 1736.

51. "Corporate Tax Breaks Enacted," 13-8.

52. Ibid.

53. Jonathan Weisman, "Proposal Seeks Wider Tax Cuts for Industries," *Washington Post,* October 1, 2004, E1.

54. Ibid.

55. "Corporate Tax Breaks Enacted," 13-7.

56. Weisman, "Proposal Seeks."

57. Jonathan Weisman, "Tobacco Rider Adds Fire to Debate over Corporate Tax Bill," *Washington Post,* October 6, 2004, A4; "Conferees Agree on Corporate Tax Bill," *Washington Post,* October 7, 2004, A5; "Corporate Tax Breaks Enacted," 13-8.

58. "Corporate Tax Breaks Enacted," 13-8.

59. That measure (H.R. 1779) had not been acted upon when the Senate session ended.

60. "Corporate Tax Breaks Enacted," 13-3, 13-8.

61. Jonathan Weisman, "Senate Vote on Tax Bill Cleared; La.'s Landrieu Had Sought a Tax Benefit for Reserve, Guard Employers," *Washington Post,* October 11, 2004, A7.

62. Weisman, "Conferees Agree."

63. Dan Morgan, "House Passes Corporate Tax Bill," *Washington Post,* October 8, 2004, A5.

64. Weisman, "Senate Vote."

65. Paul Blustein, "E.U. Set to Lift Sanctions for Now," *Washington Post,* October 25, 2004, A11.

66. Warren Giles, "WTO Says U.S. Still Violates Export Subsidy Ruling," *Washington Post,* July 23, 2005, A18.

67. European Union news release, "FSC: WTO Condemns U.S. Subsidies to Exporters; Recipient of Illegal Support Include Boeing," No. 79/05, September 30, 2005, www.eurunion.org/News/press/2005/2005079.htm.

68. Australian Chamber of Commerce and Industry, Issues Paper, "Export Subsidies: A Blight on World Trade," May 2006, www.acci.asn.au/text_files/issues_papers/Trade/May%2006%20-%20Export%20Subsidies.pdf.

69. Jill Barshay, "Boeing Loses Tax Wind beneath Its Wings." *CQ Weekly Online,* May 12, 2006, 1285, http://library.cqpress.com.ezproxy.tcu.edu/cqweekly/weeklyreport109-000002177925.

70. See thomas.loc.gov, 109th Congress, for details on the Thomas bill.

71. Barshay, "Boeing Loses."

13 The Kyoto Protocol and Beyond: The Politics of Climate Change

Rodger A. Payne and Sean Payne

Before You Begin

1. What is the U.S. national interest regarding climate change? Can the United States achieve its short-term and long-term goals? How do leaders balance economic concerns against environmental issues?
2. Will the United States likely play a pivotal role in future negotiations about climate change? Will the results of the 2008 elections prove decisive?
3. Is the United States likely to reduce its greenhouse gas emissions without formal ratification of the Kyoto Protocol? What policy processes might lead to a reduction in emissions?
4. What are the competing interests in the climate change debate? Which organizations, coalitions, and leaders most influence climate change policy in the United States?
5. What role do cities and states play in shaping American policy on climate change? Can they regulate changes that the federal government will not pursue?
6. To the extent that American opposition to the Kyoto Protocol has been rooted in domestic politics, what are the prospects for future U.S. compliance given recent shifts in public and business perspectives?

Introduction: The U.S. Stands Alone on Kyoto

The scientific evidence linking carbon dioxide and other so-called greenhouse gases to global warming is now viewed as overwhelming. That was made abundantly clear as recently as February 2007, when the 2,500 scientists from over 130 countries who make up the Intergovernmental Panel on Climate Change (IPCC) released a very troubling "Summary for Policymakers." The panel's fourth assessment report found that the data about global temperature increases are "unequivocal." Moreover, the IPCC declared that "most of the observed increase in globally averaged temperatures since the mid-20th century is *very likely*"—defined as greater than 90 percent likely—"due to the observed increase in anthropogenic greenhouse gas concentrations." The report specifically finds that human fossil fuel consumption and "land-use change," caused by deforestation, for example, are primarily responsible for an "atmospheric concentration of carbon dioxide in 2005 [that] exceeds by far the natural range over the last 650,000 years."[1]

Unsurprisingly, global climate change is now recognized as a very high political priority item on the international agenda. Sir David King, Britain's top scientific adviser has written, for instance, that "climate change is the most severe problem that we are facing today—more serious even than the threat of terrorism."[2] Numerous countries are now debating the most effective and affordable means of heading off disastrous consequences. It is generally agreed that the problem simply must be addressed collectively, since neither the causes nor consequences of climate change can be isolated even to a small set of nation-states.

The first major step was taken in February 2005, when the Kyoto Protocol to the Framework Convention on Climate Change went into effect after ratification by 168 countries and the European Union (EU). The agreement is the initial international treaty to require meaningful reductions in greenhouse gas emissions. Parties to that agreement are committed to reducing emissions by 5.2 percent by 2012 and will be trying to negotiate much deeper future reductions. In March 2007, the twenty-seven nations of the EU agreed to cut their carbon dioxide emissions 20 percent by 2020.[3]

The Kyoto agreement was reached in 1997, but the presidential administration of Bill Clinton never forwarded it to the Senate for ratification. At that time, U.S. negotiators aggressively and openly sought some significant changes to the agreement. George W. Bush's administration, however, considers the Kyoto Protocol "fatally flawed" and refuses to partake in the ongoing talks.[4] Because the United States emits nearly one-fourth of the pollutants that contribute to global warming, it is nearly impossible to imagine an international treaty that can successfully address this worldwide problem without U.S. endorsement and cooperation.[5]

Domestic and international politics in large part explain President Clinton's reluctance to embrace the Kyoto Protocol and President Bush's decision to repudiate the international political process throughout his presidency.

Background: The Emergence of the Global Warming Issue

In 1827 French scientist Jean-Baptiste Fourier recognized that Earth's atmosphere traps significant amounts of the sun's heat in much the same way that

The Kyoto Protocol

1896 Swedish scientist Svante Arrhenius publishes "On the Influence of Carbonic Acid in the Air upon the Temperature of the Ground."

1957 American oceanographer Roger Revelle warns that humans are conducting a "large-scale geophysical experiment" on the planet by emitting substantial quantities of greenhouse gases.

October 1985 The findings of the first major international conference on global warming, held at Villach, Austria, warn, "As a result of the increasing concentrations of greenhouse gases, it is now believed that in the first half of the next century a rise of global mean temperature could occur which is greater than any in man's history."

June 1988 NASA's James E. Hansen testifies before Congress that "the greenhouse effect is here and affecting our climate now."

November 1988 The first meeting is held of the Intergovernmental Panel on Climate Change, an interdisciplinary group of scientists, scholars, policymakers, and diplomats that regularly issues reports about climate change science, the effects of those changes, and possible means of mitigating the consequences of global warming.

May 12, 1989 President George Bush announces U.S. support for climate change negotiations.

June 1992 The United Nations Framework Convention on Climate Change (FCCC) is presented to the "Earth Summit" at Rio de Janeiro, Brazil. The treaty does not require states to make binding commitments to reduce greenhouse gas emissions.

October 1992 The United States becomes the first industrialized nation to ratify the FCCC.

March 21, 1994 The FCCC becomes international law three months after the fiftieth ratification.

July 5, 1997 The U.S. Senate passes the Byrd-Hagel Resolution (95–0) opposing U.S. acceptance of any climate change commitment that excludes the developing world or would seriously hurt the U.S. economy

December 11, 1997 More than 150 nations, including the United States, agree to the Kyoto Protocol to the FCCC. The agreement commits industrialized nations to an average 5 percent reduction in greenhouse gas emissions, using 1990 levels as the base.

November 12, 1998 President Bill Clinton signs the Kyoto Protocol.

continued on the next page

continued from the previous page

March 2001 Bush administration officials declare the Kyoto Protocol "dead" and announce U.S. withdrawal from international negotiations.

February 14, 2002 The Bush administration announces the voluntary Climate Leaders program to reduce greenhouse gas "emissions intensity" by 18 percent over the coming decade. By this measure, total greenhouse gas emissions would increase 12 percent.

June 2002 The European Union and Japan ratify the Kyoto Protocol. Canada joins them six months later.

July 2002 California becomes the first U.S. state to restrict greenhouse gas emissions from motor vehicles.

February 12, 2003 The Bush administration announces its voluntary Climate VISION program under the auspices of the Energy Department. The program is aimed at encouraging public-private cooperation to develop technological innovations.

October 31, 2003 By a 55–43 vote, the U.S. Senate rejects climate change legislation sponsored by Sens. John McCain, R-Ariz., and Joseph Lieberman, D-Conn.

November 2004 Russia ratifies the Kyoto Protocol.

February 2005 Kyoto Protocol goes into effect.

August 2005 Hurricane Katrina devastates New Orleans and the Gulf coast.

December 20, 2005 New York and six other states sign a Memorandum of Understanding outlining a Regional Greenhouse Gas Initiative to reduce greenhouse gas emissions in the northeastern U.S.

August 2006 California becomes the first U.S. state to require industry to lower greenhouse gas emissions. The state commits to 25 percent cuts in current levels by 2020.

January 2007 President Bush declares global warming a "serious challenge" in his State of the Union address. An industry-backed coalition, the United States Climate Action Partnership, releases a report calling for mandatory reductions in greenhouse gas emissions.

February 2007 California and four neighboring states form the Western Regional Climate Action Initiative to reduce greenhouse gas emissions.

April 2007 U.S. Supreme Court rules that carbon dioxide and other greenhouse gases are pollutants, the EPA has the authority to regulate them, and the states have the right to sue the EPA to force such decisions.

glass panels trap heat in a greenhouse. It is now well-established science that carbon dioxide (CO_2), methane, nitrous oxide, and especially water vapor create a greenhouse effect, which modulates the planet's climate. Without this atmosphere, Earth would be cooler by at least 60 degrees Fahrenheit, and life as it is known today would not exist. In the 1890s, however, Swedish scientist Svante Arrhenius and American P.C. Chamberlain identified a potential problem: the buildup of carbon dioxide in the atmosphere because of the burning of fossil fuels. Since the beginning of the Industrial Revolution, the combustion of coal, oil, and natural gas and other human activities have increased carbon dioxide concentrations in Earth's atmosphere by about 35 percent. Over the same period, nitrous oxide and methane concentrations have increased 15 percent and 140 percent, respectively, also as a result of human behavior. In 1957 oceanographer Roger Revelle noted, "Human beings are now carrying out a large-scale geophysical experiment of a kind that could not have happened in the past nor be reproduced in the future."[6]

Half a century has passed since Revelle made his observation, and the scientific community now believes that it has a solid understanding of the results of this grand experiment in atmospheric science. By the mid-1980s, scientists had reached consensus regarding the phenomenon now commonly known as global warming. They arrived at their conclusion after decades of research and over the course of a number of global conferences. The cumulative result of the research is genuinely impressive, as the latest IPCC assessment notes "a *very high confidence* that the globally averaged net effect of human activities since 1750 has been one of warming."[7]

Scientists expect global warming to become even more apparent and pronounced through the twenty-first century. As economies and population grow worldwide, energy consumption (and thus the burning of fossil fuels) increases. By the year 2100, carbon dioxide concentrations in the atmosphere are expected to be at least double the levels present at the beginning of the Industrial Revolution, in the late 1700s. If population and economic growth rates reach high-end expectations, current models estimate carbon dioxide concentrations up to 250 percent greater than they were in the preindustrial age.

Although no one can be certain of the effects of these changes, many scientists have long warned of the polar ice caps melting at rapid rates, ocean currents changing dramatically, and precipitation and storm patterns shifting significantly. The consequences of these changes could include severe flooding of low-lying coastal areas, disruption of worldwide agricultural patterns, emergence of new and threatening disease patterns, creation of hundreds of thousands (if not millions) of "environmental refugees," and great damage to the planet's biological diversity. In other words, the effects of global warming are likely to be numerous, adverse, costly, and potentially severe.[8]

International Negotiations

The ten warmest years of the twentieth century occurred during its last fifteen years. Eleven of the twelve years between 1995 and 2006 rank among the dozen warmest years recorded since 1850. Thus, with ever-increasing urgency, many national governments behave as if global warming is an extremely serious ecological threat to the planet.

In 1988, global warming emerged as a major issue in many countries, including the United States: Temperatures were much warmer than normal, North America experienced major drought, and forest fires raged through Yellowstone National Park. On June 23, 1988, James E. Hansen, director of the National Aeronautics and Space Administration's (NASA) Goddard Institute of Space Studies, made headlines in the United States when he declared to the Senate Committee on Energy and Natural Resources, "The greenhouse effect is here and affecting our climate now."[9] Many scientists were publicly critical of that comment, arguing that the assertion was not clearly supported by the available evidence. Nonetheless, after Hansen's testimony, "media coverage of global warming ignited."[10] Many political figures in the United States and around the world soon began recommending that nations pay more attention to the problem. Prime Minister Margaret Thatcher of the United Kingdom, for example, worried that human activity was "creating a global heat trap which could lead to climatic instability."[11]

In late June 1988, Canada sponsored the Toronto Conference on the Changing Atmosphere, which was attended by more than one hundred government officials and two hundred other scientists, environmentalists, and industry representatives from forty-six countries; among those attending were the prime ministers of Canada and Norway. Through the meeting, scientists and policymakers established important relationships, as its organizers intended. Later that year, the United Nations Environment Program (UNEP) and the World Meteorological Organization, following the wishes of many governments—and with the strong support of the United States—created the Intergovernmental Panel on Climate Change. Holding its first meeting in November 1988, the IPCC engaged nearly two hundred top-notch scientists in assessing global warming by creating working groups on science (chaired by the United Kingdom), impacts (chaired by the Soviet Union), and response strategies (chaired by the United States). In addition to the impressive pool of atmospheric scientists, hundreds of economists, diplomats, and public servants also ultimately participated in these IPCC working groups.

Momentum for international action continued to build. In March 1989, France, Norway, and the Netherlands cosponsored a meeting on global environmental issues that was attended by representatives from two dozen countries, including seventeen heads of state. That month, twenty-two nations, including Canada, France, Italy, and Japan, called for the negotiation of a climate change convention; on May 12, 1989, during the first months of George Bush's presidency, the U.S. announced its support for such negotiations. In July, the leaders of the Group of Seven (G-7) industrialized countries (Canada, France, Germany, Italy, Japan, the United Kingdom, and the United States) met in Paris, and for the first time they directed major attention to environmental issues—some observers called it the "environmental summit." The resulting G-7 declaration "strongly advocate[d] common efforts to limit emission of carbon dioxide and other greenhouse gases."[12]

The IPCC working groups reported their initial findings to the UN General Assembly and the Second World Climate Conference in fall 1990 at Geneva. These first reports reflected a scientific consensus that the greenhouse effect was real and was being exacerbated by human activity. This paid immediate policy dividends: On December 21, 1990, the General Assembly adopted Resolution 45/212 establishing the Intergovernmental Negotiating Committee (INC) to serve under its auspices and coordinate bargaining among nations.

Many observers believed that international negotiators intended to model a climate change treaty on the Montreal Protocol. During the 1980s, a series of negotiations led to an agreement to address the environmental problems associated with a class of man-made chemicals known as chlorofluorocarbons (CFCs), which were thinning the ozone layer in the atmosphere. Under the 1987 Montreal Protocol, a baseline emissions year was established, and then production and use of CFCs were first reduced in relation to this base year and then ultimately banned. Following the precedent set by the Montreal Protocol's CFC reductions, the 1988 Toronto Conference statement recommended that global carbon dioxide emissions be reduced by 20 percent from 1988 levels by the year 2005.[13] In 1990, Prime Minister Thatcher promised that the United Kingdom had "set itself the demanding target of bringing carbon dioxide emissions back to this year's level by the year 2005."[14] Similarly, "a large majority of the industrialized states represented at the conference" meeting in Bergen,

Norway, in May 1990 "agreed that they would stabilize the emission of CO_2 and other important greenhouse gases at 1990 levels by the year 2000."[15]

Knowledgeable onlookers realized that despite such commitments, it would be very difficult to duplicate the success of the Montreal Protocol.[16] The stage for that agreement was set in 1985, when a British Antarctic Survey report made worldwide news by establishing the existence of a dramatic "hole" in the ozone layer.[17] The news media helped build public awareness and concern by describing the many potential dangers of the exposure to ultraviolet radiation resulting from ozone depletion. The agreed cause of the ozone hole was CFC emissions. By the mid-1980s, those chemicals were used primarily in the manufacture of foam insulation (about 25 percent of all CFC uses), as aerosol propellants (another 33 percent), as refrigerants (25 percent), and as cleansers in the electronics industry (16 percent).[18] These uses were not centrally important to the global economy; a small number of countries produced and consumed the overwhelming majority of the chemicals, and only about twenty companies manufactured billions of dollars worth of CFCs. Developing countries produced just 4 percent of CFCs—and China and India together consumed only about 2 percent of the world total. The U.S. Environmental Protection Agency (EPA) had already banned nonessential CFC use in 1978, and in 1986 U.S. industry leader DuPont announced that it could likely develop and market substitutes for CFCs within a decade. The United States even assumed an international leadership role in the negotiations. In all, this was a welcoming context in which to negotiate an agreement.

The economic and political situation facing the INC participants in the 1990s was dramatically different, and negotiators were aware of the substantial barriers to international cooperation on the issue of global warming. Despite evidence backed by a fairly strong scientific consensus, the United States continued to contest the need to act upon what it considered uncertain information. Scientists willing to challenge the assembled evidence pointing toward global warming quickly assumed prominent positions in the public debate. Additional resistance stemmed from the consumption of fossil fuels by virtually every nation and the expense and difficulty of adopting substitutes. Coal and petroleum use was and remains integral to the economic livelihood of dozens of countries. Fossil fuels provide power for electricity generation, heating, nearly all automobiles, and a substantial proportion of worldwide industrial activity. Politically potent business interests in these areas have strong stakes in the status quo, as do national producers of fossil fuels, such as the members of the Organization of Petroleum Exporting Countries (OPEC).[19]

Despite these challenges, during the 1990s negotiators worked toward a meaningful climate change treaty after the General Assembly created the INC. From February 1991 through May 1992, the INC met five times to draft a Framework Convention on Climate Change (FCCC) in advance of the UN Conference on Environment and Development, which was held in June 1992 at Rio de Janeiro, Brazil. Because INC negotiators knew that the Earth Summit, as the gathering is popularly known, was symbolically important, they effectively operated under a deadline and made rapid progress in the sessions leading up to the June conference. During the negotiations, however, the United States refused to agree to make the targeted emission reductions and timetable legally binding; therefore, the FCCC did not include provisions requiring nations to reduce emissions of greenhouse gases. As the world leader in emissions, the U.S. could effectively block such requirements by threatening not to go along with the treaty.

In the final FCCC agreement presented at the Rio conference, the industrialized nations (listed in a document designated "Annex I") agreed merely to "aim" to return their greenhouse gas emissions to 1990 levels by the year 2000. The Annex I countries were also charged with developing national policies to mitigate greenhouse gas emissions, although they were allowed the option of "joint implementation." In practice, this meant they could obtain credit for emissions reductions by helping other nations, potentially including those in the developing world, reduce their emissions. The convention also created transparency measures requiring countries to provide to the FCCC secretariat inventories of greenhouse emissions and reports on their development of national emission reduction plans. Poor countries had attempted to secure pledges of increased development assistance to help them acquire the means to reduce their emissions, but the agreement did not include a provision for such aid. Yet the world's richest nations were required "to provide new and additional financial resources to meet the agreed full cost" for developing countries to meet their transparency requirements. At the Earth Summit, the Global Environment Facility was named as the interim agency to pool and distribute these financial resources for the FCCC. In 1999, after significant restructuring, the Global Environment Facility became the FCCC's permanent financial mechanism.

More than 150 states signed the treaty in Rio. The United States was the first industrialized nation to ratify the convention, which entered into force on March 21, 1994, three months after the fiftieth ratification. As of March 2007, 190 countries had ratified the agreement. The FCCC established a Conference of the Parties (COP), composed of all member states, which met formally on a number of occasions in the mid-1990s to discuss the key unresolved issues. At the spring 1995 COP-1 meeting in Berlin, the Alliance of Small Island States (AOSIS) pressed mightily for a protocol that would require emission reductions. AOSIS leaders had strong interests in global warming issues because their nations are vulnerable to future increases in sea level caused by melting polar ice caps. No agreement on emissions reductions emerged from COP-1, however, as very few states were prepared to make a commitment. In December 1995, the Intergovernmental Panel on Climate Change released its Second Assessment Report, which bolstered the arguments of countries seeking firm reduction requirements in the FCCC.[20] Nonetheless, the 1996 COP-2 meeting in Geneva also failed to reach an agreement on this issue. The Clinton administration, however, made an important concession by agreeing to commit the United States to legally binding reductions on greenhouse gas emissions; the precise figures had yet to be negotiated.

The December 1997 COP-3 meeting in Kyoto, Japan, yielded the first legally binding commitments by countries to reduce greenhouse gas emissions. Under the Kyoto Protocol to the FCCC, countries were assigned varying reduction goals, and the timetable for reaching the goals was expressed as an average over the five years from 2008 to 2012. The United States agreed to a target of a 7 percent reduction in greenhouse gas emissions from the 1990 base year. The actual U.S. obligation to reduce emissions was mitigated significantly by the acceptance of its plan to credit countries for the successful management of so-called carbon sinks (mainly forested areas that absorb carbon dioxide) by employing environmentally friendly land-use techniques and innovative forestry practices. The major negotiating parties remained deeply divided about many proposed provisions, and as a result the Kyoto Protocol actually reflected only limited agreement. To their credit, the states overcame most divisions about the specific emissions reductions that would be required and the various gases that the treaty would cover.

The Kyoto deal did not, however, successfully resolve two key U.S. concerns, which were influenced as much by domestic as by international political factors. First, the agreement did not address the U.S. demand that developing countries be required to reduce greenhouse gas emissions. The United States worried that developed states might make significant and costly reductions but see their efforts diluted by states such as China and India substantially increasing their fossil fuel consumption and greenhouse gas emissions.[21] Poorer countries argued that they should be exempted from making reductions: they had not contributed much to the atmospheric changes that dated back to the start of the Industrial Revolution, and they expelled only a small fraction of the emissions of wealthier countries on a per capita basis.[22] Many nongovernmental organizations agreed that it was unjust for wealthy countries to demand reductions in the use of fossil fuels by the world's most impoverished inhabitants.

Second, the United States strongly favored market-friendly emissions trading and joint implementation plans. Economists often argue that such approaches reduce the costs of pollution abatement because they encourage greater efficiency as compared with regulatory approaches. Most American businesses vulnerable to environmental regulation prefer market-based mechanisms, such as "cap-and-trade" approaches, which typically allow businesses to buy and sell pollution permits in order to meet local, regional, or national caps on pollution. However, influential environmental groups, such as Friends of the Earth, argue against global adoption of such mechanisms. These groups fear that industrialized states will refuse to make any technological or resource-use changes if they have the option of "joint implementation." Polluters from advanced countries might merely build new factories in nonindustrial nations to offset their treaty obligations.[23] In the end, the resolution of this particular dispute was deferred until future COP negotiations.

Domestic politics influenced U.S. positions on these points. Congress seemed determined not to allow the Clinton administration to commit the United States to any real emissions reductions. On July 25, 1997, the Senate voted 95–0 in support of S.Res. 98, cosponsored by Democrat Robert Byrd, from coal-rich West Virginia, and newcomer Chuck Hagel, R-Neb. The nonbinding resolution indicated the sense of the Senate that the United States should not sign any protocol that would "result in serious harm to the economy" or that would "mandate new commitments to limit or reduce greenhouse gas emissions for the Annex I Parties, unless the protocol or other agreement also mandates new specific scheduled commitments to limit or reduce greenhouse gas emissions for Developing Country Parties within the same compliance period."[24] The resolution also required that any future protocol or other agreement forwarded to the Senate for approval be accompanied by a detailed explanation of regulatory or other legal action that would be needed for implementation, as well as a detailed financial analysis of the costs to the U.S. economy.

The Clinton administration signed the Kyoto accord on November 12, 1998, but pointed to the Byrd-Hagel resolution and indicated that it would not submit the agreement to the Senate for its "advice and consent" until the United States negotiated commitments to reduce the greenhouse gas emissions of developing countries not yet covered by the treaty obligations. This delay was significant; for the Kyoto Protocol to become binding, it had to be ratified by at least fifty-five countries "which accounted in total for at least 55 per cent of the total carbon dioxide emissions for 1990 of the Parties included in Annex I."[25]

While countries debated whether to ratify the Kyoto Protocol, they continued to meet to address unresolved issues. In several successive COP meetings through the late 1990s, representatives from the United States and other countries engaged in ongoing talks about enforcement of the Kyoto-mandated emissions reductions, emissions trading proposals, and possible credits for greenhouse gas "sinks." In the various meetings, the United States continued to argue for both joint implementation and developing-country participation. The parties were apparently close to a deal concerning implementation questions at the November 2000 COP-6 meeting at The Hague, but the negotiations collapsed over the issue of carbon "sinks" and "reservoirs." The United States, Canada, and Japan wanted generous credits for various land uses and forestry practices, whereas the European Union nations wanted to limit such credits.[26] The meeting was widely viewed as a failure, and environmental groups largely blamed the United States, which some argued was trying to gain climate protection credits for ordinary agricultural practices.

Thus, as the Clinton presidency ended, many environmentalists hoped that a new administration would be able both to convince the next Senate to ratify the Kyoto Protocol and to negotiate a follow-on compliance and implementation agreement with the rest of the world.

Bush Takes the Helm

Republican George W. Bush, the governor of Texas, entered the White House in 2001 after narrowly defeating Vice President Al Gore in a drawn-out and contentious political process. Sierra Club Executive Director Carl Pope had hailed Gore as "the strongest environmentalist"[27] ever nominated for the nation's highest office—and Gore was a strong supporter of the Kyoto Protocol. President Bush, by contrast, had worked in the oil industry before running for governor of Texas. His vice president, Dick Cheney, was the former chief executive of the giant global oil services company Halliburton, and several appointments to his cabinet, including Commerce Secretary Donald Evans and National Security Advisor Condoleezza Rice also had strong ties with the oil industry.[28] Bush opposed the Kyoto accord, claiming that it unfairly regulated industrial nations like the United States, while states like China and India were exempt.[29] Those countries would thus have a comparative trade advantage.

On the day of President Bush's inauguration, the IPCC released a new report on the scientific basis of global warming that predicted temperature increases substantially greater than prior reports had expected.[30] The next round of negotiations on Kyoto was delayed from May until July at the new president's request, so that his administration would have time to evaluate and develop U.S. climate policy.[31] Internally, there was some support in the White House for regulating carbon dioxide, but support for the Kyoto Protocol was weak. Secretary of the Treasury Paul O'Neill circulated a memo promoting a comprehensive domestic approach to global warming, but he thought the treaty was poorly negotiated.[32] The new Environmental Protection Agency (EPA) administrator, Christine Todd Whitman, appeared on CNN advocating a new regulatory approach, which would include CO_2, and by March reports were emerging on the possibility that the administration might announce a plan to regulate greenhouse gas emissions from power plants.

However, the prospect of a new regulatory scheme met strong opposition from conservatives who were skeptical about climate science and from industry groups that opposed the creation of new environmental standards. Faced with the risk of alienating Republican support in an evenly divided Senate, the White House simply removed the regulatory proposal from the agenda.[33] Furthermore, the president announced in a letter to key Republican senators, "I do not believe . . . that the government should impose on power plants mandatory emissions reductions for carbon dioxide, which is not a 'pollutant' under the Clean Air Act."[34]

Two weeks after abandoning the domestic plan to regulate carbon dioxide, EPA Administrator Whitman announced that the United States considered the Kyoto Protocol "dead." She told reporters that the U.S. had "no interest in implementing that treaty."[35] Environmentalists were quite displeased with that decision. The head of the National Environmental Trust, for instance, said that the U.S. was sacrificing credibility with its allies and that "declaring the Kyoto negotiations dead rather than proposing changes which would make it acceptable will delay action on global warming for years and years."[36]

The International Community Moves Forward

With the U.S. withdrawal from the climate negotiations, the European Union grabbed the leadership mantle in hopes of ensuring the Kyoto Protocol's implementation. Early in June 2001, EU environment ministers unanimously passed a resolution affirming their countries' intent to ratify the treaty, and they began to court Russia and Japan in an effort to put the treaty into practice without the United States. At the July 2001 COP-6 meetings at Bonn, the strategy seemed to work, as the EU was able to bring the parties together on a compromise over implementation rules. Tough negotiations led to new standards describing how industrial states would limit greenhouse gas emissions, and a last-minute decision by Japanese Prime Minister Junichiro Koizumi saved the treaty. To reach a deal, the Europeans acceded to the Japanese position on carbon-trapping "sinks" and compromised on a Russian desire for emissions trading. Although these developments would have pleased Clinton-era negotiators, the Bush administration still worried that binding reduction targets would harm the U.S. economy. U.S. officials reiterated complaints that the treaty did not go far enough to require action by developing countries, such as China and India.[37] Paula Dobriansky, under secretary of state for global affairs, was booed when she claimed that the United States was committed to action on climate change.[38]

Europe's ability to move forward and isolate the United States on this issue was viewed by many observers as a significant diplomatic setback for the administration. Jennifer Morgan of the World Wildlife Fund Climate Change Campaign, for example, called the breakthrough agreement to implement the Kyoto Protocol a "geopolitical earthquake."[39] Some delegates to the Bonn meeting voiced their belief that the rest of the world could get along perfectly well without U.S. participation in the negotiation process. John Gummer, a conservative member of the British Parliament, said that "the rest of the world doesn't need the U.S. in quite the same way" that it did during the cold war. Gummer further noted that "countries enjoy a greater freedom of action, and the growth of power in the EU extends that."[40]

The European Union nations collectively ratified the Kyoto Protocol in May 2002. Japan and Canada followed in June and December 2002, respectively. After a lengthy bargaining period, President Vladimir Putin was able to extract Europe's backing for Russian accession to the World Trade Organization in exchange for his commitment to ratify Kyoto.[41] This meant that the agreement had a sufficient number of industrial states, and the treaty became binding on parties in February 2005. Meanwhile, later that same year, the United States partnered with Australia, China, and India to form the Asia-Pacific Partnership on Clean Development and Climate. The plan emphasized voluntary measures to promote new investments and technologies but did not require emissions reductions.[42]

In sum, the international community proved capable of negotiating and ratifying a climate deal without U.S. cooperation. However, they cannot ensure American reductions in greenhouse gas emissions because the United States is not bound by the terms of Kyoto. International treaties typically apply only to those nation-states that agree to obey. Interstate relations occur in a condition of anarchy; they are not governed by anything like world government. Even though climate change potentially affects the entire globe, the planet lacks any kind of central political authority that can pass and enforce universal laws. Therefore, given the contribution of United States emissions to the earth's atmosphere, its position on this issue remains centrally important to other states.

States Take the Lead

After the Bush administration pronounced Kyoto "dead," many members of Congress pursued legislative means to limit U.S. greenhouse gas emissions. In fact, over thirty separate bills and amendments to existing laws were introduced in the Senate or House during the 107th Congress alone, between January 3, 2001, and November 22, 2002.[43] For example, the proposed Clean Power Act attempted to do what the Bush administration refused to do in March 2001—regulate carbon dioxide emissions from power plants. While the bill narrowly cleared the Senate Environment and Public Works Committee (by a 10–9 vote) in 2002, it never became law. In June 2005, by a 53–44 vote, the Senate for the first time passed a Sense of the Senate resolution urging that the United States adopt a mandatory program to limit greenhouse gas emissions. Though nonbinding, the resolution did enjoy bipartisan support.[44] Binding legislation languished in committee or failed to pass. Indeed, more than two hundred other bills, resolutions, and amendments were offered during the four years of the 108th and 109th Congresses, but the body did not produce legislation requiring reductions in U.S. greenhouse gas emissions.[45]

Absent federal action on emissions reductions and global warming, many states and local governments have taken the lead in combating climate change, much of their action modeled after the goals and mechanisms in the Kyoto Protocol. These state, local, and regional initiatives have offered a variety of plans for action and have been widespread throughout the country. The Pew Center on Global Climate Change reports that as of March 2007, twenty-nine states had adopted climate action plans, with fourteen of those establishing statewide emissions targets.[46] On this policy issue, states have been leading the way toward a national climate change policy.

California has been at the forefront of policy to combat global warming. In July 2002, then-governor Gray Davis signed into law the first legislation in the United States to restrict greenhouse gas emissions from noncommercial vehicles.[47] The statute required that new "maximum" but "economically feasible" auto emission standards be set by 2005, so as to be incorporated into new car models sold in California by 2009.[48] "California led the nation with the introduction of the catalytic converter, unleaded gasoline, hybrid vehicles, and now we will lead on global warming," boasted Russell Long of the environmental group Bluewater Network.[49] California is in a unique position among states because it had air quality regulations predating the Clean Air Act. This means it is the only state in the nation free to establish its own tougher air standards, though other states can match California's requirements rather than those set by the federal government.[50]

Discharges from 24 million vehicles in California account for 40 percent of the state's greenhouse gas emissions. Rules issued in 2004 under the new clean cars law require a 30 percent cut in emissions of vehicles sold in the state by 2016. Industry, to say the least, is not pleased with the new regulations.[51] "The California legislation would hurt the most the people that rely on large cars, pickups, SUVs and minivans," claimed Gloria Bergquist, a spokesperson for the Alliance of Automobile Manufacturers.[52] Nonetheless ten states, including New York, have announced plans to follow California's auto emissions rules, leading David Doniger of the Natural Resources Defense Council to comment, "That is so much of the market it should reach a tipping point. . . . It won't make sense for the automakers to build two fleets, one clean and one dirty."[53] California broadened its strategy in 2006, by filing a lawsuit against six automakers for creating a "public nuisance" through the carbon dioxide emissions of their vehicles. The state explicitly claims that the vehicles are contributing to global warming and harming public health.[54] It may be years before the case is resolved.

Building on the advances made by California's clean car law, many other states began to look for regional solutions to combat global warming. The first regional plan to gain national attention involved northeastern U.S. states and was initiated by Governor George Pataki, R-N.Y. In April 2003, Pataki invited the governors of eleven states to participate in developing a "cap-and-trade" regional program for reducing carbon dioxide emissions.[55] Eight states—Connecticut, Delaware, Maine, Massachusetts, New Hampshire, New Jersey, Rhode Island, and Vermont—joined New York in forming the Regional Greenhouse Gas Initiative (RGGI) and began negotiating a plan loosely based on the Kyoto Protocol to lower emission levels. The RGGI set up working groups in each state to develop action plans; a preliminary agreement was leaked to the *New York Times* in August 2005.[56] The plan would stabilize power plant emissions at the 2005 level from 2009 through 2015, and then lower them by 10 percent by 2019.[57] Just before the deal was to be signed, however, the governors of two participating states, Massachusetts and Rhode Island, refused to join. To explain his decision, then-governor Mitt Romney, R-Mass., a presidential candidate for

2008, specifically cited corporate and consumer concerns about costs.[58] Nonetheless, on December 20, the seven remaining states announced the agreement and released the Memorandum of Understanding signed by the governors, which outlined the overarching framework for the states' action plans.[59]

The announcement of the RGGI in spring 2003 was followed soon by several similar regional proposals on the other side of the country. The leaders of California, Oregon, and Washington announced the West Coast Governors Global Warming Initiative in September 2003 to coordinate their efforts to reduce greenhouse gases. In November 2004, the group released a report on strategies the states should pursue to reduce emissions.[60] In 2006, Arizona governor Janet Napolitano and New Mexico governor Bill Richardson signed the Southwest Climate Change Initiative to coordinate the policies of the two states. Governor Napolitano said in a press release, "In the absence of real action at the federal level, states are stepping forward to address the serious issues presented by climate change."[61]

In February 2007, the governors of the five states involved in these separate agreements joined forces to form the Western Regional Climate Action Initiative. Within six months of that date, the states intended to announce regional targets for reducing greenhouse gas emissions. The initiative limits the importation of coal-fired power from other states and will develop an implementation mechanism—such as a cap-and-trade, market-based system—within eighteen months of the deal.[62] Governor Arnold Schwarzenegger, R-Calif., lauded the agreement as showing "the power of the states to lead our nation."[63]

Jeremiah Baumann, of the Oregon State Public Interest Research Group, pointed out that the western initiative should transmit a very strong signal to industry: "With the Western states you've got a huge part of the U.S. economy . . . beginning to regulate greenhouse gases[;] that should send a message to business that national regulations are coming."[64] Though the specific targets had not yet been negotiated at the time of this writing, California's most recent initiative provides a clear indicator of what is likely to follow. In August 2006, California became the first state in the nation to require industry to lower greenhouse gas emissions. The Global Warming Solutions Act of 2006 aims to reduce emissions by 25 percent of their current levels by 2020, a reduction below even Kyoto's 1990 target levels. The law requires reductions as early as 2012. Governor Schwarzenegger explicitly acknowledged that the law aims to influence national policy, declaring that "our federal government will follow us—trust me."[65] Schwarzenegger, in fact, predicted that developing countries such as Brazil, China, India, and Mexico would follow California's lead. The bill was signed in a highly publicized ceremony in September 2006, which featured British prime minister Tony Blair in a live video message. New York Governor Pataki, who was at the celebration, agreed that the law was of national significance: "As more states take these type of actions, as more people become aware that this is right not just for the environment but also for the economy, Washington will follow."[66]

In January 2007, California's Public Utilities Commission passed new rules aimed at meeting the emissions goals. The rules ban power companies from buying energy from highly polluting sources, including out-of-state coal-fired plants. This unprecedented move directly affects power produced outside of California. Governor Schwarzenegger said of the rules, "We've made a commitment in the state to clean up our environment, and that commitment extends to what we buy from other states."[67]

The gathering momentum of action on global warming has not been limited to state-based plans. Cities and local governments have pursued policies to combat global warming as well. In February 2005, Seattle's Mayor Greg Nickels began contacting other mayors around the nation to join him in a cities-based climate agreement. After Nickels circulated a letter to more than 400 mayors, the U.S. Conference of Mayors unanimously passed an agreement on global warming. In the U.S. Mayors Climate Protection Agreement, local governments commit to work independently to meet the standards of the Kyoto Protocol, to influence their state governments to adopt climate legislation, and to promote national legislation.[68] The actual impact the agreement will have on global warming is likely to be small, but many of the signatories embraced the agreement to send a political message to Washington.[69] The initiative originally had the signatures of 132 mayors, but by February 2007 the list of signatories had grown to include 376 mayors from every state and the District of Columbia.[70] In an editorial penned for *BBC News,* Mayor Nickels celebrated the diverse approaches cities are pursuing under the agreement. "Across the country, cities are trying new approaches to reducing emissions. . . . If an idea works well, it can be quickly adopted by other cities. If it fails, others can avoid the mistake."[71]

States and cities recently had a significant victory. The legal landscape changed when the U.S. Supreme Court issued its first decision regarding carbon dioxide. The matter began in 1999 when a group of environmental scientists petitioned the EPA to regulate carbon dioxide and other greenhouse gases. The EPA rejected the petition in 2003 and questioned the relationship between automobile emissions and global climate change. The EPA's decision was upheld in 2005 by a 2–1 ruling in the U.S. Court of Appeals for the District of Columbia. California, New York, ten other states, and three cities joined the environmentalists to challenge the ruling. In April 2007, the Supreme Court ruled 5–4, in the case of *Massachusetts v. Environmental Protection Agency,* that carbon dioxide and other greenhouse gases are pollutants, that the EPA had the legal authority to regulate such emissions, and that states had the right to sue EPA over its refusal to make a decision to do so.[72]

The White House, Science, and Big Oil

It is certainly not surprising that the Bush White House, which openly proclaims its "business-friendly" views, shuns regulatory approaches to climate change. After all, businesses generally oppose regulations, and even the Clinton administration sought market-based mechanisms when negotiating the implementation of the Kyoto Protocol. However, the Bush administration has altogether avoided any kind of greenhouse gas emission standards, even ones, such as cap and trade, based on market principles. Officially, the White House encourages voluntary industry efforts, with an emphasis on the development of new technologies and achievement of greater economic efficiency.

In February 2002, for example, the administration announced a Climate Leaders program under the EPA. The plan promotes joint efforts by industry and government, encouraged by tax incentives, to develop and commercialize new technologies to increase energy efficiency. The plan aims to reduce "emissions intensity"—a measure of greenhouse gas discharges expressed as a ratio of emissions to economic output by U.S. industry—by 18 percent over the succeeding decade.[73] Environmentalists have criticized the program because the efficiency improvements nonetheless allow a 12 percent increase in total emissions during that time.[74] Corporate partners included Bethlehem Steel, CINergy Corporation, General Motors, and Miller Brewing, but participation has been spotty at best. The program has grown to include 109 partners, though only fifty-nine companies have established emission reduction goals, and merely five have met their own targets.[75]

In February 2003, the administration announced its Climate Vision program under the Energy Department, to facilitate public-private cooperation in the voluntary development of cleaner technology. The program encourages greater energy efficiency in the private sector, as well as targeted federal research and development spending that might hasten emissions reductions. Environmentalists have been very skeptical about the potential for success with merely voluntary approaches, and EPA data would appear to confirm their skepticism. U.S. greenhouse gas emissions continue to increase, as they have since 1990, at the rate of about 1 percent annually.[76] In 2006, a Government Accountability Office report requested by senators John McCain, R-Ariz., and John Kerry, D-Mass., on the Climate Leaders and Vision projects found that the administration had failed in both endeavors to ensure that participating firms both set emission reduction targets and then met their goals.[77] Senator Kerry blasted the administration about the findings, saying, "This report makes clear that letting the fox guard the henhouse is not working."[78]

Many political observers have also been very concerned that the Bush administration has intentionally tried to manipulate the public debate about the scientific evidence. For instance, consider the political hullabaloo surround the *Climate Action Report 2002,* which was prepared by the EPA and submitted to the United Nations by the State Department.[79] The report clearly says that human actions contribute to global warming and warns about some of the potentially dire consequences of climate change, but it does not call for concerted U.S. action to reduce emissions. In fact, to the great dismay of environmentalists, the report emphasizes adaptation to climate changes.[80] However, the document also angered conservative climate skeptics. The Competitive Enterprise Institute (CEI), for example, a think tank that has described global warming as a myth,[81] petitioned the EPA to cease disseminating the report. CEI argued that the report contained "fatal data flaws" and relied "upon computer models and data that upon scrutiny are demonstrably meaningless."[82] President Bush himself dismissed the report as a product of "the bureaucracy," and the administration stripped the entire global warming section from the 2002 EPA report on air pollution.[83]

Indeed, the administration seems to have responded to conservative criticisms primarily by suppressing information about the science of global warming. In June 2005, the *New York Times* reported that Philip A. Cooney, the chief of staff for the White House Council on Environmental Quality, edited the drafts of several climate reports issued in 2002 and 2003. The reports were changed in such a way as to produce doubt about the "robust" findings of climate experts.[84] Before serving in the White House, Cooney worked as a lobbyist for the American Petroleum Institute, the largest trade group representing oil companies. The administration's Climate Change Science Program officially issued the edited documents. Rick S. Piltz resigned as a senior associate in that office in March 2005 and stated that he "had not seen a situation like the one that has developed . . . politicization by the White House has fed back directly into the science program in such a way as to undermine the credibility and integrity of the program."[85]

James E. Hansen, NASA's top-notch climate scientist, charged the Bush administration with censoring science in 2006. Hansen accused the White House of pressuring officials from NASA and the National Oceanic and Atmospheric Administration (NOAA) to silence researchers and monitor their contact with journalists. The allegations were denied by NOAA officials, but NASA administrator Michael D. Griffin responded by saying he would draft an agency policy to support "scientific openness."[86] Other officials in the organization denied that political pressure had been applied. To investigate the charges, the House Oversight and Government Reform Committee, newly under Democratic control, held a public hearing in January 2007. At the hearing, the Union of Concerned Scientists (UCS) and the Government Accountability Project presented the results of a survey of 279 federal scientists. The study found that many had been subjected to political pressures to downplay the risks of global warming. Francesca Grifo, a senior scientist for the advocacy group, testified that the survey "has brought to light numerous ways in which U.S. federal climate science has been filtered, suppressed and manipulated in the last five years."[87] Rep. Henry Waxman, D-Calif., the committee chair, concluded, "It appears there may have been an orchestrated campaign to mislead the public about climate change."[88]

The Bush administration has certainly not been alone in trying to shape the domestic debate to its liking. Numerous think tanks and lobbyists funded by major oil companies have been especially aggressive in climate policy discussions. The leading British scientific academy, the Royal Society, released survey results finding that Exxon Mobil Corp., the largest company in the United States, distributed $2.9 million dollars to thirty-nine groups that the society said "misrepresented the science of climate change by outright denial of the evidence."[89] Science journalist Chris Mooney similarly reported that the oil behemoth spreads millions of dollars worth of contributions among forty groups, including some with broad policy aims, such as the American Enterprise Institute, and others with more specific agendas, like the Competitive Enterprise Institute. Mooney notes that Exxon Mobil increasingly stands alone in financing groups that challenge global warming. Such companies as British Petroleum, Ford, General Moters, Shell Oil, and Texaco have abandoned their comparable efforts.[90] Exxon Mobil's economic interests provide it with overwhelming incentive to remain "the poster child of denial."[91] According to the Union of Concerned Scientists, the end users of Exxon Mobil's products are estimated to emit more carbon dioxide than all but five countries.[92]

Exxon Mobil's policy influence also seems quite apparent. In 2001, for example, the company pressed the Bush administration to remove an outspoken chairperson from the IPCC. Dr. Robert Watson, the chief scientist for the World Bank and a world-renowned atmospheric scientist, was ousted from his key post in 2002.[93] Moreover, evidence emerged in 2005 that oil companies, particularly Exxon Mobil, may have been directly involved in forming the Bush administration's climate policies. Greenpeace released State Department briefing papers from the period 2001–2004, obtained through a Freedom of Information Act request, revealing that the Bush administration had thanked Exxon Mobil executives for its "active involvement" in shaping climate change policy and that U.S. officials sought the company's advice on acceptable policy options. One briefing note written for Under Secretary of State Dobriansky revealed that the president "rejected Kyoto in part based on input" from an industry group substantially funded by Exxon Mobil.[94]

In 2006, Exxon Mobil began to seek changes in its public image on climate change, though it seems safe to conclude that it has not altered its goals. In an interview in the *New York Times,* new chairman and CEO Rex Tillerson said, "We recognize that climate change is a serious issue. . . .We recognize that greenhouse gas emissions are one of the factors affecting climate change."[95] Yet despite that acknowledgment, Exxon continues to issue documents, such as its *2005 Corporate Citizenship Report* and the 2006 report *Tomorrow's Energy,* that cast great doubt on recent climate science. The former report says that IPCC conclusions "rely on expert judgment rather than objective, reproducible statistical methods,"[96] while the latter asserts that "gaps in the scientific basis for theoretical climate models and the interplay of natural variability make it very difficult to determine objectively the extent to which recent climate change might be the result of human actions."[97] After issuing these public expressions of doubt, Exxon Mobil announced in 2007 that it was cutting its funding to the Competitive Enterprise Institute. Spokesperson Mark Boudreaux claimed that the company's position on climate change has been "widely misunderstood and as a result of that, we have been clarifying and talking more about what our position is."[98]

The apparent zigzag can perhaps best be explained by considering the new political situation that the state initiatives have created. Vice president for public affairs Kenneth P. Cohen acknowledges that the the company finds these efforts worrisome: "One thing heavy industry cannot live with is a patchwork quilt of regulations."[99] Compared to the alternatives that have been bubbling up at the subnational level, Exxon Mobil prefers a single national policy, likely based on market mechanisms such as cap and trade.

A Tipping Point?

On August 29, 2005, an unusually intense storm, Hurricane Katrina, devastated New Orleans, Louisiana, and much of the Gulf Coast. The widespread and catastrophic destruction, combined with the obvious failures of the federal, state, and local governments to respond adequately, received massive media attention. The storm killed more than 1,500 people[100] and is estimated to have caused at least $81.2 billion in damages.[101] Shortly after the storm, researchers published data revealing a sharp increase in the incidence of severe hurricanes over the past fifteen years—and the study's author concluded that this was "probably . . . a manifestation of global warming."[102] One year after the storm, on August 31, 2006, a documentary about global warming, *An Inconvenient Truth,* was released to critical acclaim. The film, which featured a slide show about climate change that former vice president Al Gore has delivered hundreds of times, ultimately became the third-highest-grossing documentary released since 1982 and won the Academy Award for Best Documentary.[103] These developments, together with the news coverage of the latest IPCC report and a series of unusual weather events, have helped create a heightened sense of public urgency about climate change.

In political terms, momentum seems to be building for the United States to adopt a serious climate policy. In November 2006, Democrats rode the growing unpopularity of President Bush and the Iraq war to electoral victory, taking control of both the House and Senate for the first time in twelve years. Key members of the new Congress quickly placed global warming–related legislation on the agenda and held a number of public hearings, featuring testimony from Gore, scientists, and various interest groups.[104] Even President Bush, who previously raised doubts about the scientific evidence, called global climate change a "serious challenge" in his January 2007 State of the Union speech, which marked the first time he had referenced the problem in his annual agenda-setting address.[105]

Immediately, the new Congress began to consider mandatory programs to limit greenhouse gas emissions, as well as other bills related to climate change. The Democratic leadership, topped by Senate Majority Leader Harry Reid, D-Nev., and Speaker of the House Rep. Nancy Pelosi, D-Calif., publicly announced an intention to pass a climate policy before July 4, 2007. For her part, Pelosi agreed in 2006 to cosponsor climate legislation introduced by Representative Waxman that aims to reduce emissions 80 percent by 2050. Pelosi's press secretary says she will continue to support that bill.[106] However, many alternative plans were up for consideration in the new Congress. Sen. Jeff Bingaman,

D-N.M., who assumed the chair of the Senate Energy and Natural Resources Committee, described the changed atmosphere on Capitol Hill: "We have an opportunity to put an emphasis on issues of clean energy, renewable energy, global warming, climate change, in a way that wasn't possible during the last several years."[107] Bingaman introduced a cap-and-trade proposal designed to slow the growth of greenhouse gas emissions, but his bill was viewed as one of the most modest.[108]

One ambitious and widely supported bill introduced in the Senate has been cosponsored by some prominent 2008 presidential hopefuls. Sen. Barack Obama, D-Ill., joined senators John McCain, R-Ariz., and Joe Lieberman, I-Conn., to reintroduce their Climate Stewardship and Innovation Act. The legislation aims to cut greenhouse gas emissions by 2 percent per year. The October 2003 version of the McCain-Lieberman bill was the first legislation introduced in the Senate to require mandatory U.S. emission targets, to be implemented through an emissions trading plan. That bill was defeated 55–43; the 2005 proposal lost 60–38.

The latest version of the bill calls for mandatory caps for power plants, industry, and oil refiners—and requires a reduction of U.S. emissions to 2004 levels by 2012 and 1990 levels by 2020.[109] In a joint press release issued in January, Senator McCain called global warming "the preeminent environmental issue of our time" and noted that "the national security concerns related to our inaction cannot be ignored."[110] The bill was endorsed by an array of environmental interest groups, including Environmental Defense, the National Wildlife Federation, and the Pew Center on Global Climate Change. Early efforts to count potential votes indicate that some senators who previously opposed mandatory greenhouse gas emissions limits, such as Max Baucus, D-Mont., and Arlen Specter, R-Pa., could now reverse course and side with the new Democratic majority.[111] Even with these votes, however, a potentially winning margin is likely to be insufficient to overcome a minority filibuster or presidential veto.

Although it is too early as of this writing to determine whether global warming legislation will pass in the new Congress, one clear political victory has already been achieved. By winning electoral majorities, Democrats were able to assume control of an important committee previously chaired by the staunchest critic of global warming science and policy. Sen. Barbara Boxer, D-Calif., became chair of the Senate Environment and Public Works Committee, replacing Sen. James Inhofe, R-Okla., a longtime skeptic who calls global warming "a cruel hoax" and who previously blocked all climate legislation from being considered by the committee.[112] Senator Boxer, in stark contrast, considers climate change policy one of her "top priorities" and claims that there is no "greater threat to future generations than the disastrous effects of global warming."[113] Boxer wants to model federal legislation on the new California law.

Many political observers believe that the Bush White House will likely veto any climate-related legislation emerging from Congress, but some signs indicate that it too is responding to the shifting political environment. In December 2006, for example, the Department of the Interior for the first time identified climate change as harmful to a particular species—and proposed listing polar bears as "threatened" under the Endangered Species Act. Global warming is melting the Arctic ice, which is the bear's native habitat.[114] Near the same time, President Bush held private talks with British Prime Minister Blair about climate change, leading many analysts to speculate that the administration might reverse its policy course.[115] However, the 2007 State of the Union address fell far short of those expectations, as the president merely referenced climate change and proposed a modest cut in gasoline consumption. Nonetheless, given the prominence of the address, some analysts claimed that even these gestures could signal a turning point in the U.S. approach to the issue.[116]

If the administration does change its course, one major reason could be the new and dramatically more flexible view of the issue on the part of business. In the mid-1980s, the Montreal Protocol negotiations gained momentum once DuPont and other chemical companies abandoned their all-out opposition to an ozone accord and signaled their willingness to live with regulation—and to research and develop potentially profitable substitutes for CFCs.[117] In 2006, ten major corporations, including Alcoa, BP America, Caterpillar, DuPont, General Electric, and Wal-Mart, joined with environmental groups to form the United States Climate Action Partnership (USCAP). USCAP released a report in January 2007 advocating mandatory greenhouse gas reductions. The chairman of Duke Energy, Jim Rogers, said at their press conference, "It must be mandatory, so there is no doubt about our actions. . . . The science of global warming is clear. We know enough to act now. We must act now."[118]

Companies outside of USCAP are also beginning to advocate for a new national policy. As in the 1980s, industry's bottom-line concerns help explain their course reversal. In a speech at the National Press Club in 2006, the president of Shell Oil, John Hofmeister, said, "From Shell's point of view, the debate is over. When 98 percent of scientists agree, who is Shell to say, 'Let's debate the science'?"[119] Hofmeister, like Exxon executives, pointed to diverse state actions as justifying a uniform national policy.[120]

Conclusions: Climate Change Policy into the Future

While the U.S. federal government has pursued only voluntary national measures to limit greenhouse gas emissions, even as the volume of pollution increases annually, much of the rest of the world has crafted mandatory emissions controls in the form of the Kyoto Protocol. In addition to the 5 percent global reductions required by that agreement, many other nations are already moving forward on new and greater emissions limits.

It now seems possible, however, that domestic political changes could bring U.S. policies into alignment with most of the rest of the international community. Numerous state governments, including giants California and New York, have alone and together started to take meaningful steps to reduce emissions. More and more businesses have announced support for a national plan, and the new Democratic leaders in Congress have expressed their intent to pass one, likely based on cap-and-trade principles. Additionally, American public opinion seems to support some kind of formal U.S. action. Poll results reveal that the overwhelming majority (88 percent) of Americans consider global warming a threat to future generations. Nearly half (49 percent) also say that the issue is "extremely important" or "very important" to them personally. Almost 70 percent of Americans think that their government should do more to address global warming.[121]

With apparently broad public support for action, some further movement in the United States on global warming seems likely. Whether through a return to the Kyoto Protocol, legislative action in Congress, or continued state-by-state rule making, reductions in greenhouse gas emissions will remain on the U.S. political agenda. Future outcomes will hinge on the results of ongoing domestic and international political battles.

Key Actors

Barbara Boxer Senator, D-Calif., favored limits on greenhouse gas emissions modeled after California's law.

George H. W. Bush President, favored participation in the negotiation of the Framework Convention on Climate Change but refused to agree to specific emissions reductions.

George W. Bush President, rejected the Kyoto Protocol because of concerns about the cost of compliance and because it required emissions reductions from advanced countries but not from less-developed nations.

Robert Byrd Senator, D-W.Va., cosponsored S.Res. 98, which warned that the United States should not abide by a climate agreement that exempted developing countries.

Bill Clinton President, favored the Kyoto Protocol but did not forward the agreement to the Senate because he knew it would likely meet defeat.

Paula Dobriansky Under secretary of state for global affairs, represented the Bush administration at international meetings of the FCCC after the U.S. rejected the Kyoto Protocol.

Albert (Al) Gore Vice president, featured in documentary *An Inconvenient Truth;* supported national and international action to limit greenhouse gas emissions.

James E. Hanson Director, NASA's Goddard Institute for Space Studies, spoke out about the threat of global warming twenty years ago and now accuses politicians of trying to censor government scientists from participating in public debate.

Joseph Lieberman Senator, I-Conn., cosponsored legislation to impose limits on greenhouse gas emissions using a pollution trading system.

John McCain Senator, R-Ariz., was the first Republican senator to support aggressive domestic action to fight global warming; cosponsors legislation that would cap greenhouse gas emissions.

George Pataki Governor, R-N.Y., worked with governors of other northeastern states to join New York in developing a regional initiative to reduce greenhouse gas emissions.

Arnold Schwarzenegger Governor, R-Calif., negotiated deals with his state legislature and neighboring states to cut greenhouse gas emissions and develop a regional cap-and-trade plan.

Notes

1. "Contribution of Working Group I to the Fourth Assessment Report of the Intergovernmental Panel on Climate Change," *Climate Change 2007: The Physical Science Basis, Summary for Policymakers* (Geneva: Intergovernmental Panel on Climate Change, February 2007), 2, 4, and 8, www.ipcc.ch/SPM2feb07.pdf. Emphasis in the original.

2. David A. King, "Climate Change Science: Adapt, Mitigate, or Ignore?" *Science* 303, January 9, 2004, www.sciencemag.org/cgi/content/full/sci;303/5655/176.

3. BBC News, "EU Agrees on Carbon Dioxide Cuts," March 9, 2007, http://news.bbc.co.uk/1/hi/world/europe/6432829.stm.

4. White House, Office of the Press Secretary, "President Bush Discusses Global Climate Change," June 11, 2001, www.whitehouse.gov/news/releases/2001/06/20010611-2.html.

5. Energy Information Administration, U.S. Department of Energy, *Emissions of Greenhouse Gases in the United States* (Washington, D.C.: U.S. Department of Energy, November 2006), 2, ftp://ftp.eia.doe.gov/pub/oiaf/1605/cdrom/pdf/ggrpt/057305.pdf.

6. Spencer Weart, "Roger Revelle's Discovery," *Discovery of Global Warming,* American Institute of Physics, August 2003, www.aip.org/history/climate/Revelle.htm.

7. "Contribution of Working Group I," 5. The study defines this as at least a 9 out of 10 chance. Emphasis in the original.

8. See IPCC, "Working Group II, Third Assessment Report, Summary for Policymakers," *Climate Change 2001: Impacts, Adaptation and Vulnerability* (Geneva: IPCC, 2001), www.grida.no/climate/ipcc_tar/wg2/pdf/wg2TARspm.pdf.

9. Robert H. Boyle, "You're Getting Warmer," *Audubon,* November–December 1999, http://magazine.audubon.org/global.html.

10. Craig Trumbo, "Longitudinal Modeling of Public Issues: An Application of the Agenda-Setting Process to the Issue of Global Warming," *Journalism and Mass Communication Monographs* 152 (August 1995): 1–57.

11. Margaret Thatcher, "Speech to the Royal Society," Fishmongers' Hall, London, September 27, 1988, www.margaretthatcher.org/speeches/displaydocument.asp?docid=107346.

12. David Bodansky, "Prologue to the Climate Change Convention," in *Negotiating Climate Change: The Inside Story of the Rio Convention,* ed. Irving M. Mintzer and J. A. Leonard (New York: Cambridge University Press, 1994), 52.

13. Information Unit on Climate Change, UN Environment Program, "The Toronto and Ottawa Conferences and the 'Law of the Atmosphere,'" May 1, 1993, www.cs.ntu.edu.au/homepages/jmitroy/sid101/uncc/fs215.html.

14. Margaret Thatcher, "Speech at the 2nd World Climate Conference," Geneva, November 6, 1990, www.margaretthatcher.org/Speeches/displaydocument.asp?docid=108237&doctype=1.

15. Information Unit on Climate Change, UN Environment Program, "The Bergen Conference and Its Proposals for Addressing Climate Change," May 1, 1993, www.cs.ntu.edu.au/homepages/jmitroy/sid101/uncc/fs220.html.

16. See Marvis S. Soroos, *The Endangered Atmosphere: Preserving a Global Commons* (Columbia: University of South Carolina Press, 1997), chap. 6.

17. Richard Elliot Benedick, *Ozone Diplomacy: New Directions in Safeguarding the Planet* (Cambridge: Harvard University Press, 1991), 18–20.

18. Ibid., 119.

19. OPEC's eleven member countries collectively produce about 40 percent of the world's oil and hold about 75 percent of the world's proven reserves of petroleum.

20. IPCC reports are available on the organization's Web site, www.ipcc.ch.

21. The Chinese government recently released a report suggesting that China will overtake the U.S. in total emissions in 2007 or 2008. See Robert Collier, "A Warming World; China about to Pass U.S. as World's Top Generator of Greenhouse Gases," *San*

Francisco Chronicle, March 5, 2007, http://sfgate.com/cgi-bin/article.cgi?file=/c/a/2007/03/05/MNG18OFHF21.DTL&type=printable.

22. On a per capita basis, the United States emits six times as much carbon dioxide as China and twenty times as much as India. See Worldwatch Institute, "State of the World 2006: China and India Hold World in Balance," January 11, 2006, www.worldwatch.org/node/3893.

23. Peter Zollinger and Roger Dower, "Private Financing for Global Environmental Initiatives: Can the Climate Convention's 'Joint Implementation' Pave the Way?" 1996, http://pubs.wri.org/pubs_content_text.cfm?ContentID=372.

24. S.Res. 98—"Expressing the Sense of the Senate Regarding the United Nations Framework Convention on Climate Change," *Congressional Record,* June 12, 1997, S5622.

25. See Article 25 of the Kyoto Protocol, http://unfccc.int/resource/docs/convkp/kpeng.html.

26. See Hermann E. Ott, "Climate Change: An Important Foreign Policy Issue," *International Affairs* 77 (2001): 277–296.

27. *PBS Online NewsHour,* "Gore and the Environment," August 21, 2000, www.pbs.org/newshour/bb/election/july-dec00/gore_environment.html.

28. Katty Kay, "Analysis: Oil and the Bush Cabinet," *BBC News,* January 29, 2001, http://news.bbc.co.uk/2/hi/americas/1138009.stm.

29. *PBS Online NewsHour,* "The 2nd Presidential Debate," October 11, 2000, www.pbs.org/newshour/bb/election/2000debates/2ndebate5.html.

30. IPCC, "Working Group I, Third Assessment Report, Summary for Policymakers," *Climate Change 2001: The Scientific Basis,* (Geneva: IPCC, 2001), www.ipcc.ch/pub/spm22-01.pdf. The IPCC meetings in Shanghai ended on January 20.

31. CNN.com, "Plea to Delay Climate Talks," January 26, 2001, http://archives.cnn.com/2001/WORLD/europe/01/26/global.warming/index.html.

32. Paul H. O'Neill, Memorandum for the President, Department of Treasury, "Global Climate Change," February 27, 2001. See Ron Suskind, "The Bush Files: Environment, From the Book," *The Price of Loyalty* (author's Web site), http://thepriceofloyalty.ronsuskind.com/thebushfiles/archives/000051.html.

33. Douglas Jehl and Andrew C. Revkin, "Bush, in Reversal, Won't Seek Cut in Emissions of Carbon Dioxide," *New York Times,* March 14, 2001, A1.

34. George W. Bush, "Text of a Letter from the President to Senators Hagel, Helms, Craig, and Roberts," White House, Office of the Press Secretary, March 13, 2001, www.whitehouse.gov/news/releases/2001/03/20010314.html.

35. Eric Pianin, "U.S. Aims to Pull out of Warming Treaty," *Washington Post,* March 28, 2001, A1.

36. Ibid.

37. William Drozdiak, "U.S. Left out of Warming Treaty; EU-Japan Bargain Saves Kyoto Pact," *Washington Post,* July 24, 2001, A1.

38. Charles Clover, "Pollution Deal Leaves U.S. Cold," [London Daily] *Telegraph,* July 24, 2001, www.telegraph.co.uk/news/main.jhtml?xml=/news/2001/07/24/wkyot24.xml.

39. Drozdiak, "U.S. Left Out."

40. Peter Spotts, "Global Climate Treaty Moves Ahead, without U.S.," *Christian Science Monitor,* July 24, 2001.

41. Peter Baker, "Russia Backs Kyoto to Get on Path to Join WTO," *Washington Post,* May 22, 2004, A15.

42. Office of the Press Secretary, "Fact Sheet: The Asia-Pacific Partnership on Clear Development and Climate," January 11, 2006, www.whitehouse.gov/news/releases/2006/01/20060111-8.html.

43. Pew Center on Global Climate Change, "107th Congress Proposals," www.pewclimate.org/what_s_being_done/in_the_congress/107th_proposals.cfm.

44. Twelve Republicans voted for the resolution. Bill Wicker, press release, U.S. Senate Committee on Energy and Natural Resources, "Climate Momentum: In Senate, Common Sense, Good Science Trump Scare," June 23, 2005, http://energy.senate.gov/public/index.cfm?FuseAction=PressReleases.Detail&PressRelease_Id=234716.

45. Pew Center on Global Climate Change, "What's Being Done in Congress," www.pewclimate.org/what_s_being_done/in_the_congress/.

46. Pew Center on Global Climate Change, "Learning from State Action on Global Climate Change," March 2007, www.pewclimate.org/docUploads/States%20Brief%20Template%20%5FMarch%202007%5Fjgph%2Epdf.

47. BBC News, "California Gets Landmark Green Law," July 22, 2002, http://news.bbc.co.uk/2/hi/americas/2143615.stm.

48. William Booth, "Calif. Takes Lead on Auto Emissions," *Washington Post,* July 22, 2002, A1.

49. Ibid.

50. Danny Hakim, "Battle Lines Set as New York Acts to Cut Emissions," *New York Times,* November 26, 2005, A1.

51. In January 2005 a group of nine automakers and the Association of International Automobile Manufacturers sued California in federal court to block the new regulations, charging that the statute would unfairly raise costs of new vehicles and would not have a positive effect on health. See "Carmakers Sue California over Groundbreaking Clean Cars Law," Environmental Defense Fund, February 9, 2005, www.environmentaldefense.org/article.cfm?contentid=4192. The case was set for a January 30, 2007, trial date but was postponed until a related Supreme Court case, *Massachusetts v. Environmental Protection Agency,* is resolved.

52. Hakim, "Battle Lines Set."

53. Ibid.

54. Sholnn Freeman, "Calif. Sues Six Automakers over Global Warming," *Washington Post,* September 21, 2006, D2.

55. Regional Greenhouse Gas Initiative, "About RGGI," www.rggi.org/about.htm.

56. Anthony DePalma, "9 States in Plan to Cut Emissions by Power Plants," *New York Times,* August 24, 2005, A1.

57. RGGI, "Memorandum of Understanding in Brief," December 20, 2005, www.rggi.org/docs/mou_brief_12_20_05.pdf.

58. Anthony DePalma, "Greenhouse Gas Pact Is in Disarray," *New York Times,* December 16, 2005, B3.

59. RGGI, "Multi-State RGGI Agreement," www.rggi.org/agreement.htm.

60. Governor's Initiative on Global Warming, "West Coast Report on Global Warming," November 18, 2004, www.oregon.gov/ENERGY/GBLWRM/Regional_Intro.shtml.

61. Jon Goldstein, "Governors Napolitano and Richardson Launch Southwest Climate Change Initiative," Office of New Mexico Governor Bill Richardson, February 28, 2006, www.governor.state.nm.us/press.php?id=179.

62. Juliet Eilperin, "Western States Agree to Cut Greenhouse Gases," *Washington Post,* February 27, 2007, A8.

63. Timothy Gardner, "Western States United to Bypass Bush on Climate," *Reuters,* February 26, 2007, www.reuters.com/article/politicsNews/idUSN2636822120070226.

64. Ibid.

65. Adam Tanner, "Schwarzenegger Signs Landmark Greenhouse Gas Law," *Environmental News Network,* September 28, 2006, www.enn.com/today.html?id=11342.

66. Ibid.

67. Associated Press, "California Bans Purchase of 'Dirty' Power," *CBS News,* January 25, 2007, www.cbsnews.com/stories/2007/01/25/tech/main2400259.shtml.

68. Office of the Mayor, "U.S. Mayors Climate Protection Agreement," www.seattle.gov/mayor/climate/.

69. Eli Sanders, "Rebuffing Bush, 132 Mayors Embrace Kyoto Rules," *New York Times,* May 14, 2005, A9.

70. Haya El Nasser, "Mayors Unite on the 'Green' Front," *USA Today,* February 1, 2007, www.usatoday.com/news/nation/2007-01-31-greencities_x.htm.

71. Greg Nickels, "Climate of Hope: U.S. Cities Lead the Way," *BBC News,* February 15, 2007, http://news.bbc.co.uk/2/hi/science/nature/6366349.stm.

72. Robert Barnes and Juliet Eilperin, "High Court Faults EPA on Inaction on Emissions; Critics of Bush Stance on Warming Claim Victory," *Washington Post,* April 3, 2007, A1; David Savage, "Justices Take Up Climate Debate," *Los Angeles Times,* June 27, 2006, A1.

73. Climate Leaders, "About Climate Leaders," U.S. Environmental Protection Agency, www.epa.gov/stateply/aboutus.html. Using the "intensity" measure, U.S. carbon dioxide emissions per unit of gross domestic product declined by 15 percent during the 1990s. Report of the National Energy Policy Development Group, *National Energy Policy: Reliable, Affordable and Environmentally Sound Energy for America's Future* (Washington, D.C.: Government Printing Office, 2001), 3–11, www.whitehouse.gov/energy/Chapter3.pdf.

74. Pew Center on Global Climate Change, "Analysis of President Bush's Climate Change Policy," www.pewclimate.org/policy_center/analyses/response_bushpolicy.cfm.

75. Climate Leaders Program, "Climate Leaders Fact Sheet," U.S. Environmental Protection Agency, January 2007, www.epa.gov/stateply/docs/partnership_fact_sheet.pdf.

76. Environmental Protection Agency, "Executive Summary," *U.S. Greenhouse Gas Inventory Reports,* April 2006, ES-3, www.epa.gov/climatechange/emissions/downloads06/06ES.pdf.

77. Juliet Eilperin, "GAO Report Faults Voluntary Program to Cut Air Pollution," *Washington Post,* May 26, 2006, A3.

78. Ibid.

79. U.S. Department of State, *U.S. Climate Action Report,* May 2002, http://yosemite.epa.gov/oar/globalwarming.nsf/content/ResourceCenterPublicationsUSClimateActionReport.html.

80. Ibid., 82; Andrew C. Revkin, "U.S. Sees Problems in Climate Change," *New York Times,,* June 3, 2002, A1.

81. David Adam, "Royal Society Tells Exxon: Stop Funding Climate Change Denial," *The Guardian,* September 20, 2006, http://environment.guardian.co.uk/climatechange/story/0,,1876538,00.html.

82. Christopher C. Horner, "CEI's Petition against Further Dissemination of EPA's 'Climate Action Report 2002,'" Competitive Enterprise Institute, February 10, 2003, www.cei.org/utils/printer.cfm?AID=3375.

83. Jeremy Symons, "How Bush and Co. Obscure the Science," *Washington Post,* July 13, 2003, B4.

84. Andrew C. Revkin, "Bush Aide Edited Climate Reports," *New York Times,* June 8, 2005, A1.

85. Ibid.; Cooney was later hired by Exxon Mobil.

86. Juliet Eilperin, "Censorship Is Alleged at NOAA," *Washington Post,* February 11, 2006, A7.

87. Associated Press, "Panel Hears Climate 'Spin' Allegations," *ABC News,* January 30, 2007, http://abcnews.go.com/Politics/wireStory?id=2836034&page=1.

88. Ibid.

89. Adam, "Royal Society Tells Exxon."

90. Chris Mooney, "Some Like It Hot," *Mother Jones,* May/June 2005, www.motherjones.com/news/feature/2005/05/some_like_it_hot.html.

91. Steven Mufson, "Exxon Mobil Warming up to Global Climate Issue," *Washington Post,* February 10, 2007, D1.

92. Ibid.

93. BBC News, "Climate Scientist Ousted," April 19, 2002, http://news.bbc.co.uk/2/hi/science/nature/1940117.stm.

94. John Vidal, "Revealed: How Oil Giant Influenced Bush," *The Guardian,* June 8, 2005, www.guardian.co.uk/climatechange/story/0,12374,1501646,00.html.

95. Jad Mouawad, "The New Face of an Oil Giant; Exxon Mobil Style Shifts a Bit," *New York Times,* March 30, 2006, C1.

96. ExxonMobil, *2005 Corporate Citizenship Report,* 23, www.exxonmobil.com/Corporate/Files/Corporate/ccr05_fullreport.pdf.

97. ExxonMobil, *Tomorrow's Energy: A Perspective on Energy Trends, Greenhouse Gas Emissions and Future Energy Options,* February 2006, 10, www.exxonmobil.com/Corporate/Files/Corporate/tomorrows_energy.pdf.

98. MSNBC, "Exxon Cuts Ties to Global Warming Skeptics," January 12, 2007, www.msnbc.msn.com/id/16593606/.

99. Quoted in Mufson, "Exxon Mobil Warming up to Global Climate Issue."

100. Michelle Hunter, "Deaths of Evacuees Push Toll to 1,577," *New Orleans Times-Picayune,* May 19, 2006, www.nola.com/news/t-p/frontpage/index.ssf?/base/news-5/1148020620117480.xml&coll=1&thispage=1.

101. NOAA's National Weather Service, "Service Assessment: Hurricane Katrina: August 23–31, 2005," June 2005, 1, www.weather.gov/om/assessments/pdfs/Katrina.pdf.

102. Helen Briggs, BBC News, "'Warming Link' to Big Hurricanes," September 15, 2005, http://news.bbc.co.uk/2/hi/science/nature/4249138.stm.

103. Beverly Keel, "Oscars: 'An Inconvenient Truth' Wins Best Documentary," *Nashville Tennessean,* February 25, 2007, http://tennessean.com/apps/pbcs.dll/article?AID=/20070225/ENTERTAINMENT2004/70225026.

104. Edward Luce, "U.S. Lawmakers Take to Cuts in Emissions with Zeal of Converts," *Financial Times,* February 16, 2007, www.ft.com/cms/s/95f0139a-bd5e-11db-b5bd-0000779e2340,dwp_uuid=728a07a0-53bc-11db-8a2a-0000779e2340.html.

105. White House, Office of the Press Secretary, "President Bush Delivers State of the Union Address," January 23, 2007, www.whitehouse.gov/news/releases/2007/01/20070123-2.html.

106. Amanda Griscom Little, "A Capitol Idea: How Green Will the 110th Congress Be?" *Grist,* November 17, 2006, www.grist.org/news/muck/2006/11/17/boxer/.

107. Nick Miles, "U.S. Democrats Mull Climate Change," *BBC News*, December 2, 2006, http://news.bbc.co.uk/2/hi/americas/6200748.stm.

108. H. Josef Herbert, Associated Press, "Emission Caps Unlikely without Bush Help," *Kansas City Star*, March 12, 2007, www.kansascity.com/mld/kansascity/news/politics/16888962.htm.

109. Associated Press, "Congress to Reconsider Caps on Carbon," *MSNBC*, January 12, 2007, www.msnbc.msn.com/id/16593468/.

110. Joe Lieberman, "Lieberman, McCain Reintroduce Climate Stewardship and Innovation Act," January 12, 2007, http://lieberman.senate.gov/newsroom/release.cfm?id=267559.

111. Zachary Coile, "Congress Moving on Climate Change," *San Francisco Chronicle*, January 29, 2007, http://sfgate.com/cgi-bin/article.cgi?f=/c/a/2007/01/29/MNGP0NQQOQ1.DTL.

112. Robert Collier, "Dems Staking out Role in Foreign Policy," *San Francisco Chronicle*, November 10, 2006, A18.

113. Little, "A Capitol Idea."

114. Juliet Eilperin, "U.S. Wants Polar Bears Listed as Threatened," *Washington Post*, December 27, 2006, A1.

115. Gaby Hinsliff, Juliette Jowit, and Paul Harris, "Bush Set for Climate Change U-Turn," *Observer*, January 14, 2007, http://observer.guardian.co.uk/world/story/0,,1989997,00.html.

116. Peter Baker and Steven Mufson, "Bush's Climate Remarks Weighed for Policy Shift," *Washington Post*, January 27, 2007, A1.

117. Soroos, *The Endangered Atmosphere*," 159–161.

118. "Companies Spell out Warming Strategy," *MSNBC*, January 23, 2007, www.msnbc.msn.com/id/16753192/.

119. Steven Mufson and Juliet Eilperin, "Energy Firms Come to Terms with Climate Change," *Washington Post*, November 25, 2006, A1.

120. Ibid. Not all industry groups support mandatory programs, of course. The power industry's main trade association, Edison Electric Institute (EEI), has continued to lobby against mandatory programs. Brad Foss, Associated Press, "Power Execs Foresee Carbon Emission Caps," *Washington Post*, October 21, 2006, www.washingtonpost.com/wp-dyn/content/article/2006/10/21/AR2006102100345.html.

121. *Time*/ABC News/Stanford University poll, "Poll: Americans See a Climate Problem," *Time*, March 26, 2006, www.time.com/time/nation/article/0,8599,1176967,00.html.

14 The International Criminal Court: 105 Nations Join, but Not the United States

Donald W. Jackson and Ralph G. Carter

Before You Begin

1. What is the International Criminal Court (ICC), and why do many countries believe that it is needed?
2. What motivated the key American participants in the effort to shape the ICC?
3. Why was the U.S. position so contrary to positions its allies took? In the U.S. view, what was wrong with the principle of complementarity?
4. What does this case say about the U.S. commitment to the rule of law or even about moral principles in U.S. foreign policy?
5. In your view, is there merit to the position the United States has taken in this case? If so, why?
6. Are there principles of universal human rights that should be enforced wherever those principles are violated? If not, what is the implication for international law?
7. In this case, is the United States acting like an imperial power? If so, is that objectionable? If not, why not?
8. What does this case suggest about the future of international law or tribunals in the twenty-first century?

Introduction: The Rise of International Law

From 1989 to 1991, a remarkable change occurred in international politics. A process of disintegration began that led to the dissolution of the Soviet empire and ultimately of the Soviet Union itself. Some of the early beneficiaries of this change seemed to be international institutions and international law, as was illustrated by Soviet-U.S. cooperation during the 1990–1991 Persian Gulf crisis and war. With the apparent end of the cold war, the U.S.-led international coalition that drove Iraqi forces from Kuwait justified and coordinated its actions through the United Nations and the application of international law. Events in the late 1980s and early 1990s led President George H. W. Bush to declare that an increasingly democratic "new world order" had arrived, a time when "the international system would be based on international law and would rely on international organizations such as the United Nations to settle international conflicts." [1]

An illustration of this trend toward international institutions—though perhaps not of the new world order envisioned by Bush—occurred on July 17, 1998, when 120 states voted at a UN diplomatic conference in Rome to create the International Criminal Court (ICC), with powers to try perpetrators of genocide, crimes against humanity, and war crimes. Only seven states voted against creating the ICC: China, Iraq, Israel, Libya, Qatar, Yemen, and the United States. Within four years, by April 2002, more than the sixty nations needed for implementation of the court had ratified the agreement. On July 1, 2002, the Rome Statute for the International Criminal Court entered into force, despite the persistent opposition of the United States. How did the United States come to find itself on "the other side" of international law and abandoned by most of its traditional allies?

Background: The Rise of International Tribunals

International courts are not unique to the twenty-first century. The Hague Peace Conference of 1899, convened for the primary purpose of promoting peace and stability by limiting or reducing armaments, also created the Hague Convention for the Pacific Settlement of International Disputes and the Permanent Court of Arbitration.[2] With the League of Nations in 1920 came the Permanent Court of International Justice, which rendered thirty judgments and issued twenty-seven advisory opinions from 1922 to 1946.[3] After World War II, the United Nations created the International Court of Justice (or World Court), but two exceptions to this international court's jurisdiction remained: the court's decisions generally applied only to states, not individuals, and, moreover, it was possible for states, through reservations, to avoid the court's obligatory jurisdiction.[4] The idea for the International Criminal Court did not arise in a political vacuum and was not a dream of idealistic abstractions; rather, it followed a series of precedent-setting tribunals. Between 1919 and 1994, five ad hoc international commissions, four ad hoc international criminal tribunals, and three international or national prosecutions of "crimes" arising during World Wars I and II were convened. The first commission sought to prosecute German and Turkish officials and military officers for war crimes and crimes against humanity during World War I. Crimes against humanity generally consisted of the abusive or murderous treatment of civilians by military personnel. This com-

International Criminal Court

1946 The UN General Assembly passes Resolution 95, recognizing the principles contained in the 1945 London Charter as binding precedents in international law. It also passes Resolution 96(I), making genocide a crime under international law. Trials are held in Nuremberg and Tokyo of Germans and Japanese accused of crimes against peace, war crimes, and crimes against humanity. In the U.S. Senate, the Vandenberg and Connally amendments ensure congressional support for U.S. acceptance of the jurisdiction of the new International Court of Justice (or World Court).

1989 Sixteen Caribbean and Latin American nations propose a permanent international criminal court for the prosecution of narco-traffickers.

1991 The International Law Commission prepares a draft code of international crimes.

1993 The UN Security Council passes Resolution 808, providing for the establishment of the International Criminal Tribunal for the Former Yugoslavia.

1994 The UN Security Council passes Resolution 955, creating the International Criminal Tribunal for Rwanda. The International Law Commission prepares a draft statute for an international criminal court.

1995 The UN General Assembly creates the Preparatory Committee for the Establishment of an International Criminal Court.

March 26, 1998 Sen. Jesse Helms, R-N.C., sends a letter to Secretary of State Madeleine Albright vowing that any agreement that might bring a U.S. citizen under the jurisdiction of a UN criminal court would be "dead on arrival" in the Senate.

March 31–April 1, 1998 Defense Department leaders meet in Washington with military attachés of more than 100 countries to warn them of the possible jurisdiction of an international criminal court over their soldiers.

June–July 1998 At a conference in Rome, delegates discuss and then vote 120–7 to establish the International Criminal Court (ICC).

June 14, 2000 Helms introduces the American Servicemembers' Protection Act (S. 2726), which would prohibit U.S. officials from cooperating with the proposed ICC. Majority whip Tom DeLay, R-Texas, introduces the same measure in the House of Representatives (H.R. 4654).

continued on the next page

continued from the previous page

December 31, 2000 The Clinton administration signs the Rome Statute establishing the ICC, so the United States can be considered an original signatory and participate in decisions about implementation of the new tribunal.

May 6, 2002 The administration of George W. Bush formally declares that it does not intend to submit the Rome Statute to the Senate for ratification and renounces any legal obligation arising from the Clinton administration's signing of the treaty.

July 1, 2002 The Rome Statute for the International Criminal Court enters into force without the participation of the United States.

August 2, 2002 The American Servicemembers' Protection Act becomes law with the signature of Bush.

March 11, 2003 The first judges of the ICC are inaugurated, and Philippe Kirsch of Canada becomes the court's first president.

March 24, 2003 Luis Moreno Ocampo of Argentina is elected the first chief prosecutor of the ICC.

July 1, 2003 The Bush administration announces its intention to eliminate military aid to the thirty-five countries that have not signed bilateral agreements exempting U.S. citizens from being rendered to the jurisdiction of the ICC.

January 29, 2007 The ICC announces its first case for prosecution. Thomas Lubanga Dyilo of the Union of Congolese Patriots is charged with three counts of enlisting, conscripting, and using children under fifteen as combat soldiers in the Democratic Republic of Congo.

mission's efforts resulted in a few token convictions in the German supreme court.[5]

After the ineffective United Nations War Crimes Commission was created in 1942, the Allies signed the London Charter for the Prosecution and Punishment of the Major War Criminals of the European Axis, in August 1945. The principles contained in the 1945 agreement were later recognized as binding precedents in international law by UN General Assembly Resolution 95, of December 11, 1946. The London Charter created the International Military Tribunal (IMT), consisting of four judges (one from each of the four powers—France, the Soviet Union, the United Kingdom, and the United States). The jurisdiction of the IMT included the following crimes:

- crimes against peace—Article 6[a] of the London Charter: planning, preparation, initiation or waging a war of aggression or a war in violation of international treaties or agreements;
- war crimes—Article 6[b] of the London Charter, though the most definitive statement appears in the Charter of the International Military Tribunal (annexed to the London Charter): violations of the laws or customs of war, to include murder, ill-treatment, or deportation to slave labor of civilian populations in occupied territory, murder or ill-treatment of prisoners of war or persons on the seas, killing of hostages, plunder of public or private property, wanton destruction of cities, or devastation not justified by military necessity; and
- crimes against humanity—Article 6[c] of the London Charter: murder, extermination, enslavement, deportation, and other inhumane acts committed against any civilian population, or persecutions on political, racial or religious grounds in execution of or in connection with any crime within the jurisdiction of the tribunal.[6]

The IMT's role concluded with the Nuremberg trials in 1946. The tribunal found eighteen of twenty-one prominent Nazi defendants guilty; twelve of the eighteen were given the death penalty, and the other six were imprisoned for terms ranging from ten years to life.[7]

With the occupation of Japan, the International Military Tribunal for the Far East (IMTFE) was created in Tokyo in 1946. Its list of punishable crimes was essentially the same as that for the IMT in Germany.[8] The results were generally similar as well: all twenty-five defendants were found guilty; seven were executed, sixteen were given life imprisonment, and two were given shorter prison terms.[9]

The London Charter and the Nuremberg precedent were affirmed in 1946 by the UN General Assembly in Resolution 95 (I). In December 1946 the assembly unanimously adopted Resolution 96 (I), which expressly made genocide—derived from the London Charter's definition of crimes against humanity—a crime under international law. Two years later the General Assembly adopted the Convention on the Prevention and Punishment of the Crime of Genocide.[10] In the United States, the genocide convention was submitted to the Senate for ratification in 1949, but U.S. ratification (with reservations) came almost forty years later, in 1988.

Much of the substantive international criminal law as applied by the IMT at Nuremberg was expanded and codified in the Geneva Conventions of 1949.

In 1948 the UN General Assembly invited the International Law Commission to study the possibility of creating an international criminal court with jurisdiction over the crime of genocide and other crimes that might be defined by international conventions. Because of the cold war, however, it was not until 1989 that the idea of an international criminal court was again brought before the General Assembly.[11]

U.S. Concerns

The protection of U.S. sovereignty vis-à-vis international law has been a long-standing issue. In 1945 President Harry Truman had to reassure the Senate that Article 43 of the UN Charter, which obligated members to make available to the Security Council "armed forces, assistance, and facilities," would not rob Congress of its right to declare war. In 1946 it took two amendments to ensure Senate support for U.S. acceptance of the jurisdiction of the World Court. The Vandenberg amendment specified that the court's jurisdiction would not apply to "disputes arising under a multilateral treaty, unless (1) all parties to the treaty affected by the decision are also parties to the case before the court, or (2) the United States specially agrees to jurisdiction."[12] The more famous reservation was the Connally amendment, which drew the line of the World Court's obligatory jurisdiction at "disputes with regard to matters which are essentially within the domestic jurisdiction of the United States of America as determined by the United States of America."[13] In the eyes of its critics, this amendment essentially said that the United States would obey the World Court when the U.S. government happened to agree with it. In 1959 the Connally amendment was revisited, when the American Bar Association's Committee on World Peace through Law tried to repeal it. That effort died when the Senate Foreign Relations Committee voted to postpone the matter indefinitely.[14]

These were not the only instances of U.S. unwillingness to be bound by international law. For example, in 1977 the United States and Panama reached agreement on two treaties that returned sovereignty of the Panama Canal and the canal zone to Panama and guaranteed neutral operation of the waterway. In approving the treaties, however, the Senate added the DeConcini amendment, which reserved the right of the United States to intervene militarily in Panama to keep the canal open if the United States (not Panama) decided that such a step was necessary.[15] Not surprisingly, the Panamanians were outraged by this infringement on their national sovereignty, and it nearly scuttled the treaties. More recently, in 1984, when the World Court ruled that the United

States was illegally trying to overthrow the government of Nicaragua, the United States announced its rejection of the court's jurisdiction, for a period of two years, regarding any of its actions in Central America. Like most countries, the United States has continued to reject the obligatory jurisdiction of the World Court, and many states that have accepted obligatory jurisdiction have attached reservations to their acceptance.[16]

Creation of the ICC

Unlike the Nuremberg and Tokyo trials, the idea for the permanent International Criminal Court was not something that victors in a war imposed on the vanquished. Instead, the genesis of the ICC came from smaller powers in the international system. In 1989 sixteen Caribbean and Latin American nations suggested international criminal prosecutions for narco-traffickers.[17] In 1990 a committee of nongovernmental organizations, including the World Federalist Movement, prepared a draft statute for an international court and submitted it to the Eighth United Nations Congress on the Prevention of Crime and the Treatment of Offenders. In 1991 the UN International Law Commission prepared a draft code of international crimes. These events culminated in November 1994, when the commission produced its draft statute for an international criminal court.[18]

At that time, the international legal community was reacting to allegations of horrendous human rights violations in civil wars in Yugoslavia and Rwanda. In 1993 UN Security Council Resolution 808 provided for the establishment of the International Criminal Tribunal for the Former Yugoslavia, to "prosecute persons responsible for serious violations of international humanitarian law committed in the territory of the former Yugoslavia since 1991."[19] The International Criminal Tribunal for Rwanda was established by UN Security Council Resolution 955, with jurisdiction starting January 1, 1994. The mandate of the Rwanda tribunal was to prosecute genocide and crimes against humanity.[20] These tribunals were temporary, however, and dealt only with specific conflicts.

In December 1995 the UN General Assembly created a Preparatory Committee for the Establishment of an International Criminal Court. The committee, known as PrepCom, first met in March 1996. Its membership was open to all the member states of the United Nations, UN specialized agencies, and the International Atomic Energy Agency.[21] The Clinton administration had been a strong supporter of the temporary tribunals for Yugoslavia and Rwanda and had pushed the general issue of criminal prosecution for persons accused of war crimes. In 1997 it created the position of ambassador-at-large for war crimes, in the State Department, and named David Scheffer to the post, thereby making him the top U.S. representative to PrepCom. In his September 1997 address to the UN General Assembly, President Clinton endorsed the establishment of a permanent international criminal court "to prosecute the most serious violations of international humanitarian law."[22]

By April 1998, six PrepCom sessions had been held. The aim of the last meeting was to prepare for an international conference in Rome in summer 1998 to conclude a treaty that would establish the permanent court.[23] The working draft at the last PrepCom meeting was the Zutphen Text, which had been produced during a January 1998 meeting in the Netherlands. That document called for a court that would complement national criminal courts. The crimes within the proposed jurisdiction of the international court were not yet determined, but the proposals included genocide, aggression, war crimes, and crimes against humanity. The definition of these crimes varied in different proposals. The draft statute included bracketed language wherever PrepCom had been unable to reach consensus. Near the completion of the last PrepCom meeting, the 175-page draft statute contained 99 articles and about 1,700 bracketed words or provisions.[24]

The proposals included a listing of sexual offenses under war crimes, including rape, sexual slavery, enforced prostitution, enforced pregnancy, and enforced sterilization. One proposal included war crimes against children, for example, forcing children under the age of fifteen to take part in hostilities, recruiting them into the armed forces, or allowing them to take part in hostilities. Another proposed the inclusion of terrorist actions, while another would have included narco-trafficking. A further issue discussed was criminalizing the use of certain weapons likely to cause "superfluous injury or unnecessary suffering," such as expanding bullets, chemical and biological weapons, land mines, and nuclear weapons.[25]

The most difficult issues touched on in Rome involved delimiting domestic criminal jurisdiction relative to the criminal jurisdiction of the international court and the means by which cases would reach the ICC. The domestic–international jurisdictional issue involved "complementarity," which is the idea that international prosecution ought to occur only when a state fails to take responsibility for its own good faith investigation and prosecution of crimes defined by the statute. The statute provided that a case would be admissible before the ICC only when a domestic judicial system was "unwilling or unable" to conduct the proper investigation or prosecution. In addition, a U.S. proposal on complementarity required the prosecutor for the international court to notify state parties and to make a public announcement when a case had been referred. A state could then step forward and inform the prosecutor that it was taking responsibility for prosecution. In the U.S. proposal, the assertion of domestic responsibility for prosecution would delay international criminal jurisdiction for a period of six months to one year, thus giving home governments more time to try accused individuals. One of the concerns expressed before the PrepCom was the length of this delay.[26]

Other issues concerning the means by which cases might come to the court were more vexing. The draft statute provided that the ICC prosecutor would initiate an investigation only when the UN Security Council referred a case or when a state party that had accepted the jurisdiction of the ICC filed a complaint with the prosecutor. Those favoring a strong ICC wanted the prosecutor to have independent authority to investigate and file charges. At the other end of the controversy were those who, like the United States, preferred that the Security Council determine the agenda of the prosecutor and the ICC. That, of course, would give the United States and the other permanent members of the Security Council a veto over the ICC's jurisdiction. As former president Jimmy Carter noted, "Such a move rightly would be seen by many nations as a means for serving only the interests of the permanent members of the Security Council rather than as an independent arbiter of justice."[27]

The U.S. Reaction

In February 1998 Ambassador Scheffer, who was acting as chief negotiator for the United States on the creation of an international court, identified three issues involving the relationship between a court and the UN Security Council that needed to be addressed. The first was the need for the two institutions to operate compatibly, with neither undermining the legitimate pursuits of the other. The second issue involved the council's power to refer situations to the ICC, and the third was the council's role in assisting the court with the enforcement of its orders. Scheffer also made note of the unique position of the United States in the world. Either alone or in concert with its NATO allies and the United Nations, the U.S. military often "shoulders the burden of international security." As he put it, "It is in our collective interest that the personnel of our militaries and civilian commands be able to fulfill their many legitimate responsibilities without unjustified exposure to criminal legal proceedings."[28] State Department spokesman James Rubin followed up on Scheffer's view, adding, "We need to ensure that, in pursuit of justice, a permanent court does not handcuff governments that take risks to promote international peace and security and to save lives."[29]

In August 1997 Singapore had presented a compromise proposal requiring the Security Council to take an affirmative vote to delay ICC proceedings, so the United States, for example, would have to have the consent of the rest of the council to delay a case. The United Kingdom accepted Singapore's proposal, and for a while it appeared that the United States might be moving in that direction as well.[30] However, Sen. Jesse Helms, R-N.C., chairman of the Senate Committee on Foreign Relations, stopped any such momentum. In a March 26, 1998, letter to Secretary of State Madeleine Albright, he vowed that any compromise that might bring an American citizen under the jurisdiction of a UN criminal court would be "dead on arrival" in the Senate. He declared that there should be no flexibility with respect to a U.S. veto over the court's power to prosecute U.S. citizens.[31] A week later, Helms again publicly encouraged the State Department to take aggressive actions to block the establishment of the ICC.

Helms's letter and public statements were the first warning shots. On March 31 and April 1, 1998, in Washington, Defense Department leaders held meetings with military attaches of more than 100 countries. Their message was that an international criminal court could "target their own soldiers—particularly when acting as peace keepers—and subject them to frivolous or politically motivated investigations by a rogue prosecutor or an overzealous tribunal." It was by all accounts quite an unusual briefing for Pentagon officials. According to Frederick Smith, deputy assistant secretary of defense for International Security Affairs, "It was not lobbying; there was no arm-twisting—it was awareness raising."[32]

A contrasting take on the court's ability to prosecute appeared in the *Times of India.* Having read the State Department's comment that "the permanent court must not handcuff governments that take risks to promote peace and security," an Indian columnist considered the conduct of U.S. forces in the My Lai massacre in Vietnam and an alleged massacre of 1,000 civilians by U.S. Army Rangers in Mogadishu, Somalia: "Shouldn't the ICC be allowed to prosecute those involved in such crimes? . . . Or, like the Security Council, will it become a victim of double standards?"[33] Going into the 1998 Rome meeting to draft the ICC statute, about forty-two so-called like-minded countries—including Canada, most European nations, and many countries in Africa, Asia, and Latin America—favored a stronger and more independent international court and prosecutor.[34] According to the *Economist,*

> After nearly four years of intense negotiations among some 120 countries, the effort to set up the world criminal court has run smack into the ambivalence that has always been felt by the world's biggest powers about international law: they are keen to have it applied to others in the name of world order, but loath to submit to restrictions on their own sovereignty.[35]

The Rome Conference

In June 1998 representatives from 162 nations gathered in Rome to see whether they could agree on the creation of a permanent international criminal court.[36] The five-week Rome Conference opened with four days of speeches, during which U.S. ambassador to the United Nations Bill Richardson reiterated the U.S. position that the Security Council should control the work of the ICC by referring critical situations for investigation and by instructing countries to cooperate. The ultimate goal, he said, would be to create a court that "focuses on recognized atrocities of significant magnitude and thus enjoys near universal support."[37] At that time, the United States' position put it in the company of China, France, and Russia, three of the other permanent members of the Security Council; only the United Kingdom had come out in favor of a stronger and more independent court. On the other side with respect to the most critical issues, the group of like-minded countries had by then grown to about sixty members. They were especially intent on creating an independent prosecutor and a court with sufficient jurisdiction and authority to actually bring those who committed human rights crimes to account. More than 200 accredited nongovernmental organizations monitored the conference. A coalition of these organizations had been working for years in the interest of creating a permanent court. The most prominent were Amnesty International, Human Rights Watch, and the European Law Students Association.

During the conference, an enormous amount of time was spent pursuing the elusive goal of consensus among the 162 nations. In part, consensus was sought because each nation had a single vote in the conference, which meant a simple majority vote would not take into account the relative size, power, or influence of individual countries. Hours were sometimes spent on one clause of one section of one article, with delegates from country after country making statements that usually were repetitive and often only seemed to serve the purpose of giving that delegate the chance to claim a few minutes at the microphone. The U.S. delegation worked hard to persuade its traditional allies to accept U.S. conditions for the treaty, especially during the final week of the conference. Indeed, the behind-the-scenes "buzz" was that the United States was actually threatening poor states with the loss of foreign aid and its NATO allies with a reduction of U.S. military support, including the withdrawal of troops.[38]

Motivated by Senator Helms's "dead on arrival" letter, throughout the conference the "U.S. delegation seemed increasingly gripped by a single overriding concern"—that no American could be tried before the court without the consent of the U.S. government.[39] Philippe Kirsch of Canada, chairman of the Committee of the Whole of the conference, noted about the U.S. delegation,

> It was amazing. Nothing could assuage them. . . . They seemed completely fixated on that Helms/Pentagon imperative—that there be explicit language in the Treaty guaranteeing that no Americans could ever fall under the Court's sway, even if the only way to accomplish that was going to be by the U.S. not joining the treaty. . . . Clearly, they had their instructions from back home—and very little room to maneuver.[40]

Most of the world's countries, however, were more willing than the United States to be subject to the international rule of law. Even the country's most powerful European allies, who had also participated in military "humanitarian" interventions, were far friendlier to the idea of the court than was the United States. The reasons for such differences were no doubt complex, but among them was the fact that since World War II European countries had been moving from the tradition of individual sovereignty toward "European" institutions transcending nationhood. Examples of this trend were the adoption of the European Convention on Human Rights (1950)—and the subsequent empowerment of a European Court of Human Rights—and the emergence of the Court of Justice of the European Union (EU) as a powerful force.

In the last days of the Rome Conference Ambassador Scheffer issued a public plea:

> We stand on the eve of the conference's conclusion without having found a solution. We fear that governments whose citizens make up at least two-thirds of the world's population [chiefly China and the U.S.] will find the emerging text of the treaty unacceptable. The world desperately needs this mechanism for international justice, but it must be a community, not a club.[41]

The final draft document for an international criminal court was distributed early on July 17 by Chairman Kirsch. It appeared to offer more to the sixty or so like-minded countries that favored a strong court than it did to the United States. The draft provided for obligatory jurisdiction of the court upon ratification of the treaty by a country for the crime of genocide, crimes against humanity, war crimes, and the crime of aggression. The United States was willing to accept obligatory jurisdiction only for the crime of genocide. Jurisdiction over war crimes was limited by a new draft article allowing states that signed the Rome Statute to opt out of the court's jurisdiction over war crimes for a period of seven years following the creation of the court. Consistent with its objective of blocking the creation of an institution that it could not control, or whose jurisdiction it could not veto, the United States sought a comprehensive opt-out provision that would allow it to be permanently exempt from the court's jurisdiction over war crimes. France agreed to support the draft proposal when the seven-year opt-out provision was added. The United Kingdom also supported the draft.

The United States again voiced its opposition to a criminal tribunal in essence beyond its control in the Committee of the Whole on July 17, when it offered an amendment to the proposal. India offered amendments that would have made the use of nuclear weapons a war crime and that limited the power of the Security Council over the court. Norway, however, moved to table the proposed amendments, and its motions were adopted. The vote against taking up the U.S. amendment was 113–17. The United States could not even muster the support of its closest allies. In the final conference plenary session, the United States demanded a vote on the draft treaty. The Russian Federation joined France and the United Kingdom in voting for the statute, leaving China and the United States the only permanent Security Council members in opposition. Israel also voted against the draft, in part because it made the relocation of a civilian population in an occupied territory a war crime, a provision too close for its comfort. Iraq, Libya, Qatar, and Yemen also voted against.

The conference came to an end just before its scheduled deadline of midnight. The United States was clearly the big loser. The final vote was 120 countries for the treaty, 7 against, and 21 abstentions. As approved, the court would exercise its jurisdiction over individuals suspected of treaty crimes if the country where the alleged violation occurred or the country of which the accused was a national was a party to the treaty (Article 12). States would accept the jurisdiction of the court on a case-by-case basis. The United States strongly opposed these provisions because they might—as the United States had feared all along—subject American troops to prosecution for alleged crimes committed in countries that had accepted the jurisdiction of the court, without first requiring the consent of the U.S. government.

Most countries felt that there were sufficient safeguards in the treaty to address U.S. concerns. The new court would only take cases involving major human rights violations carried out as part of a plan, policy, or widespread practice, not actions by individuals acting on their own. The court would act only when the appropriate domestic jurisdictions were unable or unwilling to deal with alleged crimes themselves (the complementarity principle).

Early on, the United States had favored a proposal that would have charged the Security Council with referring cases to the court, in part so the U.S. veto in the council could be used to protect U.S. citizens from prosecution. Most countries, however, eventually supported the compromise put forth by Singapore that would allow the Security Council to defer a case for a period of twelve months, with the possibility of extension. The United States eventually accepted this proposal, a version of which was included in the final draft.

The final draft called for a prosecutor with independent power to investigate and initiate prosecutions, as well as for the initiation of cases by a state party or by referral of the Security Council. The United States had fought hard against this provision, but a strong and independent prosecutor was one of the fundamental requirements of the sixty or so like-minded countries. The draft statute did call for a court review panel that would have the power to reject cases arising from an abuse of prosecutorial power, but that safeguard was not enough to satisfy the United States.

The draft also provided for jurisdiction over internal armed conflicts, such as that in Bosnia, which most delegations, including the United States, believed to be absolutely essential for a credible international court. Further, the draft included among war crimes and crimes against humanity the crimes of rape, sexual slavery, enforced prostitution, enforced pregnancy, and enforced sterilization. Aggression was made a treaty crime, but it was left to be defined at later preparatory meetings. This decision was a concession to the members of the Non-Aligned Movement, but the draft did not include the prohibition of nuclear weapons, which the movement also strongly supported. The draft also left out chemical and biological weapons, as a concession to several Arab countries.

The Rome Statute provided that when ratified by at least sixty nations, the new International Criminal Court would enter into force, to be located at The Hague, in the Netherlands, where the ad hoc tribunal for the former Yugoslavia also is located. By April 11, 2002, sixty-six countries had ratified the treaty, and July 1, 2002, was set as the date that the agreement would enter into force.

The rift between the United States and its major European allies over the creation of the court widened and deepened following the Rome Conference and the July 2002 entry into force of the ICC. As of March 2004, ninety-two countries had ratified the Rome Statute, including Afghanistan, Argentina, Australia, Austria, Belgium, Brazil, Canada, Denmark, Finland, France, Germany, Greece, Hungary, Ireland, Italy, Luxembourg, the Netherlands, New Zealand, Nigeria, Norway, Poland, Portugal, the Republic of Korea, Romania, Serbia and Montenegro, Slovakia, Slovenia, South Africa, Spain, Sweden, Switzerland, and the United Kingdom.[42]

Although Europeans, like the Americans, put their troops in harm's way as peacekeepers in global hot spots, the general consensus among Europeans seems to be that the principle of complementarity protects them from unwanted or unwarranted international prosecution. U.S. government officials have been unwilling to put their trust in this principle. Thus the ICC has been added to a growing list of issues on which the United States and its European friends significantly disagree, among them U.S. dominance of NATO, the sizes and roles of tariffs and trade subsidies, U.S. exports to Europe, capital punishment in the United States, and U.S. withdrawal from the 1972 Anti-Ballistic Missile Treaty so the United States can develop a national missile defense system. Among the most recent differences of opinion have been the efforts of European Union (EU) members to create a rapid-reaction military force independent of NATO and the opposition (led by France and Germany) to the U.S.-led war against Iraq. The latter had the added effect of creating divisions among EU governments and in some cases splits between official government positions for war and the will of the citizenry, as popular majorities across most of Europe opposed an attack.

Many of the institutional details of the ICC were not finalized at the Rome Conference. Follow-up PrepCom sessions in 2000 sought to complete the rules of evidence and procedure and the specifications for the elements of crimes recognized in principle by the Rome Statute. The United States had to sign the statute by December 31, 2000—the last day for nations to become signatories of the original treaty—in order to participate in future PrepCom meetings. On the last day of 2000, President Clinton instructed Ambassador Scheffer to sign the treaty on behalf of the United States. In a press release, Clinton noted that he still had concerns about "significant flaws" in the treaty, but he hoped that they could be overcome in subsequent negotiations before the court became a reality. He said it was important for the United States to sign the treaty to "reaffirm our strong support for international accountability. . . . With signature, we will be in a position to influence the evolution of the court. Without signature, we will not."[43]

Reaction to the U.S. signature was swift. Human rights groups praised it. Richard Dicker, associate counsel of Human Rights Watch, said Clinton's action had "offered the hope of justice to millions and millions of people around the world by signaling United States' support for the most important international court since the Nuremberg tribunal." On the other hand, Senator Helms warned that the president's "decision will not stand."[44] The incoming administration of George W. Bush also opposed the signature. In a May 6, 2002, letter from U.S. Under Secretary of State John Bolton to UN Secretary General Kofi Annan, the Bush administration formally declared that it would not submit the Rome Statute for Senate ratification and renounced any legal obligations arising from the previous administration's signing of the treaty.[45]

The ICC at the Turn of the Twenty-First Century

UN Secretary General Kofi Annan hailed the adoption of the Rome Statute as a "giant step forward."[46] One of the proponents of U.S. participation in the court has argued that

> America does not commit genocide, war crimes, or crimes against humanity. Nor do our NATO allies. . . . We thus have nothing to fear from the prosecution of these offenses, nothing to make us hesitate when the pleas of the victims of mass slaughter fill our television screens and their plight hounds our conscience.[47]

Furthermore, proponents have pointed out that should American troops cross the line, the principle of complementarity would protect them from international prosecution as long as the United States took action against them.[48] Nonetheless, others have disagreed. One opponent called the treaty "a pernicious and debilitating agreement, harmful to the national interests of the United States."[49] On July 23, 1998, Ambassador Scheffer spoke at a hearing before the Senate Committee on Foreign Relations and outlined the U.S. objections to the Rome Statute. The four main concerns of the United States were as follows:

- U.S. military personnel could be brought before the ICC prosecutor;
- the degree of Security Council control over prosecutions initiated by the ICC prosecutor;
- the ambiguity of the crimes over which the ICC would exercise jurisdiction, particularly the crime of aggression, which could conceivably extend to some U.S. troop deployments, and the alleged crime of settlement in an occupied territory, which would arguably implicate Israeli leaders for activities in the West Bank and the Gaza Strip; and
- the relationship between the ICC and national judicial processes.[50]

Not only did Republican senators Helms and Rod Grams of Minnesota praise Scheffer's remarks, but so did Democratic senators Joseph Biden of Delaware and Dianne Feinstein of California. Republicans and Democrats alike on the committee congratulated Scheffer's resolve to protect U.S. interests in Rome and expressed their contempt for the ICC as created by the Rome Statute.[51] At the hearing, Senator Helms made his position clear: the United States should block any organization of which it is a member from providing funding to the ICC; renegotiate its status of forces agreements and extradition treaties to prohibit treaty partners from surrendering U.S. nationals to the ICC; refuse to provide U.S. soldiers to regional and international peacekeeping operations when there is any possibility that they will come under the jurisdiction of the ICC; and never vote in the Security Council to refer a matter to the ICC.[52]

These concerns about protecting individual members of the U.S. armed forces may have been a stalking horse for another, broader concern. At the end of the hearing, "Helms picked off the examples defiantly[;] he was going to be damned if any so-called International Court was ever going to be reviewing the legality of the U.S. invasions of Panama or Grenada or of the bombing of Tripoli and to be holding any American presidents, defense secretaries, or generals to account."[53] Still, by early August 1998 more than twenty editorials and op-eds had run in major U.S. newspapers broadly supporting the creation of the ICC. These were written by a number of leaders of nongovernmental organizations, as well as by former president Jimmy Carter.[54] One of the treaty's defenders argued that the United States had managed to have powerful national security safeguards added to the treaty:

> First, Rome provides for "complementarity," the idea that the primary responsibility for enforcing the law of war must remain with each nation-state and with national military justice systems. . . . On another point of concern, the Rome Statute provides complete protection for sensitive national security information. . . . Isolated incidents of military misconduct that occur in wartime will not be prosecuted by the court. Rather, the tribunal is charged to focus on war crimes committed "as part of a plan or policy" or as part of "a large-scale commission of such crimes." . . . The Rome Statute also respects our bilateral treaty agreements protecting American troops stationed abroad against any attempted exercise of foreign criminal jurisdiction—the so-called Status of Forces Agreements.[55]

Countering the pro-ICC forces, on the op-ed page of the *Financial Times* Senator Helms wrote, "We must slay this monster. Voting against the International Criminal Court is not enough. The US should try to bring it down."[56]

Another opponent suggested the treaty's wording would have found the United States guilty of war crimes for the bombing campaigns against Germany and Japan during World War II.[57] Others raised the possibility of international prosecution for air strikes such as those against Libya in 1986 and Sudan in 1998.[58]

Controversy continued over who was to receive blame for genocide and other war crimes and what to do after such crimes had occurred. On June 14, 2000, Senator Helms introduced the American Servicemembers' Protection Act (S. 2726), which would prohibit U.S. officials from cooperating with the ICC. That same day, Majority Whip Tom DeLay, R-Texas, introduced the measure in the House of Representatives (H.R. 4654). It mandated that the president ensure that any Security Council resolution authorizing a peacekeeping operation exempt U.S. personnel from prosecution before the ICC. Additionally, it required the president to certify to Congress that U.S. personnel are immunized by each country participating in the operation. The bill proposed that no U.S. military assistance be provided to governments that are parties to the ICC (with the exception of the NATO allies and Israel), although the president could waive this provision. With these "big sticks," Senator Helms denounced "the ICC's bogus claim of jurisdiction over American citizens."[59]

In July 2000 a seven-member panel created by the Organization of African States issued a report blaming Belgium, France, the United States, the Catholic Church, and the UN Security Council for the 1994 slaughter of more than 500,000 Tutsis and moderate Hutus by more radical, xenophobic Hutus during the Rwandan civil war. Canadian panel member Stephen Lewis said the United States knew what was going on in Rwanda, but prevented the Security Council from deploying an effective force to stop it, because of the political fallout that ensued after eighteen Americans were killed in the Somalia intervention in October 1993. As Lewis said, "It's simply beyond belief that because of Somalia hundreds of thousands of Rwandans needlessly lost their lives. I don't know how Madeleine Albright lives with it."[60]

Also in July 2000, U.S. military personnel figured prominently in two criminal trials. In the murder trial of three Serbs accused of killing two ethnic Albanians in Kosovo, the U.S. Army requested the Yugoslavian court to drop the charges against the Serbs. The army said it had discovered that the two Kosovars had been killed by U.S. troops. In the case of one of the deceased, the army said U.S. troops fired back in self-defense after first being fired upon, which was permitted under their rules of engagement. In the case of the other decedent, however, justification for U.S. actions was far less clear-cut. It was reported that the second Kosovar fled the scene and was killed by a pursuing U.S. soldier, who fired multiple shots through the door of the shed where the man was trying to hide.[61]

In the second case, involving the death of an ethnic Albanian girl in Kosovo, a U.S. soldier formerly assigned to peacekeeping duty in Kosovo pled guilty to charges of murder, forcible sodomy, and three counts of indecent acts with a child before a U.S. military court in Germany.[62] The event played into the hands of those who argued that U.S. troops are just as likely to commit such crimes as are the troops of other states. Because of complementarity, however, this case would not have fallen under the jurisdiction of the ICC if the court had been in operation, because it was prosecuted by U.S. authorities. In fact, for a case to be tried by the ICC over the wishes of the United States,

> the United States would have to be so biased that it could not evaluate the question of international crime, had no intention of investigating the claim, or was investigating only to protect an individual. The seriousness with which the modern U.S. military justice system treats international humanitarian law makes this a virtual impossibility in the case of a military investigation.[63]

Despite the protection that complementarity offered the United States and other nations, Senator Helms wanted to leave nothing to chance. On November 29, 2000, his spokesman held a press conference at UN headquarters in New York. There he said Helms would make passage of the American Servicemembers' Protection Act a top priority in the Congress convening in January 2001. On that same day, a letter signed by a dozen former U.S. foreign policy officials was released, supporting Helms's bill; the letter claimed that U.S. world leadership "could be the first casualty" of the new ICC.[64] Among the signatories were former U.S. secretaries of state James Baker, Henry Kissinger, and George Shultz and former U.S. ambassador to the UN Jeane Kirkpatrick. As the writer James Carroll concluded in the *Boston Globe,* "That James Baker is a party to the Helms campaign signals that an incoming [George W.] Bush administration would prefer to be shackled by a xenophobic Congress than to be constrained by multilateral and equitable agreements with other nations."[65]

On July 12, 2002, shortly after the ICC entered into force and at the behest of the United States, the UN Security Council passed Resolution 1422, which restricted the ICC from commencing or proceeding with investigations or prosecutions of "peacekeepers" and other officials of states not then part of the ICC for a period of twelve months. The U.S. ambassador to the UN, John Negroponte, announced that the United States would continue to seek bilateral agreements exempting U.S. citizens from the jurisdiction of the ICC.[66]

On August 2, 2002, President Bush signed into law the American Servicemembers' Protection Act (ASPA), which had been included as part of the 2002 supplemental appropriations bill. It provided that the United States cut off military assistance to countries that had not signed bilateral agreements with the United States by July 1, 2003, ensuring that they would not surrender a U.S. citizen to the jurisdiction of the ICC or cooperate with the ICC in the apprehension or rendition of them. The law also, however, authorized the president to waive this provision on grounds of "national interest." The ASPA specifically exempted NATO members and a few other allies but potentially applied to more than fifty other countries. As of June 2003, forty-five countries had signed bilateral agreements; but few of these were adherents to the Rome Statute.[67]

In February 2003, the first eighteen ICC judges were elected, after as many as eighty-five state adherents to the Rome Statute cast thirty-three ballots. The judges took their seats on March 11, 2003, and on that same day career diplomat and attorney Philippe Kirsch of Canada, who had led the Rome Conference in 1998, was elected as the first president of the ICC. On March 24, 2003, Luis Moreno Ocampo of Argentina was elected the first chief prosecutor of the ICC. Ocampo, a lawyer experienced in criminal and human rights law and anticorruption programs, participated in the 1980s in the prosecution of the Argentine military leaders alleged responsible for the Falklands War. He also served as president of the Latin American section of Transparency International.[68]

On July 1, 2003, the Bush administration announced its intention to cut off military aid to thirty-five countries that had failed to sign bilateral agreements. At the same time, it granted waivers for varying periods of time to twenty-two countries. As of May 2005, the State Department reported that one hundred bilateral agreements had been signed. However, by January 1, 2007, one hundred and five countries had ratified the Rome Statute, including twenty-nine African, twelve Asian, fifteen Eastern European, twenty-two Latin American/Caribbean, and twenty-six Western European and other states. The most notable absences were of countries from North Africa and the Middle East, all with majority-Islamic faith traditions except for Israel; of these only Jordan, Djibouti, Comoros, and Yemen (which by now had signed and ratifed the treaty) were members. Indonesia, the Asian country with the largest Islamic population in the world (with an aggregate population of two hundred forty-two million) is also absent from the ICC, as are both Pakistan and India. One encouraging development came in December 2006, when the Japanese prime minister announced that Japan planned to join the ICC in 2007. Japan did so on July 17, 2007.[69]

It was also notable that the first situations before the International Criminal Court, including the first projected trial, were from Africa: the Central African Republic, Sudan, the Democratic Republic of Congo, and Uganda.[70] At an address before the New York City Bar on December 14, 2005, the chief ICC prosecutor responded to a question which asked whether it was a failure of the court that its only cases, so far, have involved African countries. His reply was that in the short term it was not, for African countries had been among the greatest supporters of the ICC. However, he acknowledged that in the longer term, it would not do to have ICC prosecutions only of offenders in relatively weak or failed states.

By the end of 2006, commentators were noting that the United States may have warmed slightly toward the International Criminal Court. One indicator was secretary of state Condoleezza Rice's March statement that the U.S. decision to withhold military aid and training because of a recipient's ICC stance might be "shooting ourselves in the foot" if those states were helpful on issues like the war on terror, the war on drugs, or the conflicts in Afghanistan and Iraq.[71] Other examples cited were the failure of the United States to oppose the UN Security Council's referral of issues involving Sudan's Darfur region to the ICC and U.S. support for ICC indictments in 2005 of five Ugandans who were leaders of the "Lord's Resistance Army," a group which President Bush called a "barbaric rebel cult." Nonetheless, State Department legal adviser John Bellinger stated, "Our policy toward the ICC has not changed. We are strongly opposed to the ICC's covering us. In that regard our policy is crystal clear."[72]

Conclusion: The United States and International Law

Israeli diplomat Abba Eban once said international law was "the law which the wicked do not obey and the righteous do not enforce." Whether the United States has lined up on the side of the wicked or of the righteous in this case probably lies in the eye of the beholder. There is no question that U.S. political culture values the rule of law: Presidents George H. W. Bush and Bill Clinton saw reliance on international law as a mainstay of the post–cold war era. Clinton wanted to use international law to punish war criminals and those guilty of genocide and crimes against humanity, and he said so when he endorsed the creation of the ICC in his UN General Assembly address in September 1997. Yet by the time of the Rome Conference the following summer, U.S. diplomats were swimming against the international tide by trying to ensure some degree of U.S. control over the ICC or its prosecutor. The inability to prevail on this issue produced the final vote that placed the United States in the somewhat unusual company of China, Iraq, Israel, Libya, Qatar, and Yemen (although Yemen subsequently signed and ratified the treaty). What accounts for this seeming about-face? The U.S. Congress.

In 1946 prominent senators had ensured that the World Court would not act contrary to U.S. interests, as defined by the United States. Congressional emphasis on U.S. national sovereignty at the expense of international law, the United Nations, and a host of nongovernmental organizations reappeared in the ICC case. Once powerful legislators staked out the priority of preserving U.S. sovereignty, the nature of policymaking on the issue changed for the Clinton administration. The question was no longer whether the United States could agree with its friends and allies on an important issue in international law but whether any set of procedures could be found that could ensure Senate ratification of such a treaty. Moreover, the George W. Bush administration seems to have embraced unilateralism as its preferred method of operation. Although the United States is content to work through the United Nations when that suits U.S. purposes, or with those of its allies who consent to U.S. leadership, its actions fail to demonstrate any fundamental concern for the international rule of law as enforced through institutions that it may not be able to control.

Key Actors

James Baker Former secretary of state, signed a public letter opposing U.S. participation in the ICC.

George W. Bush President, rescinded the Clinton administration's signature of the Rome Statute, signed the American Servicemembers' Protection Act, and ordered the cutoff of military aid to thirty-five countries that refused to sign bilateral agreements protecting U.S. service personnel from possible prosecution by the ICC.

Bill Clinton President, unexpectedly ordered Ambassador David Scheffer to sign the ICC treaty so the United States could be considered an original signatory.

Jesse Helms Senator, R-N.C., the chairman of the Committee on Foreign Relations, was an early and active opponent of U.S. participation in the ICC.

Jeane Kirkpatrick Former U.S. ambassador to the United Nations, signed a public letter opposing U.S. participation in the ICC.

Henry Kissinger Former secretary of state, signed a public letter opposing U.S. participation in the ICC.

Donald Rumsfeld Secretary of defense for Presidents Gerald Ford and George W. Bush, signed a public letter opposing U.S. participation in the ICC.

David Scheffer Ambassador-at-large for war crimes, led the U.S. effort to modify the ICC treaty so the United States would have some control over the court's future actions.

George Shultz Former secretary of state, signed a public letter opposing U.S. participation in the ICC.

Notes

1. John T. Rourke, Ralph G. Carter, and Mark A. Boyer, *Making American Foreign Policy,* 2nd ed. (Guilford, Conn.: Brown and Benchmark, 1996), 87.
2. Sir Arnold Duncan McNair, *The Development of International Justice* (New York: New York University Press, 1954), 4.
3. George Schwarzenberger, *International Law, as Applied by International Courts and Tribunals* (London: Stevens and Sons, 1986), 4:138.
4. Ian Brownlie, *Basic Documents in International Law,* 4th ed. (Oxford: Clarendon Press, 1995), 446. Reservations are legal statements of the conditions under which parties will agree to a treaty. Often during a debate over the ratification of a treaty, states will declare in advance certain circumstances under which they say a treaty will not apply to them or their actions. Accepting these conditions is the political cost of getting that state to agree to the treaty. "Obligatory jurisdiction" means that states are obliged to obey a court's jurisdiction. With obligatory jurisdiction, the states cannot deny that a court has jurisdiction in a case or matter. Through reservations, states can set the terms and conditions under which they will accept a court's jurisdiction.
5. M. Cherif Bassiouni, "From Versailles to Rwanda in Seventy-Five Years: The Need to Establish a Permanent International Criminal Court," *Harvard Human Rights Journal* 10 (1997): 11–62; Gerhard von Glahn, *Law among Nations: An Introduction to Public International Law* (New York: Macmillan, 1992), 878.
6. Von Glahn, *Law among Nations,* 880.
7. John E. Findling, ed., *Dictionary of American Diplomatic History,* 2nd ed. (New York: Greenwood Press, 1989), 260.
8. Bassiouni, "From Versailles to Rwanda," 34.
9. Findling, *Dictionary of American Diplomatic History,* 259.
10. Von Glahn, *Law among Nations,* 354–357.
11. Michael P. Scharf, *Balkan Justice: The Story behind the First International War Crimes Trial since Nuremberg* (Durham, N.C.: Carolina Academic Press, 1997), 13–15.
12. *Congressional Record,* August 1, 1946, 10618.
13. Von Glahn, *Law among Nations,* 615–616.
14. *Congress and the Nation,* vol. 1, *1945–1964* (Washington, D.C.: Congressional Quarterly, 1965).
15. John T. Rourke, Ralph G. Carter, and Mark A. Boyer, *Making American Foreign Policy* (Guilford, Conn.: Dushkin Publishing Group, 1994), 209–210.
16. Von Glahn, *Law among Nations,* 192.
17. Scharf, *Balkan Justice,* 15.
18. Bassiouni, "From Versailles to Rwanda," 55–56.
19. Ibid., 43.
20. Ibid., 46–47.

21. See the Rome Conference/PrepCom document at www.un.org/law/icc/prepcomm/prepfra.htm.

22. Anne-Marie Slaughter, "Memorandum to the President," in *Toward an International Criminal Court?* ed. Alton Frye (New York: Council on Foreign Relations, 1999), 7.

23. See the Rome Conference/PrepCom document.

24. James Bone, "U.S. Seeks to Limit War Crimes Court," *Times* [London], March 30, 1998.

25. More information on these issues can be found at the Web site of the Coalition for the International Criminal Court, www.iccnow.org.

26. Human Rights Watch, "Justice in the Balance: Recommendations for an Independent and Effective International Criminal Court," 1998, www.hrw.org/reports98/icc.

27. Jimmy Carter, "For an International Criminal Court," *New Perspectives Quarterly* 10 (1997): 52–53.

28. David Scheffer, "An International Criminal Court: The Challenge of Enforcing International Humanitarian Law," address to the Southern California Working Group on the International Criminal Court, February 26, 1998, www.unausa.org/issues/scheffer.asp.

29. Agence France-Presse, "Paris, Washington in Agreement on UN Genocide Court," April 4, 1998.

30. John R. Bolton, "Why an International Court Won't Work," *Wall Street Journal*, March 30, 1998; John M. Goshko, "A Shift on Role of UN Court? Envoy Suggests U.S. May Alter Demands on Proposed Tribunal," *Washington Post*, March 18, 1998; Barbara Crossette, "U.S. Budges at U.N. Talks on a Permanent War-Crimes Court," *New York Times*, March 18, 1998.

31. Senate Committee on Foreign Relations, "Helms Declares UN Criminal Court 'Dead on Arrival' without U.S. Veto," press release, March 26, 1998.

32. Eric Schmitt, "Pentagon Battles Plans for International War Crimes," *New York Times*, April 14, 1998.

33. Siddharth Varadarajan, "Imperial Impunity: US Hampers World Criminal Court Plan," *Times of India*, April 23, 1998.

34. Alessandra Stanley, "Conference Opens on Creating Court to Try War Crimes," *New York Times*, June 15, 1998, A1.

35. "A New World Court," *Economist*, June 13–19, 1998, 16.

36. Bertram S. Brown, "The Statute of the ICC: Past, Present, and Future," in *The United States and the International Criminal Court: National Security and International Law*, ed. Sarah B. Sewall and Carl Kaysen (Lanham, Md.: Rowman and Littlefield, 2000), 62. Donald Jackson was an accredited correspondent at the Rome Conference. Statements not otherwise attributed in this section are based either on direct observation or on contemporaneous conversations with conference participants, nongovernmental organization representatives, or journalists.

37. UN press release, L/ROM/11, June 17, 1998.

38. Alessandra Stanley, "U.S. Presses Allies to Rein in Proposed War Crimes Court," *New York Times*, July 15, 1998.

39. Lawrence Weschler, "Exceptional Cases in Rome: The United States and the Struggle for an ICC," in Sewall and Kaysen, *The United States and the International Criminal Court*, 91.

40. Ibid., 105.

41. David Scheffer, press release distributed at the conference, July 15, 1998.

42. Coalition for the International Criminal Court, *ICC Update,* October 2003, www.iccnow.org/publications/update.html.

43. Steven Lee Myers, "U.S. Signs Treaty for World Court to Try Atrocities," *New York Times,* January 1, 2001.

44. "War Crime Pact OK'd by Clinton," *Dallas Morning News,* January 1, 2001, 10A.

45. Coalition for the International Criminal Court, *ICC Monitor,* September 2002, www.iccnow.org/publications/monitor.html.

46. "Permanent War Crimes Court Approved," *New York Times,* July 18, 1998.

47. Kenneth Roth, "Speech One: Endorse the International Criminal Court," in Frye, *Toward an International Criminal Court?* 31–32.

48. Ibid., 31.

49. John Bolton, "Speech Two: Reject and Oppose the International Criminal Court," in Frye, *Toward an International Criminal Court?* 37.

50. Slaughter, "Memorandum to the President," 8.

51. Weschler, "Exceptional Cases in Rome," 110.

52. Michael Scharf, "Rome Diplomatic Conference for an International Criminal Court," *ASIL Insight,* June 1998, www.asil.org/insights/insigh20.htm.

53. Weschler, "Exceptional Cases in Rome," 111.

54. For example, see the op-eds in the *Los Angeles Times,* July 17, 1998, B-9; *New York Times,* June 14, 1998, WK14; and *Washington Post,* May 2, 1998, A17; May 13, 1998, A17; May 27, 1998, A-17.

55. Ruth Wedgwood, "Speech Three: Improve the International Criminal Court," in Frye, *Toward an International Criminal Court?* 63–64.

56. "Personal View: Jesse Helms," *Financial Times,* July 31, 1998.

57. Bolton, "Speech Two: Reject and Oppose the International Criminal Court," 39–40.

58. William L. Nash, "The ICC and the Deployment of U.S. Armed Forces," in Sewall and Kaysen, *The United States and the International Criminal Court,* 156.

59. Coalition for the International Criminal Court, August 29, 2000, www.cicclegal@iccnow.org; United Nations Association–USA, June 20, 2000, www.unausa.org/dc/info/dc062000; http://frwebgate.access.gpo/cgi_bin/getdoc.cgi?dbname=107_cong_public_laws&docid=f:publ206.107

60. "U.S., Others Blamed for Not Halting Slaughter in Rwanda," *Dallas Morning News,* July 8, 2000, 21A.

61. "Judge: U.S. Troops Admitted Killings," *Dallas Morning News,* July 22, 2000, 19A.

62. "Soldier Pleads Guilty in Albanian Girl's Death," *Dallas Morning News,* July 30, 2000, 28A.

63. Sarah B. Sewall, Carl Kaysen, and Michael P. Scharf, "The United States and the International Criminal Court: An Overview," in Sewall and Kaysen, *The United States and the International Criminal Court,* 10–11.

64. Myers, "U.S. Signs Treaty for World Court to Try Atrocities."

65. James Carroll, "How Helms Is Sparking a Real Crisis," *Boston Globe,* December 5, 2000, A23.

66. Coalition for the International Criminal Court, *ICC Monitor,* September 2002.

67. Ibid.

68. Coalition for the International Criminal Court, *ICC Monitor,* April 2003, www.iccnow.org/publications/monitor.html.

69. *Japan Times,* December 7, 2006, http://search.japantimes.co.pp/print/nn20061207a9.html (accessed December 12, 2006); the news of Japan's accession to the treaty, as well as updates on other states' accessions to the Rome Statute of the International Criminal Court are posted at www.iccnow.org (accessed July 18, 2007).

70. On January 29, 2007, the ICC announced the first trial would involve Thomas Lubanga Dyilo, of the Union of Congolese Patriots (UPC), for his enlisting, conscripting, and using children under the age of fifteen as combat soldiers in the Democratic Republic of Congo. See Coalition for the International Criminal Court, www.iccnow.org/?mod=drc (accessed February 14, 2007). On February 27, 2007, the ICC prosecutor announced that sufficient evidence had been found to refer two Darfur cases to the judges for further action. According to the prosecutor, Ahmad Muhammad Harun (Sudan's Interior Minister and head of the Darfur Security Desk) and Ali Muhammad Ali Abd-Al Rahman (better known as Ali Kushayb, a commander of the Jangaweed militia) were criminally responsible for 51 counts of crimes against humanity and war crimes. These crimes included summary executions, mass murder, and mass rape of civilians. See the ICC Web site, www.icc-cpi.int/press/pressreleases/228.html (accessed March 15, 2007).

71. Anne Gearan, "International Criminal Court—Rice: U.S. May Need to Soften Some of Its Policies," Associated Press, *Fort Worth Star-Telegram,* March 11, 2006, 17A.

72. Associated Press, "Four years later, U.S. Sees International Criminal Court in Better Light," *International Herald Tribune,* December 27, 2006, www.iht.com/bin/print.phb?id=4037631 (accessed December 29, 2006).

15 The Rights of Detainees: Determining the Limits of Law

Linda Cornett and Mark Gibney

Before You Begin

1. Why is there so much political contention over the rights of detainees held in connection with the war on terrorism?

2. Why, and on what basis, did the administration of George W. Bush act so aggressively to assert executive privilege in defining the rights of detainees in its war on terrorism?

3. Why, and on what basis, have critics challenged the executive branch's authority to define the rights of detainees without "interference" from Congress or the judiciary?

4. Is the war on terrorism equivalent to other wars—such as World War II or the Vietnam War—that the United States has fought? Does it justify the president's claims to exceptional war powers and military jurisdiction over detainees, or is the "war on terrorism" better understood rhetorically, like the "war on drugs" or the "war on poverty," and better fought in the criminal court system, as with the Oklahoma City bombings?

5. How does the separation of powers play out in this case?

6. What deference, if any, should the courts show the president in executing the war on terrorism? What would constitute the "end of hostilities" in this war and mark the expiration of the president's "war powers"?

7. What role did such nongovernmental organizations as the Center for National Security Studies and the American Civil Liberties Union play in defining the rights of detainees?

8. What role have the news media played in shaping the political controversies surrounding the detainees? Should media outlets have published the classified materials leaked to them, in the interest of transparent government and informed debate?

Introduction: Responding to Terrorism

On September 11, 2001, members of the al Qaeda network hijacked four commercial airliners: Two were flown into the World Trade Center towers in New York, one dived into the Pentagon outside Washington, D.C., and one crashed in a field in Pennsylvania, after passengers attempted to wrest control of the plane from the hijackers. The attacks killed approximately three thousand people, unsettled the economy, and shook Americans' sense of security. Shortly thereafter, President George W. Bush promised that the United States would "direct every resource at [its] command, every means of diplomacy, every tool of intelligence, every instrument of law enforcement, every financial influence, and every weapon of war to the disruption and to the defeat of the global terror network . . . before they strike [again]."[1] Under the assumption that extraordinary times call for extraordinary measures, the administration set out to expand its capabilities to execute what it called the "war on terrorism."

On September 14 the president declared a national emergency and requested that Congress give the administration the authority and tools to act decisively on all fronts of this new war.[2] Four days later, Congress responded to Bush's call with S.J. Res. 23, granting the executive branch broad authority to act against those responsible for the attacks of September 11 and to act to prevent future attacks, which the administration interpreted as the authority to combat terrorism whenever and wherever the threat arose. A short four weeks later, on October 24, Congress passed the USA Patriot Act—formally the Uniting and Strengthening America by Providing Appropriate Tools Required to Intercept and Obstruct Terrorism Act—to enhance the executive branch's law enforcement and intelligence-gathering capabilities, as well as its authority. Although it is multifaceted, the primary thrust of the act was to broaden the power of executive agencies to define, investigate, detain, and punish terror suspects with lower thresholds of evidence and less judicial oversight.

The administration moved equally aggressively in the international arena. On September 21, in a nationally televised address before Congress, Bush demanded that the Taliban government in Afghanistan immediately and unconditionally surrender any and all al Qaeda members on its soil, dismantle al Qaeda training camps, and give the United States unfettered access to suspected al Qaeda facilities. On October 7 the United States initiated a military campaign against Afghanistan, aided by Afghan forces of the Northern Alliance, to depose the Taliban government and root out al Qaeda. On March 19, 2003, the Bush administration carried its war on terrorism to Iraq, largely based on the claim that Iraq

Rights of Detainees and the War on Terror

September 11, 2001 Al Qaeda members hijack commercial airliners and crash them into the World Trade Center towers and the Pentagon. One plane believed destined for Washington, D.C., crashes in rural Pennsylvania.

September 12, 2001 The Justice Department begins using federal immigration laws to detain aliens suspected of having ties to the September 11 attacks or connections to terrorism, or who are encountered during the course of an investigation conducted by the Federal Bureau of Investigation.

September 14, 2001 President George W. Bush declares a state of emergency and vows to devote the full resources of the United States to the "war on terrorism."

September 18, 2001 Congress passes S.J. Res. 23, "Authorizing Use of United States Armed Forces against Those Responsible for Recent Attacks against the United States."

October 7, 2001 The United States attacks Afghanistan to overthrow the Taliban government and root out al Qaeda.

October 24, 2001 Congress passes the USA Patriot Act, expanding the executive branch's intelligence-gathering and law enforcement powers.

December 6, 2001 A broad coalition, led by the Center for National Security Studies, files a lawsuit under the Freedom of Information Act to compel the U.S. government to release information about September 11 detainees.

January 11, 2002 The Defense Department begins transporting prisoners captured in the course of the war in Afghanistan to U.S. bases in Cuba. Among the prisoners is Yaser Esam Hamdi, a U.S. citizen.

January–February, 2002 Memoranda from the White House counsel and Justice Department lawyers argue that the prisoners taken in Afghanistan do not qualify for protections under the Geneva Conventions. State Department lawyers strongly dissent. The White House announces that although the prisoners do not merit these legal protections, the Geneva Conventions would govern the actions of U.S. military personnel toward them and in Afghanistan.

continued on the next page

continued from the previous page

February 19, 2002 In *Rasul et al. v. Bush,* the Center for Constitutional Rights files a writ of habeas corpus in the U.S. District Court for the District of Columbia on behalf of Shafiq Rasul and other foreign nationals held at Guantanamo Bay.

March 3, 2002 The U.S. District Court for the District of Columbia dismisses *Rasul* and other Guantanamo Bay suits for lack of jurisdiction. The case is appealed.

May 8, 2002 Jose Padilla, a U.S. citizen, is arrested as he enters the country at Chicago's O'Hare International Airport. He is detained as a material witness in the September 11 investigations.

June 9–11, 2002 Padilla is designated an "enemy combatant" by order of Bush and is transferred from the U.S. criminal justice system to a navy brig in South Carolina. Lawyers for Padilla and Hamdi file petitions for a writ of habeas corpus in the U.S District Court for the Eastern District of Virginia.

August 2, 2002 Judge Gladys Kessler of the U.S. District Court for the District of Columbia orders the Justice Department to release the names of the detainees and their attorneys but allows the department to keep other details of their cases secret.

August 16, 2002 The U.S. District Court for the Eastern District of Virginia rules in *Hamdi v. Rumsfeld* that the "Mobbs declaration," an affidavit by a government official, is insufficient basis for detaining Hamdi as an enemy combatant.

October 2, 2002 Congress passes a joint resolution authorizing the use of U.S. armed forces against Iraq.

January 8, 2003 The U.S. Court of Appeals for the Fourth Circuit overturns the lower court finding in *Hamdi v. Rumsfeld* and rules that the president can designate U.S. citizens enemy combatants and hold them without access to counsel, if the president believes a person's behavior constitutes a threat to national security. The case is appealed to the U.S. Supreme Court.

March 19, 2003 The United States attacks Iraq based on Bush administration claims that Iraq possesses weapons of mass destruction and maintains ties with terrorists who might use such weapons against the United States.

June 17, 2003 The U.S. Court of Appeals for the District of Columbia accepts the Bush administration's contention that "disclosure of even one name could endanger national security" and reverses the lower court ruling requiring the government to release limited information about the September 11 detainees. The U.S. Supreme Court declines, without explanation, to take up the case on appeal.

December 18, 2003 In *Rumsfeld v. Padilla,* Michael Mukasey, chief judge of the U.S. District Court for the Southern District of New York, rules that although the president can hold persons deemed enemy combatants without charge until the end of hostilities, Padilla had the right to meet with counsel and offer evidence contesting the government's allegations against him. The government refuses to comply with the decision and appeals it to the Supreme Court.

April 5, 2004 The Center for Constitutional Rights directly files two habeas corpus briefs with the Supreme Court and one in district court on behalf of Rasul and his co-plaintiffs.

April 28, 2004 The Supreme Court begins hearing oral arguments in *Hamdi v. Rumsfeld, Rumsfeld v. Padilla,* and *Rasul et al. v. Bush.*

June 28, 2004 The Supreme Court hands down rulings in *Hamdi v. Rumsfeld* and *Rasul et al. v. Bush* that essentially affirm the rights of detainees to due process before a neutral judge to challenge their detention as enemy combatants. The Court rejects Padilla's petition for due process on a technicality.

October 11, 2004 Hamdi is released from U.S. custody and flown to Saudi Arabia.

December 30, 2005 Congress passes the Detainee Treatment Act, which drastically curtails the courts' habeas corpus jurisdiction over detentions at Guantanamo.

June 29, 2006 In its decision regarding *Hamdan v. Rumsfeld,* the Supreme Court strikes down the military commissions President Bush established to try suspected members of al Qaeda.

September 28, 2006 Congress passes the Military Commissions Act, which provides statutory authorization for military commission trials for Guantanamo Bay detainees and eliminates judicial jurisdiction, effectively stripping detainees of the right to file habeas corpus petitions in federal court.

possessed weapons of mass destruction. The consequences of the administration's actions have been many and complex; however, one of the most immediate effects of the executive's expanded law enforcement, intelligence, and military efforts and capabilities has been a dramatic expansion in the number and variety of people detained by the government. The nature of these detentions raises the question: What legal rights do detainees in the war on terrorism have? What follows is a depiction of the continuing struggle to answer that question.

Background: Detainees in the War on Terror

Detainee, by definition, refers to "any person deprived of personal liberty except as a result of conviction for an offense."[3] The rights of detainees are intrinsically important in a democracy that has traditionally privileged liberty above virtually all other values. The rules governing the state's authority to deprive individuals of their liberty are a central theme in the U.S. Constitution. In addressing issues related to detainees, the Court of Appeals for the Fourth Circuit noted in January 2003 that, indeed, the "Constitution is suffused with concern about how the state will wield its awesome power of forcible restraint. And this preoccupation was not accidental. Our forebears recognized that the power to detain could easily become destructive 'if exerted without check or control.'"[4] The Bush administration's war on terrorism has significantly expanded the number and variety of detainees under the authority of the U.S. government to include the September 11 detainees; foreign "enemy combatants" at Guantanamo Bay, Cuba; Yaser Esam Hamdi and Jose Padilla, two U.S. citizens arrested and detained separately as "enemy combatants" and held in military detention in Charleston, South Carolina; Iraqis held in U.S.-run prisons in Iraq; and foreign nationals who have been detained and interrogated as part of a policy known as "extraordinary rendition." An examination of some of the controversies surrounding the rights of detainees brings into stark relief a number of broader, enduring debates about the appropriate balance between national security and civil liberty; the relationship between national interest and international law; and the responsibilities of each of the branches of government in balancing competing interests and values in the making of national security policy.

September 11 Detainees

In the months following the September 11 attacks, U.S. authorities detained approximately twelve hundred foreign nationals, most on visa violations.[5] Many were arrested by the Immigration and Naturalization Service at the direction of

Attorney General John Ashcroft and detained as "special interest cases." Some were held for days, weeks, and even months without being charged with a crime. All were denied the opportunity to post bond and given very limited opportunities to communicate with family members or seek legal counsel. The government refused even to release their names, arguing that disclosing such information "would give terrorists a virtual roadmap to [the government's] investigation that could allow terrorists to chart a potentially deadly detour around [its] efforts."[6] Ashcroft further directed chief immigration judge Michael Creppy to close proceedings in deportation hearings of the special interest cases, a policy later ruled unconstitutional by the Court of Appeals for the Sixth Circuit. A broad coalition of civil liberties advocates, led by the Center for National Security Studies, sought to compel the Justice Department to release information about the detainees under the Freedom of Information Act (FOIA). In August 2002 Judge Gladys Kessler of the U.S. District Court for the District of Columbia agreed that although the government's national security concerns were legitimate, "the public's interest in learning the identity of those arrested and detained is essential to verifying whether the government is operating within the bounds of the law."[7] The judge ordered the Justice Department to release the names of the detainees and their attorneys but allowed the department to keep the details of their cases secret.

In June 2003 the U.S. Court of Appeals for the District of Columbia overturned that decision on appeal, accepting the administration's contention that "disclosure of even one name could endanger national security"[8] and in general deferring to the executive on questions of national security. The court asserted that "when government officials tell the court that disclosing the names of the detainees will produce harm, it is abundantly clear that the government's top counterterrorism officials are well suited to make this predictive judgment. Conversely, the judiciary is in an extremely poor position to second guess the government's views in the field of national security."[9] The U.S. Supreme Court declined, without explanation, to take up the case on appeal.

The government never charged any of the September 11 detainees with terror-related crimes, and most of them have been released or deported. Regardless, the USA Patriot Act substantially increased the Justice Department's authority to detain noncitizens without charge or counsel and, in fact, prescribes mandatory detention for "certified" aliens, that is, people whom the attorney general "has reasonable grounds to believe" represent a security threat or are found by the attorney general and the secretary of state to associate with "foreign terrorist organizations" to commit, incite, prepare, plan, gather information for, or provide material support for terrorist activities.[10] The legislation also explicitly limits judicial oversight of the executive branch's decisions, but it allows detainees to petition the attorney general for a reconsideration of their status every six months.

Critics warned that the administration's increasingly broad authority to secretly arrest and detain terror suspects is a dangerous precedent and provides opportunities for abuse. An internal Justice Department investigation by Inspector General Glenn Fine seemed to lend credence to those fears. In April 2003 Fine reported "significant problems" with the treatment of the September 11 detainees. For example, while recognizing that the Justice Department was operating under extremely difficult circumstances, he charged that the Federal Bureau of Investigation (FBI) in New York had made too little effort to distinguish between aliens who might have knowledge of terrorist threats and aliens encountered coincidentally, resulting in the detention of minor visa violators under very restrictive conditions. The report decried the FBI's "hold-until-cleared" and blanket "no bond" policies, which kept many of these detainees in confinement for extended periods. Fine also found evidence of a disturbing "pattern of physical and verbal abuse" by some correctional officers.[11]

Guantanamo Bay Detainees: Foreign Nationals, Enemy Combatants

The war in Afghanistan produced another category of detainee. During the war, the United States rounded up or captured some ten thousand people. Beginning January 11, 2002, the military started transferring several hundreds of those considered the most dangerous to a prison and interrogation facility dubbed "Camp X-Ray," at Guantanamo Bay, Cuba. Arguing that these detainees represent the "worst of the worst," General Richard B. Myers, chairman of the Joint Chiefs of Staff, described the Guantanamo Bay detainees as "people who would gnaw through hydraulic lines at the back of a C-17 to bring it down."[12] Many of these inmates, some of whom have now been detained for years, were subjected to constant interrogation, surveillance, and severe restrictions on their physical movements. Although the great majority were captured in Afghanistan during or immediately following hostilities there, a sizable number arrived after being turned over to the United States by other governments based on suspected ties to al Qaeda.[13] As of March 2007, approximately 385 men remained imprisoned at Guantanamo. About the same number (390) have been released or transferred to other countries (usually to their home governments).[14]

The Bush administration maintained that the detainees at Guantanamo Bay should not have access to U.S. courts or constitutional protections. It based its argument on the grounds that the facility where the detainees were being held is outside the territorial boundaries of the United States and that constitutional protections do not apply extraterritorially. Memos written by Deputy Assistant Attorneys General Patrick Philbin and John Yoo laid out the administration's view that the base at Guantanamo Bay, as one former administration lawyer described it, "existed in a legal twilight zone"—or "the legal equivalent of outer space." [15] Moreover, the government argued, the unprecedented threat that global terrorist networks posed required a suspension of the usual rules governing detainees. Holding prisoners without rights, Solicitor General Theodore Olson argued before the Supreme Court, "serves the vital objectives of preventing combatants from continuing to aid our enemies and gathering intelligence to further the overall war effort." [16]

The Bush administration also claimed exemption from judicial oversight based on the president's powers as commander in chief. The U.S. government classified all of the detainees as "enemy combatants" and steadfastly maintained that only the president can determine who is an enemy combatant and the conditions under which such detainees will be held. In a reply brief in *Rasul et al. v. Bush,* the case challenging the Guantanamo Bay detentions, the government spelled out its position:

> The detained petitioners are aliens held abroad. Accordingly, none of their claims—including their premature challenges to the Military Order—are within the subject matter jurisdiction of this Court, or *any* United States court. . . . The extraordinary circumstances in which this action arises and the particular relief that petitioners seek implicate core political questions about the conduct of the war on terrorism that the Constitution leaves to the Commander-in-Chief.[17]

In effect, the administration argued that the chief executive has total discretion over the designation of enemy combatants, that it can hold enemy combatants without benefit of counsel and with no right to challenge their detention until the "end of hostilities." Moreover, the administration argued that its judgments could not be second-guessed by the judiciary. Allowing detainees access to the federal courts, Olson argued before the Supreme Court, would "place the federal courts in the unprecedented position of micromanaging the executive's handling of captured enemy combatants from a distant zone." [18]

In addition to the position that the Guantanamo detainees were without protection under domestic law, the Bush administration also maintained that as enemy combatants, they were not protected under the Geneva Conventions. In early 2002 Secretary of State Colin Powell and State Department attorneys argued within the administration that the case of each detainee would need to be individually reviewed to determine if the conventions applied to that person. A January 9, 2002, memo from the Justice Department's Office of Legal Counsel argued, however, that the Geneva Conventions did not apply to the detainees. It also stated that the detainees were not covered by the 1996 War Crimes Act, a measure specifying the conditions under which U.S. citizens, including U.S. officials, can be prosecuted for war crimes. In a January 25, 2002, memo, White House Counsel Alberto Gonzales agreed with the Justice Department's interpretation that the Geneva Conventions (as well as the War Crimes Act) did not apply to al Qaeda or Taliban detainees. Following protests by Secretary Powell and his primary legal aide, William Howard Taft IV, the White House responded with a compromise position in February 2002: Although the protection of the Geneva Conventions did not apply to captured al Qaeda and Taliban fighters, the United States would adhere to the conventions in its conduct of the war in Afghanistan "to the extent appropriate and consistent with military necessity."[19] Regardless, the government did hold out the promise that at least some of the Guantanamo Bay detainees would receive trials before a military tribunal, although at the same time it maintained that it would not be bound to release any detainees even if the tribunal acquitted any of them.

The conditions under which the Guantanamo detainees were held and interrogated attracted renewed attention when gross abuses of detainees in Iraq's Abu Ghraib prison—where the Geneva Conventions ostensibly *did* apply—came to light in early 2004. Investigations into the Iraqi prisoner abuse scandal suggested that more aggressive interrogation techniques that Defense Secretary Donald Rumsfeld had approved for use at Guantanamo Bay were "exported" to Iraq when officials became frustrated by the paltry quantity and quality of intelligence being generated during a sustained Iraqi insurgency.[20] Of particular interest were a set of interrogation rules developed under Major General Geoffrey Miller that were first employed in Guantanamo Bay but later migrated to Iraq.[21] The " '72-point matrix for stress and duress' . . . laid out the types of coercion and the escalating levels at which they could be applied. These included the use of harsh heat or cold; withholding food; hooding for days at a time; naked isolation in cold, dark cells for more than 30 days, and threatening (but not biting) by dogs. It also permitted limited use of 'stress positions' designed to subject detainees to rising levels of pain."[22] The Red Cross reportedly delivered several reports to U.S. military authorities warning of the conditions at the Guantanamo Bay prison. In addition to potential abuses, the Red Cross specifically stated that the indeterminate nature of the detentions at Guantanamo was taking a heavy psychological toll on detainees and had resulted in thirty suicide attempts since the prison opened.[23]

Reports subsequently revealed that the purported danger and intelligence value of the Guantanamo detainees may have been systematically overstated by the Bush administration. According to the *New York Times,*

> In interviews, dozens of high-level military, intelligence, and law-enforcement officials in the United States, Europe, and the Middle East said that contrary to the repeated assertions of senior administration officials, none of the detainees at the United States Naval Base at Guantanamo Bay ranked as leaders or senior operatives of Al Qaeda. They said only a relative handful—some put the number at about a dozen, others more than two dozen—were sworn Qaeda members or other militants able to elucidate the organization's inner workings. While some Guantanamo intelligence has aided terrorism investigations, none of it has enabled intelligence or law-enforcement services to foil imminent attacks, the officials said.[24]

The article further charged that based on a top secret study conducted at Guantanamo by the Central Intelligence Agency (CIA), the administration knew as early as September 2002 that "many of the accused terrorists appeared to be low-level recruits who went to Afghanistan to support the Taliban or even innocent men swept up in the chaos of the war."[25]

Yaser Esam Hamdi and Jose Padilla: U.S. Citizens, Enemy Combatants

A handful of U.S. citizens have also been detained as enemy combatants, including Yaser Esam Hamdi, who was born in Louisiana, raised in the Middle East, and captured in 2001 during the Afghan war. In support of the decision to declare Hamdi an enemy combatant, Michael Mobbs, a special adviser to the under secretary of defense on policy, drafted a declaration (the "Mobbs declaration"—which the government would be present in court) asserting that Hamdi was arrested when the Taliban military unit he was fighting with in Afghanistan surrendered to the Northern Alliance.[26] When he surrendered, Hamdi was carrying an AK-47, according to his captors, and admitted having trained with and fought for the Taliban.[27] What makes Hamdi's case different from that of the other Guantanamo Bay detainees is his U.S. citizenship. After being captured, Hamdi was first taken to Guantanamo Bay, then transferred to a naval base in Norfolk, Virginia, and later sent to a naval brig in South Carolina. The change in his confinement was apparently made after his U.S. citizenship became known, but the government has steadfastly denied that U.S. citizens classified as enemy combatants have any more rights than do alien enemy combatants.

On June 10, 2002, Attorney General Ashcroft announced the arrest and detention of another U.S. citizen: Jose Padilla, also known as Abdullah al Muhajir. Ashcroft declared that Padilla's arrest resulted from the Justice Department's having "disrupted an unfolding terrorist plot to attack the United States by exploding a radioactive dirty bomb." Ashcroft maintained that his department had evidence from "multiple and corroborating sources" that Padilla "was closely associated with al Qaeda, and that as an al Qaeda operative he was involved in planning future terrorist attacks on innocent American civilians in the United States." As the Supreme Court was considering Padilla's case, the Justice Department publicized its case against him, alleging that he first became involved with al Qaeda in March 2002, during a pilgrimage to Saudi Arabia. According to the administration, Padilla attended training camps in Afghanistan, where he came into contact with high-level al Qaeda figures. In June 2001 Padilla was assigned to Adnan al-Shukrijurnah, an al Qaeda weapons expert, and prepared to travel to the United States and blow up several office buildings in a city of Padilla and Shukrijurnah's choosing. The two men were unable to work together, so the plan was scrapped. In fall 2001 Padilla came up with the idea to detonate a bomb with radioactive components. In March 2002 Padilla was introduced to Khalid Sheikh Mohammed, a top al Qaeda operative in Afghanistan later captured by Pakistani forces. After having received authorization from al Qaeda's leadership to proceed with his dirty bomb attack, Padilla flew from Pakistan to Chicago's O'Hare International Airport, where he was taken into custody on May 8, 2002, as he attempted to enter the country.[28]

When Padilla's arrest was made public, Ashcroft announced that both the Justice and Defense Departments had recommended to the president that Padilla be designated an enemy combatant and that the president had agreed. As a consequence, Padilla was transferred from the custody of the Justice Department to that of the Defense Department, which sent him to the naval brig in Charleston, South Carolina, without charges and for most of the time without access to an attorney.

Although presidents have commonly claimed expanded powers during wartime, lawyers for Hamdi and Padilla characterized the authority that the executive branch was claiming for itself in their cases as an unprecedented and dangerous departure from U.S. constitutional traditions. Jennifer Martinez, Padilla's attorney, argued that the government was claiming "unlimited power to imprison any American anywhere at any time without trial by labeling him an enemy combatant."[29] By that logic, Hamdi's lawyer, Frank Dunham Jr., argued, "We could have people locked up all over the country tomorrow without any due process and without the opportunity to be heard."[30] Likewise, Martinez objected to the government's claim "that military forces may seize a citizen and stow him away on a brig, without charges and without access to counsel, whenever the Commander-in-Chief concludes on 'some evidence' (regardless of its dubious character) that a citizen has 'associated' with an enemy."[31] The Bush administration policy, they charged, invited abuse.

Not only was the policy subject to abuse, it was also vulnerable to error or intelligence failure. Critics of the government's position raised several cautionary examples. Captain James Yee, a Muslim American providing religious counseling at Guantanamo Bay, was arrested September 10, 2003, on suspicion of espionage and aiding the enemy. The military detained him for seventy-six days, while it continued its investigation. All charges against him were ultimately dropped. "Yee is a free man today," one editorial pointed out, "with all mention of the fiasco removed from his military file because at least he had recourse to the military justice system. The government wants to deny Hamdi and Padilla their day in court, civil or military, even though no neutral party has been able to examine the strength of the case against them."[32]

In hearings before the Senate Committee on the Judiciary, Sen. Russ Feingold, D-Wis., raised the example of Brandon Mayfield, a U.S. citizen erroneously implicated and detained in connection with the March 11, 2004, train bombings in Spain: "But for the fact that he had access to counsel and judicial review, Mr. Mayfield might still be in jail today. [If] held as an enemy combatant, Mr. Mayfield would be in a military jail without the right to an attorney. And his truthful statements of innocence would be taken simply as failure of his interrogators."[33] Even more worrisome, the Red Cross has reported that "some military intelligence officers estimated that 70 percent to 90 percent of 'the persons deprived of their liberty in Iraq had been arrested by mistake.'"[34] Even in the Padilla case, "administration officials [eventually] concede[d] that the principal claim they have been making about Padilla ever since his detention—that he was dispatched to the United States for the specific purpose of setting off a radiological 'dirty bomb'—has turned out to be wrong and most likely can never be used against him in court."[35]

The Iraqi Detainees

The United States has held an estimated 34,000 Iraqi detainees during its occupation of Iraq.[36] Of all the detainees during the Bush administration's campaign against terrorism, their treatment has garnered the most notoriety. Photos of prisoners being humiliated and tortured in Abu Ghraib prison were first shown on *60 Minutes II* on April 28, 2004, and they quickly made their way onto the front pages of newspapers worldwide. The administration immediately protested that the acts depicted were nothing more than the work of a few "bad apples" and vigorously denied that the abuses had deeper roots in policy. Faced with growing public criticism, Bush issued an apology for these atrocities a few days later. After meeting privately with King Abdullah II of Jordan, President Bush told a group of reporters and journalists what he had told the king: "I told him I was sorry for the humiliation suffered by Iraqi prisoners and the humiliation by their families."[37] There followed immediately a veritable flood of apologies from members of his cabinet, including Secretary of State Powell, National Security Advisor Condoleezza Rice, and Secretary of Defense Rumsfeld.

As the scandal unfolded and investigations into its causes strengthened, particularly in Congress, a paper trail began to emerge tracing the evolution of Bush administration policies regarding the status and treatment of detainees. A number of legal memoranda from Justice Department lawyers and the White House counsel surfaced that interpret the limitations on the detention and interrogation of prisoners in the war on terrorism extremely narrowly. Indeed, in a leaked memo dated January 25, 2003, White House Counsel Alberto Gonzales advised the president on how to preserve the government's flexibility in the detention and interrogation of suspects:

> As you have said, the war on terrorism is a new kind of war. . . . The nature of the war places a high premium on other factors, such as the ability to obtain information from captured terrorists and their sponsors in order to avoid further atrocities against American civilians, and the need to try terrorists for war crimes such as wantonly killing civilians. In my judgment, this new paradigm renders obsolete Geneva's strict limitation on questioning enemy prisoners and renders quaint some of its provisions.[38]

Other legal memos appear to explore ways to circumvent domestic and international laws prohibiting torture. One emphasizes the evidentiary hurdles to the prosecution of torture:

> To convict a defendant of torture [under federal criminal law], the prosecution must establish that: (1) the torture occurred outside the United States; (2) the defendant acted under the color of law; (3) the victim was within the defendant's custody or physical control; (4) the defendant specifically intended to cause severe physical or mental pain and suffering; and (5) that the act inflicted severe mental pain and suffering.[39]

Each of these requirements presented new opportunities to further narrow the definition of torture. For example, the intent clause was interpreted to require that inflicting severe pain or suffering contrary to the law be the primary *intent* of the defendant. "Thus, even if the defendant knows that severe pain will result from his actions, if causing such harm is not his objective, he lacks the requisite specific intent . . . ; a defendant is guilty of torture only if he acts with the express purpose of inflicting severe pain or suffering." Likewise, the memo argues, federal law "makes plain that the infliction of pain or suffering per se . . . is insufficient to amount to torture. Instead, the text provides that the pain or suffering must be 'severe,'" which government lawyers interpreted to mean "death, organ failure, or the permanent impairment of a significant bodily function."[40] The memorandum further maintains that under the president's authority as commander in chief, torture is lawful as long as it is carried out to protect U.S. national security and that interference by Congress or the courts would be unconstitutional. Another memo, prepared by the Justice Department, explains,

> Even if an interrogation method [might arguably constitute torture under these narrow definitions], and application of the statute was not held to be an unconstitutional infringement of the President's Commander-in-Chief authority, we believe that under current circumstances certain justifications [including military necessity or self-defense] might be available that would potentially eliminate criminal liability.[41]

That memo also draws a legal distinction between torture, which is illegal, and lesser forms of cruel, inhuman, or degrading treatment or punishment, which are to be deplored and prevented but are not so universally and categorically condemned as to be illegal. A lengthy portion of the memo goes on to explore a range of cruel, inhuman, and degrading actions, just short of torture, which Justice Department lawyers argue would not violate domestic and international prohibitions on torture if applied. For example, forcing someone onto their hands and knees and kicking them in the stomach might not be construed as torture, but rape or sexual assault would.[42]

Some groups within the administration were offended by these arguments. There was, reportedly, "almost a revolt" by the military's judge advocates general, or JAGs, including lawyers who report to the chairman of the Joint Chiefs of Staff. In frustration, they took their concerns public, charging that there was "a calculated effort to create an atmosphere of legal ambiguity" about how the [Geneva C]onventions should be applied."[43] State Department lawyers also objected. Taft, the State Department's legal adviser, hastily added his own memo to the debate, arguing that the Justice Department's legal advice to President Bush was "'seriously flawed,' its reasoning 'incorrect as well as incomplete,' and all of it 'contrary to the official position of the United States, the United Nations and all other states that have considered the issue.'"[44]

Although the administration argued that these memos were "theoretical" rather than operational, it has become increasingly clear that the secretary of defense did expand the scope and nature of permissible interrogation techniques and admitted that he hid some detainees from the Red Cross at the request of Director of Central Intelligence George Tenet.[45] It is also undeniable that gross abuses, reported by the Red Cross and confirmed in detail in a report by Major General Antonio Taguba,[46] were rife in Iraq prisons. Although the administration vigorously denied that it in any way condoned torture, some observers have concluded that the atmosphere of legal ambiguity at the very least opened the door for abuses. One report, prepared by three senior army generals and commonly known as the Fay report, after its chair, General George R. Fay, asserts that "a list of interrogation techniques approved by Defense Sec[retary] Rumsfeld for use at the US detention facility at Guantanamo Bay, Cuba, migrated improperly to Abu Ghraib and contributed to some of the abuses there."[47] A four-member independent panel headed by James A. Schlesinger reiterated that "leadership failures at the highest levels of the Pentagon, Joint Chiefs of Staff and military command in Iraq contributed to an environment in which detainees were abused at Abu Ghraib prison and other facilities."[48] Public trust in the administration's appeal for wide latitude in dealing with detainees in the war on terror reached new lows in the wake of these revelations.

Extraordinary Rendition and Secret Prisons

Although information has been difficult to obtain, there is now strong evidence that the executive branch has also held prisoners in a number of secret detention facilities offshore. Some of those detainees were taken into custody through a process known as "extraordinary rendition," in which the U.S. government has abducted persons suspected of supporting international terrorism—often in collusion with friendly governments—and taken them to other foreign countries for "interrogation" purposes.

The two best known cases involve Maher Arar and Khaled El-Masri. Arar is a dual citizen of Syria and Canada. He was living in Canada when he took a family vacation to Tunis in September 2002. Responding to his employer's request to return, Arar took a plane that had a stopover in New York. There, he was taken aside by immigration authorities and interrogated for more than a week. Following this, Arar was flown to Syria, where he was detained for ten months, and subjected to torture throughout the period, before finally being released and allowed to return to his family in Canada. After a full inquiry, the Canadian government exonerated Arar of having any connection to terrorism and awarded him nearly $10 million in restitution. The United States has refused to acknowledge any wrongdoing, and to this day Arar remains on the government's terrorist watch list.

Khaled El-Masri is a German citizen of Lebanese descent, who was arrested by Macedonian authorities during a family vacation and turned over to CIA operatives. He was flown to Kabul, Afghanistan, and detained there for five months. While in detention, he was tortured. Ultimately, he was flown to a remote area of Albania and released. El-Masri then filed suit in U.S. district court against former Director of Central Intelligence Tenet, three corporate defendants, ten unnamed employees of the CIA, and ten unnamed employees of the defendant corporations. The government sought dismissal of the suit on the basis of the "state secrets" doctrine—namely, that to defend itself in the case, the government would be forced to disclose sensitive military secrets and operations. This district court ruled in favor of the United States and dismissed his case. On appeal, El-Masri claimed that the both the Council of Europe and President Bush himself had publicly acknowledged the existence of the extraordinary rendition program. Thus, there was no longer any "secret" that the "state secrets" doctrine could be applied to. The Fourth Circuit Court of Appeals disagreed and upheld the dismissal, on the grounds that pursuit of El-Masri's claim might still involve the disclosure of some sensitive military information.

Enter the Courts

The U.S. courts have been left to untangle the competing claims about the rights of detainees in the war on terrorism. A number of questions have been raised:

- How broad is the latitude that the president can expect in the execution of the war on terrorism? Does the doctrine of separation of powers limit judicial oversight of the president's treatment of various categories of detainees, or demand it?
- Do the courts have jurisdiction over enemy combatants on territory outside the United States but effectively and fully under U.S. military control?

- Do U.S. citizens retain all of their constitutional rights even when they are found (or thought to be) serving the enemy? What (if any) are the rights of detainees in Afghanistan and Iraq? What (if any) protections are available for targets of extraordinary rendition?

Hamdi v. Rumsfeld

Among the first major challenges to executive branch claims to broad authority in the war on terrorism was the case of *Hamdi v. Rumsfeld.* The U.S District Court for the Eastern District of Virginia, where Hamdi's habeas petition was filed, ruled against the government's detention on the grounds that the so-called Mobbs declaration—which laid out the factual case for Hamdi's designation as enemy combatant—was "far short" of supporting it. The court ordered not only that Hamdi be allowed access to counsel, but also that the government turn over evidence to him, such as notes of previous interrogations, that he could use in preparing his defense.[49] The U.S. Court of Appeals for the Fourth Circuit overturned the district court's ruling, charging that the district court had failed to exercise the level of "caution" or deference necessary in a case involving national security. For the majority, at least, it was "undisputed" that Hamdi was captured in a zone of active combat in a foreign theater of conflict; on this basis the court held that Hamdi was not to be allowed to challenge the facts presented in the Mobbs declaration.[50]

Yet what the majority thought was "undisputed" was most certainly disputed by two of the circuit court judges. Separate dissenting opinions by Judge J. Michael Luttig and Judge Diane G. Motz expressed strong concerns about the administration's efforts, with the support of the lower court, to allow for "the elimination of protections afforded a citizen by the Constitution solely on the basis of the Executive's designation of that citizen as an enemy combatant, without testing the accuracy of the designation. Neither the Constitution nor controlling precedent sanction this holding."[51] The dissenters argued that the administration and lower court had overstepped their authority:

> The Constitution gives the Congress, not the Executive and not the courts, the power to suspend the writ of habeas corpus when the public safety requires it. U.S. Const. Art. I, Sec. 9. Absent a suspension of the writ, the Constitution demands that we strike the proper balance between ensuring the Executive's ability to wage war effectively and protecting the individual rights guaranteed to all American citizens. Without such a balance, our system of ordered liberty will indeed ring hollow.[52]

The Supreme Court's treatment of *Hamdi* was equally fraught with tensions and disagreements about the appropriate checks and balances in the war on terrorism. The ruling of the Court, announced in a plurality opinion written by Justice Sandra Day O'Connor, was that while the president was authorized to detain enemy combatants (by virtue of the resolution Authorizing Use of United States Armed Forces), the due process clause also demanded a "meaningful opportunity to contest the factual basis for that detention before a neutral decisionmaker."[53] The Court rejected the government's contention that the Constitution afforded the president virtually unlimited discretion in the conduct of the war on terrorism in favor of a more "balanced" approach to the requirement of due process in wartime:

> [W]hile we do not question that our due process assessment must pay keen attention to the particular burdens faced by the Executive in the context of military action, it would turn our system of checks and balances on its head to suggest that a citizen could not make his way to court with a challenge to the factual basis for his detention by his government, simply because the Executive opposes making available such a challenge. Absent suspension of the writ by Congress, a citizen detained as an enemy combatant is entitled to this process.[54]

Justice Souter's opinion (joined by Justice Ruth Bader Ginsburg) explicitly highlighted, again, the separation of powers issues raised by this case, as well as delicate balance between security and liberty:

> The defining character of American constitutional government is its constant tension between security and liberty, serving both by partial helpings of each. In a government of separated powers, deciding finally on what is a reasonable degree of guaranteed liberty whether in peace or war (or some condition in between) is not well entrusted to the Executive Branch of Government, whose particular responsibility is to maintain security. For reasons of inescapable human nature, the branch of the Government asked to counter a serious threat is not the branch on which to rest the Nation's entire reliance in striking the balance between the will to win and the cost in liberty on the way to victory; the responsibility for security will naturally amplify the claim that security legitimately raises.[55]

Following the Court's decision, in October 2004, Hamdi was released from U.S. custody and flown to Saudi Arabia. He remains there under house arrest.

Rumsfeld v. Padilla

Like *Hamdi, Rumsfeld v. Padilla* bounced up and down the judicial system. Two days after Padilla was turned over to officials of the Defense Department in New York and taken to the naval brig in South Carolina, his attorney, Donna

Newman, filed a habeas corpus petition with the Southern District Court of New York. Ruling on this habeas petition, the district court held that Congress had provided the executive the authority to detain enemy combatants through its joint resolution of September 18, 2001, granting the president the power to "use all necessary and appropriate force." The court also ruled, however, that Padilla must be allowed to challenge his detention and have access of counsel in doing so.[56]

The district court's order directed the parties to set conditions under which Padilla could meet with attorney Newman, but Secretary Rumsfeld refused to do so, and the government then moved to have this part of the order set aside. Relying on the so-called Jacoby Declaration—named after Vice Admiral Lowell Jacoby, director of the Defense Intelligence Agency—the government argued that access to counsel would severely retard interrogation efforts. Once again, however, the district court found these arguments speculative.[57]

The case then moved to the Court of Appeals for the Second Circuit, which ruled that the president did not have the authority to detain Padilla.[58] This court held that under the provisions of the Non-Detention Act,[59] the president could not imprison an American citizen on U.S. soil without congressional authorization. The joint resolution of September 18, 2001, the court held, could not be read as the basis of such authority. The Second Circuit's approach was primarily based on a separation of powers analysis, relying heavily on Justice Robert H. Jackson's discussion of presidential power in *Youngstown Sheet and Tube Co. v. Sawyer* (1952).[60] In his now-famous concurring opinion in that case, Jackson argued that presidential power in the realm of foreign affairs is at its greatest when the executive acts with congressional authorization, but at its "lowest ebb" when acting against the wishes of Congress. The court of appeals held that in Padilla's case the president was acting without congressional authority.

The Supreme Court reversed the Second Circuit ruling, but it did so on the basis of a technicality—that the habeas petition was filed in the wrong court; Padilla was in custody in South Carolina at the time that the petition was filed in New York. Padilla remains in custody today, but in 2006 the government declared that Padilla was no longer an enemy combatant. Instead, it transferred him to civilian custody and filed conspiracy charges against him unrelated to the original "dirty bomb" claim.

Rasul et al. v. Bush

Rasul et al. v. Bush was a consolidated action brought by a group of British, Australian, and Kuwaiti nationals being detained by the U.S. government at

Guantanamo Bay. Relying primarily on the Supreme Court's decision in *Johnson v. Eisentrager* (1950),[61] the U.S. District Court for the District of Columbia dismissed their suit for want of jurisdiction, holding that aliens detained outside the sovereign territory of the United States may not invoke a petition for a writ of habeas corpus.[62] The Court of Appeals for the District of Columbia affirmed the dismissal, holding that "the 'privilege of litigation' does not extend to aliens in military custody who have no presence in any territory over which the United States is sovereign."[63]

The Supreme Court reversed the court of appeals decision.[64] The majority opinion emphasized the historic purpose of the writ to justify and reaffirm "the federal courts' power to review applications for habeas relief in a wide variety of cases involving Executive detention, in wartime as well as in times of peace."[65] Traditionally, the writ has been seen as the primary protection against executive restraint. The Court affirmed that "[a]t its historical core, the writ of habeas corpus has served as a means of reviewing the legality of Executive detention, and it is in that context that its protections have been strongest."[66] Congress has generally supported this broad interpretation, the Court noted, "extending the protections of the writ to all cases where any person may be restrained of his or her liberty in violation of the constitution, or of any treaty or law of the United States."[67] The fact that the petitioners are aliens and are located outside the United States did not matter to the Supreme Court.

For the Court, the crux of the matter was the proper scope of *Eisentrager* in defining the rights of detainees. That case arose during the close of World War II. The plaintiffs were a group of twenty-one German nationals who had been captured in China for engaging in espionage against the United States. Following a trial and conviction by a U.S. military commission sitting in China, the prisoners were shipped to the Landsberg prison in Germany. Their legal challenges ultimately reached the Supreme Court, which ruled that the detainees were not entitled to any legal remedy under U.S. law.

The Supreme Court in 2004 found important distinctions between the detainees in *Eisentrager* and *Rasul et al.*:

> Petitioners in [*Rasul et al.*] differ from the *Eisentrager* detainees in important respects. They are not nationals of countries at war with the United States, and they deny that they have engaged in or plotted acts of aggression against the United States; they have never been afforded access to any tribunal, much less charged with and convicted of wrongdoing; and for more than two years they have been imprisoned in territory over which the United States exercises exclusive jurisdiction and control.[68]

Justice Anthony M. Kennedy, in a concurring opinion, added that also unlike the *Eisentrager* case, Guantanamo Bay is in every practical respect a U.S. territory, and it is one far removed from any hostilities.[69] Moreover, the detainees at Guantanamo Bay face the possibility of indefinite detention, and without any benefit of a legal proceeding to determine their status, whereas the Germans were tried and convicted by a military tribunal.

Justice Scalia filed a dissenting opinion, joined by Chief Justice Rehnquist and Justice Thomas. For Scalia, the crux of the case was that the Guantanamo Bay detainees are not located within the territorial jurisdiction of *any* federal district court, and thus the protections afforded under the habeas statute do not extend to them. Scalia went on to describe the "breathtaking" and, in his view, frightening consequences of the majority's decision:

> It permits an alien captured in a foreign theater of active combat to bring a Sec. 2241 petition against the Secretary of Defense. Over the course of the last century, the United States has held millions of alien prisoners abroad. . . . A great many of these prisoners would no doubt have complained about the circumstances of their capture and the terms of their confinement.[70]

For good or for ill, the major thrust of this and the other Supreme Court decisions regarding the detainees was to reassert the judiciary's authority in defining and defending due process in the administration's war on terrorism. However, the decisions also highlighted the role of Congress in defining the reaches of both the administration and the judiciary through the legislative process. Because many of the legal controversies that made their way to the courts depended on differing interpretations of previous laws, breaking the stalemate between the executive and judiciary would require new legislation. The legislature was quick to respond to the call. Before the Guantanamo detainees could take advantage of the Court's ruling, Congress passed new legislation that took away the very rights that the courts had granted detainees. Furthermore, the Justice Department has asked the federal appeals court to restrict Guantanamo detainees' access to their lawyers, who the administration charges have "'caused Intractable problems and threats to security at Guantanamo'" by "caus[ing] unrest among the detainees and improperly serv[ing] as a conduit to the news media."[71]

Congress Responds

Following the Supreme Court's decisions in *Rasul* and *Hamdi,* in December 2005, Congress passed the Detainee Treatment Act (P.L. 109-148, 119 Stat. 2680), which added a new subsection (e) to the habeas statute, which reads: "[e]xcept as provided in section 1005 of the [DTA], no court, justice, or judge" may exercise jurisdiction over:

> (1) an application for a writ of habeas corpus filed by or on behalf of an alien detained by the Department of Defense at Guantanamo Bay, Cuba; or
> (2) any other action against the United States or its agents relating to any aspect of the detention by the Department of Defense of an alien at Guantanamo Bay, Cuba who
> > (A) is currently in military custody; or
> > (B) has been determined by the United States Court of Appeals for the District of Columbia Circuit . . . to have been properly detained as an enemy combatant.

The Detainee Treatment Act attempted to limit the judiciary's role to the D.C. Circuit Court, and then only for the purpose of determining whether the designation of "enemy combatant" was supported by the evidence that the administration provided. The only reason the federal courts were able to take up these issues again stemmed from ambiguity in the act about whether or not it would apply to cases pending when the legislation was passed.

And the Supreme Court Responds

In June 2006 the Supreme Court took up the matter of the Detainee Treatment Act. Salim Ahmed Hamdan was being detained as an enemy combatant at Guantanamo Bay, Cuba, and challenged the legality of the military tribunals the administration created to try the detainees. The Court agreed with the substantive claim that the proposed military commissions were inconsistent with the procedures established under both the Uniform Code of Military Justice and the Geneva Conventions. It also affirmed the Court's authority to hear the case, despite provisions in the DTA that eliminated most avenues for judicial oversight in matters related to the detainees. Although the government claimed that the DTA had removed the Supreme Court's jurisdiction, the Court disagreed. Rather, it pointed to a provision of the DTA that stated that subsections (e)(2) and (e)(3) of section 1005 "shall apply with respect to any claim . . . that is pending on or after the date of the enactment of this Act [DTA Sec. 1005(h)]." No provision of the DTA stated whether subsection (e)(1) applied to pending cases. However, the Court found evidence in the legislative record that the omission of pending cases from the exemption from judicial review was purposeful. The Court therefore refused to dismiss the suit brought by petitioner Salim Ahmed

Hamdan, a Yemeni national in detention at Guantanamo Bay, and purportedly Osama Bin Laden's former driver.

Congress Responds to the Hamdan Decision

The tug of war between Congress and the president, on the one hand, and the Supreme Court, on the other, recommenced after the Court's decision in *Hamdan v. Rumsfeld.* Congress responded to the decision by passing the Military Commissions Act of 2006 (P.L. 109-366, 120 Stat. 2600) (2006) (MCA), which the president signed into law on October 17, 2006. Subsection 7(a) of the MCA, entitled "Habeas Corpus Matters," added a new amendment, which reads:

> (1) No court, justice or judge shall have jurisdiction to hear or consider an application for a writ of habeas corpus filed by or on behalf of an alien detained by the United States who has been determined by the United States to have been properly detained as an enemy combatant or is awaiting such determination.
> (2) Except as provided in [section 1005(e)(2) and (e)(3) of the DTA], no court, justice, or judge shall have jurisdiction to hear or consider any other action against the United States or its agents relating to any aspect of the detention, transfer, treatment, trial, or conditions of confinement of an alien who is or was detained by the United States and has been determined by the United States to have been properly detained as an enemy combatant or is awaiting such determination.

Furthermore, a new subsection (b) provides:

> The amendment made by subsection (a) shall take effect on the date of the enactment of this Act, and shall apply to all cases, without exception, pending on or after the date of the enactment of this Act which relate to any aspect of the detention, transfer, trial, or conditions of detention of an alien detained by the United States since September 11, 2001.

Congress again clearly and consistently favored executive privilege in the conduct of the war on terrorism.

Tipping the Balance?

As of this writing, it remains unclear whether Congress has (finally) removed the ability of the judiciary to hear habeas corpus petitions brought by those designated "enemy combatants." In *Boumediene v. Bush,*[72] the U.S. Court of Appeals for the District of Columbia held that through the Military Commissions Act, Congress had removed such jurisdiction from the federal courts. Referring to the long-standing battle between Congress and the courts on this matter, as well as the MCA's language referring to "all cases, without exception," the Court of Appeals declared: "It is almost as if the proponents of these words were slamming their fists on the table shouting 'When we say "all," we mean all—*without exception!*' " (emphasis in original).

Interestingly enough, however, Judge Judith Rogers filed a dissenting opinion that agreed that Congress had shut off habeas relief for enemy combatants—under federal statute. However, Rogers claimed that under the Constitution, Congress cannot suspend the writ of habeas corpus without providing an "adequate alternative," and this the Congress had failed to do. Indeed, the first cases before the military tribunal in Guantanamo raised serious questions about the adequacy and integrity of the process. For example, in the case against David Hicks, an Australian national, the judge unexpectedly disqualified two of his three lawyers—one of them for not signing a form committing himself to conform to regulations governing the proceeding, which had not yet been created by the Secretary of Defense. Then, in another surprise move, Hicks was given a nine-month sentence to be served in Australia, as the result of a secret plea agreement that effectively bypassed the panel of military officers ostensibly presiding over the case. Heavy lobbying by the Australian government is widely believed to have influenced the plea agreement, raising serious concerns about the independence of the court from political influence from the administration. In any case, it seems certain that *Boumediene* will soon make its way up to the Supreme Court, which will then have yet another opportunity on the matter.

Of course, the democratic process ensures that the incumbents in Congress and the presidency will change with some regularity, and with them the priorities and policies of the government. Already, Democratic control of the House of Representatives has created more resistance in Congress to extending the president's already broad powers in the war on terrorism. For example, a number of recent congressional hearings have focused on charges of abuses of power by the FBI, the Justice Department, and other executive agencies.

Moreover, presidential elections in 2008 have already generated a full field of contenders, all seeking to distance and distinguish themselves from public disappointment with the Bush administration's handling of the war on terror. It is clear, however, that the problems generated by the war on terror and now the war in Iraq are not going away anytime soon. Thus the proper ends and means of the government's engagement will continue to be a source of intense debate.

Conclusion

The debate over the rights of detainees has raged so furiously and on so many fronts because the stakes are so high. The fundamental interests and values of the United States hang in the balance. Does terrorism represent a clear and present threat to U.S. national security? Does the threat terrorism poses necessitate limitations on legal rights and freedoms? What is the appropriate trade-off between security and freedom? Does the nature of the threat render international institutions and laws obsolete? What are the proper roles of the president, Congress, and the courts in striking the right balance between competing interests and values? What does it mean to say that the United States is a nation that follows the rule of law?

Key Actors

John Ashcroft Attorney general, fundamentally reoriented the Justice Department after September 11 to give priority to security and to emphasize prevention over prosecution; had primary responsibility over the September 11 detainees.

George W. Bush President, sought expanded powers for executive agencies based on "war footing" of the country after September 11 and the president's constitutional role as commander in chief.

Colin Powell Secretary of state, offered views on U.S. obligations under international law that were often contrary to the views of the Justice Department and the Defense Department.

Donald Rumsfeld Secretary of defense, had primary responsibility for the detention and interrogation of all persons designated "enemy combatants."

U.S. Supreme Court Court of last resort, ruled on the legal limits of the executive branch's detention policies in the Bush administration's war on terrorism.

Notes

1. "Address to a Joint Session of Congress and to the American Public," September 20, 2001, www.whitehouse.gov/news/releases/2001/09/20010920-8.html.

2. Ibid.

3. "Imprisoned persons," by contrast, refers to people who have been "deprived of personal liberty as a result of conviction for an offense." UN General Assembly, "Body of Principles for the Protection of All Persons under Any Form of Detention or Imprisonment," General Assembly Resolution 43/173, passed December 9, 1988.

4. Opinion written by Chief Judge T. Harvie Wilkinson III, *Hamdi v. Rumsfeld,* 316 F. 3rd 450, 464 (4th Cir. 2003).

5. The number is approximate because the government has never released complete information about the detainees.

6. Steve Fainaru, "Court Says Detainees' IDs Can Be Kept Secret; Panel: 9/11 Realities Outweigh Disclosure," *Washington Post,* June 18, 2003.

7. *Center for National Security Studies et al. v. Department of Justice,* No. 01-2500, www.cnss.org/discoveryopinion.pdf.

8. Fainaru, "Court Says Datainees' IDs Can Be Kept Secret."

9. Neil A. Lewis, "Threats and Responses: The Detainees: Secrecy Is Backed on 9/11 Detainees," *New York Times,* June 18, 2003.

10. USA Patriot Act, sec. 41-412.

11. Office of the Inspector General, Justice Department, "The September 11 Detainees: A Review of the Treatment of Aliens Held on Immigrations Charges in Connection with the Investigation of the September 11 Attacks," Washington, D.C., April 2003.

12. Tim Golden and Don Van Natta Jr., "U.S. Said to Overstate Value of Guantanamo Detainees," *New York Times,* June 21, 2004.

13. Neil A. Lewis, "Bush's Power to Plan Trial of Detainees Is Challenged," *New York Times,* January 16, 2004.

14. U.S. Department of Defense, Office of the Assistant Secretary of Defense (Public Affairs) News Release, no. 253-07, March 6, 2007, "Guantanamo Bay 2006 Administrative Review Board Results Announced."

15. John Barry, Michael Hirsh, and Michael Isikoff, "The Roots of Torture," *Newsweek International,* May 24, 2004.

16. *Rasul et al. v. Bush,* No. 03-334, Brief for the Respondents in Opposition, www.usdoj.gov/osg/briefs/2003/0responses/2003-0334.resp.html.

17. Respondent's Motion to Dismiss Petitioner's First Amended Writ of Habeas Corpus, U.S. District Court for the District of Columbia, March 18, 2002, *Rasul et al. v. Bush,* No. 02-0299 (CKK), www.ccr-ny.org/v2/legal/september_11th/docs/Government ResponseToRasulPetition.pdf (accessed April 23, 2004) (emphasis in original).

18. Patti Waldmeir, "Court Tries to Balance Guantanamo Detainee Rights with Security Goals," *Financial Times,* April 21, 2004.

19. Michael Isikoff, "Memos Reveal War Crimes Warnings," *Newsweek,* May 17, 2004, www.msnbc.msn.com/id/4999734/site/newsweek/site/newsweek.

20. Under mounting pressure from human rights groups as well as Congress, the Defense Department has released a number of previously classified documents outlining the government's interrogation policies. See "Working Group Report on Detainee Interrogations in the Global War on Terrorism: Assessment of Legal, Historical, Policy, and Operational Considerations," March 6, 2003, http://i.a.cnn.net/cnn/2004/images/06/09/pentagonreportpart1.pdf, and an untitled and incomplete report at http://i.a.cnn.net/cnn/2004/images/06/09/pentagonreportpart2.pdf.

21. General Miller assumed command of the Guantanamo base after interrogators complained that his predecessor was too soft on the detainees.

22. Barry, Hirsh, and Isikoff, "The Roots of Torture."

23. Associated Press, "Guantanamo Suicide Bids May Be Tied to General," MSNBC, June 22, 2004, www.msnbc.msn.com/id/5261632.

24. Golden and Van Natta, "U.S. Said to Overstate Value."

25. Ibid.

26. The government recognized that Mobbs had no firsthand knowledge of the facts surrounding Hamdi's surrender. Rather, his knowledge was based on information provided by the Northern Alliance.

27. Michael H. Mobbs, special adviser to the under secretary of defense for policy, filed in *Hamdi v. Rumsfeld*, No. 2:02CV439 (E.D. Va.), www.pbs.org/wgbh/pages/frontline/shows/sleeper/tools/mobbshamdi.html.

28. "Statement of Attorney General John Ashcroft Regarding the Padilla Case," www.fas.org/irp/news/2004/02/doj022004.html.

29. Oral arguments before the Supreme Court, *Rumsfeld v. Padilla*, No. 03-1027, April 28, 2004, www.supremecourtus.gov/oral_arguments/argument_transcripts/03-1027.pdf.

30. Oral arguments before the Supreme Court, *Hamdi v. Rumsfeld.*

31. Reply brief, U.S. Court of Appeals for the Second Circuit, *Padilla v. Rumsfeld*, No. 03-2235; 03-2438, www.cnss.org/Padilla_Reply_Brief.pdf.

32. "A Threat to All Citizens," editorial, *Boston Globe*, April 30, 2004.

33. Senate Committee on the Judiciary, *DOJ Oversight: Terrorism and Other Topics*, hearings, June 8, 2004.

34. Rajiv Chandrasekaran and Scott Wilson, "Mistreatment of Detainees Went beyond Guards' Abuse," *Washington Post*, June 11, 2004.

35. Michael Isikoff and Mark Hosenball, "Facing Defeat," *Newsweek* online, MSNBC.com, June 16, 2004, www.msnbc.msn.com/id/5175105/site/newsweek.

36. Walter Pincus, "U.S. Holds 18,000 Detainees in Iraq; Recent Security Crackdown in Baghdad Nets Another 1,000," *Washington Post*, April 15, 2007, A24.

37. Elizabeth Bumiller and Eric Schmitt, "President Sorry for Iraq Abuse: Backs Rumsfeld," *New York Times*, May 7, 2004.

38. Alberto Gonzales, memorandum for the president, "Decision Re: Application of the Geneva Conventions on Prisoners of War to the Conflict with Al Qaeda and the Taliban," www.library.law.pace.edu/research/020125_gonzalesmemo.pdf.

39. "Working Group Report on Detainee Interrogations in the Global War on Terrorism: Assessment of Legal, Historical, Policy, and Operational Considerations," March 6, 2003, www.ccr-ny.org/v2/reports/docs/PentagonReportMarch.pdf. See also the Memorandum for the General Counsel for the Department of Defense, www.dod.gov/news/Jun2004/d20040622doc8.pdf.

40. "Working Group Report on Detainee Interrogations in the Global War on Terrorism: Assessment of Legal, Historical, Policy and Operational Considerations," April 4, 2003, available at www.defenselink.mil/news/Jun2004/d20040622doc8.pdf.

41. Jay S. Bybee, "Memorandum for Alberto R. Gonzales: Re Standards of Conduct and Interrogation under 18 U.S.C.§§ 2340–2340A," August 1, 2002, http://news.findlaw.com/wp/docs/doj/bybee80102mem.pdf.

42. Ibid.

43. Barry, Hirsch, and Isikoff, "The Roots of Torture."

44. R. Jeffrey Smith, "Military Legal Advisers also Questioned Tactics," *Washington Post*, June 24, 2004, A7, quoting from Taft, memo to White House counsel regarding

comments on the applicability of the Geneva Convention to al Qaeda and Taliban prisoners, February 2, 2002. The Taft memo is available at www.fas.org/sgp/othergov/taft.pdf.

45. Memos are available at www.dod.gov/releases/2004/nr20040622-0930.html.

46. Antonio Taguba, "Article 15-6 Investigation of the 800th Military Police Brigade," made available to the public in May 2004, http://news.findlaw.com/hdocs/ docs/iraq/tagubarpt.html.

47. Greg Jaffe, "Army Blames Confusion in Iraq for Iraqi Abuse," *Wall Street Journal,* August 27, 2004, A3.

48. Eric Schmitt, "Defense Faulted by Panel in Prison Abuse," *New York Times,* August 24, 2004, 1.

49. *Hamdi v. Rumsfeld,* 243 F. Supp. 2d 527 (E.D. Va. 2002).

50. *Hamdi v. Rumsfeld,* 316 F. 450, 459 (4th Cir. 2003).

51. Id. at 369, Judge Motz dissenting.

52. Id.

53. Syllabus, *Hamdi v. Rumsfeld,* No. 03-6696, 2004 U.S. LEXIS 4761, at ***5 (U.S. Sup. Ct., June 28, 2004). The case is available at http://caselaw.lp.findlaw.com/cgibin/getcase.pl?court=US&navby=case&vol=000&invol=03-6696.

54. *Hamdi v. Rumsfeld,* 124 S. Ct. 2633, 2650 (2004).

55. Id. at 2655, Justice Souter concurring in part and dissenting in part.

56. *Padilla v. Rumsfeld,* 233 F. Supp. 2d 564 (S.D.N.Y. 2002).

57. *Padilla v. Rumsfeld,* 243 F. Supp. 2d 42 (S.D.N.Y. 2003).

58. *Padilla v. Rumsfeld,* 352 F. 3d 695 (2d. Cir. 2003).

59. The statute, 18 U.S.C. Sec. 4001 (a) (2000), reads, "No citizen shall be imprisoned or otherwise detained by the United States except pursuant to an Act of Congress."

60. *Youngstown Sheet and Tube Co. v. Sawyer,* 343 U.S. 579 (1952).

61. *Johnson v. Eisentrager,* 339 U.S. 763 (1950).

62. *Rasul v. Bush, Habib v. Bush,* and *Al Odah v. Bush,* 215 F. Supp. 2d 55 (D.D.C. 2002).

63. *Rasul v. Bush, Habib v. Bush,* and *Al Odah v. Bush,* 321 F. 3d 1134 (D.C. Cir. 2003).

64. *Rasul et al. v. Bush* is available at http://caselaw.lp.findlaw.com/cgi-bin/getcase.pl?court=US&navby=case&vol=000&invol=03-334.

65. 124 S. Ct. 2692-93.

66. Id. At 2692 (citation omitted).

67. Id. (referencing Habeas Act of February 5, 1867).

68. *Rasul et al. v. Bush,* 124 S. Ct. 2686, 2693 (2004).

69. Id. at 2700, Justice Kennedy concurring.

70. Id. at 2706, Justice Scalia dissenting.

71. William Glaberson, "U.S. Asks Court to Limit Lawyers at Guantanamo," *New York Times,* April 26, 2007, A1.

72. 476 F. 3d 981 (D.C. Cir. 2007).

Conclusion

Ralph G. Carter

These case studies illustrate the array of external challenges and opportunities, substantive issues, internal political situations, and policy-making dynamics likely to confront U.S. foreign policy makers well into the early twenty-first century. Although each of the fifteen cases offers a unique perspective on policy-making, patterns can be discerned in the internal and external policymaking environments.

On the Outside: Shifts in External Challenges

Foreign policy is made by individuals who act in the name of the state, and they do so in relation to the external and internal environments. Although the concept of viewing "the state as an actor in a situation" may not be new, it continues to be helpful.[1] The external environment can present opportunities to embrace or problems to solve. How foreign policy makers react to such external situations often depends on the internal environment. Why they become involved in a situation makes a difference, and how their preferences correspond to those of the people, opinion makers, and the news media plays a major role in decision making.

The cold war era was dominated by the politics of national security. To U.S. foreign policy makers, the Soviet threat overrode all other foreign policy issues. Persistent images of a relentless enemy and the potentially catastrophic costs of a policy mistake typically led administration officials neither to seek nor to encourage input from others who might know less about the external situation.[2] Although some observers perceived that the policymaking preeminence of the president ended with the Vietnam War,[3] most would agree that such presidential preeminence ended with the end of the cold war. Without the threat of nuclear annihilation looming over policy discussions, reasonable people could disagree about what the United States should do in foreign affairs.[4] So in the post–cold war and post-September 11 era, the external situation neither stifles foreign policy debate nor deters the participation of potential policymaking actors. While during the cold war many "realists" seemed to think that only the external environment mattered, there now seems little question that both the external and the internal political situations significantly influence U.S. foreign policy makers.

In the present era, fewer external challenges and opportunities that confront U.S. foreign policy makers are the traditional ones. Terrorism on a global scale, combatants unaccountable to any state, regime change and nation-building, rogue regimes, nuclear proliferation, genocidal civil wars, financial crises, drug smuggling, and global environmental degradation are but a few such examples of the challenges policymakers face. Other examples are more positive, such as the structuring of beneficial trade relations, helping people and states through multilateral assistance, and creating new, cooperative international institutions to handle complex problems. For U.S. policymakers, the difficult questions are whether the United States should respond to a particular situation and, if so, how.

On the Inside: The New Foreign Policy Challenges

The answers to whether and how the United States should respond are usually found in the internal political situation. As James Scott sums it up, "A changing agenda and increasing interdependence and transnational ties make foreign policy making more like domestic policy making: subject to conflict, bargaining, and persuasion among competing groups within and outside the government."[5] This statement echoes a remark made by President Bill Clinton: "The more time I spend on foreign policy . . . the more I become convinced that there is no longer a clear distinction between what is foreign and domestic."[6] During the cold war, the president and his advisers directed foreign policy, but in the present era members of Congress and other powerful groups have become highly visible participants in the process. There are now numerous actors clamoring to act in the name and best interest of the United States.

Interbranch Leadership: Presidential-Congressional Interactions

In the present period some actions remain clearly presidential, such as decisions to go to war. In other instances, Congress seems to be calling the tune, such as in establishing Cuba policy through the Helms-Burton Act, telling the president not even to consider sending the Kyoto Protocol or the International Criminal Court treaty to the Senate for ratification, or telling the president he cannot have the immigration reform legislation he wants.

Today presidents and members of Congress openly vie for influence over many policy issues, with each branch doing its best to shape the outcome. The possible results of this pattern of interbranch leadership include cooperation, constructive compromise, institutional competition, or confrontation and stalemate.[7] The cases in this volume illustrate all four of these variants. For example, the Colombian drug case reflects institutional cooperation; the China trade case reveals constructive compromise; institutional competition is at the heart of the port security case; and confrontation and stalemate mark the immigration reform case. The judicial branch also occasionally becomes a major actor in these policy disputes, as the National Security Agency (NSA) eavesdropping case and the detainees case demonstrate.

Each branch of government uses direct and indirect tactics to accomplish its goals. Direct tactics reflected here include the introduction by members of Congress of legislation to change U.S. policy (as in the NSA eavesdropping, immigration reform, Helms-Burton, China trade, World Trade Organization (WTO) trade subsidy, International Criminal Court (ICC), and detainees cases) and presidents' using the military (such as in the terrorism, Iraq, and Colombian aid cases) and promoting diplomatic negotiations (as in the Iranian, North Korean, and ICC cases). Sometimes, when both branches want to "frame" issues in a favorable way, indirect tactics are chosen. Thus, from President Clinton's point of view, Plan Colombia was not about getting the United States into another Vietnam War, but about protecting Americans from the ravages of illegal drugs. Similarly, from Sen. Jesse Helms's perspective, the International Criminal Court was not about the United States being a law-abiding member of the international community, but about threats to U.S. sovereignty. Once issues are successfully framed in the negative, as in the latter case, no one wants to be depicted as supporting them. The executive and legislative branches try to anticipate the reaction of the other, whether it be an administration trying to gauge congressional reaction in cases such as immigration reform and ICC participation, or Congress testing how much it can press the administration, as in the port security case.

The actions of other administration officials, and occasionally the courts, also complicate interbranch leadership. Senior administrative officials played pivotal roles in the decisions to pursue war with Iraq, change port operations companies, eavesdrop without warrants, and detain enemy combatants. The decisions of the courts were pivotal in deciding the ability of the administration to pursue warrantless wiretaps or to detain enemy combatants and U.S. citizens and immigrants in the war on terror.

New Influences: The Societal Actors

Government officials do not act in a political vacuum. They are often the targets of interest group representatives, who usually believe that their concerns are identical to those of the collective nation (as in the steel tariffs, Cuban trade, Chinese trade, trade subsidies, and detainees cases). How the news media report the political news can sway public opinion (for example, in the cases of NSA eavesdropping and the detainees). The public's opinion is then used to impress a policy preference on policymakers (as with the Colombian, port security, immigration reform, and Helms-Burton cases). In most of these cases, experts who serve as opinion leaders line up on one or both sides of an issue, trying to have their preferred policies enacted.

Stimuli: Underlying Factors

Governmental and nongovernmental actors often disagree on foreign policy issues because they respond to different stimuli and thus frame issues differently.[8] For example, in the case of Colombia, one person's "new Vietnam" is another person's "war on drugs." To one person, the China trade issue is a human rights problem, while to another it is a jobs issue. At other times agreement can be reached on the definition of an issue but not on the policy solution. For instance, nuclear proliferation concerns virtually everyone, but should Iran and North Korea be the targets of "hard" or "soft" power responses? As the product of a political process, foreign policy is influenced by what government officials think they should do—enact good policy or garner institutional prestige and stature—and what they think they must do—address the potential preferences of citizens and voters.[9]

Sometimes these differences are simply the products of partisanship and ideology. In the late 1940s and early 1950s, politics seemed to stop "at the water's edge."[10] The last two decades, however, have brought increasingly ideological partisanship to foreign affairs.[11] Cases such as warrantless eavesdropping, immigration reform, and how to get out of Iraq tend to pit more liberal Democrats against the more conservative Republican administration. This ideological divide shows no signs of narrowing anytime soon.

Looking to the Future

Each case in this collection touches on the unifying theme that the U.S. foreign policy making process is generally becoming more open, pluralistic, and partisan. More and more governmental and nongovernmental actors are becoming involved for various reasons. As foreign policy becomes increasingly intermestic and more like domestic policy, reasonable people can be expected to disagree and try to shape policy based on their own values and attitudes. Such behavior has long been commonplace for "low politics," that is, such intermestic issues as immigration, weapons procurement, and foreign trade. Without the overriding fear of global annihilation, there seem to be few reasons for congressional and societal actors to defer to the president or other officials of the executive branch for many "high politics" issues involving core national interests. These other actors bring their ideas, attitudes, passions, ideological beliefs, and partisanship with them as they try to affect policymaking. In terms of any search for consensus, the short-term trends do not look promising, as the foreign policy process continues to become more political.

The internal situation facing George W. Bush in 2001 provides an interesting illustration of the challenges likely to face presidents well into the near future. Like other former governors elected to the presidency, Bush entered office with little foreign policy experience, as did his predecessor, Bill Clinton. The comparison of the two stops there, however. Clinton was widely acknowledged as a "policy wonk," someone who immersed himself in every detail of policy. With the exception of relying on Vice President Al Gore on environmental issues and Russian relations, Clinton was not known for policy delegation. He wanted to make decisions and initially sought appointees who would follow his lead, such as his national security advisor, Anthony Lake, secretary of defense, William Cohen, and secretary of state, Warren Christopher.

During the 2000 presidential campaign, Bush promised to run his administration like the chief executive officer of a major corporation. As CEO, he promised, he would set broad strategies and then delegate to others the job of realizing the goals established. Thus he sought "experts" who would be loyal to him but who, within the administration, would press for their preferred policies. Many of those chosen to serve in top positions were veterans of prior Republican administrations. According to one close observer, "There has been a special effort to get really good people who sometimes disagree with each other. They are strong-willed people who might well create sparks in the inner circle."[12]

With a more open and pluralistic foreign policy making process, those who oppose the president's policy preferences will seek to exploit any internal divisions within an administration. Members of Congress, interest groups, nongovernmental organizations, and media pundits will seek to find policy allies in the administration. It is interesting to observe to what degree officials' loyalties to the president outweigh their occasional differences with his policy preferences.

Future presidents will have to find policy positions that feel right to them, keep their administration's officials "on message," and convince the country that their policy prescriptions are the best for the nation.

Bush's relations with Congress were initially more difficult than most new presidents'. The November 2000 elections produced a slim Republican majority of only eleven seats in the House, and a tenuous, fifty-fifty partisan split in the Senate allowed Republicans to control the chamber only by virtue of the tie-breaking vote of the vice president.[13] When Vermont senator James Jeffords defected from the Republicans to become an independent in June 2001, the Republicans' narrow margin in the Senate disappeared. Democrats regained control of that chamber for the first time since January 1995, and Democratic leaders took charge of the Senate's policy agenda. As important, if not more so, Republicans lost their chairmanships. Jeffords's defection thus also allowed the Democrats to set the agendas and activities of committees, the most influential being the Committees on Foreign Relations, Appropriations, and Armed Services and the Select Intelligence Committee. The transfer in control of the Senate put pressure on the Bush administration to shift its foreign policy toward more centrist positions. Later in the administration, when the White House adopted such positions—for example, concerning the Iraq occupation and reconstruction and working with international organizations—it put congressional Republican leaders in a bind, as they had to decide whether to support the president or to pursue ideological consistency with past, more conservative policy preferences. After the 2006 elections, congressional Republicans were freed of the majority status and thus could support or oppose the lame duck president as they saw fit. Congressional Democrats came under scrutiny as the opposition party now responsible for both chambers of Congress.

In the future, presidents can be expected under the best of circumstances to have difficulties with Congress regarding foreign policy. As a noted congressional scholar argues,

> The Constitution establishes a fluid decision process that cannot ensure a creative governmental response to issues that confront the country. The system of separation of powers, with its checks and balances, works to constrain the enactment of public programs. Partisanship (embodied in divided or unified government), the responsiveness of government to electoral considerations, the character of congressional organization, and the quality and commitment of presidential leadership conspire in distinctive ways to create a policy process prone to delay and deadlock.[14]

In such an environment, anything controversial will further complicate policy-making and lessen the president's ability by weakening his credibility. The multiple scandals that plagued the Clinton administration undermined Clinton's ability to act by diverting his energy to managing them. As illustrated by a number of cases in this volume, at times the attention of the president and other top officials in his administration were distracted from policymaking. Scandals not only disrupted the normal policymaking process; they also gave Clinton's opponents ammunition in opposing administration initiatives by discrediting his leadership.

George W. Bush has not been immune from controversy, either. His presidency is the product of a controversial election. His opponent, Al Gore, won the popular vote, while Bush won the Electoral College vote. When a president wins fewer popular votes than his opponent, there are bound to be questions about the legitimacy of the victory. Some observers believe that electoral irregularities in Florida and the hotly contested Supreme Court decision in *Bush v. Gore* (2000) allowed Republicans to "steal" the election. Bush narrowly prevailed in a contest marred by allegations of improprieties involving vote counts, recounts, and the denial of voting rights. In the words of Congressional Black Caucus chair Eddie Bernice Johnson, D-Texas, "There is overwhelming evidence that George W. Bush did not win this election."[15] To dramatize her point, she led the members of the caucus in walking out of the joint session of Congress when Florida's electoral votes were certified. The controversy surrounding Bush's declared victory hampered his ability to work with congressional Democrats early in his administration.

Another point of controversy for the incoming Bush administration was its corporate ties. Liberals, populists, and others perceived the administration as a tool of big business. When critics reflected on the oil industry backgrounds of President Bush and Vice President Cheney, and they saw former heads of major corporations such as Alcoa (Secretary of the Treasury Paul O'Neill) and Searle (Secretary of Defense Donald Rumsfeld) in the cabinet, they questioned whose interests the administration would represent. Such concerns were also voiced when the president announced his national energy policy. It was widely reported initially that the focus would be on producing energy, not on conserving it. The oil industry backgrounds of the president and vice president were rehashed widely in the media.[16] With the decisions to invade Iraq, topple the regime of Saddam Hussein, and reconstruct the Iraqi oil industry, the concerns over the ties of top executive branch officials to the U.S. oil industry arose again.

Finally, President Bush "bet his presidency" on the Iraq war. When military victory proved far easier than the subsequent occupation and attempts at Iraqi reconstruction, the Bush administration found its reputation tarnished and its political influence "inside the Beltway" substantially diminished. According to the conventional wisdom at the time, Bush's foreign policy mistakes appeared to be the primary reason Democrats recaptured control of Congress in 2006. When Bush later joined with congressional Democrats in pushing immigration reform legislation, he could not command the support of members of his own party.

In short, U.S. foreign policy making continues to grow more pluralistic, partisan, and political in the twenty-first century. The good news is that U.S. foreign policy is becoming representative of more organized interests and points of view, more democratic in nature, and somewhat more transparent in process. The bad news for policymakers is that the road to foreign policy enactment and successful foreign policy implementation shows all the signs of being an increasingly bumpy ride. To paraphrase Winston Churchill's seafaring analogy, democracies are like rafts—they are virtually unsinkable, but they proceed slowly, and one's feet always get wet. In this more open process, foreign policy making will almost always be slower, but one hopes that it will be surer in its outcomes.

Notes

1. See Richard C. Snyder, H. W. Bruck, Burton M. Sapin, Valerie M. Hudson, Derek H. Chollet, and James M. Goldgeier, *Foreign Policy Decision Making (Revisited)* (New York: Palgrave Macmillan, 2002).

2. See Richard Melanson, *American Foreign Policy since the Vietnam War,* 2nd ed. (Armonk, N.Y.: M.E. Sharpe, 1996).

3. See Thomas Franck and Edward Weisband, *Foreign Policy by Congress* (New York: Oxford University Press, 1979); James M. Scott and Ralph G. Carter, "Acting on the Hill: Congressional Assertiveness in U.S. Foreign Policy," *Congress and the Presidency* 29, no. 2 (Autumn 2002): 151–169; and Ralph G. Carter, "Congressional Foreign Policy Behavior: Persistent Patterns of the Postwar Period," *Presidential Studies Quarterly* 16, no. 2 (Spring 1986): 329–359.

4. For a good discussion of these themes, see James M. Scott and A. Lane Crothers, "Out of the Cold: The Post–Cold War Context of U.S. Foreign Policy," in *After the End: Making U.S. Foreign Policy in the Post–Cold War World,* ed. James M. Scott (Durham, N.C.: Duke University Press, 1998), 1–25.

5. James M. Scott, "Interbranch Policy Making after the End," in Scott, *After the End,* 401.

6. Quoted in Ralph G. Carter, "Congress and Post–Cold War U.S. Foreign Policy," in Scott, *After the End,* 129–130.

7. Scott and Crothers, "Out of the Cold," 11.

8. James M. Lindsay, *Congress and the Politics of U.S. Foreign Policy* (Baltimore, Md.: Johns Hopkins University Press, 1994).

9. For more on congressional policy motivations, see R. Douglas Arnold, *The Logic of Congressional Action* (New Haven: Yale University Press, 1990); Aage Clausen, *How Congressmen Decide* (New York: St. Martin's, 1973); Richard F. Fenno, *Congressmen in Committees* (Boston: Little, Brown, 1973); or John W. Kingdon, *Congressmen's Voting Decisions,* 3rd ed. (Ann Arbor: University of Michigan Press, 1989).

10. See Carter, "Congressional Foreign Policy Behavior."

11. Carter, "Congress and Post–Cold War U.S. Foreign Policy," 128.

12. Bruce Buchanan, a University of Texas at Austin political science professor, quoted in the *Financial Times,* January 8, 2001, 22.

13. The congressional partisan breakdown can be found at http://clerkweb.house.gov/mbrcmtee/stats.htm.

14. Leroy N. Rieselbach, "It's the Constitution, Stupid! Congress, the President, Divided Government, and Policymaking," in *Divided Government: Change, Uncertainty, and the Constitutional Order,* ed. Peter F. Galderisi (Lanham, Md.: Rowman and Littlefield, 1996), 129.

15. *Dallas Morning News,* January 14, 2001, 11A.

16. For example, see *Washington Post,* May 20, 2001, A3; *Newsday,* May 20, 2001, B1; and *U.S. News and World Report,* May 21, 2001, 29.

Index

Surnames starting with "al" or "el" are alphabetized by the following part of the name. Alphabetization is letter-by-letter (e.g., "Bayh, Evan" precedes "Bay of Pigs").

Abdullah II, 430
Abizaid, John, 49, 50
Abu Ghraib prison scandal, 48, 426, 429–432. *See also* Detainees, rights of
ACI. *See* Andean Counterdrug Initiative
Adeli, Mohammad Hossein, 99, 100
AEDPA (Antiterrorism and Effective Death Penalty Act (1996)), 228–229
Afghanistan
  al Qaeda in, 418–419
  authorization of force and war on terrorism and, 13–19. *See also* Terrorism
  Bin Laden in, 2. *See also* Bin Laden, Osama
  detainees, rights of. *See* Detainees, rights of
  funding of operations in, 52
  Iran and, 99, 114
  Taliban in, 4, 15, 17, 28
  war in, 1, 419
AFL-CIO, 321, 328
Africa and trials before ICC, 410–411
Agreed Framework, 113, 124, 135–145. *See also* North Korea
Agriculture and Cuba policy, 295–296
Ahmadinejad, Mahmoud, 92, 93, 104, 106–110, 115. *See also* Iran
AI. *See* Amnesty International
AIG (American International Group), 351–352
Air Bridge Denial Program, 79
Airbus, 343, 350
  downing of (Iran), 97
Albright, Madeleine, 134, 393, 400
Alcoa, 381, 453
Allawi, Iyad, 29
Alliance for Progress, 223
Alliance of Automobile Manufacturers, 372
Alliance of Small Island States (AOSIS), 366
American Bar Association, 396
American Electronics Association, 326
American Enterprise Institute, 377
American Farm Bureau, 295
American International Group (AIG), 351–352
American Iron and Steel Institute, 274
American Jobs Creation Act (2004), 337, 338, 344, 351–352
American Servicemember's Protection Act (ASPA, 2002), 393, 408, 409–410
Amnesty International (AI), 319, 328, 329, 401
Andean Counterdrug Initiative (ACI), 80–81, 83
Andean Regional Initiative (ARI), 60, 61, 79–80
Andean Trade Preference Act (1991), 62, 71, 82, 87*n*35
Annan, Kofi, 406
ANSP (South Korean Agency for National Security Planning), 131
Anti-Ballisitic Missile Treaty, 405
Antiterrorism and Effective Death Penalty Act (AEDPA, 1996), 228–229
AOSIS (Alliance of Small Island States), 366
Ara, Maher, 432–433
Arcelor Mittal, 274
Archer, Bill, 342
Argentina, 253
ARI. *See* Andean Regional Initiative
Armey, Richard, 39, 43
Armitage, Richard, 33, 37
Army of National Liberation (ELN), 63, 67, 77–78

Aronson, Bernard, 287
Arrhenius, Svante, 359, 361
Article II authority, 193, 204, 206, 209
ASEAN (Association of Southeast Asian Nations), 329
Ashcroft, John
Cuba policy and, 296, 298
detainees' rights and, 423, 427, 442
immigration policy and, 218
NSA eavesdropping and, 194–196
Asia-Pacific Partnership Clean Development, 370
ASPA. *See* American Servicemember's Protection Act
Aspin, Les, 132
Association of Southeast Asian Nations (ASEAN), 329
Asylum, 226–227, 228, 229–230. *See also* U.S.-Mexican relations
AT&T, 198–199
AUC. *See* United-Self Defense Groups of Colombia
Australia, 126, 329
Authorization for Use of Military Force (2001), 193–194, 200–201, 210. *See also* Bush Doctrine and U.S. interventions in Iraq; National Security Agency (NSA) eavesdropping
Automobile industry and China, 317
"Axis of evil" speech. *See* Bush, George W.

Baber, Catherine, 328
Bahrain, 16
Baker, James, 48, 127, 165, 409, 412
Baker, Stewart A., 159
"Baker plan," 228
Ballenger, Cass, 77, 84
Bani-Sadr, Abolhassan, 96
Bankruptcy of steel manufacturers, 257, 268–269
El Baradei, Mohamed, 101, 109
Barco Vargas, Virgilio, 63, 66
Basic Agreement, 123, 129. *See also* North Korea
Baucus, Max, 345, 350, 380
Baumann, Jeremiah, 373
Bayh, Evan, 43
Bay of Pigs, 18
Bechtel, 345
Beijing Auto Works, 317
Belgium, 339
Berger, Oscar, 218
Berger, Samuel "Sandy," 3, 7, 8, 14, 18, 19
Bergquist, Gloria, 372
Bergsten, C. Fred, 169
Beschloss, Michael, 26, 29
Betancur, Belisario, 66
Bethlehem Steel, 256, 257, 268, 375
Biden, Joseph, 12, 42, 407
Bilkey, Edward H., 166, 172, 178
Bingaman, Jeff, 236, 379–380
Bin Laden, Osama. *See also* al Qaeda
background, 2, 4–5, 19
Clinton and Bush administration strikes against, 1–11, 13–19, 27, 31. *See also* Terrorism
current status of, 17, 31
Blair, Tony, 374, 381
Blix, Hans, 130–131
Bluewater Network, 372
"Boat people," 226
Boehner, John A., 175
Boeing, 340, 342, 343, 346, 350–352
Bolton, John, 143–144
Bonjean, Ron, 174
Border Protection, Antiterrorism, and Illegal Immigration Control Act (2005), 220, 243
Boren, David, 13
Bosnia, 6, 404
Bouchard, Joe, 164
Boudreaux, Mark, 378
Boumediene v. Bush (2007), 441
Boxer, Barbara, 166, 380–381, 382
BP America, 381
Bracero program, 219, 221–223, 224, 240. *See also* U.S.-Mexican relations
Brazil, 252, 253, 259, 266, 329
Breaux, John, 326
Bremer, Paul, 29, 47
Bretton Woods economic system, 336
Britain. *See* United Kingdom
British Petroleum, 377
Brooks, David, 169
Brothers to the Rescue, 282, 284, 292, 299
Brownback, Sam, 233
Brzezinski, Zbigniew, 96
Burns, Nicholas, 110
Burton, Dan, 70, 72, 84, 292, 299. *See also* Cuba policy
Bush, George H. W.
China policy of, 324
climate change policy of, 359, 382

Colombia drug policy of, 60, 61, 68
Cuba policy of, 283, 286, 287, 297
immigration policy of, 228, 230–236
international law and, 411
Iran policy of, 98
Kuwait, response to invasion of, 27
new world order and, 391–392
North Korea policy of, 122, 127–130, 134
steel industry and, 262
Bush, George W.
approval ratings of, 18
authorization of force and war on terrorism, 1–2, 10–19, 31, 418, 419, 420, 422. *See also* Bush Doctrine and U.S. interventions in Iraq; Terrorism
"axis of evil" speech of, 28, 34, 91–92, 93, 100, 101, 112, 139
China policy of, 305–306, 307
climate change policy of. *See* Climate change
Colombia drug policy of. *See* Colombia and drug trade
Congress, relationship with, 452
corporate ties of, 453
Cuba policy of, 284–285, 294, 296–297
detainees' rights and, 430, 442. *See also* Detainees, rights of
Dubai Ports World takeover controversy and, 154, 162, 169, 175–176, 178. *See also* Dubai Ports World takeover controversy
foreign policy and, 29–30, 451
ICC and, 394, 412. *See also* International Criminal Court
immigration policy of, 218, 219, 228, 238–239, 242. *See also* U.S.-Mexican relations
Iran policy of, 98–113, 115, 144. *See also* Iran
Iraq War. *See* Bush Doctrine and U.S. Interventions in Iraq
North Korea policy of. *See* North Korea
NSA eavesdropping and, 185, 190–191, 196, 205. *See also* National Security Agency (NSA) eavesdropping
as post-imperial president, 26, 29
on Rice, Condoleezza, 14
September 11, 2001, and, 10
steel import tariffs and, 249, 251, 261–271, 272*f*, 274, 343
tax subsidies for exports and, 338, 351
Bush Doctrine and U.S. interventions in Iraq, 25–58
home front and case for war, 39–44
final preparations, 44
search for support, 40–43
imperial presidency, rise of, 26, 29
international community and impending war, 44–45, 270
Iraq War, 17, 45–46, 418, 420, 422, 454
decision making and, 30–38
ending of, 46–53
key actors, 53
postwar occupation of Iraq and, 47–52
timeline of U.S. interventions in Iraq, 27–29
troop surge, 50
U.S. foreign policy after September 11, 29–30
Bush v. Gore (2000), 453
Business Roundtable, 316
Byrd, Robert, 11, 20*n*17–18, 39, 173, 367
Byrd-Hagel Resolution (1997), 359, 367–368

CAFTA. *See* Central American Free Trade Agreement
Calderon, Felipe, 218
Cali cartel, 64, 67
California, 228, 360, 371–374
Canada, 126, 265, 362, 363, 368
CANF. *See* Cuban American National Foundation
Carbon dioxide, effect of increase in. *See* Climate change
Card, Andrew, 14, 31, 165, 194–196
Carroll, James, 409
Carter, Jimmy
China policy of, 324
Cuba policy of, 282, 311
ICC and, 399, 407
immigration policy of, 224–225
Iran hostage crisis, 6, 8, 16, 20*n*17–18, 96–97, 111
North Korea and, 124, 134, 146
Shah of Iran and, 96
Casey, George, 49, 50
Castañeda, Jorge, 218
Castaño, Carlos, 63, 64, 73
Castro, Fidel, 282, 285, 291, 298. *See also* Cuba policy
Castro, Raul, 285, 298–299
Casualties in Iraq, 47, 53

Caterpillar, 343, 344, 346, 381
CDA. *See* Cuban Democracy Act (1992)
CEI. *See* Competitive Enterprise Institute
CENTCOM, 35
Center for National Security Studies, 419, 423
Central African Republic, 410
Central America and immigration issues. *See* U.S.-Mexican relations
Central American Free Trade Agreement (CAFTA), 266–267, 272
Central Intelligence Agency (CIA)
  Afghanistan, attack on, 15
  air strikes on Bin Laden, 9, 10
  embassies, investigation of bombing of, 6
  extraordinary rendition and secret prisons and, 433
  Guantanamo Bay study of, 427
  Iran and, 102
  9/11 Commission on, 10
  North Korea and, 123, 131
  U.S. intervention in Iraq and, 34
CFCs. *See* Chlorofluorocarbons
CFIUS. *See* Committee on Foreign Investment in the United States
"Chairman's mark," 232
Chalabi, Ahmed, 32
Chamberlain, P. C., 361
Chambliss, Saxby, 235
Chandler, Ben, 18
Chavez, Hugo, 298, 299
Cheney, Dick
  authorization of force and war on terrorism, 14
  climate change policy and, 386
  corporate ties of, 453
  decision making for Iraq War and, 30, 31, 32, 33, 35, 38, 53
  election of 2000 and, 261
  hunting accident of, 161
  Iran and, 100, 108
  neoconservatives and, 32
  North Korea policy and, 127
  on presidential power, 13
  September 11, 2001, and, 10
  steel import tariffs and, 265
  vice presidency and, 33
Chernick, Marc, 65
Chertoff, Michael, 153, 162, 166, 220, 242
China
  climate change and, 364, 366, 368, 370
  humanitarian migration and, 245*n*31
  International Criminal Court (ICC) and, 392, 411
  Iran and, 106, 107, 108, 114
  Korean War and, 126
  North Korea and, 122, 125, 141, 143, 145, 323
  U.S.-China trade relations, 305–333, 449
    background, 305, 311–314
    Chinese challenge, 305, 308–311, 310*f*
    Clinton's engagement policy, 307–310, 313, 314–321, 315*b*, 316*b*, 330, 450
    Congress and support for, 310*f*
    final debates and congressional action, 321–327
    key actors, 329–330
    PNTR debate in Congress, 324–327
    privatization of foreign policy, 327–329
    steel import tariffs and, 252, 259, 265, 266
    timeline of, 307–308
    WTO membership for China, 305, 307, 308, 313, 316–324, 326
China Telecom, 318
China Unicom, 318
Chlorofluorocarbons (CFCs), 363–364, 381. *See also* Climate change
Christian Coalition, 238
Christopher, Warren, 282, 288, 290, 451
Chrysler Corporation, 317
Church Committee, 186
CIA. *See* Central Intelligence Agency
CINergy Corporation, 375
Cisco Systems, 340
CITAC. *See* Consuming Industries Trade Action Coalition
Clarke, Richard A., 9
Clean Power Act (2002), 371
Cleland, Max, 39
Climate change, 357–389
  background, 358–362
  future policy on, 382
  global warming issue, emergence of, 358–362
  international community action on, 369–371
  international negotiations, 362–368
  key actors, 382
  Kyoto Protocol
    Bush (George W.) policy toward, 358, 360, 368–369, 375–382

international community action on, 369–371
negotiations and, 366–368
timeline on, 358, 359–360
U.S. policy on, 357–358, 365–369, 448
overview, 357–358
states' action on, 371–375
tipping point on, 379–381
White House, science, and big oil and, 375–378, 453–454
Climate Change Science Program, 376
Climate Leaders program, 360, 375, 376
Climate Stewardship and Innovation Act (2007), 380
Climate Vision program, 375–376
Clinton, Bill
assassination attempt on, 4
Berger and, 14
Bin Laden, air strikes against, 1, 3–4, 6–8, 11, 15–19, 27. *See also* Terrorism
China policy of. *See* China
climate change policy of, 358, 359, 367
Colombia drug policy of. *See* Colombia and drug trade
Cuba policy of, 283–284, 286–296, 299
foreign policy and, 448, 451
ICC and, 394, 397–398, 405–406, 411, 412. *See also* International Criminal Court
immigration policy of, 228–230
Iran and, 93, 115
NAFTA and, 228
North Korea policy of. *See* North Korea
PNAC letter to, 32
scandals of, 7, 8, 324, 453
steel import tariffs and. *See* Steel import tariffs
tax subsides on exports and, 340, 342
use of military force by, 6
Clinton, Hillary Rodham, 173
Coalition Provisional Authority, 47
Coast Guard, 154, 163, 174
Coburn, Tom, 165
Coca Cola, 344
Code Division Multiple Access, 318
Cohen, Calman J., 346
Cohen, Kenneth P., 378
Cohen, William, 7, 32
Colombia and drug trade, 59–90
background, 60, 63–77, 449, 450
Bush (George W.) drug policy, 60, 62, 77–83, 84, 85
Andean Regional Initiative and Andean Counterdrug Initiative, 79–83
insurgency as new terrorism, 77–83, 84
challenge of, 59–60
Clinton drug policy, 61–62, 68–77, 83–89, 449
congressional passage, 74–77
Plan Colombia, aid in 2000–2001, 72
resistance, 72–74
key players in, 84–85
producer state, Colombia as, 60, 63–77
control of drug trade, 66–68
politics and drugs, 63–65
pre-Clinton U.S. policy, 67–68
U.S. aid to Colombia, timeline of, 61–62
"Colonel's Coup" (Greece, 1967), 226
Comey, James, 194–196, 211
Commerce Department, 259, 260
Committee on Foreign Investment in the United States (CFIUS), 158–160, 162, 165, 166, 171, 177. *See also* Dubai Ports World takeover controversy
Competitive Enterprise Institute (CEI), 376, 377, 378
Comprehensive Immigration Reform Act (2006), 118, 220–221, 234, 242
Conference of Parties (COP), 365–370
Congressional Anti-Terrorism Caucus, 18
Congressional-presidential interactions, 448–449
Connecticut, 372
Constitution, war powers under, 5–6
Consuming Industries Trade Action Coalition (CITAC), 264, 267, 275
Container Security Initiative (CSI), 152, 163, 164
Contract with America, 228
Convention on the Prevention and Punishment of the Crime of Genocide, 395
Cooney, Philip A., 376
COP-1 meeting (1995), 366
COP-2 meeting (1996), 366
COP-3 meeting (1997), 366
COP-6 meeting (2000), 368
COP-6 meeting (2001), 369–370
Cornyn, John, 231–234, 236
Corporations and foreign trade. *See* China; Tax subsidies for exports
Corzine, Jon, 347

Counterinsurgency and counternarcotics aid, 60, 77–83, 84. *See also* Colombia and drug trade
Counterterrorism. *See* Terrorism
Counterterrorism Evaluation Group, 32
Court of Justice of the European Union, 402
Courts, FISA, 186, 189–191, 201–209. *See also* National Security Agency (NSA) eavesdropping
Coverdell, Paul, 294
Cramer, Bud, 18
Crane, Philip, 337, 343, 345, 352
Creel, Santiago, 218
Creppy, Michael, 423
Crimes against humanity, 392, 394. *See also* International Criminal Court (ICC)
Crouch, J. D., 49
CSI. *See* Container Security Initiative
C-TPAT (Customs-Trade Partnership against Terrorism), 163–164
Cuban American National Foundation (CANF), 285–286, 287, 289, 297, 299
Cuban Democracy Act (CDA, 1992), 283, 286–288, 290, 291, 297
Cuban Liberty and Democratic Solidarity Act (LIBERTAD, 1996) (Helms-Burton Act). *See* Cuba policy
Cuba policy, 281–303
  background, 282–285
  Congress and Helms-Burton Act, 288–292, 448, 449
  crafting of, 281–282
  Cuban Democracy Act, 286–288
  Helms-Burton's second chance, 292–294
  immigration policy and, 225, 226–227, 228, 450
  key actors, 299–300
  politics since Helms-Burton, 294–297
  post–cold war, 286–288
  struggle to control, 297–299
  timeline of Cuban relations and Helms-Burton Act, 283–285
  U.S. cold war policy and, 282, 285
Curtiss-Wright; *United States v.* (1936), 192–193
Customs-Trade Partnership against Terrorism (C-TPAT), 163–164

Daalder, Ivo H., 30
Daley, William, 324
Daniels, Mitch, 265
Dar es Salaam, Tanzania embassy bombing, 5, 6
Darfur, Sudan, 411
Daschle, Tom
  air strikes on Bin Laden and, 8
  authorization of force and war on terrorism and, 11–12
  Colombia drug policy and, 81
  Cuba policy and, 298
  support efforts for Iraq War by, 41–42, 43
  tax subsidies for imports and, 345, 353
Davis, Gray, 371
Defense Policy Board, 32
Deficit Reduction Act (1984), 337, 340
Delahunt, William, 297
De la Madrid, Miguel, 225
Delaware, 372
DeLay, Tom, 346, 349, 393, 408
Democratic People's Republic of North Korea (DPRK). *See* North Korea
Democratic Republic of Congo, 410
Deng Xiaoping, 307, 308, 311–312, 315
Detainees, rights of, 417–445
  background, 422–432
  Congress, response by, 438–439, 446
  courts, response by, 433–438, 449
    Boumediene v. Bush (2007), 441
    Hamdan v. Rumsfeld (2006), 421, 439–440
    Hamdi v. Rumsfeld (2004), 419, 421, 427–429, 434–435, 438
    Rasul v. Bush (2004), 420, 421, 425, 436–438
    Rumsfeld v. Padilla (2004), 420, 421, 427–429, 435–436
  definition of detainee, 422
  enemy combatants, U.S. citizens as, 422, 427–429
  extraordinary rendition and secret prisons, 432–433
  future policy on, 440–442
  Guantanamo Bay, foreign national enemy combatants, 422, 424–427, 436–438
  Iraq war, 422, 429–432
  key actors, 442
  September 11 detainees, 422–424
  terrorism, response to, 418–422
  timeline of, 419–421
  war on terror, 422–432
Detainee Treatment Act (DTA, 2006), 421, 438–440

Deutch, John, 293
DeWine, Mike, 72, 348
DHS. *See* Homeland Security, Department of
Diaz-Balart, Lincoln, 286, 290–293, 295, 299
Dicker, Richard, 405–406
Director of national intelligence (DNI), 18
"Dirty bomb," 152, 164, 428
DISCs. *See* Domestic International Sales Corporation
Displaced Persons Acts (1948 & 1950), 223
DNI (director of national intelligence), 18
Dobbins, Jim, 99
Dobbs, Lou, 153, 161
Dobriansky, Paula J., 378
Dodd, Christopher, 74–75, 165, 293–294
Doha Round, 262
Domenici, Pete, 175
Domestic International Sales Corporation (DISCs), 336, 337, 339–340, 341
Domestic surveillance. *See* National Security Agency (NSA) eavesdropping
Doniger, David, 372
Dorgan, Byron, 235
Dowd, Maureen, 169
Downing, Wayne, 32, 35
Drug certification policy, 81, 82
Drug trade. *See* Colombia and drug trade
DTA. *See* Detainee Treatment Act (2006)
Dubai Ports World (DP World) takeover controversy, 151–183
  aftermath, 176–178
  background (late 2005 to January 16, 2006), 155–160, 449
  bipartisan opposition to Bush veto threat (February 16 to February 21, 2006), 164–168
  from Coast Guard report to House vote announcement, 173–175
  House Appropriations vote and DP World pullout (March 8 and 9, 2006), 175–176
  key actors, 178
  national spotlight (January 16 to February 16, 2006), 160–164, 450
  from opposition activities to 45-day investigation offer, 168–173
  overview, 152, 154
  timeline of, 153–154
Dukakis, Michael, 288
Dulles, Allen, 18
Dunham, Frank, Jr., 428–429
Dunn, Jennifer, 342
DuPont, 364, 381
Durbin, Dick, 233

Eagle Forum, 238
"Earth Summit" (Rio de Janeiro), 359, 365
East Asia Summit, 329
Eavesdropping. *See* National Security Agency (NSA) eavesdropping
Echeverría, Luis, 224
Edwards, John, 41
EFVS (electronic eligibility verification system), 241*b*
Eggen, Dan, 206–207
Eisenhower, Dwight, 222–223, 282, 283
Election of 2000. *See* Presidential election of 2000
Elections, midterm. *See* Midterm elections
Electronic eligibility verification system (EFVS), 241*b*
Electronic surveillance. *See* National Security Agency (NSA) eavesdropping
Eller and Company, 160
ELN. *See* Army of National Liberation
El Salvador, refugees from, 227, 228, 229
Emanuel, Rahm, III, 161
Embassies, bombing of, 5, 6
Emergency Committee for American Trade, 346, 352
Emergency Wartime Supplemental Appropriations Act (2003), 79
Emission standards, 371–372, 374, 375, 380. *See also* Climate change
Endangered Species Act (1973), 381
Enemy combatants. *See* Detainees, rights of
Energy Department, 375
English, Phil, 344
Ensign, John, 235
Environmental Defense Fund, 380
Environmental issues. *See also* Climate change in China, 319–320
Environmental Protection Agency (EPA), 360, 364, 369, 374–376. *See also* Climate change
"Environmental refugees," 362
Ervin, Clark Kent, 169
Escobar, Pablo, 64
ETI. *See* Extraterritorial income
European Convention of Human Rights (1950), 402
European Court of Human Rights, 402

European Law Students Association, 401
European Union (EU)
China and, 323–324
Court of Justice of, 402
creation of, 337
defined, 341
Iran and, 114
Kyoto Protocol and, 358, 360, 370
steel import tariffs and, 259, 266, 270, 275
tax subsidies for foreign exports and, 346, 350, 352
trade competition with U.S., 336, 338
WTO and, 340, 342–343
Evans, Donald, 265, 386
EVD. *See* Extended voluntary departure status
Exon-Florio amendment procedure, 154, 158–159
Export Freedom to Cuba Act (2007), 285
Exports, tax subsidies for. *See* Tax subsidies for exports
Extended voluntary departure (EVD) status, 227, 228
External challenges, shifts in, 447–448
Extraordinary rendition and secret prisons, 432–433. *See also* Detainees, rights of
Extraterritorial income (ETI), 337, 341, 342, 345, 348–349, 350
Exxon Mobil Corp., 344, 377–378

FAIR (Federation for American Immigration Reform), 238
Fair trade laws, 260
Falun Gong, 320
FARC. *See* Revolutionary Armed Forces of Colombia
"Fast track" authority, 262
Fatwa, 3, 4
Fay, George R., 423
FBI. *See* Federal Bureau of Investigation
FDI. *See* Foreign direct investment
Federal Bureau of Investigation (FBI), 6, 424
Federation for American Immigration Reform (FAIR), 238
Feinberg, Richard, 288
Feingold, Russ, 209, 429
Feinstein, Dianne, 407
Fine, Glenn, 205, 424
FISA. *See* Foreign Intelligence Surveillance Act
Fisk, Dan, 289
Flake, Jeff, 297, 298, 299
Fleischer, Ari, 165
Flynn, Stephen, 161, 163, 164, 178
FOIA. *See* Freedom of Information Act
Foley, Mark, 161, 165
Ford, Gerald, 158, 224, 282, 283, 324
Ford, Harold, 162
Ford Motor Company, 317, 344, 377
Foreign Assistance Act (1961) procedures, 70–71, 82
Foreign direct investment (FDI)
China and, 313, 318, 327
Dubai Ports World and, 154, 157–158, 169, 170. *See also* Dubai Ports World takeover controversy
Foreign Intelligence Surveillance Act (FISA, 1978), 185–187, 189–190, 194, 197, 203, 206–210. *See also* National Security Agency (NSA) eavesdropping
Foreign nationals, detention of. *See* Detainees, rights of
Foreign Operations Act, Export Financing, Related Programs for Fiscal Year 1998 amendment, 71–72
Foreign policy. *See also specific countries*
after September 11, 2001, 29–30
future options, 450–454
interbranch leadership, 448–449
new challenges, 448–449
privatization of, 327–329
shifts in external challenges and, 447–448
societal actors, 450
underlying factors, 450
Foreign Sales Corporations (FSCs), 337, 340, 341, 342
Fossella, Vito, 161–162, 165
Fourier, Jean-Baptiste, 358–359, 361
Fourth Amendment, 188–189
Fox, Vincente, 217–218, 231, 242
France
GATT and, 339
ICC and, 403
Iran and, 93, 102–104, 105, 107, 109
Kyoto Protocol and, 363
Franco, Rodrigo, 64
Franks, Tommy, 15, 17, 34, 35, 36
Frechette, Myles, 81
Freedom House, 319, 328
Freedom of Information Act (FOIA, 1996), 419, 423
Freedom to Travel to Cuba Act (2007), 298, 299

Free Trade Area of the Americas (FTAA), 262, 266, 270, 272
Frist, William (Bill) H.
Dubai Ports World takeover controversy and, 153, 166, 173, 175–176, 178
immigration policy and, 233, 235
tax subsidies for foreign exports and, 348, 353
Frost, Martin, 43
FSC Repeal and Extraterritorial Income Exclusion Act (2000), 337, 342
FTAA. *See* Free Trade Area of the Americas

G-7 (Group of Seven), 363
Gaddis, David, 64
Galán, Luis Carlos, 68
"Gallegy amendment," 229
Gallucci, Robert, 135, 137, 146
"Gang of Eight," 191, 202
Garner, Jay, 36, 47
Gates, Robert, 127, 130
GATT. *See* General Agreement on Tariffs and Trade
Gaviria Trujillo, César, 66
Gelbard, Robert, 287
General Agreement on Tariffs and Trade (GATT), 322, 337, 339–340, 341
General Electric, 347, 351–352, 381
General Motors Corporation (GM), 317, 330, 344, 375, 377
Geneva Conventions, 419, 426, 430
Genocide Convention, 395
Gephardt, Richard, 41–42
Gerecht, Reuel Marc, 99
Germany, 93, 102–104, 105, 107
Gerson, Michael, 100
Gilman, Ben, 70, 85
Gingrich, Newt, 8, 98, 290
Ginsberg, Ruth Bader, 435
Global Environmental Facility, 365
Global markets, politics of. *See* China; Steel import tariffs
Global warming. *See* Climate change
Global Warming Solutions Act (2006), 373–374
GM. *See* General Motors Corporation
Goldsmith, Jack, 195
Gonzales, Alberto
detainees' rights and, 426, 430
NSA eavesdropping and, 191–192, 194–195, 203–208, 211
Gore, Al, 7, 259, 261, 368, 451, 453
Gorton, Slade, 74
Graham, Bob, 166, 300
Graham, Lindsay, 233, 235, 239
Gramm, Phil, 291
Grams, Rod, 407
Granger, Kay, 18
Grassley, Charles, 338, 344–345, 346–347, 352
Greenhouse gases. *See* Climate change
Greenhouse Gas Initiative, 360
Greenpeace, 319–320, 378
Greenspan, Alan, 324
Griffin, Michael D., 377
Grifo, Francesca, 377
Group of Seven (G-7), 363
Grupo Domos, 294
Guam, 340
Guantanamo Bay detainees, 422, 424–427, 436–438. *See also* Detainees, rights of
Guatemala, refugees from, 227, 229
Guerrilla operations in Colombia, 65
Guest worker program, 224. *See also* Bracero program
Gulf War, 39, 391
Gutierrez, Carlos, 220, 242

Haas, Richard, 33
Habeas corpus, 421, 435–438, 440–441. *See also* Detainees, rights of
Hadley, Stephen, 32, 50, 53, 173
Hagel, Chuck, 39, 231–232, 235, 296, 367–368
Hague Convention for the Pacific Settlement of International Disputes, 392
Hague Peace Conference (1899), 392
Haiti, 6, 289
Haitian immigrants, 225–227, 229–230, 286
Haitian Refugee Immigration Fairness Act (HRIFA, 1998), 230
Halliburton, 345, 386
Hamas, 100
Hamdan, Salim Ahmed, 421, 439–440
Hamdan v. Rumsfeld (2006), 421, 439–440
Hamdi, Yaser Esam, 419, 427–429, 434–435, 438
Hamdi v. Rumsfeld (2004), 419, 427–429, 434–435, 438
Hamilton, Lee, 48, 294
Hansen, James E., 359, 362, 377, 383
Harkin, Tom, 347, 350, 352

Hastert, Dennis
Colombia drug policy and, 70, 72, 74, 76, 81, 85
Dubai Ports World takeover controversy and, 166–167, 171, 172, 174, 175–176
tax subsidies for foreign exports and, 342, 343, 344, 353
Hayden, Michael V.
North Korea and, 142
NSA eavesdropping and, 196–198, 209–210, 211
Helms, Jesse
China policy and, 325–326
Colombia drug policy and, 71, 85
Cuba policy and, 283, 289, 296, 300
ICC and, 393, 400, 402, 407–409, 412, 449
Helms-Burton Act. *See* Cuba policy
Hezbollah, 100
Hicks, David, 441
Hinchey, Maurice, 205
Hofmeister, John, 381
Hollings, Ernest "Fritz," 345
Homeland Security, Department of (DHS), 159, 176
Hoover, J. Edgar, 186
HRIFA (Haitian Refugee Immigration Fairness Act (1998)), 230
Hubbard, R. Glenn, 265
Hubbard, Thomas C., 139
Humanitarian migration, 223–224, 225–227
Human rights
in China, 310, 312, 314, 315, 319, 320, 322, 328, 450
in Colombia, 73, 75–77, 79–80, 81–82
European Convention of Human Rights (1950), 402
European Court of Human Rights, 402
Human Rights Watch, 73, 319, 330, 401, 405–406
Hurricane Katrina, 360, 379
Hussein, Saddam. *See also* Bush Doctrine and U.S. interventions in Iraq
Iran, war with, 96–101
Iraq War and, 30, 31, 33, 45
Kurd revolt, brutal response to, 27
al Qaeda and, 42, 45
WMDs and. *See* Bush Doctrine and U.S. interventions in Iraq
Huston, Tom Charles, 186
Huston Plan, 186
Hutchinson, Kay Bailey, 236

IAEA. *See* International Atomic Energy Agency
ICC. *See* International Criminal Court
Illegal Immigration Reform and Immigrant Responsibility Act (IIRIRA, 1996), 229
Immigration Act (1990), 228
Immigration and Nationality Act (INA, 1952), 219, 223–224, 225–226
Immigration policy. *See* U.S.-Mexican relations
Immigration Reform and Control Act (IRCA, 1986), 219, 225, 227
Imperial presidency, return of. *See* Bush Doctrine and U.S. Interventions in Iraq
IMT (International Military Tribunal), 394–396
IMTFE. *See* International Military Tribunal for the Far East
India
climate change and, 364, 366, 368, 370
ICC and, 400, 403
Indochinese "boat people," 226
Industry groups and China, 316–318, 326
Inhofe, James, 380–381
Integrated steel companies, 256, 257
Intellectual property issues in China, 306, 315, 321, 328
Intelligence Reform and Terrorism Prevention Act (2004), 18, 231
Intergovernmental Negotiating Committee (INC), 363
Intergovernmental Panel on Climate Change (IPCC), 357–363, 366, 368–369, 378. *See also* Climate change
International Atomic Energy Agency (IAEA)
Iran and, 93–94, 101–105, 109–112. *See also* Iran
North Korea and, 122–137, 140–142, 146. *See also* North Korea
International Criminal Court (ICC), 391–416
background, 392, 394–396
creation of, 397–406

Rome Conference, 401–406
U.S. reaction, 399–401
current status of, 406–411
international law, rise of, 391–392
international tribunals, rise of, 392, 394–396
judges of, 410
key actors, 412–413
timeline of, 393–394
United States and concerns over ICC of, 396–397
international law and, 411–412
reaction to creation of ICC by, 411–412, 448, 449
International Law Commission, 393
International Longshoremen's Association, 156
International Maritime Organization, 163
International Military Tribunal (IMT), 394–396
International Military Tribunal for the Far East (IMTFE), 392, 395
International Negotiating Committee (INC), 364–365
International Ship and Port Facility Security Code (2004), 163
International Steel Group (ISG), 268, 272
IPCC. *See* Intergovernmental Panel on Climate Change
Iran
Afghanistan and Iraq destabilization and, 114
in "axis of evil," 28, 34, 91–92, 93, 100, 101, 112
hostage crisis, 6, 8, 16, 20*n*17–18, 96–97, 111
Iraq, war with U.S., 96–101
nuclear standoff with
Agreed Framework-style compromise, 113–114
Iran's nuclear program, 101–102
key actors, 114–115
lost opportunities, 99–101
negotiations and standoff (2003–2007), 102–110, 449, 450
patterns of intervention and mutual antagonism, 92–101, 144
policy options and conclusions, 111–114
rush to confront Iran over WMDs, 91–92
timeline of U.S.-Iranian relations and nuclear issue, 93–94
Iran Freedom Support Act (2006), 98
Iraq. *See also* Bush Doctrine and U.S. interventions in Iraq
in "axis of evil," 28, 34, 91–92, 93
Clinton's use of military force against, 6
detainees, 429–432
ICC and, 403
International Criminal Court (ICC) and, 392, 411
Iran and, 96–101, 114
military strikes by Bush prior to September 11, 2001 on, 10–11
Persian Gulf War, 39, 391
weapons of mass destruction (WMDs) and, 30–31, 34, 38, 42–44, 46, 105–106
Iraqi National Congress, 32, 35
Iraq Liberation Act (1998), 32, 98–99
Iraq Postwar Planning Office, 36
Iraq Study Group (ISG), 29, 48, 49, 51
Isakson, Johnny, 234, 235
ISG. *See* International Steel Group; Iraq Study Group
Islamic Group, 4
Israel, 31, 392, 411
Italy, 363
ITC. *See* U.S. International Trade Commission

Jackson, Robert H., 187
Jacoby, Lowell, 436
Jacoby Declaration, 436
Japan
China and, 328
climate change and, 363, 366, 368, 370
Kyoto Protocol and, 360
North Korea and, 125, 135–136, 138, 140, 141, 145
steel import tariffs and, 252, 253, 259, 265, 266
Jeffords, James, 266, 452
Jiang Zemin, 307, 315
Jihad, 4, 20*n*8
Job Protection Act (2003), 337, 343
JOBS. *See* Jumpstart Our Business Strength Act
John Paul II, 4, 295

Johnson, Eddie Bernice, 453
Johnson, Lyndon, 5, 224
Johnson, Nancy, 344
Johnson v. Eisentrager (1950), 437, 438
Joint Declaration on the Denuclearization of the Korean Peninsula, 123
Jumpstart Our Business Strength Act (JOBS, 2003), 338, 345

Kang Sok Ju, 135
Kanter, Arnold, 130
Karimov, Islam, 16–17
Karzai, Hamid, 99
Kattouf, Theodore, 172
KEDO. *See* Korean Peninsula Energy Development Organization
Kelly, James, 124, 140–141
Kennedy, Anthony M., 438
Kennedy, Edward, 231–236, 239, 241, 242, 348, 350
Kennedy, John F., 223–224, 282, 283
Kennedy, Patrick, 292
Kenya embassy bombing, 5, 6
Kerrey, Bob, 8
Kerry, John, 376
Kessler, Gladys, 20, 423
Khalilzad, Zalmay, 31
Khamenei, Ali, 99, 104, 109, 110, 115
Khan, A. Q., 93, 101, 108, 111
Khatami, Mohammad, 93, 98, 100, 104, 115
Khomeini, Ayatollah Ruhollah, 6, 93, 94–95, 115
Kim Dae Jung, 136
Kim Gye Gwan, 145
Kim Il Sung, 126, 134, 146. *See also* North Korea
Kim Jong Il, 126, 136, 141, 143, 146. *See also* North Korea
Kim Yong Sam, 133
Kimmitt, Robert M., 165, 166, 173
King, David, 358
King, Joseph, 171–172
King, Peter T., 165, 171–176, 178
Kirkpatrick, Jeane, 409, 412
Kirsch, Philippe, 402, 410
Kissinger, Henry, 96, 308, 409, 412
Klein, Israel, 160
Koizumi, Junichiro, 370
Korean Peninsula Energy Development Organization (KEDO), 124, 135–136, 138, 140, 141, 146
Korean War, 125–126, 311
Kosovo, 6, 325, 408–409
Kreitzer, Michael, 160–161
Kristol, William, 32
Kuwait, 97, 111
Kyl, Jon, 231–236, 239, 241, 242, 345
Kyoto Protocol. *See* Climate change

Labor groups and China, 320–321, 328
Lake, Anthony, 288, 293, 451
Lamy, Pascal, 347, 350, 352
Landrieu, Mary, 350
Latin America and immigration issues. *See* U.S.-Mexican relations
Lautenberg, Frank, 165
Leach, Jim, 82
League of Nations, 392
Leahy, Patrick, 71, 73, 81, 85, 185, 233
Lee, Barbara, 12
Legacy costs in steel industry, 256
Levin, Carl, 12, 196–197
Levin, Mark, 207–208
Lewis, James, 161
Lewis, Jerry, 174–175
Lewis, Ron, 349
Lewis, Stephen, 408
Libby, I. Lewis, 31
LIBERTAD (Cuban Liberty and Democratic Solidarity Act). *See* Cuba policy
Libya, 6, 8, 392, 403, 408, 411
Lindsay, James M., 30
Local and state action on climate change, 371–375
London Charter for the Prosecution and Punishment of the Major War Criminals of the European Axis, 393, 394, 395–396
Long, Russell, 372
Lopez Portillo, Jose, 224
Lott, Trent, 8, 12, 74, 171, 326
Lowry, Clay, 174
LTV, 257, 268
Lucent Technologies, 318
Lugar, Richard, 39, 42, 43
Luttig, J. Michael, 434

Maastricht Treaty, 323–324
Mack, Connie, 287
Maine, 372
Majahedin-e-Khalq (MEK), 100
al-Maliki, Nouri, 29, 50, 51
Mancusco, Salvatore, 62

Mandelson, Peter, 351
Manzullo, Donald, 70, 171, 175, 345–346
Mao Zedong, 126, 307, 311
Mariel boatlift, 226
Marshall, John, 193
Martinez, Jennifer, 427–428
Martinez, Mel, 235, 285
Mas Canosa, Jorge, 287
El-Masri, Khaled, 432–433
Massachusetts, 372–373
Massachusetts v. Environmental Protection Agency (2007), 375
Mayfield, Brandon, 429
McCaffery, Barry, 65, 70, 83, 85
McCain, John
  climate change policy and, 376, 380
  immigration policy and, 231–235, 239, 242
  tax subsidies for foreign exports and, 350
  U.S. intervention in Iraq and, 39
McClellan, Scott, 167, 173
McConnell, Michael, 187, 208–210, 211
McCrery, Jim, 345
McCurry, Michael, 8, 134
McGovern, Jim, 78, 81, 82–83
McIntyre, Michael I., 347
McLaughlin, Brookly, 165
Medellín cartel, 64, 67, 78
MEK (Majahedin-e-Khalq), 100
MEM (Multilateral Evaluation Mechanism), 82
Menendez, Robert, 174, 239, 286, 292
Mexico
  steel import tariffs and, 265
  U.S. relations. *See* U.S.-Mexican relations
MFN. *See* Most favored nation trade status
Microsoft, 342, 343
Midterm elections
  of 2002, 261–262
  of 2006, 48–49
Migration and Refugee Assistance Act (1962), 225
Military Commissions Act (2006), 421, 440–441
Military tribunals. *See* Detainees, rights of
Miller, Geofrey, 426
Miller Brewing, 375
Minaret tracking system, 186
Minimills, 256
Minuteman, 238
Mittal, Lakshmi N., 272
Mittal Steel USA, 272, 274
Mobbs, Michael, 427
Mobbs declaration, 427, 434
Monsanto, 340
Montreal Protocol, 363–364, 381
Mooney, Chris, 377
Moreno Ocampo, Luis, 410
Morgan, Jennifer, 370
Mossadeq, Mohammad, 94–95, 100, 111
Most favored nation (MFN) trade status, 311–312, 313
Motorola, 318, 343
Motz, Diane G., 434
Mueller, Robert, 195, 196
al Muhajir, Abdullah. *See* Padilla, Jose
Muldoon, Joe, 160
Multilateral Evaluation Mechanism (MEM), 82
Munich syndrome, 130
Musharraf, Pervez, 16
Myers, Richard, 47–48, 424
Myrick, Sue, 18, 153, 171

NACARA (Nicaraguan and Central American Relief Act (1997)), 229–230
NAFTA. *See* North American Free Trade Agreement
Nairobi, Kenya embassy bombing, 5, 6
Napolitano, Janet, 373
National Aeronautics and Space Administration (NASA), 359, 362, 377, 383
National Association of Manufacturers, 326
National Commission on Terrorist Attacks Upon the United States. *See* 9/11 Commission
National Council for U.S.-China Trade, 316
National Endowment for Democracy (NED), 286
National Environmental Trust, 369
National Foreign Trade Group Council, 342
National Foundation for American Policy, 177
National Oceanic and Atmospheric Administration (NOAA), 377
National origin quotas for immigration, 219, 223–224. *See also* U.S.-Mexican relations
National Security Agency (NSA) eavesdropping, 185–215
  administration's response to leak, 185, 187, 190–192, 450

National Security Agency (NSA) eavesdropping (*continued*)
background, 186–187
executive self-investigations, 205
FISA statute, 185–186, 187, 189–190
Hayden's testimony and, 196–198, 209–210, 211
hospital visit to Ashcroft and, 194–196
key actors, 210–211
legislative remedies, 202–204
McConnell's testimony, 208–210
mid-course correction, 205–208
overview, 185–186
previous illegal NSA activities, 186–187
setbacks in court, 198–202, 449
sole-organ doctrine, 192–194
timeline, 187
wiretaps, establishment of limits on, 187–189
National Security Council (NSC), 10, 35
National Wildlife Federation, 380
NATO, 6, 44
Natural Resources Defense Council, 372
NED (National Endowment for Democracy), 286
Negroponte, John, 18
Neoconservatives ("neocons"), 32, 37
Netherlands, 339, 363
New Hampshire, 372
New Jersey, 372
Newman, Donna, 435–436
New Orleans and hurrican relief, 360, 379
"New Way Forward," 29, 51
New York, 360, 372
New York Time's reports on NSA eavesdropping, 185, 187, 190–192, 199, 202, 207–208, 450
NGOs. *See* Nongovernmental organizations
Nicaragua, 227, 228, 397
Nicaraguan and Central American Relief Act (NACARA, 1997), 229–230
Nickels, Greg, 374
Nickles, Don, 345
9/11 Commission, 9–10, 18
Nineteenth of April Movement, 63
Nixon, Richard
China-U.S. relations and, 307, 308
domestic surveillance and, 185, 186, 197
foreign trade and, 337
resignation of, 26
war powers and, 5
NOAA (National Oceanic and Atmospheric Administration), 377
Non-Aligned Movement, 404
Non-Detention Act (1971), 436
Nongovernmental organizations (NGOs), 310, 314, 318–319
Nortel, 318
North American Free Trade Agreement (NAFTA), 228, 230, 237, 258, 265
Northern Alliance, 99
North Korea, 121–149
in "axis of evil," 28, 34, 91–92, 93, 139
China and, 306, 323
U.S. relationship, 121–149, 449, 450
Agreed Framework and KEDO, 124, 135–136
background of North Korea's nuclear quest, 125–127
Bush (George H. W.) policy, 127–130, 146
Bush (George W.) policy, 91–92, 94, 109, 113, 124, 138–146, 450
critics and, 137–138
intelligence, 122, 125–127
key actors, 146
policy from Bush to Clinton, 115, 124, 130–138, 144, 146
policy options, 144–145
timeline of, 123–125
withdrawal from NPT and reactor refueling, 132–133
Norway, 362, 363
NPT. *See* Nuclear Non-Proliferation Treaty
NSC. *See* National Security Council
Nuclear Non-Proliferation Treaty (NPT)
Iran and, 98–99, 102, 103, 106, 108, 111, 112
North Korea and, 123, 125, 132–133, 136, 141, 142
Nuclear standoff between the U.S. and Iran. *See* Iran
Nucor, 268
Nuncio, Richard, 292
Nuremberg trials, 392, 393, 395–396

OAS (Organization of American States), 82
Obama, Barack, 380
Obey, David, 74, 79
Ochoa, Fabio, 64, 78
Ochoa, Jorge, 64
O'Connor, Sandra Day, 435

Office of Legal Counsel (OLC), 192–194, 426
Office of Professional Responsibility (OPR), 205
Office of Special Plans, 32, 46
Office of the United States Trade Representative, 312, 327
Office of the U.S. Coordinator for Mexican Affairs, 224
Oil industry, 375–378, 453–454
OLC. *See* Office of Legal Counsel
Olmstead v. United States (1928), 187–188
Olson, Ted, 195
Oman, 16
Omar, Mullah, 15, 17
Omnibus and Competitiveness Trade Act (1988), 158
O'Neill, Paul, 265, 369, 453
OPEC (Organization of Petroleum Exporting Countries), 364
Operation Blockade, 219, 229
Operation Desert Fox, 27
Operation Enduring Freedom, 1, 4, 13
OPR (Office of Professional Responsibility), 205
Oregon, environmental policy and, 373
Organization of African States, 408
Organization of American States (OAS), 82
Ortega, Jaime, 297
Outsourcing by steel manufacturers, 258
Ozone hole, 364. *See also* Climate change

Pace, Peter, 172
Padilla, Jose, 420, 421, 427–429, 435–436
Pahlavi, Mohammad Reza, 93, 95–96, 100, 101, 111
Pakistan, 34, 101
Panama Canal, 396
P&O (Peninsular and Oriental Steam Navigation Company). *See* Dubai Ports World takeover controversy
Panetta, Leon, 293
"Paragate" scandal, 62, 82
Partnership for Prosperity, 219
Pastrana, Andrés, 67, 85
Pataki, George, 372, 374
Patiño Fómenque, Victor, 67
Patriot Act. See USA Patriot Act (2001)
PBGC (Pension Benefit Guarantee Corporation), 268
Pelosi, Nancy, 79, 191, 379
Pence, Mike, 236
Peninsular and Oriental Steam Navigation Company (P&O). *See* Dubai Ports World takeover controversy
Pension Benefit Guarantee Corporation (PBGC), 268
Pentagon's Office of Special Plans. *See* Office of Special Plans
People's Republic of China (PRC). *See* China
Perino, Dana, 175
Perle, Richard, 32
Permanent, normal trade relations (PNTR), 306–308, 320, 321, 324–327. *See also* China
Permanent Court of Arbitration, 392
Perry, William J., 136, 146, 293
Persian Gulf War, 39, 391
Petraeus, David, 50
Pew Center on Climate Change, 371, 380
Philbin, Patrick, 195, 425
Piltz, Rick S., 376–377
Piracy issues in China. *See* Intellectual property issues in China
Plan Colombia, 60–62, 67, 72, 79–83, 449. *See also* Colombia and drug trade
PNAC (Project for the New American Century), 32
PNTR. *See* Permanent, normal trade relations
Pope, Carl, 386
Portillo, Lopez, 224
Portman, Rob, 308
Port security. *See* Dubai Ports World takeover controversy
Postwar occupation of Iraq, 47–52
Powell, Colin
  authorization of force and war on terrorism, 15, 16, 28
  on Cheney, 33
  Colombia drug policy and, 77
  detainees' rights and, 425–426, 442
  immigration policy and, 218
  international community and impending war and, 44
  Iran and, 100
  North Korea policy and, 138, 140
  steel import tariffs and, 265
  U.S. intervention in Iraq and, 27–28, 30, 37, 38, 53
PRC (People's Republic of China). *See* China

Predator unmanned aerial vehicle, 9
Preemption. *See* Bush Doctrine and U.S. interventions in Iraq
Presidential-congressional interactions, 448–449
Presidential Directive NSPD-24, 36
Presidential election of 2000, 261, 268, 453
Presidential powers
  NSA eavesdropping and, 193, 204, 206, 209, 210. *See also* National Security Agency (NSA) eavesdropping
  terrorism and, 5–10
  war powers, 5–6
Project for the New American Century (PNAC), 32
Pryce, Deborah, 175
Putin, Vladimir, 16, 110, 370

Qadhafi, Mu'ammar, 6
al Qaeda
  in Afghanistan, 418–419
  authorization of force and war on terrorism, 1, 2, 8–9, 14–17, 28, 31. *See also* Terrorism
  detainees and enemy combatants. *See* Detainees, rights of
  Hussein, Saddam and, 42, 45
  Iran and, 100
  Iraq and, 33. *See also* Bush Doctrine and U.S. interventions in Iraq
  port security and, 171–172
  Saudi Arabia, bombings in, 4
  September 11, 2001, terrorist attacks, 418, 419
  USS *Cole* attack and, 9
Qanooni, Yunus, 99
Qatar, 392, 403, 411
Qualcomm Corporation, 317–318, 330
Quotas for immigration, 219, 223–224, 226, 228. *See also* U.S.-Mexican relations

Radiological attacks, 152, 164
Radio Marti, 283, 285–286
Rafsanjani, Akbar Hashemi, 100
Rangel, Charles, 293, 299, 337, 343–344, 345, 350, 352
Rasul v. Bush (2004), 420, 421, 425, 436–438
RCA Global, 186
Reagan, Nancy, 60
Reagan, Ronald
  Colombia drug policy of, 60
  Cuba policy and, 282, 284, 285–286
  foreign direct investment (FDI) and, 158
  immigration policy of, 227
  Iran and, 97, 111
  Libya bombing by, 6, 8
  North Korea and, 134
REAL ID Act (2005), 230–231
Refugee Act (1980), 219, 226, 227
Refugee-Escapee Act (1957), 223
Regime change
  "axis of evil" and, 92
  foreign policy challenges and, 448
  Iran and, 98, 100, 101, 104, 108, 111, 113
  Iraq and, 28, 32, 34, 37, 38, 43, 45, 105
Regional Greenhouse Gas Initiative (RGGI), 372–373
Rehnquist, William, 438
Reid, Harry, 236, 241, 379
Religious freedom. *See* Human rights
Reno, Janet, 293
Republic of Korea (ROK). *See* South Korea
Revelle, Roger, 359, 361
Revenue Act (1971), 337
Revolutionary Armed Forces of Colombia (FARC), 62, 65, 66, 67, 72, 77–78, 80
RGGI (Regional Greenhouse Gas Initiative), 372–373
Rhode Island, 372
Ricchetti, Stephen, 324
Rice, Condoleezza
  authorization of force and war on terrorism and, 14, 18, 19
  climate change policy and, 386
  decision making and Iraq War and, 35, 38
  detainees' rights and, 430
  foreign policy after September 11 and, 29–30
  human rights in Colombia and, 81
  ICC and, 411
  Iran and, 100, 107, 108
  U.S. intervention in Iraq and, 44, 53
Richardson, Bill, 373, 401
Roberts, Judith, 441
Roberts, Pat, 204
Rockefeller, John D., IV, 203
Rogue states, 33, 36, 91, 137, 314
Rome Conference, 401–406

Rome Statute, 394, 404–405, 406, 410. *See also* International Criminal Court (ICC)
Romney, Mitt, 372–373
Roosevelt, Franklin D., 187
Ros-Lehtinen, Ileana, 286, 292, 294, 295, 300
Rothman, Steven, 79
Rove, Karl, 265
Royal Society, 377
Rugh, William, 157
Rumsfeld, Donald
  Afghanistan and, 15–16
  authorization of force and war on terrorism and, 13–14, 17
  corporate ties of, 453
  Counterterrorism Evaluation Group and, 32
  detainees' rights and, 426, 430, 432, 436, 442
  ICC and, 412
  Iraq War and, 14, 30, 31, 32, 35–36, 38, 42, 53
  postwar occupation of Iraq and, 47, 49, 50
  Uzbekistan and, 16–17
Rumsfeld v. Padilla (2004), 420, 421, 427–429, 435–436
Russia
  China and, 306
  ICC and, 403
  Iran and, 106, 107, 108, 109–110, 114
  Kyoto Protocol and, 370
  North Korea and, 125, 141, 145
  steel import tariffs and, 252, 253, 259
Rwanda, 393, 397, 408

Safeguard tariffs, 261–271. *See also* Steel import tariffs
Safe Port Act (2006), 154, 176
Salazar, Ken, 239, 242–243
Salinas, Carlos, 228, 229, 230
Samper Pizano, Ernesto, 61, 64, 71, 85
Saudi Arabia, 2, 4, 19*n*1, 111
Al Sauds, 2, 19*n*1
Savage, Michael, 161–162
SAVAK (Iran), 95
Scalia, Antonin, 438
Schakowsky, Jan, 81
Scheffer, David, 398, 399–400, 402, 406–407, 412
Schiff, Adam, 203–204
Schlesinger, Arthur M., Jr., 26
Schlesinger, James A., 423
Schumer, Charles E., 153, 160–161, 165, 174, 175, 178
Schwab, Susan C., 308, 328
Schwarzenegger, Arnold, 373–374
Science and Bush (George W.) administration, 376–378
Scott, James, 448
Scowcroft, Brent, 37, 127, 130
Searle, 453
Second World Climate Conference, 363
Secret prisons, 432–433. *See also* Detainees, rights of
Secure Borders, Economic Opportunity, and Immigration Reform Act (2007), 220, 239, 240–241*b*, 241–243
Secure Fence Act (2006), 220, 236
Self-defense of nations, 11
Sensenbrenner, James, 204, 232–233, 241*b*, 243
September 11, 2001, terrorist attacks, 10, 418, 419
Sessions, Jeff, 236
Seymour, Michael, 167
Shaerf, Peter S., 172
Shah of Iran. *See* Pahlavi, Mohammad Reza
Shalikasvili, John M., 293
Shanghai Automotive Industry Corporation, 317
Shaw, Clay, 174
Shays, Chris, 165
Shell Oil, 377, 381
Shelton, Hugh "Henry," 7, 14, 15, 19
Sheridan, Brian E., 72–73
Sherritt International, 294
al-Shifa pharmaceutical plant bombing, Sudan, 7
Shiite Dawn Party, 29
Shultz, George, 409, 413
Sierra Club, 386
Simpson, Alan, 225
Singapore, 400, 404
Sino-Soviet friendship treaty (1950), 311
Sires, Albio, 285
Skelton, Ike, 78
Smith, Frederick, 400
Snow, John W., 162, 171
Solarz, Stephen, 287
Sole-organ doctrine, 192–194
Somalia, 6, 408

Souter, David, 435
South Korea
North Korea and, 125–132, 136, 140, 141. *See also* North Korea
steel import tariffs and, 252, 253, 259, 265, 266
South Korean Agency for National Security Planning (ANSP), 131
Soviet Union, 122, 126
Specter, Arlen, 39, 232–234, 239, 243, 380
Stand Up for Steel, 262
State and local action on climate change, 371–375
Steel Caucus, 262
Steel import tariffs, 249–280
background, 252–258
Bush's tariff decision and safeguard investigation, 261–271, 272*f*, 274
economic effects and political responses, 266–269
WTO decision and Bush's reversal, 269–271, 275
Clinton's response and fair trade laws, 249, 251, 253*f*, 254*f*, 258–261, 274
key actors, 274–275
origins of, 252–258, 253–255*f*
overview, 249, 251–252
steel politics after tariffs, 255*f*, 271–274, 273*f*
timeline of, 250–251
Steinmeier, Frank-Walter, 106
Stephanopoulos, George, 288, 293
Stet International, 294
Strategy of Strengthening Democracy and Social Development (Colombia), 67, 83
Sudan, 2, 5, 7, 329, 408, 410–411
Summit of the Americas (1994), 228
Supreme Court and detainees' rights. *See* Detainees, rights of
Sutherland, George, 193
Sweeney, John, 162, 321, 330

Taft, William Howard, IV, 426
Taguba, Antonio, 432
Taiwan, 252, 265, 307, 311, 323
Talbott, Strobe, 288
Taliban
Bin Laden and. *See* Bin Laden, Osama
detainees and enemy combatants. *See* Detainees, rights of
insurgency of, 17
Iran and, 99
terrorism and, 2, 4, 15–17, 28, 31. *See also* Terrorism
UAE and, 156
Tanzania embassy bombing, 5, 6
Tariffs. *See* Steel import tariffs
Tarnoff, Peter, 288, 290
Tax Increase Prevention and Reconciliation Act (2005), 338, 351
Tax subsidies for exports, 335–355
background, 336–340
congressional conflict over corporate tax breaks (2003), 343–346
EU and WTO, 340, 342–343
key actors, 352–353
key terms, 341*b*
last stage, 348–351
overview, 335–336
resolution of differences and final passage, 346–348, 449
resolution of question of, 351–352
timeline of, 337–338
U.S.-EU trade competition, 336, 339–340
Taylor, Anna Diggs, 200–202
Taylor, Francis X., 77
Team Spirit Military Exercise (U.S.-South Korea), 129, 131–132, 133
Telecommunications in China, 317–318
Tenet, George
authorization of force and war on terrorism and, 14, 18, 19
detainees' rights and, 432, 433
Iraq War and, 30, 33, 44, 53
National Security Agency (NSA) eavesdropping and, 197
9/11 Commission testimony of, 9
September 11, 2001, and, 10
on terrorism threats, 13
Terrorism, 1–24
authorization of force and war on terrorism, 3, 10–19, 31
when to attack, 15–17
whom to strike, 13–15
background on Bin Laden, 2, 4–5
counterinsurgency and counternarcotics aid, 60, 77–83, 84. *See also* Colombia and drug trade
detainees, rights of. *See* Detainees, rights of
eavesdropping. *See* National Security Agency (NSA) eavesdropping

foreign policy challenge of, 448
key actors, 19
port security. *See* Dubai Ports World takeover controversy
presidential leadership in war on terrorism, 17–19
presidential powers and, 5–10
Clinton's strikes against Bin Laden, 1, 3, 6–8, 11, 15–19, 27
Congress, consulting of, 8–10
striking back at, 1–2
timeline of Clinton and Bush administration strikes against Bin Laden, 3–4
wiretaps. *See* National Security Agency (NSA) eavesdropping
Terrorist Surveillance Program (TSP). *See also* National Security Agency (NSA) eavesdropping
Aschcroft and Gonzales and, 194–196
authorization of, 187
Bush (George W.) defense of, 191
court review of, 199–202
FISA courts and, 206, 207
Hayden and, 198
OPR inquiry into, 205
purpose of, 210
Texaco, 377
Texas Instruments, 344
"Texas proviso," 222, 225
Thailand, 265
Thatcher, Margaret, 362, 363
Thomas, Bill, 337, 342–349, 351, 352
Thomas, Clarence, 438
Thompson, Fred, 325
Tiananmen Square massacre, 245*n*31, 307, 319
Tillerson, Rex, 378
Title III authority and wiretaps, 188–189
Toronto Conference on the Changing Atmosphere, 362, 363
Torricelli, Robert, 287–288, 292, 293, 300
Torture memos, 430–432. *See also* Detainees, rights of
TPA. *See* Trade promotion authority
Trade Act (1974), 249
Trade promotion authority (TPA), 262, 266, 271–272
Trade relations. *See specific countries*
Travel ban to Cuba, 297, 298, 299
Treasury Department, 177, 297
Troop surge in Iraq, 50
Truman, Harry, 219, 222, 223, 396
TSP. *See* Terrorist Surveillance Program
Turbay Ayala, César, 66
Turkey, 126

UAE. *See* United Arab Emirates
UAW (United Auto Workers), 321
UCS (Union of Concerned Scientists), 377
Ueland, Eric, 175
Uganda, 410
Ukraine, 252, 253
UN Convention against Illicit Traffic in Narcotic Drugs and Psychotropic Substances (Vienna Convention), 71
UNEP (United Nations Environmental Program), 362
Union of Concerned Scientists (UCS), 377
Unión Patriótica, 66
United Arab Emirates (UAE), 16, 156–157, 160, 162, 168, 170. *See also* Dubai Ports World takeover controversy
United Auto Workers (UAW), 321
United Iraqi Alliance, 29
United Kingdom
ICC and, 400, 403
Iran and, 93, 94, 102–104, 105, 107
Iraq and, 10
Korean War and, 126
United Methodist Church, 320, 330
United Nations. *See also specific conventions*
Ahmadinejad, Mahmoud speech to, 106
Bush (George W.) speech to, 40
Charter
Article 43, 396
Article 51, 11
International Criminal Court. *See* International Criminal Court (ICC)
Iran and, 93
Kyoto Protocol. *See* Climate change
Resolution 95 (I) (London Charter), 393, 395
Resolution 96 (I) (London Charter), 393, 395
Security Council
ICC and, 399, 400, 401, 404. *See also* International Criminal Court (ICC)
Iran and, 103–110, 113
North Korea and, 125, 133, 141
Resolution 687 (Iraq), 27
Resolution 808 (Yugoslavia), 393, 397

United Nations (*continued*)
Resolution 955 (Rwanda), 393, 397
Resolution 1422 (ICC), 409
Resolution 1441 (Iraq), 28, 45
Resolution 1695 (North Korea), 141–142
Resolution 1718 (North Korea), 142
Resolution 1747 (Iran), 110
United Nations Environmental Program (UNEP), 362
United Nations Framework Convention on Climate Change (FCCC), 359, 365–366. *See also* Climate change
United-Self Defense Groups of Colombia (AUC), 62, 63–64, 67, 73, 77–78
United States Climate Action Partnership (USCAP), 360, 381
United Steelworkers of America (USWA), 258, 268–269, 275
United Technologies, 88*n*50, 343–344
Uribe Vélez, Alvaro, 62, 67, 81, 83, 85
Uruguay Round, 322
U.S. Chamber of Commerce, 169, 296, 298, 316, 328
U.S.-China Business Council, 316, 330
U.S.-China trade relations. *See* China
U.S. citizen enemy combatants, detention of, 427–429
U.S. Conference of Mayors, 374
U.S. Customs and Border Protection Agency, 163–164
U.S. Customs-Trade Partnership against Terror, 152
U.S. embassies, bombings of, 5, 6
U.S.-EU trade competition, 336, 339–340
U.S. Grains Council, 295
U.S. International Trade Commission (ITC), 250, 251, 260, 263–269, 272
U.S. Mayors Climate Protection Agreement, 374
U.S.-Mexican Consultative Mechanism, 224
U.S.-Mexican relations, 217–247
background, 221–230
immigration policy since September 11, 230–236
bicameral deadlock, 236
Bush's agenda, 230–231
debate over reform, 240–241*b*
enforcement, 241*b*
legalization of undocumented immigrants, 240*b*
legal permanent visas, 240–241*b*
obstacles to reform, 237–239, 241–242
Senate floor (Spring 2006), 234–236
Senate Judiciary Committee (Spring 2006), 231–234
temporary workers, 240*b*
key actors, 242–243
overview, 217–221
timeline in, 219–220
U.S. policy (1940–2001), 221–230
bracero program, 219, 221–223, 224, 240
humanitarian migration (1965–1980s), 225–227
Immigration and Nationality Act and humanitarian admissions, 219, 223–224
immigration policy after cold war, 227–230
relations (1965–1980s), 224–225
U.S. Steel Corporation, 256, 268, 272
USA Patriot Act (2001), 190, 210, 230, 418, 423–424
USCAP. *See* United States Climate Action Partnership
USS *Cole* attack, 9
USS *Samuel B. Roberts*, 97
USS *Vincennes*, 97
USWA. *See* United Steelworkers of America
Uzbekistan, 4, 16–17

Vance, Cyrus, 20*n*17, 96
Venezuela, 329
Vermont, 372
Vienna Convention, 71
Vietnam War, 5, 186, 336, 447
Virgin Islands, 340
Vita, David, 235

Wahhabism, 19*n*1
Wal-Mart, 381
War Crimes Act (1996), 426
Warner, John, 172, 175–176
War on terrorism. *See* Terrorism
War powers, 5–6
War Powers Resolution (1973), 5–6, 8, 17–18, 42
Warren, Robert, 378
Washington Treaty, 44, 373
"Watch list," 186
Watergate scandal, 26
Waters, Maxine, 74
Watson, Robert, 378

Waxman, Henry, 377
Weapons of mass destruction (WMDs)
Iran and, 91–92, 98, 105. *See also* Iran
Iraq and, 30–31, 34, 38, 42–44, 46, 105–106. *See also* Bush Doctrine and U.S. interventions in Iraq
North Korea and. *See* North Korea
Weekly Standard article on Iran (April 2006), 99
Welfare Reform Act (1996), 228
Wellstone, Paul, 74, 75, 85, 325
West Coast Governors Global Warming Initiative, 373
Western Regional Climate Action Initiative, 360
Western Union, 186
White House Council on Environmental Quality, 376
White House Steel Action Program (1999), 259–260
Whitman, Christine Todd, 369
Wilson, Pete, 228
Wiretaps. *See* National Security Agency (NSA) eavesdropping
WMDs. *See* Weapons of mass destruction
Wolfowitz, Paul
authorization of force and war on terrorism and, 14, 19
Iraq War and, 14, 29, 30, 31, 32, 35, 53
North Korea policy and, 127
on WMDs, 44
Woolsey, James, 32, 172
World Court, 396–397, 412
World Meteorological Organization, 362
World Trade Center bombing (1993), 4
World Trade Organization (WTO)
Agreement on Safeguards, 249
Appellate Body, 251, 252, 269
China
membership of, 305, 307, 308, 313, 316–324, 326
trade issues, 308, 327. *See also* China
defined, 341
Doha Round, 262
Russia, membership of, 370
steel import tariffs and, 249–252, 258–263, 266, 269–271, 274–275
subsidies and, 260
tax subsidies for exports. *See* Tax subsidies for exports
Uruguay Round, 322
World War II, 392, 393
World Wildlife Fund Climate Change Campaign, 370
WTO. *See* World Trade Organization

Yee, James, 429
Yemen, 2, 9, 392, 403, 411
Yoo, John, 425
Youngstown Sheet and Tube Co. v. Sawyer (1952), 436
Yugoslavia, 393, 397

Zarif, Javad, 99
Zedillo, Ernesto, 229
Zinni, Anthony, 33
Zoellick, Robert, 263, 265, 275, 308, 342
Zutphen Text, 398